MEDICAL NEGLIGENCE
A Practical Guide

MEDICAL NEGLIGENCE

A Practical Guide

THIRD EDITION
Revised and Enlarged

CHARLES J. LEWIS MA,
of the Middle Temple, Barrister,
former open classical scholar of
Oriel College, Oxford

Tolley Publishing Company Ltd

 A United News & Media publication

First published 1988
by Frank Cass & Co. Ltd.

Second Edition published 1992
by Tolley Publishing Company Limited

Third Edition 1995

Published by
Tolley Publishing Company Limited
Tolley House
2 Addiscombe Road
Croydon CR9 5AF England
0181-686 9141

ISBN 1 86012 073-3

The law is stated as at 1 June 1995

Typeset by Letterpart Limited, Reigate, Surrey

Printed and bound in Great Britain by
Mackays of Chatham plc, Chatham, Kent

To my children, Ben and Janet,
and to my mother,
and to my father, who would dearly have loved
to see this book in print

Foreword to the Third Edition

Just three years have passed since the second edition of this work, yet the new text is considerably longer, much has been added, some entirely re-written, and a wealth of new case law slotted into place. The truth is that in this fast developing area of law, text books of this nature are either kept up-to-date or they die.

The author's object has always been to provide a practical and accessible guide to the pursuit of a medical negligence claim. His was the first book to do so. It has been followed but never bettered. Now, with this new edition, it is once again pre-eminent in the field. Anyone entering or considering entering this field of litigation would be well advised to have it beside them.

Nor is the value of this book confined to the immediate needs of the litigant and his lawyer, although these are comprehensively met. It contains in addition stimulating discussion on other related questions; on, for example, the right to live and the right to die, on the problems of recovering damages for nervous shock, and, in the new Epilogue, on the way ahead, a topic realistically set in its political context – for there can be little doubt that the future of this part of our law will be dictated at least as much by political considerations (including those of public expense) as by jurisprudential ones.

Writing the Foreword to the second edition, Lord Donaldson of Lymington congratulated the author for his industry and his achievement. I do too, but I congratulate him above all upon the striking readability of his prose. This is a text book one can actually enjoy.

The Rt Hon Lord Justice Simon Brown
10 May 1995

Author's Preface to the Third Edition

Tempora mutantur, nos et mutamur in illis . . .[1]

I have said in previous editions that no branch of law undergoes such continuous change in outlook as well as in procedure and – though to a lesser extent – law as the field of medical negligence. There is now a fairly large body of lawyers who can expertly process the medical negligence action and develop, within reasonable limits, the potential of a claim. But this hard-won position is under threat on a number of fronts.

Legal aid has been drastically reduced. Lawyers are being forced to take work on the basis that they only get paid if they win, which does not help patients because initially difficult cases, many of which turn out in the end to be successful, will not be taken. The medical negligence panel, created by the Law Society in a justified attempt to ensure that only experienced solicitors take medical negligence actions – thus avoiding the all too familiar horror stories of cases ruined and clients, traumatised already by medical incompetence, hurt further by legal incompetence – has criteria for acceptance, devised by Action for Victims of Medical Accidents (AVMA), that are very hard for all but a few solicitors to meet. This may mean, if exclusivity is introduced (by the Law Society or the Legal Aid Board), that only a small number of firms, in a restricted number of locales, will be available to do the work, thus denying the patient choice.

The Court of Appeal, since the departure of Lord Donaldson, is showing itself to be no friend to patients. Witness its recent decisions on limitation and nervous shock.[2] There is a fear that judges as a whole are being infected by a current wave of feeling against the increase of medical litigation and consequent large awards against health carers, though few, if any, are likely to match the record of one High Court judge, experienced in medico-legal litigation, who, as far as can be determined by those acting for patients, has never given judgment for a patient.

---

[1] Times change, and we with them.
[2] But see Chapter 28 for the court's recent limitation judgment in the Lloyd's Names litigation.

If no-fault compensation, or arbitration (with or without fault), or even mediation, is introduced for patients' complaints, it may be followed by legislation precluding the right of action through the courts. Another suggestion, which may be recommended in due course by Lord Woolf, is to have the merits of the medical claim adjudicated by a court-appointed expert. If that ever became the practice, the patient could bid farewell to any chance of a proper and unbiased investigation and a just outcome.

Behind most of these manoeuvres, effected or threatened, is the desire of the Government to save money, whether in claims upon legal aid funds or in the payment of costs or damages out of NHS funds. This is often expressed as a desire to give the litigant a better deal. Sometimes the two are not mutually incompatible.

It remains to be seen what reforms the various current reviews will suggest and what changes, if any, they will lead to. There is the review of civil procedure being carried out by Lord Woolf. There is a review being carried out by the Legal Aid Advisory Committee into the cost of personal injury litigation. There is a similar review being carried out by the Lord Chancellor's Department (this is the review that may lead to a no-fault scheme). There is the Wilson Committee review on complaints procedures. There is also the new NHSE-generated Clinical Negligence Scheme for Trusts, designed to improve risk management and create a pooling arrangement for the payment of successful claims. It is to be hoped that this will lead to quicker recognition and settlement of valid claims.[3]

Charles Lewis
Gray's Inn
June 1995

---

[3] The Practice Direction (Civil Litigation: Case Management) of January 1995 [1995] 1 WLR 262 requires the parties to state what they have done or could do towards resolving the dispute in some other way, i.e. by alternative dispute resolution. It remains to be seen if the courts will appreciate what can and, more significantly, what cannot be done in that respect for a patient's claim consistent with a just resolution.

A note on some lesser known acronyms in the text:

BMLR   the new series of Butterworths' *Medico-Legal Reports*, published from June 1992.

MLJ   the bi-monthly *Medical and Legal Journal* published by Action for Victims of Medical Accidents.

HALL   *Health and Law Letter*, which was produced, amusingly enough, as are the Medical Law Reports, by Geoffrey HALL.

Med LR   (originally MLR, which was confusable with the entirely dissimilar *Modern Law Review*): this is the extremely good, useful and highly professional, in fact indispensable series, the *Medical Law Reports*. They contain much material that is not available elsewhere.

N-J & B   *Medical Negligence Case Law* by Nelson-Jones and Burton (second edition to be published by Butterworth in mid-1995), often the best source for a case apart from the very expensive transcript.

PILS   Butterworths' *Personal Injury Litigation Service*.

PMILL   the *Personal and Medical Injuries Law Letter*.

Contents

PROCEDURE

EPILOGUE

Appendices

Table of Cases

Table of Statutes

Table of Statutory Instruments

Table of Health Circulars and Notices

Table of Rules of the Supreme Court

*Physicians of all men are most happy; what good success soever they have,
the world proclaimeth, and what faults they commit, the earth covereth.*
                                        Francis Quarles (1592–1644)

*I must say that, as a litigant, I should dread a lawsuit beyond almost
anything else, short of sickness and death.*
                                              Judge Learned Hand

*The definition of the duty of care is a matter for the law and the courts.
They cannot stand idly by if the profession, by an excess of paternalism,
denies their patients a real choice. In a word, the law will not permit the
medical profession to play God.*
                                          Sir John Donaldson M.R.

*In the practice of surgery particularly, the public are exposed to great
risks from the number of ignorant persons professing a knowledge of the
art, without the least pretensions to the necessary qualifications, and they
often inflict very serious injury on those who are so unfortunate as to fall
into their hands.*
                                              Baron Garrow (1822)

The doctor is often more to be feared than the disease.
                                              Old French proverb

*I would make it compulsory for a doctor using a brass plate to have
inscribed on it, in addition to the letters indicating his qualifications,
'Remember that I too am mortal'.*
                                          George Bernard Shaw

*The parson shows the way to heaven,
    and then with tender care
The doctor consummates the work
    and sends the patient there.*
                                        Joseph Jekyll (1754–1837)

*Take a case where a sterilisation operation is done so as to enable a man
to have the pleasure of sexual intercourse without shouldering the
responsibilities attached to it. The operation is plainly injurious to the
public interest. It is degrading to the man himself. It is injurious to his
wife and any woman whom he may marry, to say nothing of the way it
opens to licentiousness, and unlike other contraceptives, it allows no
room for a change of mind on either side. It is illegal, even though the
man consents to it.*
                          per Lord Denning in *Bravery* v. *Bravery*
                                      ([1954] 3 All ER 59, 67–8)

Doctors are men who prescribe medicine of which they know little to human beings of whom they know nothing.

Voltaire

Doctors are just the same as lawyers; the only difference is that lawyers merely rob you, whereas doctors rob you and kill you, too.

Anton Chekov

It is so hard that one cannot really have confidence in doctors and yet one cannot do without them.

Goethe

Proper treatment will cure a cold in not more than seven days, but left to itself it will hang on for a week.

H. G. Felsen

And to show the doctors also have a sense of humour (from a medical journal on gastro-enterology)

When the sun rose a year ago nothing was known about the causes of or cure for Crohn's disease or ulcerative colitis. Over the ensuing year more than a thousand articles were published on the subject. When the sun set last Sunday the causes of and cure for Crohn's disease and ulcerative colitis were still unknown. This is widely referred to as medical progress.

And the old chestnut

The operation was a success, but unfortunately the patient died.

A distinguished surgeon presented himself one day shortly after his death, at the gates of Heaven, striding to the head of the long queue that was waiting patiently in front of the entrance.

'I am Sir Reginald . . .', he said to Saint Peter, 'be good enough to let me in'.

'My dear Sir Reginald', said Saint Peter, 'I have no doubt that you will qualify for admittance, but you must take your place at the end of the queue. Everyone must take his turn, even distinguished men of medicine'.

Grumbling, the surgeon walked to the end of the queue. A few moments later a man in a white coat with a stethoscope round his neck came hurrying along the line, to be admitted through the gate with much bowing and scraping. Incensed, Sir Reginald demanded an explanation: 'One moment you're telling me there is no preference for members of my profession, and the next moment you're admitting that fellow. What's the meaning of it, please?'

'Ah, well', said Saint Peter, looking a little sheepish, 'actually, that's God. He just likes to play doctor from time to time'.

1 · Introduction

SUMMARY

Everyone is interested in medical negligence, and has his own ideas on it. It is clearly an area of growth in English litigation but it is unlikely to give rise to the sort of difficulties faced by many United States jurisdictions as our system of law differs from theirs in several important respects. A balance needs to be struck which, while recognising the excellent care that is normally afforded by our doctors to their patients, confirms the rights of the injured patient to compensation where appropriate.

A FASCINATING SUBJECT

There is probably no area of law that provokes such interest, and so immediately, from the non-lawyer as medical negligence. The lawyer has only to mention in conversation with non-lawyers, whether professional people or from any other walk of life, that he does that sort of work for him to be met with interested and informed opinions, the most striking aspect of which is the enthusiasm with which they are offered. His companions will tell him of the experiences they, their relatives and friends have had with the medical profession, usually those that have left the patient unsatisfied (the other sort is less memorable and not so much of a talking point); everyone will have a view on whether doctors are by and large a good or a bad thing; the spectre of American medical malpractice law will be raised – everyone seems to 'know' that vast sums are awarded at the drop of a hat to plaintiffs in US courts, insurance premiums for the doctors are astronomical and not a few are driven or choose to go out of business. 'We don't want to get like America', one hears.

Why does this branch of the law attract such interest and evoke so keen, often so emotional, a response from the lay person? It is partly because it is almost everyone's experience to have at one time or another been in the hands of the doctors, but I think it stems above all from the nature of the doctor's role. The healer is an archetype, just as the judge is. He is part priest, part parent; he is the object of an unstated love–hate relationship. The patient looks to the physician with one part of his mind as the comforter and healer who will make him well and happy; he has the learning and the magic that will bring relief from fear and pain. The patient, whether consciously acknowledging it or not, longs to be relieved or comforted. All this gives the physician a hierophantic status. The other side of the coin is that the adult part of the patient resents his dependence and is not averse to debunking the myth, a myth, be it noted, that he has himself created. This relationship is not entirely dissimilar to the emotional duality that a child feels towards his father. There is perhaps something of a temptation when specialising in cases against the medical profession to regard it as a sort of crusade, as do many of those who specialise in actions against the police, as if not only policeman but also doctor represent some sort of authority figure with which one has not within oneself completely come to terms; and when that happens one forgets too easily the marvellous skills and devoted care that generally characterise the practice of medicine. But this is not a textbook on psychology; I merely suggest an explanation for the fascination that lawsuits against the medical profession have for the ordinary member of the public and for the almost emotional response that they can arouse in lawyer and non-lawyer alike.

THE GROWTH OF LITIGATION

According to a recent authority, Professor Robert Dingwall,[1] assertions of a litigation crisis have been vastly exaggerated. He says there was a sharp increase in the number and size, hence in the cost of settlement, of medical claims during the 1980s, but this levelled off in about 1987 after something like a five-fold increase in the number of claims and a three-fold increase in average size over the previous 5–7 years. Thereafter the rate of increase in both size and number substantially diminished. The rate of claims in 1990–1 was 12.11 per 100,000 of population, compared with a US rate in excess of 30 per 100,000. Only 20–25% of claims (about 1,600 a year in England) result in any payment, with an average closure cost of about £30,000. So the total bill is about £50 million, to be compared with the operating cost of the NHS of about £15.5 billion.

None of this looks like a litigation crisis. True, insurance premiums for doctors rose exponentially in earlier years (some 2,700% between 1978 and 1988), but so did the premiums for other professions, barristers for example. With the introduction of Crown indemnity the medical protection societies have been

---

[1] *Challenging Medicine* (Routledge 1994), pp. 46 *et seq.*

relieved from contributing to damages awarded in respect of mismanagement by a hospital doctor, and so premiums have assumed less demanding proportions. Hospital doctors are only required to subscribe a basic sum towards the advisory facilities provided, while GPs, who still require to be fully indemnified, pay subscriptions fixed at a level that reflects the likely cost of any defence.

The amount of compensation awarded has been increasing significantly, though again nowhere near the figures regularly awarded by American juries.[2] Here the highest award in 1983 was £270,000; it is now nearly £3.5m, but awards over £2m are still very rare.

We can briefly summarise recent awards since the first edition of this book. The award exceeding three-quarters of a million pounds is common (it matters not for present purposes whether the accident is due to medical negligence or some other form of negligence such as bad driving or unsafe industrial practices, for the injuries caused are going to be commensurable in gravity and the compensation for them is going to be calculated in the same way). In July 1987 the psychological barrier of the £1m mark was crashed by Hirst J. who awarded £1,032,000 to a gifted student who at the age of 19 was reduced by a medical blunder to a sub-human zombie-like existence (*Abdul-Hosn* v. *Italian Hospital Trustees* (1987) PMILL Vol. 3 No. 7). In April 1990 Nicholas Almond received what were then record damages for medical negligence, namely £1,156,348 for cerebral palsy sustained through negligent care at his birth in 1980 (reported at [1990] 1 Med LR 370). On 27 July 1990 former airline pilot, John Lambert, aged 42, was awarded £1,571,282 against Devon County Council for injuries suffered in April 1981 when his motorbike went out of control on an inadequately maintained road-surface (life expectation was only 20 years, so it seemed clear one could expect much higher awards where the life expectancy of the injured person was longer). On 22 December 1990 Hugo Cassel achieved a new record amount of damages for medical negligence, £1,198,110, having been born severely handicapped due to perinatal hypoxia in September 1982 ([1992] PIQR Q168).

At this point the recording and comparison of awards became confused by the structured settlement (as to which see Chapter 27). Newspapers tended to give (only) the figure that was got by adding up all the payments the plaintiff would receive over her lifetime, which is not proper accounting practice (!) and of course

---

[2] See below under 'The USA'.

produces a far higher figure than the actual quantum assessed for the injury. Thus to report that Heidi Everett, a teenage road-crash victim, was awarded £8.9m in June 1991 can mislead unless one adds that the quantum as a lump sum award, i.e. by the conventional method of assessment, was £981,000. This misleading way of reporting appears to have stopped – largely, perhaps, due to the fact that structured settlements are not currently in favour (they are not very attractive in periods of low interest rates).

Rebecca Field, aged six, who was left brain-damaged and paralysed by perinatal trauma, was offered £1.7m by the health authority in June 1991, the case then being adjourned for the creation of a structured settlement. This, the highest award then for medical negligence and the first structured settlement in a medical negligence action, was reported as worth £100m if Rebecca lived to 76! In December 1991, 30-year-old Alan Tombs obtained a settlement of £1.65m – he suffered catastrophic brain damage through an anesthetic error during a minor operation for hemorrhoids.

In March 1994 Christine Leung was awarded a record lump sum of £3.4m for catastrophic injuries received in a traffic accident in 1989. She had been a high earner with a bright future and was now paralysed from the waist down and was in need of 24-hour care from two attendants. In October 1994 Richard Miles, aged 14, was awarded nearly £2m for perinatal brain damage.

Large awards against doctors inevitably led, as we have seen, to large increases in insurance premiums; large awards against health authorities or hospitals lead to a substantial reduction in the amount of money available to provide health care in the area. The secretary of a medical defence society said after the *Abdul-Hosn* award that, if a health authority should have to pay, say, half of the amount, it could well lead to the closing of a ward. He also said that the financial pressure on the NHS meant that patients perceived themselves now as getting less than optimum care – fewer doctors and nurses looking after them, worse food, too early discharge – and to blame also for the increase in litigation were the long hours worked by junior doctors without adequate senior cover in positions to which their experience did not yet fit them. In *M. (a minor)* v. *Newham London Borough Council* [1994] 2 WLR 554 Staughton L.J. said that the danger of overkill was very important in medical negligence cases, and that high standards of duty and vast awards of damages resulted in unnecessary tests and other procedures at great expense.

It is still too early to know how the introduction of Crown indemnity will affect the overall picture, that is to say what financial or social effects it will have. The possible effects are dealt with in Chapter 22. It may be that the financial burden now falling on the shoulders of the under-funded health authorities and hospitals in respect of mistakes by their doctors (when before the medical protection societies would have paid half the damages) will force some sort of insurance scheme to be introduced (see Stop Press p. 15). It may even be used, amid closures of wards and cutbacks in facilities, as an argument for abolishing a patient's right to sue and creating a no-fault scheme (see Chapter 30).

THE TRADITIONAL VIEW

As long ago as 1953 an English judge said:

It is the duty of a doctor to exercise reasonable skill and care, but a simple mistake in diagnosis or treatment is not of itself negligence. The court is not bound to shut its eyes to the fact that there are quite a few cases at the present time in which doctors are sued for negligence. That may arise from the changing relationship between doctor and patient, but it matters not. There is a considerable onus on the court to see that persons do not easily obtain damages simply because there is some medical or surgical mistake made. But the court will not shrink from facing the issue if it finds that the doctor has failed to give to a case the proper skill and care which patients have a right to expect (*per* Finnemore J. in *Edler* v. *Greenwich and Deptford Hospital Management Committee, The Times*, 7 March 1953).

That represents the traditional view: insistence that medical mistakes do not necessarily involve negligence, regardless of the consequences (but why not?), and a friendly nod in the direction of the patient.

GROWING PUBLIC AWARENESS

Certain it is that over the last few years the patient has become increasingly willing to scrutinise her position with an eye to her legal rights and the possibility of legal action. She no longer regards the doctor as beyond criticism. A shift in the public consciousness of this sort, a greater awareness of the patient's rights to proper standards of treatment, leads to an increase in litigation, and the litigation in its turn heightens public awareness. But it should not be thought that the patient's growing desire to be treated like a responsible adult, to be listened to and consulted and given full explanation, must always or even mostly lead to litigation. As we see in Chapter 4, her real objective in many cases is for a sympathetic account and explanation of what has happened and what has gone or may go wrong. If the medical profession as a whole had understood that basic fact sooner and devoted a little more time to explanation and reassurance instead of attempting, as so often, to fob off a distressed patient with a short letter from the hospital administrator, they would have found themselves with far fewer claims on their hands. It is only very recently that the medical protection societies have permitted their members to apologise when something goes wrong (one might have thought previously that being a doctor meant never having to say you're sorry) – though it is fair to recall here what one read in the annual report as long ago as 1985.

The Society and its sister organisations are often accused in the media of adopting defensive attitudes, of making obstinate denials of liability which fly in the face of reason, or of retreating behind walls of silence. Such comments are inaccurate and misleading. Members are encouraged to discuss as fully as possible problems that occur in clinical practice, with patients and their relatives. On such occasions discussions about fault or blame, which require cool, dispassionate analysis, are not appropriate but, by common consent, there is no place for secrecy. The Society does not encourage members to withhold objective factual information or expressions of sympathy.

And in their advice to members the MDU have repeatedly said:

When something has gone wrong in practice, explain the facts to the patient, parent or relative and strive to rectify the problem sympathetically –

adding that 'care, communication and courtesy are all-important'. The Medical Protection Society advises its members that they:

. . . advocate a policy of full and proper communication with patients. In circumstances where errors and complications arise it is proper that objective, factual information with appropriate clinical reassurance, is provided. Adequate explanations, ideally from the responsible consultant or principal, assist in reducing fear and uncertainty which may give rise to complaints and claims . . .

And:

Be ready and willing to provide factual information and appropriate assurance and guidance to patients at all times, but do not admit *legal* liability without reference to the Society.

It may also be that, following from the Hospital Complaints Procedure Act 1985 and the Wilson Committee review, the new complaint procedures (see Chapter 4) will result in satisfaction being given more often than before (where, that is, satisfaction rather than compensation is the objective), though it is rather the initial, informal stage, where the patient first pens his cry of distress to the hospital, that calls for the sensitive response which could avert the threat of litigation (see p. 15 Stop Press).

TEXTBOOKS

This is what I wrote at the end of 1986 for the first edition:

The lack of books on this branch of the law is strange. For American lawyers there are many. For us, at the time of writing, none. In so far as medical negligence is treated at all it is given the odd few sections in books on professional or general negligence; and there the treatment is usually highly academic, with references to assault and battery and cases in obscure US courts.[3] But the medical negligence action has many special characteristics and should not be approached as if it were just another negligence suit. It can go very wrong. The opponents are usually tough and experienced, particularly if a medical protection society is involved, and the solicitor inexperienced in medical negligence work can find himself, and his client, very much at a disadvantage. One of the reasons that these cases can take so long to come on for trial is that the solicitor does not feel confident about them and so tends to drag his feet; another is that they are difficult to prepare, particularly as regards securing appropriate expert evidence; they are also in any event likely to be complex.

But now I can write somewhat differently. The rate at which this field of law is growing and changing is reflected in this as in so many other areas: the position has now altered. We now have Powers and Harris on *Medical Negligence* (in its second edition), Nelson-Jones and Burton on *Medical Negligence Case Law* (second edition 1995), books on the subject by academic writers such as Michael Jones and Ian Kennedy, and a more practical guide by lawyers Stephen Irwin, Claire Fazan and Richard Allfrey. In addition there are the indispensable Medical Law Reports and the *Medical and Legal Journal* published by Action for Victims of Medical Accidents (now incorporated in *Clinical Risk*).

The expertise among plaintiffs' solicitors has grown also, and vastly, so that many are more than a match for the other side. There is therefore now less and less excuse (if there ever were any) for not knowing the ropes inside and out. The all too familiar horror stories of yore, involving incompetent solicitors ruining potential claims, are far less frequent now, and their final relegation to the realm of mythology may well be achieved by the new Law Society medical negligence panel.

SECURING A BALANCE

The balance of power between doctor and patient needed to be redressed. The work of groups such as Action for Victims of

---

[3] Lord Nathan's well-known volume is now completely outdated, so that there is only the odd chapter in general works on the law relating to the practice of medicine. True, one can read with profit books such as *The Doctor and Negligence* by Leahy Taylor, *Medical Malpractice*, which Dr Taylor edited, and the stimulating recent volume, *Mishap or Malpractice* by Clifford Hawkins, but these are written more from the medical than the legal angle, are produced for the doctor, not for the plaintiff, and do not aim to be legal guides to the medical negligence action.

Medical Accidents (AVMA) has helped to do this. Perhaps this book has helped in a small way. The medical profession should be no less answerable for the way in which it offers and performs its services to the public than any other profession. But a correct balance needs to be struck. A finding of negligence should not lightly be made against a professional person, particularly where his profession is not only by its inherent nature dedicated to the benefit of mankind (we cannot easily say that about lawyers!), but furnishes us constantly with evidence that such dedication is not merely theoretical.

THE USA

We certainly do not wish to imitate the extremes of some US jurisdictions, where legislation has been introduced to control the size of awards, and some physicians have found it impossible, or at any rate unattractive, to continue in practice. But for my part I do not think there is the slightest chance of that. Awards in America are large and frequent for a number of reasons that do not apply here.

Juries

The main reason is that they have juries.[4] Juries are prone to find for the plaintiff wherever possible, and to leave the insurers to

---

[4] The English litigant in a personal injury action is entitled to apply for jury trial under s.6(1) of the Administration of Justice (Miscellaneous Provisions) Act 1933 and RSC O.33 r.5(1) (but now see Supreme Court Act 1981 s.69), but the effect of this provision has been nullified by the decision of the Court of Appeal in *Ward* v. *James* [1966] 1 QB 273, to the effect that juries may be ordered only in exceptional cases, and the severity of the injuries suffered does not render a case exceptional. This ruling was based on the need to preserve some sort of reasonably uniform tariff for compensation, which trial by jury clearly would not. An example of an 'exceptional' case is *Hodges* v. *Harland & Wolff Ltd* [1965] 1 WLR 523, where the plaintiff's penis had been torn off by a revolving spindle (though it is hard to see why a jury would be better suited to decide liability or quantum in such a case than a judge). The High Court refused a jury trial on 18 July 1989 in an action by a retarded girl arising out of alleged unlawful sexual intercourse by her instructor, employed by the local authority defendants. Jury trial was sought unsuccessfully on a claim seeking damages for nervous shock, including aggravated and exemplary damages, arising out of the King's Cross underground fire (*Singh* v. *London Underground, The Independent*, 25 April 1990), the main factor influencing the judge's decision being the complex technical nature of some of the issues involved. The Court of Appeal refused jury trial in the case of *H* v. *Ministry of Defence* [1991] 2 QB 103 where it was alleged medical negligence had resulted in amputation of the plaintiff's penis, and the House of Lords refused leave to appeal. The Court of Appeal added that a jury trial might be ordered in a personal injury action where exemplary damages could be an issue, e.g. if the defendants might be found to have deliberately abused a position of power or authority. It is of course absurd that juries still assess damages in some other actions such as libel, where damage to a reputation receives compensation many times higher than personal injury.

pick up the bill; and also to award very large sums,[5] which strike our conservative minds as indefensibly high (they are aware that a large part of the damages goes to the plaintiff's lawyer). The power of the trial judge to interfere on liability is very limited, and though on the whole he has a general discretion to reduce the damages awarded that will usually lead to an appeal and is not frequently exercised.[6] Our judges, on the other hand, will only find for the plaintiff where professional negligence is clearly proved – and, as we all know, it is a hard matter to get the evidence to establish that; and furthermore our courts are singularly parsimonious in awarding compensation – at any rate for the general head of pain and suffering and loss of amenity. Where the man in the street might wish to award half a million pounds for a catastrophic injury, the judicial tariff is much more likely to be not much more than a hundred thousand. It is true that our maximum total award now not infrequently exceeds £1m, but that is after taking into account the other heads of damage such as cost of care, new home, loss of earnings over a lifetime etc. The maximum currently for pain, suffering and loss of amenity for catastrophic injuries is less than £130,000. I do not therefore see any great danger to society in the current growth of claims against the medical profession. I do not envisage them, or any part of them, being forced out of business, nor even forced into defensive medicine out of fear of potential lawsuits if they do not cover themselves for every possible test and every possible diagnosis. Their defence against extravagant and unjustified

---

[5] These sums will often include aggravated or exemplary (i.e. punitive) damages, which have no place in medical negligence actions in this country (see *Barbara* v. *Home Office* (1984) 134 NLF 888; *G.* v. *North Tees Health Authority* [1989] FCR 53, N-J & B; *Kralj* v. *McGrath* [1986] 1 All ER 54). In *H.* v. *Ministry of Defence* (*supra*) the Court of Appeal did suggest that exemplary damages might be awarded if the defendants had abused their authority. In *AB* v. *South West Water Services Ltd* [1993] 2 WLR 507 the Court of Appeal, rejecting a claim for exemplary or aggravated damages where the cause of action lay in public nuisance, emphasised the narrow ambit of such a claim as laid down by the House of Lords in the two leading cases of *Rookes* v. *Barnard* [1964] AC 1129 and *Broome* v. *Cassell and Co* [1972] AC 1027 (only relevant for torts where the claim had already been recognised before 1964 and only available where there had been oppressive conduct by the executive or similar body, or the defendant had sought to make a profit from his wrongdoing).

In *Daley* v. *Ramdath, The Times*, 21 January 1993, the Court of Appeal held that in a case of unlawful eviction exemplary damages could not be ordered against a defendant acting as the landlord's agent unless it was established that he himself stood to benefit from the eviction.

In *Treadaway* v. *Chief Constable of the West Midlands, The Independent*, 23 September 1994, where the plaintiff had been, in effect, deliberately tortured by the police when in custody, McKinnon J., assessing compensatory damages for personal injury at £2,500, awarded in addition aggravated damages of £7,500 and exemplary damages of £40,000.

[6] At the same time it can be said that the more extravagant awards are usually trimmed if appealed, though still leaving sums vast by our standards.

claims lies in the good sense of our judges. In 1987 a middle-aged woman who lost both her breasts through unnecessary surgery after an admittedly negligent diagnosis of cancer was awarded for the pain and suffering of a number of operations and for loss of amenity, i.e. for the actual loss of her breasts, £25,000 (*Vaughan* v. *Paddington & N. Kensington Area Health Authority* (1987) PMILL Vol. 3 No. 9). We might expect an American jury to have awarded at least a million dollars. In *Bagley* v. *North Herts Health Authority* (1986) 136 NLJ 1014 a woman who gave birth to a still-born child instead of a living one due to the defendants' failure of medical care was awarded only £18,000 for loss of satisfaction in bringing her pregnancy to a successful conclusion, and the physical loss of the child, and illness and suffering caused by the loss of the child. Another million dollars, at least? Loss of the ability to have children for a young woman is worth only about £25,000 here (see *Morgan* v. *Gwent Health Authority* [1987] CA transcript 8 December, [1988] 2 *The Lancet* 519); one can only guess at the astronomical sum that would fetch over there.

A US plaintiff aged 61 was awarded over $8m for the death from Opren of his 82-year-old mother – most UK plaintiffs have accepted settlements averaging about £2,500. In 1989 one US plaintiff was awarded $76m for health problems caused by asbestos exposure, an 11-year-old quadriplegic was awarded $30m, and a plaintiff who lost both legs $58m. As Michael Ogden QC wrote in *The Times* for 5 June 1990: 'Even allowing for contingency fees for the lawyers of perhaps 30 to 40% the victim in each case was left with a sum which in England would be a dream.' The average award in the United States in 1975 was $494,000; ten years later it was $1,850,000. In 1987 a jury awarded $95m to a child born with deformed arms, allegedly due to Debendox, the morning sickness drug, of which $20m was compensation and $75m punitive damages (this last element was deleted on appeal). Other Debendox awards in different States have ranged from $160,000 to $1m, for fairly similar injuries. In October 1991 a US jury awarded parents of a child born handicapped through the mother's use of the anti-nausea drug Benedictin during pregnancy $33.8m, of which $30m was punitive damages. In November 1991 a US jury awarded $127m damages, of which $124m was punitive, against the pharmaceuticals manufacturer Upjohn for failing to warn the medical profession about improper use of the anti-inflammatory drug Depo-Medrol. As already noted, many of the very high awards are reduced on appeal (though they still remain astronomical by our standards). Recently the family of a teenager who had been killed as a result of a design fault in a lorry was awarded $73m; and a mother and baby crippled when hit by a police car were awarded $67m. And, to really enter the realms of farce, a sexually harassed secretary was awarded over $7m dollars by a Californian jury, all but $50,000 of which was punitive damages.

American jurisprudence

Another important reason is the adventurous and innovative ethos of American jurisprudence. Their law admits all sorts of claims and recognises all sorts of duty situations which to the conservative English mind are little short of bizarre: for example, the imposition of a duty of care owed by the management and staff of a restaurant to users of the highway not to permit an intoxicated guest to drive away, so that a person injured by the careless driving of the diner will have a claim against the restaurant (this duty is even owed by your host at a private party!). Lovers sue each other over the transmission of infections.[7] A motel chain must compensate a female guest who is raped, on the ground that their locks were not strong enough (haven't they heard of *novus actus*?). A Californian court has imposed a duty on a psychotherapist to warn not only the police but also the intended victim when his patient utters death threats against her, and a duty on a hospital to report to the appropriate agency signs in a child patient of the battered child syndrome, so as to make the hospital liable to the child when she returns home to a beating (*Tarasoff* v. *Regents of the University of California* 551 P (2d) 334 (Cal. 1976), *Landeros* v. *Flood* 551 P (2d) 389 (Cal. 1976)).[8] In March 1987 a Californian court ordered an

---

[7] *R.* v. *Clarence* (1897) 22 QBD 23 involved an unsuccessful prosecution of a husband under the Offences against the Person Act 1861 for transmitting gonorrhoea to his wife. It was held that as she had consented to intercourse, albeit in ignorance of his ailment, of which he himself was well aware, the necessary assault had not taken place. The matrimonial offence of cruelty has in the past been adjudged proved in a number of cases by the insistence on sexual intercourse by a husband who knew he was infected. In *Hegarty* v. *Shine* (1878) 14 Cox CC 124 an action by a woman against her lover for infecting her with a venereal disease was held inadmissible, but only on the ground of *ex turpi causa non oritur actio* (see also *Hales* v. *Kerr* [1908] 2 KB 601).

[8] However, the US Court of Appeal, 7th Circuit, robustly rejected a claim by a boy, who had been seriously injured by his father, against the local authority for failing to protect him. The court stated: 'To place every state welfare department on the razor's edge where, if it terminates parental rights, it is exposed to suit by the parent and if it fails to terminate those rights it is exposed to a suit by the child, is unlikely to improve the welfare of American families and is not grounded in constitutional text or principle'. One would expect English law to impose a duty of care on the local authority in such circumstances and to award damages if negligence in the ordinary sense was proved.

On the other hand, it was reported in June 1991 that a health authority had settled for £45,000 an action in which the plaintiff alleged that they had contributed to his killing of his mother by turning him away from their hospital shortly before the murder as they did not have a psychiatrist available, a result described by a Conservative M.P. as 'ludicrous'.

American construction company to pay compensation to an employee after he had contracted AIDS in Zaire from a prostitute supposedly supplied to him by the company. A US plaintiff was awarded $1m by a Philadelphia jury as damages for the failure of her doctor to tell her that a CT scan might harm her psychic powers. A Kentucky woman serving a 20-year sentence for suffocating her nine-month-old daughter sued her psychiatrist for failing to stop her. A Massachusetts jury awarded $750,000 for a doctor's failure to diagnose AIDS in a young woman (it was not suggested he could have altered the course of the disease). Half a million dollars was awarded to the wife of a man who contracted AIDS through a blood transfusion, to compensate her for the loss of sexual relations. The English press widely reported in August 1994 the award of some $2.7m against McDonald's to a woman who was scalded when a take-away cup of coffee spilt over her legs (it appears she had placed the cup between her knees when travelling in a car). Presumably liability was found on the basis that, whatever the woman had done with the cup or should be presumed to know about hot cups of coffee, McDonald's had not lidded it securely enough! The award was cut on appeal to a paltry $480,000.

Such claims would be most unlikely to succeed in an English court. The judge would say that there was no duty owed to the plaintiff or that the damage was too remote, or find some similar legal peg on which to hang his rejection of a claim that he, brought up in the conservative (but not necessarily for that reason admirable) traditions of the English law, found outlandish. In this way the unrestrained enlargement of the tort of negligence is prevented. True, it has widened over the years, but gradually and not dramatically. Witness the brakes recently put by the House of Lords on the widening process that seemed to be under way as a result of the principle enunciated by Lord Wilberforce in *Anns* v. *Merton London Borough Council* [1978] AC 728 (see Chapter 15).

The contingency fee

Another reason why American awards are so high is the contingency fee system, whereby the lawyer is paid a proportion of the damages he recovers. He therefore has an interest in pressing for large awards and not settling until the steps of the courthouse, where the sums offered are likely to be at their zenith.

So for all these reasons we should not lightly accept any contentions from lobbyists who urge us to create public funded compensation schemes for victims of medical accidents on the basis that, unless we do, the practice of medicine, as we know it, will grind to a halt.

Is there a crisis in the USA?

In any event we should not exaggerate the dangers of the American position. Most doctors do very well there, despite the insurance premiums. The Association of American Trial Lawyers deny that there is any current emergency. They say that the crisis was caused in the 1970s when most insurers stopped offering physicians cover, which left the field open to one particular company to charge wildly excessive premiums, and that subsequent legislation ensured that about 80% of medical negligence claims failed. This legislation, enacted in some States, was designed to reduce the opportunities for judicial activism, to discourage the presentation of claims lacking merit, and to help the insurers by killing stale claims with short limitation periods. But although this had some effect, it did not last. Between 1975 and 1983 the number of malpractice claims per doctor tripled. Now it is thought by some that a second crisis is imminent. Lawyers and doctors are at odds. They each maintain registers, revealing for the benefit of doctors which prospective new patient has presented a previous medical malpractice action and, for the patient, what proposed defendant has been sued before. There is a popular car sticker: 'Support a lawyer. Send your child to medical school.'

But some argue that the crisis scenario is generated by the health industry for its own ends. When, for example, it was publicised that the average jury award in the US medical malpractice action was over $1m, it was fairly enough pointed out that that statistic ignored the cases that had settled and usually settled for far less (remember that there is no incentive under the contingency fee system to take a smaller case all the way to the court room), and that, what is more, it did not take into account the 50% and more of cases filed that resulted in no award at all, by reason of defeat or discontinuance. Again, though it is true that over the years 1976–84 the average insurance premium for a physician doubled (at a time of low inflation), his average earnings more than doubled, so that, as a proportion of gross income the premium went down from 4.4% to 4.2% (*Time*, 24 February 1986, p. 60). Nevertheless the health industry, i.e. the insurer's lobby, is powerful, and it continually ululates over rising premiums, defensive medicine and the imminent collapse of the medical services; and the current trend of reform is towards the containment of tort compensation to avoid 'damage to the body politic' (to borrow the striking phrase used by Lord Denning in the *Lim Poh* case [1979] QB 196).

Further differences

It is important to bear in mind, whenever transatlantic spectres are raised, that the whole ethos of litigation in the USA is worlds away from what we are used to. It may well be that an American trial lawyer would find the medical negligence suit as portrayed in the film *The Verdict* as unrealistic as we find many film and television depictions of the English legal system. In that film the hospital's attorney got a pretty employee of his firm to get into a relationship with the patient's attorney in order to spy on his preparation of the case, one result of which was that the plaintiff's medical expert was suborned. Attorney and judge conducted a slanging match in chambers, each threatening to see the other man 'finished' (it is perhaps not altogether easy to envisage that happening with a barrister and a High Court judge!). The judge was ludicrously biased in favour of the defendants, even to the point of refusing to admit as evidence a photocopy of a medical record that proved the 'original' had been altered, on the basis that where the court had the original there was no jurisdiction to admit a copy!

But, regardless of Hollywood licence, the differences between the system there and here are enormous. A textbook on one aspect of the personal injury claim (*Handling Soft Tissue Injury Cases*) was advertised with these words in a legal journal:

Winning . . . winning big, that's what *Handling Soft Tissue Cases* is all about. Taking the cases that other lawyers reject, lose or compromise short of an adequate award – and turning them into six figure settlements and verdicts for the injured and disabled – that's what the Preisers specialise in. And that's just what they'll show you how to do in this exciting, authoritative, new work.

That medical malpractice is big business is demonstrated, if demonstration were needed, by the fact that there exists a legal journal devoted solely to such litigation, *Medical Malpractice Verdicts, Settlements and Experts*, which, as well as reporting trial verdicts and settlements, lists with their speciality the medical experts who have testified, together with names of counsel, and also offers subscribers a database of pending cases for reference.

The press, understandably, highlight the exceptional stories: 25% of physicians in Florida stopped practising obstetrics because of the cost of insurance, one among them having to pay $84,000 a year, topped only by a New York neurosurgeon at $100,000. The American Medical Association campaigns, as I have said, for reform – limiting awards, proscribing punitive damages, modifying the contingency fee system, or shortening the limitation period.

It is not in any event the size of premiums that is important, but whether sufficient physicians are willing and able to practise despite the premium. That appears to be the case. In particular there is no shortage of physicians in the high-premium areas of

New York, New Jersey, Massachusetts and the District of Columbia, where the rate of physician per capita of the population is in fact higher than the national average.

CONCLUSION

Whatever the truth of the American medical malpractice 'crisis', for the reasons I have stated I do not apprehend any sort of similar position emerging here, and I urge caution in attempting to draw from the experience of a very different system conclusions which would be valid for us. Nor is it only their legal system that is a horse of a different colour. The world of American medicine, with its limited public medical care and its extremely high charges to the patient (charges that must be provided for, if possible, by private insurance), and the need to prove the physician himself liable rather than the hospital (because they do not have our law of accountability – see Chapter 22), combines to present a very different picture from the English scene. In point here are the words of the Canadian judge, Arnup J.A., in *Yepremian* v. *Scarborough General Hospital* (1980) 110 DLR (3d) 513. Rejecting the contention that a primary non-delegable duty of care should be imposed on a hospital in line with the English law, he said that great care had to be taken when considering the English cases as the interrelationship of the State, the medical profession, the hospitals and their patients had developed in England along different lines from those it had followed in Ontario. One does not need to be a sociologist to appreciate how much greater the difference would be if we read 'the USA' for 'Ontario'.

Nevertheless it is important to be aware of developments as they arise across the Atlantic over the coming years. Although it is certainly not a case of 'what America thinks today England thinks tomorrow', developments in transatlantic legal experience, procedure and jurisprudence will always provide us with food for thought.

STOP PRESS (ref pp. 5, 6)

The Department of Health is setting up a financial pooling scheme to spread the cost of compensation across NHS Trusts.

The special health authority to be set up to administer this scheme will also work to promote better claims handling by putting the stress on explanations and apologies to patients, quicker compensation in clear-cut cases of negligence and resolution of disputes through mediation.

2 · The structure of the book

SUMMARY

The book is in two main parts: first, procedure, which should help the patient to decide what he wants to do by way of seeking information or redress, and help the solicitor to conduct the action. The second part sets out the principles of negligence and rules for the recovery of damages which are relevant to a medical negligence action and refers them to the medical context wherever possible. The appendices contain useful legislation, some further information and a number of precedents.

The purpose of this book has always been to provide a practical guide to the pursuit of the medical negligence action. Even though far fewer lawyers are now substantially in need of advice as how to conduct a medical negligence action than when I wrote the first edition, experience suggests that advice on the finer points of procedure, and sometimes even on fundamental points, is likely still to be useful to a considerable number of practitioners. As for the law, it is thought that it remains useful, even to an experienced practitioner, to have the relevant law set out in a reasonably accessible way together with all the pertinent cases up to date.

In one sense the law takes a back seat to procedure. We all have a fairly good idea of the law of negligence, of the duty of care and foreseeability, and of quantum of damages. There are of course things to be said on the law, memories to be refreshed, grey areas to be explored, but by and large we all know that one needs above all a good expert witness to state, first in his report and then in court if necessary, that this or that aspect of the medical handling of the patient fell below accepted standards, and that through the failure to take the right action the patient ended up worse off than he would otherwise have been. But how to get to that stage in practice? How to start the ball rolling? What to do next? How to get the medical records? How to read them? How to select an expert? How to handle the legal aid side? How to get from the expert what you want to hear (where possible)? How to progress the case at all stages? In other words, how to run the action from the practical point of view? This needs experience; it cannot and should not be guessed at, if one is to avoid criticism.[1] So the book is intended in the first place to enable a patient to decide in what manner he wants to make his complaint (this will depend on whether he is basically looking for an explanation and a sympathetic hearing from the doctors or whether he is asking for or at any rate considering financial compensation), and then to select one of the courses of action that are open to him; and after that it is intended to assist the solicitor to whom the patient may have recourse in the preparation and pursuit of his case. For that reason procedure is allocated to the first part of the book and the law to the second. I have summarised the law in the opening paragraphs, so that only those who want to consider it in detail need go on to the explanatory and more digressive sections.

The first part of the book deals with the way to get a claim on its feet. It starts at the point where the patient feels dissatisfied with the medical treatment he has received, though he may not yet be able to say precisely what is troubling him. So the chapter on the initial complaint is written for and addressed to him. If he decides to seek financial compensation he must go to a solicitor. At that point the book turns to address the lawyer, though it remains, I hope, both intelligible and useful to the layman. Thereafter we look at the various stages in the preparation of the claim, concentrating on those that offer particular difficulty or require particular attention in the medical negligence suit. It is these stages that the solicitor needs to get right. Later he will have the assistance of counsel, who may perhaps also find useful what I have written. The second part of the book deals with the law. I have sought to avoid writing a general treatise on the law of negligence, but I have deliberately set out in each section by way of preliminary exposition the general principles, so that they may the more easily be referred where appropriate to our particular context. I have then selected particular aspects of the law that are likely to be relevant to our theme. Medical negligence is, after all, only negligence in the medical context.

I have made as few references as possible to cases decided in abstruse courts in foreign jurisdictions because, although that gives a (usually undeserved) impression of great learning acquired and research undertaken, your High Court judge is usually immune to the call of the Minnesota district court or the blandishments of the Alberta Court of Appeal (one only has to

---

[1] It is certainly not the same as running a personal injury action!

consider the almost contemptuous way Lord Diplock in the *Sidaway* case [1985] AC 871 dismissed the reasoning of the Supreme Court of Canada on the doctrine of informed consent to appreciate that I am not merely being flippant[2]) – though for some reason Australian judicial thought is usually accorded a degree of respect. Moreover, medical negligence actions are decided very much on the facts; the scope for usefully adducing English precedent is small, unless a legal principle is involved (which is not very often); the assistance that can be got from a perusal of the fact-situations which have given rise in foreign jurisdictions to medical liability is minimal.

I have deliberately included many quotations from the judgments in English cases. This is because it is there that one finds the *fons et origo*[3] of the common law. The expositions of the law in those judgments are not only the basis of the common law, and therefore the most authoritative statements of it (subject of course to contrary rulings in later cases), but are usually the most lucid and the best expressed that one can find. Many of our judges have been masters of the English language, or at any rate masters of the art of using it to express legal thought, to a degree which academic writers do not often achieve.

The concept, structure and writing (save for Chapter 8) of the book are my own. Therefore there is bound to be substantial scope for improvement, whether by way of addition, amendment or correction. I would welcome suggestions and would hope to include them in the fourth edition. In the first edition I bowed to convention, though somewhat reluctantly, in using the masculine form throughout when referring to a patient, or to a doctor for that matter, except in obviously unsuitable contexts such as obstetrics. I excused myself by saying that 's/he' was easy enough to type and to read, but the objective case raised problems. However, for the next edition I managed an intellectual leap and realised that I could simply, and relatively painlessly, replace some of the *he*s and *him*s with *she*s and *her*s.

Two last points: I have occasionally used the word 'physician' as Americans do, by way of elegant variation. It should of course be understood in its general and not its specialised sense. And I have declined to use the quaint and outdated ligature for e.g. fetal, hemorrhage, anesthetist, orthopedic.

---

[2] It was Lord Diplock, as legend has it, who during an appellate hearing in 1982 refused to look at a textbook on declaratory judgments by a leading Israeli professor of law, saying 'The author isn't even English'.

[3] For the benefit of a reviewer of the first edition, I translate this now as 'fount and source'.

3 · The structure of the National Health Service

It may be of interest, and even helpful (though it is not essential), when considering action against hospital or physician, to have some idea of the overall structure of the NHS. You don't want to be left wondering what has happened to the Area Health Authority, or, following its imminent demise, the Regional Health Authority, or whether you should sue Region or District or the governing body of a NHS Trust, or what indeed the meaning and function of the different levels of the Service are.

SUMMARY

Before 1982 there was a three-tier structure in the NHS: Region, Area and District (this last was not of statutory status). Now we have Region (for the time being) and District, but we also have NHS Trusts which are outside health authority control. Region is responsible to the Secretary of State and he to Parliament. His policy decisions are not subject to challenge in the courts (unless appearing clearly unreasonable). NHS Trusts are directly responsible to the Department of Health, of which the Secretary of State is the head. The NHS is a Crown service and its employees are Crown servants; although coercive orders and prosecutions do not lie against the Crown (unless specifically authorised by Parliament), this general rule has been abrogated by the NHS and Community Care Act 1990. Further substantial changes are in the offing.

ORIGINS

The NHS is a statutory creation. It came into force on 5 July 1948, by virtue of the National Health Service Act 1946, following from the Beveridge Report of 1942. It brought into being a social benefit unique in Europe. Its purpose was to provide free medical services wherever needed, nationalising the voluntary and the local authority hospitals, and achieving a more efficient distribution over the country of general practitioners, specialists, doctors and opticians.

The 1946 Act was an excellent start. But it needed in time to be amended and improved, particularly in respect of the division of management between local authorities and health authorities. So Parliament enacted the National Health Service Reorganisation Act of 1973, which came into force on 1 April 1974. All services where the main skill necessary was that of the health professions were placed under the control of the health authorities; local authorities (previously responsible for various specific health and care services) were left with those services of which the hallmark was care and support. The three levels of Region, Area and District were created. Various advisory committees were set up by the 1973 Act (they are still in existence), and both statutory health authorities and Family Practitioner Committees (now Family Health Services Authorities) are under a statutory duty to consult them. The Area Health Authorities were required to set up Family Practitioner Committees, which would make contracts for services with (but not 'employ') general practitioners, prepare lists of practitioners, pay them, and deal with complaints arising out of the performance of those contracts. The Act also created Community Health Councils (FHSAs and CHCs are considered in the next chapter). The district level was the operational level of the 1973 reorganisation. The Area Health Authority had a supervisory role; the district management team were the workers on the ground. The National Health Service Act 1977 consolidated this position.

This three-tier organisation, into Region, Area and District, was criticised from the outset, for over-administration and for delay in the provision of services to the consumer. As a result the Health Services Act 1980 was enacted, which gave the Secretary of State the power to make certain changes in the organisation of the NHS, principal among which was the abolition of the Area Health Authorities and the creation in their place, without loss of the operational role of the district management team, of a new statutory body, the District Health Authority. This was done by statutory instrument as from 1 April 1982.

Although the National Health Service and Community Care Act 1990 gives hospitals the right to opt out of health authority control and become self-governing trusts, this is more a matter of (hopefully) improved efficiency and economy within the NHS, for such units as opt out will nevertheless remain firmly within the framework of the NHS (see below). The new funding arrangements, which create the dichotomy between purchasers of health care (principally health authorities and GPs) and providers of health care (the hospitals), and which were designed to create a market economy in the field of care provision, do not directly affect the medical negligence scene; they are the subject of continual criticism, and may be abolished by a later government.

The names, boundaries and very existence of the District Health Authorities have been subject to constant change recently. The latest moves appear designed to facilitate the present government's intention to abolish the previous 14 regional health authorities (they are down to 8 already), merge FHSAs into health authorities, and create 'a central management structure which better serves the new NHS'. Thus will be created (in NHS-speak) 'a single authority at local level with responsibility for implementing national health policy, integrating purchasing across primary and secondary care boundaries'. Main revenue allocations to the new health authorities will be made direct from the Secretary of State. All this is, of course, dependent on the present government retaining power.[1]

AT GOVERNMENTAL LEVEL

The widest issues, including national health policies and the general organisation of the NHS, are decided by Parliament. The Secretary of State for Health is the cabinet-level minister who is in charge of health matters, assisted by a Minister of State for Health. The Secretary of State is in charge of the work of the Department of Health, which is responsible for central planning of the health services and for monitoring their performance.[2] Two select committees in Parliament deal with health matters – the Select Committee on Health and the Select Committee on the Parliamentary Commissioner for Administration, which examines the reports of the Ombudsman (see Chapter 4).

The Secretary of State has the basic responsibility for providing a national health service. Duties are imposed on him by the consolidating statute, the National Health Service Act 1977.

Section 1 imposes the duty to continue to promote a free, comprehensive health service designed to improve our physical and mental health and to improve the prevention, diagnosis and treatment of illness, and the Secretary of State has the duty to provide for that purpose services in accordance with the Act.

---

[1] If you wonder what became of the new NHS Management Executive the answer is that they decided that title was not user-friendly and so, at great public expense, the logo, letterheads and anything else displaying the offending word were changed.

[2] He is also Chairman of the NHS Policy Board (the other important organ is the NHS Executive chaired by the NHS Chief Executive). The Policy Board and the NHS Executive are intended to provide clear leadership of the NHS at the centre.

Section 2 gives him power to provide such services as he considers appropriate for the purposes of discharging any of his statutory duties, and to do anything calculated to facilitate, or conducive or incidental to, the discharge of any of his duties.

Section 3 imposes the particular duty to provide, to such extent as he considers necessary to meet all reasonable requirements:

(1) hospital accommodation;
(2) other accommodation for the purposes of any service provided under the Act;
(3) medical, dental, nursing and ambulance services;
(4) facilities for the care of expectant and nursing mothers and young children, such as he considers appropriate as part of the health service;
(5) facilities for the prevention of illness and the care and after-care of patients, such as he considers appropriate;
(6) such other services as are required for the diagnosis and treatment of illness.

Section 4 requires the Secretary of State to maintain special security hospitals for dangerous, violent or criminal patients. Section 5 requires him to arrange for medical and dental inspection and treatment of schoolchildren, and, in an unhappy juxtaposition, to provide advisory and medical services and appliances to those interested in contraception.

THE RECENT NHS CHANGES

The recent radical changes in the structure and management of the NHS are primarily a matter of re-allocation and redefinition of responsibilities. District Health Authorities no longer have the role of providers of services, but of purchasers. Responsibility for the funding and for the provision of services is being separated. The main function of the DHAs is to assess the health of the resident population, determine its health needs and purchase services to meet those needs. Responsibility for service provision increasingly rests with hospitals and other units. NHS contracts are negotiated between health authorities as purchasers of care and hospitals and units (including NHS Trusts) as providers of care. The funds allocated to the DHAs are now for the purchase, not the provision, of health care. The establishment of a funding system for hospitals in which money follows patients is intended to create a stronger incentive for hospitals to treat people as consumers and to agree contracts with purchasers.

The providers of services are the hospitals. It is intended that all hospitals will move gradually towards the status of NHS

Trusts. Until a hospital achieves that status it is a directly managed unit (DMU), still within the control of the DHA, who provide its services.

NHS Trusts are not within DHA (or RHA) control but are answerable to the Department of Health, remaining as they do within the NHS (a similar position to that already enjoyed by the special health authorities, e.g. those responsible for our main teaching hospitals). They are free to determine their own management structures, to employ their own staff and set their own terms and conditions of service, to acquire, own and sell their own assets, to retain surpluses, and to borrow money subject to annual limits. Each Trust is run by its own board of directors, independent of district and regional management. As Chris Ham says, 'The underlying aim of establishing Trusts is to improve the quality of care provided to patients by giving real power and responsibility to those people – managers, doctors, nurses and other staff – who work in the unit and by harnessing their skills and commitment for the benefit of patient care'.[3]

Even the directly managed unit enjoys greater autonomy, e.g. over operational decision-making – including probably personnel and financial matters and information services. 'Changes are being made to ensure that doctors and nurses take more control over the management of resources and greater responsibility for many of the day-to-day management processes'.[3]

Funding: RHAs are allocated resources by the Department of Health according to a formula based on the size, age and health of their resident populations. The RHAs have been funding the DHAs on the same basis when the latter's position as purchasers rather than providers of services has been consolidated. From April 1991 RHAs have also been responsible for funding FHSAs. Priority setting is, as we have seen, a subject which naturally arouses strong responses, especially from those whose legitimate needs are not given priority. As the 1979 Royal Commission Report on the NHS said:

The demand for health care is always likely to outstrip supply and the capacity of health services to absorb resources is almost unlimited. Choices have therefore to be made about the use of available funds and priorities have to be set.

Guidance is given to health authorities from time to time by the Department of Health in health circulars and executive letters from the NHS Executive, fundamental matters of policy having been decided at governmental level. As we see below, it is unlikely that the courts will accept a challenge to decisions of

[3] Chris Ham, *The New National Health Service*, published by NAHAT.

priority setting. Some current priorities are reduction in waiting lists, expansion of coronary artery bypass grafts, hip
replacements and cataract operations. It may be that in
deciding priorities more use will be made of the QALY (the
quality adjusted life year), which costs an operation or health
service in terms of the quality of each year of life achieved for
the patient.

Family Health Services Authorities come within the jurisdiction of their respective Regional (soon, District) Health Authority, whereas Family Practitioner Committees were responsible
directly to the Department of Health (note for a marvellous
example of bureaucratic mumbo-jumbo that GPs' budgets are
now called 'indicative prescribing amounts'). The key tasks of the
FHSAs are to assess the need for primary health care services of
their residents and ensure that these services are provided by
family doctors, dentists, pharmacists and opticians, and in so
doing they operate through the terms of the contracts negotiated
nationally with family practitioners. They discharge their responsibilities by visiting surgeries, approving the hours of contact with
patients, allocating funds for the employment of practice staff and
the improvement of doctors' premises, ensuring that those providing specialist services (such as minor surgery) have the necessary experience, training and facilities, approving and monitoring
the use of deputising services, providing information to the
public, carrying out consumer surveys and hearing patient
complaints.

SUING THE MINISTER

The question has arisen to what extent a member of the public,
dissatisfied with the manner in which the Secretary of State is
carrying out his statutory duties, can make him accountable in
the courts. In R. v. *Secretary of State for Social Services, ex
parte Hincks* (1979) 123 SJ 436, four orthopedic patients at a
Birmingham hospital, who were being obliged to wait longer
than was medically advisable for treatment because of a
shortage of facilities due in part to a policy decision not to
build a new hospital block for economic reasons, applied for
declarations against the Minister, and Regional and Area
Health Authorities, that the statutory duties imposed by ss.1
and 3 had not been discharged. The patients needed to
establish in the first place that they had a *locus standi* to bring
the action; if they had, they asked for a declaration that the
authorities were in breach of their statutory duties, and they
sought both an order requiring them to perform their duties,

and also damages for the pain and suffering caused to them by the delay in treatment. They failed. Wien J. said that the Minister's duty was to provide such services as he considered necessary and that such a wording gave him a discretion as to how financial resources were to be used. If there was not enough money then all needs could not be met. In those circumstances it was impossible to say that the Minister, or any other body, was in breach of statutory duty. The court would only interfere where the Minister had acted as no reasonable Minister could possibly act, or had acted so as to frustrate the policy of the Act. Nor did he take the view that the Act gave any right of action to the individual patient to sue in respect of an alleged breach of the Minister's general duties.

The Court of Appeal agreed with the trial judge, and Bridge L.J. pointed out that the Minister must be entitled to make policy decisions about the allocation of financial resources in the light of overall long-term planning or he would be called upon to disburse funds that were not in fact available.

In *Department of Health and Social Security* v. *Kinnear* (1984) 134 NLJ 886, sufferers from the whooping cough vaccine brought an action against the Department in relation to the manner of promoting the vaccine. Stuart-Smith J. struck out their claim in so far as it involved an attack on the exercise by the Department under s.26 of the National Health Service Act 1946 of their discretion as to whether arrangements should be made for immunisation against such a disease. The judge said that it was in the *bona fide* exercise of that discretion that the department had adopted a policy of promoting immunisation against whooping cough. That policy, being within the limits of the discretion and the result of its *bona fide* exercise, could not give rise to a cause of action (though one may note that that part of the claim that regarded actions of an operational rather than a policy nature, allegations *inter alia* that negligent or misleading advice had been given by the Department as to the manner and circumstances in which immunisations were to be performed, was not struck out).

The *Kinnear* decision was followed in part in the Scottish Court of Session in *Ross* v. *Secretary of State for Scotland* [1990] 1 MLR 235, where a pursuer's direct case against the Scottish Home and Health Department alleging that she suffered brain damage as a result of being vaccinated against smallpox was dismissed because it was based on considerations of ministerial policy and matters of discretion and was, therefore, irrelevant in the absence of averments of bad faith. The *Kinnear* decision was distinguished in part in that the judge,

Lord Milligan, said that that part of the *Kinnear* claim that was permitted to proceed appeared to be of an 'operational' nature and so not of assistance in his case. A similar decision on the main issue had been reached by Lord Grive in the Scottish case of *Bonthrone* v. *Secretary of State for Scotland* 1987 SLT 34, where the pursuer's claim for injury allegedly sustained as a result of vaccination against whooping cough, diphtheria and tetanus without there having been given adequate warning of the risk of encephalopathy or other side effects had been struck out as attacking the ambit of exercise of a discretion rather than action taken to implement a discretionary decision.

In *Re HIV Hemophiliac Litigation, The Independent*, 2 October 1990, Ralph Gibson L.J. said that in appropriate circumstances a duty of care might be imposed in regard to the discharge of functions under the Act of 1977.

In *R.* v. *Central Birmingham Health Authority, ex parte Walker, The Independent*, 26 November 1987, an unsuccessful application was made for judicial review of the health authority's decision that, although it was agreed that baby Walker needed a certain operation, it could not carry it out at that time for resource reasons. The Master of the Rolls said:

It is not for this court, or indeed any court, to substitute its own judgment for the judgment of those who are responsible for the allocation of resources. This court could only intervene where it was satisfied that there was a prima facie case, not only of failing to allocate resources in the way in which others think that resources should be allocated, but of a failure to allocate resources to an extent which was 'Wednesbury unreasonable', to use the lawyers' jargon, or, in simpler words, which involves a breach of a public law duty. Even then, of course, the court has to exercise a judicial discretion. It has to take account of all the circumstances of the particular case with which it is concerned.

(Under the well-established 'Wednesbury' principle the court will only intervene if it is shown that the decision taken was one which no reasonable body could have arrived at if it had been taking into account all relevant matters – in other words, the decision must be shown to be irrational (see *Associated Provincial Picture Houses* v. *Wednesbury Corporation* [1948] 1 KB 223).)

In another case against the same health authority less than two months later the father of four-year-old Matthew Collier failed to persuade the Court of Appeal to intervene where desperately needed open-heart surgery was delayed for months, even though Matthew had been placed at the top of the waiting list, due to shortage of intensive care beds and nurses. The court said that there was no evidence that the health authority had acted unreasonably or in breach of any public duty (*R.* v. *Central*

Birmingham Health Authority, ex parte Collier [1988] CA transcript 6 January).[4]

In *R.* v. *North West Thames Regional Health Authority, ex parte Daniels, The Times,* 22 June 1993, the Divisional Court, despite sympathising with the predicament of the boy, Rhys Daniels, and actually finding that the District Health Authority had failed, contrary to Regulation 19(1) of the NHS (Community Health Council) Regulations (SI 1985/304), to consult the community health council before closing the bone marrow unit at Westminster Children's Hospital, was, predictably, unwilling to order the reopening of the unit because making an order would not benefit the boy. The court said it was sure that the unit at Bristol would do all it could. And indeed one understands that the proceedings had the useful effect of getting the NHS to ensure that appropriate treatment was speedily made available.

In *Seale* v. *Sheffield Health Authority,* 17 October 1994, unreported, Auld J. held that it was not unreasonable for the health authority to limit IVF treatment to women between the ages of 25 and 35 in view of their limited budget. He said that although they had undertaken to provide such treatment for patients within their area, that did not mean they were bound to provide the service on demand and regardless of financial and other concerns. And on the fringe of this 'resource' question we can note *R.* v. *Secretary of State for Health, ex parte Keen* [1990] 1 Med LR 455 where Professor Keen, director of the Unit for Metabolic Medicine and director of Clinical Services/Medicine at Guy's failed in an application for judicial review of the expenditure of resources on the preparation, before the National Health Care and Community Service Bill became law, for a change of the hospital's status to that of a self-governing NHS Trust.

We may also note in this connection *Wilsher* v. *Essex Area Health Authority* [1987] 2 WLR 425 which is authority for the proposition that the employment through lack of funds of relatively inexperienced young doctors in responsible positions does not reduce the level of the standard of care which the patient has

---

[4] Reference may also be made to *R.* v. *Hillingdon Area Health Authority, ex parte Wyatt* (1978) 76 LGR 727, where it was held that as provisions in the Chronically Sick and Disabled Persons Act 1970 gave default powers over the health authority to the Minister that precluded the remedy sought from the courts.

In *R.* v. *ILEA, ex parte F, The Times,* 28 November 1988, the Court of Appeal declined to review a consultant psychiatrist's decision to transfer a patient. In *R.* v. *Ealing District Health Authority, ex parte F* (1992) 11 BMLR 59 the court made it clear that it would not compel psychiatric supervision of a patient.

In *X.* v. *A, B and C* (1991) 9 BMLR 91 the court declined to order treatment requested by a pedophile, stating that wrongful acts within the context of public law afforded no remedy to the individual.

a right to expect. And even though the Secretary of State would not himself be responsible, it appears from the judgments of Glidewell L.J. and Sir Nicolas Browne-Wilkinson V.C. that in an appropriate case a hospital management committee might be itself directly liable in negligence for failing to provide sufficient qualified and competent medical staff, it being said that there was no reason in principle why a health authority should not be liable if its organisation were at fault in that way.[5] Consider *Bull and Wakeham* v. *Devon Health Authority* [1993] 4 Med LR 117 where the Court of Appeal, upholding the judge's decision in favour of the plaintiff, said that the system of obstetric cover provided by the hospital had given rise to a real inherent risk that an obstetrician might not attend reasonably promptly. What if the hospital had alleged that its budget could not cover any better system?

This whole question of the allocation of resources, whether at ministerial, health authority or, under the NHS etc. Act 1990, self-governing hospital level, is likely to assume increasing importance as funds get tighter. Who is to say whether it is 'worth it' to purchase expensive new dialysis machines when the money could be used far more cost effectively for more hip or shoulder replacement operations? Do we consider the quality of life that is offered by the competing operations?[6] Is 'glamorous' heart surgery of any real benefit, or at any rate sufficiently worthwhile when you consider what it has actually achieved in terms of quality and number of the 'extra' months or years afforded, that it can justify (usually under pressure from an influential unit and a charismatic consultant) pushing other more mundane treatments out of the way? I suppose one's view depends on whether it is you (or your loved one) or someone else who needs the expensive treatment.

As we went to press the case was reported of the 10-year-old girl with fatal leukemia whose father sued the health authority for refusing to fund expensive, dangerous and experimental treatment that had only a very small chance of success. Not surprisingly the Court of Appeal, though sensitive to the agony of the protagonists, described the proceedings as misguided, the Master of the Rolls saying that the health authority had acted fairly and rationally and that the courts were not arbiters to the merits of cases of that kind (*R.* v. *Cambridge District Health Authority, ex parte B., The Times*, 15 March 1995). How the plaintiff's legal

---

[5] The Court of Appeal decision was reversed by the House of Lords, but not so as to affect this point ([1988] AC 1074).

[6] The QALY – quality adjusted life year – has been invented as an aid towards measuring the value of any given treatment.

advisers convinced themselves, and the Legal Aid Board, that they had a reasonable chance of showing that the decision of the health authority, taken with the full backing of its doctors on the clinical issue, as well as after its own consideration of the resource issue, was totally unreasonable is a mystery (the further mystery is how Laws J. allowed himself to give judgment at first instance for the plaintiff, speaking of a 'fundamental right to life' and suggesting that the health authority should have provided full details to support its decision as to the proper deployment of its limited resources – good media material, but bad law!). It appears, however, that the proceedings attracted a benefactor to pay for the treatment.

It has also been reported that Gavin Gerrard, an eleven-year-old boy with cystic fibrosis, is planning to sue Northumberland Health Authority for declining to fund treatment on the basis that it is experimental. One can only hope that this trend will be effectively stopped by the courts before every patient who does not agree with the decision of his health authority sues (stopped perhaps by wasted costs orders).[7]

THE NHS AND THE CROWN

The NHS is a Crown body. The NHS authorities exercise their functions on behalf of the Crown. By virtue of the Crown Proceedings Act 1947 the Crown may be sued in the ordinary way in tort and contract. But legislation does not bind the Crown unless expressly so stated, or necessarily implied. Coercive orders, such as execution of a judgment or an order for specific performance or an injunction, cannot issue against the Crown. Before February 1987 the Crown could not be prosecuted for breach of safety or health regulations. There was a procedure, in use since 1978, whereby inspectors could issue improvement or prohibition notices to Crown undertakings, including NHS hospitals, and these would not be ignored. Under the National Health Service (Amendment) Act 1986 Crown immunity was removed, to the extent that health authorities may now be prosecuted for breaches of the food, health and safety legislation.[8]

The House of Lords decision in *Pfizer Ltd* v. *Ministry of Health* [1965] AC 512 established that the NHS was a Crown service. It

---

[7] In the unlikely event of the decision of the health authority being demonstrably flawed – for example, if it could be shown to have been taken on racial grounds – then clearly it would be reviewable by the courts.

[8] Within a few weeks the local authority had collated evidence, launched the first prosecution under the Act, and obtained an order for closure of cockroach-infested kitchens at Hammersmith Hospital.

was held that the use of drugs in the NHS was a use 'for the service of the Crown', and therefore a patented drug could be made use of under the Patents Act 1949 subject to appropriate payment to the owner of the patent. In *Wood* v. *United Leeds Hospitals* [1974] ICR 535 the National Industrial Relations Court held that a NHS employee was a servant of the Crown and that therefore he could not take advantage of the Contracts of Employment Act 1972. In *Dory* v. *Sheffield Health Authority* (1988) 11 BMLR 93 the health authority's use of patented medical equipment was held to be use by the Crown for the purposes of s.55 of the Patents Act 1977. Compare *British Medical Association* v. *Greater Glasgow Health Board* [1989] AC 1211 where the House of Lords held that proceedings for an interdict against a health board (the Scottish version of a health authority) did not constitute 'proceedings against the Crown' within the meaning of s.21(1) of the Crown Proceedings Act 1947.

Section 60 of the National Health Service and Community Care Act 1990, now provides that from the appointed day no health service body shall be regarded as the servant or agent of the Crown or as enjoying any status, immunity or privilege of the Crown. It therefore follows that, whether or not the matter was arguable before, by virtue of this section a health authority can now be made subject, for example, to an injunction, to summary judgment, and to contempt proceedings.[9]

THE ARMED FORCES

The position in respect of matters arising before 1987: members of the armed forces, pursuant to s.10 of the Crown Proceedings Act 1947, may not be sued, nor may the Crown, for causing death or personal injury when on duty to another member of the armed forces, provided the injured party was on duty at the time *or* was on premises for the time being used for the purposes of the armed forces. So a soldier may not sue for mistreatment he received in an army hospital. In *Bell* v. *Secretary of State for Defence* [1986] QB 322 an injured serviceman, stationed in West Germany, was transferred from an army medical reception centre to a civilian hospital where he died, allegedly as a result of totally inadequate notes provided to the hospital by the army doctor. On a preliminary

---

[9] It may be noted that in *R.* v. *Licensing Authority established under the Medicines Act 1968, ex parte Smith Kline and French Laboratories Ltd (No.2)* [1989] 2 WLR 378 the Court of Appeal said that the prohibition in the Crown Proceedings Act 1947 against granting declaratory and injunctive relief against the Crown did not apply to judicial review proceedings.

issue the Secretary of State for Defence was held not to be entitled to immunity from the suit brought by the dead soldier's father because, said a majority of the Court of Appeal, the failure to provide proper notes had occurred at the civilian hospital and not on Crown premises (a decision which is a little difficult to understand on the facts).[10]

This immunity only applies if the Minister certifies that the injury will be attributed to service as a member of the armed forces for the purposes of disablement or death benefit (it is intended that a serviceman who has the benefit of the service pension scheme should not also have a right to sue at common law). Immunity is not to be accorded if the court is satisfied that the alleged negligence was not 'connected with' the execution of army etc. duties.

In *Pearce and others* v. *Secretary of State for Defence* [1987] 2 WLR 782, Caulfield J. ruled on a preliminary point in a claim backed by the Nuclear Test Victims Association. The plaintiff, then an NCO in the Royal Engineers, had been exposed in the late 1950s to radiation from the atomic tests carried out on Christmas Island. The tests had been carried out by the now defunct Atomic Energy Commission, which had not been a Crown body, though its functions were transferred in 1973 to the Ministry of Defence. The judge said that s.10 of the Act of 1947 did not afford immunity to the Crown upon the claim, because sub-s.(1) was restricted to acts by members of the armed forces, and sub-s.(2), which included a prohibition on legal action by members of the armed forces for death or personal injury arising out of the nature or condition of military equipment being used in connection with the armed forces, was not in point because the 'thing suffered' by the plaintiff within the meaning of the provision was the continuing omission of the Authority to warn of the hazard (the actual injury was not the 'thing suffered' but the consequence of it), and so the 'thing suffered' was not by or in consequence of the nature or condition of land, premises, ship, aircraft, vehicle, equipment or supplies (the result may be attractive, but the argument is strained). The Court of Appeal by a majority dismissed the defendant's appeal on the basis that the plaintiff's accrued right to sue the Atomic Energy Commission survived as against the Ministry of Defence ([1988] 2 WLR 144) and the House of Lords upheld their decision on the same ground, while holding also that the construction given by the trial judge to the words 'thing suffered' was wrong. That construction

---

[10] In *Pearce* v. *Secretary of State for Defence* (see below) the House of Lords said *Bell* was wrongly decided.

had followed the reasoning of the Court of Appeal in the *Bell* case, which therefore had been wrongly decided ([1988] AC 755).

It was said in *Trawnick* v. *Lennox* [1985] 1 WLR 532 that there was no right of action against the Crown in tort apart from that arising by virtue of the Act of 1947.

The position after May 1987: this immunity was repealed by the Crown Proceedings (Armed Forces) Act 1987, which received the Royal Assent on 15 May 1987, but the statute does not have retrospective effect (the Crown accepts ex gratia claims arising after 8 December 1986).

FOREIGN FORCES

In *Luttrell* v. *United States of America* [1994] PIQR P141 the court declined to exercise jurisdiction over the complaint by an American staff sergeant that he had been injured by negligent medical treatment carried out in 1987 at the military hospital at the United States air base at Lakenheath. It is surprising that the plaintiff's advisers thought they had any chance of defeating a plea of *acta iure imperii* (i.e. that, in respect of the acts complained of, the defendant state was acting in the exercise of its sovereign power and was therefore not subject to the jurisdiction of our courts – see *Lewis* on *State and Diplomatic Immunity*, Lloyd's of London Press, 3rd edition 1990).

PROCEDURE

4 · The initial complaint

SUMMARY

You, the patient, need to decide as soon as possible whether you wish to seek financial compensation or just moral satisfaction. If the former, go to a solicitor experienced in this sort of work. If the latter, or if you are not sure, you can get help initially from Citizens' Advice Bureaux, Community Health Councils, the Patients' Association, or Action for Victims of Medical Accidents (though the latter are primarily concerned with litigation). Complaints which do not concern the clinical treatment you received or did not receive may be made to the Ombudsman; complaints about treatment in hospital or clinic through the hospital's complaints procedure; complaints about any doctor to the General Medical Council; complaints about your GP or non-hospital dentist or optician to the Family Health Services Authority (formerly Family Practitioner Committee). But only legal action offers financial compensation. The private patient must think in terms of the General Medical Council or a solicitor. You can always write, initially at least, to hospital or doctor to ventilate your complaint or uncertainty.

THE PATIENT FEELS UNHAPPY

Let us assume that you or someone under your care has received treatment at the hands of the medical profession (and in 'treatment' I include non-treatment such as refusal to visit, give an appointment, treat, prescribe, etc.), with which you are not satisfied, and you are not sure what you can or what you should do about it. This chapter is intended to clarify the choices you have and what each of them involves.

You need first to decide, if you can, whether you are looking for financial compensation or for satisfaction of another sort, e.g. by way of explanation, reassurance or apology.[1] If you know that you have not suffered more than minimal damage, or if for any reason you are not interested in launching a claim for financial reparation, then there are a number of courses you can follow, depending on the type of complaint you wish to make, i.e. against

---

[1] It cannot be emphasised enough how important it is to a patient to get an explanation of what went wrong. This is often her chief, sometimes her only, objective.

whom and in relation to what. These courses will not get you compensation; they are investigations into the conduct of the medical service, with a view to correcting any mistake, maladministration or misconduct for the future. This correction may also involve offering you further treatment as well as explanations and, where appropriate, apologies. As we shall see, the investigating body in relation to some of these courses will not pursue your complaint if it is thought that you are considering legal action.

If on the other hand you wish to claim compensation, or at any rate to take advice to see if you have a claim for compensation, you should go to a solicitor (one experienced in this sort of work – see p. 46) straight away. You can, if you wish, write an informal letter to the hospital or practitioner first, to see if that gets you anywhere (when you go to your solicitor take all such correspondence with you).

Let us now look in detail at these various courses of action.

POSSIBLE COURSES OF ACTION

There are various organisations who will help you in the first place decide how you want to make your complaint.

Citizens' Advice Bureaux will point you in the right direction, probably towards the Community Health Council in your area. The CAB will give you general advice and if necessary would contact your CHC for you, or AVMA (see below), or other agencies. The CAB address can be found under 'Citizens' Advice Bureaux' in the telephone book, or your Town Hall or local library will tell you, as they will for the CHC address.

The Community Health Council

The National Health Reorganisation Act 1973 established the CHCs. They represent to the health authority the view of the 'consumer', i.e. the patient. Each health district has its own Council, consisting of 18–24 members. The meetings of the CHCs are open to the public. The CHC has a number of statutory rights: it may visit any of the institutions for health care within its district. It must be consulted by the health authority on 'any substantial development of the health service in the Council's district and on any proposals to make any substantial variation in the provision of such service' (NHS (Community Health Councils) Regulations 1973, SI 1973/2217 reg. 20(1)),[2] and the CHC is entitled to be present at meetings of the health authority, where, though not entitled actually to vote, its members may speak. It publishes an annual report, to which the health authority is obliged to make detailed and specific reply. In this way the council can oblige the health authority to consider any suggestions for change or improvement that the council on behalf of the patient thinks appropriate, and to give reasons if the suggestions are deemed unacceptable. On behalf of an individual patient the Council can help him to make his complaint through official channels, whether the NHS complaints procedure, the Ombudsman or legally, though the degree of assistance they will feel able to give will vary according to the course chosen (they cannot do more in a legal claim than perhaps suggest a solicitor or AVMA – see below). CHCs are usually listed under 'Community' in telephone books or under the individual, i.e., the district name of the CHC. The Association of Community Health Councils for England and Wales (362 Euston Road, London NW1, tel. (0171) 388 4814) serves the CHCs of England and Wales, acting as a forum for their views and recommendations, providing an information service for them, and publishing a monthly newspaper called the *CHC News*.

The Patients' Association

This body also represents the interests of the consumer, and will assist as far as it can a patient who feels aggrieved. Its motto is 'puts patients first'. It is an advice service and collective voice for the patients, independent of government, the health professions and the drug industry, and is financed by members' subscriptions, donations and a government grant. Its aims are to represent and further the interests of patients; to give information and advice to individuals; to acquire and spread information about patients' interests; to promote understanding and goodwill between patients and everyone in medical practice, and related activities. Founded in 1963, its campaigns have led or contributed to action in such areas as the appointment of a NHS Ombudsman; a code of practice for the medical profession in using hospital patients for teaching; improved hospital visiting hours; improvements in drug safety; reductions in hospital waiting lists. It does not, be it noted, give medical advice. The subscription is minimal, and the

---

[2] For judicial criticism of a health authority's failure to consult the CHC before closing a unit, see *R.* v. *North West Thames Regional Health Authority, ex parte Daniels, The Times*, 22 June 1993.

Association's address is 8 Guilford Street, London WC1N 1DT, tel. (0171) 242 3460.

The Ombudsman

The Office of Health Service Ombudsman (or Health Service Commissioner as it is officially known) was established by the Act of 1973, and the relevant statutory provisions are now found in the NHS Act 1977 Part V. His function is to investigate and report and make recommendations on complaints about the activities of health authorities and those for whom they are responsible. There are separate offices for England, Wales and Scotland, i.e. the posts are legally separate, but the same person may, and does currently, fill all three positions. He is the Parliamentary Commissioner, too, so he has a lot on his plate! He will consider and investigate your complaint if you feel that you have suffered injustice or hardship as a result of a failure in a service provided by certain authorities, or a failure by one of those authorities to provide a service which it has a duty to provide, or maladministration which has affected any other action taken by or on behalf of such an authority. The authorities whose actions he may investigate are Regional Health Authorities, District Health Authorities, boards of governors, Family Health Service Authorities and a few other specialised bodies. But he is not permitted to investigate grievances for which there is or has been a remedy in the courts or some other legal tribunal (although they can be investigated if the Ombudsman thinks it unreasonable for you to go to court). He may not investigate – and this is important – any action taken in connection with the diagnosis of illness or the care or treatment of a patient, if, in the Ombudsman's opinion, it was taken solely in consequence of 'the exercise of clinical judgment'. Complaints about the actual medical treatment you received, if they do not go to a solicitor for legal redress, can be directed through the NHS's own complaints procedure (see below).

The Ombudsman also cannot investigate the actions of family practitioners, dentists, opticians and pharmacists in connection with the services they provide under contract with Family Health Service Authorities (these complaints can be made to the FHSA or to the GMC – see below). So complaints about medical treatment and about GPs are the main areas from which the Ombudsman is excluded. These are the areas in which fall most complaints of medical negligence, as we usually use the term. If your dissatisfaction stems from the actual medical treatment you have been given or denied the Ombudsman is not the man to go to.

In relation to the various limits on his jurisdiction the Ombudsman has in the past suggested that his power to investigate a matter should not be limited to complaints actually made by an aggrieved i.e. an injuriously affected party, but that he should be able to investigate any matter that in his judgment calls for investigation in the public interest. He has also suggested that he might be empowered to investigate matters of clinical judgment provided that the patient were given a mutually exclusive option of either asking the Ombudsman to investigate or taking legal action. This aspect of his jurisdiction has been under scrutiny by a Select Committee of the House of Commons.

Other matters he cannot investigate are: personnel matters, such as staff appointments or removals, pay, discipline and superannuation; contractual or other commercial transactions; properly taken discretionary decisions which an authority has a right to take (but the Ombudsman can look at whether the authority has followed proper procedures and considered all relevant aspects in reaching its decision); action which has been or is the subject of an enquiry set up by the Secretary of State in any circumstances where he thinks it advisable to do so, such as a serious incident or major breakdown in service.

Before asking the Ombudsman to consider your complaint you must first give the health authority, or FHSA, an adequate opportunity to investigate it and reply. This is done by letter (Health Circular (81)5, 88(37)), though the Department of Health envisages a letter of explanation as the usual response by the health authority to complaints of a non-clinical nature. Then you approach the Ombudsman yourself if you are not satisfied with the answer. Write to 'The Health Service Commissioner for England' at Church House, Great Smith Street, London SW1, tel. (0171) 212 7676; for Wales the address is Pearl Assurance, Greyfriars Road, Cardiff, tel. (01222) 394621. Give a full account of what the problem is, enclosing any documents you have.

There is a time limit: complaint should be made within one year of the date on which the matter first came to your notice (though the Ombudsman may if he thinks fit waive this requirement). You will discuss your complaint with the Ombudsman's representative, and at the end of the investigation you and the 'other side' will receive his written report.

Family Health Services Authorities[3]

Health authorities are statutorily obliged to set up these committees, and their function (see the Act of 1977, s.15(1)) is

---

[3] Formerly called Family Practitioner Committees.

to administer, on behalf of their health authority, the arrangements for the provision of general medical, dental, ophthalmic and pharmaceutical services within the area, and to perform such other functions relating to those services as may be prescribed. The health authority's duty to arrange for the provision of general medical services is found in Part II of the Act of 1977. The procedure for investigation of a complaint against a practitioner is found in the National Health Service (Service Committees and Tribunal) Regulations 1974 (SI 1974/ 455, amended by SIs 1974/907, 1982/288, 1985/39 and 1987/ 445). Practitioners are engaged upon contracts for services by the FHSA, i.e. they are independent contractors and not employees. The FHSA is limited to investigating complaints which may reveal a breach of that contract. The complaint is made to the administrator of the FHSA. The terms of the service for general medical practitioners are found in the NHS (General Medical Services) Regulations 1992, SI 1992/635. For example, GPs must give their patients (usually between 2,000 and 3,000 on a doctor's list) 'all necessary and appropriate personal medical services of the type usually provided by general medical practitioners'. They must, unless prevented by an emergency, see any of their patients who come during surgery hours (in a group practice this requirement is satisfied if any of the partners sees the patient). If there is an appointment system the patient may be asked to return within a reasonable time, as long as this does not endanger his health. The GP has to ensure alternative facilities when he is away or off duty.

The administrator of the FHSA must receive your complaint within 13 weeks of the event that gave rise to it. If your complaint is about a dentist the time limit is six months from the end of treatment or 13 weeks from your becoming aware of the matter that is the subject of your complaint, whichever is the sooner. The investigating committee may pursue a late complaint if satisfied that the reason for the delay was illness or some other reasonable cause, and the practitioner consents to the investigation. If he does not consent the Secretary of State has power to overrule him. The complainant has a right of appeal to the Minister where the committee refuses to investigate a late complaint.

Less serious complaints may be dealt with by informal means, where they do not raise questions concerning an alleged breach of a doctor's terms of service: a layperson of standing is appointed by the FHSA, assisted by a doctor who explains the medical aspects. The layperson may use any method of dealing with the complaint he thinks appropriate.

The substantive investigation of a complaint that goes to a possible breach of contract by the practitioner is entrusted to the relevant service committee, composed of an equal number of members of the relevant profession and of lay members of the FHSA. It is chaired by a non-practitioner. Under the rules of procedure there are three stages. First the Chairman considers the complaint, asking for further information if desired. If his opinion is that there are no reasonable grounds for believing the practitioner to be in breach of his terms of service, then the matter may stop there with the service committee endorsing his opinion and reporting back to that effect to the FHSA. But if the Chairman or the committee wishes to take the matter further, stage two involves the practitioner being asked to comment on the complaint and a reply from the patient. A report may be prepared at that point if the committee does not think a hearing is necessary, but if it considers that a hearing is required the parties will attend with witnesses. Parties may be represented, but not by a lawyer, e.g. they can be represented by someone from a Community Health Council.

The third stage is the written report giving the committee's findings, both on the facts and as to possible breaches of the terms of service. It also makes recommendations as to what should be done, which may include dismissal of the complaint, limiting the number of patients on the doctor's list, recommendation to the Secretary of State that the doctor should be warned to follow more closely the terms of service or that part of his pay should be withheld. Their findings of fact, but not their recommendations, must be accepted by the FHSA. Reasons must be given by the FHSA if it does not act upon the service committee's recommendations. Provision is made for appeals by either party against the decision of the FHSA to the Minister.

It goes without saying that before complaining to the FHSA you are at liberty to write to the practitioner concerned for an explanation. If he responds sympathetically you may wish to let the matter rest there.

The General Medical Council

Complaints about serious professional misconduct by a GP or hospital doctor may be addressed to the GMC (44 Hallam Street, London W1, tel. (0171) 580 7642). You are likely to have to swear an official declaration to support your complaint. In its publication *Professional Conduct and Discipline*, 1981, the GMC gives examples of serious professional misconduct, including serious neglect or disregard of responsibilities to patients for their care and treatment, abuse of professional privileges in prescribing drugs or issuing medical certificates, abuse of professional confidence, abuse of the financial opportunities of medical practice, abuse of the doctor/patient relationship, and personal behaviour that could bring the profession into disrepute. On a complaint the GMC can refer the matter to the professional conduct committee for a formal inquiry, send the doctor a warning letter, refer the matter to the Health Committee of the GMC (where it appears that a doctor's fitness to practise is impaired by a physical or mental condition), or take no action. The hearing is governed by the formal rules of evidence. Sanctions where the complaint is adjudged proved range from issuing a warning to striking off. The doctor has a right of appeal to the Privy Council. The GMC will exonerate the doctor unless his conduct is shown to be grossly improper. See Stop Press, p. 47.

The statutory enquiry

An individual complaint may, though rarely, bring to the attention of the Secretary of State matters into which he decides to hold an enquiry. He has power to do this in relation to any matter arising from the NHS Act 1977 (by s.84). If the Minister thinks that any health body, including regional, district, and FHSAs, has failed to carry out any of its functions under the relevant legislation he can declare it to be in default and replace its members.

Your Member of Parliament

This can be a useful avenue of complaint, particularly where you are getting no response to your enquiries or letters. It can be used at any time to stir things up.

Hospital complaints procedure

This line of action does not preclude a legal claim being made later, though, as we shall see, the inquiry may be aborted if legal action appears imminent.

The procedure for formal complaints (recently reviewed by the Wilson Committee) was first set out in HC(81)5 but it was not compulsory. That Circular now forms part of the present procedure under HC(88)37:HN(FP)(88)18[4] which was issued in June 1988 in pursuance of the Secretary of State's duty under the Hospital Complaints Procedure Act 1985 to give directions for establishing and publishing a complaints procedure in every hospital. It gives directions to District Health Authorities on how to deal with patients' complaints.

Arrangements are to be made at every hospital for the staff to seek to deal informally with any complaint to the satisfaction of the complainant. Usually open discussion with the consultant concerned or with a senior member of the staff in the relevant department will be the preferable course. As has so often been noted by all parties concerned with patients' complaints, in many cases all the patient wants is a sympathetic ear and a fair explanation. This often disposes of the complaint without rancour, whereas lack of sympathy and explanation will on many occasions give rise to a legal action.

However, there must of course be a formal complaints procedure. For this a senior officer is designated in each hospital or group of hospitals for which the health authority is responsible to discharge the duty of receiving complaints and ensuring that appropriate action is taken. Complaints should be received within three months of the matter complained of arising, but there is discretion to admit a late complaint. Complaints about medical treatment, that is to say about the exercise of clinical judgment by a hospital doctor or dentist, where the complaint cannot be resolved by discussion with the consultant concerned, must be brought by the designated officer to the attention of his senior officers or, if appropriate, the Regional Medical Officer, for proper action to be taken in accordance with established procedures, i.e. pursuant to HC(81)5.

---

[4] Health Circulars do not have the force of law, but they can assume importance in establishing negligence, as guides to proper conduct and practice. The distinction between Health Circulars (HC) and Health Notices (HN) has been explained in a 1975 circular HSC(IS)219 as follows:

Health Circulars will be the formal means of conveying instructions, guidance, or information to health authorities (and, where appropriate, to local authorities on a 'for information' basis). The general aim is that communications covering policy matters or giving long-term guidance, and specifically those intended for circulation to organisations outside the NHS, will be issued as Health Circulars, whilst matters of an ephemeral nature will normally be appropriate to Health Notices. Health Notices will provide an informal means of communicating with health authorities, usually on matters of a short-term or routine nature; they will not normally be distributed outside the NHS. A main purpose of Health Notices will be to permit the speedy issue of guidance or information, e.g. statistical or costing returns, from all health authorities or all of one type or category of authority. The scale of distribution will be considerably lower than that for Health Circulars. They will not be used to cancel or modify advice issued in a Health Circular.

As we have noted, it was HC(81)5 that created a procedure whereby the NHS patient could complain if dissatisfied with the exercise of clinical judgment by hospital medical or dental staff. These are called 'clinical' complaints, and concern the standard of medical care the patient has received (so they do not include, for example, complaints about hospital food, ambulance transport or waiting lists, nor do they include complaints about a doctor's non-medical treatment of you, e.g. his general behaviour or the time you were kept waiting – unless of course these relate directly to the medical care he gave or failed to give you). The complaint must be about a doctor or dentist, not any other sort of NHS employee, and he must have been working in a hospital or clinic run by a health authority. You must have been a NHS patient (there is no set procedure for private patients, even in a NHS hospital: they can only complain to the doctor involved, and, if dissatisfied, see a solicitor).

You may make your complaint by word of mouth to the person in charge of the place where you were treated, but it is better if you write to the hospital administrator or the district administrator of the health authority which is responsible for the relevant hospital or clinic. Assuming yours is a 'clinical' complaint you will then enter on the first of three stages. You will be invited to see the senior doctor in charge of your care, who may or may not be the doctor who has actually treated you (if he thinks the risk of legal action is significant he will inform the District Administrator and the relevant medical defence society is likely to be consulted and to assist in the response to the complaint).

The meeting will be informal and should take place within a few days of the complaint being received. Afterwards you will receive a letter confirming the explanation you were given at the meeting and if you are satisfied the matter ends there. You must reply to say whether you are satisfied or not. If not, you go to stage two. Put your complaint into writing, if you have not already done that (the Community Health Council can help with this; so can the staff of the District Administrator). You may then have a second interview with the consultant if it is felt that that might serve a useful purpose. If there appears no point in that, or if you remain dissatisfied after such a second interview, your complaint will be referred to the Regional Medical Officer, who then decides (stage two) whether your complaint should be investigated by an independent professional review. The RMO does not concern himself with the merits of your complaint as such, but he does need to satisfy himself of a number of things: that everything possible has been done in the way of giving you a full explanation and that you are still not satisfied; that the complaint is of a substantial nature (otherwise it is not worth the time and expense of setting up a review); that the complaint does not open up wider issues that would be better dealt with by the health authority setting up an enquiry or taking disciplinary action against the doctor concerned; *that* (this is important) *you are not intending to take legal action to claim compensation* – if it was thought you were using the review procedure to assist a legal claim the doctors would not participate[5]; that a review is practicable, that you want one and that you would attend (all these matters will be canvassed by the RMO with the consultant and with you; the RMO may suggest another meeting with the consultant if the parties agree, where he thinks it might avoid the necessity of a review).

If these preconditions are satisfied you will be offered a review. The RMO will be given the names of two independent consultants in the same specialty by the Joint Consultants Committee (i.e. the RMO does not himself choose the experts). The experts are sent all the details of the case. They meet and talk with the parties on an informal basis (the consultant will not be present when you meet the experts, but you may take a friend, or your GP). They then prepare a report, with recommendations, which is communicated through the RMO to the District Administrator and then to you (the experts have probably told you their conclusions already at the review). And that is the end of the procedure. You have received an independent opinion, and, even if it seems as though the doctors have 'closed ranks' the procedure offers you no further remedy (you are not, however, legally precluded from suing if you so desire).

It is to be noted that a doctor cannot be forced to co-operate with this procedure; the patient is not represented; she will not be shown the report of the experts (only be told as much as the Administrator chooses to reveal); and action cannot be enforced upon the findings of the experts. So the procedure has its shortcomings, to say the least.

---

[5] In *R. v. Canterbury and Thanet District Health Authority* [1994] 5 Med LR 132 the Divisional Court upheld the discontinuance by the defendants of an independent review when it became clear that the complainants were contemplating legal proceedings (the complaints were against a psychiatrist for negligent diagnoses of sexual abuse). The court said that the procedure depended upon the co-operation of the consultant whose actions were the subject of the enquiry and that his co-operation would clearly not now be forthcoming. The primary purpose of the procedure was either to get a second opinion and thereby a change of diagnosis or treatment, or to enable the health authority to change its procedures in the light of what transpired at the enquiry. Further, if the matter was likely to go to court that would provide a far more searching enquiry than the independent review procedure.

The Wilson Committee recommended (*inter alia*) in May 1994 that there should be a uniform user-friendly procedure for all NHS complaints; that complaints should be dealt with informally wherever possible, within days if possible, three months at the most; that all purchasers and providers of health care should see that information about the procedure was made readily available to patients; and that training in handling complaints should be given to all NHS practitioners and staff.

Action for Victims of Medical Accidents (AVMA)

So far we have been considering courses to follow that do not, or do not initially, involve legal action. AVMA has already been mentioned as a charitable organisation that exists to help those who have been injured as a result of medical treatment (an outline of AVMA's work can be found in Appendix III below). In an appropriate case AVMA may give advice that does not involve legal proceedings. But in the main the cases that are referred to it call for the intervention of a lawyer, and to that end AVMA is able to refer the patient, or his representative, to a suitably qualified solicitor.

Going to a solicitor

If you are thinking from the outset of making a claim for financial compensation, or if you remain dissatisfied after having tried the non-legal channels, you will need a solicitor. You should not delay. You have basically three years from the time you suffered (or knew that you had suffered) the injury at the hands of the medical staff to issue your writ (i.e. start proceedings). If you are out of time for whatever reason you are likely to have lost all chance of suing (the position is actually not quite as simple as that, and is explained in detail in Chapter 28).

The question is: how do you find a solicitor who will best handle your case? These claims are usually complex and difficult to pursue. They are likely to involve in the first place technical factors which will not be understood except with medical assistance. They have a number of peculiarities which do not apply to the ordinary personal injury or negligence action. They create a lot of anxiety and stress for the plaintiff, who may not be in the best of health. The other side knows the ropes, and is unlikely to make concessions. The vital factor in the claim, the evidence of your experts establishing negligence in your treatment, is in most cases hard to obtain: the papers are likely to go to and fro between expert, solicitor and counsel for quite a time before anything really useful emerges, even if, as may well not be the case, your solicitor has gone in the first place to a suitable expert (see Chapter 9 on selecting an expert). These claims need to be continually pressed forward, and for that the solicitor requires expertise, energy and enthusiasm. Many claims have in the past been allowed to drag their heels, languishing in a pending tray, because through a lack of one or more of these three factors the solicitor, perhaps feeling nervous or oppressed about the case, allows it to doze, if not actually sleep. In some cases inexperience or somnolence may actually ruin your case.[6]

This book was originally written primarily to enable any solicitor properly to pursue a medical negligence action. Since that time, early 1988, the expertise of solicitors in this field has grown enormously, so that it should not be hard to find, after appropriate enquiries, a capable solicitor in your area.[7] If you have a solicitor in whom you have confidence of old, you could instruct him. But if you have no such predilection your best course by far is to ask AVMA, at 1 London Road, Forest Hill, London SE23 3TP, tel. (0181) 291 2793, to recommend one, and they will send you to a solicitor who is both experienced and concerned.

STOP PRESS (ref. p. 42)

The Medical (Professional Performance) Act (when passed) will, by amending the Medical Act 1983, empower the GMC to impose penalties where they find a doctor's standard of professional performance to have been seriously deficient.

---

[6] Every so often just such a horror story is revealed in the daily papers – solicitors who do nothing for years, or who get a negative report from an unsuitable expert and drop the case. Then, sometimes years later, an experienced solicitor revives it and wins substantial damages.

[7] This situation may change if entitlement to process these cases is restricted by the Law Society or the Legal Aid Board to the few solicitors who will satisfy the stringent criteria of the new Law Society medical negligence panel.

5 · First steps: funding the claim, legal aid, going to counsel

SUMMARY

Medical negligence actions are very expensive. If you are not legally aided you will be paying up to £2,000 to find out if your claim is worth pursuing (if it is not one of those rare cases that are obviously valid). If you qualify for legal aid your solicitor will obtain authority to get the medical notes, submit them to an expert for a report, and then go to counsel for an opinion on the merits of the claim.

WITHOUT LEGAL AID

If you do not qualify for legal aid you will have to think very carefully whether it is worth pursuing the claim and taking the risk of having to pay the other side's costs as well as your own if you lose. Although no case should be brought under the provisions of the legal aid scheme unless it is more likely to succeed than to fail, I would suggest a more rigorous test for a privately funded claim: it should not be pursued, at least beyond the initial stages, unless it appears unlikely to fail. Litigation is always uncertain. If you lose you could be left, after an average trial of some three days, with an overall bill for about £60,000. If you succeed you will recover a large proportion but not all of your own costs. Up till recently the expected proportion was usually between two-thirds and three-quarters, because the items, and the cost thereof, that the solicitor charged the client were not allowed in full on taxation by the taxing master. This did not make much sense, but it had always been the case. However, a new basis for taxation of the bill of costs of successful parties has been introduced, the standard basis, which permits recovery of all costs reasonably incurred, so one may hope that, although the unsuccessful party will still be protected from extravagant bills, the winner should now recover more than 80% of his costs.

You will run up a fair-sized bill, perhaps about £2,000,[1] before you can sensibly decide if your case is worth pursuing, because you will need to get an expert's report, perhaps a second if you do not like the first, and then take counsel's advice if things are not appearing manifestly hopeless.

Liability for costs in the growth area of group litigation is a problem. A privately funded plaintiff needs to be quite clear about what costs he may be liable for at any stage (i.e. before/after issuing a writ) or he may be in for a nasty surprise. Our judges are still working out various types of order to cover this situation, e.g. limiting the costs which a privately funded plaintiff may be liable for if he has not and does not start proceedings. But the basic principle is that he must bear his share *pro rata* of the costs and cannot be carried on the shoulders of the legally aided claimants.

The Lord Chancellor is currently introducing rules to allow lawyers to take cases for conditional fees, i.e. they get nothing if they lose and a small uplift (to come out of the patient's damages) if they win. This is not being done to help victims of injury to sue, but simply as a financial measure to reduce the legal aid bill. At the same time he has drastically limited legal aid eligibility. These changes are not good for patients. Solicitors cannot be expected to take any but the most obvious winners, of which in the medical negligence context there are few. Even a fair prospect can suddenly change dramatically at any time, including during trial. All that can be said is that some patients who would not have qualified for legal aid even before it was slashed and who have a good case may in this way get compensation.

LEGAL AID: FROM THE PATIENT'S POINT OF VIEW

You are on a much better wicket if you are granted legal aid. You are liable only for whatever contribution is assessed upon your means (though a contribution is now required for each year that the case is still proceeding instead of, as formerly, a one-off payment). That may be nil. You are not liable, if you lose the case, for the other side's costs, though you may have to make the same contribution to their costs that you pay to your own legal aid costs. The tactical advantage of being on legal aid is usually considerable. The other side knows that its costs are not in any event going to be recovered; so your nuisance value is much increased. The medical protection societies have said that when they are involved, i.e. in defence of their members, cases are

---

[1] Some solicitors warn that the cost could be £3,000–£5,000 in the more complex cases.

handled strictly according to their merits, and legal advisers to health authorities may well take the same view. It is easy to see why defendants would not want to give the impression that cases might be settled for their nuisance value, particularly where the allegation is one of professional negligence, but the fact remains that in practical terms it may pay defendants to offer the legally aided plaintiff a reasonable settlement (or, sometimes, even a better than reasonable one).

LEGAL AID: FROM THE SOLICITOR'S POINT OF VIEW

So far I have been addressing the patient, trying to help him decide how to air his dissatisfaction and, if he so chooses, how to approach the law. We are now entering the world of the lawyer and it is primarily for her that I now write, to assist her in the preparation and pursuit of the medical negligence claim from the moment she first sees the client.

SUMMARY

You may use the green form to obtain legal aid, which will usually be limited to obtaining the medical records, by s.33 application if necessary, submitting them to an expert, and then getting counsel's opinion on the merits. Going to counsel for a preliminary opinion, i.e. before instructing the expert or even before asking for the records, can be useful, particularly if you are not familiar with this type of case.

THE GREEN FORM

If the client is financially eligible the solicitor can use the green form to give two hours' preliminary advice on the strength of the case, during which he can get a fair idea of the proposed claim, sufficient at any rate for the purpose of filling in the application for legal aid.[2] At this stage all that is needed is to show to the legal aid authority the possibility of a case. This may amount to no more than that the patient seems to have been injured during or as a result of medical attention or inattention. In many cases the question whether injury has in fact been suffered, whether it is connected with medical treatment received, and whether there is cause for blaming the doctors, will not be known until a medical expert has given his opinion. For that reason, the legal aid certificate will usually be limited to procuring from expert and

---

[2] The green form scheme is known as 'Legal Advice and Assistance'.

counsel an assessment of the proposed claim (see below). Extensions to the work authorised under the green form may, where necessary, be applied for in advance of the extra work to the appropriate legal aid area office. Note that this green form scheme can cover areas that legal aid proper (strictly now called 'representation') does not cover, e.g. advice on preparing for an inquest, though not for representation there.

In *R. v. Legal Aid Board, ex parte Higgins, The Times*, 19 November 1993, the Divisional Court said that it was not an abuse of the legal aid scheme to fund costly expert reports, under extensions to the green form scheme, to investigate a claim that would otherwise be outside the scope of legal aid (the case concerned a claim that the Council of Legal Education had wrongly refused to pass students in the Bar examinations).

APPLYING FOR LEGAL AID

It is important, to save duplication and avoid rejection, to apply in proper form. A Leeds legal aid area office noted that in January 1986 they had to write 712 letters and make 158 telephone calls simply as a result of being given insufficient information on the original application. The *Legal Aid Handbook*[3] contains all the information a solicitor needs to apply for legal aid, as well as the relevant regulations and lucid and helpful notes for guidance. New application forms have recently been issued, which, it is hoped, are clearer and easier to complete.

The rules for computing disposable capital and income are contained in the Civil Legal Aid (Assessment of Resources) Regulations 1989, as amended – the *Handbook* includes these. Legal aid will not be granted unless the applicant can show that he has reasonable grounds for taking, defending or being a party to proceedings and, in addition, he may be refused legal aid if it is unreasonable that he should receive it in the particular case.

Eligibility limits from April 1995 are as follows. Green form: basically income of £72 a week or capital of £1,000. Civil legal aid for personal injury claims: basically a lower income limit of £2,425 (no contribution required) and an upper income limit of £7,920 (no legal aid available above that amount); the limits for capital are £3,000 and £8,560. Allowances are made for dependants and pensioners. Contributions are payable if you fall between the limits. Quite apart from the drastic reduction in availability created by these limits, there is now no once-for-all

[3] The 1990 edition was the first to be prepared by the Legal Aid Board, who took over the Law Society's function of administering legal aid.

contribution; the party on legal aid will continue to be liable for contributions as long as the case goes on. This will, as intended, scare off many injured people who have valid claims.

The means of a child plaintiff are no longer aggregated with his parents'. This, *inter alia*, puts an end to the anguish of parents wondering how they can possibly afford to try to get justice for their handicapped baby.[4]

Counsel should not advise the continuation of legal aid proceedings unless he is sure that he has before him all the available material, that that material is reasonably reliable and makes it more likely than not that the action will succeed (*Hanning* v. *Maitland (No. 2)* [1970] 1 All ER 817 *per* Salmon L.J.). In *Holmes* v. *National Benzole Co.* (1965) 109 SJ 971 Lyell J. said that where clients are legally aided, 'there is a heavy duty on counsel and solicitors to test their client's case with the same anxious care that they would bring to one where they looked to their clients for the costs'. The solicitor, and counsel, even where there is a full certificate, should keep under constant review the reasonableness of the proceedings continuing at public expense, and report back to the Area Director if in doubt about that. Costs may be disallowed where the proceedings have not been conducted with reasonable competence and expedition; and in some cases where he should have realised the case was not strong enough to continue, the solicitor may be ordered to pay all the costs of both sides from the date when he should have so realised (see p. 114). This can be particularly important in medical negligence actions because, in order to be able to come to such realisation where appropriate, the solicitor needs to understand the case and assess its strength and he can only do this if he has read and understood the medical records, which are the main source of evidence in such a case, and the expert reports (this is an argument for restricting the conduct of medical negligence actions to firms that have shown themselves medically educated).

Guidance on the interpretation of the provisions can be found in the notes for guidance on the criteria for granting legal aid (also contained in the *Handbook*).

In the unlikely event of legal aid being refused by the general committee there is a right of appeal to the appropriate area committee (except where the applicant's income has been assessed as over the limit for legal aid). There is no further right of appeal, but it is possible to seek judicial review from the

---

[4] This was an attractive development. What is not so attractive is that between 1979 and 1992 14.8 million people and 5.5 million households became ineligible for civil legal aid, and the new cutbacks have made the situation a great deal worse.

Divisional Court of such a refusal. You will need to show that the decision was irrational, i.e. one which no reasonable tribunal could have come to if it had directed itself properly, or that it failed to take into consideration matters that it should have considered or took into consideration matters that it should not have done. In *R. v. Legal Aid Area No. 10 (East Midlands), ex parte Mackenna* [1990] 1 Med LR 375, the Court of Appeal, in quashing a decision of the legal aid committee to withdraw legal aid from one of the claimants in the Opren litigation because she had refused to accept the settlement offered by the drug company, said that the fact that the costs of the litigation were immense as against the small amount of damages likely to be recovered if the plaintiff was successful (in the area of £2,000) was a very important but not the sole nor necessarily the decisive factor in considering whether to continue legal aid. If it were, then the multinationals would be placed in a position of unmerited advantage *vis-à-vis* individual claimants.

In *R. v. Legal Aid Area No. 8 (Northern) Appeal Committee, ex parte Parkinson* [1990] 1 Med LR 394, Simon Brown J. quashed decisions of the legal aid committee to withdraw legal aid from a number of whooping cough vaccine claimants, saying that the committee had misunderstood the joint opinion of counsel in the *Loveday* case (he added that he was not at all sure that he was doing the claimants a kindness in keeping the spark of hope alive for them).

THE LEGAL AID CERTIFICATE

Check the name and the capacity in which the plaintiff is entitled to sue (e.g. authorisation to a widow to sue as administratrix would not, strictly, include a claim by her in her own right for nervous shock).

Check that you and the certificate have got the right name of any proposed defendant (for getting the correct name, see Chapter 22).

And, of course, check the limitation. The first stage of the limitation is likely to permit you to obtain the medical records, by summons if necessary, to obtain a medical report (sometimes one per specialism), and then counsel's opinion. You are entitled to a conference with counsel before his opinion is prepared (this may or may not be necessary, depending on the case). Any work after counsel's opinion has been received must be further authorised. Often, to save time and expense, authority will be given for counsel to settle proceedings if so advised, but not for service. Occasionally authority is included for counsel to settle the letter of instruction to the expert, but you should really be able to do that yourself.

Assuming counsel gives a positive opinion, the limitation that is then imposed has generally been up to but not including setting down. A more appropriate limitation is up to and including setting down, exchange of witness statements and medical evidence, because it is only at that stage that one can make a meaningful reassessment of the strength of the case. Occasionally one has recently seen the requirement for a solicitor's opinion at that stage, which is odd, as counsel's opinion is what is required.

The final stage of the certificate is unlimited, so as to permit the trial.

GOING TO COUNSEL

The solicitor handling a medical negligence action these days should be able herself to write appropriate letters to obtain all the records, to proceed by summons and affidavit if necessary, and to get the records properly sorted. She may also be able to select appropriate experts, and draft appropriate questions for them both before and after receipt of their reports. But counsel should make himself available at all stages to help if needed.

Sometimes a preliminary opinion from counsel on limitation may properly be sought, and for this it is advisable to get specific legal aid authority.

Remember to send copies of the certificate and any amendments to counsel when you instruct him (see reg. 59 of the Civil Legal Aid (General) Regulations 1989).

CONFERENCES

A conference with counsel may or may not be necessary at an early stage. If the claim is clear, there is little justification in incurring the expense of bringing the doctor(s) to a conference (the patient/client should, of course, always be invited to attend any conference). A conference without an expert present (even if only by telephone) is unlikely to serve any justifiable purpose (except if at a later stage non-medical special damages are being clarified).

The main conference will usually take place after exchange of witness statements and before exchange of expert reports (see Chapter 13). At this point you will have received the statements of the treating doctors, which may help to redefine the strength and the direction of the case, and with them in mind the final draft of your expert reports can be prepared. There may be a need for a further conference shortly before the trial, or, at least, a meeting between counsel and the main expert(s), i.e. after receipt of the defence expert reports.

THE PATIENT'S STATEMENT

Ensure that every statement you take from the patient or any witness is dated. This seems obvious, but it is often overlooked, with the result that one does not know what period of time the statement is referring to or valid for, and so it can easily produce confusion, even mislead.

ALTERNATIVE FUNDING

Due to the drastic reductions in financial eligibility for legal aid pushed through by the present government, patients – and lawyers – are being forced to consider other methods of funding claims. A comprehensive legal fees insurance scheme could be worked out. Or claims could be financed by a charge on damages awarded to successful legally aided plaintiffs (the irony is that the Lord Chancellor does not seem to get the message that personal injury litigation is largely self-financing, i.e. claims brought for the most part succeed). Individual insurance cover is possible, but the policy usually involves a ceiling which does not cover the patient's own costs of prosecuting a case to trial, let alone the defendants' costs if the plaintiff loses (also, it creates a lot of extra work to have to report back at every stage to the insurance company).

The Lord Chancellor thinks he has found the answer in the conditional fees scheme, referred to above. This would have the advantage to the Government of not requiring any administration or financial support by the state. It does not mean that the successful lawyer would, as in the USA, take a cut from the damages (that is one reason why juries award such large sums there, because they know the lawyers will take 40% of it). All it means is that the lawyers get nothing if they lose, but an uplift to their fees if they win, which will have to be paid out of the damages. The uplift originally proposed by the Lord Chancellor was absurdly small and he soon realised he would have to do a lot better if he was to have any takers. It has now been increased to 100%; however, one can be sure that capping will be introduced once the scheme has been accepted. The disadvantages of such a scheme to the patient are obvious. She will still have to pay the defendants' costs if she loses (it is said that after the event insurance – i.e. in the event of failure – is available at a modest premium, but that is most unlikely to be the case for medical negligence claims unless the insurance companies are unfamiliar with their totally unpredictable nature); she will have the uplift taken out of her damages if she wins; lawyers are unlikely to take any cases but obvious winners; there will be pressure on the lawyers to get a settlement accepted by the client because if they lose one or two substantial trials they will be bankrupt. None of this, of course, matters to the Government, so long as public expenditure is restrained.

CHECKLIST

- If the legal aid position looks tricky, is there any useful work you can do under the green form scheme?
- If legal aid is not available, have you warned the client of the likely cost of the various stages and, as far as you can see, the likely amount of compensation? If you have in mind proceeding on a conditional fee basis, have you warned the client of all that that entails? (Have you warned yourself?!)
- Have you taken as full a statement from the client as you can? Have you dated it?
- If legal aid is offered, have you warned the client of all the likely costs implications?
- Have you clarified as far as you can the correct name(s) of the likely defendant(s)?
- Have you checked the parties named on the certificate, and the limitation?
- Are you aware of what you have to do next, e.g. obtaining all the records (including GP records), getting them properly sorted, attending any inquest, selecting the right expert to report etc? For these matters see the next chapters.
- Have you worried sufficiently about limitation? Do you understand the law, in so far as it is intelligible? (See Chapter 28.)

6 · The inquest

SUMMARY

The inquest provides an important opportunity for the bereaved at an early stage to hear the doctors' account of the relevant events from the witness box and, to an extent, to cross-examine them on it. Do not set your heart on achieving anything else, such as a verdict of lack of care. The right preparation for the inquest is essential. This may include getting in on the post-mortem and must include obtaining the medical records.

An opportunity not to be missed

If there is going to be an inquest efforts should be made to make the most of the opportunity to find out what the hospital says about the circumstances surrounding the death. It is, of course, not a trial, and you are very much at the 'mercy' of the coroner as to what may be asked of the doctors, by him and by you. Although legal aid is not available for representation at an inquest, a solicitor can give two hours (or more with an extension) of advice for the preparation for the inquest. The green form can cover a 'Mackenzie' adviser in the appropriate case, though not for representation. I would think that the green form could therefore cover the Mackenzie adviser sitting in on the inquest and advising *sotto voce*. Why not? Without help the relatives are likely to be floundering. The solicitor could be of substantial help, but what is really needed to make the most of the inquest is expert medical advice. Assuming the relatives do not have links with a friendly doctor, they should ask AVMA for help (Action for Victims of Medical Accidents); their staff are very well informed on both medical and legal matters. Best of all would be to get a copy of the medical records before the inquest, whether by asking the coroner to call for them (this is a bit chancey) or by demanding them, if there is time for this before the inquest (or any adjournment), by way of pre-action disclosure. In *Stobart* v. *Nottingham Health Authority* [1993] PIQR P.259 Rougier J. held that it was a proper use of the pre-action disclosure provisions to seek the medical records prior to the inquest (on pre-action disclosure see the next chapter).

Note also that a lot of work useful for the inquest can without impropriety be done under the legal aid certificate authorising the prosecution of a civil action.

Actual representation: I am afraid this has to be paid for, but it may be worth it. I am doubtful how far an advocate can get without any medical input, either by way of the records or from a suitably informed party (assuming the advocate is not medically knowledgeable himself) e.g. the said friendly doctor, or AVMA. Unfortunately opportunities are often lost at the inquest for lack of preparation – the advocate does his best to cope with a grieving and (understandably) emotional family, but, as I say, without medical input the hospital doctors and pathologist, who may be covering up for them, will have a clear field, at any rate unless the coroner is both medically expert and resolutely determined to ferret out the truth.

The law

The Coroners Act 1988 requires an inquest to be held where information has been received upon which there is reasonable cause to suspect that the deceased died (*inter alia*) an unnatural death, or a sudden death of which the cause is unknown. That information may come from any person, e.g. doctor or relative of the deceased. It is often difficult to define the relevant cause of death, particularly in a 'medical' context (it is not necessarily the proximate or terminal cause): the 1954 Regulations speak of a death which is 'unnatural or directly or indirectly caused by any sort of accident, violence or neglect or . . . attended by suspicious circumstances'. In *R.* v. *Poplar Coroner, ex parte Thomas* (1992) 11 BMLR 37 the Court of Appeal said that the late arrival of the ambulance following a terminal asthmatic attack did not make the death 'unnatural' within the meaning of s.8(1)(a) of the Act of 1988, even though the evidence indicated that if it had arrived earlier the deceased, a 17-year-old girl, could probably have been saved. Simon Brown L.J. added that if the late arrival had constituted a more extreme failure of the service than in fact it had, common sense would dictate that the death be deemed unnatural.

Among the coroner's duties is that of informing the interested relatives about the time and place of the post-mortem and the inquest. Note, all advocates, that it is the coroner's function to examine the witnesses on oath – the right to cross-examine or otherwise intervene on the part of others is within the coroner's discretion; but he must exercise that discretion judicially. The inquest is intended to ascertain not culpability for the death, but, principally, who the deceased was, and how, when and where he came by his death.

A coroner has power to order the production of the hospital records, by a *subpoena duces tecum* (the Latin denotes an order 'that you bring with you . . .', i.e. the specified documents to the court), and he can be criticised if he ignores the relatives' request for them (see *R.* v. *Southwark Coroner, ex parte Hicks* [1987] 1 WLR 1624, DC).

Among the verdicts that can be returned are (relevant for our purposes) 'want of attention at birth', and 'accident or misadventure' (it appears to be the better view that these last two verdicts are not distinguishable and that 'accident' is the preferable term). The 'lack of care' verdict can cause problems: it is unclear whether it is a verdict in its own right or a rider which may be added to some or all of the other verdicts (refer to *Cases on Coroners* by Knapman and Powers (Barry Rose, Chichester 1989)). In any event no verdict should be framed in such a way as to determine any question of civil liability (rule 42 of the Coroners Rules, SI 84/552) though, as the court said in the *Linnane* case (see below), the issue of lack of care can properly be raised so long as no one is identified in the verdict as being responsible for it.

Recent cases on 'lack of care'

Croom Johnson J. said in the *Hicks* case (*supra*) that the prime meaning of 'lack of care' was that of a failure of physical attention, such as a failure to prevent death from starvation or exposure, bad nursing or medical care, there being no difference between a failure to give enough nourishment and a failure to give enough medicine.[1]

In *R.* v. *Inner London North District Coroner, ex parte Linnane (No.2)*, 26 July 1992, the Divisional Court said that a coroner had erred in refusing to call a particular doctor as a witness: although it was up to the coroner to decide whom he wished to hear, his reasons for refusing to hear this witness were invalid, they being that the doctor had been selected by the deceased's family and that he, the coroner, being a doctor himself with experience of

---

[1] In *R.* v. *Birmingham Coroner, ex parte Secretary of State for the Home Department, The Times,* 31 July 1990, the Divisional Court said that if on the facts of a particular death the coroner took the view that there was evidence that could justify a jury in concluding that lack of care aggravated the cause of death, it would be appropriate to leave to the jury a verdict that the cause of death was so aggravated; but they should be carefully directed as to the meaning of such a verdict and the need for a clear causal connection between the lack of care and the death.

infectious diseases, did not need the assistance of any other doctor. Further, the issue of death from acute myocarditis aggravated by lack of care should have been left to the jury. However, in view of the fact that the death had been some 21 months earlier and that the doctor's report in fact gave little support to the contention that lack of care on the part of the police had been responsible for the death of the deceased in police custody, the court refused to exercise its discretion to order a new inquest.

And in *R.* v. *Birmingham Coroner, ex parte Secretary of State for the Home Department, The Times*, 31 July 1990, the Divisional Court quashed a verdict of lack of care following the suicide by hanging of a prisoner in police custody, on the ground that there was no evidence to support the causal connection.

In *R.* v. *North Humberside and Scunthorpe Coroner, ex parte Jamieson* [1994] 3 WLR 82, the Court of Appeal, emphasising the limited ambit of the inquest (solely directed to establishing the identity of the deceased, and where, when and how he came by his death) said that 'lack of care' or 'neglect', as it should more appropriately be expressed, is the obverse of self-neglect and connotes gross failure to provide sustenance, shelter or necessary medical attention for a person who was dependent by reason of age, illness or incarceration. Neglect could rarely, if ever, be a free-standing verdict and only is appropriate as ancillary to any verdict where there was a direct causal connection between the relevant conduct and the cause of death. Where, as here, a person had killed himself (while in prison), neglect could not form part of a verdict of suicide merely because he had been given an opportunity to kill himself.

On the other hand, in *R.* v. *East Berkshire Coroner, ex parte Buckley, The Times*, 1 December 1992, the Divisional Court said that counsel should have been allowed to ask the jury for a verdict of lack of care, the deceased having died at Broadmoor mental hospital after injections of Phenothiazine.

A suggestion

Instead of worrying about obtaining a particular verdict, it is probably more sensible when attending an inquest into a death that may furnish grounds for a medical negligence action to limit one's objective to getting as full an account as possible from the doctors of their version of the events. This will give you their story at an early stage, and any later deviations from it will be material for cross-examination.

Further points of interest

The post-mortem: in the appropriate case the relatives or their solicitor, if she is contacted in time,[2] should ask the coroner to confirm that he is not instructing a pathologist on the staff of or associated with the hospital where the deceased died, on the ground (a relative swearing an affidavit, if necessary, to the effect that s/he believes that the death was due to improper medical treatment – see ss.20 and 21 of the Act) that the conduct of members of that hospital is likely to be called into question at the inquest (see the Coroners Rules 1984 r.6(1)(c)(iii)), and should inform the coroner that the relatives require to be represented at the post-mortem, i.e. by a 'legally qualified medical practitioner' (which actually means no more than a doctor) (see rule 7(3)), or that they will require their own, i.e. a second, post-mortem (see *R. v. HM Coroner for Greater London, ex parte Ridley*, 4 September 1985 (Knapman and Powers (*supra*)).

The duty to hold an inquest: as we have seen the coroner must hold an inquest as soon as practicable where (*inter alia*) there is reasonable cause to suspect that the deceased has died a violent or unnatural death or a sudden death of which the cause is unknown (Coroners Act 1988 s.8(1)).

The jury: the coroner is obliged by s.8(3) of the Act to sit with a jury if (*inter alia*) there is reason to suspect that the death occurred in circumstances the continuance or possible recurrence of which is prejudicial to the health or safety of the public or any section of it.

It can probably be argued in every case of death by suspected medical negligence that a jury is compulsory, e.g. because proper procedures have not been established for checking drugs, instruments, etc., supervising staff, recording or disseminating the result of investigations, monitoring, following up, referral to and consultation with other specialities etc. (on this see *R. v. Coroner for Hammersmith, ex parte Peach* [1980] 2 WLR 496, 508, 509 and the *Linnane* case (*supra*), where the coroner's initial refusal to call a jury was successfully challenged on appeal).

If the relevant suspicion within s.8(3) arises during the course of a hearing begun without a jury the coroner must start again with one.

Refusal to summon a jury can be challenged by judicial review (for which legal aid can be sought).

Before the hearing: I have already said that the medical records should be obtained, i.e. by applying for pre-action disclosure

---

[2] Some solicitors place advertisements in the local hospital or mortuary, which seems both sensible and helpful.

from the proposed defendants. If the coroner will give disclosure of the statements of witnesses or any other documents that he obtains, so much the better, but he cannot be compelled to, and so in many cases neither the solicitor for the family nor the jury will see them (see the *Blair Peach* case at p. 503). However, the coroner will normally provide in advance of the hearing a list of the witnesses he proposes to call. He should be careful to call all relevant witnesses as by rule 24 he must give proper notice of the inquest to anyone whose conduct is likely to be called into question and, by rule 25, if that has not been done that person can demand that the inquest be adjourned.

Although the pathologist is permitted to supply his report only to the coroner (rule 10(2)), it can be argued (under rule 57(1)) that the coroner is obliged to supply a copy for an appropriate fee to any properly interested person who asks for one.

Do not be shy about communicating with the coroner before the inquest. You are likely to find him and his officers sympathetic and helpful. Make sure that you give him an estimate of the time needed for the hearing.

The funding: where legal aid has been granted with a view to an action for medical negligence, it would seem not improper in an appropriate case to bill the work done in preparing for the inquest (though not of course any representation at it) under that certificate as such work must surely be also properly referable to the necessary preparation for any civil action.

Legal aid is of course available for any appeal to the Divisional Court by way of judicial review.

At the inquest: as I have said, and as advocates, and family, often discover to their irritation/dismay/consternation, the coroner is very much the sole master of his court. He must by law disallow any question that he thinks irrelevant or otherwise not a proper question (rule 20(1)(b)). He will, in view of the limited purposes of an inquest (i.e. merely to establish the identity of the deceased and the fact, place and cause of death) not allow questions that appear to seek merely to allocate blame and will remind the questioner that his is an inquisitorial and not an accusatorial court (for guidance see the *Blair Peach* case (*supra*) at p. 504 and *In re the death of Adam Bithell (deceased)* (1986) 150 JP 282).

The advocate may not address coroner or jury on the facts (rule 40), but she may address the coroner on the law.

The verdict: 'lack of care' is dealt with above.

Occasionally it will be proper to aim for a verdict of unlawful killing. Witnesses need not answer questions where to do so may tend to incriminate them (rule 22). The criminal standard of proof applies (see *R.* v. *HM Coroners Court for Hammersmith, ex parte Gray*, 19 December 1986 DC (Knapman and Powers (*supra*)). If a charge of manslaughter appears possible the inquest must be adjourned for the view of the Director of Public Prosecutions to be sought about proceeding further with the inquest.

It was said in the *Gray* case (*supra*) that for a verdict of manslaughter by negligence to be returned the jury had to be satisfied that the doctor had failed to do what he ought to have done for the health and welfare of a patient in his care, that that failure had been at least a substantial cause of death, and that in so failing he had acted recklessly, i.e. that he had appreciated there was an obvious and serious risk to the health and welfare of the patient, or that he had chosen to turn a blind eye to that risk, and that he had deliberately elected to run that risk of doing nothing about it.[3,4]

CHECKLIST

- Will there be an inquest?
- Do you need to press for one?
- Are you trying to get the medical records first?
- Can you get some medical advice/input first?
- Have you explained to the family the limited objectives of an inquest?

---

[3] It would be churlish of me not to acknowledge the help I have received in drafting this chapter from the authoritative lectures and writings of Michael Powers, Q.C.

[4] For cases on manslaughter see the last sections of Chapter 17.

7 · Obtaining the medical records

In respect of medical records made after October 1991 the Access to Health Records Act 1990 gives a largely unfettered right to a plaintiff to inspect and obtain copies of his medical records. In respect of records pre-dating November 1991 the 'old' rules for pre-action disclosure still apply. These are dealt with first. The last part of this chapter explains the working of the Act of 1990.

SUMMARY

Obtain the medical records as soon as possible. They will probably be disclosed voluntarily if you write in proper form. Never accept disclosure to nominated expert only. Read them. Sort them. Paginate and index them. Check them later against the originals.

If you have to apply to the court under s.33 of the Supreme Court Act 1981 and RSC O.24 r.7A make sure that the supporting affidavit establishes the conditions that need to be satisfied before the court will make an order for disclosure. If you have made a proper request you are unlikely to have to pay the defendants' costs of the application. Examine any claim to privilege with the greatest care, as the courts are more and more inclined, in the area at least of legal professional privilege, to attribute more weight to the public interest in disclosure than the private interest in confidentiality.

It is essential that *all* the patient's medical notes be obtained and *put in good order* as soon as possible. All sorts of difficulties arise if you try to progress the action without seeing them. You, the solicitor, must read them and note anything that you think to be relevant. They must be sorted into good order, by a paralegal if necessary. After that they will be sent to the expert.[1] The entitlement to pre-action disclosure arises from s.33 of the Supreme Court Act 1981 and rules of court made thereunder. We shall look at the legislation in a moment. But as health authorities,

---

[1] Where appropriate, get the client to go through them first.

and even general practitioners, are almost invariably ready to disclose the records voluntarily these days if they are approached in the right way, we deal first with the way to obtain disclosure without recourse to the courts.[2]

VOLUNTARY DISCLOSURE

As soon as you have obtained legal aid, or earlier if you wish, you should write to the hospital, or practitioner, asking for disclosure. These records contain the evidence upon which the claim will be based. So they must be complete. You must put them in good order, and you must read them, and, so far as possible, understand them (see Chapter 8). You have the duty, to client, legal aid fund and to the expert, to ensure that the evidence upon which the expert is to report is complete. At some time you must check the copies you have been sent against the originals in the hospital's possession. It is by no means unknown for a less than full complement to be sent to the solicitor. Sometimes the hospital takes the view that this or that document is not part of the medical records. You must be alert to this. Your paralegal who sorts the records should alert you to any missing documents. Your expert may mention in passing that he has not seen such and such a record. You can specifically ask him whether he is satisfied that he has all the relevant records. For example, it has been known for a hospital to be reluctant to produce the fetal monitor charts in an obstetric case. They are unlikely to mean much to you, but, read by an expert, they could indicate a failure to react to early signs of fetal distress. Unless it is clearly inappropriate (and that will not be the case very often) the patient should be given the opportunity to look at and comment upon the records. The expert should be sent a full statement from the patient, whether or not he is going to see him in person, so that the patient's account can be matched by the expert against what appears in the notes. Do not be slow to chase up missing records, as advised by your paralegal or expert. It is amazing what records defendants can find when they are put under pressure by a summons and a forthcoming hearing, often after stoutly protesting in the correspondence that they are untraceable despite every effort made. Remember that you need *all* the records. For example, it is a rare case where the GP records are not of some relevance. The records of treatment at other hospitals earlier or

---

[2] In *Stobart* v. *Nottingham Health Authority* [1993] PIQR P259 Rougier J. held that it was a proper use of the pre-action disclosure provisions to seek the medical records prior to an inquest.

later than the impugned treatment may well cast light on the
pathology and on causation. Unless you are sure that any records
are irrelevant to the case, get them all. Occasionally an inexperienced defence solicitor offers limited disclosure of only the
records that in his unwisdom he considers relevant. Put him wise
without delay. Strictly, you are not entitled to pre-action disclosure of pre-November 1991 records from a non-party, but a
suitably framed request is rarely refused.

Period of retention of records

HC(80)7 advises a minimum retention period of 25 years for
obstetric records; until the 25th birthday or eight years after the
last entry for children and young people; for mentally disordered
persons 20 years from the date of cure; and in any other case eight
years.

DISCLOSURE TO 'NOMINATED MEDICAL ADVISER ONLY'

Previous editions at this point contained a lengthy section warning the solicitor not to accept disclosure limited to the medical
expert, explaining the solicitor's duty to read and understand the
records herself, and pointing out that such a condition was wrong
in law and in practice and should never be accepted. I do not
believe that any defence solicitor would now think in terms of
such disclosure. Therefore it will now suffice simply to emphasise
the importance of the solicitor getting all the records, sorting
them into order (or having that done by a paralegal), reading
them herself and, as far as possible, understanding them.

DISCLOSURE AGAINST NON-PARTY

As already noted, your right to pre-action disclosure lies only
against a likely party to the action; so if you want a health
authority that is not the one you propose to sue to disclose
records you should accept whatever terms they offer and/or apply
after issue of the writ for full disclosure (under s.34 of the
Supreme Court Act 1981). One may not join a party just to get
discovery (*Douihech* v. *Finlay* [1990] 1 WLR 269).

THE SCIENTIFIC CO-ORDINATOR

In one of the *Opren* cases (*Davies (Joy Rosalie)* v. *Eli Lilly & Co.*
[1987] 1 WLR 428 CA) Hirst J. said that in a suitably complex

case it would be permissible to allow someone who was not a prospective witness and who was neither a party to the action nor a party's legal adviser to inspect documents in the capacity of a scientific co-ordinator entrusted with the task of collating documentary evidence. The defendants, however, satisfied the judge that they had a reasonable objection to the particular person put forward as co-ordinator. On appeal ([1987] 1 WLR 428) the Master of the Rolls, approving disclosure to the particular scientific co-ordinator, said that in the light of the evidence available to the court it was clear that the fact that the co-ordinator might be an unwelcome critic of the pharmaceutical industry was no reason to think that he might breach his obligations of confidentiality and misuse information that was made available to him.

THE LETTER REQUESTING DISCLOSURE OF THE RECORDS

If you are not sure of the identity of the proposed defendant you can get help from the *Medical Directory*. This contains *inter alia* a list of hospitals and health authorities at the end of the second volume. The administrator of a hospital will always tell you the correct name of his managing body. The General Medical Council (153 Cleveland Street, London W1P 6DE) will provide details of the registration of any practitioner, which include name, qualification, address and range of employment for which registration is held.

The letter should include the name and address, and if possible, hospital number of the client, and give details of any legal aid certificate.[3]

Unless the records requested were made after October 1991, in which case the Access to Health Records Act 1990 applies, you must set out in reasonable detail, as far as you can, the allegations of negligence; but do not commit yourself to anything that could prove to be inaccurate or too restrictive, as it could be used to your disadvantage at a later date. It you can identify any practitioner who may have been negligent, this will help the Authority to process your request (by contacting him and his defence union). Letters have been written by solicitors which simply ask for the notes because 'our client is considering action arising out of his treatment at . . .'. Not surprisingly the defendants (particularly if you are writing to a doctor represented by a medical defence society) then ask for details of the allegations before they consider releasing the records, and this wastes time,

---

[3] See the precedent in Appendix II.

and money. The requirement for some sort of case to be spelt out arises, as we see below, from the provisions of the legislation. Clearly there will be many cases where it is not possible to do more than give all the facts within the client's knowledge and indicate areas of dissatisfaction. This should not be seen as the 'fishing expedition' that the courts have always disapproved of. If it is a case where the injuries appear to have arisen under anesthetic and you have no idea what was done that might be negligent, say that you rely on 'res ipsa loquitur' and refer to *Saunders* v. *Leeds Western Health Authority and Robinson* [1993] 4 Med LR 355. The commonsense approach of the judges in this context may be illustrated by the (non-medical) case of *Shaw* v. *Vauxhall Motors Ltd* [1974] 1 WLR 1035. The plaintiff there could not say whether or not he was alleging inadequate maintenance of the relevant vehicle until his expert had seen the records of maintenance. After some dissension below, the Court of Appeal approved the application for disclosure of those records. Lord Denning M.R. said:

One of the objects of the section is to enable the plaintiff to find out before he starts proceedings whether he has a good cause of action or not. That object would be defeated if he had to show in advance whether he already had a good cause of action before he saw the documents. If the reports did show a want of proper maintenance or repair of this truck, an action would no doubt be brought. Whereas if they show that there was proper maintenance and repair, an action would not be brought.

And

All that should be required is that the potential plaintiff should set out in an open letter in general terms his own knowledge, however vague, of how his accident happened. If he does so, and gives information which shows that the reports may well be material, then I think the court may properly order disclosure of them before action [is] brought. That should, I think, be the general practice. It enables each side to know the strength or weakness of the case before embarking on litigation. It is particularly useful in a legal aid case, because it gives the solicitors and counsel better material on which to advise.

And *per* Buckley L.J.

But there is an important aspect of the matter which I think it is right for any court before whom such an application comes to bear in mind. That is the public interest where the plaintiff is qualified for legal aid. Where the plaintiff is qualified for legal aid, his advisers are under a duty to inform the legal aid committee of their view of his prospects of succeeding in the action and to keep the committee informed from time to time throughout the progress of the proceedings of any change in that respect; it is undesirable that proceedings should be brought or continued with legal aid beyond the point at which it is reasonably clear that the plaintiff has got no substantial prospect of success; and therefore there is a special ground for saying that the advisers of legally aided parties should have as early information as possible on matters which may affect that aspect of a legally aided party's position in the litigation.

Ask that the hospital agree to disclose to you all the medical records therefore as soon as possible. Ask for the documents to be listed (in categories if not by item) before they are sent: it is arguable that the legislation imposes such an obligation on them (under s.33(2)(a) of the Act of 1981 – see below)[4]; and it is not very helpful to receive, as often, an unnumbered, unlisted, unstapled bundle of single sheet copies (it is at least something if you can get them to staple together sheets that comprise a single document; otherwise it is often hard for the layman to know where one document ends and another begins). The sheets are frequently badly copied so that the all-important date and time on the left-hand side of the nursing log do not appear(!).

It is best to state the documents you require in wide terms; if, for example, you simply ask for the medical notes, you may not get some or all of the clinical correspondence, X-rays, nursing notes, fetal monitor charts, laboratory reports, reports of special investigations etc. In most cases you will cover all relevant material if you ask for:

all medical, nursing, anesthetic, surgical, and medication records and notes together with the records and notes from any other investigation and treatment undertaken; all laboratory and other test reports, X-ray films, records and reports, all accident reports and memoranda, all consent forms and all clinical and other correspondence.

Or you can send a schedule (as set out in Appendix II).

Undertake to preserve the confidentiality of the records and to use them only for the purpose of the proposed claim. Say that you will in the first instance accept legible photocopies, for which you will pay their reasonable copying charges,[5] but that you would be willing to do your own copying and to return the documents straight away. Reserve your right, if you receive copies, as you probably will, to inspect them later against the originals. You may also add, formally, that they should inform you if any of the relevant documents are in the power, custody or possession of someone else, and, if so, to identify that person. And you may ask for their undertaking that the relevant documents and X-rays

---

[4] However in *M.* v. *Plymouth Health Authority* [1993] 4 Med LR 108 Brooke J. held that for pre-action discovery defendants were not required to make an itemised list of documents supported by affidavit. It was sufficient if an index identified relevant categories. This case shows that it is best practice for the plaintiff's solicitor to make her own list of the documents disclosed, if only to protect herself from any later allegation that she had been sent a copy of such and such a record at the outset (for an object lesson illustrating this principle see *Locke* v. *Camberwell Health Authority* [1990] 1 Med LR 253 and *infra* p. 115).

[5] HC(87)13 permits health authorities to fix their own copying and administrative charges for supplying information and copying records.

will be preserved in their entirety pending production, inspection and trial.

Say that you must have their consent to disclosure within 28 days or you will apply to the court (a six-week period was approved by the court in *Hall* v. *Wandsworth Health Authority, The Times*, 16 February 1985, but that seems unnecessarily long, except perhaps where the health authority has to consult a number of doctors and they their medical defence societies). A health authority is bound by agreement with the medical protection societies to consult them before producing the medical records (where at any rate one of their members is involved, or which used to be almost always, but will now, thanks to Crown indemnity, be seldom), but you should not allow this to be used as an excuse by them to drag their feet. Remind them that refusal or even delay could result in them paying the costs of an application to the court, and you may refer here to *Hall* v. *Wandsworth Health Authority* (*supra*) and *Jacob* v. *Wessex Regional Health Authority* [1984] CLY 2618 (see RSC O.62 r.6(1) and (9)). Ask them to nominate solicitors for service.

Do not forget to enclose a letter of authority from the client for disclosure of his records. (See Appendix II for a precedent.)

The health authority has a duty to give proper disclosure. Where a health authority had grossly misled the plaintiff's medical and legal advisers in their disclosure of X-rays, the Court of Appeal ordered a new trial (*Cunningham* v. *North Manchester Health Authority, The Independent*, 15 February 1994 (to be reported in the Medical Law Reports)).

Also worth noting, for the obverse side of the coin, is *Dunn* v. *British Coal Corporation* [1993] PIQR P275, in which the Court of Appeal held that where a claim for damages for an industrial accident included a substantial claim for loss of earnings the plaintiff was obliged to disclose all his medical records and not just those relating to the accident (the Court of Appeal has confirmed that the duty to disclose medical records in this type of situation was a duty to disclose not only to the medical advisers for the other party but also to the legal advisers – *Hipwood* v. *Gloucester Health Authority, The Times*, 21 February 1995).

OTHER DOCUMENTS

Note that the right to pre-action disclosure is not limited to medical records. Any document in the possession of the defendants that would be disclosable on discovery and relates to a potential issue in the case should be obtained, e.g. records made by medical staff, memoranda etc. about the accident, that were prepared before the expectation of litigation became the dominant motive.[6]

THE LEGISLATION

SUMMARY

In the increasingly unusual event of voluntary disclosure being refused, the court has power under the Supreme Court Act 1981 to order pre-action disclosure, provided certain conditions are satisfied. Medical reports are privileged, as are other documents prepared with the dominant purpose of submission to legal advisers in anticipation of litigation, and documents whose disclosure would be contrary to the public interest.

Introduction

The right of patients to see their medical records has been increasingly recognised in recent years, culminating in the Access to Health Records Act 1990,[7] giving the patient a virtually unfettered right to inspect and obtain copies of any records made after October 1991.

Computer files: more and more files are likely to be held on computer as the medical services modernise their record-keeping, but for the time being the vast bulk of personal medical data is hard copy. Under the Data Protection Act 1984 an individual has a general right of access to his or her personal data held on computer file. However, by statutory order pursuant to s.29 of the Act personal data about the physical or mental health of a data subject (i.e. for our purposes a patient) held by a health professional (as defined in the Act, including of course any doctor or hospital or health authority administrator), or by any other person provided that the information was first recorded by or on behalf of a health professional, may be withheld from a 'data subject' (e.g. a patient) in any case in which giving access to the data would be likely to cause serious harm to the physical or mental health of the data subject (or, less importantly for our purposes, lead to the identification of any other person (other than a health professional who has been involved in the care of the data subject) who has not consented to the disclosure of his or

---

[6] A computer database may be a disclosable 'document' (*Derby & Co.* v. *Weldon (No.9)* [1991] 1 WLR 652); and so may a photocopy (*Dubai Bank Ltd* v. *Galadari (No.7)* [1992] 1 WLR 106).

[7] The effect of this important Act is explained at the end of this chapter.

her identity). The decision as to whether serious harm is likely to result is to be made by an appropriate health professional, usually the doctor or dentist who is responsible for the clinical care of the subject.

What of *hard copy files*? Limited recognition of the patient's right to see his medical records is found in the Access to Medical Reports Act 1988. This gave a person, from the beginning of 1989, the right to see any report on him prepared by a medical practitioner which has been or is to be supplied for employment or insurance purposes. For employment purposes includes a report for an existing or potential employer. The subject has a right of access to the report before it is supplied and a right to correct errors, although access may be denied if in the opinion of the medical practitioner that would be likely to cause serious harm to the physical or mental health of the subject or of anyone else, or would indicate the intentions of a practitioner in respect of the subject, or information would be likely to be revealed about another person or the identity of an informant.

The Access to Personal Files (Social Services) Regulations 1989 (SI 89/206), which were made under the Access to Personal Files Act 1987 and came into force on 1 April 1989, provide access for individuals, subject to similar safeguards, in respect of information about them held by housing and social service authorities, information which may include reports provided to the authorities by medical practitioners about their patients.

All these developments were put in the shade, however, by the valiant and successful effort by the Campaign for Freedom of Information in getting onto the statute book, with effect from November 1991, by way of private member's bill, the Access to Health Records Act 1990, which provides a general right of access to one's medical records such as were made after October 1991 (this piece of legislation is dealt with in detail at the end of this chapter).

But for the ordinary case, at the time of writing, where the patient wants to see the GP records or the hospital file, the position in law has not changed in recent years. In *R.* v. *Mid-Glamorgan Family Health Services Authority, ex parte Martin* [1994] 5 Med LR 383 the Court of Appeal confirmed that there was no right at common law for a patient to see his medical records (the irony that the patient would have had such a right under the Data Protection Act 1984 if the records had happened to be computerised was not lost on the court). This decision was not followed by an Australian court in *Breen* v. *Williams* (1994), to be reported in the Medical Law Reports. Why are the Australian (and Canadian) judges almost always so much more imaginative and forward-looking than our conservative judiciary? However, one can be thankful that it is now generally accepted by defendants that, provided some inkling of a case is notified to them, they should offer pre-action disclosure (though it may well be slow in materialising and is likely at first assay to be less than complete).

The relevant provisions

The power of the court to order discovery against a prospective party before the issue of the writ was created by the Administration of Justice Act 1970. The relevant provisions are now contained in ss.33 and 35 of the Supreme Court Act 1981.

s.33(2): On the application, in accordance with rules of court, of a person who appears to the High Court to be likely to be a party to subsequent proceedings in that court in which a claim in respect of personal injuries to a person, or in respect of a person's death, is likely to be made, the High Court shall, in such circumstances as may be specified in the rules, have power to order a person who appears to the court to be likely to be a party to the proceedings and to have or to have had in his possession, custody or power any documents which are relevant to an issue arising or likely to arise out of that claim –

    (a) to disclose whether those documents are in his possession, custody or power; and

    (b) to produce such of those documents as are in his custody, possession or power to the applicant or, on such conditions as may be specified in the order –

        (i) to the applicant's legal advisers; or

        (ii) to the applicant's legal advisers and any medical or other professional adviser of the applicant; or

        (iii) if the applicant has no legal adviser, to any medical or other professional adviser of the applicant.

The court of appeal ruled in the 1970s on several occasions that the court had power under the Act of 1970 to restrict disclosure to medical and legal advisers, i.e. to exclude the patient from a sight of the records, where such sight might be detrimental to him. But the House of Lords overruled these decisions in *McIvor* v. *Southern Health and Social Services Board* [1978] 1 WLR 757, holding that no such restriction was permissible under that Act (in that case disclosure was in fact sought in a highway accident action by a plaintiff who was not the patient, so that it was understandable that the defendants should wish to exclude him from seeing the medical notes). The present legislation (the Act of 1981) has reversed the decision in *McIvor*'s case. But only the specified restrictions are permissible. Note that there is no power to exclude the legal advisers and order disclosure only to the medical adviser. The only purpose of the three 'restriction' provisions is to enable the court to exclude the patient himself, where it might be detrimental to him if he read the notes (the provisions are apt to cover a *McIvor* type case, too, but that was not their main purpose). 'Legal advisers' is not defined; fears were at one time expressed that it could cover any person without qualifications who chose to call himself a legal adviser, but it is most unlikely that the court would order disclosure to any legal adviser other than a qualified lawyer (or a scientific co-ordinator in the appropriate case – see above). Note also that, when making a restricted order, the court has power under s.33(2)(b) to attach such conditions as it thinks fit (such conditions could specify the time, place and manner of disclosure and inspection). The section enables rules of court to be made specifying the procedure. We look at those rules below.

The conditions

There are a number of conditions in the section which have to be satisfied (it is because these conditions exist that, as I said above, it is necessary to give certain details in your letter asking for voluntary disclosure):

(1) The patient must appear to the court to be a likely party to proceedings. In other words he must satisfy the court that he is seriously and reasonably contemplating action. In *Dunning* v. *United Liverpool Hospitals' Board of Governors* [1973] 1 WLR 586, the first case to come before the Court of Appeal under the new pre-action disclosure procedure, the applicant patient's expert had reported that discovery of the notes would probably allay the patient's suspicion that her condition had been aggravated by medical treatment. By a majority the Court of Appeal upheld the judge's order for disclosure. Lord Denning said 'likely to be made' and 'likely to be a party', should be understood as 'may' or 'may well be made', and he said:

> One of the objects of the section is to enable a plaintiff to find out – before he starts proceedings – whether he has a good cause of action or not. This object would be defeated if he had to show – in advance – that he had already got a good cause of action before he saw the documents.

James L.J., agreeing, said that ill-found, irresponsible and speculative allegations or allegations based merely on hope would not provide a reasonable basis for an intended claim in subsequent proceedings, and he construed 'likely' as equating with 'there being a reasonable prospect'. Stamp L.J., dissenting, said there were no grounds for thinking that the discovery sought was 'likely to disclose that the patient had a *prima facie* case'. (This view seems to be more consistent with the particular facts of that case, in the sense that the other members of the court harped on the fact that if the notes disclosed evidence of negligence the applicant would sue, whereas, as I have said, the indication from the expert was not that there was a possibility of negligence but rather that the notes were likely to put her fears at rest.)

(2) The 'likely' claim must be 'in respect of personal injuries', or 'in respect of a person's death'. In *Paterson* v. *Chadwick* [1974] 1 WLR 890, where the plaintiff was suing her solicitors for not processing her medical negligence action timeously, Boreham J. held that there was a clear and firm connection between her professional negligence claim and her personal injuries, so that she was entitled to (non-party) disclosure of her medical records from the relevant health authority as being a 'party to proceedings in which a claim in respect of personal injuries to a person is made' (the words of the earlier legislation).

Personal injuries: pre-action disclosure is only available in actions for personal injuries or death. Not every medical negligence claim will necessarily be in respect of personal injuries – for example, negligent failure to advise termination of a pregnancy of a woman contracting rubella may not cause any personal injury to her but may result in the birth of a handicapped child; a claim against a doctor for negligent diagnosis of dysfunction in an actually healthy patient might give rise to an action for mere economic loss when that patient is advised to give up work for a period. 'Personal injuries' are defined in s.35(5) identically with the interpretation section of the Limitation Act 1980 s.38, so that they include any disease or impairment of a person's physical or mental condition. It would include a claim for nervous shock, which, to be admissible, must involve an actual psychiatric disorder (see *McLoughlin* v. *O'Brian* [1982] 2 WLR 982 and Chapter 20). There may be contexts where it is not clear whether the experience undergone by the patient amounts to injury, e.g. where a mother claims for wrongful birth after an uneventful pregnancy, has she suffered 'injury'? In *Ackbar* v. *Green & Co.* [1975] 2 WLR 773 it was held that a claim against an insurance broker for failing to obtain cover for the plaintiff was not a claim for damages for personal injuries although the claim in fact arose out of the plaintiff's having suffered personal injury.

A decision similar to that in the *Ackbar* case had been reached by a Scottish court in *McGahie* v. *Union of Shop Distributive and Allied Workers* 1966 SLT 74.

However, *Ackbar*'s case was distinguished in *Howe* v. *David Brown Tractors (Retail) Ltd* [1991] 4 All ER 30 where a claim was made on behalf of a farming business for loss of profit as a result of the supply of allegedly dangerous machinery that injured the farmer and so caused financial loss to the business. The distinction was drawn that in this case the same facts gave rise to the breach of duty as to the personal injury as a result of which the financial loss was sustained, and so the action included a claim for damages 'in respect of personal injuries'.

In *Pattison* v. *Hobbs, The Times*, 11 November 1985 (to be reported in the Medical Law Reports), the Court of Appeal held that where, following an allegedly negligently performed vasectomy, damages were claimed only for the cost of raising a healthy child, the action was not one which included a claim for personal injuries. This can be understood on the limited basis that a pregnancy is not an injury (though possibly a wasted sterilisation would be). The better view is that the claim for the upkeep of the child, unlike the farming case above, is economic loss dissociate, or at any rate relatively remote, from any personal injury or any claim for personal injury – this seems to have been the view of Brooke J. in *Allen* v. *Bloomsbury Health Authority* [1992] 3 Med LR 257.

In *Walkin* v. *South Manchester Health Authority*, 19 May 1994, noted in Supreme Court Practice News 17 June 1994, Potter J. reached an opposite conclusion from the *Pattison* case, distinguishing the Court of Appeal decision on the spurious ground that his case involved a female sterilisation and the *Pattison* case a vasectomy.[8]

(3) The person against whom disclosure is sought must be 'likely' to be a party to the proceedings (note that he does not have to be likely to be a defendant; he could therefore be, for example, a likely third party).

(4) He must be 'likely' to have or have had relevant documents, i.e. relevant to an issue arising or likely to arise out of the prospective claim.

(5) He may be ordered to disclose whether he has 'those documents', i.e. documents relevant to the proceedings; and to produce them. It is arguable that in order to comply with an order to disclose he has to list what he has that is relevant; or, at least, that he has to list what he has that falls within the terms of the order. It is not clear on the words of the statute

---

[8] In *Stubbings* v. *Webb* [1993] 2 WLR 120 the House of Lords said that a claim for assault or trespass to the person was not a claim for personal injuries.

how specific the order need be; it must, like any order, be sufficiently specific to permit compliance without unreasonable effort, and, further, the wording of the section ('any documents', . . . 'those documents') suggests that the order should name the documents or class to which they belong. In other words it is probably not permissible to seek or order the disclosure merely of 'any document relevant to the issues of 'such and such'. This view is strengthened by the rules (see below) which provide that the supporting affidavit must 'specify or describe' the documents sought to be disclosed; but it remains uncertain how wide or general the description is permitted to be – the usual request for 'all medical records and notes relating to the applicant's treatment by the defendants at . . . during . . .', though somewhat general in its terms is clearly unexceptionable.

(6) The Act speaks of an application by a likely party to 'subsequent proceedings' so that, once an action has been started, which probably means as soon as the writ has been issued, even if not yet served, this section cannot be used.[9] If for limitation reasons you have to issue the writ before an originating summons under s.33 could be heard, you can nevertheless ask the court for the identical discovery by going by summons in the action under RSC O.24 r.7, which gives the court a general power in proceedings to order discovery of specified or described documents or classes of documents 'at any time'.

Section 35(1) provides that the court is not to make an order for disclosure if it considers that compliance with the order would be likely to be injurious to the public interest. As the court has anyway a general discretion whether to exercise its power to order disclosure or not, this provision seems otiose.

Disclosure should not be refused on the ground that the claim is time-barred unless that is clear beyond reasonable argument, particularly as discovery might reveal material which would affect the position (*Harris* v. *Newcastle upon Tyne Health Authority* [1989] 1 WLR 96).

In *Barrett* v. *Ministry of Defence, The Times*, 24 January 1990, Popplewell J. said that it was not necessary for the defendants to give pre-action disclosure of the report of a naval board inquiry into the death of the plaintiff's husband *because there was in that*

---

[9] Any application for pre-action disclosure where the writ had already been issued would presumably have to be entitled with the title of the writ, or one could be accused of misleading the court. Therefore the 'proceedings' in which the personal injury claim would be made could hardly be called 'subsequent', but rather 'the same' proceedings.

*particular case ample material otherwise available to the plaintiff to
enable her case to be pleaded* (this restriction should be noted).

Note that the test of relevance on the question of discovery of
documents is not the probative value of the documents in an
action but the question whether they might or could reasonably
be expected to provoke a line of enquiry which would be of
assistance to a party (*The Captain Gregos, The Times*, 21
December 1990): this was an Admiralty case but the principle is
universal; it could be useful in a medical negligence action if
defendants are baulking at full discovery for some reason.

Costs

Section 35(4) directs that rules be made whereby the 'defendants'
shall have their costs of the application 'unless the court otherwise directs', and the relevant rule, framed in no uncertain terms,
is RSC O.62, r.6(9). The thinking behind this provision was that,
as the defendant was being obliged to disclose when he was not
yet a party to any proceedings, his 'rights' were being curtailed
for the benefit of the applicant and so he should be indemnified
for the trouble he was being put to. This attitude is not defensible
in the context of medical negligence where the patient must
surely have a right to know what treatment he has received and
what exactly was done (often when he was unconscious) – see the
comments of Sir John Donaldson M.R. at the end of his
judgment in *Lee* v. *South West Thames Regional Health Authority*
[1985] 1 WLR 845 and in *Naylor* v. *Preston Area Health Authority*
[1987] 1 WLR 958. Fortunately the courts now appear to accept
that in a meritorious case it is the patient's right to see the
records, i.e. it is not a concession[10] – particularly, as we have
seen, in a legal aid case, but also in a privately funded action. The
unappealing common law tradition whereby parties are encouraged to play some sort of forensic game and keep their cards as
close to their chest as possible is increasingly – one notes with
pleasure – being replaced by a more practical and sensible
approach. This is well illustrated by the *obiter* observations of Sir
John Donaldson M.R. in *Lee* v. *South West Thames RHA*
referred to above, where he said that a patient should have a right
to be told after treatment exactly what treatment he had in fact
received, whether or not litigation was afoot (see below, where
this case is further considered); and by the forthright comments
of the Court of Appeal in *Wilsher* v. *Essex Area Health Authority*

---

[10] This must surely be the case now that the Access to Health Records Act is on the statute
book.

[1987] 2 WLR 425 on the unsuitability of the old rule that permitted defendants not to disclose their experts' reports in medical negligence actions (see Chapter 13). The judges may be persuaded to make no order for costs where the health authority has dragged its feet, and may even award costs against them where they have been guilty of unreasonable conduct amounting to misconduct (see *Jacob* v. *Wessex RHA* [1984] CLY 2618, where an unreasonable refusal by the defendants to comply with the properly made request of the plaintiff's solicitors resulted in an order that they pay the plaintiff's (applicant's) costs; see also *Hall* v. *Wandsworth Health Authority, The Times*, 16 February 1985, and RSC O.62 r.6(1) and (9)). It is specifically provided by s.35(4) that these provisions for pre-trial disclosure bind the Crown.

PRIVILEGE

Nothing in the section requires the 'defendants' to disclose what they would not have to disclose in the ordinary way (this is specifically enacted by RSC O.24 r.7A(6) – see below). In particular, there is no need to produce a privileged document (though it should be disclosed in the sense of mentioned as being in the health authority's possession).

RSC O.24 r.5(2) contains the provision applying to general discovery that any claim for privilege must be made in the party's list of documents with the ground of privilege there sufficiently stated. There seems every reason to suppose that a health authority wishing to claim privilege in pre-action disclosure should be equally explicit.

The two classes of privilege that are likely to be relevant to disclosure of medical records are legal professional privilege and public interest privilege.

Legal professional privilege

Correspondence and other communications between a solicitor and his client are privileged from production even though no litigation was contemplated or pending at the time, provided that they are of a confidential nature and the solicitor was acting in his professional capacity for the purpose of giving legal advice or getting it on behalf of the client, as from counsel. If a document to which legal professional privilege attaches does find its way into the hands of the defendant, he may use it as desired, regardless of the privilege, but if he has not yet made use of it he can be restrained from so doing (*Goddard* v. *Nationwide Building Society* [1986] 3 WLR 734,

English and American Insurance Co. v. *Herbert Smith & Co., The Times*, 22 January 1987 and see also *Guinness Peat Properties* v. *Fitzroy Robinson Partnership* [1987] 1 WLR 1027 – and see below the section 'Documents obtained by mistake').

But it is in the class of documents that are only privileged if made when litigation was contemplated or pending that any problems on disclosure of medical records are likely to arise. The general principle is that communications between a solicitor and third party, whether directly or through an agent, which come into existence after lit:gation is contemplated or commenced and are made with a view to such litigation, either for the purpose of giving or obtaining advice in regard to that litigation, or of obtaining or collecting evidence to be used in it, or obtaining information which may lead to the obtaining of such evidence, are privileged. This privilege includes documents which are obtained by a solicitor with a view to enabling him to prosecute or defend an action, or to give advice with reference to existing or contemplated litigation, but does not include copies he obtains of documents that are not themselves privileged. It is with reference to reports of accidents and similar documents which are made before litigation is commenced and generally have the purpose of putting the senior personnel or the solicitors of the potential defendants fully in the picture that problems have arisen. Such reports have a dual purpose at least, that of producing as clear an account of the incident as possible and as soon as possible so that the facts may be ascertained and any necessary action taken, and that of providing a basis on which solicitors may be instructed if necessary and proceedings defended (or settled) if they are instituted. It is not easy to discern in the shifting sands of the law what the legal rules are for defining the test of 'made with a view to litigation'. Similarly it is not clear at what point litigation may be said to have begun to be 'contemplated'.[11]

Dominant purpose

In *Waugh* v. *British Railways Board* [1980] AC 521, the defendants sought privilege for an internal report that was made in accordance with their usual practice after an accident. It contained contemporary accounts from witnesses. The defendants

---

[11] Privilege does not attach to pre-existing documents obtained, but not created, for the purposes of litigation (*Ventoris* v. *Mountain* [1991] 1 WLR 607, CA). Note also that the Court of Appeal stated that just because a document had to be disclosed it did not automatically follow that production or inspection would be ordered. Privilege, as opposed to admissibility, becomes irrelevant once a document has in fact been disclosed (*Black and Decker Inc.* v. *Flymo Ltd, The Times*, 21 November 1990).

deposed that one of the principal purposes in preparing it had been so that it could be passed to their chief solicitor to enable him to advise the Board on their legal liability and defend any proceedings if so advised. After considerable dissension below, the House of Lords, agreeing with Lord Denning M.R.'s judgment in the Court of Appeal, said that the due administration of justice strongly required that a contemporary report such as this, which would almost certainly be the best evidence as to the cause of the accident, should be disclosed, and that for that important public interest to be overridden by a claim of privilege the purpose of submission to the party's legal advisers in anticipation of litigation must be at least the dominant purpose for which it had been prepared; that in that particular case that purpose had been of no more than equal weight with the purpose of facilitating proper railway operation and safety. Therefore, the claim to privilege failed. The court added that the fact that the report stated on its face that it had finally to be sent to the solicitor for advice could not be conclusive as to what in fact the dominant purpose of its creation was.

This principle was applied to a health authority report in *Lask* v. *Gloucester Health Authority, The Times*, 13 December 1985. The Court of Appeal held that a confidential accident report which NHS circulars required to be completed by health authorities both for the use of solicitors in case litigation arose in respect of the accident, and also to enable action to be taken to avoid a repetition of the accident, was not privileged since the dominant purpose of its preparation had not been for submission to solicitors in anticipation of litigation, and this was so decided even though both health authority and solicitor had deposed that that had in fact been its dominant purpose and the report itself referred only to that purpose (the court saw in the wording of the relevant Health Circular material which enabled it to reject the sworn statements in the affidavits). This may be contrasted with *McAvan* v. *London Transport Executive* (1983) 133 NLJ 1101 in which reports that had been prepared by a bus crew and an inspector after an accident had occurred were held by the court to be privileged as the dominant purpose in their preparation was to ascertain blame in the event of a claim being made.

In *Green* v. *Post Office*, 15 June 1987, unreported, the Court of Appeal ordered disclosure of an accident report brought into existence by an employer for the dual purpose of providing information not only on which legal advice could be obtained if a claim for personal injuries was made by the employee but also on which the employer could consider whether any remedial action was required to avoid a repetition of the accident at work.

Medical reports

Medical reports, whether on liability or prognosis, and indeed
any expert report that a party has commissioned, are privileged
and he cannot be required to produce them (*Worrall* v. *Reich*
[1955] 1 QB 296, *Causton* v. *Mann Egerton (Johnsons) Ltd* [1974]
1 WLR 162). If you want a sight of the defendants' doctor's
report when you show them yours or agree to send the client to a
medical examination you must get their agreement first. It is not
safe to rely on an implied agreement, even though Lord Denning
M.R. said in the *Causton* case in a strong dissenting judgment:

> . . . I hope that in future the solicitors for every plaintiff will refuse to allow any
> defendants to have any medical examination of the plaintiff except on the terms
> that the defendants will disclose the medical reports following the examination.
> This has become so usual in practice that I think it may be said to have become
> the 'usual terms'. This is most desirable. We know that the medical men of this
> country give their reports honestly and impartially by whichever side they are
> instructed, and it is only fair that if one side shows his the other should
> reciprocate.

The usual order for disclosure of medical reports on the
plaintiff's condition and prognosis means only that if a party does
in fact intend to produce such evidence in court he must disclose
it first. (For further discussion of medical examination and
reports see Chapter 13.)

If the reports are not prepared in anticipation of litigation, e.g.
where they have been made by an employer in order to establish
whether an employee is able to return to work, the court may
order disclosure if that is necessary for the fair disposal of the case
(*Ford Motor Co.* v. *X. Nawaz, The Times,* 10 February 1987,
CA).[12]

Proceedings contemplated

The other question, at what point can one say that proceedings
are contemplated, can also give rise to difficulties. It can be said
that as soon as any accident has occurred there is a prospect of
litigation. Some cases have endorsed that approach, principally
Seabrook v. *British Transport Commission* [1959] 1 WLR 509 ('I
think that, whenever a man is fatally injured in the course of his
work on the railway line, there is at least a possibility that
litigation will ensue', *per* Havers J.); but it is doubtful if that case
is authority for anything any more in view of *Waugh* v. *British
Railways Board* (*supra*); and *Alfred Crompton Amusement*

---

[12] An example of a privileged medical report, along with other privileged papers, may be
found in *Teece* v. *Ayrshire and Arran Health Board* 1990 SLT 512.

Machines Ltd v. *Commissioners of Customs and Excise (No.2)* [1974] AC 405, which would appear to be authority for the proposition that, where a decision needs to be taken by a potential defendant before solicitors are instructed, documents coming into existence before that decision is taken cannot be said to have been made when litigation was in contemplation and are therefore not privileged. There would appear to be scope for arguing on that basis for the disclosure of a great many accident reports (the documents in the *Alfred Crompton* case comprised material collected for the purpose of preparing a valuation of the plaintiff's goods for an assessment to purchase tax, but the principle is equally applicable to accident or medical reports).

Whose privilege?

The general rule is that the privilege is that of the client and of no-one else; only the client can waive the privilege (though the privilege is not lost by reason of the death of the client). The somewhat complex facts of *Lee* v. *South West Thames Regional Health Authority* [1985] 1 WLR 845 illustrate what appears to be an exception to the principle that privilege may be claimed only by the party for whose benefit the document was prepared, or at any rate a limit upon that principle.

Pre-action disclosure was sought on behalf of a small boy who suffered brain damage, probably through lack of oxygen when he was on a respirator either in hospital or in the ambulance. The health authority for the hospital had, after litigation was contemplated against them, required from the defendants, who were responsible for the ambulance service, a report on what had or might have happened. That report was agreed by the parties to be privileged as far as the hospital health authority was concerned; but its disclosure was sought against the defendants, it being argued that the privilege was not theirs to assert. The Court of Appeal refused to order disclosure, saying that, although the defendants appeared to be advancing the other authority's claim to privilege, the cause of action being asserted against the defendants was not a wholly independent cause of action, but arose out of the same incident as that which rendered the hospital authority a likely defendant. However, that conclusion was 'reached with undisguised reluctance because we think that there is something seriously wrong with the law if Marlon's mother cannot find out exactly what caused this brain damage'.

Public interest privilege

It is all too easy for a public body that wishes to avoid embarrassing disclosures, or to create or preserve a sense of mystique, to claim that disclosure of certain important documents would be damaging to the public interest. Where the claim is based on the ground of national security it may well succeed, as that is an argument which our courts take very seriously. So, too, where the interests of children are involved. But in all cases such a claim must be carefully scrutinised so that public bodies that are seeking to take the easy way out should not be encouraged to expect to succeed.

Strictly, this is not a claim for privilege that a party may advance, but rather an immunity from production that the court should invoke of its own accord if the party does not, on the basis that such production would be injurious to the public interest, i.e. that withholding the documents is necessary to the proper functioning of the public service. If features most frequently in the area of governmental decisions or policy, and police or similar investigations, but it could be found occasionally in the medical negligence action. Every potential claim to immunity will be considered on its own facts, but a decision as to a particular type of document is likely to be of persuasive authority when a similar situation occurs later. We may note here some examples outside the area of governmental or police activity.

Examples

In *D.* v. *NSPCC* [1978] AC 171, information as to ill treatment of children given to a charitable body having statutory authority to bring proceedings was held to be protected; whereas the confidentiality of the records of a local education authority was insufficient ground for protecting them from disclosure in *Thompson* v. *Inner London Education Authority* (1977) 74 LS Gaz 66. In *Campbell* v. *Tameside Metropolitan Borough Council* [1982] QB 1065 the Court of Appeal, in an action by a teacher who had been assaulted by a violent pupil against the education authority employing her, ordered disclosure of psychiatric and other reports on the boy. Lord Denning M.R. referred to the line of cases in which the court had refused disclosure of reports on children in the care of local authorities. He said that in every case the task was to hold the balance between the public interest in keeping the reports confidential and the public interest in seeing that justice was done. In the 'children' cases the court had always found that justice could be done in the individual case without compelling disclosure of the documents. But in the instant case the significance of the documents to the plaintiff's claim outweighed the interest in keeping them confidential. Lord Denning said he saw no difference between that case and

the ordinary case against a hospital authority for negligence. The reports of nurses and doctors are, of course, confidential; but they must always be disclosed . . .

A claim for immunity should indicate whether it is based on the nature of the contents of the documents, or the class of document to which they belong, and if the latter should specify what that class is. The judge, if not satisfied with the information given, may examine them himself without the other party seeing them.

In *Barrett* v. *Ministry of Defence, The Times*, 24 January 1990, it was held that a naval board of enquiry report into the death (caused or contributed to by an excessive intake of alcoholic beverage) of a naval airman stationed in northern Norway did not attract public interest immunity.

In September 1990 hemophiliacs seeking compensation for having been infected with the HIV virus from contaminated clotting agents secured in the Court of Appeal the release of many important documents that the Government were unjustly trying to withhold from them on the factitious ground, so dear to government, that the public interest demanded that they remain secret (see *Re HIV Hemophiliac Litigation, The Independent*, 20 October 1990).

In *Balfour* v. *Foreign and Commonwealth Office* [1994] 1 WLR 681, a complaint by a member of the diplomatic service that he had been unfairly dismissed, the Court of Appeal said that the court must always be vigilant to ensure that a claim of public interest immunity was raised only in appropriate circumstances and with appropriate particularity, but, once a certificate of a Minister of State demonstrated that the disclosure of documentary evidence posed an actual or potential risk to national security, a court should not exercise its right to inspect that evidence. The trouble with this decision is that those who give such certificates are likely to have decided to give them (or to have been persuaded by their civil servants to give them) for reasons which have less to do with state security than the convenience of the government or the department involved. But, of course, the courts cannot proceed on that understanding.

One recent, and welcome, decision on 'police' matters should be noted as it is of the greatest significance to the current development of the law on this important issue. In *R.* v. *Chief Constable of West Midlands Police, ex parte Wiley* [1994] 3 WLR 433 the House of Lords, overruling earlier decisions, held that there was no public interest immunity on a class basis for police complaints files and the witness statements contained therein. Immunity could be claimed on a 'contents' basis for a specific document, which the court would then look at to see if the claim was justified, but there was no overall 'class' immunity for such files. Perhaps we can hope that we are generally moving into a

time of greater freedom of information, as witness the ruling of
the Divisional Court in November 1994 to the effect that the
Home Secretary must disclose expert reports and other relevant
evidence to convicted persons seeking a review of their convic-
tions by way of a referral to the Court of Appeal.[13]

Documents obtained by mistake

It is not unusual to find among the medical records privileged
documents, such as memos or letters from the 'accused' doctor to
the hospital administrator, health authority solicitor or MDU,
which have clearly been included through oversight – someone
has simply copied everything in the file without properly scrutinising the documents. In such a case the general rule is that you
cannot take advantage of their oversight and must send back the
documents and any copies, though that rule seems to admit of the
strange exception that if you did not realise when you saw the
document that it had been supplied by mistake you need not give
it back (see *Guinness Peat Properties Ltd* v. *Fitzroy Robinson
Partnership* [1987] 1 WLR 1027 and *Derby and Co.* v. *Weldon
(No.8)* [1991] 1 WLR 73).

In *Kenning* v. *Eve Construction Ltd* [1989] 1 WLR 1189
Michael Wright J. refused to order the return of a clearly
privileged covering letter from an expert which had been inadvertently disclosed along with his report, on the ground that if the
defendants were going to call that expert they were in any event
obliged to disclose all his evidence, warts and all (for further
comment on this dubious decision see Chapter 13 under 'The
New Rules').[14]

Where defendants had no reason to suspect a mistake when
certain documents had been included by the plaintiffs in the trial
bundle, they were entitled to assume that they were documents
on which the plaintiffs intended to rely, whether privileged or
not, and that any privilege had been waived (*Derby and Co.* v.
Weldon (No.10) [1991] 1 WLR 660).

Where the defendant's solicitor in a claim for industrial injury
reasonably believed that the plaintiff's advisers had waived
privilege in sending him a copy of a medical report, the plaintiff
was entitled to make use of it at the trial (*Pizzey* v. *Ford Motor
Co Ltd* [1994] PIQR P15).

---

[13] Reference may also be made to *Kaufmann* v. *Credit Lyonnais Bank, The Times*,
1 February 1995.
[14] Note that a document that is properly marked 'Without Prejudice' is not necessarily
privileged from disclosure, only from being adduced in evidence (see *Parry* v. *News
Group Newspapers Ltd, The Times*, 22 November 1990).

In *IBM Corporation* v. *Phoenix International* (reported in Supreme Court News, 17 February 1995), Aldous J. held that the question whether the disclosure was understood by the solicitor for the other party to be a mistake should be adjudged according to the likely reaction of the reasonable solicitor.

Overruling privilege

Where a *prima facie* case of fraud against a party has been made out the court may overrule an otherwise properly made claim to privilege (*Derby & Co.* v. *Weldon (No.7)* [1990] 1 WLR 1156).

THE RULES OF COURT

Order 24 r.7A provides that the procedure for obtaining pre-action disclosure shall be by originating summons, to which the other party shall be the defendant. The summons must be supported by an affidavit which must state the grounds for the allegation that the two parties to the application are likely parties to a personal injury action, and must 'specify or describe' the documents sought and show, by reference to a draft pleading if practicable, their likely relevance to a potential personal injury claim, and that the defendant is likely to have or have had them. The order of the court, if made, should require an affidavit from the defendant stating whether he has or has had any of the specified or described documents, and what has become of them. It is expressly stated that the defendant cannot be required to produce any document that would not fall within the scope of normal discovery.

There is a precedent for the summons and the affidavit in Appendix II. It is also acceptable, when asking for disclosure from the health authority and when proceeding by action, to list all the documents you can think of in a standard schedule – to include

A & E record card; GP's referral letter; admitting doctor's notes of examination; consent forms; ward doctor's clinical notes; operating and anesthetic records; intensive therapy records; Kardex (daily nursing notes); laboratory request forms and subsequent reports on blood and other bodily samples; ultrasound scan reports, photographs and videotapes; ECG (electrocardiograms) and reports thereon; temperature, pulse, blood pressure and respiration charts; fluid balance charts; blood balance charts; blood transfusion records; drug prescription records (once only and continuing sheets); heart injury charts; X-ray request forms, plates and reports; theatre registers and casualty registers; cardiac cerebral function record, perfusionist records; doctors' own files; health visitor records; all correspondence, internal memoranda, directives and circulars; accident memoranda, reports and all documents relating to any relevant untoward incident.

For particular cases there may well be additional records, e.g. in maternity cases there will be some or all of the following:

the co-operation card (if the hospital has a copy) and all antenatal records; partogram; [the vital] CTG traces (cardiotocograph); progress of labour chart; community midwifery records.

THE COUNTY COURT

Section 149(3) of the Supreme Court Act 1981 applies the provisions of ss.33–35 to the County Court. The relevant provisions are s.52 of the County Courts Act 1984 and O.13 r.7 of the Rules (see further on this Chapter 10 under 'High Court or County Court', where the new jurisdictional rules are discussed).

OTHER PRE-ACTION FACILITIES

By s.33(1) of the Act of 1981, and RSC O.29 r.7A, the court may, in any action, i.e. not just in personal injury actions, make orders for:

(a) the inspection,[15] photographing, preservation, custody and detention of property which by section 35(5) includes any land chattel or other corporeal property of any description [*possibilities of inspection of hospital premises and machines here*] that appears to the court to be property which may become the subject matter of subsequent proceedings or as to which any question may arise in any such proceedings; and
(b) taking samples of any such property and carrying out any experiment on or with it.

What I said above in the context of pre-action disclosure about disclosures which might be 'injurious to the public interest' and about costs applies here too; but this subsection (s.33(1)) only binds the Crown[16] so far as it relates to property relevant to a personal injury or a death claim. The relevant rules of court in relation to pre-action inspection etc. are found at O.29 r.7A.

In *Ash* v. *Buxted Poultry Ltd, The Times*, 29 November 1989, Brooke J. held that the court had power to order one party to a personal injury action to permit the other to make a video recording of a relevant industrial process, so as to facilitate the judge's understanding of the case. This power could be of use in

---

[15] The proposed libel action of *Huddleston* v. *Control Risks Information Services* [1987] 1 WLR 701 demonstrates an interesting interplay between ss.33(1) and 33(2).
[16] As to health authority as an arm of the Crown, see Chapter 3 under 'The NHS and the Crown'.

the odd medical case, e.g. to film the process of a machine in a hospital.

DISCLOSURE AGAINST A NON-PARTY

It is convenient to deal here with obtaining orders against a non-party, that is to say, for example, a health authority who is not and is not going to be a defendant to any action. This cannot be done before the issue of the writ, as it can against a likely party, so that, chronologically speaking, it could be dealt with at a later stage in this book. But as the statutory provisions are all lumped together it will be helpful if we consider them now.

Section 34 of the Act of 1981 gives the court power in a personal injury or a fatal accident action to order a non-party who appears likely to have in his possession documents relevant to any issue in the proceedings to disclose whether he has them, and if so to produce them to the applicant. The court has similar powers as in pre-action disclosure to exclude the applicant himself from a sight of the notes. This power to order disclosure only arises, as already noted, where proceedings have been commenced. If they have not, there is no general power to order documents to be produced. That is why a patient who wants his records from a health authority he is not proposing to sue is likely, until he issues a writ against his defendants, to have to accept whatever disclosure they offer (but see below the Access to Health Records Act 1990).

In *Paterson* v. *Chadwick* [1974] 1 WLR 890, where the plaintiff was suing her solicitors for not processing her medical negligence action timeously, Boreham J. held that there was a clear and firm connection between her professional negligence claim and her personal injuries, so that she was entitled to (non-party) disclosure and her medical records from the relevant health authority, she being a 'party to proceedings in which a claim in respect of personal injuries to a person is made' (the words of the earlier legislation).

In *Walker* v. *Eli Lilly and Co.* (1986) 136 NLJ 608, one of the Opren cases, Hirst J. held that the plaintiff was entitled to discovery of her medical records from a health authority not party to the action. The House of Lords considered the principles upon which the court should exercise its discretion to order a non-party to produce documents in *O'Sullivan* v. *Herdmans* [1987] 1 WLR 1047, when it approved the Northern Ireland Court of Appeal's order requiring the DHSS, on the defendants' application, to produce records of the findings of the Pneumoconiosis Board and the Medical Appeal Tribunal determining the plaintiff's entitlement to industrial benefit.

The court has under s.34(3) a power in *any* proceedings, similar to that which it enjoys in relation to *pre-action* inspection, to order inspection, photographing, preservation, custody and detention of property and the taking of samples from and experimenting upon property in the possession of a non-party which is the subject matter of current proceedings or as to which some question arises in current proceedings. The provisions mentioned above in the context of pre-action disclosure relating to disclosure 'injurious to the public interest', costs, and binding the Crown apply here too.

Order 24 r.7A sets out the manner in which an application for disclosure of documents against a non-party after the commencement of proceedings should be made, and Order 29 r.7A does likewise for an application for inspection etc.

ACCESS TO HEALTH RECORDS ACT 1990

This Act at long last gives a fairly unrestricted right to a patient to inspect and get copies of his records, provided they have been made after October 1991. (See Appendix I for the text.)

What is meant by a health record? It is a record consisting of information relating to the physical or mental health of an identifiable individual, made by or for a health professional in connection with that individual's care (it does not include computerised material coming within s.21 of the Data Protection Act 1984).

What is meant by a 'health professional'? The term includes any registered medical practitioner, dentist, optician, pharmaceutical chemist, nurse, midwife, health visitor, clinical psychologist, child psychotherapist and speech therapist.

Who may apply for access to the records? The patient; anyone authorised in writing to do so on the patient's behalf; for a child under 16 any person *in loco parentis*; the personal representative of a deceased.

To whom is the application made? To the holder of the records: GP, FPC (now FHSA), health body (includes health authority and NHS trust), the health professional who made the record.

How must the holder give access? By allowing inspection of the record or the relevant part and supplying a copy if asked. The holder must also provide an explanation of terms which are not intelligible without explanation. A fee can be charged to cover the cost of copying and postage; also for mere access a fee can be charged as set out in s.21 of the Data Protection Act 1984 (though not in respect of access to records not more than 40 days old when the application is made).

Within what period must access be given? Forty days (but 21 days if the record is itself not more than 40 days old).

Is access ever excluded? Yes. It will be denied to a child if the holder is not satisfied that the child is capable of understanding the nature of the application, and where a parent makes an application the holder needs to be satisfied that the child has consented or cannot understand the nature of the application and giving access would be in his best interests. More importantly, access may be denied where the holder is of the opinion that it would disclose information which would be likely to cause serious harm to the physical or mental health of the patient or any other individual, or information relating to or provided by an individual other than the patient, who could be identified from that information, unless that individual has consented to the disclosure or he is a health professional involved in the care of the patient.

N.B.: Access shall not be given in respect of any record made before November 1991 (the Act came into force on 1 November 1991) unless the holder is of the opinion that the giving of access is necessary to make intelligible the post-October 1991 disclosure that is to be made. One can surely expect that health authorities will disclose all past material in any case where the records include material recorded after October 1991.

There is provision for application to the court where it is thought that the holder has not complied with his obligations; this would cover an application to secure those vital sheets that so often just happen not to be among the records disclosed.

Note that a health authority or FHSA must consult the relevant doctors etc. before making any decision on an application (s.8).

Note also that the Act, unlike the rules for pre-action disclosure, does not afford anyone other than the patient or his representative the right of access.

Lastly, there is provision for a patient to enforce the correction of inaccurate information in the records.

CHECKLIST

- Have you written an appropriate letter to all possible sources of relevant medical records (including the GP)?
- Do you need to enforce disclosure by a summons?
- Have you taken advice on whether any relevant documents are missing?

- Have you pursued the defendants for any relevant missing documents?
- Have you had the records sorted, paginated and indexed?
- Have you read the records?
- Have you got the patient's comments on them?
- Are you going to check the copies against the originals, for accuracy and completeness? (This may be postponed a while, as it might prove unnecessary in the particular case.)

8 · Reading the medical notes

SUMMARY

You must get the medical records sorted and indexed, and then read them to see if you spot anything that might assist. This chapter is designed to tell you what the various documents are likely to be and to help you decipher them.

You are now in possession of the medical records. You must get them sorted, paginated and indexed – by a paralegal if you do not have that expertise in-house. You, and, where you think it could be helpful, the client, should read them carefully. They may contain material the potential significance of which only the legal eye is likely to spot. You will have no difficulty with some of the documents, such as correspondence between doctors, and consent forms. But the core of the bundle will be the clinical records, and these are often hard to read and understand. Their full effect is unlikely to be appreciated by the non-medical reader, but you should do your best.

THE RECORDS ARE LIKELY TO COMPRISE SOME OF THE FOLLOWING DOCUMENTS[1]

accident and emergency department record card
general practitioner's referral letter
admitting doctor's notes on examination
ward doctor's clinical notes
operating record
anesthetic record
daily nursing notes
laboratory reports on blood and other bodily samples
radiographs and reports on radiographs
electrocardiograms (ECG) and reports
electroencephalograms (EEG) and reports
temperature, pulse and respiration charts
fluid balance charts

---

[1] A fuller list can be found in the schedule on p. 87.

head injury charts
partogram (midwifery only)
fetal heart trace (maternity only)
correspondence to and from other hospitals involved in
    treatment and with the general practitioner.

A GP's notes will include medical record cards, correspondence from hospitals, and the results of tests.

NHS records belong to the Secretary of State. Records maintained by private hospitals do not include doctors' notes, which
are their own property, and may often be kept separately by the
treating doctor. Unlike NHS hospitals private hospitals may not
be responsible for the default of consultants, as opposed to
nursing staff (see Chapter 22).

The first thing to do is to get the records into good order.
This involves putting them in a file (easy), in a suitable order
(not so easy), paginating them (easy) and indexing them
(hard). Ideally you, the solicitor, should do that yourself, but,
although it is essential that you accept that, as you do this sort
of work, you will need all the time to be striving to broaden
your understanding of medical record-keeping if you are to
produce the best result (maybe one day you will even be
reading CTG traces and making wise observations about loss of
beat-to-beat variability), you can be excused, if you are as yet
not very experienced in this work, if you take the view that it
will be, for the time being at any rate, simpler, cheaper,
quicker and more effective to send them out for this ordering
to be done, for example to one of the paralegals, usually (ex-)
nurses who undertake this sort of work. It is better you do this
than make some valiant but highly idiosyncratic effort to order
the records yourself, *let alone send counsel and/or expert a
higgledy-piggledy bundle of loose sheets with an elastic band
round them!*[2]

Make sure that your copies are legible. If it is the copy that is
not legible, get another copy. If it is the writing that is not legible,
get it translated, by the defendants if necessary. If any copy still
remains illegible for any reason, get a typed version of it placed
on an adjacent sheet in the file. *Make sure that the left hand side
of the nursing Kardex, where the vital dates are written, has not
been chopped off in the copying.*

You will probably need to inspect the originals in due course,
to check the important entries and to ensure that there are no

---

[2] Very few solicitors are capable of making anything like as good a job of sorting the
records as the paralegal.

documents of which you do not have a copy. Pursue missing documents, by summons if necessary (see the preceding chapter).

The following guidance to reading the medical records has been written by Dr David Kirby.

WHAT THE DIFFERENT RECORDS ARE NOW AND HOW THEY ARE COMPILED

GP records

The notes kept by GPs are highly variable in quality. Mostly they are contained in an envelope, the design of which has scarcely changed in seven decades, on which is recorded the patient's name, date of birth and successive addresses, with the name of each GP with whom he has been registered. Inside the envelope there are cards which have the patient's name at the top, dates of consultations in the margin, with a second margin to give a column in which is recorded whether the consultation is on a visit or at the practice, and opposite each date a brief and often scarcely legible summary of the consultation. A few practices have changed their records to A4 folders, but the contents are essentially the same.

A GP who is trying to create systems which enable him to make any effective use of the records envelope will have arranged the cards in chronological order. There may also be a card at the front, usually in a different colour, on which is recorded a summary of the main health events in the patient's life; similarly there may be a treatment card which is a list of the drugs which at any one time a patient is receiving on a regular basis so that repeat prescriptions are being made.

Entries in GP records can be so brief as to be incomprehensible, and often they contain abbreviations which are idiosyncratic, as well as the more generally used ones which appear in hospital notes. Only a minority of GPs use any discernible system in their note-making, and these systems vary. Some GPs write a short diagnostic summary – a word or a phrase – in capitals or underlined, at the top of the notes of each consultation. However, it is not really possible after many typical consultations in general practice to make a 'diagnosis' that can be encapsulated in a few words; this is firstly because GP consultations are often about symptoms which can be managed and resolved – either by prescribed drugs or by the passage of a short period of rest – without the steps being taken by the GP which would allow an accurate diagnosis to be made. Secondly, illnesses as they are presented to GPs have several aspects –

there may be a pathological process going on in the patient's body, but there is also an emotional state, a desire to use or abuse the services of the GP, a social situation for the patient's family; the 'diagnosis' can reasonably be expressed in any of these contexts, but as the consultation will have taken a particular direction (a direction which should be determined by the patient but which all too often is in fact largely determined by the doctor) it is neither possible nor appropriate for the doctor to record more than one or two of them.

When things are written down in a patient's notes, the writer should bear in mind the possibilities that the future holds for that information to be read by many other people than himself, and this provides another powerful constraint on what a GP may write down in a patient's record, because of the need to respect the confidentiality of the consultation. For all these reasons, as well as because of the fact that most GPs do not have the time to write thorough reports about each consultation, medical records in general practice are inherently inadequate.

It follows that it is not the case that there is a correlation between the quality of a GP's practice and the quality of his records. Nevertheless, there are certain minimal pieces of information that should be recorded – the date of each consultation, and any prescribed drug treatment. It is in the nature of general practice that there will be occasional lapses even in these minimal requirements, but a consistent pattern of failure to record these fundamentals is highly suggestive of a low standard of medical care.

System of recording

Some GPs, especially those involved in training of aspiring general practitioners, or those who have been recently trained, may use a system of recording the consultation called the 'SOAP' system:

Sx ('subjective') – what the patient says is the problem.
Ox ('objective') – what the doctor finds on examination.
An (analysis) – formulation of what may be the essence of the problem.
Plan – what is to be done.

Even when you do not find that the GP's notes with which you are concerned use this system, I think that you still may find it helpful, when using the notes to try to understand what happened in a particular consultation, to try to divide up the doctor's written comments into these fundamental categories.

Some patients' records eventually become very large and difficult to use effectively. It is quite consistent with normal standards of general practice for the records to be 'culled' to remove redundant material, so that there may be gaps in the continuous chronological record, or copies of letters or of the results of laboratory investigations which have been thrown away.

As well as the handwritten records of a GP's consultations, the records envelope will contain letters about the patient which the GP has received: these are mostly from hospitals, and are either letters written by consultants after the patient has been seen as an outpatient, or discharge summaries sent after the patient has been in hospital for a period. In poorly-organised practices these letters are often to be found folded and stuffed willy-nilly into the envelope, but in a practice where efforts have been made to actually make effective use of the patients' records they will have been sorted into date order. As these letters and summaries are typed, and are in comprehensible syntactically organised English, they constitute a much more readily assimilable source of information about the patient's medical history than the cryptic abbreviated scrawlings of the general practitioner. Copies of the same letters will also be kept in the hospital records folders of each patient at every hospital they have attended.

The GP record folder may contain a variety of other bits of paper: there may be forms which contain information as to the results of investigations which the GP has ordered, such as blood tests or cervical smears.

An effective general practitioner in an urban practice today will be working closely with a number of other workers in the primary health care team, including health visitors, district nurses, community psychiatric nurses, psychologists, counsellors, social workers and others. These workers in general keep their own separate records, and the meetings between the different professions at which many important decisions are taken about a patient's care are often not well minuted: it is rarely clear from a GP's records which other members of the practice team are actively involved in the treatment at any one time, nor what treatment they are providing.

Hospital records

National Health Service hospital records are more ordered and more consistent in their quality than are the records kept by GPs. They are usually in A4 size folders and are divided into sections: there is some variation in the nature of these sections and their order, but the usual principles are as follows: the folder contains records kept by nurses as well as those kept by doctors, but these are usually arranged in separate bundles, each in chronological order. In the medical notes each admission to hospital is filed as a complete unit which usually opens with an 'admission sheet' on which various particulars are recorded by a clerk as soon as possible after the patient enters the hospital: these include name, address, date of birth, next of kin, and consultant responsible.

There should follow a thorough record of the patient's complaints and an appraisal of their current clinical state made by the house officer, the most junior of the team of doctors that is to care for the patient during his admission: this is called the 'clerking' and it constitutes a most important and valuable record, both because it is done at a most crucial time in a patient's care, especially in the case of emergency admissions, and because custom dictates that it is carried out with a great degree of thoroughness and in a certain order. Thus this record should allow readers, if it has been done properly, to have a full understanding of the patient's clinical state at that time, if they can 'read' the traditional system of layout and abbreviation which medical students are taught to use.

In the next section I have tried to compile an example with a glossary to help you 'translate' these records. It is possible to attempt this because house doctors throughout Britain are taught to use much the same system: the clarity and thoroughness of their clerkings of patients is one of the chief ways in which a consultant, who is responsible for their training, will assess the competence of the house officer, so the junior will wish to make his records comprehensible and useful to the consultant. In contrast to general practice notes, therefore, the adequacy of the hospital records is some indication of the quality of care patients have received: a junior doctor who is neglectful or overworked will keep less thorough and comprehensible records, and if his seniors, the registrar or consultant, are also neglectful, this failure will not be corrected.

After the house officer has thus recorded the admission of the patient to the hospital, the doctor who is immediately responsible for supervising the house officer's work may write in the notes, usually using the same format but more briefly. Thus frequently in hospital records the same clinical findings are recorded again under the same date, in a different handwriting, which may be that of a senior house officer or a registrar.

There follows a sequential series of entries by one or other of the team members, the frequency of which is in general a reflection of how acutely ill the patient is: on an intensive care unit the house officer or more senior colleagues may write in the notes several times a day, recording the hour at which they have assessed the patient; as well as the team of doctors responsible for the patient's care, other consultants whose opinion has been sought may write in the notes. On the other hand, the medical records kept in a long-stay ward, in a psychiatric hospital for example, may be written in only a few times a year.

Next will be filed the results of investigations carried out during that hospital admission, which are generally arrayed by sticking them in date sequence on a card, each card representing a different department – histology (the microscopic examination of tissues), bio chemistry (blood levels of hormones and drugs, and of compounds the levels of which are indices of the function of the liver and kidneys), hematology (the characteristics of the cells in the blood), or X-ray. If electrocardiograms have been done these too should be arranged, in a pattern which enables the trace to be interpreted, and kept in the notes.

If an operation is performed while a patient is in hospital this will be recorded by the house officer, but there will also be a separate sheet which has been filled in immediately after the operation by the surgeon and the anesthetist.

The admission notes are ended by the house officer, who should write a list of the drugs which a patient has been given to take at home. There will also be a typed discharge summary, which is usually written to the patient's GP by the registrar or the consultant; this document is often not written until several weeks or even months after the patient has been sent home.

In between hospital admission notes, but occasionally filed separately, there will be handwritten notes made in the out-patient clinic by the consultant, registrar or SHO who has seen the patient in the clinic; also there will usually be a letter sent to the general practitioner after each clinic visit, and copies of these letters will be kept in sequence in the patient's hospital notes.

Hospital records will contain many records kept by nurses, which may be of medico-legal importance: chief among these is the patient's 'Kardex' record: this is a system of notes kept in a single folder in the sister's office on the ward, each patient having a card which is folded into a specially designed folder which allows the patients' names to be displayed in the same sequence as their beds are arranged on the ward. When the patient leaves the hospital the card is removed and kept in the patient's hospital records folder. The nursing staff make an entry in the Kardex for each patient every day, noting the basic observations (temperature, pulse rate, and blood pressure) and commenting briefly on the patient's progress.

There will also be filed with the nursing records all the charts which have been kept at the end of the patient's bed during the admission: these will include a chart of recordings made of the patient's temperature, pulse rate and blood pressure, which may be done hourly, four-hourly, or daily according to how acutely ill the patient is. There may also be fluid balance charts which record the volumes of fluid which the patient has been given, orally or intravenously, and the volumes they have excreted.

With these charts will be found a 'Treatment Card', a new one of which is made out for each hospital admission; this is kept by the patient's bed, and is written on by one of the doctors whenever he wishes to prescribe a drug; the name of the drug should be written clearly, with instructions as to dose and frequency and route of administration, with the doctor's signature; then the nurse in charge of the ward, whenever she administers the drug, will sign the card again in a column which gives the date and time.

Most patients require the services of some other professional workers, whether they be social workers, physiotherapists, or occupational therapists, while they are in hospital. However, the notes of their activities kept by these other professionals are not usually assembled to be kept with the other records in the patient's hospital record folder, for reasons that are historical rather than logical.

Form and abbreviation in medical records

Medicine has its own language: in the past, when the knowledge and skill of physicians and surgeons were relatively limited, the dignity of their profession was enhanced and their distance above the patient increased by the use of terms the meaning of which was apparent only to their fellow trained doctors. It would be unwise to contend that the maintenance of the power of the medical profession is not, even today, a most important factor contributing to the incomprehensibility of medical records.

However, there are other important factors as well as the plethora of 'medical' words – many derived from Latin and Greek – which are still used in notes and make them difficult to understand. National Health Service doctors making records, whether GPs in the community or junior doctors in hospitals, often work in situations of pressure in which it is inappropriate to spend a high proportion of time in writing: this leads not only to poor legibility,[3] but also to the proliferation of a large number of abbreviations. In using these abbreviations, doctors assume that their colleagues will be able to interpret them, and they sacrifice the possibility of non-doctors being able to understand. This follows from the prevailing attitude to records throughout the medical profession, which is that they are written for the benefit of other doctors who may be treating the same patient in future; they are certainly not written for the patient to be able to understand them.

In recent decades advances in diagnostic methods and in treatment have led to a vast proliferation of specialities and of kinds of data that can be assembled about a particular patient; these are often presented using new codes and new words, which are hard to understand unless you have a thorough knowledge of the particular techniques.

To read medical records you will need a medical dictionary which is up-to-date. Even if the technical words are translated, however, there remains the problem of abbreviations. In the section which follows, I have written down what a house surgeon might typically write in the notes when clerking a previously fit woman with acute appendicitis; I hope that this will give an example, not only of commonly used abbreviations, but also of the way in which a doctor's notes are generally laid out and organised in a certain sequence.

FORM AND ABBREVIATION IN HOSPITAL RECORDS
AN ANNOTATED EXAMPLE

	DATE	NAME
	TIME	ADDRESS
		DATE OF BIRTH

Complains of . . . (Presenting Complaint) (duration)	C.O.	Abdominal pain.　　　　3 days
History of Presenting *Complaint* R.I.F. = right lower quadrant 　of the abdoment 1/52 = 1 week (1/12 = 1 month, 　1/7 = 1 day)	H.P.C.	Off food with central abdo. pain 3 days ago, then pain moved to R.I.F., and became more severe, with nausea and anorexia. Some diarrhoea, 1/52

---

[3] In *Prendergast* v. *Sam & Dee Ltd* [1989] 1 Med LR 36 CA, a GP was held 25% liable for injury caused when the pharmacist (held 75% liable) misread his prescription and dispensed Daonil instead of Amoxil.

Previous Medical History	P.M.H.	Tonsillectomy age 12

Previous Obstetric History
P = Parity (number of
  pregnancies). Figures
  represent no. of births
  followed by no. of
  miscarriages or abortions
  (= T.O.P.s)
L.S.C.S. = cesarean section
	P.O.H.	P 1 + 1 (T.O.P. 1980)
		
		L.S.C.S. (elective) 1983 for pre-
		eclampsia

Social History	S.H.	Mother and part-time worker Non-smoker Drinks socially
Family History A & W = alive and well Ca. = cancer	F.H.	Mother A & W, age 67 Father died age 68 Ca. lung 2 sibs A & W Daughter aged 4 well

Systematic enquiry
Gastro-intestinal system
  (tract)
B.O. = bowels open
° Diarrhoea = no diarrhoea
° Melaena = no blood in
  motions that is black
P.R. = per rectum
Weight → = weight constant
	S.E.
	G.I.T.
		
		Appetite normal until 3 days ago
		
		B.O. regular
		° Diarrhoea previous few months
		° Melaena
		
		° Fresh blood P.R.
		Weight →

Genito-urinary tract Dysuria = pain on urinating Nocturia = arising from sleep to urinate	G.U.	° Haematuria ° Dysuria ° Frequency ° Nocturia
Gynaecological K = menstrual cycle – no. of days of bleeding no. of days of whole cycle	Gynae.	K 5/27–32

Cardiovascular system
S.O.B.O.E. = short of breath
  on exertion
Orthopnoea = short of breath
  on lying flat
P.N.D. = paroxysmal nocturnal
  dyspnoea (attacks of waking
  up very breathless)
Oedema = swelling with fluid
  esp. of ankles
Respiratory system
	C.V.S.
	
	R.S.
		° Palpitations
		° S.O.B.O.E.
		
		° Orthopnoea
		
		° P.N.D.
		
		° Oedema
		
		° Cough

° Haemoptysis = coughing
  blood

Neurological system · · · · · · · · · · · · Neuro.

L.O.C. = episode of loss of
  consciousness

Vision ✔ = no problem with
  vision

List of regular medication · · · · · · · · *Drugs*

List of drugs to which the · · · · · · · *Allergy*
  patient thinks she is allergic

ON EXAMINATION · · · · · · · · · · · · O/E

General description

Not anaemic, cyanosed or
  jaundiced
No clubbing (deformity of nails)
No palpable lymph nodes

Cardiovascular system · · · · · · · · · · C.V.S.

Pulse rate and rhythm
Blood pressure (arterial)
J.V.P. = venous pressure
  estimated by observing
  jugular vein

H.S. = heart sounds (diagram
  used as visual representation
  of the sounds)

Ⓡ = Ⓛ = findings same on
  both sides, i.e. normal

Respiratory system · · · · · · · · · · · · R.S.
T⊙ = trachea in centre
  (normal)

P.N. = findings on percussion of
  chest
B.S. = breath sounds, heard
  with stethoscope. (Added
  sounds may be crackles
  (= creps, crepitations) or
  wheezes)

Abdominal examination · · · · · · · · · Abdo.
L.S.K.K.° = liver, spleen and
  kidneys not palpable (i.e. not
  enlarged)
° Masses = no lumps in
  abdomen

° Haemoptysis
° Wheezing
Headaches – occasional
° Fits
° L.O.C.

Vision ✔
Hearing ✔

nil

Penicillin

Distressed

° An, ° Cy, ° J

° Cl
° L.N.s
Temp 37.8°C

p 90 reg.
B.P. 120/70
J.V.P. →

H.S.

° Oedema
Pulses in feet Ⓡ = Ⓛ

T⊙

Expansion Ⓡ = Ⓛ
P.N. resonant Ⓡ = Ⓛ

B.S. vesicular, nil added

L.S.K.K.°

° Masses

Guarding = reflex muscle spasm
  on pressure

tender, with guarding & rebound

Rebound = pain on removal of
  pressure

B.S. = bowel sounds   B.S. ✔

P.R. = rectal examination   P.R.   N.A.D.

N.A.D. = nothing abnormal
  detected

P.V. = per vaginam   P.V.
  examination of the pelvis   Uterus N/S A/V

N/S = normal size (if abnormal,   Adnexae N.A.D.
  uterine size is often expressed
  as equivalent to a certain
  gestational age in   Cervix N.A.D.
  pregnancy, e.g. 14/40
  meaning the same as the size   V/V – N.A.D.
  of a normal pregnant uterus at
  14 weeks after the last period
  began)

A/V = anteverted (alternative
  uterine positions are axial or
  retroverted)

V/V = vulva and vagina

Adnexae = areas at either side
  of uterus

Central nervous system   C.N.S.

Examination (this part of the
  examination is often highly   Cranial nerves
  abbreviated or omitted)

P.E.R.L.A. = pupils are equal   P.E.R.L.A.
  and react to light and
  accommodation

Fundi = contents of the eyeballs   Fundi N.A.D.
  are seen by the
  ophthalmoscope

Motor = examination of the   Motor   Power
  motor aspect of the nervous   Tone   Ⓡ = Ⓛ
  system in each limb   Co-ordination N.A.D.
                                   Reflexes

Sensory = examination of the   Sensory   Pain
  different modalities of   Light touch   Ⓡ = Ⓛ
  sensation in the limbs and   Temperature N.A.D.
  trunk   Position sense
                                   Vibration

SUMMARY   ANALYSIS Previously fit mother aged —
                                years with acute abdominal
                                pain and fever

Δ = diagnosis

N.B.M. = nil by mouth

hourly obs. = instructions to nursing staff to record pulse, temp. and b.p. every hour

I.V.I. = intravenous drip

N. saline = salt solution of similar concentration to that of plasma. (Other fluids are Dextrose saline, or 5% dextrose, which contain a sugar for energy)

F.B.C. = full blood count (haematology)

U&E = urea and electrolytes (biochemistry)

L.F.T. = liver function tests (biochemistry)

Plan	Δ appendicitis
	N.B.M.
	hourly obs.
I.V.I.	N. saline 1L in 6 hours
F.B.C.	
U&E	
L.F.T.s	

Abbreviations and hieroglyphs

For a list of common abbreviations and hieroglyphs, see Appendix IV.

9 · Instructing an expert

SUMMARY

You must go to the right person (i.e. the right specialty and the right specialist). Ask AVMA (or specialist counsel) if you are at all uncertain who to go to. Instruct the expert properly.

This is the Becher's Brook of your action. We could even say, a little unkindly, that it can be the *pons asinorum*! It is all too easy to go to the wrong person, get an unfavourable report and then be obliged to tell the client that he has no case. Even if you persuade the legal aid authority that a second opinion is justified you have wasted one go, i.e. half your chances. The expert may be wrong for a number of reasons: she may be unsympathetic to plaintiffs, and so demonstrate the 'closing ranks' syndrome; she may be little interested in this sort of work; she may not come from the exact specialty you want (e.g. you may need a cardiology rather than a cardiac surgeon); she may not be able to substantiate attractive-looking conclusions when cross-examined; she may not cut a good figure in court. You need an expert of the right speciality, who can write a thorough and intelligible report that can withstand cross-examination, who achieves a happy mean between seeking to exculpate a colleague and, on the other hand, over-egging the plaintiff's pudding in an effort to come up with the goods, who is familiar with the requirements of litigation and appearing in court and who will make a good witness. These conditions cannot always all be met. Some are more important than others. At least if the report is favourable you can get the action on its feet and hope for a settlement. In due course you may strengthen your position by recruiting a second expert, and you may then hope that between them a forensically strong position will emerge.

So how do you select the right person? You may know of a suitable expert from your own previous experience, or you may seek to be referred to one. If you ask to be referred you need a referor who will understand your needs and know from his previous experience of a suitable person. It is unlikely that a name picked at random from a list of those in the relevant specialty, i.e. from lists supplied by the Law Society, the medical organisation or the medical defence bodies, will be your best bet, though such references are of course compiled and made available with care and concern. You need to ask those who make it their business, from the patient's point of view, to keep tabs on and lists of suitable or possible experts in the various specialties. So you should consult AVMA (Action for Victims of Medical Accidents) to get your expert, if you are otherwise at a loss, or ask your counsel, assuming he has access to AVMA's lists (which he should have if he is himself specialising in this sort of work, which he should be), or perhaps he has built up his own list from previous experience. For an annual subscription a member may ask for as many references from AVMA as he needs (see further under Appendix III).

A few further words on specialties

If the specialty is not an esoteric one – if, for example, you need an orthopedic surgeon because a fracture may have been missed or weight-bearing may have been prescribed too early, or you need an obstetrician or a gynecologist – you should be able to find your way to someone who is known to have provided good reports for patients in the past. If the issues to be investigated are more esoteric, such as microbiology or metabolic disturbances, or an unusual form of cancer, or an unusual tropical disease (examples could be multiplied), you will have to strike a balance between using the top doctor in the field, who may know nothing about medical negligence work and may not be inclined to help, and using a proven expert who may perhaps not really be sufficiently specialised. In this sort of situation you are likely to try more than one expert before you feel that a fair and full investigation of the potential claim has been achieved.

You will need to be careful, as I have said, that you select the right specialty, so that your card is not trumped at trial: e.g. for a brain-damaged baby case you will need an obstetrician to tell you if there was any obstetric negligence, a neonatologist to tell you if there was any neonatal negligence and also to speak as to causation, and a pediatric neurologist and/or a developmental pediatrician on condition and prognosis (the first can also help on causation, but not alone). If there is a question of anesthetic fault you will need an anesthetist. If the injury is partly neurological you will need a neurologist (a neuro-surgeon if it arises out of a neurological operation). If you want to allege a psychological injury, you will need a psychiatrist. You may need an immunologist on allergies and a skin specialist if the allergic reaction is dermatological.[1]

The possibilities are legion, and sometimes, as I say, it is not easy to know which specialty to select. A useful rule of thumb is to go to an expert whose specialty corresponds to that of the doctor whose conduct is being criticised. To an extent their status should also match. For example, if you are criticising the care of a cardiac patient by a physician in a district hospital it is likely to be unsuitable to apply the standard of care that would have been shown by a Harley Street cardiologist.

As the case progresses you would do well to fine-tune your specialties. For example, if the defendants allege that the condition of the patient is due to an underlying pathology, e.g. latent multiple sclerosis, or a fortuitous peri-operative medical emergency, such as a stroke (this is the sort of line on causation that they not infrequently dream up shortly before the trial), you should consider getting a report from a top specialist in the relevant pathology. Cases are often won or lost at trial by the stature and the particular expertise of one of the experts. You need to be alive at all times to the ways in which you might strengthen your position for trial.

Desired qualities

In *Loveday* v. *Renton* [1990] 1 Med LR 117 Stuart Smith J. identified ten attributes of an expert which assist the court in assessing the weight to be attributed to his opinion: eminence, soundness of opinion, internal consistency and logic, precision and accuracy of thought, response to searching and informed cross-examination, ability to face up to logic and make concessions, flexibility of mind and willingness to modify opinions, freedom from bias, independence of thought, and demeanour. It is advisable for the patient's advisers to explore thoroughly the profiles of all the experts, on both sides, to cover background, training experience, extent of any original research, qualifications, publications, and experience, if any, of court work, and for the purpose of evaluating comparative stature.

In *National Justice Compania Naviera SA* v. *Prudential Assurance Co, The Times*, 5 March 1993, Cresswell J. said that the expert witness had a duty to give independent evidence, uninfluenced as to form or content by the exigencies of litigation, and to provide objective unbiased opinion to the court on matters within

---

[1] And don't confuse specialties: e.g. a neurologist is different, substantively if not phonetically, from an urologist.

his expertise, never assuming the role of advocate.[2]

The court rightly looks for certain qualities in the expert. And so must the patient's solicitor. Apart from the obvious qualities of care and attention, expertise and a degree of sympathy, the solicitor has a right to expect a commitment to the case from an expert who accepts instructions to act. This means that the expert should answer letters and prepare reports within a reasonable time. If he has a long backlog he should say so. He must be willing to play his part as a member of the team. He should not think he is conferring a favour by agreeing to act. Some experts decline to have a conference unless at their premises. It may be difficult to reconcile this with the commitment I have referred to; most experts are willing to attend the lawyer's premises if given sufficient notice.

In a lighter vein: you want to avoid this sort of interchange that took place some years ago in the High Court:

Judge: Dr X, I recall you appeared before me some time ago in a matrimonial case as an expert on psychiatry, and I seem to remember you appearing before me in a road traffic case as an expert in orthopedic surgery, and here you are today in a medical negligence case as an expert in cardiology. I would like to know precisely what it is you are an expert in.
Dr X: I am an expert in giving evidence in courts of law, my Lord.

The letter of instruction

You will need to get the expert's agreement to act before you send her any of the papers. This is best done by letter. You will then send her the medical records, which will be bound, paginated and indexed, as explained in the previous chapter, together with the client's statement and any correspondence with the hospital or doctor.

In the letter you must insist that the expert set out the chronology, with appropriate extracts from the records, and refer to the pagination in her report so that her opinion can be properly understood. It is maddening if she refers to a document or an entry and you then spend 15 minutes trying to find it.[3] You should

---

[2] In the Lloyd's Names case (*Deeny* v. *Gooda Walker Ltd*, 4 October 1994, QBD) Phillips J. said of an expert witness: 'He showed a keen appreciation of his own abilities and a contempt for any challenge to his views . . . He adopted, throughout, a vigorously partisan approach and could scarcely ever be induced . . . to make a concession, however clear it might be that a concession was due.' This was not a medical witness.
[3] Also irritating is the sort of effort that immediately shows you that the writer is unfamiliar with writing reports, namely a report which proceeds to give you the expert's conclusions (it is likely to begin something like 'I have read all the records in this case and it seems to me that the only ground of criticism relates to the second operation where it appears that . . .'); it will usually contain some discussion and a degree of reasoning, but no proper reference to the history of the matter or the relevant entries in the records.

indicate the areas of concern that you or your client feel are
relevant and you may wish to formulate a number of questions for
her; but you must make it clear that you want a full report and not
just answers to your questions. Don't raise questions just to show
you have read the medical records and/or how well versed in
medical matters you are. On the other hand, do not simply send
all the papers and ask the expert if she sees any evidence of
negligence.

There are different forms for the letter of instruction currently
in use (see Appendix II). Some solicitors use a very long form,
which runs the risk, I sometimes think, of irritating, or perhaps
confusing, the recipient. Just as with pleadings, where the more
verbose your pleading the more likely it is both to obscure what
you really want or, rather, need to say, and to engender a long
and wearisome request for particulars, so the more concise your
letter to the expert the better. If she is one of the few experts who
are experienced in preparing plaintiffs' reports in the medical
negligence action she will know what to do without your telling
her, but you will not always (perhaps not often) be going to such a
person, especially if you have sought an esoteric specialty. So the
letter needs to be properly written; the expert needs to be
properly instructed.

In my opinion the most important points to get across to her
are:

– Tell her to set out the history and the important entries in the
  records, and to refer to the pagination.
– Avoid the use of the word 'negligence'.
– Make sure she understands how important causation is.

The word 'negligence' should be avoided because it can put an
expert off as it has a condemnatory ring to it. Also it can be
misunderstood (I have seen reports that exonerated the hospital
from 'negligence' because there had been no 'wilful misconduct'!). Instead ask her if she sees any evidence of sub-standard
treatment, or treatment of a standard below that which the
patient had a right to expect, or (I find this formulation particularly helpful) any treatment which she finds 'unacceptable', or to
be 'unacceptable medical practice'. Some solicitors explain the
Bolam test to her (see Chapter 17). This is of course correct in
law, but I think it is likely to confuse her when she has to ask
herself whether at the relevant time there was a body of responsible medical opinion that would have followed or approved of the
treatment given. Better, I think, to clarify that later, in conference if need be, if the report does not make it clear in one way or
another how she would answer that question.

Explain causation. It is very frustrating if you get a report that exonerates the hospital on the main issues as you saw them and then, expressing great sympathy for the patient, fulminates against the standard of post-operative nursing care or the premature discharge without telling you whether that made any difference to the outcome (when asked she probably tells you that it did not actually make any difference). Or she may explain in great detail why she criticises the GP for not referring the patient to hospital earlier, or the consultant for not operating earlier, and fail to tell you whether on the balance of probabilities the outcome would have been different if there had not been such a failure of care. Many a case of obvious, even admitted, negligence has been lost because the plaintiff has failed to show that the outcome would have been different (see Chapter 18). That is why I include a sentence to the effect 'in respect of any act or omission that you deem unacceptable please tell us what difference that made to the patient on the balance of probabilities (that means "more likely than not")'.

Some solicitors include paragraphs explaining the likely course of the action, the method of funding, the probable need to attend most of the trial, etc: all these are valid points, but I doubt the expert wants, or needs, to read all this in the initial letter of instruction.

Ask her to confirm that she has all the medical records that she would expect to be available. Tell her that, in the first instance at any rate, her report will not be seen by the other side. If she is to deal with condition and prognosis as well as liability it should be done in a separate document. This is particularly relevant now that a medical report substantiating the injuries alleged is supposed to be served with your statement of claim (see Chapter 10). Reports on liability have to be exchanged if they are to be relied on at trial[4] (see Chapter 13), but a party will still not be required to produce a report on which he does not intend to rely, unless some agreement can be spelt out between the parties whereby, for example, the plaintiff undergoes a medical examination on condition that the ensuing report be disclosed.

Ask her to support any conclusions she comes to, if possible, by reference to published texts (and let you have a copy).

I have already explained that, after receiving the expert's report, you or counsel may want the expert to clarify points, or you may want to go to a second expert. It would be unusual for the legal aid authority to refuse the patient one more attempt to

---

[4] The initial report on liability is likely to need substantial recasting when the time for exchanging eventually comes.

secure a favourable opinion where such a course is recommended in counsel's advice. Whatever you decide to do, make sure that the legal aid limitation covers it.

If you receive a favourable report there may occasionally (particularly if the case is privately funded) be advantage in communicating its findings to the health authority in the hope of securing an offer of settlement.[5]

The negative report

If a negative report is received, there are a number of options. You will want to consider to what extent the expert is known as a 'tried and trusted' expert for patients' complaints. If not at all, you may be more likely to want a second opinion. If he is clearly a reliable expert, then, provided the case is not worth a great deal of money, it is likely to be appropriate to discontinue. Remember that you are not in the business of constructing a claim by hook or by crook, but of ensuring that proper claims, and only proper claims, are presented. If the claim is worth a lot of money, it may be appropriate to seek a second opinion even if you yourself cannot see any ground for doubting, or at any rate for challenging, the opinion of the usually reliable expert.[6] Or it may be pretty clear for one reason or another that there is no valid claim. If that is the position, you should not incur further expense.

Although it is certainly useful to have, and advisable, even essential, to work at acquiring, some medical knowledge, do not become a barrack room expert, digging up texts the ambit and implications of which you do not really understand and then expecting to be able to refute the expert with them. You would not be impressed by a client who read a few pages of a legal textbook and then argued that the careful opinion you had given was wrong.

Sometimes you will be completely stuck. You cannot silence your doubts about what on the surface appears to be a careful report from a suitably qualified expert, but you do not know how to challenge it. In those circumstances you could ask AVMA's medical section to scan the report. They might be able to give you material to put to the expert or to use as argument for a second opinion.

If a statement of claim is in due course drafted it is advisable to get your expert's approval of the precise allegations of negligence, for he will have to substantiate them in court. Where the original report of the expert is clear it saves time if counsel, when

---

[5] But be careful not to be gulled into disclosing where there is no real reason to expect liability to be admitted.

[6] The Court of Appeal issued a warning against incurring costs in respect of unnecessary experts in *Rawlinson* v. *Westbrook*, *The Times*, January 1995.

advising positively on the merits, sets out in rough form the allegations of negligence that he intends to plead. The expert can then look at these before counsel produces his final draft of the statement of claim.

Conference with the expert: in a clear case it is perfectly possible to get to close of pleadings, and on to exchange of witness statements, without taking the expert to see counsel – a lot can be achieved by letter – but thereafter a conference will be necessary in the usual way well before trial. In a more complex or uncertain case it is not usually productive in terms of cost or time to have too early a conference. Better to sort out as much as possible in writing and then, with that preliminary work serving as a basis for discussion, arrange your conference. Otherwise you may be sitting in the Temple all night trying to clarify what could to a large extent have been done before by letter.

Corroborating expert: in a case of any substantive gravity or complexity you must obtain a second expert. The defendants will (technically) be at liberty, while the law remains as it is, to produce as many experts on the issue of liability as they like – within reason (though the agreed order on the summons for directions will usually limit their number). You may well be at a disadvantage with only one. It is usually best to send the first expert's report to the proposed second expert.[7] Some experienced solicitors prefer to obtain all the reports (on liability) before commencing proceedings, but I find this can delay matters unduly. It is often hard enough to obtain one expert report that supports a claim, and meanwhile time may be running out. The disadvantage of going to a second expert after you have served your statement of claim is that it may well need amending in the light of his report. Your decision as to when to seek a corroborating opinion is likely to be influenced by these considerations and by the nature, gravity and strength of your case.[8]

Whose text?

In *Whitehouse* v. *Jordan* [1981] 1 WLR 246 the House of Lords said that, while some degree of consultation between experts and legal advisers was entirely proper, it was necessary that expert

---

[7] Some solicitors prefer not to show the positive report of the first expert to the proposed second expert, but I prefer to – it certainly saves time later.

[8] The court may be entitled to overrule medical opinion. A 'guardedly expressed' opinion in a medical report, which was not countered by other medical evidence, to the effect that certain symptoms were not caused by the accident was rejected by a judge at first instance; and the Court of Appeal refused to interfere with his decision, saying that such an opinion was not of the same force as an actual medical finding (*Stevens (formerly Ludlow)* v. *Simons, The Times,* 20 November 1987).

evidence presented to the court should be, and should be seen to be, the independent product of the expert, uninfluenced as to form or content by the exigencies of litigation. This must be read together with the Bar Council's rules of conduct for counsel: from February 1989 the *Code of Conduct* for barristers stated explicitly that a barrister might settle the report of an expert witness which was to be disclosed to another party. But now there is a totally revised code, operative from 31 March 1990, which approaches the matter from another angle: it does not say explicitly that the barrister may settle the expert's report, but (at para. 606) it clearly envisages him drafting any witness statement (which must include an expert's) provided he reasonably believes that the material he includes in it is evidence that the witness would give in court. As I see it, in short, counsel is entitled to recast the report in such form as he deems best assists his case, but it must fairly represent the view of the expert, warts and all.

Bear in mind also what Lord Denning said in *Kelly* v. *London Transport Executive* [1982] 2 All ER 842, 851 about solicitors acting for legally aided clients:

> They must not run up costs by instructing endless medical experts for endless reports or by any unnecessary expenditure. They must not ask a medical expert to change his report, at their own instance, so as to favour their own legally aided client or conceal anything that may be against them. They must not 'settle' the evidence of the medical experts as they did in *Whitehouse* v. *Jordan*, which received the condemnation of this court and of the House of Lords.

Reference to other documents

Defendants' solicitors have frequently demanded to see statements of witnesses and any other documents referred to in the expert report. In *B.* v. *Wyeth (John) and Brother Ltd* [1992] 1 WLR 168, a judgment given within the benzodiazepine group litigation, the Court of Appeal said that waiver of privilege in respect of such material should not be inferred. Two months earlier (October 1991) Tucker J. had reached a similar conclusion in *Booth* v. *Warrington Health Authority* [1992] PIQR P137.

Relying on your expert

Plaintiff's solicitor to pay the costs[9] (words to strike terror into the heart of every law-abiding solicitor!).

---

[9] There is, as noted below, power to order a solicitor personally to pay costs, under the inherent jurisdiction of the court and RSC O.62 r.11 where costs have been incurred unreasonably or improperly or have been wasted by failure to conduct proceedings with reasonable competence and expedition, as well as by virtue of s.4(1) of the Courts and Legal Services Act 1990.

Section 4(1) of the Courts and Legal Services Act 1990, substituting a new s.51 in the Supreme Court Act 1981, permits the court to disallow or to make the legal or other representative concerned pay any wasted costs, i.e. costs incurred as a result of any improper, unreasonable or negligent act or omission on the part of that representative or any employee of his, or costs which, in the light of any such act or omission occurring after those costs were incurred, the court considers it unreasonable to expect the party concerned to pay.

For a while practitioners were understandably anxious about the draconian decision of Morland J. in *Locke* v. *Camberwell Health Authority* [1990] 1 Med LR 253, in which the patient's solicitor was made to pay the costs of the action from the time when he ought to have known that the case was not worth pursuing. The expert cardiologist had advised that there was no record that the patient had been given the anti-coagulant, Heparin, as she should have been and, having looked through the records on three separate occasions, repeated that assertion later in the face of the contention in the defence that she had been given Heparin. There was in fact an entry on one particular medical record (the CCPR) showing that Heparin had been given, but it was never established that that record was in front of the consultant when he advised (it would have been extremely odd if this very distinguished consultant had overlooked it on each occasion) or had ever been disclosed to the plaintiff before it was produced at the hearing of the defendants' application for the plaintiff's solicitor to be made personally liable for costs (the main action having been earlier discontinued on the advice of leading counsel).

The judge made various criticisms of junior counsel's handling of the case, in particular that he should have himself observed from scrutiny of the records that his expert had been thrice blind to the relevant record that Heparin had in fact been given, and he said that the solicitor should have realised that counsel had not properly read the records. The solicitor had therefore been guilty of 'serious dereliction of duty' in accepting what his medical expert and his counsel had said.

However, the Court of Appeal took a very different view when they reversed the judge's order. Having admitted affidavits by way of additional evidence both from Dr Sutton and from counsel for the plaintiff, the court said that it was clearly highly improbable that the CCPR (Cardiac Catheterisation Procedure Record) had been disclosed to the plaintiff's advisers, medical or legal, at any time before it was produced at the hearing and that that simply blew away the basis for the judge's order and his criticism of junior counsel and solicitor (it seems odd that counsel at the hearing did not protest strongly that the CCPR had not been disclosed earlier – presumably the records had not been indexed when received, a procedure that I have more than once in the preceding chapters strongly recommended). The Court of Appeal then not merely stated that the judge's strictures were ill-founded but also expressly approved the 'meticulous' care shown by the plaintiff's advisers in their handling of her case (the details of that exoneration need not be set out here – see [1991] 2 Med LR 249).

The Court of Appeal also made certain general observations of importance:

(1) as to the degree of misconduct required for an order under O.62 r.11 that specified costs be paid personally by the solicitor, the court was bound by *Sinclair Jones* v. *Kay* [1989] 1 WLR 114, where it was held that the words of O.62 r.11 should be given their ordinary English meaning (which means that the solicitor's conduct does not have to be shown to have amounted to 'serious dereliction of duty', as had been suggested in *Holden* v. *CPS* [1990] 2 QB 261).

(2) as to relying on your expert's reading of the medical records, the court said that it might be in some cases that counsel would need to go through the medical records line by line with the expert, e.g. when the trial was imminent and some issue had arisen on the notes so that counsel needed to be well briefed to examine and cross-examine the experts, but that situation had not arisen in the instant case.

(3) on the relationship between solicitor and counsel, the court said:
    (a) in general a solicitor is entitled to rely upon the advice of counsel properly instructed;
    (b) for a solicitor without specialist experience in a particular field to rely on counsel's advice is to make normal and proper use of the Bar;
    (c) however, he must not do so blindly but must exercise his own independent judgment. If he reasonably thinks counsel's advice is obviously or glaringly wrong it is his duty to reject it;
    (d) although a solicitor should not assist a litigant where prosecution of a claim amounts to an abuse of process, it is not his duty to attempt to assess the result of a conflict of evidence or to impose a pre-trial screen on a litigant's claim.

One thing this case shows, apart from the need for judicial caution before finding practitioners guilty of professional negligence, is that the patient's solicitor should make a list of what records she is sent (the index prepared by the paralegal may suffice).

In *Scott* v. *Bloomsbury Health Authority* [1990] 1 Med LR 214 Brooke J. severely criticised the plaintiff's legal advisers for bringing a case based on the uncorroborated medical opinion of a consultant who had long since retired. He suggested that the Legal Aid Board might take steps, perhaps in consultation with the General Medical Council and the Royal Colleges (yes, he really said that!), to prevent complex claims being supported at public expense on such evidence. But he did not make the solicitor pay the costs.

However, the Liverpool judge, Judge Lachs, did in one case that ran to five days before it came out in evidence that the plaintiff had had a drink problem, a fact that invalidated her case. The costs there were about £62,000 and solicitors had no insurance cover for a liability arising in that way.[10,11] In *Gupta* v. *Comer* [1991] 2 WLR 494 (not a medical case) the Court of Appeal said that there was jurisdiction under RSC O.62 r.11 to require a solicitor personally to pay the costs of other parties to proceedings where such costs had been incurred improperly or unreasonably or where they had been wasted by his failure to conduct the proceedings with reasonable competence and expedition, and that there was no principle in civil proceedings that gross misconduct or neglect had to be shown as a necessary precondition to the exercise of that jurisdiction.

In *Ridehalgh* v. *Horsefield* [1994] 3 WLR 462 the Court of Appeal gave detailed guidance on the correct approach to wasted costs orders, stating that, while litigants should not be financially prejudiced by the unjustifiable conduct of litigation by their or their opponent's lawyers, the courts, in the exercise of the wasted costs jurisdiction, should be astute to control the threat of a new and costly form of satellite litigation. In *Philex plc* v. *Golban, The Times,* 9 July 1993, Knox J. said that to justify a wasted costs order a court need only find that negligence by the solicitor, 'unvarnished by any pejorative adjective', had resulted in the client having to pay unnecessary costs. An order for wasted costs against counsel can only be made in respect of acts after 1 October 1991, when the amendment to the Supreme Court Act 1981 s.51(6) and (7) effected by s.4 of the Courts and Legal Services

---

[10] See also *Swedac Ltd* v. *Magnet & Southern plc* [1990] FSR 89, CA.

[11] In *Snipes* v. *USA* HALL July 1990 at p.10, a plaintiff's attorney was punished for bringing a medical negligence action to court when he had no actual expert medical evidence of negligence. Even for an American court that was a bit much to accept!

Act 1990 came into force (*Fozal* v. *Gofur*, *The Times*, 9 July 1993, CA; see also *Filmlab Systems International Ltd* v. *Pennington* [1995] 1 WLR 673 and *R.* v. *Horsham District Council, ex p. Wenman* [1995] 1 WLR 680).[12]

What if your expert has reported negligently?

It may be that the expert's original positive report is shown later to have been negligently compiled. The court would have power to make him pay wasted costs (see Supreme Court Act 1981 s.51(3) as amended by the Courts and Legal Services Act 1990, and *Aiden Shipping Co.* v. *Interbulk Ltd* [1986] 2 All ER 409). In *Landall* v. *Dennis Faulkner and Alsop* [1994] 5 Med LR 268 an orthopedic surgeon was sued in respect of advice given in a personal injury action to the effect that the plaintiff's condition could be ameliorated by a spinal fusion. The action was settled on that basis. The plaintiff contended that the advice was negligent and that the operation had damaged him further. Holland J. held that the expert was immune from suit as the report in question had been given for the purpose of assisting the lawyers to conduct the plaintiff's case and not for the purpose of advising the plaintiff about medical treatment.

Ordering the papers

Now that you have your first expert report, it is as good a time as any to order your papers, and to keep that order for the rest of the case (I am assuming that the medical records have long been sorted, paginated and indexed, as advised in the previous chapter).

Different solicitors have different ways of ordering, or in some cases disordering, the papers in a medical negligence action. Order is of course necessary for your own purposes as well as for instructing counsel – no reader would dream of simply sending all the papers they hold to counsel with the rubric 'Counsel has herewith all relevant papers', but, all the same, it has reluctantly to be said that badly ordered, even chaotic, briefs do still get delivered from time to time. The best system I have seen uses the numbered dividers in a lever arch file, the number remaining the same for the same class of document in all cases. Thus, in the first numbered section will be previous instructions to counsel and his advices, and conference notes; in the following numbered sections will be legal aid papers, plaintiff's and witness's statements

---

[12] In *Gascoine* v. *Ian Sheridan and Co. and Latham* [1994] 4 Med LR 437 lawyers prosecuting a medical negligence action agreed breach of duty through delay but denied there had been any chance of success in the proposed claim. The judge disagreed, and ruled there had been a 60% chance of success.

(all dated, marked up as 'superseded' or 'disclosed' with the date of disclosure, as appropriate) and attendance notes, pleadings, orders of the court, plaintiff's medical reports (marked up as 'superseded' or 'disclosed' with the date of disclosure) and all significant medical correspondence with the experts, discarded medical reports, defendants' medical reports and witness statements, schedules of loss with supporting documents, correspondence (with the other side, with the client, with doctors, with others); and then, if there is still room in that file, or if, as is often the case, there is not room, then in a file of their own, the medical records, paginated and indexed. This system, which is simple enough to familiarise oneself with, makes it much easier for anyone, looking at a case so prepared, to assimilate, understand and work upon it.

Tips

Check before sending the papers that the proposed expert is willing to act.

Treat your expert with care as well as with respect. Assess his 'legal' and 'forensic' experience and speak accordingly. He may be 'green', but he might develop into a useful ally.

Assess his reliability and resolution as a witness – this can only be done by meeting him in conference. Experts who give you a case at the outset are not doing you a service if it proves unsupportable or they start to vacillate when they see the defendants' expert reports.

If the case settles, tell your experts (as well as counsel) – they will be interested to hear.

Inform them of the date of the trial as soon as you know – you are likely to need most of them to be present throughout the trial. If you do not have their medical input when the defendants' experts are giving evidence you may very likely be in trouble.[13]

Don't make them ask more than once for payment. It is as well to clarify a maximum fee in advance with them and with the legal aid office for their report and their attendance at trial (it was the case, but is unfortunately no longer so, that legal aid would not put a ceiling on the cost of an expert's report).

---

[13] You will, of course, need a fixed date as doctors need to know well in advance when they will be needed. I will not believe what I have been told by a number of Newcastle solicitors, namely that the court there refuses to give any fixed dates. That would be so ludicrous and inept, and user-hostile (though, of course, court-friendly), a way to run a court that it is indeed beyond belief.

CHECKLIST

- Are you sure you have established the right specialty for your reports?
- Have you gone to a suitable referee in order to select your expert within that specialty? Have you got her agreement to act?
- Have you instructed her properly, i.e. with an appropriate letter of instruction and all relevant documents including a properly sorted bundle of records?
- Have you properly considered the effect of her report and what now to do, particularly if it is negative?
- Have you thought sufficiently about causation?
- Do you need a conference?
- Do you need a report from a further specialty?
- Do you need further legal aid authority?
- Should you now start proceedings?

10 · Issuing proceedings

SUMMARY

The basic period within which the writ (or summons) has to be issued is three years from the time the plaintiff could reasonably have known he had a cause of action. Although this period can be extended by the court the period of four months within which the writ has to be served after issue is unlikely to be extended; if you are still within the limitation period when your first writ expires issue another; if you are not within that period you have 'had it'. It is not necessary to claim interest on the writ, but it must be pleaded. Be aware of the rules as to venue.

ISSUE OF WRIT

The limitation period (the period within which the writ (or summons) has to be issued or the right to sue is – in all probability – lost) is of particular importance in medical negligence cases because (a) often the damage does not make itself felt till some considerable time after the negligent treatment, (b) it may well not be immediately apparent even when the injury is manifested that it had anything to do with the earlier treatment, (c) the patient is often in no state of mind to be decisive enough to ventilate his complaint without delay, let alone seek legal advice. So time elapses.

Put loosely for the moment, the limitation period is basically three years from the date when the patient realised or ought to have realised she had been injured by the medical treatment she received or failed to receive. (For a detailed account of the limitation rules see Chapter 28 below.) Within the limitation period the writ must be issued, though not necessarily yet served on the other side.

SERVICE OF WRIT

You used to have 12 months from the date of issue in which to serve your writ, but that was cut to four months for any writ issued after 4 June 1990 (six months if leave to serve out of the jurisdiction is required) – do not be out of time with service of the issued writ, for you are unlikely to succeed in an application to have the writ renewed (see below). This curtailing of the period of validity of a writ (and summons) was one of the new rules designed to speed litigation, rules that seem in some respects to have been devised without any thought being given to the difficulties experienced constantly by those who conduct medical negligence actions for plaintiffs.

The rules (found at O.18 r.12(1A)) provide that a plaintiff in an action for personal injuries shall serve with his statement of claim a medical report (that means a report substantiating all the personal injuries alleged in the statement of claim which the plaintiff proposes to adduce in evidence as part of his case at trial); and also a statement of the special damages claimed (that means a statement giving full particulars of the special damages claimed for expenses and losses already incurred and an estimate of any future expenses and losses (including loss of earnings and of pension rights)).[1]

One can understand how this could well speed up the progress of a simple personal injury action, but in a case of any complexity, and particularly in a medical negligence action (which will usually be 'an action for personal injuries', albeit an action for professional negligence as well),[2] these matters can rarely be clarified, let alone formulated at the stage of service of the writ, and so it is going to be almost always impossible to comply with the rule. In the simplest case, perhaps a missed fracture, it may be possible to provide a short report on condition and prognosis to substantiate the injuries alleged, but in more complex cases, where, say, brain damage has been caused, it will be quite impossible to have those documents ready at that stage. Even if it were possible they would be hopelessly out of date by the time of trial, and would need constant costly up-dating. Often the full extent of the damage is only ascertainable many months after the plaintiff's solicitor has been obliged to serve the writ, followed in due course by the statement of claim. If, as in the case of a child, there is no limitation problem, these provisions will simply serve to delay the issue of proceedings – somewhat the reverse of the intended effect!

As to service of the schedule of special damages: again, in a case of any complexity this cannot be devised and costed until well into the course of the action. Such a schedule for a handicapped person requires many reports and months of preparation. If it had to be served earlier it would only need expensive

---

[1] The County Court rules now contain similar provisions.
[2] See Chapter 28 under 'Personal injuries'.

up-dating later (such a schedule can run to 100 pages or so). Happily, defendants in complex cases by and large recognise that the rule is inappropriate and accept a general statement of the expected heads of damage.

The rules do at least provide that the Court may extend the time for service of these documents or dispense with its requirements. It can also stay proceedings if the statutory documents are not provided. To comply with the rule, I suggest that some sort of short guarded report on condition and prognosis be requested and obtained from the expert along with his original report on liability and causation (see the draft letter of instruction in Appendix II).[3] For the special damages schedule in a complex case, one could go as far as setting out the main heads of the claim. If defendants object, it is up to them to apply to the court for an 'unless' order and/or one staying proceedings – which should be firmly resisted.

Further points on the medical report served with pleading

Defendants' solicitors have frequently demanded to see statements of witnesses and any other documents referred to in the expert report served with the pleading. In *B.* v. *Wyeth (John) and Brother Ltd* [1992] 1 WLR 168, a judgment given within the benzodiazepine group litigation, the Court of Appeal said that waiver of privilege in respect of such material should not be inferred. Two months earlier (October 1991) Tucker J. had reached a similar conclusion in *Booth* v. *Warrington Health Authority* [1992] PIQR P137.

The question to what extent the medical report required to be served with the pleading should be deemed part of the pleadings was considered in *Sion* v. *Hampstead Health Authority* [1994] 5 Med LR 170. The Supreme Court Practice suggested at 18/12/4A that the report 'will operate as particulars', but Staughton L.J. said that the plaintiff was not wholly and rigidly confined to what was said in the report; it should be treated only as a general outline of the plaintiff's case.

It has been suggested from time to time, and even adjudged, e.g. by Kennedy J. in the benzodiazepine litigation, that to comply with the rule that requires the medical report to substantiate the injuries alleged it is not enough for the report to show that the alleged injuries have been sustained, but it must also

---

[3] This course will have the disadvantage that it will reveal to the defendants the identity of your expert; so sometimes one uses a separate doctor (maybe the plaintiff's GP) to prepare this short initial, probably non-contentious report. One interesting alternative is to serve, where appropriate, one of the discharge summaries from the medical records!

show that they are due to the alleged negligence, in other words it must establish causation. However, there is no good reason so to interpret the word 'substantiate'. Even if one concedes that both interpretations are possible, it is surely the case that the rule was introduced not to give defendants advance knowledge of the strength of the case on causation and of who the plaintiff's expert is but rather to give them a clear picture of the extent of the injuries for which compensation is being claimed. This, together with the schedule of loss served at the same time, enables them to make an informed offer at an early stage if they wish to settle.

Note that you do NOT serve any medical report or part of report that deals with liability, only what deals with condition and prognosis.

HIGH COURT OR COUNTY COURT?

Recent dramatic procedural changes (pursuant to the Courts and Legal Services Act 1990, s.1) have given the County Court a concurrent jurisdiction with the High Court. The purpose of these changes is said by the legislators to be to improve the administration of justice, but one has to wonder whether the predominant motive has not been, as usual, to cut legal aid costs. The County Court was already overburdened; it is not finding it easy to cope with the added workload.

Commencement of proceedings

In actions founded on contract or tort there is now no limit to the financial jurisdiction of the County Court and in all such actions both High Court and County Court have jurisdiction. A plaintiff may therefore choose where to commence proceedings, except that actions which include a claim for personal injuries the value of which is less than £50,000 must be *commenced* in the County Court (see Articles 4 and 5 of the High Court and County Court Jurisdiction Order 1991). The value of an action for unliquidated damages is the amount which the plaintiff reasonably expects to recover, disregarding interest and costs (Article 9). Further, the particulars of claim for a County Court action should state, if it be the case, that the action is worth more than £5,000. If a personal injury action is commenced in the High Court the writ must bear an endorsement as to value in the form set out in the Practice Direction at [1991] 1 WLR 642. (As I have pointed out elsewhere, most but not all medical negligence actions will include a claim for personal injuries – see further Chapter 28 under 'Personal injuries'.)

There is power under s.1(1)(d) of the Act of 1990 for the Lord Chancellor to specify types of action that should only be started in the High Court. It was hoped, vainly, that he would specify the action for professional negligence.

Transfer by the High Court

The High Court has power, under the general provisions as to transfer found in ss.40–42 of the County Courts Act 1984 as amended by s.2 of the Courts and Legal Services Act 1990, to strike out (or merely to transfer) an action wrongly commenced in the High Court, and to transfer any action which, though not wrongly commenced, it considers suitable for trial in the County Court, having regard to the criteria set out in Article 7(5) of the 1991 Order. The Practice Direction at [1991] 1 WLR 643 sets out the procedure and the forms to be used for notifying the parties and for objecting to and determining the question of transfer.

After conflicting earlier decisions the Court of Appeal finally established, in *Restick* v. *Crickmore* [1994] 1 WLR 420, that the High Court was not obliged to strike out cases which should have been begun in the County Court; it had a discretion. Stuart-Smith L.J. said:

Save where there has been a contumelious disobedience of the court's order, the draconian sanction of striking out an otherwise properly constituted action, simply to punish the party who has failed to comply with the rules of court, is not part of the court's function. No injustice is involved to the defendant in transferring an action which has been started in the wrong court to the correct court… . The ordinary sanction for failure to comply with the requirements will be in costs.

Transfer by the County Court

Any action of which the value is less than £25,000 must be *tried* in the County Court unless transfer is thought appropriate by both jurisdictions having regard to the criteria set out in Article 7(5), of which the important ones for our purposes are 'whether the action is important and, in particular, whether it raises questions of importance to persons who are not parties or questions of general public interest', and 'the complexity of the facts' (possibly sometimes also 'the complexity of the legal issues'). The Practice Direction states in paragraph 9 that actions for professional negligence 'may be considered important and therefore suitable for trial in the High Court'. A further point worth noting is that 'persons who are not parties' would appear to cover the doctors impugned but not joined as defendants in actions against health authorities. Actions worth between £25,000 and £50,000 can be tried in either court at the discretion of the County Court, the same criteria applying.[4,5]

Generally, both sides prefer the action to be tried in the High Court, largely because the standard of judging there is reckoned to be considerably higher. Defendants normally have little desire for the professional competence of their consultant to be tried by an assistant recorder in the local County Court. That said, there can probably be no objection to the less serious medical actions staying in the County Court, for example a claim for failing to prevent a bedsore. A practical disadvantage of the County Court is that, whereas in the High Court (in London at any rate) the listing of cases is very well managed and one is almost never let down, it is common form to go along to a County Court for a three-day fixture and find other cases listed in your court (just in case any one settles!) and a few *ex parte* applications in front of you, so that you are lucky if you get on by three in the afternoon, and if you overrun, the hearing is likely to be adjourned for weeks if not months (in the High Court a case runs till it finishes).

Transfer will normally be effected at the close of pleadings, when you make an application to disapply the automatic directions and substitute the directions suited to a medical negligence action (as to which see Chapter 13).

In *McLaughlin* v. *British Coal Corporation, The Times*, 16 December 1992, the Court of Appeal agreed that the question of transferring to the High Court an action worth less than £25,000 was a matter for the discretion of the County Court judge but disagreed as to whether he had in the particular case taken into account all relevant matters.[6]

Statement of value

Quite apart from the endorsement as to value that must, as I have said, be put upon the writ, for actions proceeding in the High Court, a statement of value is required on the summons for directions (it can also be required at other times), which must

---

[4] Lord Lane C.J. said in a speech in July 1991 that deputy High Court judges should not be trying medical negligence actions, i.e. a full High Court judge was required.

[5] It is interesting to note that one of the grounds for transfer, though one which must not be used to justify transfer if it stands alone, is that the trial will come on sooner – as if the Lord Chancellor was admitting that with the transfer of this large workload to the County Court it might well end up with a longer waiting list than the High Court.

[6] It was held in *Langley* v. *NW Water Authority* [1991] 1 WLR 697 that the County Court had power to issue its own enforceable practice directions. Where a case has been transferred down to the County Court, there is power to award costs on the High Court scale (*Forey* v. *London Buses Ltd* [1991] 1 WLR 327).

follow the proforma attached to the Practice Direction [1991] 1 WLR 651, certifying that the claim is worth more than £25,000 or that, though worth less, it is suitable for determination by the High Court 'by reason of one or more of the criteria mentioned in Article 7(5)'. Failure to lodge a statement of value at the right time will have the draconian result that the action will be transferred without notice to the County Court (paragraph 12 of the Practice Direction).

Limitation and the County Court

Limitation poses a particular difficulty in the County Court because there is, as yet, no provision for a protective summons. In the High Court one can issue, and later serve, a writ and then ask the defendants or apply to the court for an extension of time to serve the statement of claim. In the County Court one is, strictly, obliged to endorse the summons with the particulars of claim (as well as serving a medical report and a schedule of loss). If the expiry of the limitation period is imminent and it is not yet known what case, if any, will be pleaded, the court office is entitled to refuse to issue a summons without particulars of claim. In that event one must apply to the judge for leave to issue. However a number of courts, appreciating the injustice to the plaintiff created by the situation, will issue on condition that the necessary documents are served within the four-month period. Some courts will even encourage an application to the judge for an order that all further proceedings be stayed until further order. It is much to be hoped that the rules will make provision soon for a protective summons. Remember that you can begin in any County Court; you are not confined to the local court.

Costs penalty

The new s.51(8) of the Supreme Court Act 1981 (substituted by s.4 of the Courts and Legal Services Act 1990) gives the court a simple but effective power to reduce the costs awarded to a successful plaintiff in the High Court by up to 25% (or such other sum as may be fixed by the Lord Chancellor) where the court considers that the proceedings should have been commenced in the County Court, whether by virtue of any provision made under s.1 of the Act of 1990 or any other enactment (and see *supra* the reference to *Restick* v. *Crickmore*).

RENEWAL OF WRIT

There is power under RSC O.6 r.8, as amended, to renew the writ for up to four months from time to time and, if service is

proving impossible, for up to 12 months, but it will be exercised
with caution.[7] There must be good and sufficient reason to
exercise the discretion to renew. There is no reason to expect the
court to be any readier to grant applications to renew just because
the period of validity of a writ has been so truncated. The
principle is that in the absence of sufficient reason the court will
not exercise its discretion in favour of renewal of the writ if the
effect of doing so will be to deprive the defendant of the benefit
of a limitation period which has accrued (*Heaven* v. *Road and
Rail Wagons Ltd* [1965] 2 QB 355). In *Wilkinson* v. *Ancliff* [1986]
1 WLR 1352, CA, the court said that the defendant did not have
to show a cast-iron defence of limitation: he need show only that
if the writ were renewed there was a substantial risk or a real
likelihood that he would be deprived of a good legal defence
under the Limitation Act. And the rule is the same if you are
applying before the four months has in fact run out. Nor is it
affected by the fact that the court has a discretion under s.33 of
the Limitation Act 1980 to override all limitation periods in
personal injury cases: *Chappell* v. *Cooper* [1980] 1 WLR 958,
where a plaintiff issued a first writ in time, failed to serve it within
12 months and then issued a second writ out of time but asked the
court to permit the second action to proceed under its general
discretion afforded by s.33, alternatively to grant an extension of
time for the service of the first writ. The Court of Appeal refused
to exercise its discretion under s.33 on the ground that the words
of the Act were not apt to cover a case where a writ had in fact
originally been issued in time but had not been proceeded with
due to the plaintiff's solicitor's inaction (in not serving it), thus
creating the necessity for a second writ to be issued (out of time);
and the court said that the introduction of the general discretion
found in s.33 did not in any way affect the principles and practice
under which extensions to the period for service of a writ might
be granted.

It is not good and sufficient reason for extending that period
that the defendant knew that the writ had been issued and that a
claim existed and that he could not show any specific prejudice to
himself if the writ were to be renewed; nor that failure to serve
arose through accident or mistake; nor that the plaintiff was
awaiting the result of a pending test action; nor that there was a
delay or lack of authorisation from the legal aid angle (a case
confirming this important example is *Madron* v. *Arun District
Council*, 1986, unreported, CAT 317); nor that negotiations were
expected to reach a settlement.[8] But there may well be good
reason where the defendant has impliedly agreed to the writ

---

[7] There are similar provisions in the County Court (see CCR O.7 r.20).

being kept in abeyance (there must be a clear inference of such an agreement; merely making an interim payment does not raise such an inference), or where the defendant has contributed to the non-service in some way, even if merely by being untraceable. In *Doble* v. *Haymills (Contractors) Ltd, The Times*, 5 July 1988, CA, the fact that the plaintiff's solicitor thought that the writ expired a few days later than it in fact did was not a good reason for renewal.

In *Waddon* v. *Whitecroft Scovell* [1988] 1 WLR 309, HL, it was said, contrary to the purport of earlier authority, that one of the factors the court might take into account in deciding whether there was good reason for extending the validity of a writ were delays caused by the operation of the legal aid system.

The House of Lords has said that the power to renew is not limited to cases where there has been difficulty in effecting service of the writ, nor to 'exceptional circumstances', but that it should only be exercised where in all the circumstances, including the balance of hardship to the respective parties, there was 'good reason' to do so (*Kleinwort Benson Ltd* v. *Barbrak Ltd* [1987] AC 597). In *Goldenglow Nut Food Co.* v. *Commodin (Produce) Ltd* [1987] 2 Lloyd's Rep 569, the Court of Appeal had said that an application for extension of the validity of a writ needed to show no more than a 'good reason' why such an extension should be granted, except where, at the date of the application, the writ had already ceased to be valid and the relevant limitation period had expired. The fact that a defendant already knew of possible claims against him could be a relevant consideration in deciding whether such a good reason had been shown. But this should not be seen as any relaxation of the traditional approach, said the House of Lords in the *Waddon* case (*supra*). It was further said that a plaintiff had to establish first that there were good reasons for renewing; only then would the court go on to consider the balance of hardship (this was repeated by the House of Lords in *Baly* v. *Barrett, The Times*, 19 May 1989). It was also said in that case that the factors affecting a judge's mind when deciding whether to renew a writ were by no means necessarily the same as those he would consider when reviewing an application for leave to proceed out of time under s.33 of the Limitation Act 1980.

In *Baly* v. *Barrett* (*supra*) the House of Lords said that if a writ was to be renewed it should be renewed for the shortest period necessary and not simply every time for 12 months.

---

[8] See *The Mousa, The Times*, 7 May 1991.

In *Dagnell* v. *J.L. Freedman and Co* [1993] 1 WLR 388 the House of Lords emphasised that there had to be good reason if the validity of a writ was to be extended, and that normally involved showing good reason for the failure to serve the writ during its period of validity.

In *Barr* v. *Barr* [1994] PIQR P45 the Court of Appeal extended the time for service of a County Court summons where the court had misled the plaintiff into thinking that service had been effected. In *Singh* v. *Duport Harper Foundries Ltd* [1994] PIQR P87 the Court of Appeal, giving guidance on the general ambit of the rules for extending the validity of a writ, set aside a seven-month extension on the basis that the pre-conditions in the rules for an extension of longer than four months had not been fulfilled.

It can be seen therefore that in medical negligence cases the solicitor should work on the principle that, whatever leeway he might otherwise have under s.33 of the Limitation Act 1980, he should always ensure that he serves the writ within four months of issue. If he serves on issue he does not have the bother of remembering another deadline! There is no advantage in delaying service where service is possible; it will not, for example, reduce the chance of an offer of settlement, but increase it, if anything. Also, interest runs on general damages only from service of the writ. In some cases, however, the writ has to be issued to avoid being caught by the limitation period and the legal aid certificate, probably an emergency one, is limited to issue only. Note that under the new O.12 r.8A a defendant can call for service upon himself of a writ that has been issued which names him as a defendant.

ENDORSEMENT OF WRIT

Many writs in medical negligence cases will be generally endorsed, that is to say, not endorsed with the statement of claim, because often it is not possible to give the details of the claim within the time for the issue of the writ (also it may be tactically sound to serve the writ, as interest on general damages runs from service of the writ, or to encourage an offer, or occasionally to get disclosure against a non-party, i.e. a hospital or doctor who is not himself being sued – see p. 89). The endorsement is simple enough, giving no more than the outline and nature of the cause of action, e.g.

the plaintiff's claim is for damages for injury and loss sustained as a result of the negligence of the defendants their servants or agents in their treatment of her at the Britannia Hospital in and about September 1987, and further for interest upon such damages at such rate and for such period as the court thinks fit pursuant to s.35A of the Supreme Court Act 1981.[9]

INTEREST

Interest, which has now to be pleaded as a separate head of claim, need only be calculated as a liquidated figure up to the date of writ and thereafter on a daily basis if the claim is for a liquidated sum, which is unlikely to be the case in a medical negligence action (though it is possible, if, for example, the claim was only for loss of wages where negligent advice had caused the plaintiff to stay home from work).

The right to interest on damages in personal injury actions arises under s.35A of the Supreme Court Act 1981. The court is obliged to award interest where judgment is given in an action for personal injuries or death for a sum in excess of £200, unless the court is satisfied there are special reasons for not awarding interest. The 'judgment' may be a default judgment. In view of this mandatory provision it is not entirely clear what authority there was to make it obligatory, by RSC O.18 r.8(4), for all claims to interest to be pleaded specifically. It is nevertheless clearly advisable to include in the statement of claim, and the writ if not specially endorsed,[10] a separate claim for 'interest pursuant to s.35A of the Supreme Court Act 1981' or, in a County Court plaint or particulars of claim, 'pursuant to s.69 of the County Courts Act 1984'. If for any reason a higher rate of interest is claimed than the norm, this must be specifically pleaded; e.g. if substantial special damages accrued once and for all soon after the accident you can try for a full instead of a half rate on them. Interest is further considered below (in Chapter 27).

Interest on County Court judgments is now enabled by the County Court (Interest on Judgment Debts) Order 1991 at the rate for the time being specified in s.17 of the Judgments Act 1838 (s.106 of the County Courts Act already enabled a County Court judgment to be registered in the High Court).

An interesting difference of opinion among the lower courts was finally resolved by the decision of the House of Lords in *Thomas* v. *Bunn* [1991] 2 WLR 27 to the effect that judgment debt interest ran from the date of the assessment of damages, not from the earlier date of summary judgment. This decision should

---

[9] See above for the possibility of a protective summons in the County Court.
[10] However, the Court of Appeal has declared that, although failure to plead a claim for interest is fatal, generally endorsed writs do not need to carry a prayer for interest as r.8(4) is not applicable to them as they are not pleadings (*Edward Butler Vintners* v. *Grange Seymour Internationale, The Times*, 9 June 1987).

encourage defendants not to be reluctant in an appropriate case to admit liability and to accept judgment against themselves at a relatively early stage.

STATEMENT OF CLAIM

I would not presume to seek to instruct counsel how to draft a statement of claim in a medical negligence action, but I shall just mention one or two matters that give me some concern (particularly when I am asked to take over a case pleaded by another counsel – he having been, for example, elevated to a higher status).

First, it is not necessary to set out the whole medical history. It is always better to be as concise as possible. Do not be afraid that you will omit something – if you are thinking clearly and have confidence in your ability to express that thinking clearly, you will not omit anything. Do not believe that the more prolix you are the more effective or impressive your pleading becomes. For example, in an obstetric case you only need to set out the obstetric events that are germane to your allegations of negligence. Thus the fact that the membranes ruptured at 0900 hrs or that a Syntocinon infusion was commenced at noon may well not be relevant to an allegation that fetal distress as later shown by the CTG trace if properly read called for an emergency cesarean section, whereas the fact that the VEs (vaginal examinations) took place at intervals too far apart may be, and the fact that fresh meconium was passed early in the labour will be. So be clear what events you are relying on in support of your allegation of negligence, and plead only them.

Secondly, try not to leave the field open for the defendants to serve a long and tedious request for particulars, which wastes time and money as the questions are sent to your expert and his answers then sent on to you for you to copy them out in your draft. Tell the defendants in the statement of claim exactly what action or omission you say was negligent, when it occurred, why you say it was negligent, what you say should have been done instead, and what you say was the result to the plaintiff of that negligent act or omission. And do not put under your Particulars of Negligence sweeping allegations in the hope that you will in that way cover all possibilities, e.g. 'The defendants failed properly or at all to monitor the progress of the plaintiff's labour', or 'The defendants failed to provide an adequate system of anesthetic/obstetric cover', or 'The defendants failed properly to train and/or instruct their staff/trainees in such and such', or 'The defendants failed to observe and/or heed and/or act upon the signs of fetal distress'. These are all much too general and are just asking for the said tedious request for particulars. Be specific: e.g. 'The defendants failed properly to monitor the progress of the plaintiff's labour, in that they did such and such whereas they should have done such and such.' Sometimes the error lies simply in not adding to the general allegation words to the effect 'The facts and matters to be relied on in connection with this allegation are set out above at paras . . .'. Of course, to get this sort of clarity and particularity you have to ensure that your expert has answered the appropriate questions with sufficient precision (and that you actually understand what your case is). But nothing less will do.

On the other hand, do not omit to plead (in the main body of the claim, i.e. not simply under the Particulars of Negligence) any facts that are material. The defendants are obliged to traverse them in their defence or they will be deemed to have admitted them (see RSC O.18 r.13).

Staughton L.J. wrote in *Counsel*:

A good rule for drafting documents is to sit back at the end and ask of every phrase that one has written, whether it was necessary to write it at all.

He also said:

Unthinking copy of precedents, when nothing is ever left out as antiquated or obsolete, produces many documents which are too long, too old-fashioned and too obscure.

RSC O.18 r.7 tells us that the pleading should

contain only a statement in a summary form of the material facts on which the party pleading relies for his claim . . . and the statement must be as brief as the nature of the case admits.

In *Ashmore* v. *Corporation of Lloyd's* [1992] 1 WLR 446 Lord Templeman said that pleadings should define the issues, be brief, chronological and consistent, and that counsel should not advance a multitude of ingenious arguments in the hope that out of ten bad points the judge would be able to fashion a winner. He was expressly critical of the tendency in some cases for legal advisers to make every point, conceivable and inconceivable, without judgment or discrimination.

In *Hockaday* v. *South West Durham Health Authority* [1994] PIQR P275, which involved a highly technical analysis of the requirements for pleading a defence, the Court of Appeal gave the following guidance, which will be particularly useful when a plaintiff has to consider what to do about a holding defence, i.e. a defence which is not much more than a bare denial:

(1) The fundamental rule of pleading is that both a statement of claim and a defence must set out the material facts upon which the party pleading intends to rely.

(2) As to a bare traverse: a denial or a refusal to admit is a perfectly good plea, provided that all that is thereby intended is to put the plaintiff to proof of his case, but it may be that concealed in a traverse is an affirmative case, and that may well be so where the traverse is of a negative averment.

(3) If it is clear, either from the nature of the case or from the admission of counsel or otherwise, that it is intended to set up an affirmative case, particulars of the affirmative case ought to be delivered; otherwise the other party and the court will be in doubt as to what the issues are to be determined at the trial.[11]

We should also bear in mind that the purpose of pleading is not to play a game at the expense of litigants but to enable the opposing party to know the case against him; particularisation should not be sought when it is not necessary (*Trust Security Holdings* v. *Sir Robert McAlpine and Sons, The Times*, 21 December 1994, CA).

Make sure your expert(s) vet your draft before it is served. It is they who will have to support the allegations of negligence (and the other medical aspects of the claim) in court (for more on experts, see the previous chapter). And send any request for particulars relating to medical matters to the appropriate expert for his responses.

Order 14

If the claim seems clear and indefensible you may consider seeking summary judgment under Order 14. Unlike in other types of claim, it is probably advisable to wait for the defence, for otherwise the defendants will likely say they intend to defend but have not had time to preare their defence. Once you have the defence you can decide whether it reveals any matters which militate against a successful application. If there are none, an application for summary judgment may have the effect of forcing an early admission of liability (you could couple the application with one for an interim payment, to be heard at the same time). The disadvantage, especially in a case of modest value, is that the costs of failing in front of the Master could be taken from any award of damages. A way round this is to challenge the defendants in your affidavit to state that they have received independent expert advice exonerating them from the charge of negligence. Upon receipt of such an affidavit the application could be discontinued with minimal costs implications. Your affidavit

---

[11] The Practice Direction of January 1995 [1995] 1 WLR 262 emphasises that O.18 r.7 will be strictly enforced, and particularly that facts, not evidence, should be pleaded.

should state that you have received expert advice to the effect that the case is indefensible but avoid referring to that advice in such a way that entitles the defendants to call at that stage for your expert's report. Some lawyers favour an affidavit from the expert rather than the solicitor, but that seems unnecessary, and it reveals your hand at an early stage, which may prove embarrassing later.

CHECKLIST

- Are you aware of the limitation period?
- Can you reasonably certify the case is worth more than £50,000?
- Are you going to want it *tried* in the High Court? If so, are you aware of the available arguments for transfer?
- Have you got a suitable medical report to serve with the pleading? And a schedule of special damage?
- Have your experts vetted the draft pleading?

11 · Interim payments

SUMMARY

Where liability is admitted or manifest a plaintiff can obtain a payment on account. He must make out a case for what he needs, or what he has already lost.

A plaintiff in a personal injury action, and particularly in a medical negligence action, is likely to have to wait years before he gets judgment. There is a procedure whereby in uncontested cases or cases where the defendant is obviously liable he may obtain sums on account of damages before the issue of quantum, or even sometimes of liability, is in fact tried. Section 32 of the Supreme Court Act 1981 enabled rules to be made for the introduction of interim payments. RSC O.29 rr.9–18 provide that a plaintiff may apply for an interim payment on account of damages at any point after the time limited for acknowledgment of service has expired. He applies by summons, which may be the ordinary O.14 summons, supported by an affidavit which should verify the amount of damages, as far as this is possible, exhibit relevant documentation, e.g. medical reports, admissions by the defendants, set out the history of the suit, explain the cause of action and, if there is no admission of liability, why the plaintiff is bound to succeed. Further, if the claim is a personal injury action, as in this context our action is likely to be, the affidavit should verify that the defendant is either insured in respect of the claim (this would not be the case with a NHS body, as the Crown does not insure in this area, though it would be the case for a general or private practitioner), or is a public authority (this would include NHS bodies), or is a person whose means and resources are such as to enable him to make the interim payment (for it is only against defendants who fall into one of those categories that the court has power to make an order). Special damages and past and future loss of earnings should be set out in detail, and the affidavit should explain why the plaintiff needs an interim payment; details should be given of any special needs and hardship. In *Schott Kem Ltd* v. *Bentley* [1990] 3 WLR 397 Neil L.J. said at p. 406 that, although there was no legal restriction preventing an interim payment being made in the absence of evidence of need or prejudice on the part of the plaintiff if an order were not made, the appropriate practice was not to make such order in a personal injury case in the absence of such evidence.

However, in *Stringman* v. *McArdle* [1994] 1 WLR 1653 the Court of Appeal said that no particular need had to be demonstrated by the plaintiff beyond the general need to be paid the damages as soon as reasonably possible. In this case the judge had refused an application for funds to adapt the home. The Court of Appeal said that it was not for the judge to investigate how the money was to be used or whether the scheme was too extravagant. Tasker Watkins L.J. approved the statements in the Supreme Court Practice:

The Court readily orders payment of sufficient to compensate the plaintiff for lost wages or other financial hardship up to the anticipated date of trial, and sums needed for special treatment or equipment . . .

Where the plaintiff is a minor or patient, it is usual to confine an interim payment to sums needed by the next friend for maintenance and expenses of the plaintiff until trial.

The court may order an interim payment of such amount (including payment by instalments) as it thinks just where it is satisfied that the defendants have admitted liability, or that, if the action proceeded to trial, the plaintiff would obtain judgment for substantial damages against the defendants (or where there are two or more against any of them). The onus of proof rests on the plaintiff to satisfy the court in effect so that it is sure that the plaintiff will recover substantial damages as against that particular defendant and that he has need of an interim payment (*Breeze* v. *R. McKennon & Son Ltd, The Times*, 13 November 1985). In *Gibbons* v. *Wall, The Times*, 24 February 1988, the Court of Appeal said that the standard of proof required was the civil standard, i.e. on the balance of probabilities, but May L.J. added that that standard was flexible and in the context of an application for an interim payment the standard to be applied was at the high end of the range.

In *Trott* v. *Terry* [1975] CLY 815 a small interim payment was increased on appeal to £20,000 where the value of the claim was reckoned to be over £30,000. As with a payment into court any tribunal later trying the issue of liability should not be told of the order for interim payment, but on the application for interim payment there is no reason why the plaintiff should not tell the court of any payment in (*Fryer* v. *London Transport Executive, The Times*, 4 December 1982, CA). When or before the action is finally concluded the court has power to vary or discharge the order for the interim payment, including ordering repayment in part or whole. In one case (liability had been admitted) an interim payment of £190,000 was upheld by the Court of Appeal where the likely total damages had been assessed by the judge at first instance to be in the area of £250,000 (*Smith* v. *Glennon*, [1994] 5 Med LR 218).

After inconsistent decisions from the Court of Appeal in *Ricci Burns Ltd* v. *Patrick Toole* [1989] 1 WLR 993 and *Shanning International* v. *George Wimpey International Ltd* [1989] 1 WLR 981, it was resolved in *British and Commonwealth Holdings plc* v. *Quadrex Holdings Inc.* [1989] QB 842, that where unconditional (as opposed to conditional) leave to defend has been given on an application for summary judgment no interim payment may be ordered.

It is clear from *Van Hoffen* v. *Dawson* [1994] PIQR P101, CA, that the possibility of a finding of contributory negligence on the part of the plaintiff does not mean that an interim award cannot be made, provided that the court has regard to the net compensation likely to be obtained.

A defendant may resist the order on the ground that he does not fall within any of the categories of defendant against whom such an order can be made, or that the court should not be satisfied that the plaintiff will obtain (note that the words are not 'is likely to obtain' but 'would obtain') judgment for substantial damages. If the court is left in some doubt it can be asked as second best to certify fit for speedy trial.

Clearly there are risks in ordering large interim payments, particularly where liability remains contested. The court is likely to confine the payment to sums sufficient to compensate the plaintiff for lost wages or other financial hardship up to the prospective date of trial, and sums needed for special treatment or equipment. If the plaintiff is a minor or patient, the payment is likely to cover sums needed for maintenance and expenses.

It is expressly provided that whether or not a first application is successful the plaintiff may make a second or subsequent application for good cause, e.g. if the case suffers further or unexpected delays, or the money ordered to be paid has proved insufficient for current needs.

The facility for interim payments should not of course be confused with that which permits provisional damages to be awarded at trial with liberty to apply at a later date for further compensation, under s.32A of the Supreme Court Act 1981 (for this see Chapter 27 under 'Provisional damages').

A High Court judge (i.e. not only a Master) may hear and determine an application for an interim payment (*Smith* v. *Glennon* [1994] 5 Med LR 218).

A plaintiff who loses the trial can be ordered to repay an interim payment with interest (*Wardens & Commonalty of the Mystery of Mercers of the City of London* v. *New Hampshire Insurance Co., The Times*, 22 March 1991).

The County Court has had power since the beginning of 1983 to order interim payments where the sum claimed exceeds £500. As in the High Court this power is not confined to personal injury cases.

Practice note

If liability is contested and there is a split trial, serve a summons with affidavit in good time so that you can make an application for an interim payment as soon as you have established liability.

If you are applying for summary judgment (see Chapter 10 under 'Order 14'), you may combine it with an application for an interim payment.

Unfortunately an interim payment appears to be caught by the clawback provisions of the Social Security Administration Act 1992, so that benefits to date have to be repaid by the defendants out of the award. This is but one of the unjust results of that badly thought out legislation.

CHECKLIST

- Have you particularised past expenditure and current needs in your affidavit?
- Does the affidavit verify quantum and certify that the defendant has the means to pay?
- If there has been no admission of liability, do your affidavits 'prove' your case?

12 · Interrogatories

SUMMARY

Interrogatories should be used without hesitation if there is any matter on which further information would be helpful.

Interrogatories are generally under-used. They are likely to be of particular value in medical negligence cases for a number of reasons. First, the plaintiff may well not know exactly what treatment he received, even when the medical records have been scrutinised, or in what order the surgeon performed what actions. He is entitled to be told precisely what was done to him (in this connection reference can usefully be made, in or out of court, to the concluding observations of Sir John Donaldson M.R. in *Lee* v. *South West Thames Regional Health Authority* [1985] 1 WLR 845 where he suggested that a patient had a right, enforceable at law, whether by way of an action for discovery or for breach of contract, to be told what treatment he had had – repeated in *Wilsher* v. *Essex Area Health Authority* [1987] 2 WLR 425). Secondly, the holding defence is popular in many cases, the defendants, through uncertainty or tactical cunning, not committing themselves to any specific position. They are often slow to procure their experts' reports and thereafter to make up their minds as to whether the case is worth defending, and, if so, how. They should be obliged as soon as possible to condescend to particulars. A well-framed request for particulars can make an important contribution to the plaintiff's case, but beyond that, where the particulars are not enough or where the material sought does not arise out of the defence and so does not properly fall within the scope of further particulars, there are interrogatories.

You may, for example, be able to ascertain precisely what happened during an operation (or at any rate what the defence say happened), who was present at it, and the qualifications and relevant experience of the medical team. Or you may wish to find out what the maintenance or antiseptic precautions have been in respect of a ward or other hospital premises. It is worth asking oneself at the appropriate time, 'what would I like to find out from the other side?', and then attempting to do so by the use of suitably framed interrogatories.

Due to the limitations within which they operate, another result of the traditional common law approach to litigation whereby parties are required to disclose only the minimum about their case before trial and are actually encouraged to hold their cards close to their chest,[1] you may find yourself foiled from time to time in your efforts to find out the truth, or at least what the defence would say is the truth, about the treatment given to the patient; but the effort is certainly worth making. The particular value of interrogatories consists in forcing the defence to reveal what according to them is the factual matrix within which their defence lies. Judicial views have varied on how far plaintiffs should be encouraged to use interrogatories. At times it is said that they are not sufficiently made use of (in *Wilsher* v. *Essex Area Health Authority* [1987] 2 WLR 425 Mustill L.J. suggested that interrogatories could have helped to clarify the issues before trial). At other times the limitations on their use, as set out below, have been enforced, so that it has been suggested that in common law litigation generally their usefulness is limited to precise factual points on which information or admission is sought. As I have indicated, much of the limitation on their scope springs from our outdated adversarial approach to litigation, in which truth has often had to take second place to the rules of combat.

Order 26, as amended by SI 89/2427, provides that a party may serve on another party interrogatories relating to any matters in question between them which are necessary either for disposing fairly of the cause or matter or for saving costs, and an interrogatory which does not fulfil those conditions may not be administered even if it would be admissible as a question in cross-examination.

Interrogatories may be served on a party twice without order of the court (but not on the Crown – as to the arguments that the NHS should not be considered as part of the Crown see Chapter 3 under 'The NHS and the Crown'); the party interrogated may apply to the court if he considers that he should not be bound to answer. Note that there must be appended to the end of the interrogatories a note stating within what period they must be answered and, if the party interrogated is a body, the person who is required to answer them must be specified (he must be an 'officer or member' of the 'body' being sued).

The answer must be on affidavit; further and better particulars may be asked for if desired.

---

[1] This is much less true now that reports and statements are exchanged prior to trial (see Chapter 13).

The new right of a party to serve without order makes little real difference in the medical negligence action, as one did that anyway, and only if no satisfactory answer was forthcoming did one apply to the court. One can of course still apply to the court for leave to administer.

The point may also be made that interrogatories have probably lost some of their importance now that witness statements are exchanged before trial.

Note the following:

(1) Interrogatories relating solely to credit are not allowed.
(2) The 'fishing' interrogatory is not permitted. It must be confined to relevant issues and facts which there is some reason for believing true. It will not be allowed if it appears designed to prove a cause of action not yet pleaded. Once again, this is a rule, if strictly applied, which can be used to defeat the needs of justice, the theory being that, however culpable the defendants may be, they cannot be obliged to come clean unless the plaintiff, as luck would have it, is already in a position to make precise allegations.
(3) Interrogatories are not allowed where admission is sought of a fact peculiarly within the plaintiff's knowledge, or *which he can himself give evidence of at the trial* (my emphasis), or which is clearly denied on the pleadings.
(4) N.B.: Interrogatories are not allowed on a matter of opinion, whether expert or not. This can militate against the plaintiff getting an understanding of what the defendants' case is, i.e. what they are saying on the question of negligence – which is unsatisfactory. Why should the defendants not be obliged to state what their expert's opinion is on points raised by the plaintiff? Carefully framed questions, plus a helpful Master (or at any rate one who is not actually obstructive), could go quite a long way. For example: Did you do such and such? Do you accept that the normal practice would have been to do such and such? If so, do you say there were grounds for departing from the normal practice? If so, what were the grounds? In this way one can possibly hope to avoid the objection that one is asking about matters of expert opinion.
(5) Interrogatories are not allowed if they go to the basic question the court is being asked to decide, i.e. the issue of negligence. You may not ask: 'do you agree that if such and such was done that was negligent?', or 'do you agree that if such and such was done it was not consistent with the standard of care to be expected from a surgeon specialising in that field?' That

is why it is less objectionable to ask in such terms as: 'do you agree it would not be normal practice to do such and such?'

So it is clear that interrogatories are not admissible for conducting a cross-examination of the witnesses. If there is a matter of fact that you need to know, that you cannot find out from your witnesses, and that the defendants know (anesthetic events are the prime example), then it is appropriate to administer interrogatories. If you receive a holding defence, do not think up a long list of questions in the belief that you need to 'open the case up'. The questions are unlikely to fulfil the criteria for interrogatories, and the defendants are in any event likely to deliver a detailed defence in due course.

In order to decide whether interrogatories are needed, simply consider whether there is an obvious significant gap in your factual knowledge of the case which the defendants can fill.

As with any rules, once they are properly understood, there may be the odd case where you can break them. For example, where you have an obviously strong, perhaps an apparently indefensible, case, and the defendants have clearly not properly confronted it yet, you may be able by carefully framed questions to force them to confront the issues and perhaps realise that they have no defence to the claim. But this sort of tactic needs careful handling.

If the party interrogated makes insufficient answer he may be required to make further answer by affidavit or to submit to oral examination, under O.26 r.5. An insufficient answer is not one the truth of which may be doubted but one which is insufficient in substance (*Lyell* v. *Kennedy (No.3)* (1884) 27 Ch D 1, 16).

Witnesses: bear in mind that there is no property in a witness, so you are at liberty to seek answers to any of your questions by interviewing the medical staff – for example, a nurse present at an operation, or having the daily care of the patient, may well be able to enlighten you about aspects of the case.

You may also find it useful at a later stage (not later than 21 days after setting down) to tie the defence down to definitive answers to points by requiring admissions under the 'Notice to Admit' provisions (RSC O.27). The power of the court to penalise in costs a party who unreasonably fails to make admissions of facts or documents has recently been strengthened by amendments to O.62 r.6(7) and (8).

It used to be said that one advantage of joining the doctor(s) in the action is that the plaintiff does not then have to argue for the doctor(s) to be specified as the proper party to answer the interrogatories, rather than some administrative officer of the health authority. However (quite apart from the right recently given to the interrogating party to specify the officer or member of the health authority who is to give the replies), it should be possible to tie even an administrative officer down to precise answers, for he is under a duty to get the necessary information from the relevant medical staff (*Southwark Water Co.* v. *Quick* (1878) 3 QBD 315) and he cannot merely confine himself to his own knowledge of the facts (*Bank of Russian Trade* v. *British Screen Productions* [1930] 2 KB 90).

In the recent commercial case of *Det Danske Hedeselskabet* v. *KDM International plc* [1994] 2 Lloyd's Rep 534 Colman J. gave important guidance on the current parameters for interrogatories. Having stated that oppressive interrogatories would not be allowed, he said:

(a) the answers requested had to be essential for the preparation of the case and unlikely to emerge in due course following the usual steps of further and better particulars, discovery or exchange of witness statements (interrogatories before exchange of witness statements would probably be premature)[2];

(b) information which is essential only in the sense that it might lead to further enquiry or that questions about it could be asked in cross-examination at the trial would not be 'essential';

(c) answers needing detailed investigation not otherwise likely to be undertaken would not be required;

(d) hypothetical questions should not normally be asked;

(e) questions seeking information ascertainable on cross-examination at the trial are inappropriate unless 'essential' at the earlier stage.

We should also bear in mind that the purpose of pleading is not to play a game at the expense of litigants but to enable the opposing party to know the case against him; so particularisation should not be sought when it is not necessary (*Trust Security Holdings* v. *Sir Robert McAlpine and Sons*, *The Times*, 21 December 1994, CA).

CHECKLIST

• Have you understood the limited, but important, function of interrogatories?

• Is there a piece of factual information that you need to know in order to properly appraise or direct your case that the defendants alone can tell you? If so, ask them, but not otherwise.

---

[2] This may well not be true for the medical negligence action.

13 · The summons for directions

SUMMARY

The most important aspect of the summons for directions[1] is the timetable created for exchange of statements and reports before trial. A plaintiff must ordinarily submit to examination by the defendants' doctor and he cannot make it a condition that he see the ensuing report. Such report is privileged and need only be disclosed if the defendants are going to rely on it. The number of medical witnesses, whether on liability or condition, is usually limited in the order, though there is no judicial decision requiring that to be done.

You are likely to be asked by the other side to agree to various directions before the summons is heard, so you need to know what is appropriate. Where the Master makes an order which a party cannot or does not comply with, it may cost him dear, even to the extent of losing him the case. An example of this is the failure of the defence in *Thake* v. *Maurice* [1986] QB 644 to serve their expert evidence in time, which cost them the case.[2]

The following points should be noted:

MEDICAL TEXTS

If there are any relevant medical texts they will, one hopes, have been enumerated by the expert. An order for exchange of references, and copies, if required, should be made. This extends to unpublished material but not to individual case-notes or medical histories of third parties (see *Naylor* v. *Preston Area Health Authority* [1987] 1 WLR 958).

---

[1] See the precedent in Appendix II.
[2] RSC time limits are to be observed: *Smith* v. *Secretary of State for the Environment, The Times*, 6 July 1987.

MEDICAL REPORTS ON CONDITION AND PROGNOSIS

Where there are, or will be, reports on the plaintiff's present medical condition and his prognosis for the future, these should be exchanged in the usual way, and agreed if possible.[3] A plaintiff who unreasonably refuses to allow an examination by the defendants' expert is likely to have his action stayed (*Edmeades* v. *Thames Board Mills Ltd* [1969] 2 QB 67); but the onus of showing unreasonableness is on the defendants, who need to show, if they are to get a stay, that their case cannot properly be prepared without such an examination (*Lane* v. *Willis* [1972] 1 WLR 326). The court is unlikely to require the plaintiff to submit to an examination which is unpleasant, painful or risky, unless the interests of justice demand it (cf. *Aspinall* v. *Sterling Mansell* [1981] 3 All ER 866 with *Prescott* v. *Bulldog Tools* [1981] 3 All ER 809). Joint medical examination by doctors for each party is best if possible but is not obligatory. The plaintiff may be allowed a friend if he is nervous or if the doctor has a reputation for roughness, but he does not have a legal right to insist in every case that his own doctor be present when he is examined by the defendants' doctor (*Hall* v. *Avon Area Health Authority (Teaching)* [1980] 1 WLR 481; and see *Whitehead* v. *Avon County Council*, *The Times*, 3 May 1995). *The Times* reported on 7 November 1986 that Hirst J. had refused an application by a plaintiff suing Eli Lilly and others over the drug Opren to have her own doctor present when examined by the defendants' dermatologist; the judge said the court must give the specialist the credit of being accurate in recording his results, and the presence of an outsider would impose 'an undue constraint' on him. This is clearly most unsatisfactory: it is hard to see why a plaintiff, obviously nervous and possibly unwell, should have to walk alone into the enemy camp; and the impartiality of defendants' doctors is not sufficiently universal to warrant the judge's confidence.

If the plaintiff shows good reason for objecting to a particular doctor the court is likely to be sympathetic (*Starr* v. *National Coal Board* [1977] 1 WLR 63).

In exceptional cases, where, for example, the liability of the defendant depends largely upon his medical condition, the court has power to stay proceedings if he does not submit to a medical examination (*Lacey* v. *Harrison* [1993] PIQR P10).[4]

Then there arises the question whether a plaintiff who submits

---

[3] An initial report is likely to have been served with the statement of claim (see Chapter 10).
[4] In *Larby* v. *Thurgood* [1993] PIQR P218 May J. refused an application to stay proceedings until the plaintiff agreed to be interviewed by the defendants' employment consultant. The judge said that the report could cover all necessary issues without the need for an interview.

to an examination by the defendants' doctor is entitled to see the report. The short answer is no. Of course, if the plaintiff's solicitors made it a condition of their agreeing to the examination that the report should be disclosed the court will order disclosure, and if the defendants want to rely in court on this report as to condition and prognosis they will have to disclose it in good time, but it is a privileged document and they cannot be obliged to disclose it if they do not intend to rely on it. The court will not be quick to spell out an implied agreement to disclose even where the plaintiff has submitted to a medical examination by the defendants' doctor and shown his own doctor's reports to the defendants and they have been agreed (see *Causton* v. *Mann Egerton (Johnsons) Ltd* [1974] 1 WLR 162). In *Megarity* v. *D.J. Ryan & Sons Ltd* [1980] 2 All ER 832 the Court of Appeal refused to endorse the practice that had from time to time been followed previously of requiring the plaintiff to submit to medical examination only upon the condition that the ensuing report be disclosed to him. The view was taken that the scheme introduced by RSC O.38 rr.36–38 made it unnecessary to adopt the position urged by, principally, Lord Denning, in, e.g., the *Causton* case (*supra*) and *Clarke* v. *Martlew* [1973] QB 58, whereby it was said to be unfair that a plaintiff should submit to examination and yet not be entitled to see what the doctor said about him. The court in *Megarity* v. *Ryan* (*supra*) was much impressed with the privilege that a party enjoys not to disclose reports he is not going to rely on. Roskill L.J. said:

Now if the argument of counsel for the plaintiff be right a plaintiff would be entitled to obtain the entirety of the report at an early stage as a condition of submitting to a medical examination although, at the summons for direction stage, he would not be entitled to such wide discovery. It seems to me that that cannot have been the intention of these rules. The plaintiff is, as I see it, under no obligation, even at the present day, to disclose a report in his possession unfavourable to himself; and yet if the argument of counsel for the plaintiff be right, he could, as a condition of submitting to a medical examination, impose on the defendant an obligation to disclose the resulting medical report in the hope that the defendants' report, otherwise plainly a privileged document, would reveal in these circumstances something more favourable to him than his own medical report would reveal. That seems to me to be entirely wrong.

And *per* Ormrod L.J.:

It is perfectly easy to understand the plaintiff's feelings and his wish to know what the defendants' doctor has said about him; and in terms of ordinary human response that is perfectly comprehensible and quite natural. But the question here is whether in litigation it is fair and just not only to the plaintiff but to both sides. It means quite clearly that the plaintiff, if he is right, can insist on seeing a copy of the defendants' doctor's medical report as a condition of submitting to the medical examination, and if that report is more favourable to his case than his own doctor's, he can call, or be in a position to call, that doctor if so advised. That may be sound enough in terms of fairness, but the corollary is that he, the plaintiff, should disclose all medical reports which he has obtained even if they are unfavourable to his case. I should imagine that most plaintiffs and their advisers would think that that was a major encroachment on the privileges of a litigant in these courts.

The reasoning of the court is sound. In *McGuinness* v. *Fairbairn Lawson* (1966) 110 SJ 870 Lord Denning said that a party is not bound to produce an unfavourable report, and Russell L.J. said that an agreement to exchange medical reports only referred to those intended to be produced in evidence. The real question is whether there should be any privilege any longer for medical reports. If one side is to be obliged to disclose unfavourable reports so must the other. It depends on whether we are going to perpetuate the common law approach to litigation, whereby a party is free to call only the evidence that helps him and to jettison all unfavourable evidence he obtains, however reliable and conducive to truth (and therefore surely to justice). It is quite true, as Ormrod L.J. said, that plaintiffs' advisers would not relish disclosure of all reports they obtained, though on condition and prognosis as opposed to liability they would not often be embarrassed; but it is not easy to see why defendants should be obliged to disclose all reports if plaintiffs are not. The real answer lies in a decision whether privilege still makes sense in the context of the more investigative and less combative approach to litigation that is gradually emerging in this country (see below, where exchange of reports on liability on which parties wish to rely is considered). It may be that the questions to which these medical reports address themselves are better answered, and the purpose of justice better served, by open rather than litigious attitudes, and that for this reason all medical reports could be made an exception to the rule as to legal professional privilege.

REPORTS ON LIABILITY

Previous editions of this book contained a long exposition of the way in which the old 'trial by ambush' rules for disclosure (as exemplified by the Court of Appeal decision in *Rahman* v. *Kirklees Area Health Authority* [1980] 1 WLR 1244) fell into disrepute and were reversed under the impetus of the modern 'cards on the table' approach (following criticism in the Court of Appeal in *Wilsher* v. *Essex Area Health Authority* [1987] QB 730 and *Naylor* v. *Preston Area Health Authority* [1987] 1 WLR 958). It is not thought that such a historical analysis is directly relevant any more. Suffice it to say that with effect from October 1987 O.38 r.37 provides:

Where in any cause or matter an application is made under rule 36(1) in respect of oral expert evidence, then, unless the court considers that there are special reasons for not doing so, it shall direct that the substance of the evidence shall be disclosed in the form of a written report or reports to such other parties and within such period as the Court may specify.[5]

(See below for r.36 that provides that leave must be sought for the adduction of expert evidence.)

It is not clear what circumstances will be taken by a court to constitute special reasons for not ordering disclosure, but in the light of the observations of the Court of Appeal in the above-cited cases the Master should be very slow to see special reasons in a medical negligence action, and any refusal to order disclosure should be the subject of appeal.

The court has power to order one party only to disclose, but the circumstances would have to be wholly exceptional to justify that, and such an order is likely to be appealable. Similarly, sequential disclosure may occasionally be ordered where the circumstances justify it (in practice the plaintiff will generally have his report ready first).[6]

Rule 38 provides that in any cause or matter the court may direct 'without prejudice' meetings of experts to identify areas of disagreement. This facility is not often used in the medical negligence action, except in respect of care and quantum experts.

If a defendant himself is to give expert evidence he must disclose it under this rule (*Shell Pension Trust Ltd.* v. *Pell Frischmann and Partners* [1986] 2 All ER 911).

Some difficulty might seem to have been created by the decision of Michael Wright Q.C. in *Kenning* v. *Eve Construction Ltd* [1989] 1 WLR 1189, which, as can be inferred from the title, was not a medical case. As explained in Chapter 9 counsel is entitled to redraft an expert's report (subject to the fundamental condition that the effect of the opinion is not distorted). In this case the judge held that where a covering letter from the defendants' expert that sounded a note of disquiet had been disclosed inadvertently along with his main report the plaintiff could amend his claim based on that letter if the defendants called that witness. So far so good (except that one might have thought the letter was privileged and should go back – see Chapter 7 under 'Privilege'). But the judge went on to say that the whole of an expert's evidence must be disclosed, warts and all. This may indeed be the case where the warts are fundamental to his

---

[5] SI 89/2427 amended this slightly but not relevantly for present purposes (see Appendix I for the full text).
[6] Disclosure will normally be simultaneous; otherwise the second party can tailor his report.

opinion, but if it is possible before disclosure to excise the warts without distorting the opinion (as one might well think was possible in this case), then there can surely be no duty to disclose the warts. The medical negligence practitioner should not, I suggest, in any way be led to think that, just because his expert at one stage or another writes something that does not help the plaintiff, that has to be communicated to the other side if the expert is to be called at the trial.

The Court of Appeal have in fact thrown doubt on Michael Wright Q.C.'s decision: in *Derby and Co. Ltd.* v. *Weldon (No.8)* [1991] 1 WLR 73, the court held that there was no power to override the basic right of privilege and order the disclosure of an expert's report dealing with an issue that the party for whom the report was prepared did not intend to canvass at the trial. It was pointed out that the rules (RSC O.38 r.37) that allowed the court to order disclosure of any report that an expert was to give in evidence at the trial merely gave the court a right to impose a condition on the calling of certain evidence, and did not abrogate the principle that a document prepared with a view to litigation was privileged.

EXCHANGE OF WITNESS STATEMENTS

Pursuant to O.38 r.2A the directions should always contain an order that witness statements be exchanged. Parties appearing at trial who have not exchanged statements are not likely to be welcomed by the judge.

Statements should be signed and dated (and it seems sensible to have them witnessed, particularly in the medical action where illness might later prevent a plaintiff testifying),[7] should contain the full name and address of the maker and state that he is a party or an employee of a party if appropriate, be expressed in ordinary language and relate events chronologically, be typed double-spaced in book form on both sides of the paper and be paginated. They should not contain evidence which would by the ordinary rules of evidence be inadmissible, e.g. hearsay, opinion etc. Service of witness statements was held in *Balkanbank* v. *Taher*, *The Times*, 19 February 1994 not to waive privilege in respect of connected documents. Clarke J. also said that the party serving the statement retained an absolute right whether or not to call the witness or to put in as evidence all or part of the statement. See

---

[7] In such a case the procedure laid down by the Civil Evidence Act 1968 and rules made thereunder could be followed – note that service of a witness statement under the 'exchange' rules does not affect the Civil Evidence Act requirements (O.38 r.2A(b)), unless such service is explicitly stated to constitute service under the Act.

also *Booth* v. *Warrington Health Authority* [1992] PIQR P137. H.H. Judge Busher said in *Fairfield Mobey Ltd.* v. *Shell* [1989] 1 All ER 576 that such a statement (this appears from r.2A(4)) was not to be used unless the witness was called (or privilege waived by the other party) – in particular it could not be put to another witness unless the maker had been or was to be called (presumably counsel could ask for an assurance from the other side as to whether the maker was going to be called). However, in *Youell* v. *Bland Welch and Co.* [1991] 1 WLR 122 Phillips J. concluded, surely wrongly, that not only did a statement of a witness lose its privileged status when served (which is understandable) but also that the court had a discretion to admit it in evidence on the application of the party on whom it had been served if its maker was not called to give evidence by the serving party.[8] It was also held in *Black and Decker* v. *Flymo Ltd* [1991] 1 WLR 753 (Hoffmann J.) that once a document has been disclosed by way of exchange of witness statements a claim to privilege can no longer be asserted in respect of it. And Hobhouse J. said in *Prudential Assurance Co.* v. *Fountain Page Ltd* [1991] 1 WLR 756 that a witness statement is received subject to an implied obligation not to put it in evidence except at the trial (and then only if the maker is called), and not to use it for any other purpose. This aspect of the matter needs clarification. The Practice Direction of January 1995 [1995] 1 WLR 262 provides that, unless otherwise ordered, every witness statement is to stand as the evidence-in-chief of the witness in question.

THE TIMETABLE

The simplest form of timetable provides that witness statements be exchanged two (or three) months after setting down, and all other reports (including witnesses as to quantum) three months after that, with provision for secondary reports from experts who have already provided a report within two months thereafter or not later than two months before trial. Variations on this scheme are of course possible. The most important single factor is to allow time for exchange of statements, a full conference, preparation and then exchange of the final draft of the expert reports. (See the precedent in Appendix II.)

You must ensure that you are ready for the exchanges at the due dates, and you must ensure that the defendants keep to them,

---

[8] Section 5 of the Courts and Legal Services Act 1990 gives power to make further rules of court for compulsory service of witness statements with sanctions for disobedience, and specifically provides that the fact that such a statement might otherwise have been privileged from disclosure is irrelevant.

or your whole timetable up to trial will be thrown out of kilter and you will have to get a new order, perhaps even adjourn the trial.[9] One way of keeping the defendants up to the mark is to remind them two weeks before any exchange date and to warn them that if they are not ready you will take out a summons to debar them from calling any such evidence at the trial. As the main conference in the case will normally take place between exchange of witness statements and exchange of expert evidence, and as one of its purposes is to consider the statements from the treating doctors and any other statements provided by the defendants, that purpose will be thwarted if the defence statements have not come through by then. It may well then be necessary to postpone the conference even though a new date convenient to all is likely to be weeks ahead.

Although parties to a medical negligence action usually show each other some latitude in respect of late reports, provided that they do not feel genuinely prejudiced by them, the court may not be so complaisant. Leave to adduce expert evidence out of time was refused by the Court of Appeal in *Winchester Cigarette Machinery Ltd* v. *Payne, The Times*, 19 October 1993, on the ground that the necessary adjournment would prejudice the defendants. A similar decision was reached in *Croft* v. *Jewell* [1993] PIQR P270.

LISTS AND DISCOVERY

The significant discovery will usually have been made under the pre-action discovery facility, as explained in Chapter 7. Now is the time, however, to make sure that you have all the records and to pursue, by summons if necessary, any missing documents. If they say they are lost, put them on affidavit about it – it is amazing how much material turns up suddenly under such pressure.

Although it used to be the case that an order might be made exempting from disclosure a document for which secrecy was sought till trial, e.g. a video calculated to show that the plaintiff was lying about his injury, this appears no longer possible in view of the current 'cards on the table' approach in litigation (*Khan (Aurangzeb)* v. *Armaguard Ltd* [1994] 1 WLR 1204 CA, not following *McGuinness* v. *Kellogg Company of Great Britain* [1988] 1 WLR 913).

---

[9] Decide from which point of time you wish to date the timetable, i.e. from setting down or from the date of the order – this will depend on how soon the trial court is likely to offer a fixture (a fixture will always be necessary to secure the attendance of the doctors).

LIMITATION OF MEDICAL WITNESSES

Under O.38 r.4 the court has a general power to limit the number of medical witnesses that may be called. The practice until fairly recently was to place no restriction on the number of witnesses a party may call. That derived from *Rahman* v. *Kirklees Area Health Authority* (*supra*). In that case Cumming-Bruce L.J. said he was not prepared to restrict the defendants to any number at all, despite conceding that the history of medical negligence actions made it 'not wholly fanciful for the plaintiff to fear the prospect of litigation in which a whole string of men of medical learning might be marshalled to follow one another into the witness box to obscure the truth out of a misguided sense of loyalty to a member or members of their profession charged with negligence'. Ormrod L.J. said that if the defendants abused their position in that way they would be likely to damage their case and the judge would know how to deal with it.

But it is a simple matter in any case for the parties to decide how many experts they need (or, at any rate, the maximum number), and, if one party objects, the other can be required to justify that number to the Master. It is now usual for the parties to agree on a maximum number in the summons.

For the limited scope of O.38 r.4 see *Sullivan* v. *West Yorkshire Passenger Transport Executive* [1985] 2 All ER 134, where the Court of Appeal said there was no power under the rule or under the court's inherent jurisdiction to bar a party from calling an expert witness at the trial.

By O.38 r.36 any party intending to use expert evidence of any character at the trial must apply to the court for a direction under O.38 r.38 (or, occasionally, r.41). The effect of r.36 is that if such application is not made the party will not be permitted to adduce expert evidence at the trial (unless he can secure the consent of all parties, get it in on affidavit, or otherwise obtain the leave of the court – these possibilities are remote in a medical negligence action).

TYPICAL STEPS IN A MEDICAL NEGLIGENCE ACTION

It may be helpful at this intermediate stage to summarise the steps in the action that will usually be taken.

Bear in mind first of all that the medical negligence action is a different creature from the ordinary personal injury action. Of course, a medical negligence action may occasionally be for economic loss only, as when you claim for the cost of upkeep of an unplanned baby, so that it is not, nor does it include, a claim for personal injuries. But most medical negligence actions include a claim for damages for personal injuries, and fall within the rubric of 'action for personal injuries' (see O.1 r.4) and so, as explained elsewhere in this book, attract the provisions as to, e.g., limitation and service of reports with the statement of claim. Nevertheless the medical negligence action has its own rules and one can expect chaos at best, disaster at worst, if one tries to process it as a personal injury action.

Although the medical negligence action is for the purposes of the rules an action for personal injuries, it is more significantly an action for professional negligence. The rules for automatic disclosure do not apply:[10] a carefully drafted summons for directions is required, to create a timetable for exchange of the various expert reports and witness statements. Obtaining the medical records from all relevant sources is vital and often difficult; it is particularly difficult to spot the vital missing documents and then to get them, by summons if necessary. Pre-action disclosure is not a significant factor in non-medical cases: in the medical negligence action it is the most important step, along with instructing the right expert. To read, understand (up to a point anyway), sort, file and index the medical records, and then later prepare bundles of them for trial is unique to this sort of action, extremely difficult and time-consuming. Bear in mind, too, that our law, i.e. the judges, defer to medical practice (as explained in Chapter 17) and will not form their own views as to what is appropriate medical practice, whereas in an action, for, say, solicitors' negligence, they certainly will (believing, rightly or wrongly, that they know just as much about professional standards in that field as the expert witnesses); they will even take this robust attitude to an extent in other expert contexts, such as engineering; but they will not take this attitude in the context of medical standards.

You will also find peculiar problems of causation in the medical negligence action, where particular difficulties arise that do not usually arise in other contexts (see Chapter 18): it is fairly clear that the plaintiff in an industrial injury claim broke his leg when he fell off the scaffolding and that it was not in fact due to the progress of a pre-existing 'weak leg' condition; similarly for the motorist whose face was lacerated when his windscreen was shattered – no pre-existing condition there. But most plaintiffs in the medical negligence action had a pre-existing condition that might account for some or all of their complained of injury.

---

[10] For some reason they have not been statutorily disapplied in the County Court, so one has specifically to ask for an appropriate order disapplying them.

In the medical negligence action the expert evidence is virtually always vital, far more often than in any other form of action, both as to liability and as to causation; that is why cases are won or lost on the experts you select (see Chapter 9).

The Steps:

Stage 1

Get instructions from client (perhaps on the green form scheme). (N.B. *always* date every statement you take from a witness; it is maddening for counsel, and for you, not to know at what date the patient is writing – her complaints could be months or years out of date (and how to know which among several statements supersedes which?) – you can update and re-date on your word processor each time.)

Apply for legal aid (children (i.e. under 16 years of age) are eligible without assessment of parents' means).

Examine legal aid limitation (try/hope for authority to get 'all appropriate medical evidence', not just 'an expert report'). You will be authorised to obtain the records (by summons if necessary), instruct an (or all) appropriate expert(s) and then get counsel's advice on merits (perhaps also to get counsel to draft the letter of instruction to the expert if you wish).

Obtain the records, i.e. by writing the appropriate letter to the appropriate bodies – see Chapter 7. (N.B. for records made after October 1991 you will have a virtually unfettered right under the Access to Health Records Act 1990; for earlier records you will need to use the pre-action disclosure procedure: this cannot be used if you have issued a writ, so go under O.24 r.7; on the other hand for disclosure against a non-defendant you will have to have issued a writ. See Chapter 7.)

Read, sort, file, paginate and index the records. Chase up now, or after your expert reports, any missing ones. Inspect the originals (can also be done later, but the earlier the better). Type out any illegible pages that are important. Check that no vital edges are missing (they will be, e.g. the dates on the left margin of the nursing notes are almost always cut off). Get client's comments on the records.

Select the right expert: this is vital. Instruct her in the appropriate manner (see Chapter 9).

Read and assess her report. Get client's comments on it. Ask for further elucidation if you know what you are doing. (N.B. you may be able to get the legal aid limitation lifted without an advice from counsel if the report is clear; otherwise counsel will give (hopefully) a positive advice; he may in any event ask for further information, whether he is being asked to draft a claim or do an advice. Legal aid often extends no further than setting down and to a further advice from counsel on merits, which is unsatisfactory, as it is only *after* exchange of all reports that there is sufficient new material to warrant a reassessment of the situation.)

Stage 2

Counsel will draft the statement of claim. You may want a conference first – it may not be necessary if the report is clear. But always get the expert(s) to vet the draft.

Serve statement of claim, with short report on the alleged injuries (*not* on liability), and any schedule of loss that you can put together at that time (see Chapter 10 for the new rules).

Defence comes in: get observations from experts and client. Ask experts if they want any factual questions answered by the defendants and see if you can use a request for further and better particulars or interrogatories for that. Send all material to counsel (that may seem obvious, but I have suffered a case where I drafted the claim and the solicitor did not come back to me until a month before trial, with catastrophic results – she said that was how she handled her industrial injury practice!). If there is a request for further and better particulars of the statement of claim, ensure that your expert precisely answers each (medical) question. It is so wearing if one has to construct specific answers from an imprecisely worded letter of response from the expert.

Issue appropriate summons for directions (see precedent in Appendix II). Get order for directions, usually by consent.

Set case down (assuming legal aid authority – see comments above). Take out application to fix (having got everyone's 'dates to avoid'). Notify all concerned of fixture date.

Get counsel's approval as to the form of the factual witness statements for exchange.

When witness statements are received from defendants, send them to experts, client and counsel. Then hold a full conference to assess the current direction and strength of the case, and to put your experts' reports into proper form for disclosure – they are likely to want to amend their original reports, even rewrite them, in view of the new material. Submit the final versions to counsel for approval for disclosure. Remember that non-medical expert reports will probably have to be exchanged at the same time (e.g. accountants' reports on loss of earnings, architects' reports on housing needs).

Conferences with counsel: you will probably need two within six months or so of the trial, one on liability, and one on quantum; but the need and the timing will vary according to the nature and complexities of the case. Do not be afraid to ask for one if you want one (this applies to any stage of the proceedings – e.g. if the client wants to meet her barrister, she should be enabled to do so – she will probably have enough to worry about without wondering if he really cares about her case). (N.B. you *must* take a full note of a conference, and put a typed-up copy with your and counsel's papers as soon as possible – best to get it agreed by experts and counsel first.)

If defendants are unreasonably tardy on any exchange, take out a debarring summons; this can often result in an offer to negotiate.

Stage 3

For the trial; prepare bundles of the medical records (a real headache!). A core bundle is often the answer, as many of the records will not be important (judges like core bundles) – provided you can get agreement from everyone as to its contents, which can often prove more trouble than doing a full bundle![11] Prepare bundles of the medical reports (to be lodged before trial, even if not agreed), and of the non-medical expert reports. Bundle the witness statements (O.34 r.10 requires them to be lodged).

If not done already, serve final schedule of special and other damage. Insist on a counter-schedule from the defendants.

Trial draws near

As the trial draws nigh, do not be surprised if the defendants produce startling new medical arguments. This is a recognised ploy. It usually takes the form of 'expert' evidence designed to show that the patient's injury was pre-existing, or due to a hitherto

---

[11] Strictly speaking, the medical records are not admissible as they are hearsay unless a Civil Evidence Act notice or notice to admit has been served. In practice this is usually overlooked: it is obviously sensible if the records are put in without fuss, but it is possible that one could be faced at trial with an entry that one does not accept as accurate, only to be told by the judge that one should have objected to its admissibility in the absence of the maker. The way to avoid that situation would be for you to make it clear either by inserting an appropriate order in the summons for directions or simply recording in correspondence that the medical records are agreed in the sense that it is agreed that they were made by those by whom, and when, they purport to have been made but their contents are not necessarily accepted as being accurate. I advise that if you are proposing to challenge the truth of a particular note you should tell the defendants this (if it is not already obvious from the pleadings or elsewhere) so that they are given a chance to call the relevant witness if they so desire.

unconsidered pathology. The GP records are likely to be scrutinised to see if there is any possible indication of a pre-existing condition to which the injury could be ascribed, rather than to the treatment compained of. So a claim for substantial urinary damage following a hysterectomy may be met by the contention that, some years before, the patient complained on one occasion to her GP of a minor degree of incontinence. A claim which alleges nerve injury due to careless positioning on the operating table may be met by an allegation that, hitherto unknown to all, the patient has an underlying vulnerability to that sort of nerve damage. A claim that excessive pre- or post-operative bleeding denotes improper attention may be met by an allegation that the patient, hitherto unknown to all, has a clotting disorder. A claim that a spinal anesthetic caused permanent paralysis may be met by the allegation that the cause of the paralysis was a coincidental episode of previously latent multiple sclerosis. One cannot help getting the impression that often, where defendants decide to fight a case, the brief to the experts (at any rate, as understood by the experts) is to explain away the injury by hook or by crook. And sometimes they are successful. Reference may be made to the cases noted below in Chapter 23 of *Moore* v. *Worthing District Health Authority* [1992] 3 Med LR 431 and *Howard* v. *Wessex Regional Health Authority* [1994] 5 Med LR 57. An instance where such tactics were not successful is *Parry* v. *North West Surrey Health Authority* [1994] 5 Med LR 259, the judge describing the defendants' expert obstetrician as more of an advocate at times than an expert. And although, for other reasons, the patient was unsuccessful in *Davis* v. *Barking, Havering and Brentwood Health Authority* [1993] 4 Med LR 85 the judge made it clear that he thought the 'defence' of latent multiple sclerosis was absurd and had wasted a considerable amount of the court's time.

SETTLEMENT

Achieving a good settlement will depend on the skill and nerve of the negotiator. It is fair to say that defendants in medical negligence actions will, as a rule, fight only those cases where they firmly believe that their doctors were not guilty of misconduct, so almost all claims that are strong enough to be pursued up to trial will be settled. On the other hand, one has also to say that defendants to medical negligence actions are not known for early admissions of liability.

It is essential that you have given the defendants the impression right from the outset that you know what you are doing and that you are processing the case effectively. So be ready with your various exchanges on time and, if the defendants are not, go for an 'unless' order (within reason). Make sure if the trial is imminent that you have lodged your bundles and your witnesses are ready. If defendants get the idea that your case is not in good order they will not be likely to offer a full value settlement.

You will need to bear in mind the statutory charge, whereby such of your costs which have on the one hand been reasonably incurred and therefore allowed as against the legal aid fund, but which on the other hand are not allowed on taxation as against the defendants (e.g. to-ing and fro-ing about the legal aid certificate or excessive attendance on a demanding client) will be taken by the Legal Aid Board out of the damages agreed. Some solicitors will give up their claim to the shortfall but there is no reason why they should feel so obliged (this shortfall can, even under the new RSC O.62, be as much or more than 20% of total costs). Therefore, the best course is to prepare and agree a bill of costs if at all possible, so that the settlement will expressly include a sum by way of costs which covers all the plaintiff's costs (this will necessitate efficient liaison with your costs clerk). There is an advantage to the defendants in this in that they will avoid the costs of a taxation (about £500 each side) and the taxing fee (5% of the taxed bill). Make sure that if experts' attendance has to be cancelled they are not going to charge for their lost time, or, if they are, that they justify their charges so that you can pass them on to the defendants (in the unreported case of *Reynolds* v. *Meeston*, 24 February 1986, Bingham J. allowed a claim by experts for commitment fees where the main case had been settled 24 hours before the hearing – the judge said that each such claim had to be decided on its own merits).

Some part of any amount by way of statutory charge may be discharged from interest on the costs awarded, which runs from the date of judgment or settlement and not from the date of any agreement, taxation or allocatur. One would think that the plaintiff's solicitors should get this interest as they are the ones who have been kept out of their money, but the legal aid authority has always maintained on a technicality that the money belongs to them, which is of course an unjustified windfall for them, i.e. in respect of the substantial portion of costs and disbursements not already paid on account.

If and when conditional fee agreements are entered into, the client will have to be given different advice and the solicitor will have different considerations to bear in mind.

14 · Payment into court

SUMMARY

The most important thing about a payment in from the plaintiff's point of view is that, if he does not accept it in settlement of his claim and he then fails to secure upon judgment a sum larger than the payment in, he will get his costs only up to the date of payment in and thereafter he will have to pay the defendant's costs. If the plaintiff is legally aided, his own costs such as are not ordered to be paid by the defendant will be deducted by the Law Society from his damages before he is paid them (his solicitor has to account to the Law Society for all monies received by way of award or settlement). The plaintiff may also be ordered to pay the defendant's costs incurred after the date of payment in up to the limit of his own contribution to his legal aid (illogical, but a handy rule of thumb that the court often adopts). If he has a nil contribution the order that he pay the defendant's costs after the date of payment in will be marked not to be proceeded with without leave of the court.

After a payment into court the plaintiff is at risk as to costs. If he recovers a sum which, even including interest on the damages, does not exceed the amount in court, he will get his costs only up to the date of payment in. After that date he will have to pay the defendant's costs. If he is legally aided the Law Society are entitled to their costs out of the damages awarded. In theory the payment in is a different creature from the offer of settlement, which is more often than not an offer to buy the plaintiff off. The payment in is intended to be a genuine pre-estimate of what the plaintiff is likely to recover if he succeeds (up to a point at any rate); so paying in, say, half of what he claims in a case where his claim is valid if he is right on the law and/or the evidence but the defendants think he might not in fact succeed at all, has nothing to do with an attempt by defendants to protect themselves against costs by a genuine calculation of what the plaintiff might recover if successful. It is only an offer to settle which puts its money where its mouth is. In such a case defendants seem to think that the offer is more tempting when made in this official manner, but logically it should make no difference. Either the plaintiff will fail or he will recover more or less what he is claiming: in either event the payment in will not affect any order the court makes as to costs.

In practice, though, one must agree that the payment in is in most cases simply an offer to dispose of the claim on terms (*per* Devlin L.J. in *A. Martin French* v. *Kingswood Hill Ltd* [1961] 1 QB 96); but it is a wholly procedural, not a contractual matter (*per* Goddard L.J. in *Cumper* v. *Pothecary* [1941] 2 KB 58 at p.67).

Whether the payment in is a genuine estimate of what the plaintiff is likely to recover if he succeeds, albeit only up to a point, or is equivalent to an offer to settle, it behoves him to consider it carefully. Litigation is always chancy; the odd piece of unexpected or ill-advised evidence can lose the day.

Payment into and out of court is provided for by RSC O.22. A payment in may be made any time after issue of the writ. In *Towers* v. *Morley* [1992] 1 WLR 511 the Court of Appeal held that, as a payment in could be made after issue and before service of a writ, a defendant who paid in soon after he was informally sent a copy of the writ but was thereafter never properly served was not estopped from successfully contending that the action was a nullity as the writ had never been served. The defendant must give the plaintiff notice of any payment in or any increase in what he has already paid in, and must specify to what cause of action, if there is more than one, the payment is to be attributed (he is not obliged to split it among the causes of action, but a plaintiff who is embarrassed by it not being split may ask the court to require it to be split). Payments in may not be withdrawn or amended, except by way of 'topping up', without leave of the court (leave to withdraw may well be given where, for example, new evidence or new judicial authority has arisen which appears to damage the plaintiff's case; or leave may be given to assign a payment in already made to an interim payment when that is later ordered).

The payment in should take account of any interest that might be awarded if judgment were given at the date of the payment in (r.1(8)). The defendant is not required to assign a separate sum to the interest element, for it is not, *semble*, a separate cause of action, but he would be advised to specify, particularly if asked, whether he has allowed for interest up to the date of payment in. If an award by judgment is only a little more than the amount of the payment in, the judge will have to calculate whether the payment in exceeds the damages plus the interest that had accrued at the date of the payment in. If the defendant has already made an interim payment, voluntarily or by order, he must state in his notice of payment in that he has taken the interim payment into account (O.29 r.16) (as already stated, a defendant who has already made a payment in when the court orders an interim payment may ask that the former be applied to the latter).

The plaintiff has 21 days to accept the payment in. If it is made after the trial has begun he has only two days, and he must accept it before the court begins to deliver judgment; in such a case acceptance results in a stay of the proceedings. There seems to be a lacuna in the rules, for it is not expressly stated how a payment in which is made less than 21 days before the trial operates. It cannot put the plaintiff at risk, for it does not give him his 21 days for acceptance, and it cannot come within the two-day rule as it is not made after the trial is begun. *King* v. *Weston Howell* [1989] 1 WLR 579 CA establishes that the court is entitled to have regard to such a payment in, if it so wishes, when exercising its discretion over costs.

The plaintiff is entitled to his costs up to payment in if he accepts it (O.62 r.10(2)). He will also normally be given his costs between payment in and out such as are reasonably incurred in taking the money out. It was held in *Hudson* v. *Elmbridge Borough Council* [1991] 4 All ER 55, CA, that where a plaintiff accepted a payment in that had been made in respect of one only of a number of causes of action and abandoned the rest, he was entitled to his costs of the whole of the proceedings. This case was distinguished by Webster J. in *Q.B.E. Insurance (UK)* v. *Mediterranean Insurance and Re-insurance Co.* [1992] 1 WLR 573 where it was held that a plaintiff who accepts a payment in from one defendant is not automatically entitled to recover from that defendant the costs of pursuing the action against the other defendants, especially if their liability is alternative, not joint.

For claims under the Fatal Accidents Act 1976 or the Law Reform (Miscellaneous Provisions) Act 1934, leave of the court is required before a payment in can be taken out (the court has to apportion the money between the various claims and claimants). Leave is also required if the plaintiff is under a disability (O.80 r.13 requires the court's approval to a settlement in such a case), or if the payment in was made by one of a number of defendants.

No application to take out a payment in may be made during the trial except with the defendant's consent (*Gaskins* v. *British Aluminium Co.* [1976] QB 524).

Where it falls to the court to consider the effect of a payment in (it does not where the plaintiff accepts one timeously), the court has a complete discretion as to costs, but it is bound to exercise its discretion judicially. A successful plaintiff should not be deprived of his costs except for good reason (see *Findlay* v. *Railway*

Executive [1950] 2 All ER 969, CA, and the notes in the *White Book* at 62/2/9 *et seq.*). By O.62 r.5(b) the court must take into account the fact and amount of any payment in. The practice is, as already stated, where the payment in exceeds the award, to give the defendant his costs incurred after the payment in.

It is expressly provided by r.7 that the fact of a payment in shall not be pleaded nor communicated to the court at the trial until all questions of liability and amount of damages have been decided. If the judge inadvertently learns of the payment in, he has a discretion to continue with the trial if he considers that he can put his knowledge on one side and no injustice will be done, and such a decision affords no ground for appeal (see *Re an Action for Negligence (1992 C No.3063), The Times*, 5 March 1993). The 'secrecy' rule does not apply to interlocutory proceedings: e.g. a plaintiff applying for an interim payment will find it of advantage to point out to the court that a payment in has been made, for that may support his contention that liability cannot sensibly be disputed (*Fryer* v. *London Transport Executive, The Times*, 4 December 1982). The same principle applies to appeals to the Court of Appeal (except of course appeals on costs only) (see O.59 r.12A).

The effect of the House of Lords decision in *Legal Aid Board* v. *Russell* [1991] 2 WLR 1300 that no interest on the taxed costs was claimable where a payment in had been accepted has now been reversed by an amendment to O.62 r.5(1).

LAW

15 · Negligence and the duty of care

INTRODUCTION TO NEGLIGENCE

(This chapter deals with the general law of negligence.)

SUMMARY

The concept of legal negligence is difficult to analyse. Negligence in law always relates to a particular fact-situation, and what is decided in one case is usually little help in deciding later disputes. The incidents of life are mercurial, protean, amorphous. That, we may suppose, is what makes it so endlessly fascinating. But it also makes it hard for the lawyer to predict the outcome of a negligence suit, quite apart from uncertainties about the evidence and the likely findings of fact. The ingredients of negligence are a duty to take care owed in a particular situation by the defendant to the plaintiff, a failure to discharge the standard of care required by that duty, and a loss occasioned thereby to the plaintiff that is recognised by the law as a proper head of loss, of the same type as, if not identical with, loss that was foreseeable at the time of the wrongful act, and deemed by the law to have been caused by that act. The courts have recently made it clear that they retain an arbitrary power to decide whether a duty of care is owed in a given fact-situation and that their decision depends on whether they consider it right and fair that such a duty should exist.

Meaning of the word 'negligence'

The word 'negligence' is used in different ways. For our purposes, when we ask 'has there been negligence in the handling of this case, whether by acts of commission or omission?', or 'has the physician been negligent?', we are asking whether he has been in breach of a duty to take reasonable care with regard to our client, the patient. It is no help to us if he has been in breach of a duty to take care if that duty was not owed to our client, nor that he has been negligent in the ordinary sense of careless, unless that

amounted to a breach of duty; nor does it avail us if he has indeed
been in breach of a duty of care to our client but we cannot prove
any loss that a court will take cognisance of.

'Negligence' can mean carelessness, which is not a legal term.
One has to be careful to distinguish the two meanings. When,
years ago, Baron Alderson said:[1]

Negligence is the omission to do something which a reasonable man, guided
upon those considerations which ordinarily regulate the conduct of human
affairs, would do, or doing something which a prudent and reasonable man
would not do,

he was using 'negligence' in its ordinary non-legal sense without
reference to a duty of care. This is the way the word is used when
we speak of 'contributory negligence', which goes to reduce the
damages awarded to a plaintiff, where he has been, in a general
sense, careless of his own safety. It can also serve as a useful
definition of the standard of care that has to be shown, e.g. by a
physician, once a duty to take care has been established.

It is common knowledge among lawyers that mere negligence
in itself is not a cause of action. To give a cause of action there
must be negligence which amounts to a breach of duty towards
the person claiming. There are many cases where there has been
clear negligence, in the absence of which damage would not have
happened, and yet there is no liability under English law (*per*
Greer L.J. in *Farr* v. *Butter Bros & Co.* [1932] 2 KB 606, 618).

The ingredients

What the civil wrong, or tort, of negligence involves, insofar as it
is susceptible to analysis, is a duty of care, a breach of that duty,
and loss occasioned by that breach. But these ingredients do not
exist separately or *in vacuo*. They will always be related to the
particular facts of the case; they overlap and interact; moreover
they need to be considerably further defined before the analysis is
of any practical use.

Thus actionable negligence must involve a duty to act with
reasonable care towards the plaintiff, a failure, by act or omission, to discharge that duty (proof is called for that the standard
of care required in the particular case was not met), and loss
occasioned by that failure, which is both reasonably proximate to
the breach (proximity is measured by what should have been
reasonably foreseeable at the time of the breach) and of a type
recognised by the law. Sometimes the law does not recognise the
loss (e.g. loss of the companionship of a lover or grown-up child,

---

[1] *Blyth* v. *Birmingham Waterworks Co.* (1856) 11 Ex 781.

loss of the services of a servant, mere economic loss in some situations); so one can define the duty to take care even further: a duty towards the plaintiff to take care not to act in such a way as to cause the loss of which he complains. The breach must be a failure to discharge the duty, measured by the degree of care which the particular duty involves. The loss must come within the area of risk that was reasonably foreseeable from the defendant's acts. That sounds involved, but the point is that any attempt to keep separate and distinct the three factors – duty, breach, and loss – is bound to fail (however convenient it might seem for the purposes of jurisprudence):

... you will find that the three questions, duty, causation, and remoteness, [run] continually into one another. It seems to me that they are really three different ways of looking at one and the same problem (*per* Lord Denning in *Roe* v. *Minister of Health* [1954] 2 QB 66, 85, and *Lamb* v. *Camden London Borough Council* [1981] QB 625, 634).

Negligence does not exist *in vacuo* as some sort of clearly defined legal concept. It must always be related to a particular fact-situation. This is true of all law, but particularly so of the law of negligence. It is for that reason that judicial decisions in this field only infrequently create any precedent that will necessarily dictate the conclusion in a later case.

The ideas of negligence and duty are strictly correlative, and there is no such thing as negligence in the abstract; negligence is simply neglect of some care which we are bound by law to exercise towards somebody (*per* Bowen L.J. in *Thomas* v. *Quatermaine* (1887) 18 QBD 685, 694).

The law takes no cognisance of carelessness in the abstract. It concerns itself with carelessness only where there is a duty to take care and where failure in that duty has caused damage. In such circumstances carelessness assumes the legal quality of negligence and entails the consequences in law of negligence . . . The cardinal principle of liability is that the party complained of should owe to the party complaining a duty to take care, and that the party complaining should be able to prove that he has suffered damage in consequence of a breach of that duty (*per* Lord Macmillan in *Donoghue* v. *Stevenson* [1932] AC 562, 618, 619).

In strict legal analysis, negligence means more than heedless or careless conduct, whether in omission or commission: it properly connotes the complex concept of duty, breach and damage thereby suffered by the person to whom the duty was owing (*per* Lord Wright in *Lochgelly Iron and Coal Co.* v. *M'Mullan* [1934] AC 1, 25).

We will therefore consider at this point, from a general point of view, the three components of the tort of negligence: the establishing of a duty of care owed by the defendants to the plaintiff; the breach of that duty by failure to attain the standard of care the law requires for the discharge of that particular duty; and damage occasioned by that failure, which is (a) caused by it, i.e. not too remote – reasonably foreseeable, (b) of a sort recognised by the law, and (c) of the same type as, if not identical with, the damage that was foreseeable.

The duty to take care

SUMMARY

No formula for testing whether in a given situation a duty of care arises has proved satisfactory. There are guidelines, of which the foreseeability of harm is the most important, for it indicates a *prima facie* duty of care. However, that duty may be negatived by any number of considerations, prime among which is the general consideration of policy as it appears to the tribunal trying the case. As is the wont of the common law, the ambit of the duty of care is continually being gradually extended by ad hoc judicial decisions. In that way the scope of recovery for *inter alia* nervous shock, economic loss, negligent misstatement, and injury suffered by a rescuer, has been widened.

When does a duty of care arise? Unfortunately, the only sure, albeit unhelpful, general answer to this question is 'when a court decides that a defendant ought to compensate a plaintiff for his loss'. Sometimes the existence of a duty arises unarguably from the relationship between the parties, such as doctor and patient. In our particular context the duty is usually no problem. But not always. Is a doctor under a duty to treat when the man next to him in the theatre is taken ill? An English court would say not. What if he is your own doctor, whom you are out with for the evening? That's not so easy. What if a compassionate bystander tries to help the sick man? Must he show some, and if so what, degree of skill? Does that depend on the gravity of the situation and the availability of professional help? What are the duties on a hospital to receive an injured man who staggers in one evening? Of course if they accept him a duty arises to look after him, but can they turn him away or have they a duty to succour him? What if the hospital has/hasn't a casualty department, which is shut/open? (see *Barnett* v. *Chelsea and Kensington Hospital Management Committee* [1969] 1 QB 428).

Even if a duty exists, to whom is it owed? In the case of the patient himself there is no problem, but what if a relative or third party suffers as a result of the physician's negligence, either physically by way of nervous shock (see *McLoughlin* v. *O'Brian* [1983] 1 AC 410), or is injured by the patient (see *Tarasoff* v. *Regents of the University of California* 551 P (2d) 334 (Cal.

1976)), or suffers financial loss? (see *Evans* v. *Liverpool Corporation* [1906] 1 KB 160).

So it can be seen that, even in the medical negligence context, tricky questions as to the existence of a duty of care may arise.

There are unfortunately no clear rules to tell us when a duty of care will be implied. It is remarkable how difficult it is to find in the English authorities statements of general application defining the relations between parties that give rise to the duty.

The courts are concerned with the particular relations which come before them in actual litigation and it is sufficient to say whether the duty exists in those circumstances (*per* Lord Atkin in *Donoghue* v. *Stevenson* [1932] AC 562).

The passage of 50 years has done little to invalidate that statement, reflective as it is of the ad hoc growth of the common law. We know that the categories of negligence are never closed (*per* Lord Macmillan in *Donoghue* v. *Stevenson* [1932] AC 562 – 'the criterion of judgment must adjust and adapt itself to the changing circumstances of life'), and that precedents can be used with some effect to show that in a similar previous situation the law has recognised a duty of care, but in a novel situation – and there are forever arising from the diverse and protean vicissitudes of life novel situations – we cannot be sure if a duty will be recognised. It depends, as I said above, on the judicial hunch, almost a gut reaction – whether the judge thinks it appropriate to impose liability in a particular situation. The result of the essentially non-academic and pragmatic approach of the English judiciary is that it is made more difficult both to present a coherent analysis for jurisprudential purposes and to predict the legal conclusions that will be reached on any given set of facts. The law governing the duty owed in the tort of negligence, said Lord Asquith in *Candler* v. *Crane Christmas & Co.* [1951] 2 KB 164, 188, seems to have been built up in disconnected slabs, exhibiting no organic unity or structure.

Foreseeability as the test of duty

It has been thought at times that if there was a foreseeable risk of the plaintiff suffering harm from the defendant's activities that was enough in the normal case to create a duty of care, but that is too wide a proposition. Foreseeability has an important part to play in deciding for what damage the plaintiff can recover once a duty and a breach of that duty have been established, but it is not a *sine qua non* (see Chapter 21). In the context of establishing a duty, foreseeability of harm is a *sine qua non* (except where there is a duty to act arising simply out of the existing relationship between the parties – see below), but it is not conclusive of the existence of a duty; it is one of the several factors which the court takes into account when deciding whether or not to imply a duty.

A New Zealand judge summed up the position neatly when he said that where a case does not fall clearly within the ambit of previous decisions the proper approach

is to look at all the material facts in combination, in order to decide as a question of mixed law and fact whether or not liability should be imposed . . . it is more than Chancellor's foot justice. The courts have evolved signposts or guidelines or relevant considerations – involving such notions as neighbours, control, foresight, proximity, opportunity for intermediate examinations, deeds or words, the degree and kind of risk to be guarded against – and these are all available to be used as aids to the end result (*Rutherford* v. *Attorney-General* [1976] 1 NZLR 403, 411).

Judicial attempts to formulate a criterion for establishing a duty of care, though giving an impetus to the creation, extension and refinement of the tort, particularly in earlier days, have been expressed too widely and too generally to be acceptable as accurate reflections of what the law actually is. The two seminal formulations are, first, that of Brett M.R. in *Heaven* v. *Pender* (1883) 11 QBD 503, 509:

Whenever one person is by circumstances placed in such a position with regard to another that everyone of ordinary sense who did think would at once recognise that if he did not use ordinary care and skill in his own conduct with regard to those circumstances he would cause danger of injury to the person or property of the other, a duty arises to use ordinary care and skill to avoid such danger.

And secondly that of Lord Atkin in *Donoghue* v. *Stevenson* [1932] AC 562 – the snail in the ginger-beer bottle case – when he said that you must take reasonable care to avoid acts or omissions which you could reasonably foresee would be likely to injure your neighbour, i.e. a person so closely and directly affected by your act that you ought reasonably to have him in contemplation as being so affected when directing your mind to the acts or omissions concerned.

Clearly there are many situations where you can see you may injure your neighbour but you are under no duty to desist, e.g. opening a cut-price supermarket next to a small store, actions taken in sport (within the rules), one of two men dying of thirst in the desert grabs the last ounce of water first. One can with a little imagination add to the list at will. The formulation is particularly unsatisfactory where it suggests that one is to be liable for omissions which can foreseeably injure one's neighbour. Quite the reverse: one is not liable for any omission unless there is a pre-existing duty to act. As we have seen, even a physician is not necessarily under a duty to act, where, for example, the injured party is not his patient.

The 'Wilberforce' test

An attempt to give us a simple formula for testing whether there is a duty in a particular situation was made by Lord Wilberforce. In *Anns* v. *Merton London Borough Council* [1978] AC 728, the foremost in a long line of complex cases involving the liability of local authorities and others towards all and sundry for constructing, inspecting or certifying as adequate building foundations that turned out to be defective, Lord Wilberforce said that the position had been reached whereby a two-stage test was to be applied:

First, one has to ask whether, as between the alleged wrongdoer and the person who has suffered damage, there is a sufficient relationship of proximity or neighbourhood such that, in the reasonable contemplation of the former, carelessness on his part may be likely to cause damage to the latter – in which case a *prima facie* duty of care arises. Secondly, if the first question is answered affirmatively, it is necessary to consider whether there are any considerations which ought to negative or to reduce or limit the scope of the duty or the class of person to whom it is owed or the damages to which a breach of it may give rise.

In other words foreseeability of harm created a *prima facie* duty of care. It was then up to the defendant to negative that duty by showing that there were circumstances militating against its imposition.

This approach facilitated an important development in the law when, in *McLoughlin* v. *O'Brian* [1983] 1 AC 410, the House of Lords permitted recovery for nervous shock by a mother who did not witness the terrible accident that injured and killed members of her family but came upon the aftermath at the hospital. This was an extension to the law as to recovery for nervous shock (see Chapter 20). The mother was viewed as a person to whom, on the test of foreseeability, the defendant driver owed a duty of care. Lord Wilberforce added:

Whatever is the correct jurisprudential analysis, it does not make any essential difference whether one says that there is a duty but, as a matter of policy, the consequences of a breach of it ought to be limited at a certain point, or whether one says that the fact that consequences may be foreseeable does not automatically impose a duty of care, does not do so in fact where policy indicates the contrary.

Nevertheless the judgments in that case appear to have been based on an acceptance of Lord Wilberforce's two-stage test, it being expressly said by at least four members of the court that the injury suffered by the plaintiff was foreseeable and policy considerations did not operate to prevent recovery.

Then came *Junior Books* v. *Veitchi* [1983] 1 AC 520. This was important because it brought into juxtaposition the Wilberforce test and a claim for mere economic damage. Employers sued sub-contractors for a badly laid floor. Despite the absence of a contractual nexus the House of Lords held that there was sufficient proximity between the parties to impose a duty of care and that there were no policy considerations negativing liability. Lord Brandon dissented, on the ground that policy considerations militated against imposing liability for mere economic damage in the absence of any physical damage (this had indeed been thought up till then to be the law – see Chapter 19). It was not clear to what extent 'proximity' was to be equated with 'foreseeability of harm'. Lord Roskill thought the two were not necessarily commensurate. But

Once proximity is no longer treated as expressing a relationship founded simply on foreseeability of damage, it ceases to have an ascertainable meaning; and it cannot therefore provide a criterion for liability (*per* Goff L.J. in *Leigh and Sillavan* v. *Aliakmon Shipping* [1985] 2 WLR 289 (*infra*) at p. 327).

Following a number of decisions doubting the validity of the 'Wilberforce' test (these decisions are set out in earlier editions of this book), the Privy Council in *Yuen Kun Yeu* v. *Attorney-General of Hong Kong* [1988] AC 175, holding that no duty of care was owed by the Commissioner of Deposit-taking Companies in Hong Kong to exercise reasonable care towards potential depositors to see that they did not suffer loss through fraudulently managed companies, said that the 'Wilberforce' two-stage test had been elevated to a degree of importance greater than its merit, and should not be regarded in all circumstances as a suitable guide to the existence of a duty of care. Foreseeability was only one ingredient, though a necessary one, in establishing a duty of care in a given situation. In particular the court said that the second stage of the test would rarely fall to be considered, only where there was a genuine need to consider a matter of public policy. Approval was voiced of the passage in the judgment of Brennan J. in the Australian case of *Council of the Shire of Sutherland* v. *Heyman* (1985) 157 CLR where, disagreeing with the Wilberforce two-tier test, he said

It is preferable, in my view, that the law should develop novel categories of negligence incrementally and by analogy with established categories, rather than by a massive extension of a prima facie duty of care restrained only by indefinable 'considerations which ought to negative or reduce or limit the scope of the duty or the class of persons to whom it is owed'.

Similar observations were made by the House of Lords in *Caparo Industries plc* v. *Dickman* [1990] 2 AC 605, yet another in the seemingly endless series of important current decisions on negligence.

Lord Bridge said:

Whilst recognising, of course, the importance of the underlying general principles common to the whole field of negligence, I think the law has now moved in the direction of attaching greater significance to the more traditional categorisation of distinct and recognisable situations as guides to the existence, the scope and the limits of the varied duties of care which the law imposes.

Lord Roskill said:

. . . it has now to be accepted that there is no simple formula or touchstone to which recourse can be had in order to provide in every case a ready answer to the questions whether, given certain facts, the law will or will not impose liability for negligence or, in cases where such liability can be shown to exist, determine the extent of that liability. Phrases such as 'foreseeability', 'proximity', 'neighbourhood', 'just and reasonable', 'fairness', 'voluntary acceptance of risk', or 'voluntary assumption of risk' will be found used from time to time in the different cases. But . . . such phrases are not precise definitions. At best they are but labels or phrases descriptive of the very different factual situations which can exist in particular cases and which must be carefully examined in each case before it can be pragmatically determined whether a duty of care exists, and, if so, what is the scope and extent of that duty. If this conclusion involves a return to the traditional categorisation of cases as pointing to the existence and scope of any duty of care, . . . I think this is infinitely preferable to recourse to somewhat wide generalisations which leave their practical application matters of difficulty and uncertainty.

And Lord Oliver said:

. . . to search for any single formula which will serve as a general test of liability is to pursue a will-o'-the-wisp. The fact is that once one discards, as it is now clear that one must, the concept of foreseeability of harm as the single exclusive test – even a prima facie test – of the existence of the duty of care, the attempt to state some general principle which will determine liability in an infinite variety of circumstances serves not to clarify the law but merely to bedevil its development in a way which corresponds with practicality and common sense . . . .

Perhaps therefore the most that can be attempted is a broad categorisation of the decided cases according to the type of situation in which liability has been established in the past in order to found an argument by analogy.

In *White* v. *Jones* [1993] 3 WLR 730 the Court of Appeal, holding that a duty of care was owed to prospective beneficiaries by solicitors instructed by a testator to change his will so as to reinstate the beneficiaries, stated that the *Caparo* case had established that for the imposition of a duty to avoid particular damage to a particular person or class of persons there had to be foreseeability of damage, proximity of relationship, and a context where it was fair, just and reasonable to impose such a duty. As I have indicated, this last requirement gives the court *carte blanche* to admit or reject a duty where there has been no previous decision on similar facts. These requirements are applicable even where the damage is physical, to person or property (*Marc Rich and Co.* v. *Bishop Rock Marine Co.* [1994] 1 WLR 1071, CA). The House of Lords upheld the Court of Appeal in *White* v.

Jones, but only by a bare majority [1995] 2 **WLR** 187. The majority took the view that, on the *Hedley Byrne* principle (see below, 'The duty not to make careless statements'), the solicitor had assumed responsibility not only to the testator but also to the beneficiaries to carry out his instructions; the powerful dissenting, and jurisprudentially more convincing, judgments held that there was no principle of law upon which a duty of care could be imposed in the instant circumstances. Lord Mustill said that it did not conduce to the orderly development of the law or to the certainty which practical convenience demanded if duties were simply conjured up as a matter of positive law to answer the apparent justice of an individual case. In other words there was a complete division of opinion among our most senior judges, and it was a sheer fluke that the plaintiffs won. If the fifth judge had been more concerned with *elegantia juris* than the apparent justice of the claim, the plaintiffs would not have won.

It follows therefore that the courts have now effectively put us back at square one, where we were before Lord Wilberforce attempted to provide a formulation of a test. So much for the progress of the common law. It may well be that the above-cited passage from *Rutherford* v. *Attorney-General* [1976] 1 NZLR 403, 411 is the best one can do in attempting to express the law with some degree of precision. In the case of *Yuen Kun Yeu* (*supra*) the court used the phrase 'close and direct relations' (an echo, one may think, of the 'proximate relationship' featured in the *Junior Books* case), and held that there were no such relations between the Commissioner and the investors, and therefore no duty arose. But whatever new or not so new form of words is used it is in reality going to be just a matter for judicial impression whether a particular fact-situation is one within which a duty to compensate for damage arising should be recognised by the law.

But, although conservative by nature, the English courts do slowly increase the scope of the tort negligence. Thus, liability for negligent misstatements causing economic loss in the context of a fiduciary relationship was recognised in *Hedley Byrne & Co. Ltd* v. *Heller & Partners Ltd* [1964] AC 465; a duty of care was imposed on the Home Office towards members of the public in respect of the control of boys at a Borstal institution in *Dorset Yacht Co.* v. *Home Office* [1970] AC 1004 (and see *Vicar of Writtle* v. *Essex County Council* (1979) 77 LGR 656, where a lad of 12, whose inclinations as an arsonist were well-known to the authorities, was not stopped from walking out of a hostel and setting fire to a church in the middle of the day).

Recent cases

An example of the way in which the scope of the duty of care can be enlarged is *Al Kandari* v. *J.R. Brown & Co.* [1988] QB 665. A husband's solicitors, who had undertaken to keep their client's passport, were under a duty of care in that respect to his wife to take all reasonable steps to prevent any harm coming to her from breach of that undertaking. This was a novel situation; the court could just as easily have said that no duty was owed to the other side's client. As it was, the judge held that the damage claimed was not the foreseeable consequence of the breach of duty, so that on that basis recovery was precluded. See also *White* v. *Jones* (*supra*).

In *Ashton* v. *Turner* [1981] 1 QB 137 Ewbank J. held that a burglar driving the getaway car was not under a duty of care to his fellow criminal to drive with all due care. And in *Pitts* v. *Hunt* [1990] 1 QB 302 the Court of Appeal upheld the refusal to award damages to a pillion rider on a motor bicycle who had been actively encouraging his driver to ride recklessly, drunk and uninsured. Similarly a plaintiff who knowingly and willingly embarked on a flight with a drunken pilot was held by the Court of Appeal to have waived his rights in respect of negligent flying (*Morris* v. *Murray* [1991] 2 QB 6).

In *Chaudhury* v. *Prabhakar* [1989] 1 WLR 29 it was held, somewhat surprisingly, that a man recommending a friend to purchase a vehicle in which he himself had no financial interest was under a legal duty of care in relation to that recommendation. A school was held to be under no duty to insure against sporting accidents to its pupils (*Van Oppen* v. *Clerk to Bedford Charity Trustees* [1990] 1 WLR 235).

In *Caparo Industries plc* v. *Dickman* [1990] 2 AC 605 the House of Lords held that auditors of a public company's accounts owed no duty of care in carrying out the audit to shareholders or to members of the public who relied upon the accounts in deciding to buy shares in the company. And in *Al Saudi Banque* v. *Clarke Pixley* [1990] Ch 313 a court of first instance held that no duty of care was owed by a company's auditors to creditors to whom it was not intended that the audit would be sent (see further below under 'The duty not to make careless statements').

Contra, in *Henderson* v. *Merrett Syndicates Ltd* (and associated cases) [1994] 3 WLR 761, the House of Lords held that Lloyd's underwriting agents owed to various Lloyd's Names a concurrent duty of care in contract and in tort to carry out their underwriting functions with reasonable care and skill, and that the plaintiffs could elect which remedy to pursue.

In *Spring* v. *Guardian Assurance plc* [1994] 3 WLR 354 the House of Lords, reversing the Court of Appeal, held that an insurance company owed a duty of care to a former representative when giving a reference to a prospective employer. The court found no reason of public policy for negating such a duty.

In *Galoo Ltd* v. *Bright Grahame Murray* [1994] 1 WLR 1360 the Court of Appeal said that, although normally an auditor did not owe a duty of care to potential purchasers of shares in the company, a duty could arise where the auditor knew that particular bidders were likely to be relying on his work.

In *Anthony* v. *Wright*, *The Independent*, 27 September 1994, Lightman J. held that a company's auditors were not under a duty of care, in respect of their audit, to investors whose money was held on trust by the company. He said that *White* v. *Jones* (*supra*) was in a category of its own.

In *McCullagh* v. *Lane Fox and Partners*, *The Times*, 25 January 1994, the court held that an estate agent was under a duty of care when representing the size of a property to a purchaser who he knew was about to contract without the benefit of a survey.

Even if it could be shown that the wife of a workman did indeed die from mesothelioma caused by inhaling asbestos dust from his working clothes, the employers owed her (as opposed to her husband) no duty of care (*Gunn* v. *Wallsend Slipway and Engineering Co. Ltd*, *The Times*, 23 January 1989).[2] A provincial fine art consultant had not been negligent in failing to spot that two pictures he was asked to value were or might well be by George Stubbs (he valued them at about £50, they were then snapped up at auction for £840 and re-sold for £88,000!) (*Luxmoore-May* v. *Messenger May Baverstock* [1990] 1 WLR 1009).

In *Alexandrou* v. *Oxford* [1993] 4 All ER 328, CA, the court, following *Hill* v. *Chief Constable of West Yorkshire* [1989] AC 53, held that the police would not be liable for failing properly to inspect the security of a retail store after the alarm had been set off. This decision can be seen as simply based on the apparent policy not to involve the police in civil liability in performing their duties, as the nexus between the alleged negligence and the damage was much clearer and more direct than in the *Hill* case, and without 'policy' considerations the facts would surely raise a case of negligence (the trial judge had found for the plaintiff). Compare the liability imposed on the police to a widow for failing to notify the prison authorities that her prisoner husband whom they were transferring had suicidal tendencies – *Kirkham* v. *Chief*

---

[2] See also *Hewett* v. *Alf Brown's Transport Ltd* [1992] ICR 530, CA.

Constable of Greater Manchester Police [1990] 2 QB 283.[3] And in *Skinner* v. *Secretary of State for Transport, The Times*, 3 January 1995, it was held that the coastguard did not owe a duty of care to a mariner either when exercising its ordinary functions of listening and watching or in respect of its rescue co-ordinating activities. The judge said that the House of Lords decision in the *Caparo* case required that the duty of care be widened only by analogy with previous decisions.

In *Elguzouli-Daf* v. *Commissioner of Police of the Metropolis* [1995] 2 WLR 173, the Court of Appeal held that, in the absence of any voluntary assumption of responsibility to a particular defendant in criminal proceedings, the Crown Prosecution Service owed no duty of care to defendants in the conduct of prosecutions.

The Court of Appeal, reversing the trial judge, held that an ambulance attendant was not under a duty to warn an *un*injured passenger in an ambulance to wear a safety belt (*Eastman* v. *South West Thames Regional Health Authority* [1991] RTR 389). And in a surprising decision the Court of Appeal held in *Topp* v. *London Country Bus (South West) Ltd* [1993] 1 WLR 976, that defendants who left a minibus parked, with the key in the ignition, unlocked and unattended for hours at a bus stop in a lay-by by a public house were not liable to a pedestrian injured by someone who unlawfully took the vehicle. How they could have thought it was fair, just and reasonable to deny a duty of care in the face of such obvious negligence followed by perfectly foreseeable harm is hard to fathom.

THE DUTY NOT TO MAKE CARELESS STATEMENTS

There is no logical reason why the law should have distinguished between the duty to take care in respect of acts or omissions to act and the duty in respect of statements, but it has. Or at any rate it has where the statement inflicts, as it usually does, financial loss only; in the rare case where a careless statement leads to physical injury the court is far quicker to find a duty to take care in speaking (see e.g. *Clayton* v. *Woodman & Sons (Builders)* [1962] 2 QB 533).

But the law was for many years that in the absence of actual deceit financial loss caused by careless statements was not

---

[3] Reference may also be made to *Van Oppen* v. *Clerk to Bedford Charity Trustees* [1990] 1 WLR 235, where the Court of Appeal held that a school was not under any duty to insure a pupil against sporting injury, and to *Reid* v. *Rush & Tompkins Group* [1990] 1 WLR 212, where the Court of Appeal held that an employer was not under a duty to insure an employee against injury while motoring abroad on the employer's business.

actionable. However, the law was changed by the unanimous decision of the House of Lords in *Hedley Byrne & Co. Ltd* v. *Heller & Partners Ltd* [1964] AC 465, where a merchant bank was held to be *prima facie* liable to another bank's customer for negligently representing one of its own customers as creditworthy. The plaintiffs were customers of the second bank who, relying on the defendants' representations about their customer, entered into a commercial relationship with the customer. The customer soon went into liquidation.

The merchant bank were held on the facts not to be liable by virtue of a specific disclaimer of responsibility, but the principle was established by the House of Lords that if in the ordinary course of business one person seeks advice or information from another in circumstances where that other would reasonably know that his advice is to be relied on he is under a legal duty to take such care in giving his reply as the circumstances reasonably require. But for that duty to arise that particular relationship has to exist between the parties. It need not of course be contractual; it need not be fiduciary in the strict sense; but there does need to be a sufficient degree of proximity (that word again!) between the parties, so that the element of reasonable reliance is present.

This aspect of the duty of care has recently been exhaustively examined by the House of Lords in *Caparo Industries plc* v. *Dickman* [1990] 2 AC 605 (also in the first instance decision of *Al Saudi Banque* v. *Clarke Pixley* [1990] Ch 313). In *Caparo*, in which the judgments are extremely long, the reasoning behind the decision that auditors of a company are under no duty of care in preparing the company's accounts to non-shareholding potential investors, nor to shareholders as potential further investors, may be summarised by saying that they had no reason to suppose that their audit would be communicated to the plaintiffs, let alone relied on in deciding whether to invest (further) in the company (the auditor's statutory duty to shareholders was said to be imposed to enable them to exercise their class rights in general meeting and not to extend to assist them in making investment decisions).

Compare the House of Lords' decisions in *Smith* v. *Eric S. Bush* and *Harris* v. *Wyre Forest District Council* [1990] 1 AC 831 where a surveyor preparing a report for a mortgagee was held to be under a duty of care to the prospective purchaser, principally because he knew or should have known that the purchaser would see the report and would probably act, i.e. complete the purchase, in reliance on it. We may also see here the vital role of policy in reaching a decision: it is one thing to hold a bank or building society responsible in a limited financial context to an individual house purchaser, quite another to hold auditors responsible in a commercial context to any potential investor in the company.

In the surveyor cases Lord Griffiths said that what was required to impose liability was foreseeability of harm from any negligent advice, a sufficiently proximate relationship between the parties, and that it was just and reasonable to impose the liability (this of course gives the courts a wide (virtually unfettered) discretion to impose or not impose liability). In *Caparo* Lord Bridge said that the salient features of the cases where liability for negligent misstatement resulting in economic loss had been imposed were that the defendant was fully aware of the nature of the transaction that the plaintiff had in contemplation, knew that the advice or information would be communicated to him directly or indirectly, and knew that it was very likely that the plaintiff would rely on it in deciding whether or not to engage in the transaction.

In the *Al Saudi Banque* case Millett J. held (before the Court of Appeal decision in *Caparo* had been reversed by the House of Lords) that there was no duty of care on auditors to potential investors, whether existing creditors of the company or not, when preparing their report because there was no reasonable expectation that the report would be sent to such parties, let alone that they would act in reliance on it when deciding what action to take in relation to the company.

In *James McNaughton Paper Group Ltd* v. *Hicks Anderson* [1991] 2 QB 113 the Court of Appeal held that accountants who prepared at short notice draft accounts of their client company for the company's chairman owed no duty of care to a bidder who took the company over after inspecting those accounts.[4] Compare *Morgan Crucible Co.* v. *Hill Samuel and Co.* [1991] Ch 259 where the Court of Appeal said on an interlocutory application that, while it was clear law now that an auditor owed no duty of care to potential takeover bidders in certifying company accounts, the directors, auditors and financial advisers of a takeover target company might well owe a duty of care to bidders not negligently to mislead.[5]

In *Lancashire and Cheshire Association of Baptist Churches* v. *Howard and Seddon Partnership* [1994] All ER 467, it was held that architects' plans for a sanctuary did not amount to a statement as to the technical qualities of the proposed building.

---

[4] In *Al-Nakib Investments (Jersey) Ltd* v. *Longcroft* [1990] 1 WLR 1390 a court of first instance held that company directors in issuing a prospectus designed to help shareholders decide about a rights issue were under no duty of care if the prospectus was relied on, even by such shareholders, for the purpose of buying further shares on the open market.

[5] An insurance broker owed a duty of care to a person he knew was going to become an assignee of a policy in *Punjab National Bank* v. *De Boinville* [1992] 1 WLR 1138.

It can be seen that the commercial lawyers have over recent years been having a field day thanks to the uncertainties about the ambit of the duty of care in commercial contexts.

If a passenger on the tube sees another reading the *Financial Times* and offers advice on investments, he is not under a duty of care in giving that advice. But if he represents himself as an investment expert and perhaps suggests the other man might like to become his client, the duty might well then arise. Just as in relation to the duty of care generally, so here in relation to negligent statements, the court will effectively have a free hand to declare duty or no duty according to its own impression of the whole case and its gut reaction to the question whether the defendant in the circumstances of the case ought to be liable to compensate the plaintiff for the particular loss.

The doctor/patient relationship

In the doctor/patient relationship there will always be a duty upon the doctor to take care when he speaks. This is part and parcel of the relationship. The patient is clearly going to be relying on what he is told. Diagnosis and advice are as important as treatment. But one can envisage situations where the doctor will not be under a duty. If he is unwise enough to give a spot diagnosis at a cocktail party to a man who is not his patient but who is forcing his ailment on the doctor's attention, it is hardly likely that a court will hold him liable, unless the circumstances are very special – perhaps the doctor gave the appearance of considering the matter seriously and then told the man he must surely have cancer, as a result of which the man killed himself. Such a statement could be held to be so unwise as to attract liability. But if all he says is 'you probably need to get back to work and forget your problem' and the man then returns to work and collapses, it is likely that a court would say that the special relationship needed for the imposition of a duty to take care in respect of careless statements had not arisen. Lord Oliver gave examples in the *Caparo* case (at p. 382) of medical misstatements that would attract liability: the doctor who gives negligent advice over the telephone to the parent of a sick child, and the chemist's assistant who mislabels a dangerous medicine.

A 'statement' by a doctor to a pharmacist (i.e. a prescription) needs to be legibly written (see *Prendergast* v. *Sam & Dee Ltd* [1989] 1 Med LR 36).[6]

---

[6] For the duty of confidentiality, see the next chapter.

16 · The duty of care in the medical context

SUMMARY

The doctor's duty to take all due care of the patient arises from the relationship of doctor and patient and involves not merely a duty to take care once activity (treatment) is commenced but also a duty to initiate action, i.e. to take all steps necessary for the health of the patient. It is however confined to times when and places where the doctor can properly be expected to be 'on duty'. The cry of 'Is there a doctor in the house?' does not impose legal liability on the medical theatregoer. The duty is also confined to medical matters. It may extend, on the modern developments in the general law of negligence, to other people than the patient.

In most medical negligence contexts the duty of care is not a problem, because it is obvious that the doctor owes a duty of care to the patient. This duty arises out of the relationship. It is not based on foreseeability of harm. There would still be a duty to take care of the patient in a particular situation where as it so happened harm was not reasonably foreseeable. It is not a duty that arises from an activity undertaken, as in so many negligence situations, e.g. undertaking building works, sporting activities, care of prisoners, driving a motor vehicle etc. It arises simply from the relationship regardless of activity undertaken. This is why there is a duty to act, and not merely a duty to take care once activity is undertaken. Such a case, where there is a duty to act, is not the same, and requires different consideration from the activity situation. Without a 'relationship' based on the status of the parties, i.e. here a doctor/patient status, there is no duty, as we have seen, to act. One is permitted to do nothing. If a bleeding man comes to my door needing help I am not legally obliged to give it. Once there is a duty to act, the obligee will be in breach if he does not commence all necessary activity, quite apart from being in breach if he does not use due care in carrying out the activity (the treatment). Negligent omissions can be the failure to commence activity where there is a duty to act, as well as the failure to take some appropriate step in the course of the activity once commenced (see, on the physician's duty, *Pippin* v. *Sheppard* (1822) 11 Price 400, where an averment that the defendant had been employed to 'treat, attend to and cure divers grievous hurts, cuts & etc.' and as a result of his treatment 'the said wound became and was grievously aggravated and made worse', was held to be a good plea; see also *Edgar* v. *Lamont* 1914 SC 277).

When then is a doctor under a duty of care? Is that duty owed only to the patient? Is that duty owed only in respect of strictly medical activities? Is he liable only for losses coming within the scope of his medical activities?

As we saw earlier, a doctor is not legally obliged to assist, e.g. at a car accident (there is no duty to act where the plaintiff is not a patient or required to be accepted as a patient, as at a casualty department; see *Thompson* v. *Schmidt* (1891) 8 TLR 120). If he chooses to, as no doubt he would, he must exercise all proper skill. If he is a GP and the injured party just happens to be his patient, he might be held to be under a legal duty to act, for the court might well say that his duty to look after the patient's health was not limited to the location of surgery or home. If he happened to be the consultant who had recently operated on the now injured party, the court would be unlikely to say that his duty extended to further assistance on the highway, even if the patient was still under his care as an out-patient.[1]

A non-medical bystander is under no duty to give succour, but if he does he must act with the care that is reasonably to be expected from someone who undertakes to help. If he makes the victim worse he will be liable (there is no duty on a non-medical man who is asked to act, *Shiells* v. *Blackburne* (1789) 126 ER 94; but if he has made representations of prowess a duty of care arises, *Ruddock* v. *Lowe* (1865) 4 F & F 519, *Brogan* v. *Bennett* [1955] IR 119). In a 1988 case a motorcycle scrambler unsuccessfully sued the St John Ambulance Brigade on the ground that the volunteers who came to his aid when he fell from his motorcycle failed to spot a back injury and made it worse by getting him to stand.

Duty owed to others: if negligent medical treatment causes the death of a patient it may well be, on the 'aftermath' principle of *McLoughlin* v. *O'Brian* [1983] 1 AC 410, that liability might extend to a member of the deceased's immediate family who is present at or soon after the death and suffers nervous shock

---

[1] Ethical guidance (dated 16 May 1988) from the GMC on HIV infection and AIDS states that refusal to treat on the ground of personal risk to the treating doctor may amount to serious professional misconduct.

thereby.[2] Again, if the negligent prescription of drugs leads foreseeably to epileptic or similar attacks, a person who is injured trying to help the patient when he has endangered himself in the course of such an attack may well, on the well-known 'rescuer' principle, be able to recover damages from the physician who negligently prescribed the drugs.

In *Barnett* v. *Chelsea and Kensington Hospital Management Committee* [1969] 1 QB 428, Nield J. held that a hospital owed a duty to act *vis-à-vis* a person who presented himself at the casualty department, notwithstanding that he had not yet been received into the hospital in any way. The failure to act when he so presented himself was negligent (although on the facts it was found not to have contributed to his subsequent death). Nield J. said that, although there could be cases where the casualty officer was not required to see the caller, e.g. if he already has his own doctor whom he can attend and is merely seeking a second opinion, in general the duty of the casualty officer is to see and examine all patients who come to the casualty department. Once he has started the activity of treatment and care, by examination in the first instance, it is his duty to take all reasonable steps, which in this particular case would have required the admission of the caller to the wards. In *McCormack* v. *Redpath, The Times*, 24 March 1961, a casualty officer was negligent in permitting a patient to go home without a proper examination.

A doctor (or hospital) is under a duty of care to potential victims of a dangerous patient who is not properly contained; *Holgate* v. *Lancashire Mental Hospitals Board* [1937] 4 All ER 19, *Ellis* v. *Home Office* [1953] 2 All ER 149. The principle was explained by the House of Lords in *Dorset Yacht Co.* v. *Home Office* [1970] AC 1004, the case about the escaped Borstal boys (for an extension of this context see *Tarasoff* v. *Regents of the University of California* 551 P (2d) 334 (Cal. 1976), where a duty was recognised upon a psychiatrist to warn the intended victim if his patient uttered death threats in session). A doctor who unreasonably concludes that a child has suffered sexual abuse at home and has it taken into care is likely to be in breach of a duty of care owed to the parents and liable to them in damages for any consequent loss and suffering (e.g. loss of reputation, having to move house) – see, by way of analogy, the cases on a doctor's duty of care when recommending the admission of a patient to hospital for mental disorder: *de Freville* v. *Dill* (1927) 96 LJKB 1056, *Everett* v. *Griffiths* [1920] 3 KB 163, *Hall* v. *Semple* (1862) 3

---

[2] Since these words were written for the first edition I have settled more than one case on the basis that such a duty was owed (see further on this Chapter 20).

F & F 337. In December 1987 Eastham J. awarded £10,000 to a 6-year-old Cleveland girl and her mother after the child had been (admittedly) negligently diagnosed as sexually abused (the vaginal swab had been contaminated by a sperm sample placed on the same laboratory slide!) (*G*. v. *North Tees Health Authority* (1989)).

In *M*. v. *Newham London Borough Council* [1994] 2 WLR 554, the Court of Appeal held that no duty of care was owed to a child or her mother by a psychiatrist or social worker examining or enquiring for evidence of sexual abuse on behalf of the local authority in the exercise of their statutory child care functions.

The Master of the Rolls, dissenting in part, said that the psychiatrist was under a duty of care towards the child, who should be regarded as his patient, but he was not under a duty of care to the mother; the doctor's duty was to act in the best interests of the child, which might mean adversely to the mother's interests. He took a similar view and made a similar distinction in relation to the duty owed by the social worker. However Staughton L.J., with whom Peter Gibson L.J. agreed, took a much less imaginative view: he said the child was no more the patient of the psychiatrist than an injured motorist submitting to an examination by the insurer's doctor was a patient of that doctor. The duty of careful assessment was owed to the person who had engaged the doctor to perform the examination, not to the person being examined. Note this judge's attitude to medical negligence claims. He said that the danger of overkill was very important in medical negligence cases, and that high standards of duty and vast awards of damages resulted in unnecessary tests and other procedures at great expense.

Compare *E*. v. *Dorset County Council* [1994] 3 WLR 853, where the Court of Appeal refused to strike out claims based on a duty of care owed by a local education authority for acts or omissions of its individual psychologists, teachers or officials in failing to ascertain learning problems and provide appropriate advice and assistance pursuant to the statutory code dealing with special educational needs enacted by the Education Acts. Meeting the defendants' understandable reliance on the decision in *M*. v. *Newham Borough Council* (*supra*), the Master of the Rolls said that the circumstances were so different as to make transposition hazardous. The teaching of and making provision for children with learning difficulties could not be seen purely as a function of the state. It was hard to say that those who gave their advice to parents, or knew that their advice would be communicated to parents, owed a duty only to their employer and not to those parents and their children.

The doctor's duty of care extends, contrary to what has been popularly believed, to his handwriting, so that if he writes a prescription the illegibility of which contributes to the pharmacist dispensing the wrong medicine he will be liable for any injury suffered by the patient (*Prendergast* v. *Sam and Dee Ltd* [1989] 1 Med LR 36).

The cases where a patient inflicts injury on himself due to alleged lack of supervision provide an example of the rule that even if below-standard care is proved it has to be shown to have caused the damage complained of (see Chapter 29 under 'Self-inflicted injury').

Type of damage: the duty of care is a duty to take all reasonable steps, including, as I have said, the duty to commence activity where appropriate, for the proper medical care of the patient. The duty does not extend to other fields. If a doctor gives advice on investments to a patient he is clearly not under the same duty of care as he is when he gives medical advice. Where a factory doctor advises on non-medical matters, such as administration and economy, the high standard of care demanded of a physician in medical matters does not apply to the non-medical matters (*Stokes* v. *Guest Keen and Nettlefold (Bolts and Nuts) Ltd* [1968] 1 WLR 1776, 1784 *per* Swanwick J.).

In *Landall* v. *Dennis Faulkner and Alsop* [1994] 5 Med LR 268, an orthopedic surgeon was sued for advice given in a personal injury action to the effect that the plaintiff's condition could be ameliorated by a spinal fusion. The action was settled on that basis. The plaintiff contended that the advice was negligent and that the operation had damaged him further. Holland J. held that the expert was immune from suit as the report in question had been given for the purpose of assisting the lawyers to conduct the plaintiff's case and not for the purpose of advising the plaintiff about medical treatment.

In *Stevens* v. *Bermondsey and Southwark Group Hospital Management Committee* (1963) 107 SJ 478 Paull J. held that a doctor is not required to foresee the legal consequences of his advice. A casualty officer who negligently diagnosed a minor injury was not liable for the financial loss to the patient, when, not knowing therefore that he had suffered a serious injury, he settled his claim against the tortfeasor for a smaller sum than it was worth. The point to note here is that the physician was not examining with a view to legal liability. Had he been, one would certainly have expected him to have been found liable – the medical defence societies have in the past settled cases where a negligent medical report gave the plaintiff an underestimation of his injuries (see also *Pimm* v. *Roper* (1862) 2 F & F 783; and, to a contrary intent to the *Stevens* case, *McGrath* v. *Kiely and Powell* [1965] IR 497).

For consideration of liability for defective medical equipment see Chapter 30 under 'Consumer Protection Act 1987'.

THE DUTY OF CONFIDENTIALITY

. . . in common with other professional men . . . the doctor is under a duty not to disclose [voluntarily] without the consent of his patient information which he, the doctor, has gained in his professional capacity, save . . . in very exceptional circumstances . . .

Hunter v. *Mann* [1974] 1 QB 767, 772

The doctor is under a legal as well as a moral duty not to divulge confidential information about a patient without his consent. Until 1989 there were no English reported cases on this aspect of his duty (the best one could do was to refer to the report of *Kitson* v. *Playfair, The Times*, 28 March 1896); but it was clear that a court would be prepared to restrain the dissemination or use of such information in an appropriate case. The judgments of the House of Lords in *Gillick* v. *West Norfolk and Wisbech Area Health Authority and the DHSS* [1986] AC 112 (concerning contraceptive advice and treatment to minors) affirmed the duty of confidentiality.[3] Then came the Court of Appeal decision in *W.* v. *Egdell* [1990] Ch 359, where a mental patient, confined for having committed multiple killings under the disability of serious mental illness, complained that the psychiatrist who prepared an (unfavourable) report on him at his own request with a view to his using it in support of his application to the mental health review tribunal to secure a transfer to a regional secure unit had, contrary to his, the patient's, express instructions, disclosed it to the medical officer in charge of his detention, and also to the Home Office. The patient had withdrawn his application to the tribunal and, in effect, now wanted the report suppressed. The court stressed the importance of the duty of confidentiality, particularly to a member of the public in this plaintiff's position. But where, as so often, there was a competing interest a balancing exercise had to be carried out: in this particular case the court concluded without doubt that the public interest in being protected from those who were suffering from a mental illness that might constitute a threat to the safety of others overrode the duty of confidentiality. This was because the psychiatrist was concerned to put before those responsible for making decisions about the patient's care, transfer and discharge relevant information and opinion of which they were either not aware or not

---

[3] Reference may be made to the Scottish cases of *A.B.* v. *C.D.* (1851) 14 D 177, and *A.B.* v. *C.D.* (1904) 7 F 72.

heedful; and any such decision reached upon inadequate information could give rise to a real risk to the public at large.[4,5]

However, the doctor, unlike the lawyer, has no professional privilege which would excuse him from divulging confidential information when questioned in legal proceedings. Doctors are compellable witnesses in relation to matters within their professional knowledge, but, as Lord Denning said in *Attorney-General* v. *Mulholland and Foster* [1963] 1 All ER 767, 771, the judge will respect the confidences received by a doctor in the course of his profession and will not direct him to answer unless it is not only relevant but is also a proper and necessary question in the course of justice to be put and answered. As a corollary, the doctor's immunity from action for breach of confidence when so answering is 'settled in law and cannot be doubted' (*Watson* v. *McEwan* [1905] AC 480, 486).

The ethical duty was recognised at least as early as the fifth century B.C. 'Whatsoever in connection with my professional practice I see or hear in the life of men which ought not to be spoken of abroad I will not divulge as reckoning that all such should be kept secret' (a modern translation of the relevant part of the Hippocratic Oath – see Appendix V for the full text). The BMA in its *Handbook of Medical Ethics* states that a doctor must preserve secrecy on all he knows. However, in certain contexts the duty of confidentiality is overridden by other considerations. The *Handbook* gives five exceptions:

(1) the patient gives consent;
(2) when it is undesirable on medical grounds to seek a patient's consent but it is in the patient's own interest that confidentiality should be broken;
(3) the doctor's overriding duty to society [a doctor should surely reveal information which would show his patient to have been guilty of a serious crime, for he is under the ordinary duty imposed on every citizen not to protect offenders];
(4) for the purposes of medical research when approved by a local clinical research ethical committee . . .

---

[4] Reference may also be made to *X.* v. *Y.* [1988] 2 All ER 648 where a health authority sought to restrain a newspaper from publishing the names of doctors who were alleged to have contracted AIDS (the paper had paid someone to reveal the names that appeared in the hospital records). Rose J. held that the public interest in the preservation of the confidentiality of hospital records identifying actual or potential AIDS sufferers outweighed the public interest in the freedom of the press to publish such information because victims of the disease ought not to be deterred by fear of discovery from going to hospital for treatment. (See also *R.* v. *Crozier* (1990) 8 BMLR 128.)

[5] In a very early case action was taken to prevent publication of a diary kept by a physician to George III (*Wyatt* v. *Wilson*, see (1849) 41 ER at p. 1179).

(5) when the information is required by due legal process.[6]

In certain contexts legislation specifically requires the doctor to transmit medical information to the authorities. He must inform of notifiable diseases (nature of the disease and name and location of the patient), currently cholera, plague, relapsing fever, smallpox, typhus and AIDS (Public Health (Control of Disease) Act 1984 and SI 434/85).[7] The Abortion Act 1967 and associated regulations (1968/390, 1969/636, 1976/15, 1980/1724) require doctors to deposit with the Chief Medical Officer at the DHSS (now the Department of Health) detailed information relating to pregnancies terminated under the Act. Under the Misuse of Drugs Act 1971 and associated regulations a doctor must get in touch with the Drugs Branch of the Home Office in relation to any patient whom he attends who appears to the doctor to be drug-dependent. And a doctor may be required to disclose the identity of a patient whom he has treated after a road accident, by virtue of s.168(2) of the Road Traffic Act 1972, which requires any person to 'give any information which it is in his power to give [which] may lead to the identification of the driver'. Refusal to disclose such information has led to the conviction of a doctor of an offence under the section (see *Hunter* v. *Mann* [1974] RTR 338).[8] It has been an offence for anyone with certain information about terrorists to fail without reasonable excuse to give it to the police (Prevention of Terrorism (Temporary Provisions) Act 1984).

A Canadian case

In *Hay* v. *University of Alberta Hospital* [1991] 2 Med LR 204 a court of first instance held that by bringing a medical negligence action a patient was to be taken to have given an implied waiver of his right to confidentiality. It is to be hoped that an English court would not adopt that view. A plaintiff would be wise to reveal all, for he may otherwise be thought to be hiding something; however, he should not be compelled to disclose.[9]

---

[6] The GMC's *Blue Book* on 'Professional Conduct & Discipline' gives similar, detailed guidance at paras 79–82.
[7] Health authorities must provide reports under the AIDS (Control) Act 1987, but these, as yet, do not need to reveal identities.
[8] Peter Wright says in his book *Spycatcher* that MI5 got information from psychiatrists about their patients. This is outrageous.
[9] Plaintiffs in medical negligence actions are normally required to disclose all their medical records. This may sometimes also be the case for an ordinary accident plaintiff (see *Dunn* v. *British Coal Corporation* [1993] PIQR P275).

17 · The standard of care

SUMMARY

The degree or standard of care required by the law for the discharge of a duty of care depends on a number of factors, including how likely it is that harm will arise from the activity undertaken, how serious the harm might be, the cost of avoiding the risk and the interference that would cause to the activity, the usefulness of the activity, and a pot-pourri of prevailing social and economic conditions.

A professional is required to exercise the ordinary skill of a competent practitioner in his field. A doctor will not be adjudged to have failed to come up to the required standard if a responsible body of medical opinion, albeit a minority one, would find his actions acceptable.

Errors of judgment may or may not amount to negligence; there is no magic in that expression. Where lack of funds prevent the acquisition of staff adequate in number and experience to provide the best care it is not yet clear to what extent a patient can maintain that an inexperienced doctor doing his best in a specialised post is nevertheless negligent if he does not come up to the standard of an experienced doctor, or whether the health authority is negligent in its own right for not providing through appropriately qualified staff the proper standard of care.

There is no breach of duty unless the defendant has failed to meet the standard of care required by the law in the context of the duty that exists to take all reasonable care. Two questions arise: what is the standard of care in a particular case, and how is the plaintiff to prove that the defendant has failed to come up to that standard? We consider the first question in this chapter, and the second in Chapter 23.

THE STANDARD

The care that is required of a person undertaking an activity, that is the standard of reasonable care that he has to display, depends on a number of factors: the nature and value of the activity he is undertaking, the risk that he is creating, the seriousness of the

likely consequences if he does not exercise due care or if
something untoward happens, the expense and difficulty of
taking precautions, and the overall view of the court as to the
suitability of recovery in the particular case (this last is a mixture
of the court's views on policy and justice – see Chapter 15).

It is the duty [of an employer] in considering whether some precaution should be
taken against a foreseeable risk, to weigh, on the one hand the magnitude of the
risk, the likelihood of an accident happening [this seems tautological!], and the
possible seriousness of the consequences if an accident does happen, and, on the
other hand, the difficulty and expense and any other disadvantage of taking the
precaution (*per* Lord Reid in *Morris* v. *West Hartlepool Steam Navigation Co.*
[1956] AC 552).

It is well settled that in measuring due care you must balance the risk against the
measures necessary to eliminate the risk. To that proposition there ought to be
added this: you must balance the risk against the end to be achieved (*per*
Denning L.J. in *Watt* v. *Hertfordshire County Council* [1954] 1 WLR 835, 838).

The standard of care, in its basic form, is that care which a
reasonable person would take in the circumstances. That of
course does not get one very far. It is the court that will decide
what a reasonable person would have done. In *Bolton* v. *Stone*
[1951] AC 550 cricketers who could foresee the possibility of a
ball hitting a passer-by outside the ground were nevertheless
under no duty of care to take precautions, as the risk was not
great enough. If they had been playing baseball no doubt the
decision would have been different. Cricket is too valuable an
activity in the eyes of the English judges to be hampered by
pettifogging considerations about the possibility of hitting a child
on the head with a ball as it walks down the road outside.[1]

People must guard against reasonable probabilities but they are not bound to
guard against fantastic possibilities (*Fardon* v. *Harcourt-Rivington* (1932) 146
LT 391, 392, *per* Lord Dunedin).

The consequences of injury from flying fragments of metal to a
one-eyed workman is greater than to a two-eyed workman; so the
standard of care and the precautions to be taken, e.g. the
provision of goggles, may well be higher (*Paris* v. *Stepney
Borough Council* [1951] AC 367).

In every case of a foreseeable risk it is a matter of balancing the risk against the
measures necessary to eliminate it (*per* Denning L.J. in *Latimer* v. *AEC Ltd*
[1953] AC 643). [We may well add: 'and the importance, in the eyes of the
court, of the activity being undertaken'].

But it does not follow that, no matter what the circumstances may be, it is
justifiable to neglect a risk of such a small magnitude. A reasonable man would

---

[1] In the summer of 1994 David Lacey lost his action to enforce high netting by his house at
the side of the cricket green at Jordans in Buckinghamshire.

only neglect such a risk if he had some valid reason for doing so, e.g. that it would involve considerable expense to eliminate the risk. He would weigh the risk against the difficulty of eliminating it (*per* Lord Reid in *Overseas Tankship (UK) Ltd* v. *The Miller Steamship Co. Pty* [1967] 1 AC 617, 642).

A relevant circumstance to be taken into account may be the importance of the end to be served by behaving in this way or that. As has often been pointed out, if all the trains in this country were restricted to a speed of five miles an hour, there would be fewer accidents, but our national life would be intolerably slowed down. The purpose to be served, if sufficiently important, justifies the assumption of abnormal risk (*per* Asquith L.J. in *Daborn* v. *Bath Tramways Ltd* [1946] 2 All ER 333, 336).

The court will always pay regard to evidence of the approved common practices of the trade in deciding whether there has been lack of reasonable care; but for learned professions, as opposed to trades, the court is unlikely to conclude that any practice approved by some part of the profession involves a breach of the duty of care, and this is particularly so where a medical practice that has the sanction of a body, even a minority, of practitioners, is alleged to have been negligent (see below).

SKILLED PROFESSIONS

Every person who enters into a learned profession undertakes to bring to the exercise of it a reasonable degree of care and skill. He does not undertake, if he is an attorney, that at all events you shall gain your case, nor does a surgeon undertake that he will perform a cure; nor does he undertake to use the highest possible degree of skill. There may be persons who have higher education and greater advantages than he has, but he undertakes to bring a fair, reasonable and competent degree of skill (*per* Tindal C.J. in *Lanphier* v. *Phipos* (1838) 8 C & P 475).

If a smith prick my horse with a nail etc., I shall have my action upon the case against him, without any warranty by the smith to do it well . . . for it is the duty of every artificer to exercise his art rightly and truly as he ought (FNB 94 D).

The public profession of an art is a representation and undertaking to all the world that the professor possesses the requisite ability and skill (*per* Willes L.J. in *Harmer* v. *Cornelius* (1858) 5 CB (NS) 236, an action against a professed artisan painter).

And the seminal case for the modern law, in particular for medical negligence claims:

Where you get a situation which involves the use of some special skill or competence, then the test as to whether there has been negligence or not is not the test of the man on the top of a Clapham omnibus, because he has not got this special skill. The test is the standard of the ordinary skilled man exercising and professing to have that special skill . . . A man need not possess the highest expert skill; it is well established law that it is sufficient if he exercises the ordinary skill of an ordinary competent man exercising that particular art (*per* McNair J. in *Bolam* v. *Friern Hospital Management Committee* [1957] 1 WLR 582, 586).

MEDICAL CASES

In *R.* v. *Bateman* (1925) 94 LJKB 791 it was said that the physician

owes a duty to the patient to use diligence, care, knowledge, skill and caution in administering the treatment. No contractual relation is necessary, nor is it necessary that the service be rendered for reward . . . The law requires a fair and reasonable standard of care and competence.

If he is following approved practice the physician cannot be held to be negligent. 'A defendant charged with negligence can clear himself if he shows that he acted in accordance with general and approved practice' (*Marshall* v. *Lindsey County Council* [1935] 1 KB 516, 540 *per* Maugham L.J.). This statement was approved by the House of Lords in *Whiteford* v. *Hunter* [1950] WN 553.

A court cannot choose between two approved practices, i.e. between two schools of thought. If a respectable[2] body of medical opinion, albeit a minority one, would at the time of the alleged negligence have approved of the course taken by the defendant then he has cleared himself of the allegation of negligence (*Maynard* v. *West Midlands Regional Health Authority* [1984] 1 WLR 634).

In the realm of diagnosis and treatment there is ample scope for genuine difference of opinion and one man clearly is not negligent merely because his conclusion differs from that of other professional men . . . The true test for establishing negligence in diagnosis or treatment on the part of a doctor is whether he has been proved to be guilty of such failure as no doctor of ordinary skill would be guilty of if acting with ordinary care . . . (*per* Lord President Clyde in *Hunter* v. *Hanley* 1955 SLT 213, 217).

This statement has often been approved in the English courts – see the *Bolam* case (*supra*), *Whitehouse* v. *Jordan* (*infra*), *Maynard*'s case (*supra*), the *Sidaway* case (*infra*).

In the *Maynard* case Lord Scarman said:

A case which is based on an allegation that a fully considered decision of two consultants in the field of their special skill was negligent clearly presents certain difficulties of proof. It is not enough to show that there is a body of competent professional opinion which considers that theirs was a wrong decision, if there also exists a body of professional opinion, equally competent, which supports the decision as reasonable in the circumstances. It is not enough to show that

---

[2] The word 'responsible' appears to be interchangeable with 'respectable' (see Lord Scarman's words, cited below, in the *Maynard* case). I have heard it argued in a case that the body of medical opinion established by the defendants' evidence is not 'responsible' because it irresponsibly supports the complained of treatment, but it seems clear that the epithet refers to the general standing of the doctors comprising the body and cannot refer simply, or at all, to their attitude to the complained of treatment. If it could be understood in that limited sense, it would, in the proper sense of the phrase, be begging the question.

subsequent events show that the operation need never have been performed if at the time the decision to operate was taken it was reasonable in the sense that a responsible body of medical opinion would have accepted it as proper.

And Lord Scarman went on to commend the words above cited of Lord President Clyde.

An example of a 'two schools of thought' situation is *Pargeter* v. *Kensington and Chelsea and Westminster Health Authority* [1979] 2 *The Lancet* 1030, where the defendants avoided liability by showing that there was a respectable body of medical opinion that took the view that papaveretum should be administered after an open eye operation, even though there was an opposing school of thought. A retrial was ordered in the Irish case of *Dunne* v. *National Maternity Hospital and Jackson* (1989) HALL March 1990 p. 8: the jury should have been told that a deviation from normal practice by monitoring only one heartbeat where the mother was in labour with twins would not be negligent unless no responsible doctor would have so acted.

Note also *Hughes* v. *Waltham Forest Health Authority* [1991] 2 Med LR 155 where the Court of Appeal annulled the judge's award of £220,000 in favour of the plaintiff saying that the fact that two distinguished surgeons in a particular specialty were critical of the decision of two of their colleagues did not prove that the action of the latter was negligent, even if it had turned out to be a mistake. The proper test of negligence was said to be whether the surgeons in reaching their decision had displayed such a lack of clinical judgment that no surgeon exercising proper care and skill could have reached the same decision. A recent case illustrating the principle is *Taylor* v. *Worcester and District Health Authority* [1991] 2 Med LR 215, where the plaintiff's claim for damages for awareness during a cesarean section failed because the judge concluded that the anesthetist had followed a procedure that was acceptable at the time of the operation (1985).

A doctor's duty to exercise ordinary skill and care according to the ordinary and reasonable standards of those who practise in the same field of medicine. The standard for the specialist is the standard of the specialists. A doctor is not negligent if he has acted in accordance with a practice accepted as proper by a responsible body of medical men skilled in that particular art (*per* Sellers L.J. in *Landau* v. *Werner* (1961) 105 SJ 1008).

The Bolam principle may be formulated as a rule that a doctor is not negligent if he acts in accordance with a practice accepted at the time as proper by a responsible body of medical opinion even though other doctors adopt a different practice. In short, the law imposes the duty of care: but the standard of care is a matter of medical judgment (*per* Lord Scarman in *Sidaway* v. *Board of Governors of the Bethlem Royal Hospital and the Maudsley Hospital* [1985] AC 871, 881).

In *Ashcroft* v. *Mersey Regional Health Authority* [1983] 2 All ER 245 the judge said that the question was whether it had been established on a balance of probabilities that the physician had failed to exercise the care required of a man possessing and professing special skill in circumstances which required the exercise of that special skill. No added burden of proof rested on the plaintiff. The more skilled a person was the more care which was expected of him. That test should be applied without gloss either way (*per* Kilner Brown J.).

In *Burgess* v. *Newcastle Health Authority* [1992] 3 Med LR 224 a neuro-surgeon avoided liability in respect of his management of a right frontal craniotomy by showing that a 'widely respected body of neuro-surgeons' (*per* Turner J.) would have acted in the same way. And in *Defreitas* v. *O'Brien and another* [1993] 4 Med LR 281 both orthopedic and neuro-surgeon avoided liability by showing that their management was acceptable to a responsible body of medical opinion (see below for Court of Appeal decision).

Although the *Bolam* principle has been represented as nothing more than the general principle that applies to all skilled callings (see, for example, Lord Diplock's treatment of it in the *Sidaway* case), it is unlikely that a court would treat evidence of professional practice as conclusive in any other than the medical context. In all other professions the court is likely to be willing to declare that a practice followed by responsible members of a profession attracts legal liability if it feels strongly enough about it. And even in the medical context there has been the odd case where the court has overruled the practice of responsible physicians.

In *Clarke* v. *Adams* (1950) 94 SJ 599 the judge rejected the standard warning given by radiologists before giving heat treatment, saying that it amounted to negligence because it did not give the patient a clear enough indication as to when the danger point in the treatment might be reached. In *Hucks* v. *Cole*, a 1968 case reported at [1993] 4 Med LR 393, a doctor who failed to treat a patient with penicillin was held negligent although responsible physicians testified that they would have done what the defendant did. Sachs L.J. said that if the court was satisfied that a lacuna existed in professional practice whereby the patient was exposed to unnecessary risks the court would so declare and would expect the professional practice to be altered accordingly. It was not conclusive of proper practice that other practitioners would have acted as the defendant did; the judge was not satisfied that their reasons for so doing stood up to analysis. It is not clear how that decision (from a very strong court – Lord Denning, Diplock and Sachs L.JJ.) can be reconciled with the *Bolam* principle, though some help may be got from Sachs L.J.'s observation that it was not a 'two schools of thought' case, and see the *Bolitho* case below.

An example of the court's willingness to impose its own view of what is reasonable and what is not upon the practices of professions other than the medical is *Nye Saunders & Partners* v. *Bristow*, 8 April 1987, CA. The trial judge found on the evidence that at the relevant time there was no body of responsible professional opinion among architects that would have failed to give a warning as to inflation when estimating building costs, but that, even if he was wrong there, he was prepared to hold that no prudent architect would have omitted such a warning. He thus applied the *Bolam* test as endorsed by the House of Lords in the *Sidaway* case [1985] AC 871 but went on to apply the proviso stated by Lord Bridge, to the effect that the court could overrule (medical) practice as to non-disclosure of risk where the risk was so obvious that no prudent doctor would fail to disclose it. The Court of Appeal refused to interfere with either of those findings. Reference may also be made to the Privy Council case of *Edward Wong Finance Co. Ltd* v. *Johnson Stokes and Master* [1984] AC 296 where the court was not at all shy to find an established conveyancing practice among Hong Kong solicitors to be unacceptable. Also to the words of Phillips J. in the Lloyd's Names litigation (*Deeny* v. *Gooda Walker Ltd*, 4 October 1994, QBD):

Suppose a profession collectively adopted extremely lax standards in some aspect of its work. The court would not acquit practitioners of negligence simply because they had complied with those standards.

However, this was a commercial case. The learned judge may not have been so quick to thus express himself if he had been sitting on a medical negligence trial. We may be sure that the court will be a great deal slower to find unacceptable a practice acceptable to some part of the medical profession. For further discussion of the duty of disclosure see Chapter 24 under 'Duty of disclosure: general'.

Further discussion of the Bolam test

The comprehensive application of the *Bolam* test in the field of medical law, i.e. to every question of diagnosis, treatment, and disclosure of risks, has occasioned concern among those who act for patients, because it has seemed at times as if all that is needed for a successful defence is for one or two doctors to state on oath that they would have acted as the accused doctor acted, or, even less than that, that they find his actions to have been acceptable.

However, the following material shows that that is too facile an approach to the question.

In the first place it should be recognised that the test was originally directed to situations where there could be shown to be an accepted practice which the accused doctor had followed. It was then, without any real analysis, extended to cover single instances of a clinical decision or clinical judgment, receiving in this context the House of Lords imprimatur in the *Maynard* case (see the passage cited above). However, the judgments of the House of Lords some 25 years before in *Chapman v. Rix*, a 1960 decision reported in [1994] 5 Med LR 239, had given one to understand that a doctor could not necessarily escape liability merely by calling colleagues to say they would have done the same as he had done – although it could be argued that, as the case concerned the failure of a hospital doctor to give full information to the patient's general practitioner on discharge, it was, as Lord Keith said, 'hardly a medical question at all'. But the fact remains that Lord Goddard clearly stated that he could not agree with what Romer L.J. had said in the Court of Appeal if that judge had meant that 'if a doctor charged with negligence could find two other doctors to say they would have acted as he did, that of itself entitled him to a verdict'.

Next, as already noted, the Court of Appeal in 1968, in *Hucks v. Cole* (*supra*), was clearly not reduced to powerlessness by the evidence from other doctors that they would have acted as the defendant had. Mustill L.J. put an interesting gloss on this case in his judgment in *Bolitho v. City and Hackney Health Authority* [1993] 4 Med LR 381 when he said at p. 393:

In my judgment the court could only adopt the approach of Sachs L.J. and reject medical opinion on the ground that the reasons of one group of doctors do not really stand up to analysis, if the court, fully conscious of its own lack of medical knowledge and clinical experience, was none the less clearly satisfied that the views of that group of doctors were *Wednesbury* unreasonable, i.e. views such as no reasonable body of doctors could have held. But, in my view, that would be an impossibly strong thing to say of the honest views of experts of the distinction of Dr Dinwiddie and Dr Robertson in the present case.[3]

But two points still remain to be made.

First, the judge has to be satisfied that the defence evidence does indeed establish that a responsible body of medical opinion would have found the conduct of the accused doctor to be acceptable. He is permitted to take the view that the defence expert is simply wrong, perhaps because he has not considered all

---

[3] The phrase '*Wednesbury* unreasonable' is a reference to the well-known case of *Associated Provincial Picture Houses* v. *Wednesbury Corporation* [1948] 1 KB 223.

the factors, or that he does not speak for a responsible body but only for himself. In other words the judge can simply reject his evidence. Recent examples of such rejection can be found in *Parry* v. *North West Surrey Health Authority* [1994] 5 Med LR 259 and *Bowers* v. *Harrow Health Authority* [1995] 6 Med LR 16. And one may recall at this point the words of Oliver J. in *Midland Bank Trust* v. *Hett Stubbs and Kemp* [1979] Ch 384, 402:

Clearly, if there is some practice in a particular profession, some accepted standard of conduct which is laid down by a professional institute or sanctioned by common usage, evidence of that can and ought to be received. But evidence which really amounts to no more than an expression of opinion of a particular practitioner of what he thinks he would have done had he been placed, hypothetically and without the benefit of hindsight, in the position of the defendants, is of little assistance to the court.

Note may be taken here of *Rattey* v. *Haringey Health Authority* [1994] 5 Med LR 413 where the Court of Appeal reversed the judge's finding in favour of the patient on the ground that, given that he accepted the evidence and the standing of the defendants' experts, he was not entitled to hold that no responsible practitioner would have acted as the accused surgeon did. This case shows that to be immune from appeal the judge needs to state that he does not accept that the defence evidence establishes that a responsible body of medical opinion would have found the impugned actions to be acceptable. Even if the appeal court is anxious to support the doctor it will find it hard, if not impossible, to justify reversing the judge's rejection of the defence evidence.

Note, also, *Knight* v. *Home Office* [1990] 3 All ER 237, in which Pill J. rejected a claim that a mentally disordered prisoner who committed suicide had not been properly looked after by the prison hospital staff, on the ground that the decision to observe him at 15 minute intervals had been a decision that ordinary skilled medical staff in their position could have made. However, in the course of his judgment he said:

The reasons given by the doctors for their decision should, however, be examined by the court to see if they stand up to analysis: see *Hucks* v. *Cole*, per Sachs J.

Reference should also be made to the recent Court of Appeal decision in *Defreitas* v. *O'Brien* [1995] 6 Med LR 108, where the Court of Appeal said that it was not a question of counting heads to determine whether a body of doctors constituted a responsible body for the purposes of the *Bolam* test; in appropriate circumstances the judge could find that a small number constituted the necessary defence.

Second, the judge may take the view that, whatever the defence experts say about what they would have done at the time, they are wrong, i.e. faced with the actual situation they would not have acted as the accused doctor did. An example of this can be found in the judgment of Simon Brown L.J. in *Bolitho* (*supra*) (his was a dissenting judgment, but it nevertheless illustrates the point).

Best interests

It has been suggested in some quarters, notably by Whitfield Q.C., that the courts' attitude to the question what is in the patient's best interests when it comes to such matters as sterilisation without consent and withdrawing life support systems could be drawn on to strengthen the argument that the court has, and must exercise, the right of final judgment on medical conduct. I find the analogy unconvincing. The 'best interests' cases raise different questions from actions for medical negligence as they relate, primarily if not exclusively, to ethical questions (these cases are dealt with at other points in this book – see the discussion about the value of life in Chapter 25 and the discussion about impossibility of consent in Chapter 24).

STANDARD OF CARE AND DISCLOSURE OF RISKS

The principle that in medical negligence actions the defendant has only to show that at the time of the alleged negligence there was a body, albeit a minority one, of responsible medical opinion that would have approved his actions, has been applied to the duty of disclosure as to the risks of treatment, in the case of *Sidaway* v. *Bethlem Royal Hospital* [1985] AC 871, and *Gold* v. *Haringey Health Authority* [1987] 3 WLR 649, CA. This situation is considered below (Chapter 24 under 'Duty of disclosure: general').

ERRORS OF JUDGMENT

One particular aspect of the standard of care is the question whether an error of judgment amounts to negligence. In *Hucks* v. *Cole* (*supra*), Lord Denning M.R. said:

With the best will in the world, things sometimes go amiss in surgical operations or medical treatment. A doctor is not to be held negligent simply because something has gone wrong. He is not liable for mischance or misadventure; or for an error of judgment. He is not liable for taking one choice out of two or favouring one school rather than another. He is only liable when he falls below the standard of a reasonably competent practitioner in his field so much that his conduct may be deserving of censure or inexcusable.

And in *Whitehouse* v. *Jordan* [1980] 1 All ER 650 Lord Denning said in the Court of Appeal:

We must say, and say firmly, that, in a professional man, an error of judgment is not negligent.

But in the House of Lords Lord Edmund-Davies said ([1981] 1 WLR 246 at p. 257):

To say that a surgeon committed an error of clinical judgment is wholly ambiguous, for, while some such errors may be completely consistent with the due exercise of professional skill, other acts or omissions in the course of exercising 'clinical judgment' may be so glaringly below proper standards as to make a finding of negligence inevitable.

. . . doctors and surgeons fall into no special legal category . . . the true doctrine was enunciated . . . in *Bolam* v. *Friern Hospital Management Committee* [1957] 1 WLR 582, 586, . . . applied in *Chin Keow* v. *Government of Malaysia* [1967] 1 WLR 813 . . . If a surgeon fails to measure up to that standard [viz. the standard of the ordinary skilled man exercising and professing to have the special skill in any respect] ('clinical judgment' or otherwise), he has been negligent and should be so adjudged.

And Lord Fraser said at page 263:

. . . I think that the learned Master of the Rolls must have meant to say that an error of judgment 'is not necessarily negligent'. But in my respectful opinion the statement as it stands is not an accurate statement of the law. Merely to describe something as an error of judgment tells us nothing about whether it is negligent or not. The true position is that an error of judgment may, or may not, be negligent; it depends on the nature of the error. If it is one that would not have been made by a reasonably competent professional man professing to have the standard and type of skill that the defendant held himself out as having, and acting with ordinary care, then it is negligent. If, on the other hand, it is an error that such a man, acting with ordinary care, might have made then it is not negligent.

The question, therefore, is: would a doctor acting with reasonable care have done what the defendant did? I pointed out earlier that it is not advisable to ask your expert whether there is evidence of negligence, for that may well put him off. Much better ask whether a want of reasonable care is evident. Everyone makes mistakes. Even Homer nods. A surgeon may have been exemplary in all his work, save that on one occasion, perhaps through overwork or just human fallibility, he fell below the standard of care required. This may or may not be characterised by the expression 'error of judgment', but it is probably better not to use it as it seems to have created confusion.[4] The doctor is not

---

[4] In the Scottish case of *Phillips* v. *Grampian Health Board* [1991] 3 Med LR 16 Lord Clyde said that it was not enough for the plaintiff to show there had been an error in clinical judgment; she had to prove an error that no doctor of ordinary skill would be guilty of if he were acting with reasonable care.

to be vilified for one slip in a distinguished career, but he cannot on that account escape liability to compensate the patient for a mistake that the exercise of reasonable care would have avoided.

Counsel for the defendants referred to Professor —'s status as 'Olympian'. My recollection of classical mythology is that the gods on Olympus were no strangers to error . . .

. . . [but] I hope Professor — will take comfort in the thought that even Apollo, the god of healing and the father of Aesculapius, had his moments of weakness (*per* Pain J. in *Clark* v. *Maclennan* [1983] 1 All ER 416).

There are of course situations where even while exercising due care the surgeon can damage the patient. One example is the risk of damaging the spinal cord or the adjoining nerves when performing a laminectomy. This is a dangerous operation; the instruments can go too far even though the surgeon is using all possible care. Provided he has told the patient of the risks in accordance with the prevailing practice at the time, he is not legally liable for his damaging act.

The plaintiff in *Ashton* v. *Alexander and Trent Regional Health Authority* (29 January 1988, CA) sustained a displaced fracture of the lower left jaw when, under general anesthetic, an unerupted molar tooth was removed by hammer and chisel. The surgeon accepted that the most likely cause was either excessive force on the chisel or insufficient removal of bone from the jaw, and that would mean that he had fallen below his usual standard. On that the Recorder found negligence. However, the Court of Appeal ordered a new trial, saying that an error of judgment might or might not be negligent, the admission of a mistake does not equate with an admission of negligence, and the Recorder should have gone on to ask whether the error was one that would not have been made by a reasonably competent professional person professing to have the standard and type of skill that the defendant held himself out as having, and acting with ordinary care.

LACK OF FUNDS

What if it is difficult for a hospital to deliver as high a standard of care as it would wish or as normal standards would dictate because it does not have the equipment or doctors, and the staff it does have are overworked and tired, or lack experience? Hardly an unusual situation! We saw earlier (Chapter 3, under 'Suing the Minister') that challenges to health authority or Minister over the allocation of resources are really non-starters, but if there is a failure in care is it any defence for the hospital to say that the staff worked as hard and as long, and with as much expertise, as they could, but economies prevented further care or more experienced doctors from being provided?

Statistics produced at the end of 1989 showed that 70% of junior doctors still worked more than 72 hours a week and 11% for more than 101. The BMA claimed that some doctors worked more than 112 hours. The Government pledged to reduce the working hours of junior doctors from 83 a week in April 1993 to 72 by the end of 1994 and to 56 by the end of 1995. The Court of Appeal on an interlocutory application refused to strike out a former junior hospital doctor's claim against his employer health authority for forcing him to work 88 or more hours a week, and held that health authorities could not lawfully require junior doctors to work for so many hours that there was a foreseeable risk of injury to their health: the Vice-Chancellor said that in any sphere of employment other than that of junior doctors an obligation to work up to 88 hours in any one week would be rightly regarded as oppressive and intolerable (*Johnstone* v. *Bloomsbury Health Authority* [1992] QB 333).

The BMA's representative for junior doctors said in June 1994 that nothing in the television series *Cardiac Arrest* struck him as unrealistic. He had in mind the actual death of a doctor who collapsed in January 1994 after an 86-hour-week.

The same standard of care is expected from the learner driver as from any other driver on the road (*Nettleship* v. *Weston* [1971] 2 QB 691). However, a learner driver chooses to drive on the highway; it is not a matter of necessity. The learner doctor goes where he is put, and the health authority usually has no option, if it is to provide a service pursuant to its statutory duty, but to put him there.[5] This question was considered in the medical context at the Court of Appeal stage in *Wilsher* v. *Essex Area Health Authority* [1987] QB 730. A baby suffered from lack of oxygen after birth. Over a period of some weeks devoted care from the medical staff saved it from permanent damage other than an incurable condition of the retina, which caused permanent near-blindness. The trial judge found that there had been negligence and the Court of Appeal upheld the decision.

---

[5] In *Collins* v. *Hertfordshire County Council* [1947] 1 All ER 633 it was said that it would be no excuse that the doctor was a student; nor (*Jones* v. *Manchester Corporation* [1952] 2 All ER 125) that he was inexperienced; nor that he was unwell (*Nickolls* v. *Ministry of Health, The Times*, 4 February 1955).

You cannot get compensation for injury received as a passenger as a result of the antics of your drunken driver or pilot if you willingly embarked on the trip knowing he was inebriated (*Morris* v. *Murray* [1991] 2 WLR 195); so be wary of putting yourself in the hands of a drunken doctor as you may be taken to have willingly accepted the risk of negligent doctoring!

The claim was apparently pursued only on the basis of vicarious liability and not on the basis of a primary non-delegable duty of care resting on the health authority. During their judgments the judges of the Appeal Court made various pronouncements on the standard of care owed by young doctors in positions of considerable responsibility. Mustill L.J. said that he did not accept the notion of a duty tailored to the actor rather than the act which he elects to perform, whereby the patient's right to complain is more limited where he happens to be in the hands of a doctor who is a novice in the particular field than if he is in the hands of one who has already spent months on the ward. The judge accepted that if hospitals abstained from using inexperienced personnel they could not staff their wards and theatres and the junior staff could never learn, but

... to my mind it would be a false step to subordinate the legitimate expectation of the patient that he will receive from each person concerned with his care a degree of skill appropriate to the task which he undertakes, to an understandable wish to minimise the psychological and financial pressures on hard-pressed young doctors . . .

For my part I prefer the third of the propositions which have been canvassed. This relates the duty of care not to the individual but to the post which he occupies. I would differentiate 'post' from 'rank' or 'status'. In a case such as the present the standard is not just that of the averagely competent and well-informed junior houseman (or whatever the position of the doctor), but of such a person who fills a post in a unit offering a highly specialised service.

Glidewell L.J. said that the law required the trainee or learner to be judged by the same standard as his more experienced colleagues. If it did not, inexperience would frequently be urged as a defence to an action for professional negligence.

But the Vice-Chancellor disagreed. He said that he could not accept that the standard of care required of an individual doctor holding a post in a hospital is an objective standard to be determined irrespective of his experience or the reason why he is occupying the post in question. A doctor learning specialist skills could not be said to be at fault if, at the beginning, he lacked the very skills which he was seeking to acquire. A learner need only come up to the standards of a careful doctor with his limited qualifications, notwithstanding that the post he held required greater experience than he in fact possessed. The law was not to be distorted by making findings of negligence personally against young doctors who had done their best in the position in which they had been put.[6]

---

[6] The Court of Appeal decision was reversed in the House of Lords on grounds not relevant to this discussion (see below Chapter 18).

The Court of Appeal judgments in *Bull and Wakeham* v. *Devon Area Health Authority* [1993] 4 Med LR 117 repay study. There was a medically unacceptable delay of one hour in securing the attendance of a suitably qualified doctor to deal with an emergency arising in the delivery of a second twin, as a result of which he suffered brain damage. On the question whether the defendants should have had in place a system which guaranteed prompt attendance, Slade L.J. said the evidence pointed strongly either to inefficiency in the system for summoning the assistance of the registrar or consultant or to negligence by some individual in the working of that system. Dillon L.J. said that any hospital which provided a maternity service for expectant mothers ought to be able to cope properly with premature delivery of twins, and there should have been at the hospital a staff reasonably sufficient for the foreseeable requirements of the patient. He described the hospital's system for providing senior attendance where the need arose as 'unreliable and essentially unsatisfactory'. Mustill L.J. said that the system fell short of the required standard, which demanded at the least that a doctor of suitable experience be available within 20 minutes to handle any emergency. It was not a question of an 'ideal' solution appropriate to 'centres of excellence', nor a question of highly specialist techniques or advanced new instrumentation which it would be unrealistic to expect in provincial hospitals, but just a question of getting the right people together in the right place at the right time.

Although it does not seem to have been expressly argued on behalf of the defendants that lack of funds prevented a better system and as therefore one should perhaps assume that there were sufficient funds to ensure a proper system, the question of deployment of limited resources can surely not have been far from the defendants' mind. One still waits to see what the court's reaction would be to a plea from defendants that their funding did not permit a better system even though the care they provided placed the patient at risk.

Argument

There are certainly attractions in the view, set out above, of the Vice-Chancellor in the *Wilsher* case, but if that were the law it could be objected that the health authority would not be liable for negligent care by an inexperienced doctor who was as careful as a new doctor could be, for there would be no negligence for them to be vicariously liable for. That is why the Vice-Chancellor went on to suggest that the health authority might be made directly liable for failing to provide doctors of sufficient skill and experience to give appropriate treatment, although claims had not yet been brought on that basis. In this particular case, however, he said that he was satisfied on the evidence that even allowing for any relevant inexperience there had in fact been negligence by one of the doctors, and so the award could be upheld on the basis of vicarious liability.

The difficulty with this view is that it is hardly fair to hold a health authority liable for failing to provide specialist care when it does not have the manpower or financial resources to do that. It has to use inexperienced personnel in responsible positions because there are not enough experienced staff to fill or supervise the posts. Nor would there be enough money to pay them. The truth of the matter is that in most cases both staff and health authority have done their best in the prevailing social and economic conditions. It may be hard, but the best view may be that the patient cannot expect a higher standard of care than the Secretary of State and Government generally makes possible. As long as compensation depends on proof of fault, recovery in many cases will require a distortion of the concept of fault, and this will mean that either a young doctor who is doing all that can reasonably be expected of him is going to be declared negligent because he has not shown the skill of an experienced doctor, or the health authority is going to be declared at fault for not providing a standard of care through experienced staff that it was not in fact able to provide. In the end the answer may be for compensation to be made independent of fault, but that is a long way off yet (see Chapter 30).

PREVAILING CONDITIONS

However, the standard of care to be expected may vary with the specific circumstances prevailing at the time. One can hardly expect the same meticulous attention in a hospital that is coping with a rail disaster or an epidemic as at normal times:

. . . in what may be called 'battle conditions' . . . an emergency may overburden the available resources, and if an individual is forced by circumstances to do too many things at once, the fact that he does one of them incorrectly should not lightly be taken as negligence (*Wilsher*'s case (*supra*) *per* Mustill L.J.).

In *Wooldridge* v. *Sumner* [1962] 3 WLR 616 the Court of Appeal said that an error of judgment committed by a horseman at the National Horse Show which resulted in injury to a spectator committed 'in the agony of the moment' did not amount to negligence. In such circumstances there had to be something in the nature of a reckless disregard of the spectator's safety. Like

Bolton v. *Stone*, the cricket ball case (see p. 192), the court's view was no doubt influenced by the fact that riding is an establishment diversion.

MANSLAUGHTER (and other offences)

It seems that more doctors are being prosecuted for manslaughter these days. In 1992 two doctors were convicted at Nottingham Crown Court after prescribing a lethal cocktail of drugs to a heroin addict in police custody, some of the drugs in quantities up to five times the recommended maximum. In 1991 two junior hospital doctors were each given a nine-month suspended prison sentence at Birmingham Crown Court for the manslaughter of a 16-year-old with leukemia. He died after being wrongly injected in the spine with a cytotoxic drug that should have been injected intravenously. The verdict was quashed by the Court of Appeal on the ground that the jury should have been directed to decide whether the defendants were guilty of 'gross negligence', not merely of recklessness.

In July 1994 Dr Mahbabul Alam was given at Stafford Crown Court a nine-month suspended prison sentence for administering a grossly excessive, lethal pain-killing injection to a nine-year-old boy during a circumcision (the GMC later decided that it was a sufficient disciplinary penalty to suspend him for eight months).

In *R.* v. *Adomako* [1994] 3 WLR 288 the House of Lords, dismissing the defendant's appeal against conviction, said that the ingredients to be established to constitute the offence of involuntary manslaughter by breach of duty were the existence of the duty, breach of that duty which caused death, and gross negligence which the jury considered justified a criminal conviction. After the alarm had sounded during an operation at the Mayday Hospital in Croydon, the defendant anesthetist had failed to check the integrity of the endotracheal tube connection and the deceased had gone on to suffer a cardiac arrest. The court said that the test laid down in *R.* v. *Bateman* (1925) 19 Cr App R 8 and *Andrews* v. *DPP* [1937] AC 576 was correct.

In May 1994 at Cardiff Crown Court a GP, Dr Sinha, was acquitted of manslaughter after he had prescribed a lethally dangerous beta-blocker to an asthmatic. He maintained that he had not known the patient was asthmatic. However, he was sentenced to six months' imprisonment for doing an act tending to pervert the course of justice in that he had gone on to alter the computer records of the practice so as to delete earlier references to the asthmatic status of the patient. The Court of Appeal dismissed his appeal, on the ground that it was enough that his actions were likely to mislead the coroner's court (*The Times*, 13 July 1994).

Before leaving the criminal arena we may note that in September 1994 a Dr Gaud, who had been working in London hospitals assisting in heart and chest operations, was sent to prison for twelve months on the unusual criminal charge of causing a public nuisance, in that he had knowingly put patients at risk over a period of some three years by working when he knew he was infected with hepatitis B.

STOP PRESS

(Ref pp. 194–200). The Department of Health is to set up a special health authority concerned, *inter alia*, to impose minimum standards of risk management. A breach of such standards might, in time, be *prima facie* evidence of negligence.

(Ref p. 203). Dr Johnstone has just settled his claim for £5,000.

18 · Loss/injury: damage and causation

SUMMARY

Even given a duty of care and a breach of it, the plaintiff has to show that he has suffered some actual damage (though it may be no more than an increased vulnerability); that the damage is of a sort recognised by the law in the context in which it has arisen (e.g. economic loss is only claimable when it accompanies physical injury or arises out of a particular relationship); that it is the sort of damage that was foreseeable (though the fact that its extent is greater than was foreseeable due to the special sensitivities of the plaintiff is no defence, nor is the fact that it arose in an unpredictable manner); and that it was, in the eyes of the law, caused by the negligent act of the defendant (it must not be 'too remote', which it will be if it was not reasonably foreseeable, or if some intervening act or event broke the chain of causation, or because the court as a matter of policy takes the view that the damage falls outside what justice requires the tortfeasor to be liable for).

A causative link has to be proved between the act of negligence and the injury suffered. A plaintiff may take advantage of the rule that any significant cause may be deemed to have caused the injury in law, and of the rule of evidence that where it is not known how an injury actually occurred, but it would not normally occur in that situation without some negligence, then the court may say that negligence is proved on the basis of *res ipsa loquitur*. It seemed at one time that a plaintiff who was denied treatment need only show that the defendants' omission to treat had resulted in his losing a chance or prospect of recovery, but that approach was condemned by the House of Lords.

INTRODUCTION

The plaintiff in a negligence action has to show that as a result of the defendant's negligence, i.e. breach of a duty of care owed to him, he has suffered damage. The damage may be physical (to person or property), mental or financial, but it must be:

(1) caused by the breach of duty: a patient who cannot show that an admitted act of negligence contributed to his present condition has not proved a causative link between the negligence and his injury;
(2) a type of damage which is recognised by the law: certain types of damage are not recognised by the law, at any rate if they stand alone, e.g. distress and disappointment, mental strain or nervous shock not amounting to a psychiatric disorder or illness.[1] Mere financial loss is not recoverable if it stands alone, i.e. not accompanied by any physical injury to person or property and did not arise in the context of a fiduciary or proximate relationship between the parties;[2] and
(3) it must come within the foreseeable area of risk created by the breach of duty. The damage will not be the subject of compensation, even if directly caused by the breach of duty, if it is of a completely different type or caused in a completely different way than that which was foreseeable.

All these matters are considered in detail below.

The different factors in negligence are not clearly separate from one another. They shade off into and overlap each other. A woman who loses wages looking after a lover who has gone to bed because the doctor wrongly and negligently told him he was ill and needed bed-rest may be told by the court that her claim cannot succeed because the doctor owed her no duty of care, or that she cannot recover for mere economic loss, or that the damage she suffered was too remote, or not foreseeable, or that it was not caused by the breach of duty because her decision to look after her friend broke the chain of causation; or the court may even, as a last resort, pray in aid public policy. As I have said earlier, in the end a claim that does not clearly come within the body of case law created by the courts in the past, i.e. a claim that presents a novel quality, will be accepted or rejected by the courts according to the judge's overall view as to whether it is appropriate that it should succeed or not (what has been called the 'judicial hunch'); and if the judge feels that the claim should not succeed he will hang his decision on one or other of the legal pegs that are available.

ACTUAL DAMAGE

The plaintiff has of course to show that he has suffered some damage (negligence is not actionable without proof of damage).

---

[1] See Chapter 20.
[2] See Chapter 19.

What amounts to injury in the context of the personal injury action was considered in *Church* v. *Ministry of Defence* (1984) 134 NLJ 263, where a worker in the Chatham docks sustained from the inhalation of asbestos dust symptomless pleural plaques in his lungs together with symptomless incipient fibrosis that could possibly develop into asbestosis and consequent anxiety when he realised what had happened. Pain J. said that there was a small risk that the plaintiff might go on to suffer further incapacity and it would be wrong in the light of current knowledge about the disease to disregard the plaques as not amounting to an injury in law. He also said that the anxiety alone was an actionable injury, but this must be wrong in view of the clear authority that mental states not amounting to psychiatric disorder and not accompanied by other actionable injury give no cause of action (see Chapter 20).

In *Sykes* v. *Ministry of Defence, The Times*, 23 March 1984, Otton J. found that such plaques, involving definite structural changes, even without the incipient fibrosis that Mr Church suffered, plus the risk of the onset of separate lung complaints amounted to actionable damage. (In any event increased vulnerability must surely amount to damage, for it gives rise to the chance of injury developing.)

Asymptomatic pleural changes in the form of pleural plaques and thickening plus anxiety about his condition falling short of nervous shock were 'actionable damage' for the purposes of an award to a plaintiff of provisional damages under s.32A of the Supreme Court Act 1981 (*Patterson* v. *Ministry of Defence* [1987] CLY 1194, *per* Simon Brown J.).

CAUSATION

The plaintiff has to prove that the breach of duty caused his injury. The issue of causation can raise notoriously difficult intellectual issues, e.g. as to what was the cause or an operative or significant cause of an accident, and in what circumstances the chain is broken, but on the whole the courts give pragmatic answers depending on their assessment of the factual situation.

Causation is to be understood as the man in the street, and not as either the scientist or the metaphysician would understand it. Cause here means what a . . . man would take to be the cause without too microscopic analysis but on a broad view (*per* Lord Wright in *Yorkshire Dale SS Co.* v. *Minister of War Transport* [1942] AC 691, 706).

However, what is the commonsense answer in any situation often admits of divergent views (see, for example, the varying views of the Law Lords about the cause of an accident when an unsafe roof fell on a miner in *Stapley* v. *Gypsum Mines Ltd* [1953] AC 663).

One example where there is no causative link between breach of duty and damage is when an employer, who is in breach of his duty to his employees in not providing safety helmets, is held not liable for head injuries suffered by one of them when it is shown that the employee would not have worn a helmet even if it had been provided for him (*McWilliams* v. *Sir William Arrol & Co.* [1962] 1 WLR 295; *Wigley* v. *British Vinegars Ltd* [1964] AC 307).

In the cases of *Meah* v. *McCreamer* [1985] 1 All ER 367 and (*No.2*) [1986] 1 All ER 943, where the plaintiff had suffered injuries from the negligent driving of the defendant, including a personality change that had led him to attack women as a result of which he was sent to prison, Woolf J. held that the imprisonment was within the area of causation of the original negligence but that the damages the plaintiff had to pay to his victims were not.

Medical cases

Causation is tremendously important in medical cases, and always needs careful consideration. This is because the etiology of medical conditions is often unclear and because the situation will often be complicated by the presence of an underlying illness or other pre-existing vulnerabilities. You may be delighted to get an expert report indicating obstetric negligence, but it is a far more difficult task to prove that that negligence caused or even materially contributed to the neonate's handicap. A delay in treating timeously a fracture or a laceration affecting the nerve in a limb may, on the balance of probabilities (i.e. more likely than not – a better than 50% chance), have made no difference to the eventual outcome. A not very experienced expert will need to be directed to the question of causation because, understandably, he may think that his job is merely to review the standard of medical care provided.

(Of course you may have in a particular case no problem with causation, i.e. it is clear that certain actions of the doctor caused the injury, but your difficulty lies in proving that he was negligent (e.g. he did not merely make an error of judgment that did not amount to negligence) in taking those actions – that is a different story.)

If failure to treat a patient made no difference because he would have died anyway his death is not caused by the negligence. Thus in *Barnett* v. *Chelsea and Kensington Hospital Management Committee* [1969] 1 QB 428 a casualty officer was negligent in not treating a night watchman who complained of vomiting after drinking tea. He later died of arsenic poisoning. His widow's claim failed on the ground that the workman would have died even if he had received all due care, because the judge concluded on the evidence that there was no chance that the only effective antidote could have been administered in time.

In *Robinson* v. *Post Office* [1974] 1 WLR 1176 a doctor was found to be negligent in not administering a test dose of an anti-tetanus serum before injecting it in a patient who had cut his leg. The patient was allergic and developed encephalitis which led to brain damage and paralysis. The Court of Appeal said that the question (on this issue) was whether the negligence of the doctor had 'caused or materially contributed' to the plaintiff's injury, and that the onus was on the plaintiff of proving on the balance of probabilities that it had. The Court of Appeal said that the judge had been right to conclude on the evidence before him that even if the test dose had been administered there would have been no observable reaction in the patient and that therefore the doctor would in any event have gone on to administer the injection. So the injury would have happened anyway.[3]

In *Hotson* v. *Fitzgerald* [1987] AC 750, the House of Lords denied compensation to an infant plaintiff on the basis that his injury would not on the balance of probabilities have benefited by the treatment which the defendants negligently failed to afford him (see below for a full discussion of that case).

Recent cases

The significance of causation in medical cases is indicated by the number of times it has been an issue in reported cases since the first edition of this book. In *Gregory* v. *Pembrokeshire Health Authority* [1989] 1 Med LR 81 the plaintiff was delivered of a child suffering from Down's syndrome. She alleged, correctly, that the consultant had been negligent in not telling her that the sample from her amniocentesis had not produced sufficient cultures to determine whether her child would suffer from Down's syndrome. She contended that, had she been so informed, she would have had the test repeated, the result would have been positive and she would have arranged for an abortion. The judge accepted that she could have obtained a legal abortion, but he concluded that she would have discussed the matter first

---

[3] The old case of *Rich* v. *Pierpoint* (1862) 3 F & F 35 was to similar effect: the wrongful administration of tartaric acid made no difference to the outcome: it 'turned out to be of no consequence'.

with the consultant and would as a result have accepted what would have been his advice, namely not to undergo a second amniocentesis (amniocentesis always carries a risk to the fetus; there was no reason to suspect at that time that something was actually amiss, and the statistical chance of chromosomal abnormality was one in 800). So the outcome would have been the same even had the defendants not been negligent; therefore the claim for the cost of raising the child failed. And the Court of Appeal saw no reason to criticise the judge's conclusion, arrived at on the evidence and his assessment of the witnesses, that the plaintiff would not have proceeded to a second amniocentesis.

Compare *Rance* v. *Mid-Downs Health Authority* [1991] 2 WLR 159; [1990] 2 Med LR 27: here a mother of a child born suffering from spina bifida alleged that the defendants should have discovered the defect in the fetus and she would then have had an abortion. Brooke J. said that, even if he were satisfied that negligence had been made out, any abortion would have had to take place when the gestational age was more than 27 weeks; this would have been a crime by virtue of the Infant Life (Preservation) Act 1929 because the child would then have been capable of being born alive; and a claim for damages which depended for its success on establishing a chain of causation which included the commission of a criminal offence could not be accepted by the court. So the situation was as if the mother had failed to prove that she would have proceeded to an abortion; so the outcome would have been the same. If the facts of this case were repeated at the present time the judge would not find that the proposed abortion would be a crime, thanks to s.37(1)(d) of the Human Fertilisation and Embryology Act 1990, which permits the termination of a pregnancy at any stage where there is a substantial risk that if the child were born it would be seriously handicapped.

In *Smith* v. *Barking, Havering and Brentwood Health Authority* [1994] 5 Med LR 285 the plaintiff proved that the defendants had been negligent in not warning her of the risks of a difficult operation on the cervical canal but failed in her claim for damages for serious injury suffered in the operation because the judge was satisfied that, even if warned, she would still have agreed to the operation as it was her only chance of avoiding the onset of tetraplegia.

Then there was the House of Lords decision in the *Wilsher* case, considered in detail below, where it was held that the plaintiff had failed to prove that his injury was due to negligence rather than to one or another of various other possible causes which did not involve negligence.

Causation also proved the stumbling block for the plaintiffs who sought to allege that the pertussis vaccine caused brain damage to their children (see *Loveday* v. *Renton* [1990] 1 Med LR 121 and pp. 440 and 452 below).

In the Australian case of *H.* v. *Royal Alexandra Hospital (NSW)* [1990] 1 Med LR 297 the plaintiff, a boy born in May 1973, established negligence by the hospital in not warning his parents of the risk of AIDS infection from the blood product that was used to treat his hemophilia in September 1983, but the court found that he had failed to establish that, given the appropriate warning, his parents would have refused the treatment. Similarly, even if the manufacturers of the product had been negligent in not giving such a warning to the doctors and hospitals to whom they supplied it, the judge's conclusion was that such a warning would not have affected the attitude of the doctors to the use of the product on this patient (a conclusion which was reinforced by, if not solely due to, the fact that the treating doctors were aware of the risks in any event).

In *Ellis* v. *Wallsend District Hospital* [1990] 2 Med LR 103 the New South Wales Court of Appeal held that where the patient's evidence was that if warned of the risks of an operation she would have declined it the trial judge was not at liberty to reject that evidence unless there was contrary evidence showing the plaintiff's contention to be 'inherently incredible' or 'inherently improbable'.

Sellers v. *Cooke and East Dorset Health Authority* [1990] 2 Med LR 13 and 16, CA is interesting: although the plaintiff succeeded in persuading the Court of Appeal that certain fresh evidence suggesting a negligent termination of her pregnancy could not reasonably have been obtained by her for the trial (which she had lost), the court went on to hold that, even if that evidence were to establish that her pregnancy had been negligently terminated, that would not have affected the outcome, because the judge had found that the fetus would probably not in any event have survived.[4]

In *Marsden* v. *Bateman* [1993] 4 Med LR 181 the plaintiff failed to establish that her brain damage was due to untreated neonatal hypoglycemia rather than a congenital condition.

In *Stockdale* v. *Nicholls* [1993] 4 Med LR 190 the claim failed because the judge held that earlier admission to hospital would

---

[4] Reference may also be made to *Vernon* v. *Bloomsbury Health Authority* (1986) where it was held that, even if the defendants had been negligent in not monitoring the plaintiff during her course of gentamycin for subacute bacterially negative endocarditis, the monitoring would have had no effect on the outcome as the probability was that no danger would have been revealed.

not have affected the outcome, in that the plaintiff would still have been admitted for observation only and the unavoidable and unpredictable onset of septicemia resulting in fitting and brain damage would have occurred in hospital at the same time and with the same results.

Causation will often be an insuperable obstacle in cancer cases (apart from one or two particular manifestations, such as testicular or cervical cancer). The disease, by and large, is usually unstoppable.

An interesting application of the principle is found in the cases concerning a surgeon's failure to warn of the risks of an operation or disclose other information. Even if he was in breach of his duty in not making a certain disclosure the patient has still to show that she suffered loss thereby. If the court concludes that the plaintiff has not proved on the balance of probabilities that she would have declined the operation, and so avoided the injury, she has not made out a case (*Smith*'s case (*supra*) is an example of this). In the specific context of failed sterilisation followed by pregnancy the woman has to show that she would have declined to be sterilised and taken some other prophylactic measure, perhaps a vasectomy for her husband. In one case the court accepted, after a failed vasectomy, that the couple would have realised earlier that the woman was pregnant and would have had an abortion, but by the time they did in fact realise she was pregnant it was too late for a termination (*Thake* v. *Maurice* [1986] QB 644; see also *Buchan* v. *Ortho Pharmaceutical* [1984] 8 DLR (4th) 373; and Chapter 25 below).

In the Scottish case of *Goorkani* v. *Tayside Health Board* [1991] 3 Med LR 33 the court said the doctor should have disclosed the risk of sterility from long-term ingestion of Chlorambucil but that the patient would in any event have accepted the risk as it was the only hope of saving his sight.

The Bolitho case

In *Bolitho* v.*City and Hackney Health Authority* [1993] 4 Med LR 381 the facts can be summarised in this way: a child was ill in hospital; it was agreed that it was negligent that during the night no doctor had responded to a call made by the night sister; it was agreed that, if a doctor had come and had intubated the child, the cardiac arrest and brain damage that he went on to suffer would have been avoided. One might think that the defendants would have paid up on these facts, but no. They chose to argue (successfully) that the plaintiff could not prove that if a doctor had come she would probably have intubated.

The plaintiff's expert said that it would have been mandatory to intubate; the defendants' expert said that he would not have intubated. The doctor who should have responded to the call from the sister (Dr Horn) said that she would not have intubated. Faced with this conflict of medical opinion the judge held that the plaintiff had not proved that the outcome would probably have been different if the doctor had responded to the nurse's call.

By a majority the Court of Appeal upheld this decision. Dillon L.J. said there were clearly two schools of thought about the need to intubate and there was no material which entitled the court to say that on the balance of probabilities the child would have been intubated if the nurse's call had been responded to, nor could it be shown that not to have intubated would have been negligent.

Simon Brown L.J., dissenting, said that causation issues were not to be decided according to some sort of application of the *Bolam* test, but by deciding what would probably have taken place if proper care had been given, and he boldly stated that, on the evidence, whatever the defendants' expert and the doctor on duty at the time might say in retrospect about what would, should or could properly have been done, the only reasonable inference was that any doctor who had responded to the nurse's call would, in the circumstances prevailing in the ward at the time, have intubated.

Unfortunately, this case has given rise to a lot of misunderstanding. There have been anguished cries to the effect that it applies the *Bolam* test to causation. Perhaps that is a correct statement, but so what? It is simply a matter of common sense that the plaintiff in such a situation has to prove either that the child would have been intubated or that it would have been negligent not to intubate. If a doctor had actually come but not intubated, the plaintiff would have had to prove that it had been mandatory to intubate. The question remains the same for the scenario where the doctor did not in fact come, except that then there was a second way in which the plaintiff could have succeeded, i.e. by proving that the doctor would in fact have intubated if she had come.

Confusion seems to have arisen in part because Farquharson L.J. is reported as saying that the plaintiff had to show both that Dr Horn would probably have intubated and also that if she had not done so that would have been negligent. That is obviously wrong, probably simply a misquotation. It would make no sort of sense. It would have been enough if the plaintiff could have shown either that Dr Horn would probably have intubated (only Simon Brown L.J. made a finding to that effect) or that it would have been mandatory to intubate (as Dillon L.J. said, the expert evidence for the defendants made that a difficult – if not an impossible – finding to make).

'Material contribution'

Any contribution to the injury which is not negligible (does not fall within the *de minimis* principle) may be taken to have 'materially contributed' to the injury (see *Bonnington Castings Ltd* v. *Wardlaw* [1956] AC 613 *per* Lord Reid, and *Clarkson* v. *Modern Foundries Ltd* [1958] 1 All ER 33).

In *Hotson* v. *Fitzgerald* [1987] AC 750, Lord Bridge said that the plaintiff had to prove that the delay in treatment was 'at least a material contributory cause' of his injury.

In *Murray* v. *Kensington and Chelsea and Westminster Area Health Authority*, 11 May 1981, CA, a baby's sight was lost due to excessive oxygen. The trial judge had found one incident only of negligence on the part of the doctors, namely in administering extra oxygen in the first thirty-six hours of life, but had found for the defendants nevertheless on the basis that it was not proved that it was that particular quantity of oxygen that had caused the injury, for it could have been caused by later doses in respect of which no negligence was found. The Court of Appeal upheld his decision. It seems hard on the plaintiff that the judges were not prepared to conclude on the evidence that the initial excess had probably made a material contribution to the injury.

In the Scottish case of *Kay* v. *Ayrshire and Arran Health Board* [1987] 2 All ER 417, HL, a child suffering from pneumococcal meningitis was negligently given three times the proper dose of penicillin. Liability was admitted for the short-term effects of convulsion and temporary paralysis, but denied in respect of the permanent deafness that later occurred. The House of Lords, confirming the Appeal Court's reversal of the trial judge's award of damages for the deafness, said that there was no evidence which would support a finding that the overdose caused the deafness or even materially increased the risk of its occurring. On the evidence the probability was that it was the original meningitis that caused the deafness.

In *Wilsher* v. *Essex Area Health Authority* [1988] AC 1074, where it was alleged that administration of excessive oxygen had caused neonatal blindness, the House of Lords was unanimously of the view that there had to be a retrial for the simple enough reason that on the evidence there were a number of possible causes for the injury to the child and the judge had not at any time made any finding that excess oxygen was the actual cause, the effective cause or even the most likely cause (that omission seems to have been due to the judge's misunderstanding of part of the expert evidence). Had he made that finding his conclusion would have been unassailable. But he did not and so a retrial before another judge on the issue of causation was unavoidable (the attempt by the majority of the Court of Appeal to shore up the trial judgment was unacceptable to the House of Lords).[5]

Note also that the House of Lords judgments refuted the belief that the burden of (dis)proof shifts to the defendants where damage follows a failure to take a precaution which is designed to avoid such damage (see the next section and Chapter 23 under 'Burden of proof').

It was for a while thought that even if the plaintiff could not show that what was done materially contributed to his injury (because the state of medical knowledge at the time was not sufficiently advanced to demonstrate the connection), it was nevertheless enough if he showed that what was done materially increased the risk of injury. In those circumstances the court would be entitled to infer, as a matter of fact, that what was done did play a part in the causing of the injury:

It has often been said that the legal concept of causation is not based on logic or philosophy. It is based on the practical way in which the ordinary man's mind works in the everyday affairs of life. From a broad and practical viewpoint I can see no substantial difference between saying that what the defendant did materially increased the risk of injury to the plaintiff and saying that what the defendant did made a material contribution to his injury (*per* Lord Reid in *McGhee* v. *National Coal Board* [1973] 1 WLR 1, 5).

This principle was extended by a majority of the Court of Appeal in *Wilsher* v. *Essex Area Health Authority* [1987] QB 730, where the fact that the administering of an excess of oxygen was only one of the possible causes of loss of sight in a neonate did not preclude the court from attributing the injury to that cause. The principle was also applied in *Bryce* v. *Swan Hunter Group plc, The Times*, 19 February 1987, and *Fitzgerald* v. *Lane* [1987] 3 WLR 249. However, it is now clear from the judgment in the House of Lords in the *Wilsher* case that the interpretation put upon Lord Reid's words in the *McGhee* case was misconceived and that that case added nothing to the traditional rules on causation: it is up to the plaintiff to show on the balance of probabilities that the act or omission complained of caused or materially contributed to his injury (see below for further discussion of *Wilsher*).

---

[5] There was in fact no retrial as an amicable settlement was reached about the end of 1990 under which a proportion of the total damages claimed was paid to the plaintiff.

Failure to take precaution

It was for a while thought that where a failure to take a precaution was followed by the very damage which that precaution is designed to prevent, the court is entitled to conclude, in the absence of an explanation from the defendant, that such failure caused the injury (*per* Pain J. in *Clark* v. *MacLennan* [1983] 1 All ER 416). It is now clear from the House of Lords decision in the *Wilsher* case that that is not good law, at any rate not where there are a number of possible causes. It may still be arguable where no competing cause is present (though in that case the inference as to causation would probably be drawn anyway without recourse to any special principle).[6] It will in any event be appreciated how these various principles of causation overlap into the evidential arena and that of burden of proof and *res ipsa loquitur*. All these can be used in the appropriate case to force the conclusion that the patient's injury must be taken to have been in law caused by the breach of duty (see Chapter 23).

LOSS OF THE CHANCE OF RECOVERY

It seemed at one time (from March 1985 to July 1987) that the law was developing an interesting and important new doctrine, whereby a patient could recover a proportion of full compensation for his injury where he could do no more than show that there was a less than 50% chance, quantifiable as a percentage, that a proven or admitted negligent act or omission on the part of the medical staff had been responsible for him being in a worse condition than he would have been had the negligence not taken place. As a corollary it appeared that if the chance was, say 80% he should have 80% of his damages. But that approach has now (and certainly not to my surprise) been condemned by the House of Lords.

SUMMARY

The House of Lords held that, unless the judge concludes on the balance of probabilities, i.e. discerns a better than even chance, that negligently withheld treatment would have in fact benefited the patient, then the patient has not shown the necessary causative link between the defendants' negligence and injury suffered by him. In so holding the court overruled the Court of Appeal.

---

[6] Peter Pain J. was the trial judge in both *Clark* v. *MacLennan* and *Wilsher*.

What follows is a discussion of the arguments and decisions that led to the restatement by the House of Lords of the traditional approach to causation and loss.

We have long been familiar in various contexts with the assessment of chance by the courts. The model who is deprived in breach of contract by the impresario of her opportunity to compete in an audition will receive damages commensurate with the chance of success that she has lost (*Chaplin* v. *Hicks* [1911] 2 KB 786). The solicitor who fails to issue the writ in time will pay damages to compensate for the chance of success he has deprived his client of, and unless the court is satisfied that the claim was bound to fail something more than nominal damages will be awarded, proportionate to the court's view of the chances of success (*Kitchen* v. *Royal Air Forces Association* [1958] 1 WLR 563). In *Gascoine* v. *Ian Sheridan and Co.* [1994] 5 Med LR 437, a claim in respect of admitted culpable delay by the patient's legal advisers in processing a medical negligence action years before, the judge assessed the chance of success in the original action at 60%, and so 60% of the total damages was recoverable. The widow in a Fatal Accidents Act claim will be awarded compensation in proportion to the chances she had of financial support from the deceased; this applies even where she was separated from him at the time of his death but can show some significant possibility that they would have been reconciled (*Davies* v. *Taylor* [1974] AC 207; *Mallett* v. *McGonagle* [1969] 2 WLR 767). In your run-of-the-mill personal injury action a percentage chance (often as little even as 10%) of some further injury arising in the future (e.g., as so often, osteo-arthritis developing in an injured joint) will be assessed and a suitable addition made to the award.

But apart from the context of fatal accident claims, and claims in contract (and possibly also in negligence) for loss of the opportunity to go for a prize or an award, the courts have made it clear without exception that it has to be proved on a balance of probabilities that the injury complained of was caused by the negligence. Thousands of cases have been decided on this principle, including *Barnett* and *Robinson* and *McGhee* (*supra*). In *Sykes* v. *Midland Bank Executor* [1971] 1 QB 113 the Court of Appeal would not accept that clients who entered into an underlease after negligent advice from their solicitors could recover damages in proportion to the chance, as assessed by the court, that they would not have signed the underlease had they been properly advised. The court's task was to decide whether or not on the balance of probabilities the plaintiffs had shown that they would not have signed if properly advised:

[Counsel for the plaintiffs] contended that, even if it were probable that the plaintiffs, if properly advised, would have executed the underlease, yet if there were a chance, however slim, that they would not have done so, the plaintiffs were entitled to some damages for the loss of that chance. I cannot accept that proposition, attractively though it was put. It would lead to the strange result that, unless the defendants could prove with certainty that they had not caused damage, they would be liable for the remote chance that they had done so. This seems to me to turn the onus of proof on its head. In my view, the plaintiffs cannot succeed unless they can prove that the negligence was probably a cause of their executing the underleases. Since they failed to do so, their claim does not get off the ground (*per* Salmon L.J. *ibid*. p. 129).

This seemed no more than the exposition, in pellucid language, of a principle of law that had been operative since time immemorial. No-one had ever suggested in a case such as a claim by a workman for injury suffered through not being provided with a safety helmet that the court should assess the percentage chance that he would have worn it and award him that percentage of full damages. The judge would simply say whether or not he found on the balance of probabilities that the workman would have worn the hat if it had been provided. Similarly no-one in the cases about the surgeon's failure to warn of the risks inherent in an operation (as to which see below p. 305 *et seq*.) has ever suggested that the chance should be assessed of whether or not the patient would have accepted the treatment if he had been warned and that he should be awarded a proportion of his damages commensurate with that assessment. The judge has simply stated whether or not he was satisfied that the patient would have declined the treatment. To suggest, as we shall see has been done, that the lost opportunity cases (lost opportunity to qualify in an audition, lost opportunity to bring an action against a tortfeasor) show that the chance that an injury has been suffered is to be assessed on a proportionate basis is quite untenable and ignores several thousand precedents.

The novel concept of awarding damages in tort for loss of a chance that something would have been other than it was may have been hovering on the fringes of consciousness, shyly seeking to be admitted to the light of judicial awareness for some time. But apart from the particular contexts of fatal accident claims and solicitors' negligence we first find it in *Clark* v. *MacLennan* [1983] 1 All ER 416. There Pain J. found that the defendants were in breach of their duty in performing a certain operation prematurely and that if it had been performed at the right time the patient would have stood a two in three chance of avoiding the injury. But instead of saying that she had proved on the balance of probabilities that her injury was caused by the breach of duty he awarded her two thirds of full damages.

The *Hotson* case

The facts in the important case of *Hotson* v. *Fitzgerald* [1987] 2 WLR 287, CA; [1987] AC 750, HL, can be simply stated. The defendant physician failed to treat the plaintiff at the proper time. The plaintiff developed a disability. The evidence established that even if he had been properly treated he would still probably (three to one) have contracted the disability. The defendant said that therefore the plaintiff had not proved on the balance of probabilities that the failure to treat had caused the injury. The plaintiff said that he had been deprived of the chance of recovery and should therefore receive one-quarter of full compensation for his injury.

The traditional way to deal with this would have been for the court to say that as the plaintiff had not proved, on the balance of probabilities, that the treatment would have avoided the injury, loss was not proved. For the plaintiff to say 'Well, it might have, so I want a proportion of full damages' was a novel plea. But it was accepted. Simon Brown J. said that the issue was one of quantification rather than liability. Just as the solicitor's client is compensated for the lost chance of succeeding in an action against a tortfeasor, so the patient should be compensated for the lost chance of recovery, provided that chance was more than minimal. He declined to follow *Kenyon* v. *Bell* 1953 SC 125, a Scottish interlocutory decision at first instance where Lord Guthrie had refused to allow a claim for the loss of a chance of saving an eye.

In the Court of Appeal this decision was upheld unanimously. The Master of the Rolls said that there was no scope for assessing the chance of there having been a duty of care or a breach of that duty; those elements had to be proved on the balance of probability in the usual way. They related to past events, and there the court did indeed take the view that if something was shown to have had over 50% likelihood of having happened then it was taken to have happened. But when one was dealing with future happenings (which obviously includes hypothetical happenings, i.e. what would have happened as well as what will happen) the position was different:

. . . it is unjust that there should be no liability for failure to treat a patient, simply because the chances of a successful cure by that treatment were less than 50%. Nor by the same token can it be just that if the chances of a successful cure only marginally exceed 50%, the doctor or his employer should be liable to the same extent as if the treatment could be guaranteed to cure. If this is the law, it is high time that it was changed, assuming that this court has power to do so . . . .

. . . there is no room in justice or law for holding a defendant liable on the basis that he may have been subject to a duty. Either he was or he was not . . .

there is no room in justice or law for holding a defendant liable on the basis that there is a significant possibility, not amounting to a probability that he was in breach of this duty . . . .

. . . the essence of the plaintiff's claim is that he has lost any *benefit* which he would have derived from [timely treatment].

The Master of the Rolls said that this benefit sounded in damages, subject to proper evaluation. The categories of loss were never closed, and it was not only financial or physical injury that were fit subjects for compensation.

This was a new development. If plaintiffs were to be compensated for the chance that they might have suffered injury as a result of a proven or admitted breach of duty, extensive possibilities would be opened up. In the workman's helmet type case and the failure to warn case were we to expect the chances to be evaluated of the helmet having been worn if provided, and also the chance of its having warded off the injury if worn, and of the operation having been declined if the information had been given? And was it only in those cases where expert evidence was directed to establishing percentages that the court would apply the percentage assessment basis? The development needed careful watching. In proof of which read on.

The insurance cases

Consider the decision of the Court of Appeal in *Dunbar* v. *A. & B. Painters Ltd, The Times*, 14 March 1986: the insured party sued his brokers, whose negligent misrepresentation to the insurers had voided the policy. On a quite different ground (because the employee had fallen from a height above the 40-foot maximum covered by the policy) the insurers would have been entitled to refuse to indemnify the insured in any event. The employee recovered against the employer (the insured party). The question was whether the negligent brokers should reimburse the employer in full. The brokers argued that if there was, say, a 30% chance that the insurers would have repudiated the policy in any event they should be relieved of liability *pro tanto*. The employers said that the correct approach was to ascertain whether on the balance of probabilities the insurers would have repudiated the contract and if the answer was in the negative the brokers should reimburse them, the employers, in full. The Court of Appeal disagreed: the correct approach was not to ask if on the balance of probabilities the insurers would in fact have refused to indemnify on the 'height' ground, but to assess the chance that they would have refused and award proportionate damages. They said the judge had probably adopted the 'probability' test, but in the event it did not make any difference because he had in any case effectively assessed that chance at nil. Therefore, his decision to award full damages against the brokers, whether on a 'probability' basis or an 'assessment of chance' basis was appropriate.

This seems to take the principle of chance too far, and to run completely contrary to the reasoning in *Sykes* (see above). The court misread (deliberately?) the similar earlier case of *Fraser* v. *B.N. Furman Productions Ltd* [1967] 1 WLR 898. In that case there is nothing to suggest the Court of Appeal was there saying that the chance of the insurers repudiating the policy had to be evaluated in order for proportionate damages to be assessed. They were saying merely that the fact that the insurers would have had a right to repudiate the policy did not necessarily mean that the insured failed in his claim against the brokers, for the chance of that repudiation had to be considered to see if on the balance of probabilities repudiation would have taken place or not, *not* to see precisely what the chances were with a view to awarding proportionate damages.

The percentage approach continued

Another aspect of the percentage approach appears from the case of *Bagley* v. *North Herts Health Authority* (1986) 136 NLJ 1014, where Simon Brown J., true to his reasoning in the *Hotson* case, having found that a hospital had been negligent in not carrying out blood tests on a mother, as a result of which she gave birth to a stillborn child, knocked 5% off the damages awarded because, even had the hospital acted properly, there would still have been a 5% chance that the child would not have lived! This sort of discount was entirely unorthodox and would not have occurred to anybody a few years ago.[7]

The House of Lords decision in the *Hotson* case

This can be summarised very simply. The judge's conclusion that there was only a 25% chance that any treatment would have been beneficial, i.e. would have prevented the necrosis, was equivalent to a finding that the plaintiff had not proved on the balance of probabilities that the defendants' admitted negligence had caused the necrosis. And, therefore, said the Law Lords with complete unanimity, he could not succeed in his claim.

---

[7] In fact, I understand that the parties had already agreed a 5% discount, something which does not emerge from the House of Lords judgments in *Hotson*.

The distinction was emphasised between assessing the chance of a future hypothetical event occurring and the question whether at a particular time in the past treatment would have benefited that particular injury. That question was to be answered by deciding first as a matter of fact and in the usual way what was the condition of the plaintiff when he arrived at the hospital. In this particular case that question could be framed as: had the blood vessels running along his leg been injured to such an extent that necrosis was in any event inevitable? Clearly, said the court, the judge's findings that there was only a one in four chance that treatment would have prevented the necrosis meant that he had concluded on the balance of probabilities that the plaintiff's condition on arrival at hospital was such that treatment would not have benefited him.

Unless the plaintiff proved on the balance of probabilities that the delayed treatment was at least a material contributory cause of the avascular necrosis he failed on the issue of causation and no question of quantification could arise (per Lord Bridge).

Just as failure to get over the 'probability' hurdle meant total failure for the plaintiff, so, once over it, there was no principle of English law, said Lord Bridge, to entitle the defendants to a discount if there remained some chance that the treatment would not have prevented necrosis. It followed therefore, as Lord Ackner pointed out, that the 5% deduction referred to above given to a defendant by Simon Brown J. in *Bagley* v. *North Herts Health Authority* (*supra*) was clearly wrong. That was 'a wholly new doctrine which has no support in principle or authority and would give rise to many complications in the search for mathematical or statistical exactitude' (see footnote 7 above). And Lord Ackner said that, unless there is some special situation, there is no point or purpose in expressing in percentage terms the certainty or near certainty which the plaintiff had achieved in establishing his cause of action. Lord Mackay said that a judge deciding disputed questions of fact would not ordinarily do it by use of a calculator.

The court did not rule out the possibility of suing for loss of the chance of benefit in an appropriate case, but no help was given towards the delineation of what was an appropriate case. Lord Bridge was content to say that the analogy between the instant case and the solicitors' negligence cases as well as the cases concerning loss of a chance to secure an appointment, although superficially attractive, was very difficult to accept. Lord Mackay said that unless and until the House of Lords departed from the decision in *McGhee*'s case it was not possible to say that in no circumstances could evidence of a loss of a chance resulting from the breach of a duty of care found a successful claim for damages.

Lord Ackner pointed out that in the solicitor's negligence case the court has to put a value on an asset that has some value, namely the action that could have been brought. He said that not only actions that are bound to succeed have a value, for every action with any prospect of success has some value (we may agree, adding that at the very least it has a nuisance value, such as might provoke an offer); but, said Lord Ackner, the plaintiff in the instant case was not entitled to any damages in respect of the deformed hip because the judge had decided that this was not caused by the admitted breach by the defendants of their duty of care, but by the original accident that brought him to their hospital.

A good example of the 'correct' approach is *Gregory* v. *Pembrokeshire Health Authority* [1989] 1 Med LR 81 (see above at p. 213), where Rougier J. said that there was no question of assessing the chances that the plaintiff, had she been properly advised, would have proceeded via a second test to an abortion – he had simply to decide on the evidence whether on the balance of probabilities she would or would not.

BREAKING THE CHAIN OF CAUSATION

SUMMARY

An intervening act or event occurring after the original act of negligence may operate to break the chain of causation, with the result that the wrongdoer is not liable for loss caused by that event. There is no clear test or formula for deciding whether an act, which may be of a third party or of the plaintiff himself, and may be lawful or unlawful, voluntary or involuntary, will break the chain of causation. The most useful test is to ask whether the act was reasonably foreseeable at the time of the original negligence, but that is not conclusive of the issue. The court will in any event judge each case on its own facts and decide the question according to its own view of whether justice requires the tortfeasor to compensate the plaintiff for the additional damage suffered from the intervening act.

We have already seen that the court will adjudge an effect too remote where it regards it as inappropriate that the wrongdoer should be made liable in respect of it. In such cases it may be said that the effect is not to be regarded in law as having been caused by the original negligence. This may be so even though the effect appears to be both directly and foreseeably caused by the negligence, without any intervening act that could be said to have broken the chain of causation. Where however there is such an intervening act, whether of human agency, lawful or unlawful, voluntary or involuntary, or whether of a third party or of the plaintiff himself, or whether it be an event which is not of human origination, the court is free, if it chooses, to say that the intervening act, which in the case of a third party's act and sometimes in the case of the plaintiff is described by the Latin tag of *novus actus interveniens* (an independent supervening act), breaks the chain of causation, so that the damage flowing from it cannot be regarded in law as having been caused by the original negligence.

However, it is by no means easy to predict when such an intervening act will be regarded as breaking the chain of causation. At times the test applied seems to have been whether the intervening act was reasonable in the circumstances, but currently the question seems to turn on foreseeability, though that is not necessarily conclusive of the issue. Was it reasonably foreseeable that the intervening act would occur? On that basis the courts have several times ruled on a wrongdoer's liability for the criminal acts of third parties (*Stansbie* v. *Troman* [1948] 2 KB 48; *Lamb* v. *Camden London Borough Council* [1981] QB 625; *Ward* v. *Cannock Chase District Council* [1985] 3 All ER 537; *P. Perl (Exporters) Ltd* v. *Camden London Borough Council* [1984] QB 342; *King* v. *Liverpool City Council* [1986] 1 WLR 890, CA; *Smith* v. *Littlewoods Organisation Ltd* [1987] 2 WLR 480).

Lord Reid said in *Dorset Yacht Co.* v. *Home Office* [1970] AC 1004 that for a *novus actus* not to break the chain of causation it would have to be an act which was likely or probable to happen; but Lord Denning and Watkins L.J. took a contrary view in *Lamb*'s case (*supra*), where a judicious mix of 'reasonable foreseeability' and 'policy' was applied to deny recovery. Watkins L.J. said that a robust and sensible approach to the question of remoteness would often produce an instinctive feeling that the event or act being weighed in the balance was too remote to sound in damages (this is the 'judicial hunch' or 'gut reaction' that I have referred to from time to time). Lord Denning said:

. . . it is not every consequence of a wrongful act which is the subject of compensation. The law has to draw a line somewhere. Sometimes it is done by limiting the range of persons to whom duty is owed. Sometimes it is done by saying that there is a break in the chain of causation. At other times it is done by saying that the consequence is too remote to be a head of damage. All these devices are useful in their way. But ultimately it is a question of policy for the judges to decide . . . .

It seems to me that it is a question of policy which we, as judges, have to decide. The time has come when, in cases of new import, we should decide them according to the reason of the thing. In previous times, when faced with a new problem, the judges have not openly asked themselves the question: what is the best policy for the law to adopt? But the question has always been there in the background. It has been concealed behind such questions as: Was the defendant under any duty to the plaintiff? Was the relationship between them sufficiently proximate? Was the injury direct or indirect? Was it foreseeable or not? Was it too remote? and so forth. Nowadays we direct ourselves to considerations of policy.

But the guidelines of foreseeability, remoteness etc., must still serve a purpose. Policy is an unruly and unpredictable steed. It may tip the balance in many cases, but if it is the only criterion the law becomes fearfully uncertain, and depends only on the view of the particular tribunal. It is still necessary and appropriate for cases to be argued on the lines of the law as set out in the precedents, as far as the legal principles can be gleaned therefrom, and even if that is not very far it is better than nothing.

Where an injury is subsumed into a later injury (e.g. a broken leg is then severed in a later accident) the original tortfeasor remains liable for the damage he did, and cannot take advantage of the later event to reduce his liability (*Baker* v. *Willoughby* [1970] AC 467); but a supervening serious illness which was unconnected with the accident and which was already dormant within the plaintiff at the time of the accident will go to reduce the damages payable (*Jobling* v. *Associated Dairies* [1982] AC 794). If a car is already damaged so that a wing needs respraying, a defendant who crashes into that wing cannot be held liable for the cost of the respraying, only for any extra cost he puts the owner to (*Performance Cars Ltd* v. *Abraham* [1962] 1 QB 33).

This issue of supervening cause, like all aspects of causation, is a fruitful source of academic disputation, and for the practitioner admits of no easy formula. Lord Wilberforce said in *Jobling*'s case (*supra*) that no general, logical, or universally fair rules could be stated, which would cover, in a manner consistent with justice, cases of supervening events, whether due to tortious, partially tortious, non-culpable or wholly accidental events. The courts could only deal with each case as best they could to provide just but not excessive compensation.

In *Hogan* v. *Bentinck West Hartley Collieries Ltd* [1949] 1 All ER 588, where an injury at work to a workman's thumb was followed by an ill-advised amputation of the thumb, it was held by a bare majority in the House of Lords that that unreasonable operation broke the chain of causation (Lord Simonds said that the question of *novus actus* could only be answered on a consideration of all the circumstances and, in particular, the quality of the later act or event).

In the Australian case of *Martin* v. *Isbard* (1947) 48 WALR 52, where after being involved in an accident the plaintiff contracted an anxiety and litigation neurosis because she was wrongly told by her doctor that she had suffered a fracture of the skull, it was held that the advice given by the doctor broke the chain of causation as it was a *novus actus*.

It was held in *Robinson* v. *Post Office* [1974] 1 WLR 1176 that where the Post Office had through their original negligence caused the minor leg injury of their employee, the plaintiff, the doctor's negligence in failing to administer a test dose before injecting with an anti-tetanus serum did not break the chain of causation. They had to take the plaintiff as they found him, which included his allergy to the anti-tetanus serum.

Where the act is that of the plaintiff himself a number of other factors come into play. If that act is so unreasonable as to eclipse the defendant's wrongdoing, then it will have broken the chain of causation and the defendant will not be liable for the ensuing damage. An odd example of this is the South African case of *Alston* v. *Marine and Trade Insurance Co. Ltd* 1964 (4) SA 112, where the fact that the plaintiff, who had suffered brain injury in a motor accident, ate cheese while on a certain drug and as a result suffered a stroke, was held to break the chain of causation even though the plaintiff could not have known it was dangerous to do that.

An example of a case where the conduct of the plaintiff did not break the chain of causation is *Emeh* v. *Kensington and Chelsea and Westminster Area Health Authority* [1985] QB 1012, where the Court of Appeal in no uncertain terms reversed the trial judge's finding that the refusal of an abortion by a woman who had become pregnant after a negligently performed sterilisation was so unreasonable an act that it eclipsed the original negligence.

Another principle that falls to be considered in this context is the rule that a plaintiff is under a duty to take reasonable steps to minimise his loss; if those steps include submitting to medical examination and accepting medical treatment, then failure so to do will go to reduce the award (*Selvanayagam* v. *University of West Indies* [1983] 1 WLR 585).

A common dual liability situation for a patient's claim is where the original accident, whether road traffic, or employment or whatever, is mistreated at hospital. Are both parties liable for the full damage or is the original tortfeasor liable only for the extent of injury that would have resulted from proper medical care? I doubt that a court would hold, save in an exceptional case, that the medical negligence broke the chain of causation. More likely, it would simply apportion the damages as between the two defendants in such proportion as it considered was merited by their respective fault. The widow of the actor and comedian, Roy Kinnear, obtained £650,000 from the film company that was responsible for the fatal injury he sustained when he fell from a horse while filming in Spain. Some time later Hidden J. ordered the Spanish hospital to pay 60% of the damages for failing to treat the injury properly (reported in *The Times* for 22 December 1994).

CONTRIBUTORY NEGLIGENCE

Where some blameworthiness attaches to the plaintiff's conduct, in that he has shown a failure to take proper care for his own safety, the matter can be dealt with by a proportionate reduction in the award on the principle of contributory negligence. That is not very likely to arise in medical negligence cases, but an example is *Brushett* v. *Cowan* [1991] 2 Med LR 271, where the Newfoundland Court of Appeal held that the plaintiff, who was a registered nursing assistant with some experience in orthopedics, was 50% to blame for her injury when she fell while using crutches and broke her leg, because she had failed to seek instructions regarding the proper use of the crutches. Or a patient may be held negligent for failing to report to his GP when the hospital had advised him to do so. In the end it is simply a matter of common sense whether the patient has been irresponsible in regard to his own health and safety.

19 · Loss/injury: economic loss

SUMMARY

Mere economic loss, i.e. economic loss that is not consequent upon physical damage to person or property or the threat of it, is as a general rule not recoverable in tort, as opposed to contract. It is, however, recoverable when it arises from careless statements, provided there is a duty in the circumstances on the person making the statement to take care; that duty will arise in the context of a fiduciary relationship. Recovery is also permitted where there is a sufficient relationship of proximity between the parties to permit the court to infer that the defendant voluntarily assumed a duty of care in respect of the alleged negligent activity; but it is impossible to formulate any sort of test or even suggest guidelines for deciding whether the necessary proximity exists in a particular situation, because the courts have only just created this new concept and as yet it is hardly more than embryonic, or at any rate 'sent into this breathing world scarce half made up'. Apart from these contexts a line will be drawn by the court as a matter of policy to prevent recovery for economic loss that does not flow from, i.e. is not consequent upon, some physical damage or the threat of it.

There has never been any problem in compensating for financial loss where it accompanies injury to person or property. If your car is damaged you can hire another pending repair; if you are injured you can recover lost earnings. Nor has there been any difficulty in permitting recovery for economic loss consequent upon breach of contract. But, as regards liability in tort, carelessness, whether in act or word, which gives rise to foreseeable economic loss only is a different matter. 'The reluctance to grant a remedy for the careless invasion of financial or pecuniary interests is long-standing, deep-rooted and not unreasonable' (*per* Professor Heuston). The court might declare that there was no duty of care, as where a large supermarket setting up next door to a small competitor puts the latter out of business; or that the damage was too remote, or that public policy drew the line at recovery in respect of the loss claimed, or simply that mere economic loss was not recoverable.

I think the question of recovering economic loss is one of policy. Whenever the courts draw a line to mark out the bounds of 'duty' they do it as a matter of policy so as to limit the responsibility of the defendant. Whenever the courts set bounds to the 'damages' recoverable – saying that they are, or are not, too remote, they do it as a matter of policy so as to limit the liability of the defendants (per Lord Denning M.R. in Spartan Steel & Alloys Ltd v. Martin & Co. (Contractors) Ltd [1973] 1 QB 27, 36).

THE 'ELECTRICITY' CASES

However, when the economic loss is consequent upon physical injury it is usually recoverable. Thus in SCM (United Kingdom) Ltd v. W.J. Whittall & Son Ltd [1971] 1 QB 137 defendants who negligently cut off the electricity supply to the plaintiffs' factory were held liable by the Court of Appeal for the loss of profit which resulted from the solidifying in the furnaces of molten metals, because it stemmed from the damage to furnace and metal, but not for further economic loss which was said to be too remote. Lord Denning said that recovery for mere economic loss was not usually permitted by the law, on the ground of public policy, rather than by the operation of any logical principle; and Winn L.J. said that, apart from the special case of liability for negligently uttered false statements, there was no liability for negligent unintentional infliction of any form of economic loss which was not itself consequential upon foreseeable physical injury or damage to property.

In the similar Spartan Steels case (supra) the defendants negligently damaged the electric cable supplying the plaintiffs' factory, who had therefore to pour molten metal out of their furnaces, for otherwise it would have solidified and damaged the furnaces. They lost part of the value of the metal and their profit on its resale. In addition they claimed for loss of profit on the four further melts they could have performed in the time the power was off. Though they succeeded at first instance the Court of Appeal would not permit recovery in respect of the four melts, on the basis that whereas loss of profit on the metal that was poured out was consequential on the physical damage to that metal and the risk of damage to the furnaces, loss of profit on the four hypothetical melts was mere economic damage not consequent upon the physical damage or the risk of physical damage. Lord Denning said that the more he thought about the subject of recovery for economic loss the more difficult he found it to put each case into its proper pigeonhole:

Sometimes I say: 'There was no duty'. In others I say: 'The damage was too remote'. So much so that I think the time has come to discard those tests which have proved so elusive. It seems to me better to consider the particular relationship in hand, and see whether or not, as a matter of policy, economic loss should be recoverable or not.

In truth, as Edmund Davies L.J. pointed out in a strong dissenting judgment, there was no logical distinction between the two losses. It must simply be seen as a matter of policy that the court insisted on drawing a line to the defendants' liability.[1]

For a time, beginning with the decision of the House of Lords in *Anns* v. *Merton London Borough Council* [1978] AC 728, it seemed that economic loss which was foreseeable should be recoverable, as any other loss, unless there were policy considerations in the particular case militating against such recovery. We have already seen (in Chapter 15) how this general formulation was later whittled down by the courts; the context in which it was proposed, the liability of local authority inspectors for certifying defective foundations, was itself reduced to the situation where physical damage was created or threatened; and then the very decision itself, imposing liability for economic loss in these circumstances, was declared misconceived because the court in 1978 had failed to recognise that the damage for which it was permitting compensation was mere economic loss and to do that was to introduce a wholly new and unsuitable extension to the law (see further below on this).

In *Junior Books* v. *Veitchi* [1983] 1 AC 520 the House of Lords held that, assuming the facts pleaded were true, subcontractors who laid a defective floor would be liable to the plaintiff occupiers of the building for the cost of repair and certain financial loss flowing therefrom. This was despite the fact that there was neither a contractual nexus between the parties nor any physical damage or threat of it to the building. It was said that where there was a sufficient relationship of proximity between the parties the duty of care extended to the duty not to inflict carelessly economic loss (Lord Roskill said that the defendants, as subcontractors, were in almost as close a commercial relationship with the plaintiff as it was possible to envisage short of privity of contract).

---

[1] Economic loss can be recovered where it is claimed as part of a claim which originates in a claim for physical damage (*The Kapetan Georgis* [1988] FTLR 180).

An example where at first mere economic and then later added physical damage was sustained and the court drew a distinction between the two losses so as to find a cause of action only in respect of the second loss is *Nitrigin Eireann Teoranta* v. *Inco Alloys Ltd*, *The Times*, 4 November 1991.

Lord Brandon dissented, saying that to impose liability would be to create obligations appropriate only to a contractual relationship, and that the authorities made it clear that in the absence of physical damage or the threat of it mere economic loss was not recoverable.

RETRENCHMENT

Recovery for mere economic loss was denied in shipping contexts – by the Court of Appeal in *Leigh and Sillivan* v. *Aliakmon Shipping Co.* [1985] QB 350, where buyers sued ship-owners in contract and tort for damage to goods caused by bad stowage; and by the House of Lords in *Candlewood Corporation* v. *Mitsui Ltd* [1986] AC 1, involving a time charterer's claim for financial loss. In *Muirhead* v. *Industrial Tank Specialities* [1986] QB 507, the Court of Appeal rejected a claim for mere economic loss by the user against the manufacturer of lobster tanks. It was said that there was not a sufficiently close relationship between the two for such a duty to arise; there had to be such a very close proximity of relationship between the parties and reliance by the plaintiff on the defendant that the defendant was to be taken voluntarily to have assumed direct responsibility to the plaintiff.[2]

Then came the House of Lords' decision in *Caparo Industries plc* v. *Dickman* [1990] 2 AC 605, where it was held that auditors of a company owed no duty of care not to inflict economic loss on shareholders or potential investors who relied on the audit in deciding whether to invest (further) in the company (Millett J. had already held in July 1989 in *Al Saudi Banque* v. *Clarke Pixley* [1990] Ch 313 that no duty was owed in similar circumstances to creditors of a company). In the *Caparo* case the court said that liability for economic loss due to negligent misstatement was confined to cases where the statement or advice had been given to a known recipient for a specific purpose of which the maker was aware and on which the recipient had relied and on which he had acted to his detriment. As the auditors had no reason to think that their report would go to the plaintiff, let alone that it would be relied on by them in deciding whether to invest (further) in the company, there was no sufficient proximity between them and the plaintiffs to found a duty of care (see also Chapter 15 under 'The Duty Not To Make Careless Statements' for further cases).

The decisions of the House of Lords in July 1990 in *Murphy* v. *Brentwood District Council* and *Department of the Environment*

---

[2] See also *Virgo Steamship Co.* v. *Skaarup Shipping Corporation* [1988] 1 Lloyd's Rep 352.

v. *Thomas Bates and Son* [1991] 1 AC 499 concerned liability for economic loss caused not by misstatement but by negligent conduct. The House of Lords made it clear that, as presently constituted, they shared the disquiet that had been voiced increasingly in the last five years or so about the wholesale extension of the law of negligence, in cases where no physical injury had been sustained, that was inherent in and threatening to develop as a logical outcome from the 1978 decision of the House of Lords (as then constituted) in *Anns* v. *Merton London Borough Council* [1978] AC 728. In our present context the point to note is that the court made it clear that there can be no general formula for establishing when mere economic loss is recoverable – one can only look to decided cases and see if one's own case falls more or less within the factual matrix of any case where liability has been imposed.

There is of course scope for the court to admit a new situation, for the categories of negligence are never closed, but it would need careful argument and the court would need to be convinced that policy and justice required that liability be imposed. A recent example of the court being so convinced is *Spring* v. *Guardian Assurance plc* [1994] 3 WLR 354, where the House of Lords held that an insurance company owed a duty of care to a former representative when providing him or prospective employers with a reference (the breach of duty was by way of careless statement and the damage purely economic).

COMMENT

In the absence of a special relationship of proximity and/or a voluntary assumption of risk (it is not clear what terminology to use – see, e.g. *Reid* v. *Rush & Tompkins Group* [1990] 1 WLR 212) there is no duty of care not to inflict mere economic loss. It may well be the case that it is almost impossible to establish such a relationship where the loss is caused by conduct or omission and not by misstatement. Note, to give the example of the most common situation, that a manufacturer of defective goods is not liable in tort to the eventual purchaser who suffers economic loss because, say, he loses business when his new computer fails. He will have a claim in contract against the shop where he bought it but no court, particularly in the present climate where retrenchment is the order of the day, is going to hold that the purchaser is in a sufficiently proximate relationship with the manufacturer to impose a duty of care upon the latter not to inflict mere economic loss (of course the position is quite different if the goods cause physical injury, as the ginger beer with the decomposing snail in it taught us many years ago (*Donoghue* v. *Stevenson* [1932] AC 562)).

It is clear therefore that I was right to suggest in the first edition of this book that *Junior Books* v. *Veitchi* [1983] 1 AC 520 was a flash in the pan: if that case recurred today Lord Brandon's dissenting judgment would be followed – no court is going to dare to hold now that a subcontractor is under a duty of care in his work not to inflict mere economic loss on the building owner with whom he is not in a contractual relationship. The House of Lords had already made it clear enough in *D. & F. Estates* v. *Church Commissioners for England* [1989] AC 177 (July 1988) what they thought of the *Junior Books* decision. It should be seen now as one of the fairly numerous cases that were (wrongly) decided by accepting the general (and the specific) extension to the law of negligence proposed (the proposal being spearheaded, as the journalists say, by Lord Wilberforce) in the *Anns* case, an extension which has now been firmly ruled out of court.

MEDICAL CONTEXT

As stated elsewhere, most but not all medical negligence actions are in respect of personal injury. But one may be sure that within the doctor/patient relationship there is a sufficient proximity and reliance by the patient on the doctor to give rise to a duty not to inflict mere economic loss, so that, for example, a careless diagnosis that leads to the patient taking time off work will give rise to compensation for lost wages. Where a negligently premature discharge from hospital of an infected child causes his siblings to contract the infection, resulting in financial loss to the parents, a court would probably hold the hospital liable (see on these facts *Evans* v. *Liverpool Corporation* [1906] 1 KB 160, where the father failed in his action against the hospital, but on the basis that as the law then stood the hospital was not liable for the negligence of the discharging physician).

Claims for the cost of upkeep of an unplanned child may be for economic loss only, i.e. where there is no claim made for any personal injury. Even if the action includes a claim for the unplanned pregnancy itself (which may or may not be seen as a personal injury) the main part of the claim is for financial loss occasioned by the arrival of the unplanned child (see Chapter 25).

20 · Loss/injury: nervous shock[1]

SUMMARY

Shock, anxiety, depression, disappointment or grief, not amounting to psychiatric disorder, is not compensatable when it stands alone, but it may be taken into account to increase the award when it accompanies other, recognised injuries. Nervous shock amounting to psychiatric disorder is as much a head of damage as physical injury. To recover, the plaintiff has to be within the range of persons likely to be harmed by nervous shock; but even then the law permits recovery in the case of one who suffers nervous shock as a result of a person's death only where the shock is suffered by a close relative who either witnesses the death or its immediate aftermath.

Nervous shock is more than the normal emotions of distress, disappointment, unhappiness, grief, anxiety or depression: these do not constitute a head of damages in themselves but can serve to increase an award for a recognised loss, whether physical or financial (e.g. the 'spoilt holiday' cases where disappointment over a spoilt holiday can increase the award beyond the mere financial cost of the holiday). Nervous shock means an actual mental disorder, a 'positive psychiatric illness' (*per* Lord Bridge in *McLoughlin* v. *O'Brian* [1983] 1 AC 410).

In *Whitmore* v. *Euroway Express Coaches, The Times*, 4 May 1984, Comyn J. said that damages could be recovered for mere shock not amounting to psychiatric disorder occasioned by being in hospital with a severely injured spouse; but this is much to be doubted.

---

[1] Nervous shock claims can be worth a great deal, at any rate where the injury precludes employment. Mr Tredget, who could not return to work as a result of nervous injury sustained when he was present at the stillbirth of his child, received in the region of £300,000 by way of settlement (his case on liability is considered in detail below). Mr Peter Vernon, a successful businessman who could no longer work after seeing his daughters drown in a car accident, was awarded £1m by Sedley J. for loss of earnings (plus £37,500 for general damages and £152,000 for future care) – see *The Independent*, 31 January 1995, p. 1 (liability had been admitted).

In *Nicholls* v. *Rushton, The Times*, 19 June 1992, the Court of Appeal re-stated in the clearest terms the rule that nervous reaction falling short of actual psychological illness cannot be the subject of compensation unless it is parasitic to physical injury. And in *Hicks* v. *Chief Constable of South Yorkshire Police* [1992] PIQR P433 the House of Lords said that horror and fear for one's own safety (as the Hillsborough stadium collapsed), not amounting to recognisable psychiatric damage, do not sound in damages.

In *Reilly* v. *Merseyside Regional Health Authority, The Independent*, 29 April 1994, an unsuccessful claim for damages for extreme claustrophobia suffered by an elderly couple trapped in a lift for over an hour, the Court of Appeal said that that was not a nervous disorder but nothing more than 'excitement of normal human emotion'. Presumably the medical report failed to identify an actual psychiatric disorder consequent upon the frightening experience.

Contra, in *M. (a minor)* v. *Newham London Borough Council* [1994] 2 WLR 554, the Master of the Rolls rejected the claim that the psychiatric damage said to have been suffered by a child as a result of allegedly incompetent diagnosis of sexual abuse was not damage which the law recognised as compensatable injury. He pointed to Lord Ackner's words in the Hillsborough stadium case (*Alcock* v. *Chief Constable of South Yorkshire Police* [1992] 1 AC 310) where the Law Lord had acknowledged that future development of the law was to be expected, and to the warning given by Lord Bridge in *McLoughlin* v. *O'Brian* (*supra*) against the temptation of seeking to freeze the law in a rigid posture.[2]

Where the nervous shock is allied to a more apparent physical injury there has been no problem with recovery. But where it stands alone the courts have been reluctant to permit recovery, both, in the older cases, because knowledge of mental trauma was scanty, and also because of a feeling that public policy should draw the line at recovery for mental shock.

Thus where a level crossing attendant negligently allowed a pregnant woman to cross the railway lines in her carriage in front of an oncoming train and she suffered nervous shock and a miscarriage, the Privy Council would not permit her to succeed. But that was in 1888 (*Victoria Railway Commissioners* v. *Coultas* 13 App Cas 222). A pregnant barmaid suffered nervous shock when a negligently driven van crashed into the pub. She succeeded, but only because her shock arose 'from a reasonable fear of immediate personal injury to [herself]' (*Dulieu* v. *White* [1901] 2 KB 141). The

---

[2] In *Page* v. *Smith, The Times*, 12 May 1995, the House of Lords, overruling the Court of Appeal by a bare majority, held that where nervous shock without any physical injury was alleged as a result of an accident, it did not have to be shown that nervous injury was foreseeable, given that physical injury to a primary victim had been foreseeable.

scope of the claim was extended by the majority decision in
Hambrook v. *Stokes Bros* [1925] 1 KB 141: a mother suffered shock
through fear that her children had been injured when she saw a
runaway lorry careering down a hill from the bend round which her
children had just gone out of sight (her apprehension was unhappily
justified). The significance of this decision was twofold: first it
severed the link between nervous shock and fear of impact to
oneself; secondly, it suggested extension of the claim to cases where
the disaster had already occurred and the fear of what might be
about to occur was no longer relevant.

The only case in which the House of Lords had considered the
matter before *McLoughlin* v. *O'Brian* (*supra*) was *Bourhill* v.
Young [1943] AC 92. The plaintiff heard the noise of a road
accident as she alighted from a bus, went of her own volition to
the scene and, seeing upon the road the blood of the dead
motorcyclist (who was not known to her), suffered shock. Understandably her claim was rejected. It could be said she as passer-by
was owed no duty by the negligent driver, at least no duty as far
as the infliction of injury by shock was concerned, or that the
actual injury suffered was too remote, or unforeseeable.

In *Hinz* v. *Berry* [1970] 2 QB 40 it was agreed without dispute
that a mother could recover for psychiatric illness caused by her
witnessing a ghastly accident to her family on the other side of the
road. Lord Denning M.R. said that it was settled law that
'damages can be given for nervous shock caused by the sight of an
accident, at any rate to a close relative'.

But recovery had not always been limited to a 'close relative'.
In *Chadwick* v. *British Railways Board* [1967] 1 WLR 912, the
estate of a rescuer at the Lewisham rail disaster recovered in
respect of a psychiatric disorder caused by his work amid the dead
and dying that night. (See also *Galt* v. *British Railways Board*
(1983) 133 NLJ 870, where a train driver recovered for nervous
shock occasioned by his seeing in front of him two men on the
track whom he then thought he went on to strike and kill.) In
Wigg v. *British Railways Board, The Times*, 4 February 1986,
Tucker J. held that it was reasonably foreseeable that a train
driver who stopped the train and got down to help a passenger,
who had in fact been killed due to the negligence of the guard in
giving the starting signal, might suffer nervous shock thereby.[3]

Recovery for nervous shock was extended by the House of
Lords in *McLoughlin* v. *O'Brian* [1983] 1 AC 410, where a

---

[3] For an example of an unsuccessful claim for shock suffered by a rescuer, see the Piper
Alpha case of *McFarlane* v. *E.E. Caledonia Ltd* [1994] PIQR 154, where the Court of
Appeal held that there had been insufficient involvement or risk of involvement by the
plaintiff in the tragedy (the fire-fighting vessel he was in was never in danger).

mother was told at home by a witness that her family had just been involved in a serious road accident. She rushed to the hospital to find one child dead, two others seriously injured, and her husband in a state of shock. She herself suffered nervous shock, organic depression and a change of personality. She lost her claim at first instance and in the Court of Appeal, on the ground that her injury was not foreseeable and she herself was owed no duty of care, but the House of Lords reversed the decision. Lord Wilberforce promulgated the 'aftermath' principle. Recovery was permitted, but only where the shock came through sight or hearing of the event or its immediate aftermath. This is an example of judicial law-making – but none the worse for that. If therefore a relative visits the hospital to find a patient dying because of negligent treatment and suffers himself some psychiatric disorder as a result of nervous shock, he could recover damages. Probably also if he sees the corpse soon after, provided the relationship is sufficiently close; but not if the shock is occasioned merely by being told of the death and its circumstances, however horrible, and however close the relationship. In *Schneider* v. *Eisovitch* [1960] 2 QB 430, recovery for shock on being so informed was permitted as an additional item of damages, where a wife, injured along with her husband in a road accident, learned that he had died. (It is of interest to note that the New South Wales legislature intervened as early as 1944 to permit recovery for this sort of injury suffered by a close relative of a person 'killed, injured or put in peril', irrespective of any spatial or temporal nexus with the accident.)

So we can summarise by saying that claims for nervous shock by witnesses, or secondary victims as they appear now to be called, have had only slow and restricted acceptance in English law. The claim was first recognised where the plaintiff had been put in fear of imminent physical harm (this context should probably be seen as one of primary victim, just as if the harm had materialised), then extended to shock caused by fear that imminent harm was about to befall others, to the witnessing of a shocking event (also to shock caused to a rescuer by actually participating in a horrific event), then, by the House of Lords decision in *McLoughlin* v. *O'Brian* (*supra*) to shock caused by coming upon the aftermath of a horrific event. Recent developments have done nothing to extend the ambit of the claim.

Recent developments

In the Hillsborough stadium case (*Alcock* v. *Chief Constable of South Yorkshire* [1991] 3 WLR 1057) the House of Lords held that a plaintiff claiming for nervous shock over the death or injury of another must satisfy the test of proximity, in that it must have been foreseeable that this particular plaintiff might suffer nervous shock over the death of that particular relative or friend. The law would not define a class of qualifying relationships. The required proximity (to be based upon close ties of love and affection) was to be proved by evidence; it could in the case of obviously close familial ties be presumed (a presumption that could, however, be rebutted by appropriate evidence). The court was prepared to make the presumption in the case of plaintiffs who had lost a son or a fiancé but not, in the absence of evidence of closeness, in the case of a brother, brother-in-law or grandson. Secondly, the court re-affirmed Lord Wilberforce's limited extension of the right of recovery to the 'aftermath' principle, i.e. the witnessing of the traumatic event or its immediate aftermath. It was not possible to bring within that principle the viewing of the distressing scenes on television, emphasis being laid on the fact that the television code of ethics meant that the suffering of recognisable individuals was not broadcast. Although it was not impossible that a television viewer might be sufficiently proximate in appropriate circumstances (probably where the telecast was horrifyingly graphic), the viewing of the television scenes in this case did not create the necessary degree of proximity and could not be 'equiparated' with the position of a plaintiff at the ground. Thus there are two tests of proximity for the plaintiff to satisfy, the first relating to the victim, the second to the event – the second can be further divided into the proximity of the plaintiff to the accident and the means by which the shock has been caused. Lord Ackner said at p. 1104 that 'shock' involved the sudden appreciation by sight or sound of a horrifying event which violently agitated the mind; as the law presently stood it did not include psychiatric illness caused by the accumulation over a period of time of more gradual assaults on the nervous system. So illness caused by the stress of caring for an injured relative over a period of time would not be compensatable.

The court's decision was that none of the plaintiffs could succeed – those at the ground failed the test of proximity of relationship, those elsewhere failed the test of proximity in time and space (those who came to hospital or mortuary later were said not to be within the 'immediate' aftermath as they did not get there for some eight hours – the mother in *McLoughlin* v. *O'Brian* (*supra*) had arrived at the hospital within one hour).

A recent, disappointing example of the restrictions that the Court of Appeal is currently placing on the ambit of the nervous shock claim can be seen in *Taylorson* v. *Shieldness Produce Ltd*

[1994] PIQR P329. Parents went immediately one morning to the hospital to which their 14-year-old son, their only child, had been admitted after being crushed under a reversing vehicle. They did not see him at the hospital, but they followed the ambulance that transferred him to another hospital, the father glimpsing him in the ambulance, the mother seeing him briefly as he was being rushed into the intensive care unit on a trolley. They did not see him then for a few hours while he was being treated. The father saw him that evening, when he had black eyes, blood on his face and a tube attached to the top of his head to relieve pressure on the brain. The mother saw him the next day in a similar state. The boy remained unconscious for two days. Then the life support machine was switched off. The parents were with him throughout that time.

The court said that the shocking events were not sufficiently proximate and that the involvement of the parents did not come within the aftermath principle. It seems that the first conclusion was based on the lack of close contact in the first few hours and the second on the refusal of the court to adopt the reasoning in the Australian case of *Jaench* v. *Coffey* (1984) 155 CLR 549 and extend the aftermath period to include the two days waiting at the bedside of the dying child.

It is also to be noted that the court found that causation was not proved, in that it took the view that the real cause of the psychiatric injury was the loss of their child and that the injury would have been sustained even if there had been no question of any participation in any aftermath.[4]

An unusual case

The scope of recovery for nervous shock was widened significantly by the interesting case of *Attia* v. *British Gas plc* [1988] QB 304, where a woman had allegedly suffered positive psychiatric illness (as opposed to 'normal' grief and distress) through seeing her home burnt down before her eyes as a result of the defendants' negligence. The Court of Appeal refused to strike out the claim for nervous shock (the claim for damage to property had been settled), saying that there was in principle no reason to preclude recovery if the injury and foreseeability were proved in the usual way. In other words nervous shock arising out of damage to property rather than damage to the person is not for

---

[4] In the Canadian case of *Beecham* v. *Hughes* (1989) CLY 1266 the husband of a woman brain-damaged in a car crash was unable to recover damages for his own nervous shock as the evidence indicated that it had been caused not by his presence at the accident and its immediate aftermath but by his ongoing distress at the condition of his wife.

that reason alone to be irrecoverable. Scott J. has doubted whether shock caused by the disclosure of confidential medical information could properly be reflected in an award of damages (*W.* v. *Egdell* [1990] Ch 359).

THE MEDICAL ACCIDENT

What if a close relative suffers psychiatric damage through being present at and around the death and/or terminal illness in hospital (or elsewhere) of a loved one, the injury being due to medical negligence? There is no reason in principle why the tests of proximity (or the 'aftermath' test) should not be satisfied in this context. Until recently there was no English authority on the point, but several settlements of such claims had been achieved. In the Australian case of *Jaench* v. *Coffey* (1984) 155 CLR 549 (not a medical accident case) Deane J. permitted recovery for nervous shock where a wife came to her injured husband's bedside in hospital, and through her constant attendance upon him and her fear that he was going to die suffered severe anxiety and depression.[5] The judge said:

The aftermath of the accident extended to the hospital to which the injured person was taken and persisted for so long as he remained in the state produced by the accident up to and including immediate post-accident treatment . . . Her psychiatric injuries were the result of the impact upon her of the facts of the accident itself and its aftermath while she was present at the aftermath of the accident at the hospital.

In principle there is no difference between claims for shock due to horrific scenes at the hospital after a road accident and the same after a medical accident, so the case of *Taylorson* (*supra*) is also in point. However, the difficulty with the medical accident context is that horrific scenes are less likely, and so the question that immediately springs to mind is how the element of shock can be satisfied in such a case (assuming that there is no such shocking element as the relative finding the loved one dying or dead at home). In the Hillsborough case Lord Ackner said:

'Shock', in the context of this cause of action, involves the sudden appreciation by sight or sound of a horrifying event, which violently agitates the mind. It has yet to include psychiatric illness caused by the accumulation over a period of time or more gradual assaults on the nervous system.

---

[5] Note, incidentally, that the plaintiff's predisposition to such injury was no defence; similarly in *Brice* v. *Brown* [1984] 1 All ER 997 Stuart Smith J. held that, once nervous shock was a foreseeable consequence of a breach of duty, it made no difference that the precise nature and extent of the injury were not foreseeable (the plaintiff had suffered particularly severely due to a basic mental instability) – see Chapter 21 below under 'You must take the plaintiff as you find him'.

In *Jaench* v. *Coffey (supra)* Brennan J. said:

I understand 'shock' in this context to mean the sudden sensory perception – that is, by seeing, hearing or touching – of a person, thing or event, which is so distressing that the perception of the phenomenon affronts or insults the plaintiff's mind and causes a recognizable psychiatric illness.

There are now, besides the judgment in *Taylorson* (set out above), recent decisions in medical negligence actions, including one from the Court of Appeal, which make it more difficult for a claim of this sort to succeed.

In *Taylor* v. *Somerset Health Authority* [1993] 4 Med LR 34 Auld J. rejected a claim by a widow who had come to the hospital after her husband had suffered a fatal heart attack at work (due to earlier medical mismanagement). She had not believed that he had died, not even when she was so informed by a doctor. She then saw him lying peacefully behind curtains in the basement of the hospital. The judge said that this did not fulfil the test of temporal proximity (in other words, she was too late on the scene). He also said that there had to be an external traumatic event; however, in the *Sion* case (see below) Peter Gibson L.J. made it clear that an external horrific event was not a prerequisite as the crucial element in this sort of claim was a sudden awareness, violently agitating the mind, of what was occurring or what had occurred. It could, nevertheless, be argued that in the *Taylor* case what was absent was the necessary element of horror or sudden shock. One has to remember that one cannot claim merely for psychiatric injury caused by the death of a loved one. The claim is a claim for *shock*.

In *Sion* v. *Hampstead Health Authority* [1994] 5 Med LR 170 the Court of Appeal struck out as doomed to fail a claim by a father who suffered psychiatric injury through attending for some two weeks by the bedside of his 23-year-old son who had been injured in a traffic accident and fatally deteriorated in hospital due, allegedly, to negligent medical treatment. The court took the view on the pleadings, having regard principally to the psychiatric report that was served with the particulars of claim, that there was no evidence of 'shock', no sudden appreciation by sight or sound of a horrifying event, but rather a continuous process that ran from the father's first arrival at the hospital to a death two weeks later that was by then not unexpected – and on then to his realisation after the inquest of the possibility of medical negligence.

This seems odd. In the first place, does it make any sort of sense that there would probably have been a good claim if the father had still been hoping for recovery when death occurred and had therefore been 'shocked' when there was a sudden fatal deterioration? Secondly, there do in fact appear to have been discrete 'shocking' events during the two-week period, such as a sudden (though not immediately fatal) deterioration, sudden respiratory difficulties, cardiac arrest, and transfer to the ITU.

A more imaginative judgment (in the best sense) was given in the Central London County Court by Judge White on 4 February 1994 in the case of *Tredget and Tredget* v. *Bexley Health Authority* [1994] 5 Med LR 178. Although this was before the Court of Appeal judgment, it was after Brooke J. had struck out Mr Sion's claim at first instance, and nothing that was said in the Court of Appeal invalidates Judge White's approach.

In the first place this case concerned claims for nervous shock sustained by both parents as a result of a traumatic and frightening delivery of their fatally injured child, following negligent failure to go for an earlier cesarean section, and as a result of attending upon their son during his short life of some two days. So the case was rather different from the usual 'attending by the bedside' case.

Judge White accepted, as did the Court of Appeal in the *Sion* case, the following requisites for a successful claim:

The plaintiff must show he has suffered an actual psychiatric illness caused by shock (i.e. the sudden and direct appreciation by sight or sound of a horrifying event or events, rather than from stress, strain, grief or sorrow or from gradual or retrospective realisation of events); that there was propinquity in time or space for the causative event or its immediate aftermath; that such injury was reasonably foreseeable; and that the relationship between plaintiff and defendant was sufficiently proximate.

It is surprising that the health authority sought to argue that there had been no element of shock in the events that the parents had experienced, and quite amazing that they should have chosen to contest the mother's claim on that basis. Fortunately the judge sensibly declined to see the two day period as lacking the element of shock. He saw the traumatic birth (in which the husband had been involved, and which had been complicated by shoulder dystocia – an obstetric emergency) and the delivery of a clearly traumatised baby and the ensuing harrowing hours as a single event ('frightening and harrowing') which satisfied the requisite of a sudden shock to the nervous system. He said:

Of course, it was not in the nature of an immediate catastrophe which lasts only a few seconds – panic in a stadium or a motor accident – but one just as traumatic, for those immediately involved as participants, as each of the parents was . . .

In my judgment, if this is a new step in the development of the law, it is not only . . . within the principles that have been set out, but has its own in-built limits, being founded on the special relationship, with all that follows, of the parent with the child at the unique human moment of birth.

CHECKLIST

So, in the face of all this (negative) activity from the Court of Appeal, what does the plaintiff need to establish to succeed in this sort of claim?

- In the first place the psychiatric report must clearly certify that the plaintiff has suffered an actual psychiatric injury, i.e. going beyond the normal ambit of a bereavement reaction, grief, fear or distress.
- Next, one has to show that the circumstances were such that nervous shock was foreseeable.
- Next, the plaintiff needs to satisfy the test of familial proximity, i.e. to show that nervous shock to this relative or close friend was foreseeable. Note the arbitrary treatment of this requirement by the House of Lords in the Hillsborough case.
- Next, the plaintiff needs to satisfy the test of temporal and spatial proximity, i.e. show that the plaintiff was sufficiently close in time and space to the events that are alleged to have caused the injury.
- Next – and this is where the most recent cases come in – the report must identify a discrete shocking event (or events) that constituted a sudden assault upon the nervous system of the plaintiff and was responsible wholly or at any rate materially for the injury. It is unwise to rely on any protracted period of time as being the horrifying event unless the sights and sounds during that period were more or less continuously horrifying.
- The psychiatric report should make it clear that the injury would probably not have been sustained simply through the loss of the loved one, i.e. in the absence of the identified shocking event(s).

A final note

Before one criticises the judges for their policy, whether consciously formed or not, of restricting the ambit of the claim, one should bear in mind that nervous shock means just that, and that the claim began life as a reaction to a horrifying event, usually a motor accident or the threat of one on the part of those involved in it, at the time or in the direct aftermath when the immediate marks and traces of the shocking event were still observable and capable of evincing nervous shock in a relevant witness, e.g. victims of a motor accident at hospital but still displaying the immediate signs of their trauma.

How far these stringent conditions can be satisfied in a claim arising out of medical mismanagement remains unclear. It must depend on the precise events. If the plaintiff was present when a shocking emergency or a shocking deterioration in the patient occurred, or comes to the hospital and finds the patient in a state that reasonably shocks, or perhaps is present at an unexpected, and therefore in itself shocking, death, the claim might well be successful. But if there is a slow process of decline leading to a death that was not really unexpected at the time, or at any rate was on the cards, and the death did not involve any particularly shocking factors beyond the actual dying, the claim is likely to fail.

FATAL ACCIDENT AND BEREAVEMENT

On behalf of the deceased himself, that is to say, the estate of the deceased, a claim lies only for funeral expenses. The claim for loss of expectation of life, which used to be set at a formal figure of about £1,250, was abolished by the Administration of Justice Act 1982. And the deceased has no claim for loss of earnings during the lost years, i.e. the years when he would have earned had he been alive (see pp. 374 *et seq.*). There may be a small claim for his suffering in the interval, if there was one, between the injury and his death. Apart from that, nothing. So you can see how truer than ever is the common law saw 'It is cheaper to kill than to maim.' Had he been maimed, the deceased could have claimed a substantial sum for pain and suffering and loss of amenity, all his lost earnings, and the cost of all necessary care for the rest of his life.

The tortfeasor, or his insurance company will not, however, escape scot-free if the deceased had dependants (by virtue of the Fatal Accidents Act 1976, as amended). For full details of the fatal accidents legislation the reader is referred to the standard textbooks. What I want to point out here is this:

First, by virtue of the amendment made to the Act by the Administration of Justice Act 1982, the spouse of the deceased or a parent of an unmarried minor deceased (note: a child cannot claim for loss of a parent) killed by negligence can claim from the tortfeasor (regardless of any dependency) the statutory bereavement award of £7,500 (£3,500 for deaths before April 1991).[6] This is of course a minimal amount and is no sort of compensation for

---

[6] A deceased child must have died, not merely sustained the lethal injury, before his 18th birthday for the parents' entitlement to arise (*Doleman* v. *Deakin, The Times*, 30 January 1990).

the loss of a loved one. But it has to be remembered that at common law the general rule is that no person has a financial or indeed a legal interest in the life of another person, so that no duty of care is owed by A to B not to kill B's relative by negligence. So the statutory award represents a legislative exception to the common law rule in a context where no duty of care was owed to the plaintiff. The 'aftermath' principle represents, as we have seen, another limited exception to the rule.

Secondly, the general effect of the long-standing and important statutory exception to the common law rule effected by the fatal accidents legislation is that those who were or had an expectation of being financially supported by the deceased may claim their loss from the tortfeasor over the whole of the period during which they could have expected to be supported by him. As I have said, for the details of this legislation the reader is referred to the standard textbooks.

DEATH OF AN INFANT AND NERVOUS SHOCK

It is not easy to know how to assess damages for a stillbirth or a miscarriage. They will of course vary according to the time at which the miscarriage takes place and according to the degree of nervous shock (i.e. actual psychiatric injury) suffered by the mother. But there is little in the way of precedent.

One must first bear in mind that mental trauma unaccompanied by physical injury will not found a claim in negligence unless the mental trauma amounts to actual psychiatric damage (to be proved by a medical report). It should be possible in most cases of miscarriage or stillbirth to identify a physical injury, e.g. the pain of the abortion, or the prolongation of labour beyond the appropriate point.[7] It may well be that damaging the child *en ventre*[8] constitutes in itself a physical injury to the mother.

I would suggest that for an early miscarriage, up to a few weeks say, the award is likely to be about £1,500 – of course if any sequelae are proved, e.g. substantive psychiatric injury, or difficulty or impossibility of conception, gestation or parturition in the future, damages will be substantially increased. I am thinking of a miscarriage that leaves no substantive sequelae.

After the early days, the award will increase as the pregnancy advances until you have the stillbirth. The real question on

---

[7] In some other contexts it will be essential to prove nervous shock, e.g. where cancer is negligently diagnosed and, although the patient does not accept treatment and is therefore not physically harmed by the misdiagnosis, s/he suffers very great anxiety for a period of time until the diagnosis is corrected.

[8] The medics prefer us to say '*in utero*'.

assessing for a stillbirth (again assume no substantive nervous shock, only the normal sorrow, distress and disappointment, with some identifiable physical injury on which to hang that) is whether you take the bereavement award as a guide. However, as explained above, that is an award under the fatal accident legislation and presupposes no common law duty of care owed to the relative (the spouse or parent). So it can be viewed as a bonus added by the legislation. In the case of the stillbirth there is of course a duty of care owed to the mother. Nevertheless the old principle of the common law that no person has an interest in the life of another means that traditional learning would say that the mother cannot be compensated for the death of her child as such (apart from the bereavement award, which presumably cannot apply where the child is not born alive and so is never a 'person' within the meaning of the legislation).

Cases

There are four reported cases on damages for stillbirth. In *Bagley* v. *North Herts Health Authority* (1986) 136 NLJ 1014 Simon Brown J. acknowledged that damages could not be awarded to the mother for grief and distress as such (Lord Wilberforce had made that clear in *McLoughlin* v. *O'Brian* (*supra*)) or for loss of society, or for the statutory bereavement award, but he found other means of compensating her. He awarded damages for loss of satisfaction in bringing the pregnancy to a successful end, for disappointment at the shattering of her plans for a family and for being deprived of the joy of bringing up an ordinary healthy child, and he said that those damages would amount to not less than the statutory sum. In fact the mother got some £18,000, but a lot of that was for other heads of claim such as actual physical sequelae (she suffered a substantial nervous illness as a result). Counsel in the case has said to me that one could probably think in terms of about £6,000 for the actual stillbirth.

And in *Kralj* v. *McGrath and St Theresa's Hospital* [1986] 1 All ER 54, where £10,000 general damages were awarded after a horrendous and agonising piece of obstetric mismanagement had caused the stillbirth of one of twins, Woolf J. said that not only was the mother entitled to damages for shock at what had happened, but if her injury was aggravated by the grief she was suffering that could be reflected in the award. Having stated that it would be wholly inappropriate to introduce into the medical context the concept of aggravated damages, the judge awarded compensation also for the financial loss that would arise if the parents went on to implement their desire for a larger family; if they decided not to, then that award would be appropriate nevertheless to cover disappointment over the loss of their objective; £10,000 was awarded for pain and suffering, and £18,000 for loss of the mother's earnings. It is not possible to know how much of the total award was for the stillbirth pure and simple (if I may use that expression) – indeed I am sure the judge did not assess that aspect separately in his own mind.

In *Grieve* v. *Salford Health Authority* [1991] 2 Med LR 295 Rose J. awarded a woman with a pre-existing vulnerable personality £12,500 in respect of initial prolongation of labour, some additional pain, loss of her stillborn child and of the satisfaction of a successful conclusion to the pregnancy, plus psychological damage likely to endure for some four years from the date of the stillbirth. This could possibly be seen as about £6,000 for the stillbirth in itself and about £6,000 for the four-year nervous illness.

In *Kerby* v. *Redbridge Health Authority* [1993] 4 Med LR 178 a twin was fatally injured before birth in 1988 by admitted negligence, and survived only three days. Ognall J. said, with reference to the dicta in *Bagley* (*supra*), that damages for 'dashed hopes' would duplicate the bereavement award, but he awarded, nevertheless, in addition to the bereavement award, £10,000 for the cesarean section and consequent scar, a depressive illness of moderate severity lasting some six months, and the constant reminder of what might have been by the presence of the surviving twin.

I believe that if the matter were put to the test a court would award close to the bereavement award for a stillbirth pure and simple. One line of argument that might suggest that damages should not greatly exceed the bereavement award is as follows: what if the child dies shortly after birth, let us say through poor neonatal care? How do you justify any award other than the bereavement award in that case? In which event why should the situation be radically different if the child died just before birth? No duty of care is owed by the pediatricians to the mother in respect of their care of the neonate. The only way I see of increasing the award substantively beyond the bereavement level of £7,500 in such a context is to show that the mother suffered substantial nervous shock – i.e. an actual psychiatric injury – that comes within the 'aftermath' principle of *McLoughlin* v. *O'Brian* (*supra*).

A final note: regardless of whether 'normal' grief and distress at loss of a loved one will attract the bereavement award or no compensation at all in a given situation, the award for nervous shock should only reflect that element of suffering which is additional to 'normal' grief and distress (see the report on the Zeebrugge Ferry awards in Kemp & Kemp, *Quantum of Damages*, C4–150).

21 · Loss/injury: foreseeability and remoteness

SUMMARY

Damages are recoverable only in respect of injury of a type that was foreseeable (though no definition of 'type' is available). But this must be read subject to the important rule that the wrongdoer must take the plaintiff as he finds him, so that the fact that the injury develops unexpected complications or, through hypersensitivity, more harm is suffered than was to be expected is no bar to recovery. Nor is the fact that the injury did not arise in the precisely foreseeable manner.

Strictly, injuries which are of an unforeseeable type and do not come within the rule that the wrongdoer must take the plaintiff as he finds him are not subjects for compensation (an example would be where a brick is thrown from a window and there is a foreseeable risk from it striking someone, but in fact it hits an electricity cable and in a manner not to be foreseen causes a person in the vicinity to be electrocuted – injury from impact would seem of a different kind from injury by electrocution). A judge would be entitled to hold the wrongdoer not liable for the injury suffered, but in practice he might well find a way to implement his 'gut reaction' to the situation and award compensation, e.g. by 'finding' that there was in fact some slight degree of foreseeability of electrocution.

TOO REMOTE

Even if the plaintiff has established a duty of care, a breach of that duty, and loss of a type recognised by the law and caused by the breach, the defendants will only be liable to compensate for that loss if it was reasonably foreseeable at the time of the breach that it could arise. In other words, the basic principle (though subject, as we shall see, to substantial exceptions) is that you cannot recover for an injury that was not foreseeable.

This is sometimes expressed as a statement that the loss must not be too remote. But that catch-all expression is also used to mean that no duty was owed to the particular plaintiff (the plaintiff was too remote, not being within the area of foreseeable risk created by the defendant's actions, and therefore so was the damage he suffered); or that no duty was owed to take care not to inflict the particular sort of harm suffered, or not to inflict it in that particular way; or that the chain of causation was broken; or that policy militates against recovery. Thus a mother who suffers nervous shock on being told of the death of her son and is denied damages on the basis that she does not come within the 'aftermath' principle (see Chapter 20) may be told that the damage she suffered was too remote. This may mean that no duty was owed to her by the tortfeasor, or that the intervening act of her informant broke the chain of causation, or that the law or policy forbids recovery in the particular circumstances.

To assist clarity of thought on this issue it is better therefore to avoid the expression 'too remote' (it is in fact unhelpful in any context), and say simply that the loss must be reasonably foreseeable. We have already looked at the issue of foreseeability in connection with the establishing of a duty of care, and we concluded that although foreseeability of harm is a prerequisite for a duty of care, except perhaps where there is a duty to act (as opposed to merely a duty to take care if you choose to act) arising from the existing relationship between the parties and which therefore renders the obligee liable if he does nothing at all, it does not of itself prove the existence of a duty. It is a prerequisite for a duty of care because, if there is no reasonable foreseeability of harm arising from an act there can be no duty of care in relation to it. Here, however, we consider the essential requirement of foreseeability in the context of recoverability of loss. We assume therefore in the discussion that follows that duty and breach have been proved.

The basic principle is that a tortfeasor is liable only for the natural and probable consequences of his actions, those that he, as a reasonable man, could have foreseen as likely to occur, and which should therefore have caused him to hold his hand. Damage which occurs directly from the breach is not the subject of compensation, as a general rule, unless it was also foreseeable. This is the result of the Privy Council decision in *Overseas Tankship (UK) Ltd* v. *Morts Dock and Engineering Co. Ltd* (also known as *The Wagon Mound (No.1)*) [1961] AC 388, which overruled the long-standing decision to the contrary of the Court of Appeal in *Re Polemis* [1921] 3 KB 560.

DEGREE OF FORESEEABILITY

It is not clear how foreseeable a consequence has to be, i.e. what chance of its happening is sufficient. In *The Wagon Mound (No.2)* [1967] 1 AC 617, the Privy Council's view was that once *some* foreseeability of fire was proved that was sufficient, however remote that possibility. It was said in the Australian case of *Commonwealth of Australia* v. *Introvigne* 150 CLR 258 that 'a risk of injury is foreseeable so long as it is not far-fetched or fanciful, notwithstanding that it is more probable than not that it will not occur'. These propositions, however, are hardly consistent with what is generally understood to be the law, that the loss has to be reasonably foreseeable – unless we are being told that reasonable foreseeability of harm is appropriate for establishing a duty of care but any degree of foreseeability short of the far-fetched is enough in the context of compensation. We can well do without yet another subtle refinement in the law of negligence!

EXCEPTIONS

Policy

To the basic rule that the wrongdoer is liable for the natural and probable consequences of his wrongful act, and for no other consequences, there are a number of very substantial exceptions. In the first place the law will draw a line at some point as a matter of policy to prevent over-extensive recovery.

The law cannot take account of everything that follows a wrongful act; it regards some subsequent matters as outside the scope of its selection, because 'it were infinite for the law to judge the cause of causes' or consequence of consequences . . . In the varied web of affairs the law must abstract some consequences as relevant, not perhaps on grounds of pure logic but simply for practical reasons (*per* Lord Wright in *Liebosch Dredger (Owners)* v. *SS Edison (Owners)* [1933] AC 449, 460).

It is always difficult to predict and impossible to define the line where liability stops. It is left to the good sense of the judge in each particular case to decide where practical convenience and policy dictate that it be drawn.

It is something like having to draw a line between night and day; there is a great duration of twilight when it is neither night nor day; but . . . though you cannot draw the precise line, you can say on which side of the line the case is (*per* Blackburn J. in *Hobbs* v. *LSWR Railway* (1875) LR 10 QB 111, 121).

The legal basis for drawing the line is variously expressed:

In order to limit liability . . . the courts sometimes say either that the damage claimed was 'too remote' or that it was not 'caused' by the defendant's carelessness or that the defendant did not 'owe a duty of care' to the plaintiff (*per* Thesiger J. in *SCM (UK)* v. *Whittall* [1970] 1 WLR 1017, 1031).

Or it may simply be said that justice or social convenience demands that a limit be placed upon the defendant's liability.

'You must take the plaintiff as you find him'

The most comprehensive exception to the foreseeability principle that goes to extend a defendant's liability is the rule that a tortfeasor must take the plaintiff as he finds him, in relation both to his physical condition and to his financial circumstances. If you carelessly knock a man over in circumstances where you could reasonably expect a slight injury and a claim for average earnings lost over a relatively short period, you will nevertheless be liable for full damages if he turns out through an inherently weak physical condition to suffer far greater damage and for a longer period, and also to be a very high earner, perhaps with several extremely lucrative contracts lined up which he cannot now fulfil.

One who is guilty of negligence to another must put up with idiosyncrasies of his victim that increase the likelihood or extent of damage to him; it is no answer to a claim for a fractured skull that its owner had an unusually fragile one (*per* Mackinnon L.J. in *Owens* v. *Liverpool Corporation* [1939] 1 KB 394, 400–1).

It is not only if the foreseeable injury proves more serious than could have been anticipated that the tortfeasor must pay, but also if a different type of injury arises out of the foreseeable injury. Thus in *Robinson* v. *Post Office* [1974] 1 WLR 1176, where a plaintiff developed encephalitis as a result of an allergic reaction to an anti-tetanus injection, the defendants, whose negligence was responsible for the original slight injury that led to the need for an injection, were held liable to compensate him for the full extent of his injury.[1]

There have been very many cases where unforeseeable complications involving a different type of physical injury from that which could have been foreseen have been the subject of compensation. For example, in *Warren* v. *Scruttons* [1962] 1 Lloyd's Rep 497, a defendant had to compensate for the unforeseeable aggravation of an existing eye condition that developed after the plaintiff had hurt his finger on a frayed rope. A cancer which unforeseeably developed from a foreseeable burn on the lip was held to be a proper subject for compensation in *Smith* v.

---

[1] See also *Brice* v. *Brown* [1984] 1 All ER 997 where the nervous shock sustained was particularly severe due to a basic mental instability.

Leech Brain [1962] 2 QB 405. Where a woman had to wear a cervical collar as a result of a foreseeable physical injury she was able also to recover compensation for injury suffered when she fell down stairs due to the fact that she could not see so well with the collar on (*Wieland* v. *Cyril Lord Carpets Ltd* [1969] 3 All ER 1006). Eveleigh J. said:

in determining liability for . . . possible consequences of personal injury, it is not necessary to show that each was within the foreseeable extent or foreseeable scope of the original injury in the same way that the possibility of injury must be foreseen when determining whether or not the defendant's conduct gives a claim in negligence.[2]

'TYPE' OF INJURY SUFFERED

Of course, if no injury could be foreseen then the fact that an abnormally susceptible plaintiff suffered some injury does not give rise to a claim; there would probably be neither a duty nor a breach in those circumstances, but even if there were, there would be no liability where no injury could reasonably be foreseen from the acts in question. For an injury to be claimable, it must, if it does not accompany a foreseeable injury, at least be of the same type as the foreseeable injury (although, as we see below, it is quite unclear what is meant by 'type'). Thus in *Bradford* v. *Robinson Rentals Ltd* [1967] 1 WLR 337, a driver was negligently exposed to freezing conditions in an unheated vehicle as a result of which he developed the unforeseeable injury of frostbite. Rees J. made it clear that recovery was permissible in respect of the frostbite as the foreseeable injury, i.e. common cold, pneumonia, chilblains, was of the same type as that which was in fact suffered. In *Ogwo* v. *Taylor* [1988] AC 431 Dillon L.J. said that injury caused to a firefighter from the steam that arose when he played water on to a fire was not different in kind from injury caused directly by the flames.

The apparent necessity for a connection between the type of damage that was foreseeable and the type of damage that was suffered arises from the decision of the Privy Council in *The Wagon Mound (No.1)* (*supra*). That case arose out of the careless spillage of oil on the waters of Sydney harbour. Damage to slipways by pollution was foreseeable, but the damage by fire that occurred was not. The Privy Council said that as the damage that occurred was of a different type from what was foreseeable (i.e. damage by fire and not damage by

---

[2] Where a second injurious condition does *not* flow from the original injury, causation has to be established on the balance of the probabilities in respect of the second condition (see Lord Bridge's judgment in *Hotson* v. *Fitzgerald* [1987] AC 750).

pollution) recovery was not permitted. Ironically, in *The Wagon Mound (No.2)* [1967] 1 AC 617, which concerned the same facts, a contrary decision was reached as to liability, but that was because the evidence given in that trial established, as we saw above, that there was a slight possibility to be foreseen of damage by fire.

What is completely unclear is what is meant by 'type' of damage in the context of physical injury. A plaintiff is assisted by the rules that the defendant must take him as he finds him, and that neither the extent of the damage has to be foreseeable nor the precise manner in which it arose, and it is hard to see what practical scope is left for a rule that restricts liability by providing that the injury suffered has to be of a type that was foreseeable. In *Thurogood* v. *Van den Bergh and Jurgens* [1951] 2 KB 537, the Court of Appeal permitted recovery by an injured workman when he caught his fingers in a fan even though the foreseeable injury was by catching his necktie in it (a decision that seems good sense); but that was upon an application of the principle derived from *Re Polemis* [1921] 3 KB 560, that all damage directly caused was claimable for, and that principle was rejected by the Privy Council in *The Wagon Mound* (*supra*). In *Tremain* v. *Pike* [1969] 1 WLR 1556 Payne J. refused relief to a herdsman who contracted a rare disease from rats' urine because the only foreseeable consequence from exposure to rats was rat-bite or food-poisoning, which was said to be 'entirely different in kind'. This decision must surely have been wrong (see, to an apparently contrary intent, *Parsons (H.) Livestock Ltd* v. *Uttley Ingham & Co. Ltd* [1978] QB 791).

In *Woodhouse* v. *Yorkshire Regional Authority* [1984] 1 *The Lancet* 1306 the plaintiff suffered foreseeable digital contracture deformity from a carelessly performed operation. The defendants were held liable also for a hysterical condition that developed because they had damaged a plaintiff with a hysterical personality and they had to take her as they found her. In *H.* v. *Royal Alexandra Hospital* [1990] 1 Med LR 297 the fact that a hemophiliac given AIDS-contaminated blood products was infected with a retro-virus and not with a virus (which alone was foreseeable when the negligent act took place) was of no assistance to the defendants as the damage was of the same kind as what was foreseeable.

In *Doe* v. *USA* [1990] 2 Med LR 131 the US Rhode Island District Court held that it was foreseeable in 1983 that if a patient required through negligence an extensive blood transfusion he might contract AIDS from it.

An hypothesis (for the academically minded)

If a light plank is carelessly tossed into the hold of a ship with the foreseeable risk of it inflicting slight physical injury by hitting a workman, but in fact in a manner that could not be foreseen it strikes sparks from some material lying in the hold and the workman is burnt to death in the ensuing fire, how far will the wrongdoer's liability extend? Are we to say that there is no liability because the damage suffered was not of a foreseeable type in that it arose from burning and not physical impact, or that the manner in which it arose was so different from what was foreseeable that it is to be adjudged of a different type? Or are we to say that physical injury was foreseeable and that is what in fact occurred and it does not matter that it did not happen in the precise manner that was to be foreseen? And would it make any difference if the plank had struck the plaintiff first, doing some slight harm, and then gone on to create the unforeseeable fire?

In my view the result in a situation of this sort would depend on the court's 'gut reaction' to the claim, rather than a logical application of clear legal rules. In this particular case I would expect the wrongdoer to be held not liable for the injury by burning, even if the plank hit the workman first. The rule that you must take the plaintiff as you find him would be irrelevant; the rule that the extent of the damage need not be foreseen would be of no assistance to the plaintiff because the further extent of damage by burning did not arise out of the original injury (if there was one); and the rule that the precise manner in which the injury arose need not be foreseen would not assist the plaintiff either, because the manner in which the injury by burning arose was totally different from the manner in which foreseeable injury would have arisen (see, below, the reference to the case of *Doughty* v. *Turner Manufacturing Co.* [1964] 1 QB 518).

It has in fact been suggested that the only distinction in type to have significance is the distinction between damage to person and damage to property, so that once some physical injury is foreseeable any physical injury suffered is a subject for compensation, no matter how unforeseeable the type, extent or manner of its arising. This might be the most sensible rule, and would do away with the unnecessary subtleties in our law on this point. The courts in any event, to judge by the cases, generally apply such a 'rule' upon the facts before them under one guise or another, e.g. by applying the principle that the defendant must take the plaintiff as he finds him or by interpreting foreseeability widely. But for such a rule to apply officially *The Wagon Mound (No.1)* (*supra*) would have to be confined to damage to property.

In *Aswan Engineering Ltd* v. *Lupdine Ltd* [1987] 1 WLR 1, the Court of Appeal held that, where material packed in pails was exposed for hours to the Arabian sun so that the pails collapsed, the manufacturers of the pails were not liable to the users because the damage suffered was of an unforeseeable type. However, it would seem better to say that the manufacturers had not been negligent in the way they manufactured and marketed the pails because no loss was reasonably foreseeable from their use. It does not seem an appropriate situation to bring in the rule as to type of damage, which only applies when there has been a breach of duty resulting in some loss.

In *Wood* v. *Bentall Simplex Ltd* [1992] PIQR P332 a farmer was held not to have contributed to his own death by building a grid of a non-approved pattern across the entrance to his slurry tank because the consequence of death by asphyxiation after he entered the tank to clear a blockage resulting from the unorthodox construction was not foreseeable. All that was foreseeable was that a person entering the tank to cure the (foreseeable) blockage might slip and fall. The Court of Appeal said that the test of liability for injury by asphyxiation was foreseeability of injury by asphyxiation. See Stop Press p. 261.

THE 'PRECISE MANNER'

We have already adverted to the rule that it does not help a defendant to argue that, although the type of damage could be foreseen, the precise manner in which it arose could not. In *Hughes* v. *Lord Advocate* [1963] AC 837, where a child picked up a lighted Post Office paraffin lamp and entered an unguarded manhole, damage by burning was foreseeable, so that although the manner in which that damage arose was not foreseeable (the child was burned not by the oversetting of the lamp but by an explosion) that did not prevent recovery. In *Stewart* v. *West African Terminals* (1966) 110 SJ 688, the Court of Appeal said that as long as a result is within the general sphere of contemplation, and not of an entirely different kind, the precise chain of events need not be foreseeable.

It is not necessary that the precise concatenation of circumstances should be envisaged. If the consequence was one which was within the general range which any reasonable person might foresee (and was not of an entirely different kind which no-one would anticipate) then it is within the rule that a person who has been guilty of negligence, is liable for its consequences (*per* Lord Denning).

. . . the precise mechanics of the way in which the negligent act results in the original injury do not have to be foreseen (*per* Eveleigh J. in *Wieland* v. *Cyril Lord Carpets* [1969] 3 All ER 1006).

The question of the manner in which the damage arose overlaps with the question whether the damage was of a type that was foreseeable. The difficulties that can arise over these subtle distinctions when injury occurs in an unforeseen manner and one has then to ask whether it still remains within the type of injury foreseeable is illustrated by *Doughty* v. *Turner Manufacturing Co. Ltd* [1964] 1 QB 518, where it appears that the fact that there was a foreseeable risk only of damage from splashing when a cover was carelessly let slip from a height of a few inches into molten liquid prevented recovery for injury caused when the liquid erupted due to an unforeseeable chemical reaction a few moments later. Such subtle distinctions were eschewed in *Parsons (H.) Livestock Ltd* v. *Uttley Ingham & Co. Ltd* [1978] QB 791, where the Court of Appeal said that as long as some illness to the plaintiff's pigs was foreseeable as a result of the defendant's negligence they were liable for the unforeseen illness that did in fact develop, the consequence being of the same type as that which was foreseeable (this was a claim in contract but the court said that the law as to the amount of damages recoverable was the same in contract as in tort).

CONCLUSION

For the purposes of the medical negligence action we may sum up (remembering that we are here only dealing with the question what damage may be compensated for, given a breach of duty, and also bearing in mind that the law is far from clear in this area) as follows.

If there was no foreseeability of harm on the facts that the defendants knew or ought to have known, then recovery for any injury occasioned will not be permitted.

If there was foreseeability of physical damage, however slight the chance and however slight the injury to be foreseen, then compensation may be got for all physical injury resulting from the breach of duty that is of the same type as the injury to be foreseen, plus any injury, however unforeseeable, that is consequent upon the foreseeable injury. Unforeseeable injury not consequent upon a foreseeable injury is not compensatable, but this is subject to the rule that the tortfeasor must take the plaintiff as he finds him.

Subject to that rule, some injury must actually be suffered that falls within the type of injury to be foreseen, i.e. within the area of risk created (in *The Wagon Mound (No.1)* (*supra*) the Privy Council said that foreseeability must be of 'the damage that happened – the damage in suit'). Whether a court these days is likely in practice to say that the injury suffered was of a different type or kind from the injury that could have been foreseen and thus deny recovery to a person injured through another's admitted negligence may be doubted. If a man carelessly tosses a brick out of an upper window and it falls on to an electric cable which causes a passer-by to be electrocuted through an unforeseeable chemical reaction, it may well go against the judicial grain to hold that the injured party cannot recover because the only foreseeable injury was from being struck by the brick and electrocution was a different type of damage. Probably in such a case the court would 'find' that there was a slight degree of foreseeability of electrocution.

When all is said and done, on this aspect of negligence as on every other, the determining factor will be the judge's view as to whether justice dictates recovery. He will then find a legal peg on which to hang his decision. That is particularly easy in the field of negligence, where so much is uncertain and lacks precision. As Lord Wright said in *Bourhill* v. *Young* [1943] AC 92, 107: '. . . negligence is a fluid principle, which has to be applied to the most diverse conditions and problems of human life'. It may well be that, as R.W.M. Dias has said, 'the principles of the future will be that a negligent person shall be liable according as the court thinks reasonable in the circumstances'.[3] The progress of law within a society is always from formalism to flexibility, albeit that in the common law tradition judicial activism is usually disguised by an artfully contrived appearance of deference to authority.[4]

STOP PRESS (ref p. 259)

We may also note the decision of the House of Lords in *Page* v. *Smith* (see footnote, p. 239). Note that the dissenting judges considered nervous injury to be of a different type from physical injury, and therefore for a nervous injury claim to succeed, whether by a primary or secondary victim, it had to be foreseeable.

---

[3] This aphorism is surely validated by the recent retrenchment in the law of negligence, where the House of Lords has completely demolished its own earlier attempt to provide a generalised formula for deciding whether a duty of care lies and has reverted to (mere) categorisation (see Chapter 15).

[4] 'In previous times, when faced with a new problem, the judges have not openly asked themselves the question: what is the best policy for the law to adopt? But the question has always been there in the background. It has been concealed behind such questions as: Was the defendant under any duty to the plaintiff? Was the relationship between them sufficiently proximate? Was the injury direct or indirect? Was it foreseeable or not? Was it too remote? and so forth.' (*per* Lord Denning).

22 · Who to sue[1]

SUMMARY

An employer is vicariously responsible for the negligent acts or omissions of his servant committed within the scope of the employment, but not for the negligence of an independent contractor, provided he showed due care in selecting the contractor.

The correct defendant in respect of allegations of negligence at a hospital is the health authority at district level or, if the unit is a NHS Trust (or special authority), the governing body. It is rarely appropriate to sue the Regional Health Authority. The health authority is liable for the negligence of any of its staff, including all medical personnel it engages to carry out the necessary treatment upon the patients, because it is under a primary non-delegable duty of care to see that the patient receives proper treatment. It is therefore unnecessary to pray in aid the principle of vicarious liability. A health authority is not responsible for the negligence of a doctor who has been selected and employed by the patient.

A private clinic is probably responsible only for the negligence of its resident staff, though where it selects and engages the surgeon itself a court is these days likely to find a primary duty of care, just as with a NHS hospital.

The GP is alone liable for his own negligent acts. He is also liable for the acts of anyone he employs, and may possibly be liable for outside services he engages to look after patients in his absence.

GENERAL PRINCIPLES

The general principles of vicarious liability, that is the liability of one person for the negligence of another, are as follows (they are stated in summary form as the topic is too complex to be discussed here in detail, and our concern is with the medical negligence context; so I give merely the outline of the law and one or two useful references).

The plaintiff has first to show that the negligence complained of was due to the act or omission of an employee of the defendant. An employee is one who is engaged upon a contract of service.

---

[1] The solecism is deliberate, in the interests of euphony.

An independent contractor is not engaged upon a contract of service, but a contract for services (a nice distinction).

The test of employment has varied through the years. Basically a man is not an employee if the person who engaged him has no say in how he does his work, but only in what work he is to do. If the person engaged is subject to the control and directions of the other in respect of the manner in which the work is to be done he will be an employee (the leading case is *Mersey Docks and Harbour Board* v. *Coggins and Griffith (Liverpool) Ltd* [1947] AC 1). It is often not easy to decide on applying this test whether there is a situation of employment. A good reference point is the judgment of Mackenna J. in *Ready Mixed Concrete (South East) Ltd* v. *Ministry of Pensions and National Insurance* [1968] 2 QB 497.[2]

Secondly, the plaintiff has to show that the negligence complained of was committed within and not outside the course or scope of the employee's employment. Is the unauthorised and wrongful act of the employee one way, albeit an improper way, of discharging his obligations under the contract of employment, or is it an independent act unconnected with his employment (a useful point of reference on this question is *Century Insurance Co.* v. *Northern Ireland Road Transport Board* [1942] AC 509).[3] An employee may be acting within the scope of his employment even if he acts in express disregard of instructions or prohibitions from his employer (compare *Limpus* v. *London General Omnibus Co.* (1862) 1 H & C 526 with *Twine* v. *Beans Express Ltd* [1946] 2 All ER 202, and observe the difficulties which those conflicting lines of authority gave the Court of Appeal in *Rose* v. *Plenty* [1976] 1 WLR 141.

---

[2] Reference may also be made in this context to the House of Lords' judgment in *McDermid* v. *Nash Dredging and Reclamation Co.* [1987] 3 WLR 212.
[3] Recent cases illustrating the test of 'was it a mode, albeit an improper mode, of performing his duties under the contract of employment' are *Irving* v. *Post Office, The Independent*, 3 April 1987, CA (the Post Office was not vicariously liable for the spiteful act of a postman scrawling a racist slur on an envelope before delivering it to the home of the victim of his malice, because his act was unconnected with the performance of his duties); in *Stenner* v. *Taff-Ely Borough Council*, 15 May 1987, CA, a gymnastics coach employed by a local authority was not acting within the scope of his employment when coaching friends in the gym outside his working hours, even though he was allowed so to do. He was said to be engaged on a private venture of his own. A policeman's employer was not vicariously liable for his tort of blackmailing a woman he was investigating into yielding her body to him, as he was clearly on an adventure of his own (*Makanjuola* v. *Commissioner of Police of the Metropolis, The Times*, 8 August 1989). Members of a fire brigade who, while operating a 'go-slow' policy, took so long to reach a fire that the building and its contents were substantially destroyed, were not acting in the course of their employment, and so their employer was not liable for their default (*General Engineering Services* v. *Kingston and St Andrew Corporation* [1989] 1 WLR 69, PC). An employee travelling to work in his own car, and paid for so travelling, was within the course of his employment (*Smith* v. *Stages* [1989] AC 928).

A master may be liable for the dishonest acts of his servant, e.g. where he approbates the act or it is committed in the furtherance of his purpose; but where the act is quite outside the purpose for which the servant is employed the master will not be liable. Compare *Morris* v. *C.W. Martin & Sons Ltd* [1966] 1 QB 716, where an employer was liable when his employee stole the fur that it was his job to clean, with *Heasmans* v. *Clarity Cleaning Co.* [1987] ICR 949, CA, where the dishonest use of the telephone in an office by an employee employed only to clean that office was not something for which the employer was liable.

The 'scope of employment' principle could assume significance in a medical negligence context, in that, even though, as we shall see, there is a primary non-delegable duty of care imposed upon a health authority, negligence by medical personnel falling outside the scope of their employment would not render the health authority liable (for example, staff playing a game of cricket on the lawns and carelessly hitting the ball at a patient sitting in the sun, or an off-duty nurse running down a patient as she drives out of the grounds). In *Rosen* v. *Edgar* (1986) 293 BMJ 552, the plaintiff, acting in person, sued a consultant for acts done by his senior registrar. It was held, as one would expect, that a senior employee was not answerable for the fault of a junior employee, for he did not employ him, albeit he had overall supervision of him.

Whether an act falls within the course of employment is a question of fact in each case, and a broad view must be taken of all the surrounding circumstances.

INDEPENDENT CONTRACTOR

There is in general no liability for the acts of an independent contractor, i.e. one who is free to perform the work contracted for in his own way. Sometimes the factual matrix within which the question of 'independence' and control arises is complex. In *P* v. *Harrow London Borough Council, The Times*, 22 April 1992, a local education authority which, in furtherance of its duty under the Education Act 1981 to make provision for children with special educational needs, sent boys with emotional behavioural difficulties to an independent school approved by the Secretary of State for Education and Science, was held not liable in negligence for sexual abuse committed on the boys by the headmaster of the school while the boys were in his charge. The contact between the local authority and the boys was said by the court to have been wholly in the context of assessment and place provision and not in the context of physical control or direction, which was at all times in the charge of the parents and the staff of the school.

However, if the employer has a primary duty to perform an act, he will be liable if his agent in the performance of that act, whether independent contractor or not, performs the act negligently. It is not generally clear to what extent a person has, apart from a contractual or statutory duty, a primary duty of care in respect of an activity, although fortunately it is now beyond argument that under English law a health authority is under a primary non-delegable duty of care in respect of the treatment that is afforded the patient under its auspices.

It may be that the scope of the primary duty in law cannot as a general rule be extended beyond acts which create a source of danger. In respect of hazardous activities the employer is liable for the negligence of an independent contractor. Liability is, however, restricted in all cases to acts which fall within the duty of care of the employer: he is not liable for the collateral negligence of the independent contractor, i.e. for acts which are not in fulfilment of the activity in respect of which the primary duty of care is imposed on the employer (a leading case is *Padbury* v. *Holliday and Greenwood Ltd* (1912) 28 TLR 494). The liability of the employer for the acts of the independent contractor should not be seen as an example of vicarious liability, that is to say liability assumed by one person on behalf of another, but rather as an example of the situation where a person is himself under a primary duty of care which he cannot delegate to another (see below under 'The Primary Duty of Care').

HEALTH AUTHORITY AS DEFENDANT

The appropriate defendant when the action arises out of NHS treatment in hospital is the health authority at district level or the governing body if the hospital or unit has acquired NHS Trust status, not the Regional Health Authority.[4] Solicitors will often find themselves dealing with the legal adviser to the Regional Health Authority (while such a body still exists) to whom the hospital has passed the request for disclosure of the hospital notes, and this may give the impression that his clients are Region and it is they who should be made the defendants. This is not so. A few hospitals have for years had special constitutions, so that the hospital itself or its board of governors is the appropriate

[4] The National Health Service Act 1977 provides by Sched. 5, para. 15: 'An authority shall, notwithstanding that it is exercising any function on behalf of the Secretary of State or another authority, . . . be liable in respect of any liabilities incurred (including liabilities in tort) in the exercise of that function in all respects as if it were acting as a principal. Proceedings for the enforcement of such . . . liabilities shall be brought, and brought only, . . . against the authority in question in its own name.'

defendant, but usually a NHS hospital came within the jurisdiction of a health authority at district level, and it was that authority which had to be made the defendant. Now that hospitals can opt out of health authority control under the National Health Service and Community Care Act 1990 (though remaining of course within the NHS) there will be more hospitals with 'special' authorities (usually NHS trusts), and the appropriate defendants if you are suing in respect of treatment at a hospital that has opted out will be the new body. The hospital administrator will always tell you the correct name of the body that runs the hospital.

However, always bear in mind that the body responsible for any negligent conduct in NHS treatment is the body in charge of the hospital at the time of the alleged negligence. This body may have changed its name or even disappeared as a separate body. It may simply have a new name. Or it may have merged. Or it may have been subsumed into an existing body or into a new body entirely. Although the legislature will always have provided for some body to have taken over the pre-existing liabilities of the old body, it will *not* be the NHS trust that may now be running the hospital (a trust would not exactly be delighted to hear that its limited funds are going to be targeted to settle the health authority's liabilities!). As I have said, it is not difficult to find out the name of the body running the hospital at the time of the alleged negligence, and it is just as easy to find out, if that body is no longer extant under the same name, what body is now responsible for the pre-existing liabilities of the original body.

Action may be brought for an act or omission that is directly the responsibility of the authority, such as a failure to provide appropriate medical facilities (see, for example, *Bull and Wakeham* v. *Devon Health Authority* [1993] 4 Med LR 117, where the court found that the system of obstetric cover provided was not acceptable in that it gave rise to a real inherent risk that an obstetrician might not attend reasonably promptly); or for an act or omission that is directly the responsibility of the hospital, such as a failure to take appropriate general anti-infection measures (*Lindsey County Council* v. *Marshall* [1937] AC 97); or for specific acts of negligence by its staff. By and large all medical personnel working at the hospital may be regarded as employed by the health authority at district level. Obviously the nursing staff are and the resident doctors and technicians, but, even though, strictly speaking, senior staff and consultants are employed by the Regional Health Authority there is no need for that reason to sue Region; the health authority at district level is not going to take the point (this was confirmed in a useful book published by the National Association of Health Authorities, *Patient Complaints and Litigation* by Brian Capstick). Occasionally the Regional Health Authority is the appropriate defendant, for example where negligence on the part of the ambulance service is alleged and that service is run by Region.

There is no point in adding the particular doctor as defendant where the health authority is in any event clearly liable for any negligence on the doctor's part. It increases costs, delays the trial, and it may be unfair on a young doctor unnecessarily to turn the spotlight and put the pressure on him when he may have been doing his overworked best, perhaps also when he had been, for lack of better qualified staff, required to discharge a responsibility for which he was not yet properly trained (this is not just a matter of being gentlemanly, for it is not in anyone's interest to discourage or even destroy a young doctor in such circumstances). Note also that a ground for transfer from the County Court to the High Court is that the case is 'important, particularly to persons who are not parties' (see Chapter 10 under 'High Court or County Court?'), which could be a good reason not to join the doctors as defendants.[5]

Suing two defendants

The situation often arises that there appear to be two different parties potentially liable, for example GP and hospital, or two different hospitals run by different health authorities. Liability may be in the alternative or both may be severally liable. One is then anxious about costs in the event of succeeding against one only. The recent judgment of the Court of Appeal in *Gerdes-Hardy* v. *Wessex Regional Health Authority* [1994] PIQR P368 shows that, even where the unsuccessful defendant has not been responsible for the plaintiff having joined the successful defendant (i.e. it did not seek to cast blame in that direction), the court may, if it thinks it reasonable to do so,

---

[5] If it were true (which it appears no longer to be in the light of the decision of the House of Lords in the Scottish case of *British Medical Association* v. *Greater Glasgow Health Board* [1989] AC 1211 and s.60 of the National Health Service and Community Care Act 1990, as to which see Chapter 3 under 'The NHS and the Crown') that summary judgment under O.14 were not possible against a health authority as being 'the Crown' (see O.77 r.7), then if it were the sort of case where you were justified in going for summary judgment it would be helpful to join the doctor personally – I presume the doctor would not be held to be an 'officer of the Crown', i.e. a 'servant of Her Majesty', within ss.21(2) and 38(2) of the Crown Proceedings Act 1947.

Going for O.14 is something of a new idea among those who act for plaintiffs in medical negligence actions, so its full implications are still being worked out – note that interest on damages will not run from the date of the summary judgment but from the date damages are assessed; see Chapter 10.

order the unsuccessful defendant to pay the costs of the successful defendant. If, however, it becomes necessary to discontinue against one defendant, the best one can hope for is an agreement that each side pay its own costs, in which case the plaintiff's costs against the discontinued party may be claimable by the legal aid fund out of any damages awarded.

WHO PAYS THE DAMAGES?

The old system

The apportionment of damages or agreed damages of compensation between a health authority and a medical defence society was regulated by the government circular HM(54)32 which advised that, irrespective of which party was actually being sued, the apportionment should be the subject of agreement based upon a joint assessment of the extent to which either party, the health authority or the doctors, were responsible for the accident. Sometimes the responsibility for what happened was clearly entirely that of members of the defence society, i.e. the doctors; sometimes doctors were not involved – perhaps it arose from a failure of nursing care, e.g. out of the activities of nurses or midwives in the context of obstetric care; and sometimes it was in part due to the actions of the doctors and in part due to the actions of health authority agents or employees who were not members of the defence society. In this latter case, if agreement as to apportionment was not reached, the circular provided that each should pay one-half of the damages. If either party objected, the relevant experts might meet to come to a joint decision; failing that, arbitration might be sought and a barrister appointed as arbitrator; and, at worst, in the exceptional case, the two defendants might fight it out in court, the one having given notice to the other of such hostile intent.[6]

The new system

From early 1990 the system known as 'Crown indemnity' has come into force. The health authorities are now exclusively liable for the negligence of any of the doctors in their hospitals (apart of course from the doctor's own liability for his mistakes – but, as I have said, I see little point in suing the doctor as

---

[6] Note that the medical defence societies are not insurers (*Medical Defence Union* v. *Department of Trade* [1980] Ch 82).

well). In other words, the medical defence societies are no longer called upon to bear any share of the costs of a successful medical negligence claim in the United Kingdom except in respect of GP practice or private treatment. By amicable arrangement certain substantial funds held by the medical defence societies for satisfying medical negligence claims were, as a transitional provision, transferred to the Government, for disbursement to the health authorities. The Government has the task of deciding to what extent to increase the budgets of the health authorities to allow for their increased liability. Currently NHS trusts are setting up a pooling arrangement to meet liabilities (the Central Fund for Clinical Negligence, as from April 1995). Their budgets are obviously smaller than a health authority's, and two or three large claims could spell disaster.

In January 1991 AVMA voiced concern that there was some evidence, following the introduction of Crown indemnity, that health authorities were starting to defend unmeritorious cases and to protract the hour of judgment by any means in order to protect their budget, at the same time trying to work a sort of blackmail on potential plaintiffs by saying that every time an action succeeded a bed, or even a ward, was lost. I cannot believe that that sort of conduct will become widespread.

However, one unsatisfactory consequence of the introduction of Crown indemnity and the creation of NHS trusts that can be discerned is that some hospitals or even health authorities are, perhaps for financial reasons, instructing solicitors who, however otherwise reputable they may be, are not experienced in medical negligence litigation, with the result that claims are not properly handled; in particular these firms are often unreasonably obstructive to the investigation of a claim. It is to be hoped that they will learn the ropes in time.

NHS handling and funding arrangements

The Health Circular (89)34, published December 1989, asks health authorities with effect from the beginning of 1990 to assume responsibility for new *and* existing claims of medical negligence, to ensure a named officer has sufficient authority to make decisions on the conduct of cases on the authority's behalf, and to release medical and dental staff from their previous obligation to belong to a medical defence organisation. For claims lodged on or after 1 January 1990 health authorities are free to handle the defence as they see fit, using the services of a medical defence organisation or any other advisers or in-house expertise (for pre-existing claims the health authority is encouraged to retain the services of the relevant medical defence organisation).

The health authority in handling a claim is to pay particular attention to ('take careful note of') any view expressed by any practitioner concerned and to any potentially damaging effect on his or her professional reputation. They should also have regard to any point of principle or of wide application raised by the case and to the costs involved.

The circular explains what work by its doctors a health service body will be responsible for, e.g. not for a consultant's private practice even in a NHS hospital, not for reports written for insurance companies, not for Good Samaritan acts, though at the same time it states that a liberal interpretation should be given to the concept of acts performed within the course of employment.

As to funding: for settlement of pre-1990 claims, assistance for the health authority may be got from the transitional funds provided by the medical defence organisations (about £50m when set up), up to 80% of the excess over £300,000.

For 'new' claims (i.e. all cases of clinical negligence arising from incidents which occur after 1 April 1991) the financial liability will fall directly upon the hospital itself, whether a directly managed unit, i.e. a hospital which has not opted out of health authority control, or on the NHS Trust that is the governing body of a hospital that has opted out. In this way it is hoped that every hospital will have a direct incentive to tighten up its procedures.

Both directly managed units and NHS Trusts can get interest-bearing loans to help meet their liabilities upon claims for clinical negligence, the former by way of a cash limit addition made by the RHA to the DHA (but Region will not be given additional funds to enable this(!)), the latter by way of loan from the Secretary of State within external financing limits (for all these matters see the letters from the NHS Management Executive EL(90)195 and (91)19).

'Clinical negligence' is defined in EL(91)19 in appropriate terms referring to breach of duty of care resulting in foreseeable, cognizable loss.

Health authorities are unlikely to insure – that would need Departmental and Treasury agreement. NHS Trusts are free to make their own insurance arrangements (see EL(90)195).[7]

---

[7] I am grateful to John Pringle for advice and direction on this section.

THE PRIVATE PATIENT

The private plaintiff has to be careful. Though a private clinic is responsible for its resident staff, on the basis that they are employed by the clinic, a consultant may be an independent contractor, engaged on a contract for services rather than a contract of service. If he is not employed by the clinic the clinic will not be vicariously liable for his actions; and, furthermore, it is doubtful if a court would accept the argument that he was engaged to perform hazardous activities and for that reason the clinic must be held vicariously responsible if he is negligent in the course of performing them (one of the exceptions to the rule that a person who engages an independent contractor is not liable for his negligence, provided that due care was taken in the selection of the contractor). So the private patient will probably have to sue the consultant concerned if it is his acts or omissions that are alleged to be negligent. It is, however, arguable that, provided it was the clinic and not the patient that engaged the surgeon, albeit upon a contract for services, the clinic is under the same primary duty of care as a NHS hospital (there seems no reason to limit Lord Denning's words (see below) as to the primary duty of care to NHS institutions).

In *Ellis* v. *Wallsend District Hospital* [1990] 2 Med LR 103 the New South Wales Court of Appeal held that a public hospital was not vicariously liable for the acts of an 'honorary medical officer', a neuro-surgeon, who was treating a patient pursuant to a direct engagement between him and the patient. This case needs to be studied by anyone seeking to impose liability outside the NHS framework on a health authority or hospital for a doctor's negligence.

THE GP

If negligence is alleged against a general practitioner or anyone employed by him (e.g. nurses, receptionists, secretaries), including any locum he engages, it is the GP who is the appropriate defendant (a physician was held liable for his apprentice's negligence in *Hancke* v. *Hooper* (1835) 7 C & P 81). It is possible but, I think, unlikely that he would be held to have a primary non-delegable duty towards the patient to ensure that any alternative care he arranges for when he is 'off' comes up to appropriate professional standards.[8] The locum or doctor concerned in the alternative service is of course liable for any negligent act or omission on his part. Probably one cannot take the GP's liability for an independent locum further than to say that he must be reasonably satisfied of the competence of the deputising service he engages. GPs are engaged by the Family Health Services Authority (formerly Family Practitioner Committee) on contracts for services,[9] so that neither the FHSA nor the health authority is responsible for the negligence of GPs. Probably the GP does not have a contract with his patient either, unless the patient is a private patient. A GP is not permitted to act privately for a patient who is on his NHS list (as one knows, the GP may refer the patient to a consultant who may treat privately). It might occasionally be the case that certain services carried out upon the premises of a general practice are performed by agents of the health authority, rather than employees of the doctor, for example immunisation services, or, if it should come to this, AIDS screening and inoculation. Care always needs to be taken in identifying the employer. For example, the health visitor, the community nurse and the community midwife, though working closely with the GP, are employed by the health authority, and although they may be acting at times under the direction of the GP, it is the health authority and not the GP who will be responsible for any mistakes they personally make.

GPs are not obliged to insure, although it is likely to be a condition of any partnership agreement that participating doctors do insure. NHS hospital doctors, as we have seen, are now covered by Crown indemnity. I know of no obligation on a consultant in private practice to insure, though he would be wise to!

If the Conservative Government's plans to transfer the duty to provide GP care to the local health authority are realised, it might be possible to contend that the health authority is under a primary non-delegable duty to provide GP care, similar to its duty in respect of hospital care, and that therefore the health

[8] In *Lobley* v. *Going* (1985) it was stated that if it was brought to a GP receptionist's attention that a small child had been brought to the surgery in an ill condition, with respiratory difficulties about which the parents were concerned, it was her duty to inform the doctor immediately and if she did not do so she would be guilty of negligence. It would follow that the employer GP, or GP practice, would be vicariously answerable for that negligence (on the facts it was held that she had not been negligent).
[9] See *Roy* v. *Kensington and Chelsea and Westminster Family Practitioner Committee* [1992] 1 AC 624.

authority is liable for a GP's negligence (see below under 'The primary duty of care').

AS TO CONTRACT

It has not been decided whether a NHS patient has a contract with the doctor or health authority (or hospital that has opted out) who or which treats him. Probably not. It does not seem to be consistent with the scheme of the NHS. Even though the patient may at times come under the care of a particular doctor he has no right to demand that he be treated by any particular practitioner. The point may assume importance if it is ever of advantage to a patient to bring his claim in contract rather than tort. This is not likely often to be the case, but it may possibly arise in certain circumstances. *Charlesworth on Negligence* (7th edn) at p. 542 states:

> The duty in contract is only owed to the parties to the contract, but it would seem that there is in most cases a contract between patient and medical practitioner, even if the patient himself is not liable for payment of the services rendered, such payment being made by someone else;

but no authority is given for that proposition. In *Emeh* v. *Kensington and Chelsea and Westminster Area Health Authority* [1985] QB 1012 Slade L.J. spoke of the plaintiff 'contracting' with the health authority (though he was not concerned with this particular point). On the other hand the Master of the Rolls appears to have assumed in *Hotson* v. *Fitzgerald* [1987] 2 WLR 287 *obiter* that a NHS patient is not in contractual relation with the NHS or its staff. It is in any event clear that, given a contract, the duty of care is owed both in contract and in tort (see *Midland Bank Trust Co.* v. *Hett Stubbs and Kemp* [1979] Ch 384), and that the plaintiff can elect which remedy to pursue.[10]

THE PRIMARY DUTY OF CARE

The most important point about hospital treatment is that it is not necessary to prove the facts that would give rise to vicarious liability, because the hospital has a primary non-delegable duty of care to provide proper treatment.

---

[10] In *Lancashire and Cheshire Association of Baptist Churches* v. *Howard & Seddon Partnership* [1993] 3 All ER 467 it was held that there was no reason in principle why a duty of care in tort should not exist, and be sued upon, in the context of a contractual professional relationship. In *Henderson* v. *Merrett Syndicates Ltd* (and associated cases) [1994] 3 WLR 761, the House of Lords held that Lloyd's underwriting agents owed to various Lloyd's Names a concurrent duty of care in contract and in tort to carry out their underwriting functions with reasonable care and skill, and that the plaintiffs could elect which remedy to pursue.

While the courts were still applying the distinction between employer and independent contractor for the purpose of establishing liability on the part of a hospital for the negligence of medical personnel, the nice distinctions of the common law mentioned above (e.g. as to whether the employer could control the manner in which the work was done) were important. So in *Hillyer* v. *St Bartholomew's Hospital* [1909] 2 KB 820, Kennedy L.J. expressed the view that a hospital, though responsible for the exercise of due care in selecting its professional staff, whether surgeons, doctors or nurses, was not responsible if they or any of them acted negligently in matters of professional care or skill.

I see no ground for holding it to be a right legal inference from the circumstances of the relation of hospital and patient that the hospital authority makes itself liable in damages if members of the professional staff, of whose competence there is no question, act negligently towards the patient in some matter of professional care or skill, or neglect to use or use negligently in his treatment the apparatus or appliances which are at their disposal (*per* Kennedy L.J.).

It was even said that as soon as the nurses enter the operating theatre the health authority was no longer liable for any errors they may make because they were then under the control of the surgeon, for whose errors the health authority was not responsible.

In *Davis* v. *LCC* (1914) 30 TLR 275, a local education authority could not be held liable for a medical practitioner's negligence in carrying out an operation upon a school pupil if he had engaged a competent practitioner and if that practitioner was not in his employment.

In *Gold* v. *Essex County Council* [1942] 2 KB 293, the Court of Appeal was concerned to distinguish between different types of staff: the hospital would not be responsible for the acts of a consulting surgeon or physician, but the position of a house physician or surgeon was left open. Goddard L.J. said that responsibility for the position of doctors on the permanent staff would depend on whether the doctor was engaged on a contract for services or a contract of service. On the facts the defendants were responsible for the negligence of a radiographer who was a full-time employee.

In *Collins* v. *Hertfordshire County Council* [1947] KB 598, Hilbery J. considered that a hospital was responsible for the acts of a house surgeon but not for the acts of a part-time surgeon.

In *Cassidy* v. *Ministry of Health* [1951] 2 KB 343, it was left to Lord Denning, as ever, to direct the law onto a path more appropriate to modern social needs. In that case Somervell L.J. was prepared to hold a hospital liable for the acts of permanent medical staff, those who were employed to provide the patient with nursing and medical treatment, but not for the acts of a visiting or consulting surgeon or physician. Both he and Singleton L.J. decided for the plaintiff on the basis that, even though the plaintiff could not pinpoint the employee who had been negligent, there had clearly been negligence by one or more employees of the hospital.

Denning L.J. said that the hospital was under a duty to take reasonable care of all patients, whether private or not. They would be discharging that duty through their staff, and it was no answer for the hospital to say that the staff concerned were professionals who would not tolerate any interference with the way they did their work. When hospitals undertook to treat a patient, and themselves selected and appointed and employed the professionals who were to give the treatment (as opposed to the patient himself selecting and employing the staff – which he would be doing if he were to ask a consultant to operate on him privately), the hospital was responsible for any negligence, no matter whether of doctors, surgeons, nurses or anyone else; and 'it does not depend on the fine distinction whether the medical man was engaged under a contract of service or a contract for services'.

I take it to be clear law as well as good sense that where a person is himself under a duty to use care, he cannot get rid of his responsibility by delegating the performance of it to someone else, no matter whether the delegation be to a servant under a contract of service or to an independent contractor under a contract for services.

In *Roe* v. *Minister of Health* [1954] 2 QB 66, McNair J. at first instance held himself bound by the majority in *Cassidy's* case to find that a specialist anesthetist who carried on a private anesthetic practice but was under an obligation to provide a regular service to the hospital concerned, and on the occasion in question had been assisting the theatre staff of the hospital, was not a person for whose acts the hospital could be held liable. On appeal Somervell L.J. said that he regarded the anesthetist as on the permanent staff of the hospital and therefore it would be liable for his errors. Morris L.J. said that the hospital had undertaken to provide all the necessary facilities and equipment for the operation and the obligations of nursing and anesthetising. This was going some way towards Denning L.J.'s concept of a primary non-delegable duty of care, but Morris L.J. was still basing himself on the maxim of vicarious liability, *respondeat superior*.

Once again it was Denning L.J. who brushed aside nice distinctions with a robust and lucid exposition:

I think that the hospital authorities are responsible for the whole of their staff, not only for the nurses and doctors, but also for the anaesthetists and surgeons. It does not matter whether they are permanent or temporary, resident or visiting, whole-time or part-time. The hospital authorities are responsible for all of them. The reason is because, even if they are not servants, they are the agents of the hospital to give the treatment. The only exception is the case of consultants or anaesthetists selected and employed by the patient himself.

It is clear from *Barnett* v. *Chelsea and Kensington Hospital Management Committee* [1969] 1 QB 428, that a health authority will be held responsible for the negligent omission by a casualty department to treat a person who presents himself at the door of the department.

Although, on a strict analysis, it has been only Lord Denning who imposes on a health authority responsibility for all the medical personnel it engages to carry out treatment to patients, there can be little doubt that a court would today follow his lead. In any event it is clear that early cases should be treated with the greatest care, as they are unlikely to reflect the modern law.

Examples of such decisions

Evans v. *Liverpool Corporation* [1906] 1 KB 160, where a hospital was not liable for the negligent discharge by a physician of a boy still infectious from scarlet fever; *Hillyer*'s case (*supra*) where the hospital was not liable for the burning of a patient's arms in the operating theatre; *Strangways-Lesmere* v. *Clayton* [1936] 2 KB 11, no liability for the negligence of nurses in administering the wrong dosage (overruled by *Gold*'s case (*supra*)); *Dryden* v. *Surrey County Council and Stewart* [1936] 2 All ER 535, no liability for the discharge home after an operation of a patient with a wad of surgical gauze still inside her. *Junor* v. *McNichol, The Times*, 26 March 1959, where a house surgeon was declared not liable for the negligent treatment of a child because he was acting under the instructions of the consultant. Surgeons were not liable for negligent bathing of a patient by nurses: *Perionowsky* v. *Freeman* (1866) 4 F & F 977. A surgeon was not liable when a tube was found in the patient's body three months after surgery as it could have been put or left there by the nurses and house doctors any time since the operation: *Morris* v. *Winsbury-White* [1937] 4 All ER 494.

These cases were important in the context of vicarious liability, when it mattered on whom the plaintiff could fix liability. But, as I have said, in most cases now the hospital will be liable for the negligence of any of the medical staff. The importance of vicarious liability in the context of medical negligence has substantially diminished. It may, however, still assume significance in the case of a private clinic, where the clinic may be able to avoid liability for the mistakes of a visiting consultant, though probably only where the patient has chosen and privately contracted with him, or, if the consultant is being sued himself, he may be able to avoid responsibility for the mistakes of others not under his direct control at the time.

The interaction between vicarious responsibility and the non-delegable duty of care, and the significance of the distinction between these two bases of liability, was considered by the Court of Appeal in the case of *Wilsher* v. *Essex Area Health Authority* [1987] QB 730 (reversed on another ground by the House of Lords).

The Ontario Court of Appeal has reviewed the concept of the non-delegable duty of care and by a majority declined to follow the English cases (*Yepremian* v. *Scarborough General Hospital* (1980) 110 DLR (3d) 513). Arnup J.A. said that great care had to be taken when considering the English cases as the interrelationship of the State, the medical profession, the hospitals and their patients had developed in England along different lines from those it had followed in Ontario.

23 · The proof of negligence

SUMMARY

There are a number of difficulties a plaintiff faces in proving negligence. They include the problem of ascertaining exactly what was done in the course of treatment, of securing expert evidence which will allege and substantiate a want of due care, of proving a causative link between the treatment and the injury, and of overcoming any possible pro-doctor prejudice in the mind of the judge, and, if the matter goes further, the appeal court.

The burden of proving negligent conduct resulting in injury is upon the plaintiff. Where there is no direct or circumstantial evidence which permits a conclusion to be drawn as to how the accident happened, the plaintiff may pray in aid the maxim *res ipsa loquitur* (the matter speaks for itself). This applies where what happened is not the sort of thing that would normally happen in the absence of negligence in some form or another. The court may then find that there was negligence even though it is not known what form that negligence took. If the defendants give a reasonable explanation as to how the accident might have happened without negligence, or show that they had in fact taken every possible care of the patient, the court will not be entitled to rely on the maxim.

CLOSING RANKS

It is common knowledge that it has been extremely difficult to prove that a doctor has been negligent. The usual reason given for this is that you could not find an expert who is willing to accuse a colleague. This is known as the 'closing ranks' syndrome, and it no doubt has contributed to plaintiffs' difficulties, particularly where the specialty concerned is a narrow one, for its practitioners will almost certainly all know each other, so that the reluctance to accuse of negligence is all the more pronounced. I have already considered the question how to find and instruct a suitable expert in Chapter 9. Fortunately it is easier these days to get a fair assessment of a patient's treatment than it was, due largely to greater expertise in choosing experts.

JUDICIAL PREJUDICE

But there are other reasons why it is hard to prove medical negligence. One reason is, or at any rate has been, the anti-patient prejudice of the courts. To read some of the older cases, and even some of the more modern rulings of the appeal courts, which have not been slow, in this field more than most, to reverse the trial judge's finding of negligence, one would think that the plaintiff was virtually guilty of *lèse-majesté* in bringing an action. It must be a matter of one's own impression as to how responsive a court is to the medical negligence plaintiff: I have certainly gained the impression that the House of Lords was and is unresponsive, while the Court of Appeal, when Lord Donaldson was Master of the Rolls in place of Lord Denning, became considerably more responsive.

Unfortunately, when one looks at recent decisions of the Court of Appeal, particularly on limitation and nervous shock, one gets the impression that the trend is now the other way. Judges of first instance strive to be impartial, although there is one High Court judge, well known in medical negligence circles, who is the subject of an unusual statistic, in that, as far as the researches of those who act for patients have been able to establish, he has never given judgment in favour of the patient (we may, however, assume that this is simply because none of the claims he has heard have been valid ones).[1]

DIFFICULTIES IN CAUSATION

Another obstacle to proving a claim for compensation is that, even if you know what specific acts or omissions you are alleging to have been negligent, you need to be able to prove that not only did they constitute a less than reasonable standard of care, but also that they were the cause of injury or loss to the patient. Negligence is not actionable without proof of loss or injury arising from the negligent acts or omissions. But the etiology of medical conditions is notoriously complex and obscure. Would the correct or timely treatment have prevented death or resulted in the patient being better off than he actually is? How to prove that a particular act or omission caused any part of the plaintiff's

---

[1] Sometimes bias may be more apparent than real, e.g. where the judge is, say, chairman of an NHS Trust.

present condition? Can one give, and is it relevant to give, an estimation of the chances of proper treatment having saved or helped him? The problem of causation, of showing that what was done or omitted was not only negligent by professional standards but also caused or may have caused a deterioration in the condition of the patient that would not otherwise have occurred, is considered above in Chapter 18.

BURDEN OF PROOF

The burden of proving what needs to be proved to establish a case rests on the plaintiff. It has been said that there are no special rules about the burden or standard of proof in cases involving professional negligence, but that it must necessarily be harder to prove negligence where a case concerns the 'complicated and sophisticated professional activities of a doctor, lawyer or architect' (*Dwyer* v. *Roderick, The Times*, 12 November 1983).

In *Hucks* v. *Cole* [1993] 4 Med LR 393, Lord Denning had said:

> A charge of negligence against a professional man was serious. It stood on a different footing to a charge of negligence against the driver of a motor car. The consequences were far more serious. It affected his professional status and reputation. The burden of proof was correspondingly greater. As the charge was so grave, so should the proof be clear.

It is clear that that does not represent the modern law.[2]

In *Ashcroft* v. *Mersey Regional Health Authority* [1983] 2 All ER 245 the judge said that the question was whether it had been established on a balance of probabilities that the physician had failed to exercise the care required of a man possessing and professing special skill in circumstances which required the exercise of that special skill. No added burden of proof rested on the plaintiff. The more skilled a person was the more care which was expected of him. That test should be applied without gloss either way (Kilner Brown J.).

The plaintiff has to persuade the court that the only explanation for the injury that can reasonably be accepted is one that involves negligence. If the court cannot select between two explanations for complications following treatment, only one of

---

[2] The same thing may be said for the odd pronouncement from Lord Denning in *Bater* v. *Bater* [1950] 2 All ER 458 (approved by the Court of Appeal in *Hornal* v. *Neuberger Products Ltd* [1956] 3 All ER 970, Lord Denning being a party thereto) to the effect that the degree of probability required to establish proof could vary with the gravity of the allegation. Are we supposed to think, for example, that 51% probability is enough to prove negligence against a shopkeeper or builder but 75% is required against a doctor? Hardly!

which involves negligence, then the plaintiff has not proved his case (*per* Beldam J. in *Harrington* v. *Essex AHA, The Times,* 14 November 1984).

In *Clark* v. *MacLennan* [1983] 1 All ER 416, Pain J. said that where in the context of a general duty of care there had been a failure to take a generally recognised precaution which had been followed by damage of the kind that that precaution was designed to prevent, the burden of proof shifted to the defendant to show either that he was not in breach of duty or that the damage was not caused by the breach. In that case there had been a departure from the usual practice of not performing a certain operation for stress incontinence within three months of delivery; that departure was found to have been unjustified and therefore constituted a breach of the duty of care. It was followed by a consequence that that precaution was designed to prevent, i.e. breakdown of the repair effected in the operation, and it was therefore up to the defendants to satisfy the court that that damage had not flowed from their breach of duty to the patient. However, it was expressly denied by the House of Lords in *Wilsher* v. *Essex Area Health Authority* [1988] AC 1074 that the burden shifted in such circumstances. In *Gregory* v. *Pembrokeshire Health Authority* [1989] 1 Med LR 81, 85, Rougier J. rejected the suggestion that whenever the fault complained of was a fault in omission the burden of proving causation shifted to the defendants: 'the burden of proof on the balance of probabilities remains on the plaintiff throughout'.

It is certainly less intellectually complex if, instead of having a collection of rules and perhaps even some stab at a general formula about when the burden of proof will shift to the defendants, one simply acknowledges that the burden remains on the plaintiff, but in various circumstances where the defendants are seen to be in some regard 'in the wrong', e.g. where they have failed to take a certain precaution or they have lost the medical records, so making it hard for the plaintiff to prove his contention, the court may well be readier to find that the plaintiff has discharged the burden of proof. There will, however, always be some contexts where the burden of proof is on the defendants, but that will usually be in respect of a positive averment that they make by way of confession and avoidance (i.e. they say 'Even if the facts you allege are correct, the result would have been different for the following reason'): for example, where a mother says she would have procured an abortion had she been told of the risk of handicap to the fetus, it is up to her to prove that she would have procured an abortion, not up to the defendants to prove that she would not; but if the defendants allege that any abortion would have been illegal, it is up to them to prove that and not up to her to prove that it would have been legal. Again, if defendants allege that she would not have asked for an abortion because she would have accepted the advice of her consultant not to have one, it is up to the defendants to prove that that would have been his advice but then up to her to prove she would have rejected it. And so on. In order to prove that his injury or loss was caused by the acts of the defendants a plaintiff can take advantage of certain principles as to causation and the nexus or link between the negligence complained of and the injury suffered. These are considered above in Chapter 18. But although they assist the plaintiff to prove the link between the negligent conduct and his loss, they do not affect the principle of the burden of proof. He has to show on a balance of probabilities that he has been caused through the conduct of the defendant loss of a type recognised by the law.

RES IPSA LOQUITUR

What we consider here is a situation that often arises, where not merely is it unclear why the patient's condition has deteriorated or what the cause must have been of the injury he suffered, but where he cannot even point to any act or omission and say that that was wrong, and in all probability caused his present condition, because the only acts or omissions he knows to have taken place are unimpugnable. Therefore all he can say is that something must have been done which should not have been done, because his injury could not have arisen without something having been done wrong. This is the principle of evidence known as *res ipsa loquitur*, 'the matter speaks for itself'.

There must be reasonable evidence of negligence. But where the thing is shown to be under the management of the defendant or his servants, and the accident is such as in the ordinary course of things does not happen if those who have the management use proper care, it affords reasonable evidence, in the absence of explanation by the defendant, that the accident arose from want of care (*per* Erle C.J. in *Scott* v. *London & St Katherine Docks Co.* (1865) 3 H & C 596).

The maxim applies where 'the circumstances are more consistent, reasonably interpreted without further explanation, with . . . negligence than with any other cause of the accident happening' (*per* Kennedy L.J. in *Russell* v. *L & SW Ry* (1908) 24 TLR 548, 551).

The court is in any event entitled to make an inference as to how an accident happened upon the evidence before it. It may be that no-one can give direct evidence of how it happened, but, if the evidence that is given permits a reasonable inference to be drawn as to the cause, the court in drawing such an inference is not applying the principle of *res ipsa loquitur*, for that principle only applies where the cause cannot be specified, whether upon direct evidence or by inference.

If the facts are sufficiently known the question ceases to be one where the facts speak for themselves, and the solution is to be found by determining whether on the facts as established negligence is to be inferred or not (*per* Lord Porter in *Barkway* v. *South Wales Transport Co. Ltd* [1950] 1 All ER 392, 395).

An example of this type of inference is found in the case *Clowes* v. *National Coal Board, The Times*, 23 April 1987, in which the Court of Appeal said that, where there is no clear evidence of an accident but the court knows of habitual careless behaviour which could have caused it, the court may assume that to be the cause in the absence of any other explanation.

The maxim is also misapplied if it is sought to be used where it is known what the doctor did and the dispute is as to whether that constituted negligence. A surgeon performing a laminectomy may penetrate too far and injure the nerve or the spinal cord. One cannot say indignantly: 'Of course it was negligent; the matter speaks for itself'. That is simply a misunderstanding of what the maxim means in law. It would be up to expert evidence to establish whether or not any surgeon exercising due care could make that mistake.

The statement of claim usually pleads that the plaintiff will pray in aid the principle of *res ipsa loquitur*, but that would appear to be unnecessary if the pleading is otherwise complete as to the facts alleged (see *Bennett* v. *Chemical Construction (GB)* (1970) 115 SJ 550).

The maxim has often been applied where a defendant is carrying out lifting or building operations and the plaintiff is injured by a falling article. It is not known what made it fall, but the court declares that it would be unlikely to have happened without negligence.

In *Howard* v. *Wessex Regional Health Authority* [1994] 5 Med LR 57 Morland J. said that *res ipsa* could not help the patient where she had sustained tetraplegia following maxillo-facial surgery by way of a sagittal split osteotomy, because her injury was most likely due to a fibro-cartilaginous embolism, which would not connote negligence. Reference was made to the unreported Court of Appeal case of *Delaney* v. *Southmead Health Authority*, 9 June 1992, in which Stuart-Smith L.J. doubted that the principle was useful in medical negligence actions, at least not where 'all the evidence in the case has been adduced'[3], and Dillon L.J. said:

I cannot for my part accept that medical science is such a precise science that there cannot in any particular field be any room for the wholly unexpected result occurring in the human body from the carrying out of a well-recognised procedure.

As the helpful note by Margaret Puxon QC at the end of the report of *Howard* shows, it appears that the defendants, as not infrequently happens in medical cases, advanced their explanation for the injury very late in the day. It seems surprising that the judge accepted it.

In *Girard* v. *Royal Columbian Hospital* (1976) 66 DLR 3d 676, where the patient had suffered permanent paralysis of both legs after a spinal anesthetic, the Canadian judge, Andrews J., exonerating the anesthetist, used words similar to Dillon L.J. in the *Delaney* case:

The human body is not a container filled with a material whose performance can be predictably charted and analysed. It cannot be equated with a box of chewing tobacco or a soft drink. Thus, while permissible inferences may be drawn as to the normal behaviour of these types of commodities, the same type of reasoning does not necessarily apply to a human being. Because of this, medical science has not yet reached the stage where the law ought to presume that a patient must come out of an operation as well as or better than he went into it.

In *Bull and Wakeham* v. *Devon Area Health Authority* [1993] 4 Med LR 117, CA two of the judges differed on the question whether *res ipsa* applied to the failure of the hospital to have an obstetrician attend the mother at the vital time, Mustill L.J. taking the view (p. 142) that as the facts of the 'accident' were largely known the principle did not apply.

Rebuttal

The defendant may rebut the presumption of negligence, but not merely by showing the general precautions he had taken. It is not entirely clear on the authorities how far the defendant must go to shift the onus of proof back to the plaintiff, in particular whether he has to show a possible or a likely cause of the accident that would not involve negligence. It was said in *Moore* v. *R. Fox & Sons* [1956] 1 QB 596, that it was not sufficient for the defendants to show several hypothetical causes consistent with the absence of negligence and that the accident might have occurred without negligence on their part; to discharge the onus they had to go

---

[3] Judge Thompson QC commented on this observation in *Ritchie* v. *Chichester Health Authority* [1994] 5 Med LR 187, 206.

further and either show that they had not been negligent (it would seem to be enough in this connection if the defendants satisfied the court that all possible precautions had been taken) or give a reasonable explanation of the cause of the accident which did not connote negligence.

It was said in *Ng Chun Pui* v. *Lee Chuen Tat* [1988] RTR 298, PC that the burden of proving negligence remains upon the plaintiff, despite the applicability of the doctrine of *res ipsa loquitur*.

Whose negligence?

In some of the older cases the issue has been whether it can be shown that the negligence the court is asked to infer must have been that of the defendant himself or one of his agents and not that of someone for whom the defendant was not responsible. One would, therefore, encounter the problem as to who was the servant or agent of the surgeon and who was the servant or agent of the hospital (see Chapter 22). Now that most cases are brought against the health authority, which is responsible for all the medical personnel involved in the treatment of the patient, this particular issue is not likely often to arise (it could still be relevant in the field of private practice and in cases against a general practitioner). Suffice it to say that the plaintiff must show that the accident could not reasonably have happened without some want of care on the part of the defendant himself or his agents.

Examples

Whether or not the accident is one which the court will find would not usually happen without some negligence somewhere will depend on expert evidence. Things can go wrong in operations without there being any negligence. Denning L.J. had this to say in *Cassidy* v. *Ministry of Health* [1951] 2 KB 343, 365:

If the plaintiff had to prove that some particular doctor or nurse was negligent he would not be able to do it. But he was not put to that impossible task: he says, 'I went into the hospital to be cured of two stiff fingers. I have come out with four stiff fingers, and my hand is useless. That should not have happened if due care had been used. Explain it if you can.' I am quite clearly of the opinion that that raises a *prima facie* case against the hospital authorities: see *per* Goddard L.J. in *Mahon* v. *Osborne* [1939] 2 KB 14, 50. They have nowhere explained how it could happen without negligence. They have busied themselves in saying that this or that member of their staff was not negligent. But they have not called a single person to say that the injuries were consistent with due care on the part of all the members of their staff. They called some of the people who actually treated the man . . .; but they did not call any expert at all to say that this might happen despite all care. They have not therefore displaced the *prima facie* case against them . . .

Both Somervell L.J. and Singleton L.J. agreed that the facts disclosed a *prima facie* case of negligence on the basis of *res ipsa loquitur* (*ibid.* 348, 353).

In *Roe* v. *Minister of Health* [1954] 2 QB 66, patients in hospital for minor operations were paralysed by the spinal anesthetic each was given:

The judge has said that those facts do not speak for themselves, but I think that they do. They certainly call for an explanation. Each of these men is entitled to say to the hospital: 'While I was in your hands something has been done to me which has wrecked my life. Please explain how it has come to pass.' (*per* Denning L.J. at p. 81).

Morris L.J. said:

When [the plaintiffs] proved all that they were in a position to prove they then said *res ipsa loquitur*. But this convenient and succinct formula possesses no magic qualities: nor has it any added virtue, other than that of brevity, merely because it is expressed in Latin. There are certain happenings that do not normally occur in the absence of negligence, and upon proof of these a court will probably hold that there is a case to answer.

However, in this case, the hospital gave an explanation of the accident which was accepted by the court as absolving them from any negligence (the ampoules of anesthetic had been kept in a solution of phenol, which seeped into the anesthetic after the ampoules had developed in some way or another tiny undetectable cracks or molecular flaws. At that time such a possibility and the danger arising therefrom were totally unknown).

In this case Lord Denning also referred to the position where both hospital and private doctor deny negligence but give no explanation for the patient's injury. He said:

I do not think that the hospital authorities and [the doctor] can both avoid giving an explanation by the simple expedient of throwing responsibility on to the other. If an injured person shows that one or other or both of two persons injured him, but cannot say which of them it was, then he is not defeated altogether. He can call on each of them for an explanation.

In *Saunders* v. *Leeds Western Health Authority and Robinson* [1993] 4 Med LR 355, the heart of a 4-year-old girl stopped for some 30 minutes during an operation under anesthetic to remedy a congenitally deformed hip. The defendants agreed that did not normally happen without a want of care somewhere but they offered an explanation as to how the accident might have happened. Mann J. rejected their explanation and said:

The plaintiff's reliance on *res ipsa loquitur* makes it unnecessary for her to suggest a specific cause for the cardiac arrest. It is plain from evidence called on her behalf that the heart of a fit child does not arrest under anaesthesia if proper care is taken in the anaesthetic and surgical processes.

This decision has been thought to constitute a new and helpful departure for plaintiffs in the court's willingness to infer negligence, at any rate in the context of injury under or from anesthetic; but, though the case is certainly not without significance as a precedent, it is important to note that the defendants admitted here that the principle of *res ipsa* applied to the facts. See also *Glass* v. *Cambridge Health Authority* [1995] 6 Med LR 91.

In *Moore* v. *Worthing District Health Authority* [1992] 3 Med LR 431 Owen J. rejected a plea of *res ipsa* where a patient was left with bilateral ulnar nerve palsy following a mastoidectomy. He absolved the defendants from failing to protect the arms properly while the patient was under anesthetic by accepting their contention that the patient had been abnormally vulnerable to such an injury, despite the absence of any real evidence of such a condition. One wonders if this is an example of a contrived explanation of an injury by the defence being accepted by a judge who is reluctant to find doctors guilty of mismanagement.

Other examples

In *Mahon* v. *Osborne* [1939] 2 KB 14, where the surgeon was sued when a swab was left inside the patient, the majority of the Court of Appeal was of the view that the principle did not apply in the case of a complex operation where a number of medical staff took part, but it is now clear that the correct view was that taken by Goddard L.J. when he said:

There can be no possible question but that neither swabs nor instruments are ordinarily left in the patient's body . . . If therefore a swab is left in the patient's body, it seems clear that the surgeon is called upon for an explanation. That is, he is called upon to show, not necessarily why he missed it but that he exercised due care to prevent its being left there.

This view was endorsed by the Court of Appeal in *Urry* v. *Bierer*, *The Times*, 15 July 1955, where there was a dispute as to which of the two, surgeon or nurse, had the responsibility for seeing all the swabs were removed after an abdominal operation. As I said above, now that the hospital will be liable in almost all cases for the negligence of any of those who treat the patient this sort of tedious analysis of who had what responsibility and who was whose agent is unlikely to arise.

Reference may also be made to *Cavan* v. *Wilcox* (1973) 44 DLR (3d) 42, where the maxim was applied to the situation of a patient who developed gangrene after he had been given an injection in his arm; and to *Fish* v. *Kapur* [1948] 2 All ER 176, where it was held that the maxim did not apply where a dentist's patient's jaw was broken during an extraction.

In the Australian case of *Chisholm* v. *State Transport Authority* (1987) 46 SASR 148 the court declined to infer negligence where the plaintiff, having been struck by a train, relied on expert evidence that stated (merely) that his injuries were consistent with a negligent course of conduct by the defendants, because the proved facts were equally compatible with a 'non-negligent' explanation.

And some more medical examples:

In *Clarke* v. *Worboys, The Times*, 18 March 1952, where the patient's buttock was burnt in electro-coagulation treatment, the Court of Appeal reversed the judge's finding and held that the evidence showed that such an accident would not happen if reasonable care were used.

The maxim was successfully invoked by the widow of a man who was asphyxiated when he swallowed a dental throat pack (*Garner* v. *Morrell, The Times*, 31 October 1953).

In *Ludlow* v. *Swindon Health Authority* [1989] 1 Med LR 104, where the plaintiff alleged she had been awake during a cesarean section as a result of what must have been the negligent administration of the anesthetic, the judge said that for the doctrine of *res ipsa loquitur* to apply the plaintiff had first to establish that she had indeed been awake during the operation. As he was not satisfied of that the doctrine could not help her.

In *Leckie* v. *Brent and Harrow Area Health Authority* [1982] 1 The Lancet 634 it was held that a 1.5 cm cut on the cheek of a baby delivered by cesarean section would not happen without some lack of care. The matter spoke for itself.

Reasonable traction could have caused the plaintiff's lesion of the musculocutaneous nerve, as could also excessive traction, and so the maxim could not help him, in the case of *Levenkind* v. *Churchill-Davidson* [1983] 1 The Lancet 1452.

The plaintiff was successful in *Woodhouse* v. *Yorkshire Regional Health Authority* [1984] 1 The Lancet 1306. She was a pianist whose ulnar nerves were severely damaged in an operation for a suphrenic abscess. The judge said that the evidence established that this sort of injury would not occur if the standard precautions to avoid this recognised hazard had been taken. The Court of Appeal upheld his decision. *Contra O'Malley-Williams* v. *Governors of National Hospital for Nervous Diseases* [1975] 1 BMJ 635, where it was held that the maxim did not apply where partial paralysis was sustained by the plaintiff (who was also an accomplished pianist) because the injury sustained was recognised as an inherent risk of the treatment undergone, namely an aortagram for recurrent episodes of loss of vision in the right eye.

In *Brazier* v. *Ministry of Defence* [1965] 1 Lloyd's Rep 26 the defendants satisfied the judge that he should not infer negligence on the part of a person giving an injection to the plaintiff as the cause of the needle breaking, because the actual cause could properly be inferred to be a latent defect in the shaft of the needle (similarly in *Corner* v. *Murray* [1954] 2 BMJ 1555).

In the Scottish case of *Fowler* v. *Greater Glasgow Health Board* 1990 SLT 303, a court of first instance was unable to infer negligence in treatment from the fact that the doctors had failed later to give the parents of a dead child an explanation of what had happened.

In *Coyne* v. *Wigan Health Authority* [1991] 2 Med LR 301 the defendants agreed that *res ipsa* applied when hypoxia leading to brain damage occurred during recovery from a routine operation, but they failed to satisfy the judge that it was due to the (non-negligent) cause of silent regurgitation of gastric content. Therefore the matter did 'speak for itself' and the plaintiff succeeded.

For another recent application of the maxim, see the final part of the judgment of Waterhouse J. in *Bentley* v. *Bristol & Weston Health Authority (No.2)* [1991] 3 Med LR 1 (damage to the sciatic nerve during a total hip replacement).

And a recent non-medical case: in *Bergin* v. *David Wickes Television Ltd* [1994] PIQR P167 the Court of Appeal held that there was no arguable defence to a claim by an actor for injury sustained at Pinewood film studios while he was being carried on a sledge. The sledge was under the management of the defendants, the occurrence was not such as would ordinarily happen without negligence, and the defence was no more than a bare denial, containing no exculpatory explanation of the accident.

24 · Consent

SUMMARY

Any operation or treatment which involves an invasion of the patient's bodily integrity requires his consent, or that of his guardian. Without consent the operation is a battery, and damages can be recovered without proof of fault. If the patient would have consented if asked, and the operation has benefited him, damages are likely to be nominal. The patient must be in a fit condition, i.e. *compos mentis*, to give consent. Consent to treatment is not valid if the nature and purpose of the proposed treatment have not been explained in broad terms to the patient. Once that has been done, however, the consent will not be invalid merely because the risks of the operation were not explained, but an action in negligence may lie, provided the patient would not have accepted the treatment if he had known the risks, and no responsible body of medical opinion would have approved of the failure to disclose them.

ASSAULT AND BATTERY

We start from the premise that any contact by the physician with the patient's body, whether by laying hands on it, e.g. for an operation, for an injection, for massage, or, less directly, by the use of a machine directing electro-magnetic or other waves at the body, e.g. radiotherapy, chemotherapy, X-rays, sound or heat treatment, is *prima facie* or potentially a trespass to the person, as involving an invasion of the patient's bodily integrity.[1]

It is not significant whether the conduct complained of is termed a trespass, an assault or a battery. The nub of it is the unlawful, intentional application of force to the person of another.

If a man intentionally applies force direct to another, the plaintiff has a cause of action in assault and battery, or, if you so please to describe it, in trespass to the person . . . (*per* Lord Denning, in *Letang* v. *Cooper* [1965] 1 QB 232).

---

[1] Every human being of adult years and sound mind has a right to determine what shall be done with his own body; and a surgeon who performs an operation without the patient's consent commits an assault (*per* Cardozo J. in *Schloendorff* v. *Society of New York Hospital* 105 NE 92 (NY, 1914).

It is generally thought that the interference with the plaintiff's bodily integrity has to be by way of an intentional act; otherwise the cause of action lies in negligence (see *Fowler* v. *Lanning* [1959] 1 QB 426). An intention to injure is not essential, but the act that violates the bodily integrity of the plaintiff, i.e. the contact, must be intentional. In *Wilson* v. *Pringle* [1987] QB 237, the Court of Appeal said, in the context of the horseplay that goes on between schoolboys, that the contact must be proved to be a hostile contact. Hostility was not to be equated with ill-will or malevolence, and would be a question of fact. Clearly one cannot require any sort of hostility to be proved when a surgeon operates without consent. Yet it is a battery. The 'hostility' factor must surely be limited to situations where the contact could otherwise be one of the incidents of friendly intercourse (e.g. slapping a batsman on the back after a good innings or part of accepted horseplay among friends). One would do best to adopt the formulation of Goff L.J. in *Collins* v. *Willcock* [1984] 1 WLR 1172, when he said that there was a general exception to the illegality of intentional physical contact which embraced all physical contact generally acceptable in the ordinary conduct of daily life. Goff L.J. expressly disassociated himself from the antic notion that a battery is only committed where the action is 'angry, revengeful, rude or insolent' (Hawkins, *Pleas of the Crown*, 8th edn, 1824, Vol.1, ch.15, sec.2) – words hardly apt to describe a surgical intervention! Wood J. took this view in *In re T.*, *T.* v. *T.* [1988] Fam 52 when he said that, as the law stood, a surgeon who performed a termination of pregnancy on a mentally handicapped adult would be liable for trespass (assuming it was not a medical emergency) despite the absence of hostile intent (see below under 'Mentally Disordered Persons').

Another example of a 'friendly' (non-hostile) assault is the hairdresser who, without getting proper consent, applies a 'tone rinse' to a customer's hair (*Nash* v. *Sheen* [1953] CLY 3726).

CONSENT OF THE PATIENT

What prevents an operation, or any other invasion by the physician of the patient's bodily integrity, from being an assault is the consent of the patient.

Consent may be express or implied, oral or written. For surgical procedures a written consent is usually taken. This will refer in short form to the operation to be undertaken, and is likely to authorise 'such further or alternative operative measures as may be found to be necessary during the course of the operation'. This should probably be understood to authorise only operative measures connected with the specific treatment, i.e. it should be read, as we say, *ejusdem generis*.[2] Measures of a different nature would have to be justified by the physician's right to act in an emergency to protect the patient's health (see below).

For treatment involving little risk the consent may be oral; in appropriate cases it may be implied from the fact that the patient has consulted the doctor. It has been said that consent to such surgical and medical treatment as the doctors might think necessary is not to be implied simply from the fact of entering hospital (*Stoffberg* v. *Elliott* (1923) CPD 148). An apparent consent, oral or written, will not be valid if the physician should have seen that the patient did not realise the significance of what he was giving his consent to (*Chatterton* v. *Gerson* [1981] QB 432; *Kelly* v. *Hazlett* (1976) 75 DLR (3d) 536).

If the patient has not given his consent to the treatment and it involves an invasion of his bodily integrity the treatment constitutes an assault and the cause of action lies in assault and battery.

In *In re T (Adult: Refusal of Treatment)* [1992] 3 WLR 782 Lord Donaldson M.R. said that the principle of consent meant that *prima facie* every adult had the right and capacity to decide whether or not she would accept medical treatment, even if a refusal might risk permanent injury to health or even lead to premature death; and it mattered not whether the reasons for the refusal were rational or irrational, unknown or even non-existent.

So in *In re C* [1994] 1 WLR 290 Thorpe J. held that a 68-year-old schizophrenic was entitled to an injunction preventing the hospital from amputating his leg because it had not been established that the patient's general capacity was so impaired by his illness as to render him incapable of understanding the nature, purpose and effects of the treatment advised and so his right of self-determination had not been displaced.

---

[2] For examples of 'unrelated procedures' see *Mulloy* v. *Hop Sang* [1935] 1 WWR 714 (amputation of hand), *Allan* v. *New Mount Sinai Hospital* (1980) 109 DLR (3d) 634 (see below), and *Schweizer* v. *Central Hospital* (1974) 53 DLR (3d) 494 (operation on back not justified by consent to one on toe).

Where proposed operation was the simple removal of supposed bronchial cyst, Inner House held that the consent signed for 'any operation the surgeon considers necessary' justified the complicated procedure of removing a carotid body tumour which was in fact found, a procedure which resulted in the patient suffering paralysis (*Craig* v. *Glasgow Victoria and Leverndale Hospitals Board of Management*, 1st Division, 22 March 1974, unreported). Such a 'consent' is surely not only unwise but so wide as to be devoid of legal validity (see *Rogers* v. *Lumbermann Mutual Cas. Co.* 119 So (2d) 649 (1960)).

In *Brushett* v. *Cowan* [1991] 2 Med LR 271 the Newfoundland Court of Appeal held that a consent signed to an operation of 'Muscle biopsy right distal thigh' plus 'such further or alternative measures as may be found necessary during the course of the operation' justified a bone biopsy when during the operation an abnormal area of bone had been found.

Contrast the surprising decision of Stephen Brown L.J. in *In re S (Adult: Refusal of Treatment)* [1992] 3 WLR 806 where a cesarean section was authorised to be carried out despite the mother's objections. Although one sympathises with the judge's justified concern for the life of the child, this decision must surely be wrong in law, and probably also morally unjustifiable (unless one can invoke an argument along the lines that by becoming pregnant a woman impliedly agrees to take all reasonable steps to protect her baby).

Blood transfusion cases are a fertile source of decisions on the law of consent. In *In re T (Adult: Refusal of Treatment)* [1992] 3 WLR 782, where a 20-year-old girl was refusing a blood transfusion after a road accident, Lord Donaldson said that the right of a rational adult patient to refuse treatment was paramount and had to prevail over society's conflicting interest in upholding the concept that all human life was sacred and should be preserved if at all possible. However, the court found reasons for holding that the patient had not given a properly informed refusal which applied to the present situation, due to her inherently weakened condition, the continually changing circumstances of her medical condition, and to the degree of pressure that appeared to have been put upon her by her Jehovah's Witness mother shortly before she had refused the transfusion. Butler-Sloss L.J. said that there was abundant evidence to justify the court in concluding that the young woman was subjected to her mother's influence so as to vitiate her refusal to the transfusion.

Provided that the patient is adult and rational, the court cannot overrule her wishes (though see *Re S (supra)*). If the doctor nevertheless proceeds in the face of a refusal of treatment he will be committing an assault. In *Malette v. Shulman* [1991] 2 Med LR 162 a Canadian court ordered a doctor who gave a blood transfusion in the face of clear objection from the patient to pay $20,000 for assault, saying 'A conscious rational patient is entitled to refuse any medical treatment and the doctor must comply, no matter how ill-advised he may believe that instruction to be'.

The September 1990 NHS booklet giving guidance on consent procedures (see the end of this chapter) takes the view at 2.13 that a patient's refusal to accept a blood transfusion must be accepted by the doctor, such refusal to be recorded and witnessed if possible.

Absence of consent may also be illustrated by the example of an administrative mix-up over the identity of a patient or over the nature of his complaint. It is no defence to an action for assault that the surgeon believed, without fault on his part, that the operation he performed was the appropriate one for the plaintiff, and that the patient had consented. He may have been acting consistently with the best professional standards, but he will himself nevertheless be liable for assault (irrespective of the hospital's liability in negligence), for fault is irrelevant in assault. Either there was, as a matter of fact, consent or there was not. The administrative staff may have been negligent in marking Mr Jones's card with the operation intended for Mr Smith, or in noting a right leg amputation instead of a left leg one; but it is the surgeon who is liable in assault if he is misled.

An extension of this principle is found in *Allan* v. *New Mount Sinai Hospital* (1980) 109 DLR (3d) 364. An anesthetist who acted without negligence was held liable in battery for unforeseeable injury suffered by the patient because he administered the injection that led to the injury into the patient's left arm, the patient having expressly told him not to inject into that limb. The defendant acted in accordance with normal medical procedure, but he had ignored the plaintiff's instructions. He was accordingly liable for trespass to the person, and for all the damage that flowed directly from that trespass (see below at (2)).

In an unreported case decided in an English court in July 1983 a Mrs Potts of Salford recovered £3,000 damages for assault when the surgeon who terminated her pregnancy injected her with the controversial contraceptive drug Depo-Provera without her consent. In a number of cases damages have been recovered for a sterilisation carried out without consent (*Devi* v. *West Midlands Regional Health Authority* (9 December 1981, CA); *Wells* v. *Surrey Area Health Authority* (*The Times* 29 July 1978).

The Court of Appeal said in *Freeman* v. *Home Office (No.2)* [1984] QB 524, that a prisoner was able to give a valid consent to the administering of drugs, and whether he had actually done so was a question of fact for the trial judge, and a court had to be alive to the risk that in a prison setting an apparent consent might not be a real one. A prisoner who has not given consent to treatment may of course maintain an action for assault (*Barbara* v. *Home Office* (1984) 134 NLJ 888).

In *Davis* v. *Barking, Havering and Brentwood Health Authority* [1993] 4 Med LR 85 McCullough J. said that a separate consent was not required where, within proper medical practice, a caudal anesthetic (about which the patient had not been told) was added to her general anesthetic during an operation for marsupialisation of a Bartholian cyst. He said that sectionalising consent for every step in a procedure would lead to the 'deplorable' prospect of this type of action being brought in trespass rather than in negligence ('deplored' to a greater or lesser extent by Bristow J. in *Chatterton* v. *Gerson* [1981] 1 QB 432, Hirst J. in *Hills* v. *Potter* [1984] 1

WLR 641 at p. 653, and Lord Scarman in the *Sidaway* case [1985] 1 AC 871 at p. 883).

Some doubts

Some doubt has been cast by what was said in the House of Lords in *In re F.* [1989] 2 WLR 1025 on the traditional understanding of the limitations placed on a doctor's right to treat where, for one reason or another, consent cannot be obtained. This would seem to include the situation where the patient is already anesthetised, where the treatment is given in an emergency, and where the patient is mentally handicapped. In holding, as explained below, that there was no legal obligation on a doctor to seek permission from the court before sterilising a mentally handicapped adult, Lord Brandon said that a doctor was justified in carrying out any treatment upon a person who could not give consent that was in his best interests; and what were his best interests fell to be decided according to the classic *Bolam* test – i.e. if a responsible body of medical opinion, albeit a minority one, would have approved of the treatment given, the doctor is not in breach of his duty to the patient. This is a very dangerous rule (for the patient), and a novel one – fortunately it is probably *obiter*, in that it was not necessary to the actual decision. What it would mean is that not only is a doctor exonerated in an emergency situation as long as he acts in accordance with some accepted practice or another, which is understandable, and not only can he carry out upon a mental patient any treatment that would have the approval of any minority body of medical opinion (subject to the legislative safeguards – see below), but also, during an operation, he can perform other procedures that take his fancy as long as a minority opinion would support him. This could be seen as a(nother) failure on the part of the courts to protect the patient. A pity that the words of Lord Donaldson when the case was in the Court of Appeal were not heeded:

[Consent] is a crucial factor in relation to all medical treatment. If it is necessarily absent, whether temporarily in an emergency situation or permanently in a case of mental disability, other things being equal, there must be greater caution in deciding whether to treat and, if so, how to treat.

In the Annual Report of the MDU for 1989 at p.36 there is a note of a case where a woman was sterilised while still anesthetised for the cesarean section that delivered her second child. The reason for the sterilisation was that the uterine wall was found to be so thin that it was almost translucent and had ruptured in the midline. This put her at grave risk during any succeeding pregnancy. So clearly the doctor acted in the 'best interests' of the woman. Nevertheless the MDU recognised that it was not an emergency and consent could have been sought for a later operation (in other words they applied the established legal test). So they settled for £10,000. Would Lord Brandon have exonerated the doctor?

Consideration of what is in the patient's best interests is appropriate to the context of withdrawal of treatment, but it should not be used to give a doctor a licence to proceed in the absence of consent other than in an emergency. In *Frenchay Healthcare NHS Trust* v. *S* [1994] 1 WLR 601 Lord Donaldson M.R. said:

It is, I think, important that there should not be a belief that what the doctor says is the patient's best interest *is* the patient's best interest. For my part I would certainly reserve to the court the ultimate power and duty to review the doctor's decision in the light of all the facts.

See further the section at the end of the next chapter, 'The action for wrongful life', where the court's attitude to the question of the quality of life is discussed.

HIV infection

The GMC have stated (May 1988) that the principle that all treatment and investigation of a patient needs his or her prior consent applies to testing the blood for HIV infection (this would extend to any other virus that the scientists may tell us in due course is responsible for AIDS in place of the (?) maligned HIV). Explicit consent must be sought for such testing. They add that testing without consent may be justified where the safety of others is at risk and consent cannot reasonably be obtained. It may also be justifiable, they say, for a doctor to test a child's blood where the parent may be withholding consent in case he or she may be the infecting agent.

ASSAULT v. NEGLIGENCE

A number of factors distinguish the action for assault from that for negligence.

(1) Fault, as we have seen, is irrelevant. If the patient can show he did not consent to the treatment he will be able to recover damages without proof of negligence.
(2) Whereas in the action for negligence the defendant is only liable for loss and injury which was foreseeable at the time of the negligent act (see Chapter 21), the tortfeasor in trespass is

liable for all damage flowing directly from the assault, whether foreseeable or not. The wrongful act consists in laying hands on the plaintiff, and for that the defendant is liable in respect of all loss and injury flowing directly from the assault, however unforeseeable (see *Allan* v. *New Mount Sinai Hospital* (*supra*) *per* Linden J.). Nevertheless the injury or loss must be of a type which the law recognises, and within the rules as to remoteness of damage in the sense that it must be directly caused by the assault.

(3) Whereas negligence is not actionable without proof of actual damage or loss, trespass has no such requirement. Even if no injury is suffered, damages may be awarded to compensate for the fact of the assault (these are likely to be nominal in such a case, though one can envisage an award for, e.g., the indignity suffered). The limitation period will therefore start to run, in the absence of special factors (see Chapter 28), when the assault takes place and not when injury is suffered, as the cause of action is complete at the time of the assault. In negligence the cause of action is not complete until damage has been suffered.

(4) The limitation period for a claim for assault is six years, not three, as it has been held, oddly enough, that the provisions of s.11 (and consequently s.14) do not apply to such a claim (*Stubbings* v. *Webb* [1993] AC 498, HL).

(5) The fact that the patient would have consented if asked does not absolve the defendant from liability, but it would seem sensible to take that fact into account in reducing damages, for otherwise a person might recover damages for an operation, carried out without consent, but which benefited him and which he would have agreed to if asked. If the cause of action is in negligence the defendant is entitled to contend that the patient has suffered no injury because, even if he had not been negligent, e.g. even if he had explained the nature of the operation properly, the patient would still have agreed to it. It was probably with reference only to liability that Bristow J. said in *Chatterton* v. *Gerson* [1981] QB 432:

> Where the claim is based on trespass to the person, once it is shown that the consent is unreal, then what the plaintiff would have decided if she had been given the information which would have prevented vitiation of the reality of her consent is irrelevant.[3]

It may be that the fact that no action will lie for assault in respect of emergency treatment reasonably and carefully carried out upon a patient without his consent may be based on this

---

[3] And see *Davis* v. *Barking etc. Health Authority* (*supra*).

principle. The patient would have consented if it had been possible to ask him.

EMERGENCY TREATMENT

There is no English reported case on the right or duty of a doctor to carry out emergency treatment on a patient when consent cannot be obtained, but commentators generally agree that, where such treatment is necessary to preserve the life or the health of the patient no action lies for assault. Another possible basis for this immunity, beside that of implied consent, is the duty of the physician, albeit a moral rather than a legal one, to take all reasonable steps to preserve life.

In *Wilson* v. *Pringle* [1987] QB 237, the Court of Appeal, speaking of the 'legal rule [that] allows a casualty surgeon to perform an urgent operation on an unconscious patient who is brought into hospital' said:

The patient cannot consent, and there may be no next-of-kin available. Hitherto it has been customary to say in such cases that consent is to be implied for what would otherwise be a battery on the unconscious body. It is better simply to say that the surgeon's action is acceptable in the ordinary conduct of everyday life, and not a battery.

And see the observation of Wood J. in *In re T., T.* v. *T (supra)*.

In *Marshall* v. *Curry* (1933) 3 DLR 260, a case decided in the Supreme Court of Nova Scotia, a surgeon who found and removed a grossly diseased testicle during an operation for a hernia was found when sued for trespass to have acted properly.

'Where a great emergency which could not be anticipated arises' a doctor is justified in acting 'in order to save the life or preserve the health of the patient' (*per* Chisholm C.J.).

But the fact that it is convenient to perform the operation at the time is not sufficient to give the doctor immunity from an action for trespass; it must actually be necessary. In *Murray* v. *McMurchy* (1949) 2 DLR 442, the Supreme Court of British Columbia imposed liability on a surgeon who, while performing a cesarean section, discovered fibroid tumours on the uterus of the patient and, concerned for the hazards of any future pregnancy, tied her tubes. Here the action of the doctor, though undertaken from the best of motives, was not a necessity at that particular time (for a suitably academic treatment of this topic, see P.D.G. Skegg, (1974) 90 LQR 512, 'A justification for medical procedures performed without consent').[4]

---

[4] See also the section 'Some doubts' above.

CHILDREN

In this and the following section we consider the context where a valid consent cannot be given because the patient is under a disability. Reference should also be made to the cases on the duty to treat e.g. the terminally ill patient. Although such cases are usually put under the consent rubric, they raise ethical rather than legal questions and are unlikely to give rise to an action for damages for assault (see the next chapter under 'The action for wrongful life').

In *In re S. (Hospital Patient: Court's Jurisdiction)*, *The Times*, 6 March 1995, the Court of Appeal, assuming jurisdiction in a dispute between carer and family over the issue in which country a patient who was too ill to make his own views known should be cared for, made it clear that the court was ready, without raising technical objections about the *locus standi* of an applicant and even where, as here, the issue in question was not particularly momentous, to give declaratory judgments to ensure that the patient's best interests were protected in cases where the patient was unable for one reason or another to express any or any reliable preference.

An infant can give a valid consent to treatment if he is old enough and sufficiently intelligent to understand what is proposed and the risks involved. If he is not so capable, then, under the age of 16, consent lies with his parents or guardian. For children over 16 the Family Law Reform Act 1969 provides by s.8:

Section 8(1): The consent of a minor who has attained the age of sixteen years to any surgical, medical or dental treatment which, in the absence of consent, would constitute a trespass to his person, shall be as effective as it would be if he were of full age; and where a minor has by virtue of this section given an effective consent to any treatment it shall not be necessary to obtain any consent for it from his parent or guardian.
(2) In this section 'surgical, medical or dental treatment' includes any procedures undertaken for the purposes of diagnosis, and this section applies to any procedure (including, in particular, the administration of an anaesthetic) which is ancillary to any treatment as it applies to that treatment.
(3) Nothing in this section shall be construed as making ineffective any consent which would have been effective if this section had not been enacted.

In *Gillick* v. *West Norfolk and Wisbech Area Health Authority* [1986] AC 112, an action by a parent to get declared unlawful DHSS advice permitting a doctor to prescribe the pill to children without telling their parents, the court said that the parental right to determine whether or not a child should receive medical treatment terminated when the child achieved a significant understanding and intelligence to enable him or her to understand fully what was proposed; but it was also said that parental rights clearly existed and did not wholly disappear until majority. Lord Scarman said:

> . . . the parental right yields to the child's right to make his own decisions when he reaches a sufficient understanding and intelligence to be capable of making up his own mind on the matters requiring decision.

In *W. v. Official Solicitor* [1972] AC 24 the court was prepared to countenance the ordering of a blood test upon a minor to determine paternity if it was in the public interest that it should be so ordered. And, on the other side of the coin, a judge authorised an abortion upon a 15-year-old girl against the wishes of her parents because the court was satisfied that the girl both wanted and understood the implications of the operation (*Re P. (a minor)* [1982] CLY 2077).

In *In re R (A Minor) (Wardship: Consent to Treatment)* [1991] 3 WLR 592, CA the issue was whether a psychiatrically disturbed girl of 15 in the care of the local authority could effectively refuse consent to the administration of the anti-psychotic drugs that the treating doctors thought were essential to her condition. Waite J. had taken the view, which had been the generally understood view, that the *Gillick* decision meant that neither parent nor court could override the decision of a *Gillick*-competent child to accept or refuse treatment. However he also concluded that in fact the child was not *Gillick*-competent and so could not give a valid refusal.

In the Court of Appeal Lord Donaldson took a much wider view of the court's powers and a much narrower view of the child's. He said that the court in the exercise of its wardship jurisdiction, which was wider than, independent of, and not derived from the parental powers (and had, of course, not been in issue in the *Gillick* case), was entitled to override the wishes of a ward, and indeed also of the parents, whether consenting to or refusing treatment, and whether the child was *Gillick*-competent or not. He also said that parents could give a valid consent to treatment in the face of the child's refusal, and that if Lord Scarman in *Gillick* had meant otherwise his words were *obiter*. The farthest Lord Donaldson went was to accord the child a right to insist on such treatment as the doctors advised even if the parents objected. However, these far-reaching observations were in themselves *obiter* as the court held that this particular patient, even though she had lucid intervals when according to the medical evidence she was in her rational mind, could not be regarded in the context of her fluctuating disease as being generally of sufficient understanding to meet the criteria for *Gillick*-competence.

There is certainly ground for concern at the assumption by the court of overriding powers in the case of a *Gillick*-competent child; it can be strongly argued that the court's powers in this context should be no greater than that of a natural parent. Furthermore, what power has the court to deprive the competent child over 16 years of age of the right to consent that he has been given by Parliament?

A year later Lord Donaldson had occasion to repeat his assertion that, although a minor over 16 has a right to consent to medical treatment in defiance of his parents' wishes, that does not include an absolute right to refuse treatment. In *Re W. (A Minor) (Medical Treatment)* [1992] 3 WLR 758 the Court of Appeal, in the exercise of its inherent jurisdiction to protect minors, over-rode the refusal of a girl aged 16 to consent to necessary treatment for anorexia nervosa. Thorpe J. had held that the child was *Gillick*-competent but that the court would exercise an overriding right to order the treatment necessary to save her life. In the Court of Appeal Lord Donaldson said that the court's inherent powers under the *parens patriae* jurisdiction were theor-etically limitless and certainly extended beyond the powers of a natural parent, and it was clear beyond doubt that the court could override the wishes of a *Gillick*-competent minor, not by ordering the doctors to treat, but by authorising them to treat according to their clinical judgment of what was in the best interests of the patient.

However, in this case, too, the court doubted that the minor was able to give a valid or informed refusal because the nature of her disease would impair her judgment, in that it created a compulsion to refuse treatment or to accept only treatment that was unlikely to be effective.

Note here a disquieting decision reached by Douglas Brown J. in *South Glamorgan County Council* v. *B. and W.* (1992) 11 BMLR 162: the court authorised psychiatric treatment against the wishes of a competent 15-year-old girl.

Reference may also be made to *Re K., W. and H. (Minors) (Consent to Treatment)* [1993] 1 FCR 240 where Thorpe J. said that parents' wishes could override refusal of *Gillick*-competent minors (though all three minors in the case were in fact held not to be competent).

Blood transfusion cases: In *Re O. (A Minor) (Medical Treat-ment)* [1993] 4 Med LR 272 Johnson J. authorised a blood transfusion for a two-month-old girl born 12 weeks prematurely despite the objections of her Jehovah's Witness parents. Booth J. acted similarly to overrule the wishes of the parents of a 10-month-old girl suffering from leukemia in the case of *Camden*

London Borough Council v. *R. (a Minor) (Blood Transfusion)*
(1993) 15 BMLR 72, stating that the court could grant a specific
order to permit a transfusion under s.8 of the Children Act 1989,
and that it was not necessary to invoke the inherent jurisdiction of
the court.

Similarly in *Devon County Council* v. *S.* (1992) 11 BMLR 105
Thorpe J. authorised a non-urgent transfusion to enable chemotherapy upon a boy aged four-and-a-half where there was only an
even chance of success and his Jehovah's Witness parents
objected.

Reference may also be made to *In re E.* [1993] 1 FLR 386 in
which Ward J. authorised a life-saving blood transfusion for a
leukemic boy of 15 from a family of Jehovah's Witnesses.

Sterilisation and termination: The rules for seeking a declaration that a sterilisation procedure upon a minor (or a mentally
handicapped person) may lawfully be carried out are now found
at [1993] 3 All ER 222, dated May 1993. It has been held that a
declaration is not required for a medically indicated hysterectomy
on a minor (*In re E. (A Minor)* [1992] 2 FLR 585).

Reference may also usefully be made to ss.1–4 of the Children
Act 1989.

MENTALLY DISORDERED PERSONS

Part 4 of the Mental Health Act 1983, besides providing by s.62
that urgent treatment may be given to a patient without his
consent, permits treatments for the mental disorder from which
the patient is suffering (other than the more serious treatments)
to be given without his consent.[5] The most serious treatment,
involving interference with brain tissue or other serious treatments specified in regulations, must have the consent of the
patient. For treatments of middling seriousness, as specified in
regulations, consent is not required if a second medical opinion
advises that the treatment be given.

What if the patient is incapable of giving consent, whether to
the most serious form of treatment for mental disorder or for
routine medical treatment unconnected with mental disorder? – a
mentally handicapped person who is not mentally disordered
within the meaning of the Act may also be in this position. In *In
re D. (a minor)* [1976] Fam 185 the court was required to decide if
it should authorise the sterilisation of a mentally handicapped

---

[5] In *B* v. *Croydon Health Authority* [1995] 2 WLR 294 a declaration was obtained from the
Court of Appeal that tube-feeding a mental patient who was refusing to eat did not require
her consent as it constituted 'medical treatment given for the mental disorder' from which
she was suffering within the meaning of s.63 of the Mental Health Act 1983.

11-year-old girl. On the evidence Heilbron J. concluded that that was not an appropriate course, the court proceeding on the assumption that a parent could give consent for such an operation on a child, and that, where the child was a ward of court, the court could give that consent in place of the parent.

In *In re B. (a minor)* [1988] AC 199, the House of Lords upheld the order of the courts below, who had authorised a sterilisation upon a severely mentally handicapped girl of 17. It was said that sterilisation of a minor would always need the court's approval. The court expressly left undecided the question whether (apart from the limited context afforded by the Mental Health Act, as set out above) any person or court could authorise or give consent to medical treatment upon an adult who was not capable of giving consent himself.

In an *in camera* hearing in May 1987 (*The Times*, 27 May 1987) Latey J. authorised an abortion upon a mentally handicapped adult woman. Without expressly deciding whether the court had power to give consent on her behalf, the judge declared that the proposed abortion would not be an unlawful act. And on 3 June 1987 Reeve J. made a similar ruling in respect of a pregnant woman who suffered from Down's syndrome (*In re X., The Times*, 4 June 1987).

Then on 10 July 1987 Wood J. gave the first judgment in open court in this context (*In re T., T.* v. *T.* [1988] Fam 62) when he authorised a termination of pregnancy and sterilisation to be performed on a severely handicapped girl aged 19. He said that as the law stood neither a parent or guardian nor the court nor any person appointed under the Act of 1983 could give a valid consent for the girl (the treatments authorised by the Act were, he said, confined to psychiatric treatment). Urgent consideration should be given to the restoration of the prerogative powers invested in the Crown as *parens patriae*, particularly as the court was informed that such cases were occurring at the rate of about one a month. He would grant declarations (even though they referred to future actions) to the effect that termination of pregnancy and sterilisation would not amount to an unlawful act by reason only of lack of the patient's consent. Wood J. was content to rely on the principle that, in exceptional circumstances, where there was no provision in law for consent and no one who could give consent and where the patient was suffering such mental abnormality as to be unable ever to give consent, then a medical adviser was justified in taking such steps as good medical practice demanded.[6]

---

[6] In *In re Eve* (1981) 115 DLR (3d) 283, 31 DLR (4d) 1 a Canadian court held that it was possible for a parent to give consent to the sterilisation of a mentally retarded adult, a decision that was subjected to considerable criticism.

The House of Lords considered the matter in *In re F.* [1990] 2 AC 1. This 33-year-old patient was born in 1953 and as a result of a respiratory infection as a baby had the general mental capacity of a four- or five-year-old. She had recently formed an attachment to another patient within her hospital and ran the risk of becoming pregnant (the pill and an IUD were contra-indicated). All her carers, the judge at first instance and the Court of Appeal concluded that it was in her best interests to be sterilised. The court decided that there was a rule at common law, hitherto unknown, that a doctor was entitled, where the patient was unable to give consent, to carry out any treatment which was in the best interests of the patient; and the best interests of the patient were to be measured according to the classic *Bolam* test, namely that if there was a responsible body of medical opinion that would have supported what the doctor did, then he cannot be criticised. For a critique of this aspect of the decision see above at pp. 295, 296. As far as the actual decision is concerned, the court said that it followed that there was no legal obligation on the doctors to seek the approval of the court before sterilising a patient whose mental condition made consent impossible to obtain, but the court strongly urged the medical profession to seek that approval first (Lord Griffiths was alone in saying that the court should insist that its approval be sought first).

The rules for seeking a declaration that a sterilisation procedure upon a mentally handicapped person may lawfully be carried out are now found at [1993] 3 All ER 222, in a Practice Note dated May 1993. It has been held that a declaration is not required for a medically indicated hysterectomy on a mentally handicapped adult (*In re GF* [1993] 4 Med LR 77), nor for a termination (*In re SG* [1993] 4 Med LR 75). In *Re H (a Mental Patient)* [1993] 4 Med LR 91 Wilson QC held that there was no call for a declaration to be given to legitimate investigations for a brain tumour in a mentally handicapped 25-year-old. The judge was clearly concerned that the medical profession should not think it must be forever seeking authorisation from the court for its procedures.

In *R* v. *Kirklees Metropolitan Borough Council, ex parte C (a Minor)* [1993] 2 FLR 187 the Court of Appeal held that a local authority could give valid consent for a psychiatric admission in respect of a child in its care.

In *R.* v. *Mental Health Act Commission, ex parte M., The Times*, 27 May 1988, the Divisional Court reversed the refusal of the mental health commissioners to issue a certificate to a patient under s.57 of the Mental Health Act 1983 to the effect that he was capable of understanding the nature, purpose and likely effects of the treatment for pedophilia that he desired to undergo.

NOTIFIABLE DISEASES

A person who has a notifiable disease or is carrying an organism capable of causing one may be ordered by a Justice of the Peace to be medically examined and removed to hospital and detained there (Infectious Diseases and the Public Health (Control of Disease) Act 1984, ss.35–38; Public Health (Infectious Diseases) Regulations 1968 (SI 68/1366 as amended).

It is of interest to note that the Public Health (Infectious Diseases) Regulations 1985 (SI 85/434) did not make AIDS notifiable, the view being taken that that would impose unacceptable restrictions on sufferers (including, for example, restrictions on their use of public transport), when in fact the virus is not particularly infectious. A local authority can in any event obtain an order from a magistrate under s.38 of the Act for the detention in hospital of a patient with AIDS where it is shown that proper precautions would not be taken by him on his discharge to prevent the spread of the disease.

DUTY OF DISCLOSURE: GENERAL

So far we have looked at situations where consent was clearly not given for the operation undertaken. But what if the patient knows something, but not everything, about the treatment proposed? How much does the doctor have to reveal? And does a failure to reveal mean that no valid consent can be given, so that the doctor is liable in assault, or should it be seen as an aspect of negligence, so that the action will lie only in negligence, with the consequent limiting factors applicable to such an action (as set out above).

In *Chatterton* v. *Gerson* [1981] 1 QB 432 Bristow J. considered a claim by a woman that an operation to relieve pain in a post-operative scar area in the right groin had been carried out without consent and negligently. The operation had proved unsuccessful, and she claimed for assault, on the basis that her consent was vitiated for lack of proper explanation as to the nature of the procedure to be undertaken, and for negligence, on the basis that the defendant was in breach of his duty of care towards her because his failure to give a proper explanation of the nature and the implications of the proposed operation made it impossible for her to give an informed consent.

On the question whether there was a real consent so as to free the physician from liability for assault, and on the distinction between a claim for assault and one based on negligence, the judge said:

It is clear law that in any context in which consent of the injured party is a defence to what would otherwise be a crime or a civil wrong, the consent must be real. Where, for example, a woman's consent to sexual intercourse is obtained by fraud, her apparent consent is no defence to a charge of rape. It is not difficult to state the principle or appreciate its good sense. As so often, the problem lies in its application . . .

In my judgment what the court has to do in each case is to look at all the circumstances and say 'Was there a real consent?' I think justice requires that in order to vitiate the reality of consent there must be a greater failure of communication between doctor and patient than that involved in a breach of duty if the claim is based on negligence. When the claim is based on negligence the plaintiff must prove not only the breach of duty to inform, but that had the duty not been broken she would not have chosen to have the operation. Where the claim is based on trespass to the person, once it is shown that the consent is unreal, then what the plaintiff would have decided if she had been given the information which would have prevented vitiation of the reality of her consent is irrelevant.

In my judgment once the patient is informed in broad terms of the nature of the procedure which is intended, and gives her consent, that consent is real, and the cause of the action on which to base a claim for failure to go into risks and implications is negligence, not trespass . . . in my judgment it would be very much against the interests of justice if actions which are really based on a failure by the doctor to perform his duty adequately to inform were pleaded in trespass.

That remains the best statement of the English law on the question when an apparent consent is invalid for lack of information, so as to afford a claim for assault. Only if the physician fails to 'inform in broad terms of the nature of the procedure which is intended' will the apparent consent be vitiated and an action for assault lie.[7] Any lesser failure in giving information can give rise only to an action in negligence for breach of duty. What then is the surgeon's duty of disclosure?

The risks of the operation

Every operation is attended by its risks. So is most treatment. Every drug can produce unwanted side effects. No treatment can be guaranteed to succeed. When something goes wrong the patient first asks whether the doctor has been negligent in his treatment. Has he made a negligent diagnosis, or prescribed the wrong drugs when he should have known better? Or has he performed the operation without due care? When it appears that

---

[7] In *Slater* v. *Baker and Stapleton* (1767) 95 ER 860 it was said that 'a patient should be told what is about to be done to him, that he may take courage and put himself in such a situation as to enable him to undergo the operation' – courage is what was needed in those days, one may be sure!

in the strictly medical context the doctor's performance has been unimpugnable, the patient's complaint is likely to be: 'You never told me this might happen. If you had I would have declined the treatment'. The English courts have recently had to consider which of two tests to adopt for assessing the duty upon a physician to disclose the risks inherent in a particular treatment. The tests may be termed 'the medical standard' and 'informed consent'.

The medical standard

Under the medical standard the medical profession is permitted to set its own standards of disclosure without supervision by the court. The profession itself decides what disclosure is to be made in any particular case. It is enough for a defendant to avoid liability if he shows that at the time of the treatment there was a body of responsible medical opinion, albeit a minority one, that would have done what he did. This enables a defendant to succeed simply by producing one or two physicians who endorse his conduct, and it is of no avail for the plaintiff to produce evidence to a contrary effect. If the court accepts that there was such a body of medical opinion it will not be entitled to choose between the differing schools of thought. This is a unique advantage for the professionals. The court is forever choosing between differing expert testimonies in other fields and making up its own mind as to what constitutes negligence.

This medical standard has long been accepted as the test for assessing negligence in treatment and diagnosis (see Chapter 17 above for a full discussion), but it was not clear before the decision of the House of Lords in the *Sidaway* case (see below) that it would be applicable to the question of disclosure of risks.

Informed consent

There had grown up across the Atlantic, in some US jurisdictions and also in Canada, a different test, whereby the court had the right to assess and delineate the extent of the duty of disclosure in any particular case. This was the test of 'informed consent'. If the patient was not given sufficient information upon which he could reach an informed decision whether to accept the treatment proposed or not then he was not able to give a valid consent. It was for the court to decide whether he had been given that information, not for the doctors. The leading cases illustrating this doctrine are, in the USA, *Canterbury* v. *Spence* (1972) 464 F (2d) 772, *Scaria* v. *St Paul Fire and Marine Insurance* 227 NW (2d) 647, *Zelesnik* v. *Jewish Chronic Disease Hospital* (1975) 336

NYS (2d) 163, and in the Supreme Court of Canada, *Hopp* v. *Lepp* (1980) 112 DLR (3d) 67, and *Reibl* v. *Hughes* (1980) 114 DLR (3d) 1.

The courts have variously said:

To bind the disclosure obligation to medical usage is to arrogate the decision on revelation to the physician alone. Respect for the patient's right of self-determination on particular therapy demands a standard set by law for physicians rather than one which physicians may or may not impose upon themselves.

The duty to disclose or inform cannot be summarily limited to a self-created custom of the profession, to a professional standard that may be non-existent or inadequate to meet the informational needs of a patient.

Risk disclosure is based on the patient's right to determine what shall be done with his body. Such right should not be at the disposal of the medical community.

According to the doctrine of informed consent a risk is required to be disclosed when a reasonable person, in what the physician knows or should know to be the patient's position, would be likely to attach significance to the risk or cluster of risks in deciding whether or not to forgo the proposed therapy. The physician can plead therapeutic privilege, and show that there was a good clinical reason why a particular disclosure should not have been made.

Expert evidence of current medical practice remains cogent and persuasive evidence of the appropriate standard, but it is not conclusive. As it was neatly put in a Canadian case:

No longer does the medical profession alone collectively determine, by its own practices, the amount of information a patient should have in order to decide whether to undergo an operation (*White* v. *Turner* (1981) 120 DLR (3d) 269).

Anyone interested in recent applications of the doctrine of informed consent might wish to read some of the cases in which the Canadian reports abound: *Videto* v. *Kennedy* (1981) 125 DLR (3d) 127, *Bucknam* v. *Kostuik* (1983) 3 DLR (4th) 99, *Considine* v. *Camp Hill Hospital* (1982) 133 DLR (3d) 11, *Ferguson* v. *Hamilton Civil Hospitals* (1983) 144 DLR (3d) 214, *Casey* v. *Provan* (1984) 11 DLR (4th) 708, *Grey* v. *Webster* (1984) 14 DLR (4th) 706.

The Saskatchewan Court of Appeal's decision in *Haughian* v. *Paine* (1987) 37 DLR (4th) 624 is interesting. Although based on the doctrine of informed consent, it makes the generally valid point that a patient is entitled to be told of non-surgical alternatives to the treatment proposed.

Kitchen v. *McMullen* [1990] 1 Med LR 352, New Brunswick Court of Appeal, can be used to illuminate the difference in the law on the doctor's duty to disclose the risks of an operation or treatment between Canadian law, where the patient's rights are respected, and here, where they are not. In short, the plaintiff was given an anti-coagulant (Hemofil) to control bleeding after a tooth extraction. Like all blood products Hemofil carries a small risk of hepatitis, which materialised. The plaintiff sued for damages on the ground that he should have been warned of the risk, claiming that, if he had been warned, he would not have accepted the treatment.

Now under the Canadian doctrine of informed consent the doctor has a duty to disclose all 'material' or 'unusual or special' risks. Those risks are (more or less) such risks as the court feels would affect the mind of a patient when deciding whether or not to accept the treatment proposed. What is important here is that it is for the court to decide the status of the risk, not for the doctors. So if the court decides the risk was 'material', then it matters not that no doctor ever discloses it. A doctor is in breach of his duty in not doing so. In this way the Canadian court protects the right of a patient to be properly informed about the treatment proposed. But under English law, as explained below, there is no duty to disclose any risk unless there is no body of responsible medical opinion, not even a minority one, that would follow the course of not disclosing it. So it is left to the medical profession to decide what the patient may or may not know about the treatment s/he is being offered. So much for patients' rights.

The second aspect of the Canadian test is to decide if a reasonable patient in the plaintiff's position would have declined or accepted the treatment if warned. This issue is similarly relevant under our law: if the court decides that the risk should have been disclosed (for example it is likely to find that the risk of failure of a sterilisation should these days be disclosed to the woman), it still has to decide if the patient would have nevertheless accepted the operation or the treatment (thus it might well find that the woman would have taken the 1 in 500 risk of the sterilisation failing, rather than try some other, probably even less secure, method). Canadian law has a rather complex test of whether a reasonable patient would have refused the treatment: our test is simply to ask whether the plaintiff has satisfied the court that s/he would have refused it.

The actual decision in the *Kitchen* case was that all three judges found that the risk was one that should have been disclosed to the patient, but two of them then decided that he would have accepted the risk (the third said he would have waited to see if the bleeding got worse). So his action failed.

In *Ellis* v. *Wallsend District Hospital* [1990] 2 Med LR 103 the New South Wales Court of Appeal held that where the patient's evidence was that if warned of the risks of an operation she would have declined it the trial judge was not at liberty to reject that evidence unless there was contrary evidence showing the plaintiff's contention to be 'inherently incredible' or 'inherently improbable'.

The English test

The English test for establishing negligence in matters of treatment and diagnosis was clear. The medical standard test had been clearly set out in the direction to the jury given by McNair J. in *Bolam* v. *Friern Hospital Management Committee* [1957] 1 WLR 582. This direction had become a *locus classicus* and was expressly endorsed by the House of Lords in *Whitehouse* v. *Jordan* [1981] 1 WLR 246 and *Maynard* v. *West Midlands Regional Health Authority* [1984] 1 WLR 634. But did it apply to the duty to disclose material risks? In fact the *Bolam* case included an allegation of failure to disclose the risks inherent in the treatment undertaken, but it was generally thought that it was still arguable that the test for the duty of disclosure was not necessarily the same as the test for diagnosis and treatment. In the seminal case of *Hunter* v. *Hanley* 1955 SLT 213, a Scottish case upon which McNair J. relied, Lord President Clyde had spoken only of diagnosis and treatment:

In the realm of diagnosis and treatment there is ample scope for difference of opinion and one man clearly is not negligent merely because his conclusion differs from that of other professional men . . . The true test for establishing negligence in diagnosis or treatment on the part of a doctor is whether he has been proved to be guilty of such failure as no doctor of ordinary skill would be guilty of if acting with ordinary care . . .

In *Hills* v. *Potter* [1984] 1 WLR 641 Hirst J. rejected any form of the doctrine of informed consent as having no place in English law and adopted the medical test (though he made it clear that the plaintiff would have failed in either event). A similar approach was taken by Tudor Evans J. in *Sankey* v. *Kensington and Chelsea Area Health Authority* (2 April 1982; QBD).

The *Sidaway* case

· The most important case on this issue has been *Sidaway* v. *Board of Governors of the Bethlem Royal Hospital and the Maudsley Hospital* [1985] AC 871. The facts were that the plaintiff suffered paralysis following an operation upon her cervical vertebrae. The operation carried a small risk of untoward damage, about a 2% risk of damage to nerve root or spinal cord. Damage to the cord would produce a far more serious result, and the risk of that happening was less than 1%. The surgeon warned of the risk of damage to the nerve root but not of the risk to the spinal cord. The trial judge found that the patient had not been told of all material risks so as to be able to give a fully informed consent to the operation, but, as he was satisfied that the surgeon, in giving the limited disclosure that he did, was following a practice that had the backing of a body of responsible medical opinion at the time of the operation, the plaintiff must fail, because the test in English law was the medical standard, not informed consent.

The Court of Appeal by a majority endorsed this view ([1984] QB 493). Dunn L.J. said a contrary result would damage the doctor/patient relationship and might well have an adverse effect on the practice of medicine. Sir Nicolas Browne-Wilkinson said that the particular quality of that relationship meant that the duty of disclosure in that context should be approached on a different basis from that applicable to ordinary professional men, that the patient must have all the information he reasonably should, but that to test the reasonableness of the disclosure made one looked to the standards of the profession. However, the Master of the Rolls said that, although evidence of the medical practice was important, the definition of the duty of care was not to be handed over to the medical profession. It was a matter for the law and the courts, who could not stand idly by if the profession, by an excess of paternalism, denied their patient a real choice. In other words, he said, the law will not permit the medical profession to play God.

Although the House of Lords judgments reveal different bases for their conclusions it is tolerably clear that they, albeit by a bare majority, endorsed the medical test, though adding a proviso. Lord Diplock said that the *Bolam* test should be applied to the context of disclosure as to that of treatment and diagnosis. He pointed out that there might at any one time be a number of practices that satisfied the test, and he said:

To decide what risks the existence of which a patient should be voluntarily warned [about] and the terms in which such warning, if any, should be given, having regard to the effect the warning may have, is as much an exercise of professional skill and judgment as any other part of the doctor's comprehensive duty of care to the individual patient, and expert medical evidence on this matter should be tested in just the same way.

On the question of informed consent, Lord Diplock said that the doctrine was jurisprudentially unsound as it sought to transfer to the sphere of negligence considerations as to consent that were only meaningful in the context of assault and battery (it is indeed true that the American courts had had difficulty in reconciling the absence of 'consent' with a cause of action not in battery but in negligence).

Lord Bridge, with whom Lord Keith agreed, rejecting the informed consent approach, said that a decision as to what degree of disclosure of risks is best calculated to assist a particular patient to make a rational choice as to whether or not to undergo a particular treatment must primarily be a matter of clinical judgment, and so the issue was to be decided primarily on the basis of expert medical evidence, applying the *Bolam* test; but he added (this is the proviso I mentioned above) that the judge might in certain circumstances come to the conclusion that disclosure of a particular risk was so obviously necessary to an informed choice on the part of a patient that no reasonably prudent medical man would fail to make it. He instanced a 10% risk of a stroke from an operation, though he pointed out that there might even there be some cogent clinical reason militating against disclosure.

It still remains to be seen to what extent the courts will be prepared to overrule medical practice on the basis of this proviso. Virtually never, I would think.[8]

Lord Templeman's approach was different: he said that neither was the patient entitled to know everything nor the doctor to decide everything. The doctor was under an obligation to provide information adequate to enable the patient to reach a balanced judgment, subject always to the doctor's own obligation to say and do nothing which he was satisfied would be harmful to the patient: the court would award damages if satisfied that the doctor blundered and that the patient was deprived of information which was necessary for that purpose. Although Lord Templeman makes it clear that in his view the patient is not entitled to know everything, particularly if he does not ask, there is in his judgment no suggestion that the court is bound by medical evidence. He says more than once that it is for the court to decide whether sufficient information was given. This puts him on the same side of the conceptual fence as Lord Scarman, who effectively adopted the doctrine of informed consent, though holding against the plaintiff on the facts.

In *Moyes* v. *Lothian Health Board* [1990] 1 Med LR 463 a Scottish court of first instance rejected a claim that certain risks alleged to be inherent in an angiography procedure should have been disclosed to the patient, principally because it was shown

---

[8] The Court of Appeal indicated willingness to overrule the practice of architects in not warning of the possible risks of inflation when estimating building costs (*Nye Saunders & Partners* v. *Bristow*, 8 April 1987).

that at the time of the procedure, in 1981, it was consistent with responsible medical practice to give no warning at all.

In *Heath* v. *West Berkshire Health Authority* [1992] 3 Med LR 57, the plaintiff failed in her allegation that she should have been warned of the risk of lingual nerve damage arising from an operation to extract a wisdom tooth because the evidence accepted by the judge was that at the time of the operation there was a responsible body of medical opinion that gave no such warning.

In *Smith* v. *Tunbridge Wells Health Authority* [1994] 5 Med LR 334 a surgeon failed to inform a man of 28 sufficiently clearly before a rectopexy of the risk, sadly fulfilled, that the procedure could make him impotent. The judge held that, as his condition was not particularly serious, he would probably have declined the operation. Similarly, in *McAllister* v. *Lewisham and Southwark Health Authority* [1994] 5 Med LR 343 a neurosurgeon had failed properly to warn his female patient of the relevant risks before surgery to correct arteriovascular malformation in her leg. What is particularly of note is that the judge held that she would probably have declined the operation if she had been warned even though her evidence was to the effect that she really could not answer such a hypothetical question.

In *Smith* v. *Salford Health Authority* [1994] 5 Med LR 321 the patient failed on causation, i.e. he proved that the warnings given before surgery on his neck were inadequate but the judge concluded that proper warnings would not have put him off the operation. However, he still won the case as he succeeded in proving operative negligence.

Australia

Now the High Court of Australia has refused to follow *Sidaway*.

In *Rogers* v. *Whittaker* [1993] 4 Med LR 79 the evidence showed that a responsible body of medical practitioners would not have disclosed to the plaintiff the risk to her good left eye from sympathetic ophthalmitis if her defective right eye were removed. This would have been enough to lose her the case if *Sidaway* had been applied. However, it was held that it was for the courts to adjudicate on what was the appropriate standard of care after giving weight to 'the paramount consideration that a person is entitled to make his own decision about his life', that breach of duty of care was not to be concluded on the basis of the expert medical evidence alone, that evidence of accepted medical practice was a useful (but not a conclusive) guide for the courts, and that the factors according to which a court determined whether a medical practitioner was in breach of the standard of care would vary according to whether it was a case involving diagnosis, treatment, or the provision of information and advice: the different cases raised varying difficulties which required consideration of different factors. The finding of the courts below that the defendant had been negligent in not disclosing the risk was upheld.

It is high time that the English courts reviewed their rejection of the doctrine of informed consent and their consequent refusal to acknowledge any right in the patient to be given any information beyond what the medical profession sees fit to disclose.

The duty to answer questions

The judgments of the Law Lords in the *Sidaway* case make it clear that, when questioned specifically by a patient of apparently sound mind about risks involved in a proposed treatment, the doctor must answer as truthfully and as fully as the questioner requires. This duty to answer has been said, though *obiter*, by the Master of the Rolls to apply to questions asked *after* treatment, i.e. in an effort to find out exactly what was done and what, if anything, went wrong. This was said in the context of an application for pre-trial disclosure (*Lee* v. *South West Thames Regional Health Authority* [1985] 1 WLR 845).

Before absolving a physician, therefore, who has made only a limited disclosure, the court should at the very least be satisfied that there was a responsible body of medical opinion that would at that time have made only such limited disclosure, that the patient did not (expressly or impliedly) ask for further information, and that it could not be said that any prudent doctor would have made further disclosure.

It was said at first instance in *Blyth* v. *Bloomsbury Health Authority* [1993] 4 Med LR 151 that a health authority that receives a reasonable request from a patient as to the possible side effects of a drug that is prescribed for her (Depo-Provera in this case), but administers the drug without warning of possible dangers, will be liable to pay damages if it is proved that the patient would not have taken the drug had she been given the relevant information. However, allowing the authority's appeal, the Court of Appeal said that there was no evidence on which the judge could properly have found that insufficient information was given in answer to the plaintiff's request so as to constitute a breach of duty. The court also said, *obiter*, that even where a patient asks for information the duty to inform him is governed by the *Bolam* principle, so that in this context, too (the context of a patient actively seeking information before deciding whether or not to accept the proposed treatment), the medical standard must be applied. This reading of the observations of the Law Lords in the *Sidaway* case is, it is submitted, not only a misreading but is in itself quite unacceptable. It turns over to the medical profession the decision as to what to reveal when they are specifically asked for information, thus totally negating the right of a patient to be properly informed before deciding whether to submit to treatment.[9]

Non-therapeutic contexts

There are various references in the argument and judgments in the *Sidaway* case to the 'healing' or 'therapeutic' context in which that case was set. Is this rule, whereby the medical profession sets its own standards for disclosure, limited to such a context? It is perhaps understandable that the decision as to what should be disclosed to the patient about the risks of the operation should be viewed as a clinical decision and part and parcel of the delicate relationship between the physician and a sick patient – there may well be therapeutic considerations. But what if there are none, or none of any great substance? What if the patient needs advice about an elective procedure and the options involved in, for example, cosmetic surgery, or birth control or diet? This question arose in *Gold* v. *Haringey Health Authority* [1987] 1 FLR 125.

The facts were that when in 1979 Mrs Gold entered her third pregnancy, she and her husband decided to have no further children after that one. They reached a provisional decision that he would be vasectomised. But when she informed the consultant at the ante-natal clinic that she wanted no more children she was told that a sterilisation would be arranged for her. Nothing was said about the other contraceptive options and nothing was said about the failure rate of sterilisation. There was evidence to the effect that in 1979 there was a responsible body of medical opinion that would not have spoken of the options or the failure rate. The judge said that the *Sidaway* case was decided in a therapeutic context, and that he was concerned with a different situation, where a woman asks for advice as to methods of contraception and is told that sterilisation is right for her without being told of other options and without being given the information that there is a risk of failure. He said that in that context the adequacy of what she is told was to be determined not exclusively

---

[9] On the duty to disclose risks if asked, see also *Smith* v. *Auckland Hospital Board* [1965] NZLR 191; *Hatcher* v. *Black, The Times*, 2 July 1954.

by reference to the prevailing medical practice but by the court's view as to whether the person giving advice – who might be a hospital doctor, a general practitioner or a counsellor at a family planning clinic or a health visitor – acted negligently. He saw no reason to extend the exceptional test in respect of negligent advice given by a doctor to the context of contraceptive counselling. And he found that there was a duty upon the doctors concerned to have mentioned the options and the failure rate, a duty which they had not discharged.

However, the Court of Appeal took a different view ([1988] QB 481). They said that the distinction the judge drew between therapeutic contexts, where the *Bolam* principle applied, and non-therapeutic contexts, such as contraceptive counselling, was artificial and contrived, and ran counter to the intent of the *Sidaway* decision. The fact that medical practice as to warning was divided at the time of Mrs Gold's sterilisation meant *ipso facto* that a doctor who did not warn could not be held in breach of his duty. The result of this decision is that, even in the context of an adult and healthy woman wanting to know the best way to avoid having any more children, her right to information to help her decide is governed solely by what the profession is willing to tell her, and the court will not assert any other right to information on her behalf. As long as there are some doctors, sufficient to constitute a responsible body of opinion, who give only a limited or no disclosure (in this or any other context), such disclosure will be declared by the court to be consistent with the patient's rights.

The various factors which go to decide what should be revealed before any particular treatment, whether the professional standard rules the day or the court has an overall jurisdiction to decide whether the medical practice is appropriate, were considered in detail by Woodhouse J. in the New Zealand case of *Smith* v. *Auckland Hospital Board* [1964] NZLR 241 (overruled on other grounds [1965] NZLR 191, but Woodhouse J.'s views were specifically endorsed by the Ontario courts in *Male* v. *Hopmans* (1965) 54 DLR (2d) 592, and on appeal (1967) 64 DLR (2d) 105).

Experiments

There is a more stringent need for disclosure of risks where the treatment is to any extent experimental. In *Chadwick* v. *Parsons* [1971] 2 Lloyd's Rep 49, 322, CA, the defendant admitted liability on the basis that in his desire to find patients in need of a particular treatment he was so enthusiastic about the prospects of success that he failed to disclose the serious risks which the operation carried.

NHS GUIDANCE

In September 1990 the NHS Management Executive produced a circular HC(90)22 with a booklet explaining in clear terms the requirements of consent and exhibiting standard consent forms. Among the statements therein are:

Patients are entitled to receive sufficient information in a way that they can understand about the proposed treatments, the possible alternatives and any substantial risks, so that they can make a balanced judgment. Patients must be allowed to decide whether they will agree to the treatment, and they may refuse treatment or withdraw consent to treatment at any time.

Enough information must normally be given to ensure that they understand the nature, consequences and any substantial risks of the treatment proposed so that they are able to take a decision based on that information. The patient's ability to appreciate the significance of the information should be assessed.

A doctor will have to exercise his or her professional skill and judgment in deciding what risks the patient should be warned of and the terms in which the warning should be given. However, a doctor has a duty to warn patients of substantial or unusual risks inherent in any proposed treatment.

Care should be taken to respect the patient's wishes.

Where treatment carries substantial risks the patient must be advised of this by a doctor so that consent may be well-informed, and the doctor's advice must be formally recorded.

Oral consent may be sufficient for the vast majority of contacts with patients by doctors and nurses and other health professionals. Written consent should be obtained for any procedure or treatment carrying any substantial risk or substantial side effect.

It should be noted that the purpose of obtaining a signature on the consent form is not an end in itself. The most important element of consent procedure is the duty to ensure that patients understand the nature and purpose of the proposed treatment.

Where a patient has not been given appropriate information then consent may not always have been obtained despite the signature on the form.[10]

---

[10] This position can be divertingly contrasted (by those with a taste for the bizarre) with the recent decision of the High Court in Japan, which held that doctors are not obliged to tell patients they are suffering from cancer, and in so doing rejected a claim by the family of a woman who had died of cancer that she might well have received treatment to save her life had she or they been told. The court said that the deceased and her doctor did not share a 'relationship of mutual trust' that would have enabled him to disclose the true nature of her condition to her or members of her family (November 1990).

25 · The failed sterilisation and the action for wrongful birth

SUMMARY

Sterilisation carries a risk of failure of about 1 in 250 to 1 in 500, vasectomy much less.[1] Pregnancy after sterilisation does not therefore of itself show negligence; you need evidence, e.g. of one tube having been left uncut or unclipped, which requires an internal investigation. Without that evidence the claim may be based on the omission to warn of the failure rate. In respect of operations after about 1984 you might be able to show that no responsible body of medical opinion existed that would have considered it proper to omit such a warning; but for sterilisations carried out at an earlier date, when the practice of the profession as to warning was divided, the court will for that reason be unable to hold negligent a doctor who failed to warn.

If breach of duty is proved, it is still necessary to prove loss, by showing either that had the warning been given other contraceptive precautions, such as vasectomy, would have been taken, or that the woman would have realised she was pregnant in time to have an abortion.

Damages may be awarded so as to include the cost of keeping the child to the age of 17 or 18. There is no rule of public policy preventing an award of damages in respect of the wrongful birth of a healthy child.

A claim by the child itself for having been born at all, after a failed termination or a failed sterilisation, the so-called action for wrongful life, is a non-starter, whether the child is handicapped or not.

The topic of sterilisation and vasectomy merits a section to itself because many claims are now made in respect of the failure of such operations and patients are not content to be put off with the

---

[1] Some dispute this.

answer that it is 'just one of those things', and because such claims are to a large extent *sui generis*, they raise particular problems and need special handling.

Sterilisation is a form of birth control or family planning. So are the pill, the pessary, the coil, coitus interruptus and the rhythm method. They are none of them foolproof. Some are more risky than others. But whereas people seem well aware that all the others carry a risk of failure, many men and women who have been sterilised later avow that they had no idea the operation could be less than 100% successful. Those who so aver have found themselves to their amazement to be fertile again. The fact that the surgeon will always stress the irreversibility of the operation (because, understandably, he does not want regrets later) makes it harder for the defendants to contend that the patient must as a matter of general knowledge have known of the failure rate.

Every operation has a failure rate. Medicine is not an exact science. It does not work according to set principles, like a word processor. The risk of failure in any operation, or the risk of untoward consequences, can usually be gauged from previous experience. The question is therefore raised, to what extent must a patient be informed of the risk of failure or injury? This as a general question is dealt with in Chapter 24. Here we consider the way in which this question has been answered by the courts in the context of sterilisation operations.

There are a number of ways to perform the operation of female sterilisation: the tubes can be cut and tied (the Pomeroy method), burnt (diathermy), ligated, clipped with specially designed spring clips that go over the tube and occlude the lumen (the most common method these days), or 'ringed' with rings that achieve a similar effect. In some cases, e.g. clips, it is possible to sterilise laparoscopically rather than by an open operation. This operation has the advantage that the patient need stay in hospital only a few hours or at most a day, rather than the few days that are required for an open operation, but it needs an experienced operator, because it is obviously trickier to get the clips on in that way than when the surgeon is himself able to hold and inspect the tubes.

FAILURE OF THE OPERATION

There are two ways in which these operations can fail: the obvious one is when they are wrongly done, e.g. the surgeon clips a neighbouring structure instead of the tube, or does not occlude the tube completely.[2] This is more likely to happen where he is less experienced or less competent; therefore the chance of an operation failing for this reason will be less if it is performed by an experienced surgeon. In the English cases no distinction has yet been made between an overall failure rate and the particular failure rate of the surgeon in the case, but in the Australian case of *F.* v. *R.* 33 SASR 189, the Supreme Court of South Australia exonerated the defendant by looking to the small failure rate achieved by his department (though in fact by today's standards, if the UK figures are reliable, it was not so small, being in the area of 1%).

The other way the operation can fail is when, despite its having been properly performed, nature reasserts itself and the tube joins up again or in some way a clear passage for fertilisation is created (occasionally a new passage can grow right round the clip-occluded lumen – the central passage of the tube). After a vasectomy natural recanalisation can occur early, i.e. within a few months (that is why sterility is not assured until two consecutive specimens of semen have been found to be sperm-free), or late, i.e. at any time. After female clip sterilisation the inference, if conception takes place within a few months, is that the clips were misplaced. There are no firm separate figures for the two sorts of failure, operator and natural, and it is sometimes difficult when scrutinising the statistics to see what type of failure they are based on. It is, however, generally accepted that, although the figures for the different methods of sterilisation vary to some extent, from about 1.5 in 1,000 to as much as 10 in 1,000, the overall failure rate for the operation of female sterilisation, whether operator failure or natural failure, is to be taken as between 1 in 250 and 1 in 500. For natural failure alone the figure of 1 in 750 has been given. For the laparoscopic method by an experienced operator the overall rate is better than 1 in 500. So it can be said in one way the risk is small. On the other hand if 100,000 women are sterilised every year at least 200 of them are going to be surprised, and if you are one of them the risk is going to seem immense! In addition, the risk of failure is substantially increased where the operation is done *post partum* (i.e. within the puerperium, say a month after delivery) rather than after an interval of a

---

[2] To misidentify the tube or fail properly to occlude the lumen is substandard care (unless the operator has doubts at the time and recommends a post-operative check by way of a hysterosalpingogram). Do not be misled by the odd defence-oriented doctor who is prepared to state otherwise.

In *McLennan* v. *Newcastle Health Authority* [1992] 3 Med LR 215, a claim for negligence in not offering a hysterosalpingogram to check tubal patency after a sterilisation, the patient failed as the court held there was no reason for the surgeon to have doubted the success of his procedure at the time. It is not clear from the short note of the judgment how long after the sterilisation the plaintiff became pregnant.

few months (the *post partum* sterilisation is convenient in that the patient does not need to return to hospital at a later date, but it is not now favoured by the doctors, though principally because of the incidence of regret – a patient is unlikely soon after delivery to be in the best state of mind to make such an important decision).

Vasectomy requires slightly different consideration. It is an easy operation to perform, and is unlikely to involve operator failure (at any rate, which is provable). Its natural failure rate is overall much the same as for female sterilisation but with one important difference. Once the trial period is over (during which specimens of semen are examined to see if sterility has been achieved) and the man is pronounced sterile the chance of late recanalisation is very small, no more than 1 in 2,000 and, on some figures, as small as 1 in 7,000.[3] Nevertheless there are a number of men who have complained that they have become fertile despite an apparently successful operation (this can create for the couple a temporary anxiety as to the woman's fidelity, though that is soon resolved when tests show the man to be fertile).

QUESTIONS THAT ARISE

Where the complaint is sought to be made that the operation was negligently performed it is obviously not enough to rely on the maxim '*res ipsa loquitur*' and merely say: 'the matter speaks for itself; I was sterilised and now I am pregnant; so the operation must have been improperly performed'. That will not do for the simple reason that pregnancy can occur, as I have explained, without operator failure. So you need evidence.[4] This will usually only be available from a later operation: the woman may be re-sterilised after the unwanted pregnancy and the clips found to be in the wrong place or some other evidence of original negligence discovered (this could emerge at a cesarean), or, fortuitously, a hysterectomy may have become necessary in the passage of time, or a laparoscopy may be undertaken for the express purpose of looking for evidence of negligence, though this is asking a lot of the plaintiff (it is unlikely, unfortunately, that the easier option of X-rays would be able to detect what was wanted), and will probably be medically unacceptable.

---

[3] Some experts dispute these figures and say the late failure rate is not much better than for female sterilisation.
[4] Where conception occurs within a few months of sterilisation by clips it is reasonable to allege that the overwhelming probability is that the clips were not properly placed so as to occlude the lumen of one of the tubes.

Questions raised when the complaint is directed to the omission to warn of the failure rate include:

(1) Was the patient told of the failure rate? Over the last few years a specialised consent form has begun to be used for this operation, which makes it clear that the operation is not guaranteed of success, but before that the general consent form was used, which said nothing of the possibility of failure. The information may of course be given by word of mouth. The problem where the specialised consent form is not used is that, as always, the surgeon and nurses will be stressing the irreversibility of the operation (it can in fact sometimes be reversed but it would be most unwise to bank on that), because, understandably, they want to be quite sure, and they want the patient to be quite sure, that she really wishes to be made sterile. And so they use phrases such as 'you know you will never be able to have any more babies . . .'. It is therefore highly arguable that, if no other information is given to the patient which suggests otherwise, she is being given to understand that permanent sterility is the inevitable outcome of the operation.[5] It would be easy enough for the surgeon to tell her, and to record his telling her, that the overwhelming probability is that she will be rendered permanently sterile, but there nevertheless remains a very small chance that nature could at some later date reverse the effect of the operation.

(2) If she was not told of the failure rate, should she have been? It may be difficult for defendants to contend that the woman must have known as a matter of general knowledge that such an operation could fail, particularly where, invariably, the irreversibility of the operation has been emphasised. So that argument is not often heard and is unlikely to be accepted by the court. But what defendants do say is that there is or was no legal duty on the surgeon to warn of the failure rate. They are less likely to make that plea in respect of operations after about 1984 because the medical profession is now alert to the possibility of litigation and it has become generally recognised in the profession that surgeons should warn the patient (this is

---

[5] Stressing the irreversibility of the operation does not of itself amount to a contractual warranty that the patient will be rendered permanently sterile (*Eyre* v. *Measday* [1986] 1 All ER 488), nor to such a representation in tort (*Gold* v. *Haringey Health Authority* [1988] QB 481, CA).

In *Worster* v. *City and Hackney Health Authority*, *The Times*, 22 June 1987, Garland J. held that a consent form which included the words 'We understand that this means that we can have no more children' did not amount to a representation that the operation was bound to be successful.

not entirely logical, because a prophylactic need to warn for fear of litigation does not prove a legal duty to warn with a corresponding right to be informed on the part of the patient).

The real question, the most important one in the context of sterilisation cases, is: is a surgeon under a legal duty to warn of the failure rate, i.e. does the patient in the ordinary case have a legal right to be so informed? The Court of Appeal held (in *Gold* v. *Haringey Health Authority* [1988] QB 481) that a woman's right to information in this context is governed (just as is a patient's right to information in every other medical context) by the *Bolam*[6] principle, so that withholding information from her will not be a breach of the doctor's duty to her unless there is no responsible body of medical opinion that would have viewed such withholding as proper. In other words her right to information is governed by the lowest common denominator. This is unsatisfactory: the suggestion that a woman who is thinking of submitting herself to the non-emergency, non-therapeutic, elective operation of sterilisation because she chooses not to have any more children has no right to be properly informed about the operation, including the possibility of failure, is little short of insulting; it perpetuates the bad old paternalistic attitude of the medical profession whereby 'doctor knows best, dear', and the patient is treated as a child rather than a responsible adult. Quite apart from anything else, the risk of a post-sterilisation pregnancy being ectopic, i.e. sited in the wrong place and therefore life-threatening, is very much greater than the risk of a pregnancy being ectopic in a woman who has not been sterilised (the risk of a post-sterilisation pregnancy being ectopic is some 40%). Is a woman to be denied that information?[7]

Where the sterilisation is medically indicated, i.e. the sterilisation is being undertaken for the reason, in part or wholly, that any future pregnancy would be likely to involve serious complications, the need to inform is even greater.

(3) Assuming the woman should have been told of the failure rate and was not, has she suffered loss or injury thereby? This aspect of the matter needs to be carefully thought out. If she would nevertheless have had the operation, clearly she has not suffered from the omission to tell her of the failure rate.

---

[6] See Chapter 17.

[7] Oddly enough, urological opinion has since well before 1980 been agreed that a man should be told of the failure rate of vasectomy (sexual discrimination?).

What she must say to get over this hurdle is *either* that she would have taken other contraceptive precautions, in addition to, or in place of, the sterilisation, *or* that she would earlier have realised that she was pregnant and would have arranged for a termination or abortion, but that as she believed she had been made sterile she did not finally realise the truth until it was too late for such an operation. The first alternative can pose problems, because no other form of contraception, short of an hysterectomy, is demonstrably safer than sterilisation, though, as I said above, it should be accepted that vasectomy carries less risk (the court does not seem to have taken, in any reported case, the point that other forms of contraception may well not have been any safer).[8] If the plaintiff can say that her husband would have been vasectomised as well, and the court can be persuaded to accept that, she will be on stronger ground. Clearly, if a further pregnancy was likely to pose dangers to mother or child, double contraception could make sense. In *Gowton* v. *Wolverhampton Health Authority* [1994] 5 Med LR 432 the plaintiff established easily enough in respect of a vasectomy in 1986 that there was a duty to warn, less easily that warning was not given, and, with a lot of difficulty, that his wife would have continued on the pill as well as him having a vasectomy if they had been told of the small chance of late failure (can one sensibly imagine a couple doing that?). The second contention, that the woman would have had the pregnancy terminated if she had realised in time, was a basic plank in the successful claim in *Thake* v. *Maurice* (*infra*) (one wonders whether the child in such a case ever learns that this was said).[9]

(4) Granted breach of duty and consequent loss, what can the parents claim for? It is now clear that one can recover not only for the travail of an unwanted pregnancy, with additional compensation if it had complications (or compensation for a termination or miscarriage if that occurred), loss of wages in

---

[8] I would argue that, if the court accepts that the plaintiff would have adopted another form of contraception, it is not open to the defendants to argue that that method would similarly have failed (they would have to show a better than even chance of that, which would be impossible).

[9] On the question whether a plaintiff's assertion that she would have declined the operation if told of the risks is to be accepted, we can refer to *Ellis* v. *Wallsend District Hospital* [1990] 2 Med LR 103, where the New South Wales Court of Appeal held that when the patient's evidence was that if warned of the risks of an operation she would have declined it, the trial judge was not at liberty to reject that evidence unless there was contrary evidence showing the plaintiff's contention to be 'inherently incredible' or 'inherently improbable'.

and around the pregnancy and birth, the cost of the layette and ancillary special damages (e.g. taxis to and from the hospital etc.), but also the cost of keeping the child until it is of age, say 17 or 18, whether or not the child is healthy or handicapped, including, where appropriate, a contribution to the cost of building an extra room, or moving house, and, in the case of a handicapped child, all reasonable additional expense, as well as compensation for distress and anxiety, e.g. over the prospect of a painful pregnancy, and the extra work and care, even hardship, to be incurred in looking after the new arrival. Damages are not to be reduced because the child may or does bring joy to its parents.

Compensation for an uneventful pregnancy stands now close to £5,000[10] (see the quantums detailed below). The basis on which the cost of upkeep should be assessed is not completely clear. The cost of the layette and most other expenses of keeping the baby can usually be proved up to trial as special damage. Thereafter one can use a number of sources. Usually the figure for future care is agreed. At one time the weekly figure for supplementary benefit was taken as a basis, but it is much too low, even below the poverty line. Better to use the current figures provided by the National Foster Care Association as to the current fostering payments – these give varying figures for different ages of the child, and can yield a reasonable sum. The total figure can be worked out for the coming years (inflation is of course to be ignored), child benefits deducted, and a suitable discount made for accelerated payment and the chances of life. There is now something of a consensus that the NFCA rates are the appropriate rates for the calculation; they will usually yield a total (after deduction of child benefit) of about £40,000 (see further on this below under 'Cost of upkeep').

The cases

The cases below cover, as well as the action for failed sterilisation followed by pregnancy and sometimes the birth of a child, healthy or handicapped, other aspects of what has been called the action for wrongful birth, that is to say, the action brought to recover damages as a result of the birth of a child who would not have been born had the defendants not been negligent. The claim

---

[10] See the judgment of Alliott J. in *Akintubobo* v. *Lewisham Health Authority* (PILS X [1071]).

arises not only from a failed sterilisation followed by a birth but also where, for example, there has been a negligent failure to terminate a pregnancy, or a failure to diagnose a pregnancy in time for a termination, or, more complex, a failure to advise that the fetus, through hereditary factors or exposure to disease, was likely to be deformed, thus denying the mother the chance of a termination.

Sciuraga v. *Powell* 24 July 1980, CA (123 SJ 406), appears to be the first decided case on the subject in an English court. The defendant doctor had negligently failed to terminate the seven-week pregnancy of the plaintiff, a young unmarried woman who later, in December 1972, gave birth to a healthy boy. The judge at first instance awarded her £7,000 for agreed loss of earnings up to trial, £7,500 for future loss through having to look after the child (reduced by the Court of Appeal on their analysis of the evidence to £4,750), £3,500 for impairment of marriage prospects (reduced on appeal to £1,500 on the ground that, in all the relevant circumstances, including the fact that the plaintiff was a polio victim, albeit a courageous and optimistic one, the presence of the child did not so materially affect her marriage prospects), and £750 (only) for pain, distress, humiliation and embarrassment. There was no claim for the cost of rearing. Waller L.J. suggested in the Court of Appeal that policy considerations might well preclude compensation for the nursing years in the case of a healthy baby, as nursing a baby instead of earning money might well be seen as one of the factors in the joy of parenthood, which should not be a subject for monetary compensation (he was to be proved wrong later). And it appears that the low figure awarded by the judge (Watkins J.) for pain and distress etc., i.e. general damages, was influenced by the view he took of 'the happiness motherhood has obviously brought her'. He said: 'Indeed in the latter stage of pregnancy she found contentment, if not more – ease of mind'.

In the American cases the courts have had to operate the 'benefit' rule, whereby under the Restatement of Torts (1939) No. 920 the value of any benefit accruing to the interest harmed is considered in mitigation of damages where such a balancing process is equitable. Different courts have taken different views. The Texas Court of Appeal said in 1973:

. . . the satisfaction, joy and companionship which normal parents have in raising a child make such economic loss worthwhile. Who can place a price tag on a child's smile or the parental pride in a child's achievement . . . these benefits to the parents outweigh their economic loss in rearing and educating a healthy normal child (*per* Barrow C.J.).

However, the prevailing view is that illustrated by the Minnesota judge, Rogosheoke J., in *Sherlock* v. *Stillwater Clinic* (1977) 260 NW (2d) 169:

Although public sentiment may recognise that to the vast majority of parents the long-term and enduring benefits of parenthood outweigh the economic costs of rearing a healthy child, it would seem myopic to declare today that those benefits exceed the costs as a matter of law.

Pursuant to that view substantive sums were awarded in American courts to cover the cost of rearing (as was later to be the case in our courts).

In *Cataford* v. *Moreau* (see the *Canadian Bar Review* 1979, Vol. 57, p. 88), Chief Justice Deschenes, in awarding damages for the birth of an (eleventh!) child after a failed sterilisation, countenanced a claim for the cost of upkeep but calculated, surprisingly, that after taking into account State benefits accruing from the birth there was only a small economic deficit, which was amply compensated for by the moral benefits of parenthood.

In *Chaunt* v. *Hertfordshire Area Health Authority* (1982) 132 NLJ 1054 (Park J.), a sterilisation was negligently performed upon a woman aged 44, so that about 16 months later she became pregnant. The pregnancy was terminated and she was re-sterilised. Complications followed involving a hysterectomy, laparotomy and pelvic infection. She was awarded £2,000 for the negligent sterilisation and the unwanted pregnancy (and, it seems, the abortion). (She was also awarded £5,000 for negligent aftercare leading to septicemia and pelvic infection, but that is not in point here.)

There was in 1983/4 a division of opinion at first instance as to whether damages could be recovered for the birth of a healthy child. In *Udale* v. *Bloomsbury Area Health Authority* [1983] 1 WLR 1098, a sterilisation was negligently performed in that the clips were placed elsewhere than on the tubes. The plaintiff gave birth in November 1978 to a healthy boy. Jupp J. awarded (March 1983) £8,000 for pain and suffering (to cover the heads of damage that were not disputed – the anxiety of the unwanted pregnancy, the thwarting of the decision not to have any more children, the discomfort of the pregnancy, the real fear of the plaintiff that drugs she had taken might harm or deform the child, and the operation for re-sterilisation as well as that to remove the vestiges of the earlier one). He also awarded 11 months' loss of earnings, but he rejected the claim for the cost of upkeep in future years on the basis that it was against public policy.

But in *Thake* v. *Maurice* [1986] QB 644, Pain J. (March 1984) disagreed and awarded the plaintiff £6,677 for the cost of a layette and the upkeep of a baby daughter to the age of 17. The child was born despite the fact that her father had been earlier vasectomised and it was held that the surgeon had been negligent in not disclosing the failure rate of vasectomy (see below for more on that aspect). The judge said that he saw no ground of public policy for refusing to award damages to compensate for the cost of upkeep. By the time this case came before the Court of Appeal in November 1985 ([1986] QB 644) this issue had been ruled on by the Court of Appeal in July 1984 in *Emeh* v. *Kensington and Chelsea and Westminster Area Health Authority* [1985] QB 1012. The court agreed with Pain J. and rejected the reasoning of Jupp J., saying that it was for Parliament to legislate for public policy and the court should follow the established rules on recovery of damages.

In the case of *Emeh*, the plaintiff, on becoming pregnant with a fourth child, arranged to be sterilised following a termination. The sterilisation was admittedly performed negligently, and she thereafter gave birth in 1977 to a handicapped child. Park J. (in December 1982) said he would have awarded £1,736 for the cost of upkeep to trial (when the child was five), and £507 a year on eight years purchase thereafter, i.e. a total cost of upkeep of about £6,000. He would also have awarded damages for pain and suffering at £3,000, a layette at £248, loss of future earnings at £7,000, and an additional award of £10,000 for pain, suffering and loss of amenity in the future, including the extra care which the unlucky child would need. But he refused to award damages for any period beyond the point when she found herself pregnant, on the ground that she should reasonably have accepted another termination. This unattractive conclusion was given short shrift in the Court of Appeal ([1985] QB 1012), where the judge's contingent awards of damages were brought into effect. Slade L.J. said:

Save in the most exceptional circumstances, I cannot think it right that the court should ever declare it unreasonable for a woman to decline to have an abortion in a case where there is no evidence that there were any medical or psychiatric grounds for terminating the particular pregnancy.

And Purchas L.J. said:

. . . it would be intolerable if a defendant, admittedly by his own admission standing charged with negligence of a professional character and having, through that negligence, placed the plaintiff in a position in which a choice or decision had to be made, was able closely to analyse that decision so as to show that it might not have been the right choice, and thereby escape his liability.

I find it unacceptable that the court should be invited to consider critically in the context of a defence of *novus actus interveniens* the decision of a mother to terminate or not her pregnancy which has been caused by the defendant's negligence.

In general, though, a plaintiff has a duty to mitigate the damage that flows from the negligence by taking all reasonable steps, which include, in appropriate cases, submitting to medical treatment to alleviate his condition (*Selvanayagam* v. *University of West Indies* [1983] 1 WLR 585).

In *Jones* v. *Berkshire Area Health Authority* (2 July 1986, QBD), the mother was awarded £2,750 for a worrying pregnancy and a cesarean section.

In *Williams* v. *Imrie* (1988) PMILL Vol. 4 No. 3, a mother was awarded £4,000 for an anxious unplanned pregnancy after a failed sterilisation, and for the re-sterilisation, which led to a four- to five-inch scar on her abdomen.

In *Benarr* v. *Kettering Health Authority* (1988) 138 NLJ 179, liability for an unplanned pregnancy was admitted on the basis that the husband should have been warned that his semen might remain fertile for a while after his vasectomy, and £3,000 was awarded to the mother for the pregnancy with four years' loss of earnings at £15,000.

In *Salih* v. *Enfield Health Authority* [1990] 1 Med LR 333, a mother who gave birth to a handicapped child after the defendants had failed to facilitate a termination was awarded £5,000 for the pregnancy, although she did not suffer any psychiatric damage.

In *Akintubobo* v. *Lewisham Health Authority*, reported at PILS X [1071], Alliott J., giving judgment in 1987, said that the appropriate sum at that time for an unwanted pregnancy was £3,000.

Cost of upkeep

The usual way of calculating the cost of upkeep is as follows: for future years the National Foster Care Association current rates of payment to foster parents are taken (they do not involve any element of reward). These figures can be obtained from the Association. You will see that in the penultimate column (p. 7/8 of Part 3 of the 1994 booklet) there is a basic payment specified per week depending on the age of the child (there are two rates, one for London, one for elsewhere). To get the yearly payment you multiply by 52 *and* add four weeks' money for birthday, Christmas and holiday. In addition, the mother should prepare a list of expenses she has already been put to, such as the layette, maternity clothes, new clothes after the birth (if her figure alters), toys etc. Also for the first two or three years it helps if a list of expenses, i.e. mostly food and clothes, nappies, soaps, washing expenses etc., can be prepared which tallies with the NFCA figures, so that these figures are, as it were, 'proved'.[11] I do not accept that the figures from the Child Poverty Action Group or the DSS (e.g. income support) are relevant, for they are below subsistence level.

At the same time it is a factor of importance what sort of life style the child should expect, and this would probably explain the wide divergence in the awards made in such cases. Thus in *Thake* v. *Maurice* [1984] 2 All ER 513, where, as we have seen, Pain J. awarded only some £6,600 for all the upkeep of the child, he explicitly commented on the humble circumstances of the family. As long ago as 1986 in *Gold* v. *Haringey Health Authority* [1987] 1 FLR 125 (reversed on appeal on another ground, see below) upkeep of £11,000 was agreed, and a few days later in *Jones* v. *Berkshire Health Authority* (*supra*) £19,000 was agreed. In *Williams* v. *Imrie* (*supra*) Hutchinson J. awarded only £6,000. Yet in *Benarr* v. *Kettering Health Authority* (1988) 138 NLJ 179, Hodgson J. awarded a total of some £60,000 of which nearly £20,000 was to pay for private schooling, because that was the life style of the family (the other children had received private schooling), and, as I have been told, £18,000 was the agreed upkeep on a multiplier of eight. In *Gardiner* v. *Mounfield and Lincolnshire Area Health Authority* [1990] 1 Med LR 204 Scott Baker J. assessed upkeep, in effect, at only £20 per week from age five to 17, but it appears that he was simply guessing, no evidence having been adduced on the issue (one wonders what his wife would think of that assessment of the cost of bringing up a child!).

In a settlement based on those figures reported in MLJ (AVMA's journal) for October 1990 at p. 8 the parents got £46,000 for the cost of upkeep plus £4,200 for piano lessons and £1,730 for the cost of the baby girl's future wedding!

In the case of *Allen* v. *Bloomsbury Health Authority* [1992] 3 Med LR 257, Brooke J. accepted the relevance of the NFCA rates and assessed damages for upkeep of an unplanned baby at almost £100,000. The award for the pregnancy in itself was only £2,500, for the future cost of care from age five, £30,000, but there was an unusually large claim for loss of earnings, £17,000 to trial and nearly £30,000 thereafter to age 14 (the claim for the cost of a future wedding was rejected, but a claim for alterations to the home was allowed at nearly £3,000).

---

[11] Strictly, one may claim only actual expenditure for past years, but as it is unlikely that this can be itemised one may argue that the NFCA figures are good evidence of what probably was spent (provided that the total family income could support such sums being spent on the new arrival).

Contra, in *Robinson* v. *Salford Health Authority* [1992] 3 Med LR 270 Morland J. declined to follow *Allen* or to use the NFCA figures, stating that the social environment and condition of the two families were very different and that, unlike the *Allen* case, he had the actual family income to work from. His calculation was, however, less than subtle: he did not even alter the weekly rate as the child grew older. One other point to note: the judge said, rightly, that for the past costs of upkeep the court could award only what had actually been expended (however, as already indicated, in an appropriate case one can argue that the NFCA figures are useful evidence as to what the family probably was obliged to expend on upkeep in the past, bearing in mind that the parents can hardly be expected to itemise every item of food and clothing purchased; but watch out in case the total family income shows that it is impossible that they could have spent as much on the new baby).[12]

Currently the NFCA calculation, allowing deduction of child benefit (currently £10.40 for a first child, thereafter £8.45), is likely to come out at something over £40,000. Each period in the future where the rate is the same, e.g. from age five to age ten, should be given its own multiplier, say 4 for a five-year period, and the total for each period should be discounted as per the 4½% per annum table for each year until the period begins.

The handicapped child

We have been assuming cost of care to age 18, or perhaps 21 where further education is envisaged. But what if the unplanned child is handicapped? Can one claim for the cost of upkeep/care for the rest of his life? It is not clear whether this claim for the cost of upkeep of a handicapped child (remember the defendants did not cause the injury, only the fact of birth) can go beyond the age of 18. The opposing arguments may be of equal strength, the parents contending that they will in the event be caring and paying beyond the age of 18, the defendants contending that the legal duty on the parents ends at majority and that the presence of handicap is irrelevant to their liability to pay for the cost of upkeep. There is no authority on this as yet, save for an obiter dictum by Swinton Thomas J. in *Fish* v. *Wilcox*, High Court at

---

[12] A very odd decision was reached in the Scottish case of *Allan* v. *Greater Glasgow Health Board* (1993) 17 BMLR 135 where the judge concluded that the cost of future upkeep of a child whose parents were on benefit was £500 a year. However, he seems to have proceeded on the flawed premise that the mother was entitled to recover only what they would have been able to spend on the child if she had no claim, not what was needed if the child was to get a reasonable standard of living.

Cardiff, 9 April 1992, unreported, to the effect that, as a matter of general principle, if it is proved that the parent will render services to the injured child after the age of 18, damages are recoverable for such services.

Further heads of claim

In an appropriate case one may claim for the cost of an extension or moving house, a larger car, and, of course, for mother's loss of earnings (usually, but not necessarily, limited to the years that the child will be at school).

By and large these claims for an unplanned child tend to be settled within the range £50,000–£80,000.

Points on causation

If the plaintiff was intending to have a child or another child anyway, it would seem that damages would be restricted to cover the distress and any loss through having the child at a time when she had not intended to – if she was unmarried and only planned to have a child when she found the right man the award could be reasonably substantive. In *Salih* v. *Enfield Health Authority* [1990] 1 Med LR 333 at first instance, the breach of duty of care consisted in failing to warn the mother of the possibility that the fetus would be deformed by rubella, and the child was indeed born handicapped. The pregnancy would have been terminated had the defendants not been negligent. Now that they had a handicapped child to look after, the parents had given up their original plan to have another (a fourth) child. The Court of Appeal, reversing the trial judge, said ([1991] 2 Med LR 235) that the fact that the parents were forced, through now having a handicapped child to look after, to forgo their plans to have a further child, meant that the costs they would not now have to meet of rearing that further child must be deducted from their claim for the cost of upkeep of the handicapped child. It is really odd to think that, having forced the parents by their negligence to give up their plan for another child, the defendants should derive a financial advantage from that. I would have thought the answer would have been to equate any saving by the parents with compensation for having been thwarted in their desire for a larger family.

In *Rance* v. *Mid-Downs Health Authority* [1990] 2 Med LR 27 the claim for the cost of upkeep failed: the complaint was that the defendants should have realised the fetus was or might be damaged, and accordingly have given the mother an opportunity to procure a termination. But Brooke J. found that even if that had been done a lawful termination would not have been possible as it was too late for that, and he was not prepared to award damages on the basis that a termination which would have been a criminal act under the Infant Life (Preservation) Act 1929 would have been performed.

Limitation

The limitation period in these cases will normally run from the time the woman discovers she is pregnant again, or, in the case of a failed termination, from the time she discovers she is still pregnant. Where the claim is for failing to discover that the fetus was abnormal, the period is likely to run from the time she should reasonably have known that this could (note: not *should*, as fault is irrelevant to questions of limitation) have been discovered by appropriate tests.

The question has arisen whether this type of claim is an action for personal injuries, even where there is no claim for the 'trauma' of a pregnancy. The point at issue is whether the claim for financial loss is 'in respect of personal injuries'.[13]

In *Pattison* v. *Hobbs, The Times*, 11 November 1985 (to be reported in the Medical Law Reports), the Court of Appeal held that where, following an allegedly negligently performed vasectomy, damages were claimed only for the cost of raising a healthy child, the action was not one which included a claim in respect of personal injuries and therefore attracted the six-year limitation period. This can be understood on the limited basis that a pregnancy is not an injury (though possibly a wasted sterilisation would be). The better view is that the claim for the upkeep of the child is economic loss dissociate, or at any rate relatively remote, from any personal injury or any claim for personal injury – this seems to have been the view of Brooke J. in *Allen* v. *Bloomsbury Health Authority* [1992] 3 Med LR 257.

In *Walkin* v. *South Manchester Health Authority*, 19 May 1994, noted in Supreme Court Practice News, 17 June 1994, Potter J. reached an opposite conclusion from the *Pattison* case, distinguishing the Court of Appeal decision on the doubtful ground that his case involved a female sterilisation and the *Pattison* case a vasectomy.

Note that even where the action is not a personal injury action there is scope for postponing the commencement of the limitation

---

[13] The more general aspect of this and other issues on limitation is dealt with in Chapter 28.

period until the date the plaintiff acquired knowledge of material facts, pursuant to the provisions of the Latent Damage Act 1986 (in force from 18 September 1986). Reference may be made, especially by those who, like me, had thought this Act was applicable only to latent physical damage to property (following from the *Pirelli* case [1983] 2 AC 1), to *Iron Trade Mutual Insurance Co.* v. *JK Buckenham Ltd* [1990] 1 All ER 108 and *Société Commerciale de Réassurance* v. *ERAS (International) Ltd* [1992] 2 All ER 82.

The duty to disclose the failure rate in sterilisation or vasectomy

In *Waters* v. *Park, The Times*, 15 July 1961, the court decided that, where a surgeon had carried out a sterilisation upon a woman for medical reasons but had not told her that there was a slight risk of further pregnancy or advised the use of contraceptives, that did not amount to negligence.

But the question whether a surgeon was under a duty to disclose the relevant failure rate *before* operating seems first to have been raised in the case of *Thake* v. *Maurice (supra)*. At that time (March 1984) the test as to the duty of disclosure in this context appeared to be the same as that for establishing negligence in treatment, namely the medical test propounded by McNair J. in the case of *Bolam* v. *Friern Hospital Management Committee* [1957] 1 WLR 582, and thereafter accepted by the House of Lords in *Whitehouse* v. *Jordan* [1981] 1 WLR 246 and *Maynard* v. *West Midlands Regional Health Authority* [1984] 1 WLR 634. The House of Lords had not at that time yet given their decision in *Sidaway* v. *Bethlem Royal Hospital* [1985] AC 871, February 1985, though the Court of Appeal had more or less endorsed the medical test in their judgments (in the *Sidaway* case) in February 1984 ([1984] QB 493).

Under the test of the medical standard the plaintiff has to show that at the time of the operation there was no respectable and responsible body of medical opinion that would have endorsed the defendant's actions. That could not possibly have been shown in respect of the Thake operation, which took place in 1975; in fact most surgeons were not then in the habit of mentioning the failure rate for late recanalisation, which, as we saw above, is extremely small. How then did Mr Thake succeed in showing that Mr Maurice had been in breach of his duty, both contractual and tortious, in not warning him? There were in fact two reasons for his success: one was that the defendant's solicitors were out of time in presenting their expert evidence, the evidence that would have established that there were plenty of surgeons who would not then have disclosed the failure rate, i.e. evidence that would have won them the case; and, being out of time with it, they were not permitted to adduce it. The second reason was that the defendant himself made several surprising admissions in the witness box, to the effect that he himself considered it necessary to warn of the failure rate and that if he did not do so the patient would be left with the impression that the operation was bound to render him permanently sterile.

The Court of Appeal (December 1985, [1986] QB 644) said that the judge was entitled to exclude the tardy expert evidence and to treat the defendant himself as an expert, and accordingly to find that he was in breach of duty. They reversed by a majority his finding that the surgeon was in breach of a contractual undertaking to render the patient permanently sterile, on the basis that no operation can reasonably be expected to be guaranteed of success. Neill L.J. said that although all the parties expected that sterility would be the result of the operation, that did not mean that a reasonable patient would have understood he was being given a warranty of success.

Medicine, though a highly skilled profession, is not, and is not generally regarded as being, an exact science. The reasonable man would have expected the defendant to exercise all the proper skill and care of a surgeon in that specialty; he would not in my view have expected the defendants to give a guarantee of 100% success.

Nourse L.J. referred to the words of Lord Denning M.R. in *Greaves & Co. (Contractors) Ltd* v. *Baynham Meikle & Partners* [1975] 1 WLR 1095. Speaking of the position of the professional, Lord Denning had said:

The law does not usually imply a warranty that he will achieve the desired result, but only a term that he will use reasonable care and skill. The surgeon does not warrant that he will cure the patient. Nor does the solicitor warrant that he will win the case.

Nourse L.J. went on to say in the *Thake* case:

Of all sciences medicine is one of the least exact. In my view a doctor cannot be objectively regarded as guaranteeing the success of any operation or treatment unless he says as much in clear and unequivocal terms.

This followed the reasoning of the Court of Appeal in *Eyre* v. *Measday* [1986] 1 All ER 488, in October 1985. In that case the plaintiff was a woman who, after being privately sterilised in 1978, conceived and produced a healthy baby. For reasons that do not appear from the judgments (but probably because she could not get the expert evidence to satisfy the medical standard test, or perhaps due to the fact that she signed a consent form to the operation that mentioned the chance of it failing) she abandoned her claim for negligence in not disclosing the failure rate and pursued her claim only in contract for breach of undertaking to render her sterile. This, the sole ground of her action, did not succeed.

Slade L.J. said that the contract was to perform a sterilisation in accordance with the proper skills of the profession, not to render the patient permanently sterile. Nor was it possible to spell out, of what passed between the parties, an implied warranty to do so.

. . . the court should be slow to imply against a medical man an unqualified warranty as to the results of an intended operation, for the very simple reason that, objectively speaking, it is most unlikely that a responsible medical man would intend to give a warranty of this nature.

If the plaintiffs had wanted a guarantee of that nature, he said, they should have specifically asked for it.

It is therefore clear, and eminently reasonable, that one is virtually bound to fail in a contention that any operation was guaranteed, whether contractually or in some other manner, to produce the desired result.[14]

In *Venner* v. *North East Essex Health Authority*, *The Times*, 21 February 1987, the plaintiff alleged that the defendants had been negligent because they had told her to come off the pill one month before her proposed sterilisation, and further because she had in fact been pregnant at the time of sterilisation, a pregnancy which she said the surgeon should have discovered and terminated. However, Tucker J. found as a fact that she had been told to take other precautions for that month, and, on the second allegation, that she had herself assured the surgeon, in answer to a question from him just before the operation, that she was not pregnant. Therefore there was no negligence.

In *Cronin* v. *Islington Health Authority* [1987] 1 *The Lancet* 638, the plaintiff, who had a child after a sterilisation, failed in her claim because the court found as a fact that she had been warned of the possibility that the operation might fail. And in *Keane* v. *Plymouth Health Authority* (14 June 1988, Steyn J., PMILL, March 1989 p.13), the claim for failure to warn before a sterilisation in 1980 was dismissed for the same reason. *Palmer* v. *Eadie* (18 May 1987, CA), is an example of the failure for a similar reason of a claim in respect of the alleged omission to disclose the risk of a vasectomy failing. For a recent successful vasectomy claim see above at p. 324, *Gowton* v. *Wolverhampton*

---

[14] In *Williams* v. *McDowell and Laing*, 16 February 1987, unreported, Drake J., sitting at Winchester, rejected the contention by a woman whose breasts were mutilated in a plastic surgery operation that a guarantee of success had been given, and said that she would have realised that any expressions of hope were subject to qualification.

Health Authority [1994] 5 Med LR 432. See also *Lybert* v. *Warrington Health Authority*, *The Times*, 17 May 1995.

The non-therapeutic context

So far it has appeared to be the case that, if complaint is made about the omission to disclose the failure rate in sterilisation or vasectomy, the plaintiff has in some way or another to satisfy the court that no responsible surgeon would at the time of the operation have omitted to disclose it. This view, as I have said, stems from the *Bolam* case, and seemed to have been confirmed by the House of Lords' decision in the *Sidaway* case [1985] AC 871 (for a discussion of the issue of consent to an operation and the duty of disclosure see Chapter 24). However, the duty of disclosure was differently construed by Schiemann J. in the case of *Gold* v. *Haringey Health Authority* [1987] 1 FLR 125.

This case raised for the first time in the clearest form the question, is a surgeon obliged to disclose the failure rate of sterilisation before the operation? The day after the birth of her third child in 1979 Mrs Gold was sterilised. The defendants said she was warned of the failure rate but the judge found against them on that. She gave birth after natural recanalisation to another child in October 1982. The expert evidence made it clear that in 1979 there was a body of responsible medical opinion that did not warn; so the simple application of the *Bolam* test, the medical standard, would make it impossible for a court to hold that the surgeon had been negligent. This despite the fact that all the experts, including the consultant in question, said that they regarded it as good practice to warn and would always do so.

The significant conclusion of the judge was that the *Bolam* test, as confirmed latterly by the House of Lords in the *Sidaway* case, was confined to therapeutic situations, i.e. situations where the doctor is concerned to heal the patient and where therefore there is a real need for him to weigh carefully what he should tell the patient before the operation or other treatment. To tell too much might alarm and deter when in the doctor's opinion the patient really needed the treatment. But in Mrs Gold's case she was effectively asking for contraceptive counselling. The Golds had already considered the possibility of vasectomy and had not themselves settled on the option of sterilisation. The defendants, through their staff, failed to counsel the patient about the other options, merely saying that they would arrange for her to be sterilised, and in particular failed to inform her of the failure rate. There was clear literature to the effect that patients should receive full counselling before a sterilisation was decided on (even if the main reason for that was the desire to avoid regret) – e.g. DHSS *Memorandum of Guidance on the Family Planning Service* (May 1974); *BMJ*, 21 October 1978, p. 24; NHS *Handbook of Contraceptive Practice*, January 1979, p. 25. The judge said:

I find that there was no discussion as to vasectomies or anything that could be described as contraceptive counselling . . .

He found that there was no responsible body that would in a counselling context, that is the context of someone seeking contraceptive advice, have omitted to mention the options and the failure rate; but even if he were wrong there he went on to say that the duty of disclosure in the non-therapeutic context was to be determined not exclusively by reference to the current state of responsible and competent professional opinion and practice at the time, though both were relevant considerations, but by the court's view as to whether the person giving advice – who might be a hospital doctor, a general practitioner or a counsellor at a family planning clinic, or a health visitor – acted negligently. He said that the *Bolam* or *Sidaway* test was different from the one generally applied in actions in respect of negligent advice, and he saw nothing in the reasoning in *Sidaway* which compelled him to widen that exceptional rule so as to cause it to apply to contraceptive counselling.

However, the Court of Appeal said ([1988] QB 481) that the distinction between therapeutic and non-therapeutic contexts was artificial and contrived and ran counter to the intent of the *Sidaway* case. The court said that there was no evidence to support the judge's conclusion that there was no responsible body that would have failed to warn in the context of contraceptive counselling, and that the fact that the practice of the medical profession at the time of Mrs Gold's operation was divided on the question whether to warn of the failure rate meant that a court was not permitted to find negligent a doctor who at that time failed to warn.

Now consider *Keane* v. *Plymouth Health Authority* (14 June 1988, Steyn J., PMILL, March 1989 p. 13), where the claim was for failure to warn before a sterilisation in 1980. The evidence for the plaintiff was that in 1979/1980 there was no body of responsible medical opinion that would have found it acceptable practice not to warn, the evidence for the defendants was that there was. The judge preferred the evidence of the plaintiff's expert (though the plaintiff in fact failed in her claim as the judge found that she had been warned). He was aware that a contrary conclusion had been reached in the *Gold* case (where all the experts had agreed that the profession was divided at the time on whether to warn or not), but, as he rightly said, he had to decide the case on the evidence that was adduced before him. This is a neat illustration of how little litigation has to do with truth: it is simply a question of what evidence you can put in front of the judge and what evidence he chooses to accept.[15]

CHECKLIST

– for failed sterilisation:

    (i) Can you show operator negligence?

- Did conception take place within a few months (a year at most) after a clip sterilisation? If so, the probability is that there was operator negligence (misplacing clip) because natural recanalisation takes longer.

- If no such inference is possible, has there been, or will there be, a medically indicated opportunity for internal examination? If there has been, get the records; if there will be, have an observer present unless you can rely on the operator to observe and report.

    (ii) Omission to warn of the failure rate

- Are you misleading yourself into believing a claim for failure to warn is possible?

- Are you satisfied that none of the medical records indicates that a warning of the failure rate was given?

- Are you satisfied that your client is a credible witness?

- How can you reasonably allege that the pregnancy would not have occurred if the warning had been given?

    (iii) Quantum

- What did the apparent negligent act or omission result in, e.g. a miscarriage, termination, stillbirth, or delivery of a healthy/handicapped child?

- Have you obtained a psychiatric report? (this may not be appropriate for the healthy child case.)

---

[15] Compare the two diametrically contrary conclusions reached about the same factual situation by two different Australian courts in the *Wagon Mound* cases (see p. 253), which we all remember from our student days: in one case it was found to be unforeseeable that the oily rag would catch fire on the water and the plaintiff's property would be damaged thereby, in the other foreseeable. It simply depends on the evidence presented on the day and the whim of the judge.

- Have you worked out the cost of upkeep on the current NFCA figures? Are you satisfied that the family's standard of living has not been so low that something less than the NFCA rates should be accepted? Also, have you calculated the expenses of maternity, confinement and layette?

- What maternal loss of earnings can you prove as a result of having to look after the child? Can you reasonably allege loss of earnings (perhaps only partial) after the child starts school?

- Are there reasonable claims for extending or moving house (*Roberts* v. *Johnstone*, but only while the child is dependent)? Remember that the new arrival is entitled to the same opportunities as the siblings (e.g. piano, riding, karate, further education etc).

– peculiar to the failed vasectomy:

(i) Is there any evidence of operator failure? (unlikely.)

(ii) Was the patient properly advised about continuing with contraception until two specimens of semen had been declared sperm-free?

(iii) Was he given to understand that he was sterile when he should not have been?

(iv) Was he warned of the very small possibility of late recanalisation? If not, would it really have made any difference if he had been? (remember that the doctor's duty would surely have been owed only to him and (arguably) any known or current partner, i.e. not to any woman he might at any later time be intimate with.)

UNWANTED STERILISATION

This is the reverse side of the coin. The amount awarded for loss of fertility will depend on the age of the woman and whether she already had the size of family she wanted. There is no clear-cut case assessing the amount, but it appears that for a young woman who is deprived of the right to have a family the award will be not less than £30,000. In *Morgan* v. *Gwent Health Authority* [1988] 2 The Lancet 519 the Court of Appeal increased from £8,000 to £20,000 the award to a young woman who after a negligent transfusion of Rh+ instead of Rh− blood was now at risk as to the health of any future fetus and would find it hard to find a husband with a compatible blood group. In *Biles* v. *Barking and*

Havering and Brentwood Health Authority [1988] CLY 1103 general damages of £45,000 were awarded to a woman of 19 who was unnecessarily sterilised. This sum included compensation for much pain and suffering involved in attempts at *in vitro* fertilisation. Counsel in the case have stated (NLJ, 5 February 1988 at p. 80) that for 'probable permanent infertility' they reckon that the award, which was not divided up by the judge, was £25,000.[16] The award of £4,000 in *Devi* v. *West Midlands Regional Health Authority* (9 December 1981, CA) was for an older woman who already had a family of four. An award of £3,000 general damages for the 'somewhat remote chance' that the plaintiff would have had a third child was made in *Wells* v. *Surrey Area Health Authority*, *The Times*, 29 July 1978. And a mother of three sons was awarded £750 for a sterilisation done without her consent at the birth of the third son in *Hamilton* v. *Birmingham Regional Hospital Board* [1969] 2 BMJ 456.

THE ACTION FOR WRONGFUL LIFE

> *Never to have lived is best, ancient writers say,*
> *Never to have drawn the breath of life,*
> *Never to have looked into the eye of day.*
> *The second best's a brief goodnight and quickly turn away.*

(A free translation of some mournful observations by a Sophoclean chorus.[17])

SUMMARY

An action on behalf of a child, whether born normal or handicapped, alleging that his birth (*not* his injuries though) only came about because the doctors were negligent, is a non-starter.

The action for wrongful life, as it has been called in America (in contradistinction to the action for wrongful birth), is an action by the child himself, claiming that through the doctor's negligence he has been born, where if the doctor had not been negligent he would not have been born.

The metaphysical issues raised by this contention are impossible to resolve satisfactorily in a court of law, or elsewhere for that matter. The child does not complain that the physician's negligence

---

[16] Reference may also be made to *Parrott* v. *Redland Tile Co.* (1955) and *McGuigan* v. *Langfield* (1957) (see Kemp & Kemp F5–014 and F5–012 respectively).

[17] *Oedipus Colonaeus* 1225 *et seq.*

has caused him to be born handicapped, for the physician did nothing to cause or contribute to the handicap. But, he says, if you had sterilised or aborted my mother properly (or however the claim might arise) I would not now be living. Theoretically a healthy child could so contend, not only a handicapped one. But if there is any claim at all to be countenanced here, it obviously is even more difficult, perhaps even ludicrous, for a healthy child to contend that he has been injured by the mere fact of being born, whereas, in the case of a severely handicapped child, there is at least some superficial attraction in the contention that his quality of life is so wretched as to amount to a continuous state of suffering, and that he should be recompensed for having to endure that. The logical fallacy is, of course, as I have already indicated, that the negligence, assuming there to have been negligence, is not responsible for the difference between a life of suffering and a reasonable life (this can often be recompensed under the Congenital Disabilities (Civil Liability) Act 1976 (see the next chapter)), but between a life of suffering and a state of non-life; and how can the court possibly evaluate the state of non-being?

Transatlantic cases

The American courts have almost invariably rejected this claim. The Illinois Court of Appeal said in 1963: 'Recognition of the plaintiff's claim means the creation of a new tort, a cause of action for wrongful life. The legal implications of such a tort are vast, the social impact could be staggering . . .' (*Zepeda* v. *Zepeda* (41 L Ill App (2d) 240). In a 1977 case (394 NYS (2d) 933) a New York court, while permitting the parents of a deformed child to recover for pain and suffering over the birth, rejected the child's claim. It has been said by the Supreme Court: 'Thus, the threshold question here is not whether life with deformities, however severe, is less preferable than death, but rather whether it is less preferable than the "utter void of non-existence".'

In the Canadian case of *Cataford* v. *Moreau* (*supra*), the judge, rejecting the child's claim, said:

La naissance d'un enfant sain ne constitue pas pour cet infant un dommage, et encore moins un dommage compensable en argent. Il est bien impossible de comparer la situation de l'enfant après sa naissance avec la situation dans laquelle il se serait trouvé s'il n'était pas né. Le seul énoncé du problème montre déjà l'illogisme qui l'habite. D'ailleurs par quelle perversion de l'esprit pourrait-on arriver à qualifier comme un dommage l'inestimable don de la vie?

(The birth of a healthy baby does not constitute a loss for that child, let alone a loss that can be compensated for by money. One cannot compare the child's position after being born with what it would have been had he not been born. Merely to state the problem demonstrates its inherently illogical nature. Moreover, by what sort of warped outlook could one put under the head of loss or damage the priceless gift of life?)

There was, however, one occasion when a New York court refused to strike out the claim of a deceased child born with a fatal kidney disease after his parents had been told that the disease would not be transmitted to the fetus. It was said by the court to be 'tortious to the fundamental right of a child to be born as a whole, functional human being'. That decision was not upheld on appeal – the reasoning of the lower court seems to have fallen into the fallacy above referred to, whereby the defendant is illogically held responsible for the suffering of the child.

English cases: the quality of life

The attitude of an English court to this 'quality of life' question is illustrated by the case of In re B. (a minor) (Wardship: Medical Treatment) [1981] 1 WLR 1421, which was heard in the Court of Appeal in August 1981. The facts were that a child born suffering from Down's syndrome needed an operation to clear an intestinal blockage if she was to live. If it was carried out she stood a good chance of living 15 to 20 years. The parents refused their consent to the operation, believing that it was in the child's best interests that she be allowed to die, rather than face a short life of severe handicap. The local authority had her made a ward of court, and, when the surgeon in charge accepted the parents' decision, applied to the court. At first instance Ewbank J. refused to order the operation to be performed by another willing surgeon.

On appeal Templeman L.J. said that it was a very poignantly sad case. The child would probably not be a cabbage but would certainly be very severely mentally and physically handicapped. He said it was the duty of the court to decide whether it was in the interests of the child that the operation should take place, and while the view of the parents should be given substantial weight it was wrong to approach the matter on the basis simply that the parents' wishes should be respected. The question was, was the child's life demonstrably going to be so awful that in effect she must be condemned to die? The trial judge was clearly of the view that it was not. He said that, although there might be cases of severe proved damage where the future was so uncertain and where the life of the child was so bound to be full of pain and suffering that the court might be driven to a different conclusion (sc. to allow the child to die), the evidence in the instant case only went to show that if the operation took place and was successful, then the child might live the normal span of a mongoloid child with the handicaps and defects and life of a mongol child, and it was not for the court to say that life of that description ought to be extinguished. Dunn L.J. agreed. He said that there was no evidence that the child's short life was likely to be an intolerable one. The child should be put into the same position as any other mongol child and it must be given the chance to live an existence.

These judgments show that the parents will not be granted by the courts the right to decide whether or not their baby should live in such circumstances; that the courts are willing to consider the quality of life as a valid factor influencing their decision (they may well take the view that there is no rule that life is to be preserved at all costs); and that life would need to be proved to be utterly dreadful, to the point of being intolerable, one might say unliveable, before it should be considered not worth preserving.

In *In re C. (a minor) (Wardship: Medical Treatment)* [1990] Fam 26 the Court of Appeal were concerned with a 16-week-old baby suffering from congenital hydrocephalus (she had already been made a ward of court for non-medical reasons). A pediatrician had reported on behalf of the Official Solicitor that she was irreversibly brain-damaged, that her condition was hopeless and that the objective of treatment should be to ease her suffering and not to prolong her life. The court accepted that she should be treated within the parameters of the report but declined to give specific instructions as to that treatment.

In *In re J. (a minor) (Wardship: Medical Treatment)* [1991] 2 WLR 140; [1990] 2 Med LR 67, the Court of Appeal said that a court, acting solely on behalf of and in the best interests of a ward who was profoundly, but not terminally, ill, might in appropriate circumstances approve a medical course of action which failed to prevent death. The correct approach in determining the child's best interests was to assess the quality of life if life-prolonging treatment were given and to decide whether, in all the circumstances, such a life, judged from the child's viewpoint, would be intolerable to him. There was therefore no absolute rule that, save where a ward was terminally ill, the court should never withhold consent to treatment to prolong life regardless of its quality and of any additional suffering which the treatment itself might cause. In this case the court approved the consultant's advice that if further resuscitation by way of ventilation was required it would not be in the child's best interests unless his doctors thought so at the time.

In May 1991 Hollis J. overruled a Hillingdon mother's objection to a termination upon her 12-year-old daughter (at the time of the hearing the pregnancy was fast approaching the 24-week

limit for abortions under the Abortion Act 1967, as amended by
the Human Fertilisation and Embryology Act 1990, s.37).

In *In re J (A Minor) (Child in care: Medical Treatment)* [1992] 3
WLR 507 an infant, who was born in January 1991, had suffered
severe brain injury in a fall a year later. The local authority,
acting under s.100 of the Children Act 1989, applied to the court
to determine whether the consultants' decision was appropriate,
namely that, if the baby suffered a life-threatening event, only
ordinary resuscitative measures should be employed, not intensive therapeutic measures such as artificial ventilation. Waite J.
made an order that if a life-threatening event occurred full
resuscitative measures should be employed. The Court of Appeal
said that that order was inconsistent with established law. It was
up to the treating doctors in the exercise of their clinical judgment
to decide at any relevant time what treatment was appropriate.
Leggatt L.J. said the court was not depriving the doctors of the
right to give life support, but was merely declining to deprive
them of the power that they had always had of deciding themselves what was the appropriate treatment. Balcombe L.J. said
that it would put the doctors in an impossible position to order
them to treat in a certain way, because if they did they might be
acting contrary to what they believed was best for their patient
and if they did not they would be in contempt of court. Lord
Donaldson also made the distressing but valid point that doctors
had to have regard day in day out to the limitation of resources
when deciding what treatment to give to what patient (as we
know from the decided cases, the court will not dictate the
allocation of resources).

In *Airedale NHS Trust* v. *Bland* [1993] AC 789 the House of
Lords approved an order authorising discontinuance of life-
sustaining treatment in the case of a patient who had been in a
persistent vegetative state for some three years since the Hillsborough stadium tragedy. It was said that the principle of the
sanctity of life, which was not absolute, was not violated by
ceasing to give medical treatment and care involving invasive
manipulation of the patient's body, to which he had not consented and which conferred no benefit upon him.

In *Frenchay Healthcare NHS Trust* v. *S* [1994] 1 WLR 601 a
young adult had been admitted to hospital following an overdose
of drugs. It was clear that his condition had developed into a
persistent vegetative state with no cognitive function and no
chance of recovery. His nasogastric feeding tube had become
dislodged and the consultant considered that it was not in his best
interests to replace it. The Court of Appeal said that, although
ultimate power was reserved to the court to review a doctor's

decision as to what was in the patient's best interests, there was no reason to question the consultant's conclusion, albeit the context of acute emergency did not permit leisurely investigation, and so the court endorsed the judge's decision to grant a declaration to the defendants that they might lawfully refrain from intervention. The Master of the Rolls said in the course of his judgment:

It is, I think, important that there should not be a belief that what the doctor says is the patient's best interest *is* the patient's best interest. For my part I would certainly reserve to the court the ultimate power and duty to review the doctor's decision in the light of all the facts.

In *Re A* [1992] 3 Med LR 303 Johnson J. made a declaration that a child, who was brain-stem dead, was dead for all legal and medical purposes and that disconnecting the ventilator would not be unlawful.

In *Swindon and Marlborough NHS Trust* v. *S, The Guardian*, 10 December 1994, Ward J. declared that it was lawful for a patient in a persistent vegetative state, who was being cared for at home by her family, to be allowed to die by the discontinuance of all life-sustaining treatment.

There is a Practice Direction governing applications for leave to withdraw treatment in cases where there is a persistent vegetative state ([1994] PIQR P312). By and large the application is to follow the procedure laid down for sterilisation cases ([1993] 2 FLR 222) – the reader is also referred to Chapter 24.[18]

The *Mackay* case

The first and as far as I know the only action in which the claim for wrongful life has been considered in the English courts came before the Court of Appeal in February 1982. The facts in *Mackay* v. *Essex Area Health Authority* [1982] QB 1166 were that a child was born disabled as a result of her mother having contracted German measles during the pregnancy. It was alleged *inter alia* that the medical staff were negligent in not giving the mother proper advice and information which, had it been forthcoming, would have led to an abortion. So the mother claimed on her own account.[19] But there was also a claim on behalf of the child for her having 'suffered entry into a life in which her injuries

---

[18] The BMA has now (April 1995) issued guidelines on 'advance directives', acknowledging that patients have a right to say in advance that they do not want treatment if they are dying or mentally infirm.

[19] In *Becker* v. *Schwarz* 386 NE (2d) 807 (NY 1978) a 37-year-old mother who bore a handicapped child after the doctor failed to recommend amniocentesis was awarded the cost of institutional care for the child.

are highly debilitating', in other words for having been born, or at any rate for having been born into a life of handicap and suffering.

On a preliminary hearing the Master struck out the child's claim as disclosing no reasonable cause of action; Lawson J. restored it on the ground that it was really a claim for injuries suffered and was highly arguable; the Court of Appeal was unanimously of the view that the Master's decision was right (although, as a matter of procedure, Griffiths L.J. was not prepared to interfere with the judge's exercise of his discretion).

Stephenson L.J. pointed out the lack of success such a claim had met with in the USA, and that the Law Commission report on injuries to unborn children (Cmnd 5709), which was followed by the Congenital Disabilities (Civil Liability) Act 1976, counselled against admitting such a claim. He said that the claim must be viewed as an allegation that the defendants were negligent in allowing the child to be born at all. To impose on the medical advisers a duty owed to the child over and above that owed to the mother to give the mother the opportunity to terminate the child's existence would constitute a further inroad on the sanctity of human life, which would be contrary to public policy. In addition, the judge adverted to the impossibility of evaluating the difference between the child's handicapped existence and the non-existence it would have had had the defendants not been negligent.

Ackner L.J. said that he could not accept that the common law duty of care to a person could involve the legal obligation to that person, whether or not *in utero*, to terminate his existence. Such a proposition ran wholly contrary to the concept of the sanctity of human life. On the question of damage he said that what the doctor was blamed for was causing or permitting the child to be born at all, not for causing or contributing to her injuries; and he asked how a court could begin to evaluate non-existence. 'No comparison is possible and therefore no damage can be established which a court could recognise. This goes to the root of the whole cause of action.'

Griffiths L.J., while of the view that, procedurally, the application should fail and the matter be argued at the trial, had no doubt that the claim did not lie. 'The most compelling reason to reject this cause of action is the intolerable and insoluble problem it would create in the assessment of damages.'

All the judges expressed the view that s.4(5) of the Congenital Disabilities Act, while not applying to the instant birth – which took place in 1975, before the date upon which the Act came into force (22 July 1976) – had the effect of abolishing this cause of action for births after that date. This, with respect, is clearly wrong, in the sense that it puts an interpretation upon the section which Parliament did not intend and which the words cannot bear, however desirable the result may be thought. The Act gave a child the right to sue a tortfeasor for injuries sustained in the womb; one would therefore expect that the Act would seek to abolish, *ex abundanti cautela*, any common law cause of action that might possibly exist corresponding to the new statutory cause of action, and this is exactly what it does. Section 4(5) abolishes any law in force before the passing of the Act ('whereby a person could be liable to a child in respect of disabilities with which it might be born'). The action for wrongful life is not an action in respect of the child's disabilities at birth; as the court itself said in this case (as noted above) it is a claim for having been born at all. The section is simply concerned with actions for personal injury suffered before or possibly at birth. That the section does not apply to the action for wrongful life is demonstrated not only by the context of the Act and the obvious intended scope of the subsection, but also by the reflection that this action would in theory, if it existed, be open to a healthy child, for the essence of the complaint is 'you permitted me to be born, *sc.* into this dreadful world when, had it not been for your negligence I would have remained in the tranquil and carefree land of the unborn'. The fact that the plaintiff may be handicapped rather than healthy is not of the essence of the action, though it would of course make it even more difficult to show that he had suffered loss, i.e. that he was worse off alive than unborn (see Chapter 26 for a discussion of the Act of 1976).

26 · The Congenital Disabilities Act 1976

SUMMARY

The Act enables a child injured *en ventre sa mère* and thereby born disabled to recover damages for its disabilities from the person responsible, provided that person is in breach of duty to the parent. A doctor whose treatment, before ever conception takes place, negligently impairs the reproductive faculties of a man or a woman can be held liable by the disabled child that that man or woman later begets, provided that neither parent knew the risk they were taking when having intercourse.

THE PROBLEM

What if negligent treatment harms the fetus, so that the child is born handicapped? Perhaps drugs for the pregnant woman have been manufactured, marketed or prescribed without proper care. Or perhaps her antenatal care has been deficient. And what if, before ever conception took place, the mother's (or the father's) reproductive capacity was, unknown to her (or to him), harmed by treatment or drugs so that later she conceived a handicapped child? Or there may have been a transmission to the mother (or father) of tainted blood, years before, or tainted semen in an artificial insemination. Or a Rhesus negative mother was not given, after the birth of a Rhesus positive child, the anti-D gamma globulin injections that would immunise her, so that in her next pregnancy her blood contaminated the fetus, with the result that her second child suffered Rhesus disease.[1]

These are just a few of the possibilities where negligence towards a parent can result in the birth of a handicapped child.

---

[1] Liability was admitted in the case of *Roberts* v. *Johnstone* [1989] QB 878, CA, where the defendants, although knowing that a mother had in 1975 mistakenly been given a blood transfusion of Rhesus positive blood, failed, her husband being Rhesus negative, to protect her child when she later, in 1981, became pregnant, so that the plaintiff was born severely handicapped from hemolytic disease (she recovered some £400,000 damages (see also *Lazenvnick* v. *General Hospital of Munro City Inc*, Civ Act 78–1259, Cmnd Pa, 13 August 1980).

In the post-conception case the child is effectively saying: 'You injured me, albeit I was only a fetus then, and as a result of that injury I have been born handicapped instead of whole'. In the pre-conception case he says: 'If you had treated my mother (or my father) with proper care I would have been conceived and born hale and hearty. You are responsible for my present plight and so you must compensate me for it'.

THE COMMON LAW

Before 1990 there was no English authority which decided whether the common law recognised the right of a child injured *en ventre sa mère* to sue when born (though the Irish case of *Walker* v. *G N of Ireland* (1890) 28 LR Ir 69 gave a negative answer). The thalidomide litigation, which raised this question in the most urgent form, did not provide an answer, as a settlement was reached (see *S.* v. *Distillers Co.* [1970] 1 WLR 114), though it appears that the defendants, while hotly contesting negligence, did not deny the right of the children to recover if in fact there had been negligence. In the Canadian case of *Montreal Tramways* v. *Leveille* (1933) 4 DLR 339 the court was prepared to recognise the right of a child to recover for damages negligently inflicted upon it when in the womb, while at the same time pointing out:

The great weight of judicial opinion in the common law courts denies the right of a child when born to maintain an action for pre-natal injuries (*per* Lamont J.).

Such a claim was later recognised in the South African case of *Pinchin* v. *Santam Insurance Co.* (1963) (2) SA 254 (Supreme Court, Witwatersrand Local Division), in the Australian case of *Watt* v. *Rama* (1972) VR 353, in the Canadian case of *Duval* v. *Seguin* (1972) 26 DLR (3d) 418, and in the Australian case of *X and Y* v. *Pal* [1992] 3 Med LR 195.

Recovery by the estate of a pre-viable stillborn fetus was permitted in *Presley* v. *Newport Hospital* 365 A (2d) 748, Rhode Island (1976) (and such a cause of action was allowed in *White* v. *Yup* 458 P (2d) 617). But under English law it was thought that a child had no rights and therefore no *locus standi* as a litigant until birth (*Paton* v. *British Pregnancy Advisory Service Trustees* [1979] QB 276). This principle was not affected by the fact that, once born, the child might have under the Act of 1976 rights in respect of damage done to it in the womb or to its parent before conception. In *C.* v. *S.* [1988] QB 135, the Court of Appeal ruled that an 18-week fetus was not a 'child capable of being born alive' within the meaning of the Infant Life (Preservation) Act 1929, so that an otherwise lawful termination of pregnancy at that stage under the Abortion Act 1967 was not a crime. The Appeal Committee of the House of Lords later that day rejected all the arguments of the young father who sought an injunction to stop his girlfriend from having the abortion. It would appear therefore that their Lordships, as well as agreeing with the issue decided by the Court of Appeal, must have been of the view that the father had no standing to interfere with the mother's proposed abortion (indeed even a husband is no better placed, as was shown by the *BPAS* case above-cited), and that the fetus was not a legal person for the purposes of bringing an action through his father (or *semble* anyone) to restrain the act which would destroy it.

Then in the cases of *Burton* v. *Islington Health Authority* and *De Martell* v. *Merton and Sutton Health Authority* [1993] QB 204 the Court of Appeal held that children damaged *in utero* before the Act came into operation were nevertheless entitled to sue for damages at common law. The decision of the Supreme Court of Canada in *Montreal Tramways* v. *Leveille* (*supra*) was approved, namely that when a child not actually born at the time of the accident was subsequently born alive and viable, it was clothed with all the rights of action which it would have had if actually in existence at the date of the accident. The case of *Walker* (*supra*) was held not to be the modern law of England. The reasoning of the two judges at first instance was approved. Potts J. had said in *B.* v. *Islington Health Authority* [1990] 2 WLR 501 that there was a potential duty on the defendants towards the child who might later be born and that the cause of action was complete when the birth took place. Phillips J. had said in *De Martell* v. *Merton and Sutton Health Authority* [1991] 2 Med LR 209 (a) that the plaintiff's case accorded with the legislative policy and that the Act of 1976 recognised the possibility that the plaintiff had a valid claim at common law, and (b) that the damage was suffered by the plaintiff at the moment that, in law, he achieved personality and inherited the damaged body for which the defendants, on the assumed facts (as the issue was being decided as a preliminary point), were responsible, and that the events prior to the birth in February 1967 were mere links in the chain of causation between the defendants' assumed lack of skill and care and the consequential damage to the plaintiff (*quaere*: does one not 'inherit' the body long before birth? Science and religion would surely say so, but maybe not the law).

The decision of the English Court of Appeal was followed by the Scottish appeal court in *Hamilton* v. *Fife Health Board* [1993] 4 Med LR 201.

A claim at common law (i.e. before the Act) in respect of pre-conception negligence seems never to have come before the English courts. But such a claim has occasionally been recognised in the USA. In *Renslow* v. *Mennonite Hospital*, 351 NE (2d) 870, Ill 1976, the mother had at the age of 13 been given a transfusion of mismatched blood, so that the child she gave birth to eight years later was handicapped. In *Jorgensen* v. *Meade Johnson Laboratories*, 483 F (2d) 237, CCA 10, it was held that Down's syndrome twins had the right to maintain an action for chromosome damage against the manufacturers of the contraceptive pill their mother had been taking.[2]

THE ACT

The Congenital Disabilities (Civil Liability) Act 1976 was based on the recommendations of the Law Commission contained in their *Report on Injuries to Unborn Children* (Cmnd 5709, August 1974) (the text of the Act is set out below in Appendix I).

The right of the child to claim compensation depends on its injuries having been caused by negligence. A child born handicapped through the 'will of God' alone has no claim. Our law is based on fault; we have as yet no system, as in some other jurisdictions, notably New Zealand and Sweden, of compensation for injury without proof of fault.[3] So the parents who manage to prove medical fault connected with the birth of their handicapped child will receive a lot of money, and the parents who cannot do that, either for lack of evidence or because there was no fault, are left to struggle.

The general principle under the statute, which applies to births after but not before 22 July 1976 (s.4(5)), is that a child injured *en ventre sa mère* by the negligence (or, of course, the deliberate assault) of any person, except his mother,[4] can maintain an action for damages for those injuries after his birth. He can also sue anyone who, before ever he was conceived, tortiously injured either of his parents with the result that when he was later conceived and born he was disabled (this includes suing his father for injuring his mother, for example by infecting her with a sexually transmitted disease).

---

[2] Reference may also be made to the Canadian case of *Cherry* v. *Borsman* [1991] 2 Med LR 396.

[3] See Chapter 30.

[4] A child would have no civil claim against its mother for having injured it in the womb through drug-taking, though the mother might, under a different jurisdiction, have the child taken from her, and could in certain circumstances face prosecution under the Infant Life (Preservation) Act 1929 (see *Re D. (a minor)* [1987] AC 317).

The action can only be maintained at the suit of a child who is born alive, which means alive when it first has a life separate from its mother (ss.1(1) and 4(2)) – presumably at the moment of severance of the umbilical cord. (Section 4(4) provides that for the purpose of recovering damages for loss of expectation of life the child must live for at least 48 hours; but for deaths after 1982 the provisions of the Administration of Justice Act 1982 have now in any event abolished the right to claim under that head.)

The child has to show that he was born disabled, i.e. born with any deformity, disease or abnormality, including a predisposition (whether or not it is susceptible of immediate prognosis) to physical or mental defect in the future (ss.1(1) and 4(1)); that the defendant was in breach of his duty of care to the mother (it is irrelevant that the mother herself suffered no damage from the breach); that his having been born disabled was the result of that breach of duty; and that the breach affected either parent in his or her ability to have a normal, healthy child (i.e. pre-conception), or affected the mother during pregnancy, or mother or child in the course of its birth, so that the child was born with disabilities which would not otherwise have been present.

These results are achieved by the legislation in the following ways:

If the child is born disabled as a result of an 'occurrence' before its birth, and someone other than the mother is 'answerable' for it, the child can sue for the disabilities as damage resulting from the wrongful act (s.1(1)).

The 'occurrence' must be one which affected either parent's ability to have a normal, healthy child, *or* which affected the mother during pregnancy, or mother or child in the course of the birth, so that the child was born disabled (s.1(2)).

A person is 'answerable' to the child if he was liable in tort to the parent for the occurrence, regardless of any limitation point and regardless whether or not the parent suffered any actionable injury from the wrongful act (s.1(3)).

If the 'occurrence' preceded conception the child cannot sue if either parent knew 'at that time' (which presumably means when having intercourse) of the risk created by the 'occurrence' that any child he or she begat might be handicapped (s.1(4)). In other words, if a person knows that he or she is at risk of creating a handicapped child and nevertheless goes on to do so, the child cannot sue the person responsible for creating the risk. (But where the father is the defendant and he alone knew of the risk, the child can sue him. In other words, a man who knows he is at risk of producing a handicapped child, and does not tell the mother, can be sued by the child when it is born disabled (s.1(4)).)

It is specifically provided (it was the law anyway, but it was put in, as the Law Commission Report makes clear, to assuage the fears of the medical profession) that a medical adviser is not liable if he took reasonable care of the parent consistent with the received wisdom of the profession at the time; but that does not mean that he is to be held liable for the reason merely that he did not follow that wisdom (in other words, negligence has to be proved as against the physician in the usual way) (s.1(5)).

Liability to the child may be reduced or extinguished where the defendant could take advantage as against the parent of a term in a contract he made with the parent (s.4(6)) – this should now be read with s.2 of the Unfair Contract Terms Act 1977 which precludes a person, whether by contract or notice, from excluding or restricting his liability for death or personal injury resulting from negligence. Liability may also be reduced to the extent the court thinks just and equitable where it is shown that the parent shared the responsibility for the child being born disabled (this must refer to contributory negligence or some sort of fault on the part of the parent) (s.6(7)).

(There is in fact an exception to the rule that a woman cannot be liable for pre-natal injuries suffered by her child: she has a duty when driving a motor vehicle to take the same care for the child she knows or ought to know she is carrying as she must take for other road users (s.2). This enables the child to recover damages from the mother's motor insurers.)

CAUSATION

The 'occurrence' must be shown to have resulted in the child being born disabled. It is often difficult in the medical negligence action to show that the plaintiff's condition was caused by the treatment he received, even within the relatively wide scope the law affords to causation (which permits any significant cause, even one among many, to be taken, for the purpose of proving loss, as having caused the damage). But the difficulty is increased in the context of pre-natal injury, where

. . . often there are difficulties in separating the relative contributions of genetic and environmental effects, and interactions between them . . . There must be many pregnant women carrying a foetus with a genetic defect who are exposed to a potential teratogenic [i.e. capable of deforming a fetus] agent, and many misinterpretations in deciding the cause of damage to the child' (*per* Dr Edwards, 246 *Nature* 54 (1973)).

THE DAMAGE

The child sues in respect of the disabilities caused by the original tortious act, the 'occurrence'. This has nothing to do with the unjusticiable action for wrongful life (see Chapter 25).

The Act 'replaces any law in force before its passing, whereby a person could be liable to a child in respect of disabilities with which it might be born' (s.4(5)) (see, for one view on this provision, pp. 346–347).

LIMITATION

It is clear from s.4(3) that the limitation period will be the same as if the injuries had been suffered at birth. It will not begin while the child is still a minor (see below pp. 405–406). An action could therefore be brought as of right by a plaintiff aged 20 years in respect of an incident that injured his mother many years before he was born (though the evidence would be hard to collate).

AN EXAMPLE

Liability was admitted and compensation of over £330,000 awarded to a girl born handicapped due to the negligent transfusion to her mother seven years before her birth of blood which rendered the mother Rhesus incompatible with her husband (*Roberts* v. *Johnstone, The Times*, 26 July 1986 – the Court of Appeal's judgment on damages is reported at [1988] QB 878).

EXTENSIONS AND RESTRICTIONS

The provisions of the Act are apt to cover negligence in and around *in vitro* fertilisation and artificial insemination.

By s.6(3) of the Consumer Protection Act 1987 that Act applies to the provisions of the Congenital Disabilities Act, thus affording its protection to the unborn child (see Chapter 30).

OTHER CASES

Unborn babies cannot be made wards of court (*In re F. (in utero)* [1988] Fam 122).

A fetus is not a 'person' distinct from its mother for the purposes of the offence of threatening to kill another person under s.16 of the Offences against the Person Act 1861 (*R.* v. *Tait* [1990] 1 QB 290).

In *Rance* v. *Mid-Downs Health Authority* [1991] 1 QB 587 Brooke J. held that the words 'a child capable of being born alive' in s.1 of the Infant Life (Preservation) Act 1929 meant capable of existing as a live child, breathing and living by reason of its breathing through its own lungs alone, without deriving any of its living or power of living by or through any connection with its mother, and that, once a fetus had reached such a state of development in the womb that it was capable, if born, of possessing those attributes, it was capable of being born alive within the meaning of the Act. The point of this determination was that the parents of a child born with spina bifida were suing the health authority for not discovering the deformity and terminating the pregnancy. The judge held that, even if it had been discovered, it would have been too late for a lawful abortion as the child was then (he was some 27 weeks in gestation) capable of being born alive.

27 · Damages

SUMMARY

This chapter deals, mostly in summary form, with practical aspects of assessment and payment of damages. It is clearly impossible to provide more than a guide to the subject, and for more detailed treatment the standard textbooks should be consulted. I have chosen those points that seem to me to be most relevant to the medical negligence action and also those that have given me trouble in the past, being tricky to research, understand or remember.

We have dealt earlier with the statutory provisions for interim payment (Chapter 11) and payment into court (Chapter 14). We may now consider the facility for provisional damages and that for split trials.

PROVISIONAL DAMAGES

SUMMARY

Where the injured person wants to wait and see if he gets worse he can, instead of getting a once for all award at trial which will allow for the chance only that he may get worse, seek a provisional award at trial and apply for more later if his condition does deteriorate.

Awarding damages on the basis of the medical reports on the plaintiff's condition and prognosis at the time of trial will often involve an element of guesswork. However recent the reports, there are many cases where it is just not known whether his condition will deteriorate in the future, either by way of the further progress of his present condition or by the contraction of some new ailment of which the original injury is still the cause. For many years courts have assessed the chance of some new condition developing and awarded damages for that chance, or, better put, for the increased vulnerability of the plaintiff. This has been commonly seen in the context of the risk of osteoarthritis after a bone injury. The medical report is likely to give a percentage chance of osteoarthritis developing at a future date and the court awards damages for that prospect, adding them to the rest of the award. But this is unsatisfactory where the possible new condition is both uncertain and substantial. It had long been thought that there ought to be power in a suitable case for the court to award at trial a provisional sum, which could later be increased if it was inadequate to compensate for a condition that manifested itself after the date of the award. To allow for this situation s.6 of the Administration of Justice Act 1982 adds a section (s.32A) to the Supreme Court Act 1981, to the following effect.

Where in an action for damages for personal injuries it is proved, or admitted, that there is a chance that at some time (definite or indefinite) in the future the plaintiff will, as a result of the original negligence, develop some serious disease or suffer some serious deterioration in his physical or mental condition, then rules of court may be made to allow the court when it gives judgment in the action to award damages at the date of trial on the basis that the plaintiff will not go on to suffer the disease or deterioration *and* at a future date award further damages if he does in fact develop the disease or suffer the deterioration. The section applies to the County Court too. It came into force on 1 July 1985 and applies to causes of action arising both before and after that date.

All the plaintiff need show, therefore, is a chance that he will get worse. The court may then award him a sum to compensate for his injuries without taking that chance into account. Then if the condition does develop he will be compensated by a second award for what has actually transpired. If there is only a small chance of the condition developing he may wish to accept compensation at trial for that chance, rather than gamble on it later arising. That will depend on the degree of chance and the gravity of the potential condition.[1]

In *Ivory* v. *Martens*, 21 October 1988, PILS I [637], where the risk of deterioration was less than 2%, French J. declined to make a provisional award and added something to the general damages for the chance of the risk materialising. In *Barratt* v. *Furniss*, 13 October 1987, PILS I [648] the same judge made a provisional award to a 34-year-old woman in respect of a 10%

---

[1] Note that there is in English law no power to review a trial award at a later date in case the sum awarded should turn out to be too little or too much, due, for example, to changed financial considerations or the death of the plaintiff, a lacuna regretted by Hirst J. when he awarded over £1m in the case of *Abdul-Hosn* v. *Italian Hospital Trustees* (Kemp & Kemp, *Quantum of Damages*, A4–104).

risk of epilepsy (a risk that would reduce over the next three or four years to a continuing 3%). Provisional damages were awarded in respect of a threatened malignant mesothelioma in *Patterson* v. *Ministry of Defence* [1987] CLY 1194.

In *Hurditch* v. *Sheffield Health Authority* [1989] QB 562 the Court of Appeal said that an award may be made even if not every aspect of liability was agreed, and they made an order in the case permitting the plaintiff to seek further damages unlimited as to time in relation to an onset of pleural carcinoma or mesothelioma or the serious deterioration of his current asbestos-related condition. In *Middleton* v. *Elliott Turbomachinery Ltd, The Times*, 29 October 1990, the Court of Appeal said it was not permissible to attach a declaration to a provisional award of damages to the effect that if the plaintiff died his dependants could bring an action in respect of the fresh damage.

In *Willson* v. *Ministry of Defence* [1991] 1 All ER 638 Scott Baker J. said that 'serious deterioration' denoted a clear and severable risk and not merely the progression of the particular disease.

RSC

Rules of court have been made which define the circumstances and manner in which such awards may be made. Order 37, rr. 7–10, provide that the claim to an award of provisional damages (i.e. with the right reserved to apply later for more) *must* be pleaded by the plaintiff (though it could be pleaded with leave by way of amendment after the date of the original statement of claim). In making an award of provisional damages the court must specify the disease or deterioration which may occur, and must also, unless it determines otherwise, specify the period within which the application for a further award must be made (the plaintiff may apply to extend that period before it expires). The court may specify more than one disease or type of deterioration and may specify a different time period in respect of each.

The parties are at liberty to agree a sum by way of provisional damages where the plaintiff has applied for one; such agreement must be submitted to the court for an order to be made (in the case of a person under a disability such an agreement needs the approval of the court). When an award has been made, by consent or otherwise, the plaintiff, if he wishes to apply for a further award, must do so within the period specified by the court, and he must give the defendant three months' notice of his intention so to apply. The plaintiff can only apply once for a further award in respect of each specified disease or type of deterioration. There are provisions for making orders for the conduct of the application by way of a summons for directions.

A Practice Direction ([1985] 1 WLR 961) has specified the form the judgment to be entered should take, and made provision for the safeguarding of the case file, and for the manner in which settlements as to the award of provisional damages should be entered on the court record (see Appendix I). Another Practice Direction ([1988] 1 WLR 654) specifies the procedure to be followed where there is default in acknowledgment of service or default in serving a defence.

The County Court now has power by the rules to award provisional damages (SI 89/2426, reversing the effect of *Kennedy* v. *Bowater Ltd* [1990] 2 WLR 84).

SPLIT TRIALS

There is power under O.33 rr.3 and 4 to order the trial of liability alone, damages to be assessed later in the event of judgment for the plaintiff. The court should be ready to order separate trials of the issues of liability and damages whenever it is just and convenient to do so (*Coenen* v. *Payne* [1974] 1 WLR 984). This may arise in a personal injury action when there is an element of uncertainty about the plaintiff's future (*per* Winn L.J. in *Stevens* v. *William Nash Ltd* [1966] 1 WLR 1550), or where it is not possible to make a firm prognosis about the plaintiff's condition until some years later (*per* Winn L.J. in *Hawkins* v. *New Mendip Engineering Ltd* [1966] 1 WLR 1341). The court will consider the interests of justice in deciding whether or not to make an order, and in particular the advantage of hearing the evidence on liability while it is still relatively fresh in the minds of the witnesses.

By the new O.33 r.4(2A) (SI 89/2427) the court may, in an action for personal injuries, at any stage of the proceedings *and of its own motion* [my emphasis] make an order for the issue of liability to be tried before any issue or question concerning the amount of damages. If it makes such an order a party has 14 days to apply for the order to be varied or set aside. It remains to be seen how much use will be made by the Master of this new power. Probably a lot – and no bad thing, too: if you hive off quantum in a complex case you can concentrate on liability evidence, get the issue tried sooner, and save everyone considerable costs, time and effort in the event of your losing on liability (though it may make settlement less likely, for you may not have worked out yet what your claim is worth).

It was said in *Ashworth* v. *Berkeley Wallbrood, The Times*, 13 July 1984, that an order for a split trial will be made whenever there is a real probability that that would save time and expense and simplify the issues of fact or law. An example of an appropriate case would be where the plaintiff's case on liability is uncertain, and the issues of quantum which would have to be tried if he succeeded on liability unusually complex. A judgment for the plaintiff on liability is a final judgment (no leave to appeal needed).

Under O.33 r.4(2A) a defendant may, where an order for trial of liability only has been made, make a written offer to the plaintiff to accept liability up to a specified proportion. It is not yet clear how this provision will work in practice: it may be that its relevance is limited to cases involving contributory negligence or where there are a number of defendants who are not likely to be all jointly liable for the whole of the damages sought. Such an offer may be brought to the attention of the court after the issue of liability has been decided, so as to relieve the offeror from liability for costs if the plaintiff has failed to establish that the proportion of the damages for which the offeror is liable is more than the offer.

The proponents of split trials emphasise the advantages, namely that costly and time-consuming work on quantum need not be undertaken until the question of liability has been decided, that an earlier date for trial is likely, and that all parties can concentrate their minds on the issue of liability without being distracted by the manifold issues arising on quantum. But they overlook the disadvantage to the plaintiff that, unless work is done on quantum and a schedule presented to the defendants, no offer is likely, and, if one is made, the plaintiff will not know what to make of it. The only possibly useful offer would be one agreeing to pay a percentage of damages. Such an offer is not often made as defendants in this situation, unable to assess the case for a real offer of settlement, usually consider that they might as well have a go on liability. So it may well be best to prepare the case on quantum with a view to settling, and then, if no settlement is forthcoming, to deal at trial first with liability (the judge would want that anyway) and then, if the plaintiff is successful, damages will probably have been agreed during the course of the trial.

THE STRUCTURED SETTLEMENT

This is a way, fairly new to the United Kingdom, of setting up a settlement of a major personal injury claim. It originated in the

United States in the late 1960s in response to rapidly escalating awards that were often squandered. It was made possible by the co-operation of the US Revenue. It spread to Canada, and it is now used in several thousand transatlantic cases a year, with a value said to be in excess of a billion dollars. A structured settlement was approved for a Canadian national by an English court in *Stachnick* v. *Mitchell, The Daily Telegraph*, 30 June 1981.

In short, the defendants or their insurers will purchase a suitable annuity from an independent life office, payable to themselves, which they will bind themselves by the terms of the settlement to pay over to the plaintiff and which will serve to meet all the plaintiff's foreseeable needs for the rest of his life by way of periodical guaranteed payments. The advantages to a plaintiff are: the fund will not be overspent; through agreement reached here with the Inland Revenue about six years ago, the periodical payments are not viewed as taxable in the hands of the plaintiff;[2] the annual payment is guaranteed for his lifetime. The benefits of the structured settlement will be most obvious where the amount of compensation is over £250,000 (though in the United States it is being used in some cases for quantums as low as $100,000).

For their part, the defendants are offered a discount for agreeing to a structure (as yet, a structure cannot be ordered by the court). An example given in PILS IV [1522] shows a saving of £10,000 to the defendants upon an award of £210,000, with better security to the plaintiff. The United States experience suggests that the saving to the defendants is likely to be between 10% and 20%.

In the first UK case where settlement was effected by structured settlement[3] Potter J. approved a settlement created for a legal patient, a young woman aged 25 who was badly injured in a road accident in July 1986. The lump sum entitlement would have been £427,500, whereas by way of the settlement the insurers had to find only £410,000. Of that sum £110,000 was paid forthwith by way of lump sum and £300,000 was used to purchase an index-linked annuity for £25,562 a year, guaranteed for ten years in any event and thereafter for the rest of the plaintiff's life. There was a wide difference of medical opinion as to her life expectancy, so this form of

---

[2] The payments are viewed – though the courts have yet to pronounce on this – as payment by instalments of an antecedent debt and so as capital rather than income payments – see *CIR* v. *Ramsay* (1935) 20 TC 79.

[3] Note that the court has no power to order periodic payments by way of damages without the consent of the parties: *Burke* v. *Tower Hamlets Health Authority, The Times*, 10 August 1989. On this see Croxon Q.C.'s article in MLJ (AVMA's journal) July 1990 p.4.

settlement obviated the risk of a lump sum running out if the plaintiff lived longer than the lump sum allowed for.

The first structured settlement in a medical negligence action was achieved at the beginning of November 1991 when 6-year-old Rebecca Field, entitled to a conventional lump sum award of some £1.7m, had it structured as follows: £550,000 was paid to the family and into the Court of Protection as a lump sum, and the defendants will pay regular sums as long as Rebecca lives at £59,000 p.a., increasing after five years to £90,616 p.a., and to £148,229 p.a. after ten years, together with index-linked sums every five years based on the figure of £50,000. The monies received are tax-free; the settlement was reported in the papers as worth £100m if Rebecca lives to 76 (that figure is obtained by the amateurish device of simply adding up all the monies she might receive over the years). The Treasury was able to give its consent on behalf of the public purse as the settlement represented a significant saving to the health authority.

There would of course be scope for creating a structured settlement which admitted of a further claim if the plaintiff suffered a subsequent deterioration in his condition, i.e. it could easily enough embody the concept of provisional damages.[4]

Structured settlements look less attractive in times of low interest rates. The plaintiff may do better to make his own arrangements. Also, it seems wasteful that payments cannot be made direct to the plaintiff but have to pass through the defendants as intermediary, thus creating ongoing management expenses. It is hoped that the Treasury will authorise direct payment in due course. When that happens, there will be little reason to offer the defendants more than a token discount to afford whatever co-operation may be required.

As we went to press the Lord Chancellor announced that he would introduce legislation to implement the recommendations of the Law Commission (Report No.224), which suggested a rationalisation of the current voluntary system for creating structured settlements, so that the parties could arrange that part (or all) of the agreed damages be paid by periodic payments, the defendants then to arrange for an appropriate annuity which would be paid direct to the plaintiff free of tax. However, the Law Commission did not recommend that the court should have power to impose a structured settlement against the wish of either party. The report appends a draft Bill to that effect.

---

[4] For the procedure for obtaining the court's approval to a settlement see the Practice Note at [1992] 1 WLR 328.

INTEREST ON DAMAGES

On general damages for pain, suffering and loss of amenity the court currently awards a rate of 2% from the date of the service of the writ up until judgment. Attempts to persuade the court to increase this amount have not been successful (*Wright* v. *British Railways Board* [1983] 2 AC 773, HL).

Interest on special damages, that is to say loss that has already occurred before trial, whether by way of expenses incurred or loss of earnings or loss of dependency up to trial in Fatal Accidents Act cases, is awarded at half the short-term investment account rate from accident to trial (see RSC O.6 r.2/12). There appear from time to time in the *Law Society's Gazette* statistics on this fluctuating interest rate for preceding years (see, for example, the issue of 28 September 1994). If the loss was incurred soon after the accident, rather than over the whole period up to trial, interest at the full rate may be awarded (*Ichard* v. *Frangoulis* [1977] 2 All ER 794, *Dexter* v. *Courtaulds Ltd* [1984] 1 All ER 70) (but you need to plead your case on that).

One particular point is worth noting here, as many medical negligence actions are brought on behalf of minors many years after the injury, especially in respect of a birth injury. It used to be thought that only culpable delay in presenting or prosecuting the claim would entitle the court to reduce the period of interest on past loss,[5] but it has recently been stated that non-culpable delay can trigger the discretion (see *Nash* v. *Southmead Health Authority* [1994] 5 Med LR 74 and *Fairhurst* v. *St Helens and Knowsley Health Authority* [1994] 5 Med LR 422).

On future loss of whatever kind, including loss of earning capacity, no interest is awarded as the loss has not yet been incurred (*Joyce* v. *Yeomans* [1981] 1 WLR 549). This applies *inter alia* to loss of earnings for the 'lost years', whether claimed by the estate of the deceased for deaths before 1983, or claimed, as it may still be, by a living plaintiff whose expectation of life has been shortened (see pp. 374–375). The damages awarded for future loss take account on the one hand of the fact that by the time these future losses or expenses arise inflation will have increased the sums concerned, and on the other hand of the fact that there must be a discount for accelerated payment because the award can be invested. These two factors may well equate out, though that appears less likely in periods of rapid inflation.

The new bereavement award of £7,500 (it was £3,500) under s.3 of the Administration of Justice Act 1982 in fatal accident

---

[5] See, for example, *Spittle* v. *Bunney* [1988] 1 WLR 847, CA.

cases[6] attracted interest of 2% in *Prior* v. *Bernard Hastie & Co.*
[1987] CLY 1219, but of over 11% in *Khan* v. *Duncan* (1990),
Kemp & Kemp M3–140.

Loss of expectation of life: this is no longer a head of damages
for deaths after the beginning of 1983, as it was abolished by s.1
of the Administration of Justice Act 1982. Where applicable it
would attract a rate of 2%. But a living plaintiff can claim for
damages for suffering caused by his realisation that his life has
been shortened, with interest at 2% as being part of his general
damages.

Interest in County Court actions is similarly enabled under s.69
of the County Courts Act 1984 and O.6 r.1A of the County Court
Rules 1981.

Any settlement calculation should of course include all possible
interest claims.

There is no liability to tax in respect of interest. This is so
whether the interest is awarded upon a judgment (see the Finance
Act 1971, s.19), or whether it is included in a settlement or a
payment into court (see the Finance Act 1981, s.19(1)).[7]

MEDICAL AND OTHER EXPENSES

All additional costs to which the plaintiff has been put by reason
of his injuries may be recovered. These may include the cost of
living in an institution, the cost of any special care, whether at
home or elsewhere, including special equipment and the cost of
running and maintaining it (an unusual example would be the cost
of keeping a guide dog for a plaintiff whose sight was lost; and see
Povey v. *Governors of Rydal School* [1970] 1 All ER 841 where
the cost was recovered of obtaining and maintaining over some 25
years a lifting appliance for enabling the plaintiff to get into and
out of his motor car). The care may be expert medical care, or it
may just be cleaning and tidying. There are now a number of
expert nursing and general rehabilitation agencies who provide
expert detailed reports on all aspects of care and loss.

It has been held that a plaintiff cannot recover the cost of
acquiring special accommodation, on the ground that he retains
the asset as a capital benefit (*Cunningham* v. *Harrison* [1973] 1
QB 942). It would seem reasonable in such a case to claim, for
example, for the additional cost of mortgage interest, and the
extra expense involved in running a larger home (see *Fowler* v.

---

[6] Note that the death must occur before the child is 18 (*Doleman* v. *Deakin, The Times*, 30
January 1990).
[7] For further material on interest see Chapter 10.

Grace (1970) 114 SJ 193), Kemp & Kemp, *The Quantum of Damages*, Vol. 1 5–045. It was held that an award might be made to cover the extra cost involved in establishing a new and suitable home (see *Moriarty* v. *Mitchell* [1978] 1 WLR 155, 163), and that on the other hand where improvements had to be made to the home it might be necessary to discount their cost to reflect an element of betterment (*Udale* v. *Bloomsbury Area Health Authority* [1983] 1 WLR 1048, 1105). It is now usual to compensate for the whole of the additional capital and running costs of the new accommodation by allowing 2% per annum on the difference between the capital costs of the two accommodations (following *Roberts* v. *Johnstone* [1989] QB 878). The costs of moving and of adapting the new home to suit the handicap are extra to this.

A plaintiff is not obliged to avail himself of the facilities of the National Health Service (Law Reform (Personal Injuries) Act 1948, s.2(4)) (the Pearson Commission recommended the repeal of this provision – Cmnd 7054 (1978), pp.341–432); nor is he obliged to go into private care just because it would be cheaper than living at home (*Rialas* v. *Mitchell, The Times*, 17 July 1984).

If NHS facilities are used the plaintiff cannot claim what it would have cost him privately (*Cunningham* v. *Harrison* (*supra*), *Lim Poh Choo* v. *Camden and Islington Area Health Authority* [1980] AC 174). If a plaintiff will be obliged at some future date to use the NHS facilities because private facilities will no longer be available, no award for cost of care should be made in respect of the projected 'NHS' period. If he will, through being in a care institution, save on domestic or other expenses he would otherwise have incurred this should be brought into the calculation. By s.5 of the Administration of Justice Act 1982 any saving to a plaintiff attributable to his maintenance wholly or partly at public expense in a hospital, nursing home or other institution shall be set off against any income lost by him as a result of his injuries. In *Croke* v. *Wiseman* [1982] 1 WLR 71 the risk of overlap between the award for future loss of earnings and that for future care was considered. Griffiths L.J. said that overlap was likely to arise where the award for future care included the cost of roof and board, because if he had not been injured the plaintiff would have had to meet those costs out of his earnings.

Other recoverable expenses include Court of Protection fees on behalf of a plaintiff who can no longer look after his own affairs (*Jones* v. *Jones* [1985] QB 704).

Examples of types of loss for which compensation may be awarded will be found above in Chapter 21.

Care provided by third party

Where the plaintiff has a moral obligation to reimburse or compensate a third party, whether parent or friend, for services rendered (either because the party has given up employment to look after him or simply because he has put time and effort into the care), the court may permit recovery of an appropriate sum for those services (the benefactor himself has in general no right to claim against the tortfeasor) – *Donnelly* v. *Joyce* [1974] QB 454. The award will always be in the discretion of the court, but it should not be more than the commercial rate for the services provided, even if the benefactor has given up more lucrative employment (*Housecroft* v. *Burnett* [1986] 1 All ER 332). Such an award can properly take account of the loss of the benefactor's pension rights (*Croke* v. *Wiseman* [1982] 1 WLR 710).

A plaintiff is likely to be able to recover on behalf of those who visit him in hospital the costs they reasonably incur in attending him, at any rate where the visits may be said to aid recuperation (see *Kirkham* v. *Boughey* [1958] 2 QB 338). It is, however, doubtful whether a plaintiff confined to an institution would be permitted to recover visiting costs of his family projected over a future period of years, but on this point, as on any moot question of recoverability of expenses and loss incurred, the ultimate criterion will be the particular judge's view of what is reasonable.[8]

Expenses of divorce

The Court of Appeal originally held, in *Jones* v. *Jones* [1985] QB 704, that as the breakdown of a marriage could be a reasonably foreseeable consequence of a brain injury, the plaintiff could recover in respect of the payments he had had to make to establish his wife and children in separate accommodation (though not for the additional cost of maintenance, because the difference between the cost of maintenance before and after the divorce was too speculative to be quantifiable).

However, in *Pritchard* v. *J.H. Cobden* [1987] 2 WLR 627, the Court of Appeal took a contrary view and held, reversing the trial

---

[8] The anomalous right of a husband (not a wife) to claim for loss of an injured spouse's services (*per quod servitium amisit*) was abolished by s.2 of the Administration of Justice Act 1982. An award was made, in respect of a cause of action arising before the section came into force, in *Hodgson* v. *Trapp, The Times*, 9 May 1987, where Taylor J. held at first instance that it was not necessary for an award that there should have been total loss of consortium. Damages may still be awarded for loss of care and attention furnished by a spouse to a disabled partner, i.e. over and above the normal care and attention of consortium (*Abrams* v. *Cook*, 18 November 1987, CA, unreported); it has been said that such damages need not be limited to the commercial rate (*Regan* v. *Williamson* [1976] 2 All ER 241, but see also *Housecroft* v. *Burnett* above).

judge who had awarded the plaintiff £53,000 for the cost of creating and maintaining a separate establishment for himself, that a plaintiff cannot claim damages for any alteration in his financial position resulting from his divorce, because such damages are too remote, and it was contrary to public policy to bring matrimonial considerations into personal injury litigation. Compensation for loss of the marriage itself and the extra expense a spouse is put to in looking after the children when the other leaves may, however, be awarded (*Noe* v. *Nester* 1966 CA No.300, where compensation was awarded on the basis that there was a 50% chance that the marriage would not have broken up had the plaintiff not been injured; and *Oakley* v. *Walker* (1977) 121 SJ 619).

LOSS OF EARNINGS

The basic loss in the case of a wage earner is his net wage after tax and other deductions. 'Perks' should be valued and reflected in the figure taken as the net wage.

The tax the plaintiff would have paid is to be deducted, as he has not lost that (*British Transport Commission* v. *Gourlay* [1956] AC 185); *contra* if for some reason tax will be payable on the award (it is not payable on the ordinary personal injury award); *contra* also where it remains doubtful whether the plaintiff will be taxed on the award (*Hall & Co.* v. *Pearlberg* [1956] 1 WLR 244; *Stoke-on-Trent City Council* v. *Wood Mitchell & Co.* [1979] 2 All ER 65). A court is not entitled to take into account the higher rate of tax that the interest on a large award will attract (*Hodgson* v. *Trapp* [1989] AC 807, overruling *Thomas* v. *Wignall* [1987] 2 WLR 930); but it may increase the multiplier for an infant dependant in a fatal accident case where there has been a long delay before an award is made (*Corbett* v. *Barking Health Authority* [1990] 3 WLR 1037).

Also to be deducted are the national insurance contributions the plaintiff would have had to pay (*Cooper* v. *Firth Brown* [1963] 1 WLR 418). Any income tax rebate gained through the fall in the plaintiff's wages must be brought into account (*Hartley* v. *Sandholme Iron Co.* [1975] QB 600), as must also any reduction in his liability to tax due to diminished earnings (*Brayson* v. *Wilmot-Breedon* [1976] CLY 682). In *Dews* v. *National Coal Board* [1988] AC 1, the House of Lords held that the plaintiff's loss of earnings did not include the amounts which would have been deducted from his pay as his contribution to the company's pension scheme, on the basis that such sums would not have been his to dispose of in any event (he had in fact not lost any of his pension entitlement). A distinction was drawn between sums immediately available for spending and sums to be put into saving for a pension.

Credit to be given for certain benefits

There are currently two sets of rules in respect of deduction of state, or other, benefits from loss of earnings or damages generally. The old rules apply in respect of accident or injury sustained before the beginning of 1989. New rules, by virtue of s.22 and Sched. 4 of the Social Security Act 1989 (now found in the Social Security Administration Act 1992 ss.81 and 82, and the Social Security (Recoupment) Regulations 1990), apply to accidents or injuries sustained after the beginning of 1989.

The old rules:

(1) By virtue of the Law Reform (Personal Injuries) Act 1948 s.2 the plaintiff must give credit against any claim for loss of earnings or profits (which includes a claim for handicap on the labour market) for half of what he receives by way of sickness benefit, invalidity benefit,[9] non-contributory invalidity pension, injury benefit, severe disablement allowance, or disablement benefit, for five years from the time when the cause of action accrued.[10] This was a compromise measure to satisfy the trade unions, who were arguing for no deductions. After the expiry of the five-year period no deduction is to be made in respect of these benefits (*Jackman* v. *Corbett* [1988] QB 154) (though deduction continues as against any loss of earnings claim in respect of the other state benefits listed below).

(2) The general common law principle applied under the old rules, namely that all benefits received, with limited exceptions (as to which see below), must be deducted for as long as they might continue, but only as against like claims. So virtually all state benefits not covered by the 1948 Act have to be deducted, not as against general damages, but rather, for example, attendance and mobility allowance (or their current equivalent) must be deducted against the cost of care, and unemployment benefit against a claim for loss of earnings.

Thus credit under the old rules must be given in full for unemployment benefit[11] (*Nabi* v. *British Leyland Ltd* [1980] 1

---

[9] But see *Roderiguez* v. *Roderiguez, The Times*, 6 April 1988.

[10] Invalidity and sickness benefits are termed 'incapacity benefits' from April 1995.

[11] 'Jobseeker's allowance' from April 1996.

WLR 529, CA; *Westwood* v. *Secretary of State for Employment* [1985] AC 20, the rationale being that social security contributions are a form of taxation and not saving), supplementary benefit (now income support) (*Lincoln* v. *Hayman* [1982] 1 WLR 488), family income supplement (now family credit) (*Gaskill* v. *Preston* [1981] 3 All ER 427), and statutory sick pay (*Palfrey* v. *GLC* [1985] ICR 437). Also deductible are student maintenance or tuition grants paid by the local authority to plaintiffs who take up educational courses when unable through their injuries to retain employment (*Sully* v. *Doggett* (1984) CA No. 463; *Spittle* v. *Billington*, 3 March 1987, QBD Birmingham). Credit must be given in full for industrial rehabilitation allowance (*Cackett* v. *Earl, The Times*, 15 October 1976), any tax rebate received by reason of the plaintiff's absence from work through the relevant injury (*Hartley* v. *Sandholme Iron Co. Ltd* [1975] QB 600), and for a redundancy payment attributable to the injury (*Colledge* v. *Bass Mitchell and Butlers Ltd* [1988] ICR 125, CA) (this is not so in Scotland, by virtue of the Administration of Justice Act 1982, s.10). Overruling *Bowker* v. *Rose* (1978) 122 SJ 147 and *Gohery* v. *Durham County Council* (1978) CA No. 1236, the House of Lords held in *Hodgson* v. *Trapp* [1989] AC 807 that attendance and mobility allowances (now disability living allowance) had to be deducted. Monies paid by an employer to employee while off sick under a non-contributory permanent health insurance scheme were to be deducted, regardless of the fact that the employer recovered those sums from the insurers (*Hussain* v. *New Taplow Paper Mills Ltd* [1988] AC 514). *Contra* where the plaintiff was liable under Italian law to reimburse similar sums (*Berriello* v. *Felixstowe Dock and Railway Co.* [1989] 1 WLR 695, CA). Any saving to a plaintiff through being maintained at public expense in a hospital or similar institution must be brought into account (Administration of Justice Act 1982, s.5).

    Note that, unlike the position under the new rules, these deductions, both the half-deductions under the Act of 1948 and the full deductions, are made, as fairness would demand, only from like awards, e.g. for loss of earnings (or loss of earning capacity – see *Foster* v. *Tyne and Wear County Council* [1986] 1 All ER 567) or from awards for the cost of care, so that, if the claim is only for general damages for pain and suffering and loss of amenity, the benefits do not need to be brought into account.

(3) Credit need not be given for pension monies, whether discretionary or not, *ex gratia* or not, contributory or non-

contributory (*Parry* v. *Cleaver* [1970] AC 1; *Cunningham* v. *Harrison* [1973] QB 942), even where the employer is the tortfeasor (*Smoker* v. *London Fire Authority* [1991] 2 WLR 1052; *Wood* v. *British Coal Corporation, The Times*, 10 October 1990), nor for a State retirement pension (*Hewson* v. *Downs* [1970] 1 QB 73);[12] nor for insurance monies received where the plaintiff has paid the premiums (*Bradburn* v. *Great Western Railway* (1874) LR 10 Exch 1). Credit need not be given for an insurance payment for injuries received at work even where it is the employer alone who has paid the premiums (*McCamley* v. *Cammell Laird* [1990] 1 WLR 963, CA). Credit need not be given for monies received by the plaintiff from the bounty or benevolence of third parties motivated by sympathy for his misfortune (*Redpath* v. *Belfast and County Down Railway* [1947] NI 167). Credit need not be given for available state benefits that the plaintiff has not in fact claimed (*Eley* v. *Bedford* [1972] 1 QB 155).

In assessing loss of earnings it is, of course, the net earnings after tax and deductions that must be taken (*British Transport Commission* v. *Gourley* [1956] AC 185).

The new rules under the Act of 1989 (these rules operate from September 1990 and in respect only of causes of action arising after the end of 1988):
Section 2 of the Law Reform (Personal Injuries) Act 1948 is repealed. In short, the principle now is that all benefits paid to a plaintiff under the Social Security Acts 1975 to 1988 (or the Industrial Diseases and Injuries (Old Cases) Act 1975) must be fully deducted from general and special damages (not from costs or chattel damage, thanks to amendments made by the Social Security Act 1990), but only for five years from the accident (or, in the case of a disease, five years from the date when the plaintiff first claimed a benefit for the disease). If final settlement (except as to costs) is made before the end of such five-year period, then the benefits are deductible only up to the date of such settlement. Thereafter, no deductions. So early settlement may well benefit the plaintiff. Note that this change in the law applies only to the relevant state benefits as specified in para.2 of the 1990 Regulations, so any of the above-cited precedents that deal with other benefits remain good law.

---

[12] For the problems that can arise over pension deductibility see the *dicta* in *Parry* v. *Cleaver* [1970] AC 1 and *Cox* v. *Lancashire County Council*, 20 October 1987 at PILS I [513].

The defendant has the duty of repaying the DSS the relevant benefits. He must, before settling a case or a judgment, obtain from the DSS a certificate of total benefit received by the plaintiff, and must deduct that amount from what he pays to the plaintiff and then send it on to the DSS. In this way a tortfeasor, unlike the position under the old rules, will not profit by the amount of benefit that the plaintiff has received from the State. No deduction need be made where the sum recovered is less than £2,500 (this is termed a 'small payment' and is exempted from the operation of the Act). When making a payment into court in respect of his alleged liability the defendant should withhold the relevant deduction and file a certificate with the court to say what he has withheld, the sum paid in being deemed to include the deduction. Plaintiffs can expect delays in settlement at every stage as defendants take steps to comply with their obligations.

The deduction is to be made regardless of whether there is a head of claim for special damages or loss of earnings: in other words, unfairly as it appears, the deduction is to be made even from general damages (this should be amended, similarly to the amendment of 1990 that provided that benefits should not be deducted from an award of costs). Claims worth more than £2,500 which after the necessary deductions are worth less are therefore likely to be settled for £2,500. No regard will be had to any finding of contributory negligence which may have reduced the award. Also to be noted is that the provisions for deduction apply to any interim payment: this is likely to discourage defendants from readily agreeing to make an interim payment. At all stages of an action it will be necessary, if delays are to be kept to a minimum, for the DSS to be able speedily to provide the necessary certificate to defendants: a special office was set up in Newcastle to handle this new workload (it is hoped that the cost of running it will be no more than the benefits it recoups).

Fatal accident benefits

The new rules for deduction of state benefits do not apply to fatal accident awards.

In a Fatal Accidents Act claim, benefits accruing to any person from the deceased's estate or otherwise as a result of his death must be disregarded, by virtue of s.4 of the Fatal Accidents Act 1976 (as amended by s.3(1) of the Administration of Justice Act 1982 – this reverses finally and completely the common law principle of deductibility, as exemplified by the rules for ordinary personal injury claims). These non-deductible benefits include an allowance based on the husband's pension and paid by his former employers to his widow following his death (*Pidduck* v. *Eastern Scottish Omnibuses* [1990] 1 WLR 993, CA). Any benefit accruing to a minor after his unreliable mother was killed in a road accident from his father's subsequent marriage to a reliable woman was not to be taken into account (*Stanley* v. *Saddique* [1991] 2 WLR 459, CA). The prospect or fact of a widow's re-marriage must be ignored, by virtue of s.3 of the Fatal Accidents Act 1976. *Contra* for a widower. For further discussion of the Fatal Accidents Act context where the benefits received may not fall within the wording of exemptions in the Act the reader is referred to the very full treatment in Kemp & Kemp, *The Quantum of Damages*, Chapter 20.

Inflation

This is a vexed question. By and large the courts have adopted a rough and ready rule that no account should be taken of the rate of inflation because the opportunity for investment allows for inflation (this was the approach of the House of Lords on the last occasion they considered the question (*Lim Poh Choo* v. *Camden and Islington Area Health Authority* [1980] AC 174)). Lord Scarman said:

> . . . the correct approach should be, therefore, in the first place, to assess damages without regard to the risk of future inflation. If it can be demonstrated that, upon the particular facts of the case, such an assessment would not result in a fair compensation (bearing in mind the investment opportunities that a lump sum award offers) some increase is permissible.

But it is not easy to persuade the courts to accept that an increase is needed (*Wright* v. *British Railways Board* [1983] 2 AC 773, where the House of Lords refused to increase the rate of interest above 2% in the case of general damages for pain and suffering – see above). The assumptions upon which the rule about ignoring inflation were based have proved to be no longer tenable. This has been argued in cases in this country without success (though it has been well received in Australia – see *Todorovic* v. *Waller* (1981) 56 ALJR 59). Kemp & Kemp in *The Quantum of Damages* demonstrate in a complex argument that the practice of taking a discount rate of 4% or 5% no longer properly reimburses the plaintiff for the loss he has suffered (Vol. 1, 7-007 *et seq.*). However, the practice was approved by the Court of Appeal in *Auty* v. *National Coal Board* [1985] 1 WLR 784. The court there endorsed the trial judge's rejection of actuarial evidence for the valuation of loss of pension rights and his application in its place of a discount rate of 5%.[13]

---

[13] The House of Lords made observations thereon in *Hodgson* v. *Trapp* [1989] AC 807.

But as we went to press the Lord Chancellor announced that he would introduce legislation to implement the recommendations of the Law Commission (Report No.224) to the effect that the tables prepared by the Government Actuary's Department showing expected real rates of return (known as the Ogden tables) should be admissible in evidence on issues of future pecuniary loss and that the court should take account of the real rate of return on index-linked government securities. This is likely greatly to increase the multipliers used in such calculations.

The lost years

This is a complicated story. I will attempt to summarise it.

(1) Until the House of Lords' decision in *Pickett* v. *British Rail Engineering Ltd* [1980] AC 136, the settled law was that no damages could be recovered for loss of earnings during years when, but for the accident, the plaintiff would have been alive. This applied whether the plaintiff died immediately or had merely suffered a shortened expectation of life.

(2) It was also the law that, if the injured party commenced an action against the tortfeasor, his dependants lost the right to bring a claim on their own behalf under the Fatal Accidents Acts.

(3) The result of these two rules was that a plaintiff who was expected to die in, say, five years, instead of 30, could not get compensation to provide for his dependants when he was gone, although if he had died immediately they could have themselves got compensation for the 30 years' loss of dependency under the Fatal Accidents Acts.

(4) The House of Lords sought to remedy this unsatisfactory situation by their decision in *Pickett*. They held that an injured party may recover in respect of loss of earnings for the lost years.

(5) They then went on to hold in *Gammell* v. *Wilson* [1982] AC 27 that this right must necessarily pass to the estate upon the death of the injured party along with all his rights of action under the Law Reform (Miscellaneous Provisions) Act 1934, s.1.

(6) The result was therefore reached that not only could a life-shortened plaintiff who in fact had no dependants get compensation which was intended in theory to enable him to provide for his dependants when he was gone (that was not too bad, because in some cases there might be a chance that the plaintiff would go on to acquire dependants before he

died), but, further, the estate of an injured party could claim for the lost years, and so also could the dependants under the Fatal Accidents Acts. If the beneficiaries of the estate were the same people as the dependants, as they generally were, then all that was required was a complex calculation which set one award off against the other in respect of every dependant. But if they were not the same people there was double recovery in respect of the same loss, by estate and by dependants, which was clearly absurd.

(7) The House of Lords was inviting the legislature to intervene, which it did by s.4(2) of the Administration of Justice Act 1982; this amended s.1(2)(a) of the Law Reform (Miscellaneous Provisions) Act 1934, the section now providing that, where a cause of action survives by virtue of sub-s.(1) for the benefit of the estate of a deceased person, the damages recoverable for the benefit of the estate of that person shall not include any damages for loss of income in respect of any period after that person's death. That applies to deaths after the end of 1982.

(8) The net result of these shenanigans is that *a living plaintiff can still recover for the lost years*, whether or not he has or may go on to acquire dependants.[14] (It would also seem to be the case that the estate of an injured party could recover for any financial loss that does not come within the term 'income' in the Act.)

(9) The loss is not simply the projected net earnings. After considerable judicial uncertainty it is now established that the loss is the available surplus the injured party would have had after deductions representing the reasonable living expenses which would have been deployed to maintain him at the standard of life appropriate to his case (*Harris* v. *Empress Motors Ltd* [1984] 1 WLR 212).

For more detailed treatment of the calculation to be employed the reader is referred to the cases and the standard textbooks on the subject.

LOSS OF EXPECTATION OF LIFE

The conventional award of (usually) £1,250–£1,500 for loss of expectation of life that used to be made in the case of a deceased

---

[14] In *Jackson* v. *Telcon Metals Ltd*, 30 January 1987, unreported (Mr Kidwell Q.C. sitting as a deputy High Court judge), the 46-year-old plaintiff had contracted from his employment as a welder between 1969 and 1979 a form of beryllium poisoning that would ensure his death within a few years. He was awarded just short of £100,000. With this he could hope to provide for his wife and children after he had died.

(or in genuine cases of shortened expectation of life) is no longer available in respect of deaths after the end of 1982, but where a living plaintiff suffers through the knowledge that his life has been shortened an award may be made to compensate him for that extra suffering (Administration of Justice Act 1982, s.1).

EXAMPLES

It may be useful to consider how recent large awards have been made up, and for that purpose I take the recent £1,032,000 award by Hirst J. in *Abdul-Hosn* v. *Italian Hospital Trustees*, 10 July 1987 (see Kemp & Kemp at A4–104). The plaintiff was a gifted 19-year-old student when, due to negligent treatment, he suffered brain damage which reduced him to, as the judge said, a sub-human, zombie-like existence. He retained some awareness of his condition, but one could not know how much. For pain, suffering and loss of amenity the award was £85,000. His parents recovered for their devoted nursing care up to the date of trial at the full commercial rate (as agreed) of £16,137 p.a., which over nearly five years gave a figure of £76,650. Together with agreed out-of-pocket expenses of £23,767 the total figure for care up to trial came to £100,700.

The judge took a base multiplier of 16 and added one point for the incidence of a higher rate of tax on a large award. As life expectancy for the plaintiff was to age 60 to 65, which coincided with the normal retirement age, there was, he said, no justification in this case for taking a larger multiplier for future care than for loss of earnings. As to future care: of the 17 years of the multiplier the judge concluded that the parents would provide home care for 11, the remaining six would involve residential care. The mother would work five hours a day at the full commercial rate, and this over 11 years yielded £234,102. Residential care was agreed at £18,824 p.a., which gave £112,944 over six years. Also to be included in future care were supporting medical services, such as physio- and speech therapy, neurological checks and dietary advice. This gave an overall figure of £13,800.

The cost of residence in a rehabilitation unit, with refresher courses, for a total of 26 months was assessed at £95,000, less £40,000 for saving on home care during those months. A further deduction of £15,000 was made to avoid overlap between the lost earnings and the care heads for the periods the plaintiff would be cared for in an institution. The grand total for future care came to £400,800.

As to housing needs: the family would have to move from their £80,000 home to a house costing £150,000, which would need to be adapted to the tune of £46,000. The judge allowed the whole cost of the adaptations, saying that the money saved by the plaintiff not setting up a home of his own as he would otherwise have been expected to do was swallowed up in the extra purchase price of the new home. He added a small sum for a mini-gym and heating costs over 11 years, and awarded a figure of £48,100.

Future loss of earnings: on evidence as to the earnings of chemical engineers and the plaintiff's proven abilities the judge decided that the figure to be put on the plaintiff's lost earnings was £18,000 p.a., which over 17 years gave £306,000, plus £25,000 for the lost perk of a company car.

Court of Protection fees were agreed at £34,850, and the grand total of the claim, with interest of £31,550, came to £1,032,000.

The contractual claim by the father of the plaintiff for his own loss of earnings in having to look after his son was rejected as too remote, and his claim for damages for the great distress and vexation he had suffered was held to be bad in law (unaccompanied as it was by any physical injury to himself).

We may also look at *Almond* v. *Leeds Western Health Authority* [1990] 1 Med LR 370, Fennell J., where a (then) record-breaking award was made of £1,156,348 in favour of 10½-year-old Nicholas Almond for severe brain damage sustained when he was born and resulting in dyskinetic palsy. Liability was admitted; damages were agreed only in part. The plaintiff was not intellectually impaired (the judge, who met him, said he was highly intelligent), but he was grossly physically handicapped, with virtually no control over his bodily movements and needing constant help in every day-to-day activity. He could not speak intelligibly, but had normal sight and hearing, with an expectation of life to 61 years.

Pain, suffering and loss of amenity: the judge took as his guideline the award of £75,000 in 1985 in *Housecroft* v. *Burnett* [1986] 1 All ER 332 for a typical case of tetraplegia. He applied an uplift of 1.3 for inflation which gave £97,500. He concluded that Nicholas was worse off than a tetraplegic in view of his intelligence and his awareness of his situation and awarded £105,000. It is open to debate whether less extensive injuries should receive a larger sum on the ground that the absence of mental handicap makes the physical handicap worse for the victim. The mental anguish will certainly be worse, but the fact remains that physical handicap without mental handicap is, in terms of injury merely, substantially less handicap than the two combined.

Past parental care: this was calculated on the basis of the cost of two residential carers. The sum was halved for reasons that are not clear from the judgment, but probably relate to the fact that the parents would have been in the home anyway, so that they were not really to be considered as 'residential' carers. With state benefits deducted a total of £49,090 was reached.

Future nursing care: this was based on three periods of care – from the present (age 10) to 18 (multiplier 6), 18 to 22 (multiplier 2.3), and 22 to 61 (multiplier 9.7). The total multiplier (chosen, presumably, before the division) was the usual maximum of 18. The figures for the cost of care came from the report of the plaintiff's experts: the total, allowing for certain reductions made by the judge, was £505,000.

Future parental care: Nicholas's mother was awarded £10,000 for the extra care she would be giving him on top of the help she would receive. It seems that this sum was not a precise calculation but a figure that seemed appropriate to the judge.

Housing claim: the 2% per annum formula of *Roberts* v. *Johnstone* [1988] 3 WLR 1247 was used. The difference in value of the old and the new home was multiplied by 2% and then by the multiplier of 18. The cost of converting the new home to cater for Nicholas's needs was allowed, but less a sum for the enhanced value of the property due to the conversion. In addition the judge, interestingly, awarded a further 2% × 18 on that enhanced value. The total award here was £71,565.

Loss of earnings: this is particularly interesting, as a large sum was awarded. It was clear that Nicholas would have been well educated and would have earned a good living like his parents (his father was a manager with a water board). As it was, he would not be employable. The judge took an annual figure for earnings of 1.5 times the average national wage (as done in *Croke* v. *Wiseman* [1976] 1 WLR 71). This gave, at date of judgment, £19,000 net per annum. The multiplier used was 10. The unusually large figure, for a young person, was therefore £190,000.

The remaining £225,000 odd comprised agreed amounts, not specified by the judge. No doubt they will have included computer aids, travel costs, holidays, extra household expenses, education costs etc.

It is understood that the £1.7m record-breaking award to Rachel Field in June 1991 reached such a figure largely because the poor child needed two carers 24 hours a day for the rest of her life (as we saw earlier in this chapter, this award has now been structured).

Cassel v. *Riverside Health Authority* [1992] PIQR Q168 was a claim by a child, 8-years-old at trial, who had suffered grievous physical and mental handicap as a result of birth asphyxia. The judge assessed general damages at £110,000, past care at almost

£96,000, future care at over £0.5m, future accommodation at over £45,000, loss of earnings at £350,000, £47,000 for the fees of a receiver, nearly £33,000 for Court of Protection fees, and interest of over £53,000. With numerous other items and aids, medical, educational and social, the total award, which was subject to a 10% agreed reduction by way of compromise, was £1,192,000.

It will be appreciated that the formulation and calculation of heads of claim in cases of grave injury need special expertise, and there are experts who provide an invaluable service in preparing schedules which set out all the envisaged needs of an injured lifetime. These needs may include nursing, attendance, rehabilitation, medical and therapeutic attention, housing, education, holidays and a variety of mechanical aids for the home and for mobility, as well as items specific to the injury (e.g. in cases of incontinence, a supply of pads, a number of additional trousers and underpants, funds for the additional cost of washing, and repairing and replacing washing machines). A second line of expertise may well be required, e.g. from an architect on the cost of adapting the home. The lawyer should not attempt to prepare such a schedule himself, for he does not have the necessary expertise, neither to decide what to claim for nor to cost it.

28 · The limitation period

SUMMARY

The point of prescribing a limitation period within which an action
has to be brought if at all is to prevent stale claims, when loss of
memory and evidence will hamper justice, prejudicing, in particular, the defendant. So *prima facie* actions may not be commenced
when the period of limitation has expired. But a set and inflexible
period of limitation can lead to injustice, particularly in the case of
an action for personal injuries, because often a plaintiff may not
know he has been injured, or how, or by whom, until a considerable period of time has elapsed. Legislation has to a large extent
remedied this situation.

Where an action includes a claim for personal injuries the writ
(or summons) must be issued within three years. Time does not
begin to run until the patient knows, or would know if he had
made reasonable inquiries, that he has suffered injury and that it
may reasonably have been caused by the treatment of which he
now complains. It is irrelevant that he has no idea that those facts
give rise to a legal claim. But even if time has expired the court has
a discretion to allow him to start an action out of time where it
thinks it equitable to do so. If the delay is due to his solicitor's
negligence the court may well leave him to his remedy against the
solicitor.

THE IMPORTANCE OF LIMITATION

The period of limitation is that period within which a writ has to
be issued (though not necessarily served)[1] if the claim is not to
become time-barred. This period is of great practical importance

---

[1] As far as the County Court is concerned, proceedings are commenced when the
summons is issued by the court, at which time the plaint will be entered in the court
records (see CCR 1981, O.3). There will then be four months to serve it (the plaintiff's
solicitor can take advantage of the new provisions permitting him to serve it himself,
rather than the court – O.7 r.10A). However, strictly speaking, the court requires the
particulars of claim and, in a personal injury action, a medical report before it will issue
the summons. But some court offices are willing to issue a summons in appropriate cases
where the claim is only briefly indicated on the summons, something like an endorsement
on a writ. In any event the situation will need to be sorted out. (See Chapter 10 for the
new jurisdictions.)

in medical negligence claims. This is in part because they are almost always complex; ascertaining the facts is not easy and construing negligence from the available material takes time and expert consideration, and the temptation to let matters drift is not always resisted. Until one knows what the cause of action is, which requires a degree of precision, though not of course as much as the drafting of the statement of claim, it is not possible to endorse a writ with the appropriate wording. Further difficulty is likely to arise because often the injury itself may not become apparent for a number of years, or the connection of the injury with medical treatment received by the patient may not emerge; or the connection may be clear but it may not occur to the patient that what the doctor did or did not do could amount to negligence. This last may depend on the state of the art at the time, i.e. what was accepted as proper practice. The state of the art is changing all the time: the wonder drugs of yesteryear, and the 'in' operations (on which reputations and fortunes are made) are seen a few years later as little short of lethal.

Where a prescribed drug (to take one example) is followed by internal injury it may not be apparent that the patient has been injured, or it may not be apparent that the injury is due to the drug.[2]

We will see that legislation has acknowledged many of these difficulties that plaintiffs may face by providing for extended periods of limitation in personal injury cases and even permitting the court a general discretion to allow out of time actions to proceed.

PLEADING POINTS

Note that it is up to the defendant to plead a limitation bar (this also applies to a claim between co-defendants – *Kennett* v. *Brown* [1988] 1 WLR 582, CA; *Holland* v. *Yates Building Co. Ltd, The Times*, 5 December 1989. A defendant cannot argue that the claim is barred unless he has pleaded that. Normally the plaintiff will plead by way of reply his case as to why the limitation period had not expired by the time the writ was issued, and/or as to why the court should exercise its discretion to permit his action to proceed notwithstanding the expiry of the limitation period. He is at liberty, however, so to plead in his statement of claim (that of course makes it clear to the defendants, who might in the odd case not otherwise take the point, that there is a limitation point

---

[2] A recent example of how, in a non-personal injury case (solicitors' negligence), the limitation period can expire before the injured party realises he has been injured, is *Bell* v. *Peter Browne and Co.* [1990] 3 WLR 510 (and see *D.W. Moore & Co.* v. *Ferrier* [1988] 1 WLR 267).

to be taken).[3] Further, it is for the defendant to establish his plea that the limitation period has expired, not for the plaintiff to show that it has not (*Holland* v. *Yates Building Co. Ltd* (*supra*)) and see *infra* under 'Burden of proof').

THE BACKGROUND

Limitation is entirely statute-created. The earliest Statute of Limitation was in 1623 (21 Jac. 1, c.16). The point of limitation was well expressed by Lord Simon in the *Ampthill Peerage* case ([1977] AC 547) at p. 575:

As a means of resolution of civil contention, litigation is certainly preferable to civil violence. But it is not intrinsically a desirable activity . . . . The law itself is fully conscious of the evil of protracted litigation. Our forensic system, with its machinery of cross-examination of witnesses and forced disclosure of documents, is characterised by a ruthless investigation of truth. Nevertheless, the law recognises that the process cannot go on indefinitely. There is a fundamental principle of English law (going back to Coke's *Commentary on Littleton* [Co Litt (1809) p.303]) generally expressed by a Latin maxim [*interest reipublicae ut sit finis litium*] which can be translated: 'It is in the interest of society that there should be some end to litigation'. This fundamental principle finds expression in many forms. Parliament has passed Acts (the latest only last year [1975]) limiting the time within which actions at law must be brought. Truth may thus be shut out, but society considers that truth may be bought at too high a price, that truth bought at such expense is the negation of justice.

SIX YEARS

The Limitation Act 1939 was the first modern statute, and it brought order to the chaos that had previously prevailed. It provided a basic period of six years for all actions in contract or tort (the exceptions need not concern us). That period of six years is still the basic period for actions which do not claim damages for personal injuries. There has been a lot of movement over the last few years, both judicial and legislative, over claims for damages for latent defects in property that do not show themselves until the period of limitation has expired; it is interesting to note that the same sort of problem has arisen in that context as has confronted the personal injury plaintiff in respect of latent injury; a solution is now provided by the Latent Damage Act 1986 (see below under 'Financial loss').[4]

---

[3] It has been said that the plaintiff should wait for the defendants to raise the plea (see *Ogunsanya* v. *Lambeth Health Authority*, 3 July 1985, Bristow J., unreported), but it surely cannot be improper in a suitable case for the plaintiff to state his case on limitation in the statement of claim.
[4] For recent cases in which the period of limitation expired before any damage became evident, see *D.W. Moore & Co.* v. *Ferrier* [1988] 1 WLR 267, and *Bell* v. *Peter Browne & Co.* [1990] 3 WLR 510, claims against solicitors for alleged negligence.

THREE YEARS

You know of course that the period for personal injury actions is now three years. This change occurred when the Law Reform (Limitation of Actions etc.) Act 1954 reduced the six-year period to three years

in the case of actions for damages for negligence, nuisance or breach of duty (whether the duty exists by virtue of a contract or of a provision made by or under a statute or independently of any contract or any such provision) where the damages claimed by the plaintiff for the negligence, nuisance or breach of duty consist of or include damages in respect of personal injuries to the plaintiff or any other person.

This is now the rule for actions for personal injuries, and appears at s.11 of the consolidation statute, the Limitation Act 1980. It applies in medical negligence actions where the plaintiff has been injured whether the doctor is being sued in tort or upon a contract made with a patient treated privately.

PERSONAL INJURIES

A medical negligence action is not necessarily an action for personal injuries. The three-year period will apply where the claim includes damages for personal injuries, regardless of what other claims are included. But if the claim is, for example, in respect of negligent advice or diagnosis that caused the plaintiff to stop work and thereby lose money when he was in fact well enough to continue working, the six-year period will apply. One can envisage a case where it may be to the plaintiff's advantage to omit any claim for personal injuries and bring only the claim for financial loss, in order to take advantage of the six-year period. For example, a claim for wrongful birth (see Chapter 25) may involve only a slight personal injury element but a large claim for loss of wages and the cost of the upkeep of the child over the years. If the mother issues a writ outside the three-year period she may be advised to ask first for the court's discretion under s.33 (see below) to be exercised so as to allow her to proceed, and, if she is unsuccessful in that, to abandon the personal injury element and proceed with the claim for mere economic loss (though there can be difficulties in recovering for economic loss unconnected with personal or property injury (see Chapter 19)). It is, however, possible that the court would hold that the action nevertheless still included a claim for damages 'in respect of' personal injuries (see below).

'Personal injuries' are defined by the interpretation section of the Limitation Act 1980, s.38, as including 'any disease and any impairment of a person's physical or mental condition'. It would, therefore, include a claim for nervous shock, as that must, to be admissible, involve an actual psychiatric disorder (see *McLoughlin* v. *O'Brian* [1983] 1 AC 410). It may not always be clear whether a physical injury has been suffered. For example, where a mother claims for wrongful birth after an uneventful pregnancy it is a moot point whether compensation for her travail is compensation for an impairment to her physical condition; and the anxiety and distress she suffers over the advent of an unplanned baby, though a proper head in law for compensation, may not be of sufficient gravity to amount to an impairment of her mental condition.

In *Ackbar* v. *Green and Co.* [1975] 2 WLR 773 it was held that a claim against an insurance broker for failing to obtain cover for the plaintiff was not a claim for damages for personal injuries, although the claim in fact arose out of the plaintiff's having suffered personal injuries.

In *Paterson* v. *Chadwick* [1974] 1 WLR 890, where the patient wished to sue her solicitors for not prosecuting her medical negligence claim properly, the judge held that she was entitled to pre-action disclosure of her medical records because there was sufficient nexus between her claim against the solicitors and her personal injuries for her to be 'a person who is a party to proceedings in which a claim in respect of personal injuries to a person is made' within the meaning of s.32(1) of the Administration of Justice Act 1970 (now replaced by s.34(2) of the Supreme Court Act 1981 – see Chapter 7). This does not mean that in suing your solicitors for professional negligence for not prosecuting your personal injury claim a three- and not a six-year period of limitation applies. In *Broadley* v. *Guy Clapham & Co* [1994] 4 All ER 439 it appears to have been accepted without argument that a six-year period applied.

A decision similar to that in the *Ackbar* case had been reached by a Scottish court in *McGahie* v. *Union of Shop Distributive and Allied Workers* 1966 SLT 74. However *Ackbar*'s case was distinguished in *Howe* v. *David Brown Tractors (Retail) Ltd* [1991] 4 All ER 30 where a claim was made on behalf of a farming business for loss of profit as a result of the supply of allegedly dangerous machinery that injured the farmer and so caused financial loss to the business. The distinction was drawn that in this case the same facts gave rise to the breach of duty as to the personal injury as a result of which the financial loss was sustained and so the action included a claim for damages 'in respect of personal injuries'. Nicholls L.J. said that in the ordinary personal injury action including a claim for financial loss a plaintiff could not acquire a six-year limitation period by the simple device of suing for compensation only for his financial loss and not for the personal injury.

In *Pattison* v. *Hobbs, The Times*, 11 November 1985 (to be reported in the Medical Law Reports), the Court of Appeal held that where, following an allegedly negligently performed vasectomy, damages were claimed only for the cost of raising a healthy child, the action was not one which included a claim for personal injuries and therefore attracted the six-year limitation period. This can be understood on the limited basis that a pregnancy is not an injury (though possibly a wasted sterilisation would be). The better view is that the claim for the upkeep of the child, unlike the claim for loss of profit in the farming case above, is economic loss dissociate, or at any rate relatively remote, from any personal injury or any claim for personal injury – this seems to have been the view of Brooke J. in *Allen* v. *Bloomsbury Health Authority* [1992] 3 Med LR 257.

In *Walkin* v. *South Manchester Health Authority*, 19 May 1994, noted in Supreme Court Practice News 17 June 1994, Potter J. reached an opposite conclusion from the *Pattison* case, distinguishing the Court of Appeal decision on the doubtful ground that the *Pattison* case involved the 'personal injury' of a pregnancy. It is doubtful because, first, if a pregnancy is a personal injury, so is a wasted, or repeat, vasectomy; second, the Act speaks of a claim for damages for personal injury to the plaintiff or any other person, and so the pregnancy after a failed vasectomy would be just as relevant on this issue as after a failed sterilisation.

Financial loss

Even where the action is not a personal injury action there is scope for postponing the commencement of the limitation period until the date the plaintiff acquired knowledge of material facts, pursuant to the provisions of the Latent Damage Act 1986 (in force from 18 September 1986). Reference may be made, especially by those who, like me, had thought this Act was applicable only to latent physical damage to property (following from the *Pirelli* case [1983] 2 AC 1), to *Iron Trade Mutual Insurance Co.* v. *JK Buckenham Ltd* [1990] 1 All ER 108 and *Société Commerciale de Réassurance v ERAS (International) Ltd* [1992] 2 All ER 82, and to *Hallam-Eames* v. *Merrett Syndicates Ltd, The Times*, 25 January 1995 (this last case is dealt with more fully below).

ASSAULT

It has been held that the words 'actions for damages for . . . breach of duty' (now in s.11 of the Act of 1980) include a claim for trespass to the person, whether intentional or unintentional (though the latter is better pleaded as negligence). In *Letang* v. *Cooper* [1965] 1 QB 232, a sunbathing plaintiff was injured when the defendant drove his car over her legs. The Court of Appeal held that her claim in trespass as well as her claim in negligence attracted the three-year period. In *Long* v. *Hepworth* [1968] 1 WLR 1299 it was held that the plaintiff's claim for intentional trespass, i.e. assault, arising out of the defendant having deliberately thrown a handful of cement into her eye, was similarly governed by the three-year period of limitation.

However, the House of Lords held in *Stubbings* v. *Webb* [1993] AC 498, a claim for damages for injury suffered many years earlier by way of childhood sexual abuse where the writ was issued 12 years after the plaintiff had attained her majority, that the words of s.11 were not apt to include a claim for damages for assault. The court pointed out that the Tucker Committee, upon whose 1949 recommendations the later legislation was based, had expressly recommended that actions for trespass to the person should remain governed by the six-year period. It may also be that the court did not relish the prospect of claims for sexual abuse, which raise questions of the greatest difficulty, concern and delicacy, being brought many years after the incident. In any event, a child has until the age of 21 to present a claim.

The court did not expressly disapprove of the decision in *Letang* v. *Cooper*, where the trespass to the person had been *unintentional* and the claim had been framed in assault rather than in negligence simply in an attempt to escape the three-year rule (the Court of Appeal had felt bound to follow the *Letang* decision and hold that the three-year rule applied to claims for sexual abuse). So one then asks whether a claim for assault against a doctor for operating without consent would be subject to a three- or a six-year period of limitation. The six-year period has the disadvantage that there is no provision for extending this period such as exists in respect of the three-year period, nor for seeking the court's discretion to proceed notwithstanding the expiry of the limitation period. On the other hand, where there appear to be difficulties for the plaintiff even with the three-year period and its extended possibilities (as to this, see below), the six-year period might assist merely by virtue of the extra three years. Bearing in mind that the courts have on several occasions (in the context of consent) disapproved of suing doctors for assault where an action in negligence is possible, and that the application of a six-year rule is more likely to embarrass than assist the patient, it is perhaps to be expected that they would apply the six-year rule. On the other hand, they might follow the *Letang* v. *Cooper* line and say that the assault claim is only an action for negligence in disguise and therefore the three-year period should apply. We will have to wait and see.

Presumably the earlier case of *Halford* v. *Brookes* [1991] 1 WLR 428 (not referred to in *Stubbings* v. *Webb*) was wrongly decided. The claim there was brought by the estate of a murdered girl and was principally laid in battery against the alleged murderers, but the Court of Appeal accepted without argument the applicability of the three-year period (the actual decision was that the plaintiff had acquired the relevant knowledge several years before the writ was issued but that it was equitable to permit the action to proceed notwithstanding).

LATENT INJURY: THE FIRST ATTEMPT OF THE LEGISLATURE

The reduction of the limitation period to three years operated wholly to the plaintiff's disadvantage, and served to accentuate what was becoming an increasingly evident injustice, namely the latent defect syndrome, whereby the limitation period expired before the plaintiff knew he had been injured. Matters came to a head in *Cartledge* v. *Joplin* [1963] AC 758 when the House of Lords reluctantly held, in the case of a victim of pneumoconiosis in whom the condition had remained undetectable for many years, that the limitation period ran from the time the victim suffered injury, that is to say, more than minimal injury, regardless of whether any injury was detectable. The result was that the plaintiff's right of action was barred by limitation before he could have known that he had suffered any injury, let alone known the cause of such injury. The injustice of this position was sought to be remedied by the Limitation Act 1963 (which made it possible for an action for personal injuries to be brought outside the normal limitation period with the leave of the court where 'material facts of a decisive character' had been outside the actual or constructive knowledge of the plaintiff and the action was begun within 12 months of his acquiring such knowledge). That Act was 'obscure and difficult to construe' Lord Denning once said, and Lord Reid commented that it had a strong claim to the distinction of being the worst-drafted Act on the statute book.

One particular problem that Act left unresolved was whether time ran against a plaintiff who knew all the material facts but did not know he had a worthwhile cause of action. Opinion on this important point was divided in the House of Lords in *Smith* v. *Central Asbestos Co.* [1973] AC 518, so that the Court of Appeal was led to say in *Harper* v. *National Coal Board* [1974] QB 614 that there was no common ratio discernible in the *Smith* judgments. They held that time did not run against a plaintiff until he knew he had a worthwhile cause of action. Unfortunately the Law Reform Committee rejected that approach and the Limitation Act 1975, which was Parliament's next, and comparatively successful, attempt to resolve the situation and which is the basis for the present law, followed the recommendations of the Committee (so that it is irrelevant whether or not the patient knows the treatment that injured her was negligent).

The Act of 1975 has been incorporated into the Act of 1980, and it is to that consolidating statute that we now turn.

THE LIMITATION ACT 1980

SUMMARY

The Act postpones the commencement of the limitation period until such time as the plaintiff has the requisite knowledge as to the identity of the defendants and the connection between a significant injury suffered by him and the acts or omissions of the defendants of which he now complains (but failure to appreciate that known facts might or do represent a less than proper standard of medical care or constitute negligence in law does not operate to postpone the commencement of the period). It also gives the court a general discretion to permit an action to proceed even when the writ (or summons) has not been issued within that extended period, but the provisions of the Act do not assist a plaintiff where a writ has been issued in time but the period of limitation expires without the writ having been served.

Scheme of the Act

The legislation, which is set out below in Appendix I, assists the plaintiff in a personal injury action in two quite different ways. In the first place it postpones the date from which the limitation period of three years begins to run until the victim knows he has been injured, how, and by whom (though, unfortunately, neither justifiable ignorance on the part of a patient that the treatment he received could constitute negligence in the medical sense, i.e. a failure to come up to proper medical standards, nor that it could amount to negligence in law, enable the commencement of the limitation period to be postponed).[5] Secondly, even though the period as so defined may have expired, the court has a general discretion to permit the action to proceed.

The special time limit for actions for personal injuries is laid down in ss.11 and 14 of the Act of 1980. The limitation period is three years from the date the cause of action arose (which means, for actions in negligence, the date when injury was first suffered, and in contractual cases the date when the breach of contract occurred – that is a reason to sue in negligence wherever possible) *or* three years from the date of the plaintiff's knowledge, if that is later.

Knowledge

By s.14 of the Limitation Act 1980 the two most important factors (relevant to a medical negligence action) of which a plaintiff must have knowledge before the limitation period can commence are (i) the knowledge that she has suffered a significant injury (which means one worth suing for if liability were not contested) and (ii) the knowledge that the injury was attributable in whole or in part to the act or omission which is alleged to constitute negligence.

Significant injury

If a medical negligence plaintiff was aware of the injury at all during the limitation period it is unlikely that it would reasonably appear to him so trivial as not to warrant proceedings, given that the proposed defendants would *ex hypothesi* pay up without demur. But if it did turn more serious only after the expiry of the limitation period, much would turn on whether the plaintiff ought to have realised the trivial aspect was only the precursor of more serious damage (see, on the original provision in the Act of 1975, *Davies* v. *British Insulated Cables* (1977) 121 SJ 203, *Buck* v. *English Electric Co. Ltd* [1978] 1 All ER 271; see also *Miller* v. *London Electrical Manufacturing Co.* [1976] 2 Lloyd's Rep 284). In *McCafferty* v. *Metropolitan Police Receiver* [1977] 2 All ER 756 Lane L.J. said:

It is not altogether clear to me why the word 'would' is used ['would reasonably have considered it sufficiently serious . . .']. It may be that one must understand

---

[5] The Court of Appeal held in *Halford* v. *Brookes* [1991] 1 WLR 428 that the commencement of the limitation period was not postponed merely because the personal representative of a murder victim did not realise that a civil action was feasible against the alleged culprits; however the court exercised its discretion under s.33 to permit the action to proceed.

such words as 'if he had considered the matter'; or it may be that it is because of the possibility of knowledge being imputed to the plaintiff under [s.14(3)].

Whatever the answer to that particular problem may be, it is clear that the test is partly a subjective test, namely: would this plaintiff have considered the injury sufficiently serious? And partly an objective test, namely: would he have been reasonable if he did *not* regard it as sufficiently serious? It seems to me that [s.14(2)] is directed at the nature of the injury as known to the plaintiff at that time. Taking *that* plaintiff, with *that* plaintiff's intelligence, would he have been reasonable in considering the injury not sufficiently serious to justify instituting proceedings for damages?

Young v. *GLC & Massey* [1987] 6 CLY 2328 is an illustration of the postponement of the commencement of the limitation period where the injured plaintiff did not realise for a period of time that his whiplash injury was 'significant'.

The 'injury' refers to the first of the injuries which the plaintiff knows to be significant, not to an inquiry, albeit from the same accident, subsequently discovered after settlement of the first claim (*Bristow* v. *Grout, The Times*, 3 November 1986).

In *Stubbings* v. *Webb* [1991] 3 WLR 383, the plaintiff issued a writ 12 years after she had reached majority alleging rape when a child against her adoptive father. The Court of Appeal distinguished between her recognition at an early stage that she had suffered minor or transient distress and her later realisation that the assault may have done her a lasting (i.e. a significant) injury, and held that it was within the previous three years that she had realised this, as a result of the new awareness in public and professional understanding of these issues that had arisen largely as a result of the Cleveland inquiry, and that she had been able, with expert guidance, to appreciate the causal link between the defendant's alleged conduct and her having suffered serious long-term mental impairment.[6]

It is not infrequently the case that the patient is reassured by the hospital for a considerable period after the apparent injury that time or further treatment will put matters right. It is clear that while the patient still reasonably believes that to be true, she can properly contend that she did not know the injury was significant. It may also be possible to argue that her condition was so weakened by her illness or injury that she was not for some time in a position to appreciate that the injury was significant.

For a recent example of a plaintiff reasonably believing for some eighteen months after an accident causing back and leg pain that the injury was not significant see *Harding* v. *People's Dispensary for Sick Animals* [1994] PIQR P270.

---

[6] As explained above, the House of Lords reversed the decision of the Court of Appeal, but not so as generally to invalidate the above line of argument.

The vital 'act or omission'

The Act provides that the relevant knowledge must include knowledge that the injury was attributable in whole or in part to the act or omission which is alleged to constitute negligence or breach of duty – s.14(1)(b).

'Attributable' means 'capable of being attributed to'; it does not mean 'caused by' (*Davis* v. *Ministry of Defence, The Times*, 7 August 1985, CA, and *Wilkinson* v. *Ancliff* [1986] 1 WLR 1352). The act or omission need only be a possible, not necessarily a probable, cause of the injury, but the possibility must be real and not fanciful – *Guidera* v. *NEI Projects (India)*, unreported, 30 January 1990 (cited in the *Opren* judgment of Hidden J. in *Nash* v. *Eli Lilly* [1991] 2 Med LR 1269).

The 'act or omission which is alleged to constitute negligence' clearly means the act or omission which is alleged to constitute negligence in the particulars or statement of claim.

But how specific an interpretation should be given to the words 'the act or omission alleged to constitute negligence'? And what if there are a number of different acts or omissions alleged to be negligent? In a number of cases at first instance it had been held (prior to the Court of Appeal decision in *Nash* v. *Eli Lilly* [1993] 1 WLR 782, the *Opren* judgment) that for the limitation period to start running in the context of medical injury the patient must know not merely in a generalised way that she had been caused injury by the treatment she had received, but, far more specifically, must know that her injury was reasonably capable of being attributed to the precise act or omission that constituted her allegation of negligence. It can immediately be appreciated that in many cases she will not know that until she has received an expert report.

Earlier Court of Appeal decisions in the context of industrial injury interpreted the provision as to attributability broadly. In *Davis* v. *Ministry of Defence (supra)* it was enough to describe the acts or omissions complained of in 'compendious' terms as the failure on the part of the defendants to provide the plaintiff with safe working conditions. In *Wilkinson* v. *Ancliff (supra)* Slade L.J. said:

In a case such as the present, where the acts and omissions on the part of the defendants which are complained of are, in broad terms, the exposure of their employee to dangerous working conditions and their failure to take reasonable and proper steps to protect him from such conditions, I think that the employee who has this broad knowledge may well have knowledge of the nature referred to in s.14(12)(b) sufficient to set time running against him, even though he may not yet have the knowledge sufficient to enable him or his legal advisers to draft a full and comprehensively particularised statement of claim.

A line of medical cases in recent years has sought to clarify the 'attributability' aspect of the necessary knowledge, giving proper weight to the reference in the Act to the relevant 'act or omission'.

In *Davis* v. *City and Hackney Health Authority* [1991] 2 Med LR 366, Jowitt J. held that the relevant act or omission that allegedly caused perinatal injury to the plaintiff in 1963 was not in broad terms 'the delivery' or 'the treatment afforded his mother' but, specifically, the act of injecting his mother with the drug Ovametrin and that he did not know of that act as a possible cause of his injury until he received his expert's report in late 1986.

In *Driscoll-Varley* v. *Parkside Health Authority* [1991] 2 Med LR 346, Hidden J. found that the relevant act or omission where negligence in the post-operative treatment of a fracture was alleged, was not, in general terms, the treatment of the fracture but was, more specifically, the decision to mobilise the patient prematurely.

In *Bentley* v. *Bristol and Western Health Authority* [1991] 2 Med LR 359, Hirst J. said that the act or omission alleged to constitute negligence in operation cases was some conduct or failure which could affect the safety of the operation, and that knowledge of such act or omission would frequently depend on information derived by the patient from expert opinion. He held that the relevant act or omission in that case was not the operation itself but the specific act of (alleged) traction of a nerve during the operation, and the knowledge that that was a possible cause of the injury was only gained by the plaintiff when she received her expert report. However, this decision was disapproved of by the Court of Appeal in *Broadley* v. *Guy Clapham & Co. (infra)*.

In *Khan* v. *Ainslie* [1993] 4 Med LR 319 it was clear that the defendant optician had precipitated acute angle glaucoma by the administration of mydriatic fluid. For years the plaintiff had continued to believe, despite expert advice to the contrary, that it had been negligent to administer the fluid; it was only when he later received a further expert report that he learned that his real complaint (the complaint that his claim was later based on) should be about the failure to recognise the glaucoma and refer him to hospital immediately. The judge held that the plaintiff only knew his injury was attributable to that act or omission when he received the later report.

In *Colegrove* v. *Smyth* [1994] 5 Med LR 111 the plaintiff, born in 1959, claimed for injury arising from delay in diagnosing congenital displacement of the hip. In essence, the view of the judge was that there was no reason for the plaintiff to have suspected that she had suffered injury, i.e. impairment of her condition, through any delay in diagnosis until, applying for a job in 1984, the examining doctor suggested as much to her. As far as she knew until then, she had been born with a disability that had been treated as well as could be expected. The judge also said that what she was told by the examining doctor in 1984 would not in itself have given her the necessary knowledge but would have put her on enquiry (this distinction is of general importance when advising on limitation and should always be borne in mind). Her knowledge would not be complete until confirmed by an expert report (the Court of Appeal's judgment in *Nash* v. *Eli Lilly* (*infra*) envisaged the need for expert confirmation in appropriate cases).

In *Atkinson* v. *Oxfordshire Health Authority* [1993] 4 Med LR 18 Simon Brown J. held that a writ issued in 1989 for operative negligence in 1967 (when the plaintiff was 17) was not out of time. His reasoning is not entirely convincing, but it is interesting to note that he found it significant that the patient and his mother had been told at the time by the hospital that no one was to blame for the accident, that they had been advised in the past by solicitors that they had no case, and that the surgeons had failed to give a proper explanation to the patient and his mother at the time.

In *Baig* v. *City and Hackney Health Authority* [1994] 5 Med LR 221, a case decided after the Court of Appeal decisions set out below, Rougier J. said that a plaintiff had to have knowledge of 'what it was that was either done or not done'. That was 'the only sensible conclusion to which the words of the statute lead'. For an interesting recent example of a court carefully identifying the relevant 'act or omission' see *Gascoine* v. *Ian Sheridan & Co* [1994] 5 Med LR 437.

However, in *Hendy* v. *Milton Keynes Health Authority* [1992] 3 Med LR 114, Blofeld J. took the view that a high degree of specificity was not always required – in that case the patient had been told by one of the treating doctors what had gone wrong shortly after the operation and that was enough to start the limitation period running, though the judge went on to exercise his discretion under s.33 of the Act in her favour.

So, on the whole, decisions at first instance have been favourable to patients, by requiring a reasonably high degree of specificity, i.e. they must know specifically what act or omission could have caused their injury. However, the Court of Appeal has not been so helpful. It is necessary to examine its decisions in some detail.

In the Court of Appeal

In *Nash* v. *Eli Lilly* [1993] 1 WLR 782 (the *Opren* case) the principle of specificity was accepted by the court (i.e. for the plaintiff to be held to have the relevant knowledge so as to trigger the limitation period she must know that she had suffered a significant injury which was capable of being attributed to the (specific) act or omission alleged in the pleading to constitute negligence). However the court, reasonably enough, was not prepared to accept that the plaintiff had to know the precise terms in which it would be alleged that the negligence lay:

What is required is knowledge of the essence of the act or omission to which the injury is attributable.

Applying this test, the court rejected the submission of plaintiffs' counsel that the judge had been wrong to hold that the relevant 'act or omission' of which the plaintiff had to have knowledge was 'providing for the use of patients a drug which was unsafe in that it was capable of causing persistent photosensitivity in those patients and/or in failing to discover that such was the case so as properly to protect such patients'. Counsel submitted unsuccessfully that a further degree of specificity was required, namely that the plaintiff had to have knowledge that the marketing of an unsafe drug was due to lack of care in testing it or in informing the medical profession about it or in responding to adverse drug reaction reports.

In *Broadley* v. *Guy Clapham & Co.* [1994] 4 All ER 439 the plaintiff had undergone an operation on her knee in August 1980, which was promptly followed by foot-drop. She consulted a solicitor in June 1983, and saw an independent orthopedic surgeon in July 1983, who told her that the operation might have been negligently performed. The solicitor never got an expert report or issued a writ. Nothing was done about suing the solicitor until the writ in the present action was issued on 17 August 1990, alleging that the plaintiff had had a good claim for negligence at the original operation in that the left lateral popliteal nerve had been negligently divided and/or damaged. The solicitor-defendant pleaded limitation in respect of the claim against him, a plea that would succeed if the plaintiff's cause of action against him had accrued more than 6 years before the issue of the writ, i.e. before 18 August 1984.

The solicitor's negligence lay in not serving a writ within the limitation period for the medical negligence action. If that limitation period had expired before 18 August 1984 the cause of action against the solicitor would have accrued more than 6 years before the issue of the writ. So the vital question, tried at first instance as a preliminary issue, was 'Did the plaintiff have the relevant knowledge in respect of her medical negligence claim before 19 August 1981?'

At the trial the judge found that the patient had had constructive knowledge before August 1981 in that she must have known before then that she had suffered a significant injury as a result of the operation and should and could have reasonably discovered the cause by seeking appropriate expert advice.

In the Court of Appeal Balcombe L.J. distinguished (as suggested by defence counsel) four categories of knowledge, namely 'broad', 'specific', 'qualitative' and 'detailed', of which the latter two were not necessary to constitute 'knowledge' for the purposes of limitation. He indicated that 'broad' knowledge was not enough in itself, i.e. knowledge that the operation had been carried out in such a way that something went wrong and resulted in foot-drop. The plaintiff needed also to have 'specific' knowledge, namely that the operation had been carried out in such a way as to damage a nerve and so cause the injury of foot-drop. 'Qualitative' knowledge was not necessary, i.e. knowledge that the operation had been carried out 'unreasonably', nor, of course, was 'detailed' knowledge, i.e. sufficiently detailed to enable the plaintiff's advisers to draft the claim. In conclusion Balcombe L.J. agreed with the trial judge that the plaintiff had, constructively, the necessary specific knowledge by 19 August 1981.

Hoffmann L.J. said that plaintiff's counsel was in effect arguing that she needed to know that the relevant act or omission involved fault. It is not surprising that, viewed in that light, the submission failed. The judge said that s.14 required one to look at the way the case was put, distil what the plaintiff was complaining about and ask whether she had, in broad terms, knowledge of the facts on which that complaint was based. He said that all the *facts* pleaded in the allegation of medical negligence were known, actually or constructively, to Mrs Broadley shortly after the operation. The only factor that was not known was that what had been done was negligent, and that of course was not material to the issue of limitation.

Leggatt L.J. also endorsed the conclusion of the trial judge, saying that the plaintiff knew soon after the operation that something was wrong with her foot which was not an inevitable consequence of the operation, and one would therefore expect her to take advice and so to discover that the nerve must have been damaged in the operation in a way that was not inevitable. He said that it was not necessary that the plaintiff have knowledge of the *mechanics* of damage.

The plaintiff therefore had the relevant knowledge by a date more than six plus three years before the issue of her writ against the solicitor, and thus her claim against the solicitor was brought out of time.

This case appears to be authority for the following propositions:

(1) When a patient knows (actually or constructively) that she has been injured by an operation in a way that was not inevitable and knows in broad terms (i.e. in essence) how it arose, even though she does not know the precise mechanics, the limitation period will start.

(2) The patient should seek advice once she has reason to suppose that medical treatment has resulted in an injury which was not a normal hazard, for otherwise she runs the risk of being held to have acquired constructive knowledge (i.e. of how the accident happened in broad terms) far earlier than the time she acquired actual knowledge.

Currently defendants' counsel often seek to argue that this case supports the proposition that broad knowledge is sufficient and that the court was indorsing the test formulated by Blofeld J. in *Hendy* v. *Milton Keynes Health Authority* (*supra*). This is a wilful misreading of the judgments in *Broadley*.[7]

In *Dobbie* v. *Medway Health Authority* [1994] 5 Med LR 160 the patient had undergone in 1973 a left mastectomy for suspected cancer. She knew soon after the operation that histology showed the tissue to be benign. She did nothing about the matter until 1988. Otton J. decided in February 1992 that she had the relevant knowledge when she learned that the tissue was benign, and he declined to exercise his discretion in her favour. The Court of Appeal unanimously agreed with him on both issues.

The actual result is understandable. The patient knew in 1973 that her breast had been removed unnecessarily. The decision could reasonably be based on a finding that at that point she had been put on enquiry and should have investigated. In other words she would and should have acquired knowledge at such time as an

---

[7] A very odd decision was reached by a deputy High Court judge in *Hopkins* v. *Mackenzie* (for its reversal by the Court of Appeal see [1995] 6 Med LR 25), to the effect that where a solicitor failed to process a medical negligence action the period of limitation began with his failure rather than the date when the action was eventually struck out because of that failure, the thinking apparently being that the claim was at risk of being struck out as soon as the failure took place and therefore the financial loss which was the subject of the claim against the solicitor had already (to some extent at any rate) been sustained! See also *First National Commercial Bank plc* v. *Humberts*, *The Times*, 27 January 1995, where it was held that the cause of action for damages for financial loss incurred as a result of an advance given pursuant to a negligent valuation did not arise when the advance was given but only when the loss crystallised upon the sale of the security.

expert report, timeously sought, would have told her that pre-operative investigation (e.g. by way of fine needle aspiration or biopsy) could and probably would ('should' is irrelevant as knowledge of fault is not a necessary ingredient of the relevant knowledge) have revealed that the lump was benign. It has, *contra*, been argued (e.g. by Arnold Simanowitz in the AVMA Medical and Legal Journal) that she would not necessarily have seen the loss of her breast to be an injury even after discovering it had been non-cancerous because she could well have continued to believe that it had been necessary to remove it as part of the required medical treatment and that it was simply a matter of good fortune that it had turned out to be benign.

In all three of these cases the Court of Appeal accepted that the plaintiff had to know the essence of the act or omission alleged to be negligent to which her injury was reasonably capable of being attributed. In *Dobbie* it would appear that the act or omission that was alleged to constitute negligence was going for a mastectomy without pre-operative investigations.

The Lloyd's Names case

As this book was going to press the decision appeared of the Court of Appeal in the commercial case, part of the Lloyd's Names saga, of *Hallam-Eames* v. *Merrett Syndicates Ltd*, 13 January 1995 (reported in *The Times* on 25 January 1995). This judgment of the court vindicated the view I had taken of the earlier cases on limitation.

Put in short form, the plaintiffs claimed that the defendants were negligent for having written reinsurance contracts recklessly (exposing them to potential liabilities without having the material on which those liabilities could be properly assessed). The defendants pleaded that the claims were statute-barred (as having being commenced outside the six-year period for non-personal injury claims). The wording of the relevant provisions governing limitation in a commercial claim for economic loss is virtually identical with the provisions affecting limitation in a personal injury case. Section 14A of the Limitation Act 1980, inserted by the Latent Damage Act 1986, postpones the commencement of the limitation period until the relevant knowledge has been acquired. That knowledge includes knowledge of facts which would lead a reasonable person to consider the damage sufficiently serious to justify proceedings, and knowledge *that the damage was attributable in whole or in part to the act or omission which is alleged to constitute negligence*. The main issue in the case was the correct interpretation of the italicised words, i.e.

exactly the same issue as arises so often in medical negligence actions.

The judgment

Let us look first at the interpretation given to *Broadley* and *Dobbie*. The court said that the trial judge had been in error in interpreting those cases to mean that a plaintiff need only have known that his damage had been caused by an act or omission of the defendants. This was declared by the Court of Appeal to be 'an oversimplification' of the reasoning in the cases. 'The act or omission of which the plaintiff must have knowledge must be that which is *causally relevant* for the purposes of an allegation of negligence' (my italics). This concept of causal relevance, said the court, is what earlier judgments had been identifying when they spoke of 'the essence of the act or omission to which the injury is attributable' (the Court of Appeal in *Nash* v. *Eli Lilly*), or the 'essential thrust of the case' (the Master of the Rolls in *Dobbie*).

The court said that the plaintiff 'must have known the facts which can fairly be described as constituting the negligence of which he complains'. The relevant knowledge on the part of Mrs Dobbie was that the surgeon had removed a *healthy* breast. And for Mrs Broadley, that she knew, or should have asked and would have found out, that the hip replacement operation had caused her foot drop by damaging a nerve. In this commercial case the court rejected the contention that the relevant knowledge was merely that the defendants had written the contracts that caused the damage. They had also to know that the potential liabilities had not been capable of reasonable qualification. The court said that that was not the same thing as requiring knowledge of fault. It would be irrelevant whether or not the plaintiffs realised the defendants had been at fault. It was simply a matter of requiring knowledge of the causally relevant act: that act was not merely the writing of the contracts; it was the writing of contracts which exposed the plaintiffs to literally incalculable potential liabilities.

This judgment is of great value to those acting for patients. It gives the lie once for all to the disingenuous arguments of defence lawyers referred to above and makes it crystal clear that for knowledge to arise the plaintiff has to know with a reasonable degree of specificity how the injury arose, i.e. what as a matter of common sense was the causally relevant act or omission.

Compare *Whitfield* v. *North Durham Health Authority* [1995] 6 Med LR 32. As we went to press yet another limitation decision from the Court of Appeal appeared. The judgment of the court was given in this case in December 1994 (before the *Hallam-Eames* judgment). The basic facts were not dissimilar from the *Dobbie* case. In 1985 a surgeon removed a lump in the plaintiff's neck, notwithstanding that he knew he would have to damage the brachial plexus, because the histopathologist had declared it malignant. In fact it was not malignant, and the patient was so informed shortly after the procedure. Within a few weeks a detailed letter of complaint was written on behalf of the plaintiff. A writ was issued in 1987 against surgeon and health authority, but unfortunately the histopathologist was not made a defendant nor was it even suggested he had been negligent. This writ was never served. The solicitors decided there was no case to proceed. Some years later new solicitors established a *prima facie* case and in 1992 issued another writ against the health authority.

It was agreed that the plaintiff had the relevant knowledge in respect of the histopathologist's negligence in 1985, but it was argued that she only obtained knowledge of the surgeon's negligence shortly before the issue of the 1992 writ. At first instance the judge held that the date for 'surgical' knowledge was when the first writ was issued in 1987. It was agreed that s.33 discretion could not be exercised in respect of the claim against the surgeon because of the decision in *Walkley* v. *Precision Forgings* [1979] 1 WLR 606 (see below under 'Limits to the discretion'), but the judge exercised his discretion in favour of the plaintiff so as to permit the claim to proceed in respect of the alleged negligence of the histopathologist.

I find this concept of separating the allegations of negligence, and exercising discretion in respect of some of them, very odd. However, neither court said it was unacceptable. It has to be said that, although the decision of the Court of Appeal on date of knowledge is not in itself objectionable in view of *Dobbie* and in view of the letter of complaint written shortly after the events (the decision was that knowledge in respect of the alleged negligence of both doctors was acquired at the latest by the time the letter was written), the way the court (none of the judges of which had been involved in the earlier decisions on limitation) expressed the test of knowledge is unacceptable, principally because little attention seems to have been paid to the principle of specificity and no formulation attempted of the relevant 'act or omission'. The court said, without further particularisation, that the authorities required that the court should look to the essence of the complaint and inquire how far the plaintiff had knowledge in broad terms of the facts on which it was based. In fact the authorities, as I hope is apparent from the preceding analysis of the cases, require nothing of the sort. The court then said that the judge had allowed himself to look beyond the basic essentials and try to anticipate how the case might be put, in terms of positive act or negligent omission. That, they said, was an error. An anticipatory inquiry into the merits was not appropriate at the stage of simple inquiry into the state of the plaintiff's knowledge.

I find it hard to make sense of this. Determining what was the relevant negligent act or omission is the basic task in these cases. That has nothing to do with inquiring into the merits. The reference to 'knowledge in broad terms of the facts on which [the complaint] is based' is an unhelpful gloss on the far more specific treatment of the issue found in all four of the other Court of Appeal decisions (*Nash, Broadley, Dobbie, Hallam-Eames*).

Also worrying was the readiness of the court to reverse the judge's exercise of discretion in allowing the action to proceed in respect of the histopathologist's alleged negligent reading of the pre-operative slide. It is clear that the Court of Appeal was at pains to give itself the right, by first invalidating in one way or another the judge's approach to the question, then to substitute its own negative conclusion. One could be forgiven for thinking that the court had made a prior determination, perhaps as a matter of general policy, not to permit the action to proceed out of time. For a fuller discussion of this discretion point, see below the section 'The exercise of the discretion'.

Suspicion is not knowledge

In *Stephen* v. *Riverside Health Authority* [1990] 1 Med LR 261, Auld J. held that the plaintiff's suspicion, and her anxiety based upon that suspicion, which she had entertained from the outset despite assurances to the contrary from doctors, that she had suffered injury through an overdose of radiation during mammography, did not amount to 'knowledge' within the meaning of the Act. In *Halford* v. *Brookes* [1991] 1 WLR 428, 443, the Master of the Rolls said that 'reasonable belief' was usually enough to constitute the required level of 'knowledge'.

In *Nash* v. *Eli Lilly* (*supra*) the Court of Appeal said:

Knowledge is a condition of mind which imports a degree of certainty and . . . the degree of certainty which is appropriate for this purpose is that which, for the particular plaintiff, may reasonably be regarded as sufficient to justify embarking upon the preliminaries to the making of a claim for compensation such as the taking of legal or other advice.

Whether or not a state of mind for this purpose is properly to be treated by the court as knowledge seems to us to depend, in the first place, upon the nature of the information which the plaintiff has received, the extent to which he pays attention to the information as affecting him, and his capacity to understand it. There is a second stage at which the information, when received and understood, is evaluated. It may be rejected as unbelievable. It may be regarded as unreliable or uncertain. The court must assess the intelligence of the plaintiff; consider and assess his assertions as to how he regarded such information as he had; and determine whether he had knowledge of the facts by reason of his understanding of the information.

It is important to note that the court envisaged the possibility that a particular plaintiff might have been taking the view that, although she had received information on which knowledge could be based, she needed *expert confirmation* before her belief could attain that degree of firmness to amount to knowledge. If, however, 'the plaintiff held a firm belief which was of sufficient certainty to justify the taking of the preliminary steps for proceedings by obtaining advice about making a claim for compensation, then such belief is knowledge and the limitation period would begin to run'. It is also to be noted that the court said that once knowledge had been gained it could not then be lost, e.g. as a result of reassurances from doctors.

However, a note of warning: knowledge that something needs investigating should not *ipso facto* be equated with the specific knowledge required for the purposes of the Act.

Consulting a solicitor

The Court of Appeal said in *Nash* v. *Eli Lilly* (*supra*) that it had difficulty in perceiving how in any case where a claimant had sought advice and taken proceedings it could rightly be held that she had not then had the relevant knowledge. This is reasonable, provided that merely consulting solicitors is not deemed to be due to the relevant knowledge having been gained. That would clearly be unjust, because many a patient asks for legal assistance without having any real idea about the attributability of any injury that she may have suffered.

Other factors required for knowledge

The plaintiff needs to have knowledge of the identity of the defendant; and, where the defendant is alleged to be vicariously responsible for the negligence of another, of the identity of that other and of the facts making the defendants liable ('if it is alleged that the act or omission was that of a person other than the defendants, the identity of that person and the additional facts supporting the bringing of an action against the defendants' – s.14(12)(d)).

These last two provisions, could be useful in the context, for example, of injury at work, where it may be difficult to establish who is in charge of the site or the machinery or who is

employed by whom (see *Simpson* v. *Norwest Holst Southern Ltd*
[1980] 1 WLR 968). Time does not run while the plaintiff does not
know who caused his injury, or the connection between that person
and the defendant. But the provisions are unlikely to assume much
significance in the medical negligence context, where the identity of
the medical staff is usually ascertainable without too much difficulty,
and, even if that may not be known, the defendants are in any event
clearly liable for any breach of duty by their medical staff, whether
vicariously or by way of breach of their primary obligations (see
Chapter 22). However, it is possible that identity may be a problem
in the odd case, perhaps where the treatment occurred a long time
ago, or possibly in the private sector where the relation between
doctor and clinic or employer may not be so clear cut (perhaps also
where a locum GP cannot be traced).

Patient must show reasonable alertness

So these various provisions mean that time will not begin to run
until the patient knows both that he has suffered more than
minimal injury and that it was caused by the treatment of which
he now complains. But it is specifically provided that a plaintiff
cannot plead ignorance if he has been 'dozy' or failed to take
proper advice ('. . . a person's knowledge includes knowledge
which he might reasonably have been expected to acquire (a)
from facts observable or ascertainable by him, or (b) from facts
ascertainable by him with the help of medical or other appropriate expert advice which it is reasonable for him to seek' –
s.14(3)).

Constructive knowledge currently features prominently in
defence arguments on limitation. The patient must be as alert to
observe and infer from his observation as his level of awareness
and intelligence permits. And he must consult the medical
experts to the extent to which it is reasonable for him to do so. A
patient who does not know he has been injured cannot be
expected to seek any advice, but one who knows he has been
injured but thinks the injury is insignificant may be held to have
acted unreasonably in not asking an expert if his belief was
justified. Similarly a patient who does not know the cause of his
injury may in an appropriate case be required to ask a medical
expert if the cause can be established.

In *Nash* v. *Eli Lilly* [1993] 1 WLR 782 the Court of Appeal said
that the proper approach was to determine what the particular
plaintiff should have observed or ascertained, while asking no
more of him than was reasonable.

In *Davis* v. *City and Hackney Health Authority* [1991] 2 Med LR 366 the plaintiff, who had been born suffering from spasticity, issued when aged 24 his writ alleging that was due to medical negligence. When he had been 17 his mother had told him she thought his birth might have been mishandled, but it was only when he was 23 (in 1986) that a medical expert alleged that his handicap was due to an injection of Ovametrin administered to his mother. Jowitt J., considering the plaintiff's disabilities, which included a serious speech defect, held that he acquired the relevant 'knowledge' only on reading the expert's report:

The test is an objective one. The question is, looked at objectively, when might he, the plaintiff, reasonably have been expected to acquire those facts referred to in paragraph (b) of subsection (3)? In other words one applies an objective test, but it is an objective test applied to the kind of plaintiff I am here dealing with, with his disability, and looking at his age and circumstances and the difficulties he has faced.

In *Sergeant* v. *Lewisham Health Authority* (High Court), 6 July 1990, unreported, where the writ in respect of a muscle injury alleged to have been caused by excessive traction at delivery was issued when the plaintiff was 21 and three months, Phillips J. said that a minor was not required to take 'reasonable steps' and that he would not be fixed with any failure of his parents to take them. In this case, too, the relevant knowledge was held to arise only when the expert report was received (the plaintiff was then nearly 21).

It is often the case that the plaintiff wishes to assert that he only acquired the relevant 'knowledge' when his expert had drawn his attention to the precise act or omission that caused his injury. This case provides some ammunition for that contention in the appropriate case.[8]

In *Khan* v. *Ainslie and others* [1993] 4 Med LR 319 the plaintiff complained that both the ophthalmic practitioner and his own GP had been negligent in not referring him urgently to hospital after mydriatic drops applied to his eyes had precipitated acute angle glaucoma. Waterhouse J. said that the limitation period began when the plaintiff received the expert report that suggested culpable delay in referring, as up to that time the plaintiff had been thinking (mistakenly) only in terms of the negligent application of the mydriatic; both he and his solicitors had previously taken all reasonable steps to investigate the position and there had been nothing to alert them to the significance of the delay.

---

[8] The disadvantage in having to plead that it was the expert's report that gave the plaintiff the relevant knowledge is that you may have then to disclose the report to the other side unilaterally at an early stage (see RSC O.24 r.10). Better to allege (if it be so) that the expert gave the plaintiff the relevant knowledge first by word of mouth at an earlier conference.

In *Baig* v. *City and Hackney Health Authority* [1994] 5 Med LR 221 the plaintiff showed that he did not get actual knowledge until some 12 years after the 1977 operation on his ear, but it was held that he had reason and opportunity to start investigating the matter far earlier.

If the expert fails to inform the patient as he should, the patient is not deemed to have that information:

... but a person shall not be fixed under this subsection with knowledge of a fact ascertainable only with the help of expert advice as long as he has taken all reasonable steps to obtain (and, where appropriate, to act upon), that advice.[9]

As knowledge of the legal position is not relevant, so that a plaintiff cannot be heard to say that time did not begin to run until he knew that he had a worthwhile cause of action in law, it is no help to him to contend that he was told by his advisers, whether legal or medical, that he had little chance of succeeding in his proposed action, nor to allege that he was misled by them on any matter of law (see *Farmer* v. *National Coal Board, The Times*, 27 April 1985).

Burden of proof

It was said in *Fowell* v. *National Coal Board, The Times*, 28 May 1986, that as limitation was a matter of defence it had to be for the person setting up limitation to assert and prove that the claim was time-barred. But once it had been shown that the initial limitation period had elapsed it was for the plaintiff to assert that the date of knowledge was later than the accrual of the cause of action. If the proposed defendants wished to assert earlier knowledge either in the plaintiff himself or in his solicitors or by way of what he should have found out (under s.14(3)), it was for them to do so (and see *supra* under 'Pleading points').

At the end of his judgment in *Driscoll-Varley* v. *Parkside Health Authority* [1991] 2 Med LR 346, Hidden J. considered in detail the question of the shifting burden of proof in limitation issues.

In *Nash* v. *Eli Lilly* (*supra*) the Court of Appeal said that, where the writ was not issued within three years of the cause of action arising, the onus was on the plaintiff to plead and prove a date within three years from issue, but it was for the defendants to prove an earlier date if they wished to rely on one.

Actions by the estate of a deceased

Where the injured party dies before the limitation period has expired, whether he dies immediately upon injury or later, the limitation period for actions by his estate is three years from his

---

[9] See *Marston* v. *British Railways Board* [1976] ICR 124.

death or from the date of his personal representative's 'knowledge', whichever is the later. If he has more than one personal representative time runs from the moment when any one of them acquires the relevant knowledge (s.11(5) and (7)). These days the estate will generally have a claim only for funeral expenses and any other special damages, as, for deaths after the end of 1982, claims for loss of earnings during the lost years (i.e. the years the deceased would have been earning had he not died) do not pass to the estate upon death, and there is no longer any compensation awarded for loss of expectation of life (Administration of Justice Act 1982).

Fatal accident claims

The limitation period provided by s.12 of the Act of 1980 for actions under the Fatal Accidents Act 1976 (which was amended by s.3 of the Administration of Justice Act 1982) is three years from the date of death or the date of 'knowledge' of the dependant for whose benefit the action is brought, whichever is the later. If at the date of death the deceased's right of action was already time-barred by s.11, then the dependants' action is also barred, no account being taken of the possibility that the deceased might have got leave to proceed under s.33; but the dependants can on their own account ask for their action to be given the go-ahead under s.33 (see s.12(1) and (3)). Similarly, if they had a right of action at the deceased's death, his right not having been time-barred by then, but they thereafter permit the limitation period to expire without commencing proceedings, they can ask the court for leave to proceed under s.33.

Dependants are to be considered separately, so that one may be barred where another is within the limitation period because his knowledge arose later or because he is under a disability (s.13). The court's power to exclude a dependant from participating in the action is limited by s.13(3), which provides that no direction to exclude shall be given if it is shown that if the action were brought exclusively for the benefit of that dependant it would not be defeated by a defence of limitation.

Persons under a disability

It is not unusual for a person injured by medical treatment to be under age (or sometimes of unsound mind), and the provisions governing the limitation period in such cases of disability are accordingly of importance.

Majority at 18 is enacted by the Family Law Reform Act 1969. The other case of disability, that of unsound mind, is defined by s.38(3) and (4). A person is of unsound mind if, by reason of mental disorder within the meaning of the Mental Health Act 1959 (now the Mental Health Act 1983), he is incapable of managing and administering his property and affairs. Mental disorder is defined by s.4(1) of the Act of 1959 (now s.1(2) of the Mental Health Act 1983) as 'mental illness, arrested or incomplete development of the mind, psychopathic disorder, and any other disorder or disability of mind'.

The limitation period does not begin to run if when the cause of action accrues, i.e. the date when the injury is suffered, the patient is under a disability. It only begins to run when the disability ends. The period for personal injury claims is of course three years. If disability arises after the period has begun, i.e. by the onset of mental illness, the period is not affected; it continues to run (*Purnell* v. *Roche* [1927] 2 Ch 1420), though s.33(3)(d) of the Limitation Act 1980 enables a court to take this factor into account when deciding whether to exercise its discretion to permit the action to proceed notwithstanding the expiry of the limitation period. The section does not prevent the representatives of a person under a disability from commencing an action if they so wish.

The fact that the disability comes to an end, e.g. by majority, does not of course necessarily mean that the limitation period begins to run. If the plaintiff does not even then have the relevant 'knowledge' the period will simply begin in the normal way when he does acquire that knowledge: the postponing of the commencement of the limitation period is applicable to those cases where – to use the words of s.28(1) – 'the period of limitation has expired'.

Where an infant is injured no amount of dilatoriness on the part of his solicitors can cause the action to be struck out, for a fresh writ can be issued any time before he gets to 21 (*Tolley* v. *Morris* [1979] 2 All ER 561, but see below under 'Striking out').

An example of time not running for a mentally handicapped person is the much publicised case of *Blackburn* v. *Newcastle Area Health Authority (No.1)* (1988) PMILL Vol. 4 No. 7. The adult plaintiff suffered brain damage in 1976. Three firms of solicitors failed to pursue his case; the fourth won it for him in 1988. In *Dawson* v. *Scott-Brown* (18 October 1988, CA), the Court of Appeal held that the fact that the plaintiff, a former Royal Navy seaman, was discharged from the Navy in 1974 for mental ill-health did not mean that he was therefore incapable of managing his affairs, and so the limitation period for his action had long since expired. The Master had been right to conclude that the limitation defence was bound to succeed and that therefore the action was an abuse of the court's process (for striking out for delay where there may be a valid limitation defence, see below).

The discretion under section 33

The power of the court to permit an action to proceed even though the period of limitation, whether extended by the 'knowledge' provisions of ss.11 and 14 or not, has expired, is contained in s.33 of the Act of 1980. It is exercised by 'disapplying' the sections that lay down the limitation periods for actions for personal injuries (ss.11 and 12). It may only be exercised where the plaintiff would be otherwise barred by those sections, not where he is barred by some other limitation provision.

The court may disapply ss.11 or 12 where it considers it would be 'equitable' to allow the action to proceed having regard to the respective degree of prejudice suffered by (a) the plaintiff from the operation of ss.11 or 12, and (b) the defendants if the action were to proceed. The court is required to have regard to all the circumstances of the case and in particular to how long and why the plaintiff has delayed, the effect upon the available evidence of the delay, the behaviour of the defendant since the injury and of the plaintiff since he knew he might have a claim, including what steps he took to get expert advice, and what it was. These conditions, which are spelt out by s.33(3), follow the lines of judicial decisions on striking out actions for want of prosecution (see below). In *Taylor* v. *Taylor, The Times*, 14 April 1984, the Court of Appeal said that a judge must have regard to all the circumstances of the case when considering whether or not to exercise his discretion in favour of a plaintiff, and not just to the matters set out in the section.

In *Nash* v. *Eli Lilly* (*supra*) the Court of Appeal said that apparent weakness of a plaintiff's case could be a relevant factor. This is unsatisfactory because it invites the defendants to impugn and the court to assess the plaintiff's case prematurely and on incomplete evidence.

Limits to the discretion

The discretion is an unfettered one and the Court of Appeal will be loath to interfere with its exercise by the judge (see *Conry* v. *Simpson* [1983] 3 All ER 369, *Firman* v. *Ellis* [1978] QB 886, *Bradley* v. *Hanseatic Shipping* [1986] 2 Lloyd's Rep

34). However, the judge has to stay within the ambit of the section. Thus in *Walkley* v. *Precision Forgings Ltd* [1979] 1 WLR 606 the House of Lords held that where the plaintiff discontinued an action he had started within the limitation period the court had no power to permit him to proceed under s.33 with another action after the limitation period had expired. This was because the prejudice to the plaintiff had not been occasioned by the operation of the limitation provisions of the Act, but by his own conduct (through his solicitors). This somewhat contrived reasoning was extended by the Court of Appeal, albeit reluctantly, to a case where the plaintiff had forgotten to serve his writ within the year allowed (*Chappell* v. *Cooper* [1980] 1 WLR 958). On this particular point *Firman* v. *Ellis* (*supra*) was overruled, although that case is still good authority on the proper approach of the court generally to the exercise of its discretion, which is not limited to 'exceptional' cases.

Walkley v. *Precision Forgings* (*supra*) was followed in *Deerness* v. *Keeble & Son* [1983] 2 Lloyd's Rep 260, where the judge's exercise of discretion in permitting an action to proceed was reversed on the ground that a writ had been issued but not served within the limitation period, and that therefore there was no jurisdiction to allow a second writ to proceed (because the plaintiff had been prejudiced not by the provisions of s.11 giving him three years to issue a writ but by the failure of his solicitors to serve the writ within the 12-month period for service). So a plaintiff who issues a first writ in time but fails to serve it in time is in a weaker position than one who does not even get around to issuing one in the first place! In such a case all the plaintiff can do is ask for the writ to be renewed, but this will almost certainly not be granted (see Chapter 10), and then sue his solicitors.

The rule in *Walkley* v. *Precision Forgings* does not apply where the first action was improperly constituted (the defendants had been wrongly titled), notwithstanding that the defect could be corrected. In such a case the second action is not an abuse of the process of the court (*White* v. *Glass, The Times*, 18 February 1989).

The exercise of the discretion

It is difficult to predict when the court will exercise its discretion in the plaintiff's favour. It depends very much on which judge she gets. Some are more sympathetic to plaintiffs in the medical negligence action than others, and also the facts differ in each case. Compare *Cornish* v. *Kearley and Tonge* (1983) 133 NLJ

870, where a plaintiff who was three years out of time was allowed to proceed with his action, with *Pilmore* v. *Northern Trawlers* [1986] 1 Lloyd's Rep 552, where a plaintiff who was nine years out of time was not permitted to proceed, principally on the basis that the very long delay substantially prejudiced the defendants. In *Waghorn* v. *Lewisham and North Southwark Area Health Authority* (23 June 1987, QBD) Deputy Judge Stuart McKinnon Q.C. gave leave for the plaintiff's action to proceed by writ issued seven years after the operation to improve her sex life which, allegedly, had the opposite effect (she knew her injury was attributable to the operation within a few days of its being performed). The judge said that he did not think it would be equitable to dismiss her action despite some delay, and any resulting prejudice to the defendants would be no more than marginal. It should in the end be a matter of commonsense and what is just, but of course opinions differ on these considerations. It does appear that the factors determining the commencement of the limitation period under the 'knowledge' provisions of ss.11 and 14 are likely also to be relevant considerations in the exercise of the s.33 discretion. Thus even if the plaintiff knew his injury was 'significant' he can still argue in the appropriate case that his state of mind at the time should be taken into account (see *Miller* v. *London Electrical Manufacturing Co.* [1976] 2 Lloyd's Rep 284, *per* Lord Denning M.R.). Again, though it does not help the plaintiff in regard to the commencement of the limitation period that he did not want to 'sponge off' his employer, or that he was reluctant to go to court over what he regarded as an 'irritating nuisance', these are circumstances the court can consider under s.33 (see *Buck* v. *English Electrical Co. Ltd* [1977] 1 WLR 806, *McCafferty* v. *Metropolitan Police Receiver* [1977] 1 WLR 1073).

In *Rule* v. *Atlas Stone Co.* [1987] CLY 2335 Simon Brown J. exercised his discretion to permit an action to proceed where a widower was 18 months out of time, but had been very depressed after his wife's death, and a letter before action had been written only four months after the expiry of the limitation period.

Where there is a claim available against the plaintiff's solicitor for negligence in allowing the limitation period to expire, this, though not decisive, is a highly relevant consideration (*Thompson* v. *Brown Construction (Ebbw Vale) Ltd* [1981] 1 WLR 744). Where the scales are otherwise fairly evenly balanced between the parties, that consideration is likely to tip them in the defendants' favour. In *Davis* v. *Soltenpur, The Times*, 16 February 1983, the court refused to exercise its discretion in favour of the plaintiff, having regard to the prejudice to the defendants, the unsatisfactory nature of a trial seven years after the accident (such a time lapse is usual in medical negligence actions unfortunately), and also the potential claim the plaintiff had against his solicitors. In *Ramsden* v. *Lee* [1992] 2 All ER 204 the Court of Appeal recognised that the fact that the plaintiff would have a claim against his solicitor did not necessarily mean that discretion should not be exercised in his favour as the court recognised that such a claim involved some prejudice to the plaintiff that a claim against the tortfeasor would not.

The fact that a defendant will not recover his costs if he is successful against a legally aided plaintiff is a factor that the court may take into account on a s.33 application (*Lye* v. *Marks and Spencer plc, The Times*, 15 February 1988).

In *Waghorn* v. *Lewisham and North Southwark Area Health Authority* (*supra*), what particularly influenced the judge to disapply the limitation provisions and permit the action to proceed where the writ was issued in 1985 in respect of an operation in 1977 was the fact that the defendants had known of the plaintiff's complaint since 1978 and that most of the medical records were still extant.

An example of a case where a plaintiff should have taken expert advice is *Casey* v. *J. Murphy and Sons* [1979] CLY 1668. Such advice can be scrutinised by the court, e.g. a negative advice from counsel (*Jones* v. *G.D. Searle and Co. Ltd* [1978] 3 All ER 654).

In *Birnie* v. *Oxfordshire Health Authority* [1982] 2 *The Lancet* 281, where a writ was issued in 1978 for medical negligence in 1973, the judge weighed the prejudice to the defendant, in that he was not insured, against the reasons for the delay, which were mostly due to the plaintiff's ill-health, and he decided on balance that the action should proceed. Compare *Goodman* v. *Fletcher* (4 October 1982, CA), where the court refused to allow a claim begun by writ issued in 1978 for negligent dietary advice given in 1973 to proceed, because the case would have turned on the recollection of consultations and it was unfair to the defendant to expect him to remember so far back.

In the recent case of *Doughty* v. *North Staffordshire Health Authority* [1992] 3 Med LR 81 Henry J. exercised his discretion in favour of a plaintiff who was 11 years out of time (so that the court would be investigating matters arising 28 instead of 17 years previously), stating, surprisingly, that a fair trial was still possible even though the plastic surgeon whose conduct was being impugned had in the interim suffered a stroke and was no longer capable of giving evidence.

Although the context of *Halford* v. *Brookes* [1991] 1 WLR 428 was unique the case is worth noting: the mother of a murder victim sought to bring an action some six years out of time against the alleged murderers; the Court of Appeal said that in the particular circumstances of the case the passage of time had not prejudiced a fair trial as the matter would simply turn on the veracity of the defendants. The Court also said that the fact that a defendant might or would be unable to meet any judgment was not relevant to the exercise of the discretion.

In medical cases the important factors are likely to be when the defendants first had notice of a potential claim, whether the records are still extant (for the preservation of records see p. 66) and, if personal recollection is to play a part, whether the witnesses are still available, whether their recollection is likely to have been materially affected by the relevant delay, and whether the defendants have otherwise been prejudiced by that delay.

In *Hartley* v. *Birmingham City Council* [1992] 1 WLR 968, the Court of Appeal said that it was a clearly wrongful exercise of the judge's discretion to refuse leave to proceed where the writ was issued just one day out of time.

The decision of the Court of Appeal in the recent case of *Whitfield* v. *North Durham Health Authority* [1995] 6 Med LR 32 is a disappointing one for patients and suggests that the court may have a policy of stopping late cases by all means. The trial judge had exercised discretion to allow the plaintiff to proceed by a 1992 writ with an allegation of negligence against a histopathologist for misreading a slide in 1985 as showing a malignant tumour instead of a benign one, as a result of which it had to be surgically removed despite the certainty of serious damage to the brachial plexus. The Court of Appeal went to great pains to invalidate the judge's approach to the issue of discretion, and then substituted its own negative conclusions. Without condescending to detail, the Court of Appeal held that it was plainly inequitable on the balance of prejudice to allow the action to proceed. Yet the decision had the effect of depriving the patient of what may well have been an unanswerable claim for negligent management resulting in serious injury. The issue would have depended simply on experts' view of the appropriate interpretation of the biopsy tissue, which was extant and unchanged. The court's 'explanation' of how the passage of time would have prejudiced a fair trial of this issue is little, if at all, short of fanciful. True, some of their criticisms of the approach of the judge might be well founded (e.g. he should not have discounted the solicitors' delay on the basis that it was not the personal delay of the plaintiff; he should have given more weight to the prejudice accruing as a result of the introduction of Crown indemnity (see the reference below to *Antcliffe* v. *Gloucester Health Authority*); he should have taken more account of the fact that, if the solicitors had not neglected to make the histopathologist defendant to an earlier writ in which they had sued the surgeon, there would have been no question of asking for discretion (by virtue of the decision in *Walkley* v. *Precision Forgings* (*supra*)); but the fact remains that all these criticisms were simply an excuse to invalidate the exercise of discretion by the trial judge and substitute in its place their own contrary view.

Delay

In *Eastman* v. *London Country Bus Services Ltd, The Times*, 2 November 1985, the Court of Appeal said that the meaning of delay in s.33(3)(a) and (b) (delay by the plaintiff and the effect on the evidence of such delay) was the delay between the expiry of the limitation period and the issue of the writ (as stated by Lord Diplock in *Thompson* v. *Brown* (*supra*)); and that the date to which s.33(3)(e) refers, when the plaintiff first knew he might have a case, was not necessarily the same as, but could well be later than, the date when for the purposes of ss.11 and 14 he first had the 'knowledge' which started the limitation period running.

However, in *Donovan* v. *Gwentoys Ltd* [1990] 1 WLR 472 the House of Lords, reversing the Court of Appeal, held (this was not a medical negligence action) that although a plaintiff's inaction before the expiry of the limitation period was not one of the matters that the court was directed to have regard to under s.33(3), for that provision refers only to delay after the limitation period has expired, the court was required to take into account all the circumstances of the case, which must include the degree of prejudice suffered respectively by the parties over the whole of the case. In particular it was an important consideration when the defendants were first notified of the claim. In that case the House of Lords decided that the prejudice to the plaintiff, who had in any event an unanswerable claim against his solicitor, was far outweighed by the prejudice to the defendants if they had to face a claim about which they were first notified five years after the event.

Procedural points

Amending the statement of claim

In *Sayer* v. *Kingston and Esher Health Authority* (9 March 1989, CA) the Court of Appeal endorsed the judge's decision to permit an amendment of the claim on the eve of the trial whereby the previous case alleging mishandling of the cesarean section was replaced by allegations of mismanagement earlier in the labour and after delivery. The court said that as the new claims arose out of substantially the same facts as those already pleaded the judge had discretion to allow the amendment under s.35(5) of the Limitation Act.

Adding a new claim

In *Welsh Development Agency* v. *Redpath Dorman Long Ltd* [1994] 1 WLR 1409 the Court of Appeal held that leave could not be given to add a new claim after the expiry of the limitation period unless it fell within one of the stated exceptions in the Act and the rules of court, and that the relevant date for when a new claim should be taken to be made was not the date when the application for leave to amend was issued but when the amendment was actually made.[10] Reference may also be made to *Howe* v. *David Brown Tractors (Retail) Ltd* [1991] 4 All ER 30.[11]

In *Sion* v. *Hampstead Health Authority* [1994] 5 Med LR 170 the defendants' counsel took an obviously bad point on adding a claim after the expiry of the limitation period. It was agreed that the rules permitted a new claim to be added where it arose out of substantially the same facts as a cause of action in respect of which relief had already been claimed in the action, but he said that as the statement of claim in fact disclosed no cause of action the rule did not apply. The court gave the obvious response, namely that if the pleading could be amended to disclose a cause of action substantially on the facts as pleaded the pre-condition to adding a new cause of action was satisfied.

It often happens in medical negligence actions that the patient needs to add a new party after proceedings have been begun. Perhaps the culprit appears to be a different GP from the current defendant, or perhaps a GP or health authority needs to be added

---

[10] This judgment overruled the decisions in *Holland* v. *Yates Building Co., The Times,* 5 December 1989, and *Kennett* v. *Brown* [1988] 1 WLR 582, to the effect that s.35(3) did not automatically bar a new claim but merely offered a procedural bar for the defendant to raise if he wished. The Court of Appeal made it clear that the onus was from the outset upon the plaintiff to show that the amendment came within the relevant legislative provisions.

[11] In *Leadbitter* v. *Hodge* [1982] 2 All ER 167 the date of knowledge accepted by the court was the date when it first became apparent from a police report of a car accident that a further defendant might be liable; the plaintiff was permitted to add a second defendant (s.35 of the Act makes provision for new claims in pending actions). Where it is sought to add another defendant to the action the proper approach is for the court to ask itself this question: if at the time the writ was amended the plaintiff had instead issued a fresh writ against the same defendant, could that defendant have successfully applied to strike out the action on the ground that the limitation period had expired and the action was therefore an abuse of the process of the court? (*Leicester Wholesale Fruit Market Ltd* v. *Grundy* [1990] 1 WLR 107, CA; *Holland* v. *Yates Building Co., The Times,* 5 December 1989).

to the frame. The legislative provisions are not particularly easy
to understand, but can usefully be summarised by saying that the
judge has no general power to add a defendant (or a new cause of
action) out of time except by exercising discretion under s.33 (see
s.35(3)). Section 35(4) and (5) lay down guidelines for the
enaction of rules of court to permit new claims to be added, but
provide that the rules can be more restrictive than the guidelines.
Therefore it is to the rules of court that one has to look upon any
such application.

RSC Order 15 r.6 allows the court to add or substitute a
party where it is 'necessary for the determination of the
action', provided, of course, that an action begun against that
party at the time the main action was started would not have
been out of time (this is quite apart from the court's power
under s.33 to disapply the relevant limitation period). However, the five conditions one of which must be satisfied before
the amendment can be considered 'necessary' offer no assistance to the patient in the normal case. One then has to turn to
Order 20 r.5 which allows the name of a party to be corrected,
even by substituting a new party, provided that 'the court is
satisfied that the mistake sought to be corrected was a genuine
mistake and was not misleading or such as to cause any
reasonable doubt as to the identity of the party . . . intended
to be sued'. It is unfortunate that the restrictive words after the
words 'genuine mistake' were added to the rule. They do not
appear in the Act's guidelines.

What all this amounts to is that the patient seeking to add a
party should try to show that the relevant knowledge was not
acquired more than three years before such date as the amendment is likely to be made if it is granted; failing which, she may be
able to show a genuine mistake (on this see *Evans Construction
Co. Ltd* v. *Charrington and Co. Ltd and Bass Holdings Ltd* [1983]
QB 810); failing that possibility, discretion must be sought under
s.33.

By Order 15 r.1 the county court is governed by the same rules
as the High Court.

Preliminary issue

In *Fletcher* v. *Sheffield Health Authority* [1994] 5 Med LR 156 the
question was raised whether the limitation issue should be tried as
a preliminary issue or whether it was so closely bound up with the
evidence that would be led on the issues of liability and causation
that it was better for both matters to proceed to trial together.
The Court of Appeal said that the judge had clearly been right in

seeing too great an overlap between the limitation issues and the substantive issues to sensibly allow of a preliminary hearing.

An analysis of the facts of the case is not necessary. Suffice it to say that negligence in and around the birth of the plaintiff in 1959 and negligence in and around a series of orthopedic operations in 1975–76 formed the basis of the claim.

The lesson to be learned from the case is that it is not always the better course to go for a preliminary hearing on limitation, but only when the issues are relatively discrete.

In *Barrand* v. *British Cellophane plc*, *The Times*, 16 February 1995, the Court of Appeal drew attention to the distinctions between an application to strike out for want of prosecution and an application for the exercise of discretion under s.33. In the first the onus was on the defendant to prove that he had been prejudiced by the delay, in the second the onus was on the plaintiff. Further, under s.33 the judge had to consider the factors set out in the section, whereas there was no such obligation upon an application to strike out.

CHECKLIST

- Have you identified (in fairly broad but not too broad terms) the essence of the act or omission alleged to constitute negligence?
- Is the patient under a disability, or was she under a disability at the time of the alleged negligence?
- When did she first know that she had suffered a significant injury?
- Should she have discovered/realised that earlier?
- When did she first know that the injury was possibly caused by the act or omission?
- Should she have discovered this sooner? Particularly, were there matters to put her on enquiry and so require her to investigate and thus acquire the relevant knowledge sooner?
- If there were earlier negative reports from experts, were they negative on causation (in which case she would not have gained knowledge of attributability) or were they negative on breach of duty (which would be irrelevant to the limitation question, but which it is hoped would be relevant to the exercise of discretion)?

PRODUCT LIABILITY

Note that claims under the Consumer Protection Act 1987, e.g. against the manufacturer, importer, or supplier of a drug, are subject, by s.6(6) and Sched.1 which insert a new s.11A into the Limitation Act, to an overall limitation period of ten years from the date of the relevant supplying, regardless of the state of the plaintiff's knowledge. The Act also provides for a primary limitation period in similar terms to that affecting personal injury claims generally (see further Chapter 30).

THE LIMITATION PERIOD AND STRIKING OUT

Problems have been posed for the court by the interaction of the limitation period, the court's discretion to disapply it, and the inherent power of the court to strike out an action for want of prosecution. The court has an inherent jurisdiction to control its own process, and in addition there is power to dismiss an action under rules of court (O.25 r.1(4)).

The general principle is that the court will not strike out an action for want of prosecution while the limitation period is unexpired, because the plaintiff need merely issue another writ, which would serve to delay the trial yet further. This was established by the House of Lords' decision in *Birkett* v. *James* [1978] AC 297. There was a division of opinion as to whether the court would have power to strike out such a second writ where there had been a contumelious failure to comply with a peremptory order of the court. The general grounds for dismissing an action were said to be either inordinate and inexcusable delay on the part of the plaintiff causing a substantial prejudice to the defendant or intentional and contumelious default. In *Tolley* v. *Morris* [1979] 2 All ER 561 the infant plaintiff was injured at the age of two-and-a-half; the writ was issued when she was seven, but nothing more was done for nine years. The delay was wholly inordinate and inexcusable, but the House of Lords said that as the limitation period would not expire until the child was 21 there was no power to strike out. They were again divided on the question whether a second writ issued within the limitation period could be struck out if there had been contumelious default.

In *Janov* v. *Morris* [1981] 1 WLR 1389 the Court of Appeal said that there was indeed such power and that it was a matter of discretion in each case whether to use it or not. Where a plaintiff ignored a peremptory order of the court, failed to appeal the striking out or give any explanation for his conduct, he could expect to be adjudged guilty of 'intolerable contumely' and have his second writ struck out as an abuse of the process of the court. This case was followed in *Palmer* v. *Birks* (1985) 135 NLJ 1256. In exercising its discretion to strike out an action for want of prosecution before the limitation period had expired, the court should have regard to the state of affairs at the date of the hearing of the application and not to the state of affairs prevailing at the date of the issue of the writ (*Van Pragg* v. *Vickers Ltd*, 7 May 1987, unreported, CA).

Abuse of process: In *Hogg* v. *Hamilton and Northumberland Health Authority* [1993] 4 Med LR 369 the Court of Appeal dismissed an appeal against the striking out of a claim by a mentally handicapped patient on the ground that, although a claim would only most exceptionally be struck out within the relevant limitation period, the court had an inherent jurisdiction so to do, and would do so in this case as the action amounted to an abuse of the process of the court in all the circumstances, in particular because the alleged negligence occurred in 1976, an action in respect of that negligence had been struck out for want of prosecution in 1982 and then in 1988 a fresh action was sought to be pursued. A similar conclusion was reached at first instance in *Headford* v. *Bristol and District Health Authority* [1994] 5 Med LR 406 where a 28-year-old man sought damages for brain damage sustained under anesthesia at the age of ten months. However the Court of Appeal reversed the decision, saying that prejudice to a defendant from delay in bringing an action, even a delay of some 28 years, was irrelevant in the case of a person under a disability who had commenced the action within the limitation period as laid down by s.28 of the Act for persons under a disability ([1995] 6 Med LR 1).

And see *Turner* v. *WH Malcolm Ltd* (1992) 15 BMLR 40 where the Court of Appeal reminded practitioners of the decision in *Tolley* v. *Morris* [1979] 2 All ER 561 to the effect that there was no point in striking out within the limitation period as the plaintiff could merely start another action.

In *Hicks* v. *Newman and Newman*, 6 July 1989, unreported, Hoffmann J. said that the rule in *Birkett* v. *James* only applied where there was no advantage to a defendant in striking out a claim within the limitation period, and, finding in that case the advantage to the defendant that the plaintiff would have to settle a bill of costs from the original action before being allowed to proceed further, he struck out the claim for want of prosecution even though the limitation period had not yet expired. Then in *Wright* v. *Morris, The Times*, 31 October 1988, Millett J. said that the *Birkett* rule was a general but not an immutable principle. Where the plaintiff was seeking by injunction to regulate the future conduct of the defendant, the latter should be entitled to judge whether he wished the action to be struck out for inordinate and inexcusable delay and face the prospect of another writ.

Nevertheless, out of Chancery, the *Birkett* principle was re-affirmed, by the Court of Appeal, in *Simpson* v. *Smith, The Times*, 19 January 1989.

Where it is open to serious argument that the claim is in any event time-barred the court will strike it out, leaving it to the plaintiff to issue another writ if he chooses to (*Barclays Bank* v. *Miller* [1990] 1 WLR 343; it had earlier been said by the Court of Appeal, in April 1988 in *Leicester Wholesale Fruit Market* v. *Grundy* [1990] 1 WLR 107 that a claim would only be struck out if the plea of limitation was incontrovertible).

But this general rule does not enable a plaintiff to argue in a personal injury action that, as he is entitled to issue a fresh writ after the expiry of the limitation period in the hope of persuading the court to exercise its discretion under s.33, therefore his present action should not be dismissed for want of prosecution. In *Walkley* v. *Precision Forgings* (*supra*) the House of Lords made it clear that a sluggish plaintiff cannot avoid liability to be struck out merely because he might be able to proceed with a fresh writ if the court gave him leave (but see *White* v. *Glass, The Times*, 18 February 1989).

In *Birkett* v. *James* (*supra*) the House of Lords had said that the court should look, in assessing the prejudice that had arisen to the defendants from the plaintiff's delay, only to the delay after the issue of the writ and not to any delay in issuing it. However, the Court of Appeal in *Biss* v. *Lambeth Health Authority* [1978] 1 WLR 382 held that that rule did not apply where the plaintiff was proceeding by leave under s.33. There the writ was issued some ten years after the alleged negligent treatment, leave having been given (under the then current legislation) to proceed notwith-standing. Thereafter there was an inexcusable delay of nine months. The court said that where the writ was issued outside the normal limitation period the court would look at the totality of the delay and not just the delay arising after the issue of the writ.

Biss v. *Lambeth Health Authority* (*supra*) is the high point for defendants' success in getting a medical negligence action struck out. The court restated the general principle that to get an action struck out for want of prosecution the defendant had to show that there had been inordinate and inexcusable delay in the conduct of the action by the plaintiff, and that as a result a fair trial was no longer possible or he had been caused substantial prejudice. The court accepted that the defendants had to show that they had suffered more than minimal prejudice from inordinate and inexcus-able delay after the issue of the writ, and then decided that the further delay of nine months after the issue of the writ was inordinate and inexcusable, and that more than minimal prejudice had arisen due to the defendants' doctors and nurses having the matter hanging over their heads for that much longer. Lord Denning said: 'Prejudice to a defendant by a plaintiff's delay is not limited to the death or disappearance of witnesses or their failing memories or to loss or destruction of records. There is much more prejudice to a defendant in having an action hanging over his head indefinitely.' Lord Denning created this extra head of prejudice to counter the plaintiff's contention that all the prejudice (in the conventional terms of fading memories, untraceable witnesses and lost records) had accrued by the time the writ was issued and so no further prejudice could be identified thereafter.

Though inordinate delay in issuing a writ (i.e. one issued at the end of the limitation period) cannot be relied on by the defendants, delay after the issue of a writ can be relied on even if it occurs wholly within the limitation period (*Rath* v. *C.S. Lawrence & Partners* [1991] 1 WLR 399, CA). So to that extent, the plaintiff is better off delaying issue![12]

In *Trill* v. *Sacher* [1993] 1 WLR 1379 the Court of Appeal reaffirmed the principle that culpable delay was not a ground for striking out unless it had given rise to a substantial risk that a fair trial was no longer possible or it was likely to cause serious prejudice to the defendants. A similar approach can be discerned in *Costellow* v. *Somerset County Council* [1993] 1 WLR 256. And in *Hornagold* v. *Fairclough Building Ltd* [1993] PIQR P400 the Court of Appeal made it clear that alleged prejudice as a result of relevant delay had to be clearly identified by the defendants.

In *Dale* v. *British Coal Corporation* [1992] PIQR P373 the Court of Appeal discerned substantial prejudice to the defendants in the fact that notification of the claim was given very late. They also said that the test of reasonable conduct on the part of the plaintiff was objective, i.e. what would a reasonable workman in the position of the plaintiff have done?

In *Antcliffe* v. *Gloucester Health Authority* [1992] 1 WLR 1044 the Court of Appeal recognised as a ground of prejudice the fact that, following the introduction of Crown indemnity (as to which

---

[12] In *Westminster City Council* v. *Clifford Culpin and Partners*, 18 June 1987, the Court of Appeal said that the present legal system provided insufficient sanctions against those responsible for dilatory and inefficient conduct of litigation, and the law should be changed to provide for a stricter and more efficient system of rules. The medical negligence practitioner should therefore keep a watchful eye on any changes in the rules as he, as much if not more than anyone, is likely to be affected. This view was endorsed in *Simon Carves Ltd* v. *Costain Construction*, *The Times*, 13 November 1987.

Worth noting also is *Mansouri* v. *Bloomsbury Health Authority*, *The Times*, 20 July 1987, where the Court of Appeal said that it did not excuse inordinate delay to plead that the papers were with counsel and struck out the plaintiff's medical negligence claim.

see Chapter 22), the health authority would now have to meet the full cost of any damages awarded instead of sharing it with the medical defence body. In *Gascoine* v. *Haringey Health Authority* [1992] 3 Med LR 291 the Court of Appeal gave a similar reason as one of the grounds for striking out the action.

In *Doyle* v. *Robinson* [1994] PIQR P59 the Court of Appeal took this approach substantially further when it held in a simple accident case that increase in damages on account merely of their delayed assessment was in itself capable of constituting serious prejudice (this seems to be going too far – the plaintiff could simply agree to accept the amount he would have got if he had acted with proper speed).

Acquiescence

There have been many cases recently on the question whether defendants are precluded from applying to strike out where they have given the plaintiff to understand that the action will be going to trial and the plaintiff as a result has undertaken further expenditure. In *Roebuck* v. *Mungovin* [1994] 2 WLR 290 the House of Lords held that such conduct was not an absolute bar to an application to strike out but was merely a relevant factor for the judge to take into account when deciding how to exercise his discretion.

Further examples

In *Joseph* v. *Korn* (31 July 1984, CA), the court dismissed in 1984 for want of prosecution a writ issued in 1974 for medical negligence in 1971. The court was particularly impressed with the fact that the case would involve disputed questions of fact (the court will be quick to infer that memories and reliability of witnesses have deteriorated over the passage of time (*Leniston* v. *Phipps*, 21 October 1988, CA, unreported)).

In *Rosen* v. *Marston* (15 March 1984, CA), the court upheld the dismissal in 1984 of a claim arising from an operation in 1977 (writ issued in 1980) after two-and-a-half years of unwarranted delay which prejudiced the defendant because his recollection would have deteriorated and he would have suffered the anxiety of the case hanging over his head (similarly *Goodman* v. *Fletcher* (4 October 1982, CA)).

Compare *Westaway* v. *South Glamorgan Health Authority* (9 June 1986, CA), where the Court of Appeal, despite finding inordinate and inexcusable delay, held that, as the claim related to a failure to diagnose a fracture, the issue would turn on the records, and so the defendants were not prejudiced by the delay.

It will be noted how similar are the considerations that influence the court whether considering an application to disapply the limitation provisions and permit an action to proceed out of time or one to strike out a claim for want of prosecution. As to which way the court will decide, it is in the end a matter of the length of the Chancellor's foot, or, if you like, how the judge happens to be feeling on the day.

29 · Cases

SUMMARY

The cases summarised below are examples of decisions on medical negligence from the English reports. For the reasons given earlier (see Chapter 2) I have not included foreign decisions, neither here nor elsewhere in the book, unless a useful point of principle is involved. Cases which receive fuller treatment elsewhere in the book under specialised headings, e.g. 'Consent', 'Duty of disclosure', 'Vicarious liability' (Chapter 22, 'Who to sue'), are not all mentioned here. Remember what I said in Chapter 2 about the *ad hoc* character of most medical negligence decisions and the limited use they have, therefore, as precedents; and beware of older cases, which reflect often what is hopefully an outmoded approach to the doctor as the almost unimpugnable father-figure. Sometimes the law contained in the older cases is now irrelevant in any event, e.g. the cases that refuse to impose liability upon a hospital or resident staff in respect of a consultant's activities.

The best repository of reports of medical negligence cases is Nelson-Jones and Burton, *Medical Negligence Case Law* (2nd edition, Butterworth, 1995). One finds there a full summary of the relevant facts of all reported, and a number of unreported, cases. My objectives in this chapter are much less comprehensive: merely to give a very brief summary of potentially useful decisions.

EXAMINATION

The failure to enquire as to the patient having a possible allergy to penicillin was negligent: *Chin Keow* v. *Government of Malaysia* [1967] 1 WLR 813, PC.

A casualty officer at a hospital was negligent when he allowed a patient who had been struck on the head with a spanner to go home without the proper examination being made that would have disclosed a depressed fracture of the skull: *McCormack* v. *Redpath, The Times*, 24 March 1961.

A doctor must make proper enquiries to find out what, if any, treatment his new patient has already received: *Coles* v. *Reading and District Hospital Management Committee* (1963) 107 SJ 115.

Failure to suspect malaria and make proper tests has several times resulted in an indefensible claim for damages: *Langley* v. *Campbell, The Times*, 6 November 1975.

An ineffectual examination of a girl of 11 who had appendicitis was held to be negligent in *Edler* v. *Greenwich and Deptford Hospital Management Committee, The Times*, 7 March 1953. Similarly there was a negligently cursory examination of a man who had been kicked in the abdomen by a horse in *Payne* v. *St Helier Hospital Group Management Committee, The Times*, 12 November 1952.

A doctor's plea that it was the patient's intoxicated condition that led him to discharge him home without discovering the fractured collar bone; any of the 18 fractured ribs or the badly congested lungs did not succeed in *Wood* v. *Thurston, The Times*, 25 May 1951.

There was evidence of negligence, that should have been left to the jury, where a doctor attending a patient with severe stomach pains in the middle of the night injected morphine without making a full examination and did not advise the patient to go to hospital: *Reeves* v. *Carthy* [1984] IR 348.

A doctor who failed to treat as urgent an infant's problem with urine retraction, but left him in the care of qualified nurses, was not negligent when the infant was found the next day to have florid meningitis. No urgent treatment would have prevented that condition from arising (*Barker* v. *Nugent* [1987] 3 MLJ 182). (And see *Sutton* v. *Population Services, The Times*, 7 November 1981.)

General practitioners who were informed that a child had ingested hot tea from the spout of a teapot were negligent in failing to appreciate the potential consequences, to visit and to refer the child to hospital (*Sa'd* v. *Robinson* [1989] 1 Med LR 41).

DIAGNOSIS

A doctor will be guilty of negligence if he fails to use due care in examination or diagnosis. But he cannot be expected to use an instrument which at that time was very rarely found in this country: *Whiteford* v. *Hunter* (1950) WN 553.

In *Newton* v. *Newton's Model Laundry, The Times*, 3 November 1959, a physician was held to have been negligent when he failed to diagnose a fractured patella after the plaintiff had suffered a fall of some 12 feet on to a concrete floor.

Negligence was found in *Pudney* v. *Union Castle Mail SS Ltd* [1953] 1 Lloyd's Rep 73, where the wrong diagnosis was made and wrong treatment given based upon that diagnosis. Failure to diagnose amebic dysentery in a patient who had spent many years in the tropics was negligent in *Tuffil* v. *East Surrey Area Health Authority, The Times*, 15 March 1978.

But a wrong diagnosis is not necessarily negligent; negligence has to be proved in the usual way by expert evidence, to the effect that no doctor acting with reasonable care would have made such a diagnosis. So, in *Crivon* v. *Barnet Group Hospital Management Committee, The Times*, 19 November 1958, the diagnosis of cancer made by a pathologist, followed by treatment for that condition, was on the evidence held to have been made without negligence.

In a recent case reported in the press, liability was admitted in respect of a negligent diagnosis of cancer that led to the unnecessary removal of a woman's breasts.

An operation carried out as a matter of urgency on the basis of one diagnosis without waiting for the results of a sputum test that might invalidate it was not negligent, as there was evidence that there was a body of professional opinion that would endorse the decision to operate. The judge was not entitled to 'prefer' contrary evidence from another school of thought: *Maynard* v. *West Midlands Regional Health Authority* [1984] 1 WLR 634. In *Langley* v. *Campbell, The Times*, 6 November 1975, failure to diagnose malaria in a patient just returned from East Africa was held to be negligent.

A consultant obstetrician and gynecologist who negligently dismissed the possibility that the plaintiff was pregnant was liable in damages for the pain and discomfort of the pregnancy and birth and for the loss and expenses consequent upon the birth of the child (*Gardiner* v. *Mounfield and Lincolnshire Area Health Authority* [1990] 1 Med LR 205).

Failure to diagnose or even suspect meningitis in an infant has been a not infrequent complaint against GPs; an award of £700,000 for the ensuing brain damage after a cardiac arrest is found in *O'Donnell* v. *Khan*, unreported, 11 January 1989, HC (for a similar case where the GP was exonerated see *Barker* v. *Nugent* [1987] 3 MLJ 182).

Failure to diagnose a fracture (also an intra-ocular object), because the appropriate X-rays were not taken or were misread, is often the subject of a claim: *Patterson* v. *Rotherham Health Authority* (20 May 1987, CA) is one example.

Failure to diagnose testicular cancer was held not to have been negligent in the recent Scottish case of *Phillips* v. *Grampian Health Board* [1991] 3 Med LR 16.

In *Redmayne* v. *Bloomsbury Health Authority*, High Court, 31 January 1982 (unreported), the plaintiff failed to show negligence by the Hospital for Tropical Diseases in not diagnosing the

African filarial disease, onchocerchiasis, when she presented to them in 1975. The judge was not satisfied that she even had the disease, let alone that the hospital had negligently failed to diagnose it.

In the recent case of *Thornton* v. *Nicol* [1992] 3 Med LR 41 it was unsuccessfully alleged against a GP that, even though he could not have diagnosed the meningitis in the baby he was examining, there were sufficient indications to require immediate hospital admission.

ANESTHETICS

Keeping an anesthetic in a dangerous manner is not negligent if the state of medical knowledge at the time did not enable the danger to be recognised: *Roe* v. *Minister of Health* [1954] 2 QB 66.

A doctor was not negligent in failing to get his injection into the vein of the arm of an 'exceedingly fat' woman, thus damaging the tissues of the arm: *Williams* v. *North Liverpool Hospital Management Committee, The Times*, 17 January 1959.

A spinal anesthetic for a certain operation might have been, with hindsight, not the best course to have taken (it led to paralysis of the leg), but in view of the conflicting expert evidence the choice of that method could not be said to have been negligent: *Moore* v. *Lewisham Group Hospital Management Committee, The Times*, 5 February 1959.

During an operation to remedy a congenital displaced hip the heart of an otherwise fit little girl of four stopped for half an hour, and she suffered brain damage. Mann J. found that a fit heart does not stop under anesthesia without negligence (*Saunders* v. *Leeds Western Health Authority and Robinson* (1985) 82 LS Gaz 1491 – see further Chapter 23 under 'Res ipsa loquitur').

An anesthetist faced with difficult intubation during induction of anesthesia because of a patient's obesity and absence of teeth was not to blame for injury resulting from the plaintiff's aspiration of stomach fluid (*Chambers* v. *Southern Health and Social Services Board* [1990] 1 Med LR 231).

At the end of a very long case, anesthetic negligence was found in *Ritchie* v. *Chichester Health Authority* [1994] 5 Med LR 187 in that during labour a neurotoxic substance had been injected subdurally instead of the correct epidural injection, causing permanent disastrous saddle anesthesia.

There have been a number of recent claims for awareness under anesthetic, particularly during cesarean sections: in *Ludlow* v. *Swindon Health Authority* [1989] 1 Med LR 104 the judge was not satisfied that the plaintiff had been conscious during, as opposed to at the end of, the operation (similarly *Jacobs* v. *Great Yarmouth and Waveney Health Authority* [1984] 1 *The Lancet* 1249). In June 1985 a woman who had been conscious for over an hour and suffered therefrom enduring nervous shock was awarded £12,000 (*Ackers* v. *Wigan Health Authority* [1991] 2 Med LR 232). Margaret Ashton obtained £21,000 against Wigan Health Authority for the same sort of injury on 7 November 1989 (reference may also be made to the case of Pamela Hill (AVMA's MLJ, April 1990, p.4) where £25,000 was agreed for general damages for pain and enduring nervous shock from awareness during a hysterectomy).

In *Taylor* v. *Worcester and District Health Authority* [1991] 2 Med LR 215 the plaintiff's claim for damages for awareness during a cesarean section failed because the judge concluded both that the anesthetist had followed a procedure that was acceptable at that time (1985) and that the awareness arose *after* the operation at the reversal stage of the anesthetic.

In *Phelan* v. *East Cumbria Health Authority* [1991] 2 Med LR 418 a patient who had been aware of intense pain and fright during an operation for a serious leg injury that involved deep cutting and drilling into the bone was awarded £15,000, of which £5,000 was for the actual experience on the operating table and, it appears, the rest for the after-effects.

A claim for anesthetic negligence failed where a girl of 13 had come to while still partly paralysed from the anesthetic, the judge stating that the protocol which the anesthetist had followed had not been shown to be one which no competent hospital could have adopted (*Early* v. *Newham Health Authority* [1994] 5 Med LR 214).

OBSTETRICS, GYNECOLOGY, AND NEONATAL

Where a baby suffered brain damage at birth after a trial of forceps delivery followed by a cesarean section the trial judge was wrong to find negligence upon the evidence: *Whitehouse* v. *Jordan* [1981] 1 WLR 246 (see above under 'Errors of judgment' at p. 201, Chapter 17). This case and *Maynard*'s case ([1984] 1 WLR 634) are illustrations of the willingness of the Court of Appeal in this area of the law to interfere (at least in the early 1980s) with the findings of the trial judge. In the former, despite the fact that the judge was the one who heard and assessed the reliability of the witnesses' evidence, the Court of Appeal was prepared to say that the evidence did not support his findings, and the House of Lords agreed with them. In the latter case the appeal court reversed the decision of the trial judge on the basis that the expert evidence did not support his conclusion that the doctor had been negligent.

For an example of 'horrific and wholly unacceptable' behaviour by an obstetrician at delivery see *Kralj* v. *McGrath* [1986] 1 All ER 54, where liability was admitted before trial.

A failure to treat an expectant mother after cord prolapse led to a finding of negligence in *Mitchell* v. *Hounslow and Spelthorne Health Authority* [1984] 1 *The Lancet* 579.

There is no duty involved, breach of which could give rise to judicial review, when *in vitro* fertilisation was refused to a prostitute (*R.* v. *Ethical Committee of St Mary's Hospital, ex parte Harriott* [1988] 1 FLR 512).

In *Bovenzi* v. *Kettering Health Authority* [1991] 2 Med LR 293 negligence was proved where the uterus was perforated *and* bowel was pulled down during a dilatation and curettage for evacuation of retained products of conception (note that it is generally the case that it is not negligent merely to perforate the uterus during a D & C).

In *Hendy* v. *Milton Keynes Health Authority (No.2)* [1992] 3 Med LR 119 (the trial of the main action, not the limitation issue), Jowett J. held that, although it was just possible for the anatomy of a ureter to be so irregular as to excuse a surgeon from injuring it when performing a hysterectomy, the defendants had not shown that that was the case in the hysterectomy carried out on the plaintiff.

In *Hinfey* v. *Salford Health Authority* [1993] 4 Med LR 143 the defendants were held not to have been negligent in going for a vaginal delivery and not for an earlier cesarean section.

In *Parry* v. *North West Surrey Health Authority* [1994] 5 Med LR 259 the court found that the attending doctor negligently attempted a forceps delivery when the fetal head was too high and so precipitated a period of severe hypoxia which led to brain damage and cerebral palsy.

In *Marsden* v. *Bateman* [1993] 4 Med LR 181 a claim for negligent neonatal attention resulting in brain damage from hypoglycemia failed as the judge concluded that the injury was caused by a prenatal developmental defect.

James v. *Camberwell Health Authority* [1994] 5 Med LR 253 is interesting. The plaintiff appeared to have a reasonable case for alleging negligent obstetric delay leading to perinatal asphyxia and brain damage. However, shortly before the trial the defendants announced that the readings on the CTG trace were out by some 33 minutes, thus destroying the basis of the plaintiff's case. What is extraordinary is that the defendants had either not discovered this before or had not so informed the plaintiff.

GENERAL PRACTITIONERS

In *Stockdale* v. *Nicholls* [1993] 4 Med LR 190 a GP was held
not to have been negligent in not visiting an infant but sending
a practice nurse instead. In *Durrant* v. *Burke* [1993] 4 Med LR
258 the infant plaintiff failed in a claim against a GP for failing
to visit quickly enough as a result of which it was alleged the
child suffered brain damage from an excess of sodium in the
blood.

In *Bova* v. *Spring* [1994] 5 Med LR 120 a GP was found
negligent in respect of a plaintiff's death for not suspecting that
his chest pain might be pleural in origin and therefore a sign not
of a pulled muscle or viral enteritis but of lobar pneumonia (the
critical comments by Margaret Puxon QC which follow the case
report are of particular interest).

DEPARTING FROM USUAL PRACTICE

This is not of itself proof of negligence. That principle is given
statutory force in the context of actions for pre-natal injury by
s.1(5) of the Congenital Disabilities Act 1976 (see Chapter 26). A
doctor is entitled to use his common sense, experience and
judgment in the way he decides to treat any patient; a slight
departure from the textbook does not establish negligence (*per*
Streatfeild J. in *Holland* v. *Devitt & Moore Nautical College, The
Times*, 4 March 1960). It has to be shown that the defendant took
a course which no physician of ordinary skill would have taken if
acting with reasonable care.

It was alleged in *Slater* v. *Baker and Stapleton* (1767) 95 ER 860
that the defendant, an apothecary and chief surgeon at Bart's,
had been negligent in treating a broken leg, in that he had
re-broken it and then attempted to straighten it through extension rather than compression, using some new-fangled machine.
The jury found for the plaintiff, and, affirming the verdict, the
court said:

For anything that appears to this court, this was the first experiment made with
this new instrument; and if it was, it was a rash action, and he who acts rashly
acts ignorantly: and although the defendants in general may be as skilful in their
respective professions as any two gentlemen in England, yet the court cannot
help saying, that in this particular case they have acted ignorantly and
unskilfully, contrary to the known rule and usage of surgeons.

In *Cooper* v. *Nevill, The Times*, 24 March 1961, where a
surgeon had left an abdominal pack in the patient's body, the
Privy Council said there was no justification for any departure
from the normal routine.

A psychiatrist had social contacts with his female patient. He was found negligent by the trial judge. In the Court of Appeal Sellers L.J. said:

. . . a doctor might not be negligent if he tried a new technique, but if he did he must justify it before the court. If his novel or exceptional treatment had failed disastrously he could not complain if it was held that he went beyond the bounds of due care and skill as recognised generally. Success was the best justification for unusual and unestablished treatment. Here the medical evidence was all one way in condemning social contacts and the doctor had failed to convince the judge that his departure from accepted practice was justified (*Landau* v. *Werner* (1961) 105 SJ 257, 1008, CA).

Where there was a departure from normal practice in performing a colporrhaphy operation (to remedy stress incontinence) within three months of birth, which proved to be unsuccessful, it was held that such a departure had not been shown to have been justified and therefore constituted a breach of the duty of care owed to the patient: *Clark* v. *MacLennan* [1983] 1 All ER 416.

In *Wilsher* v. *Essex Area Health Authority* [1987] QB 730 Mustill L.J. said:

. . . where the doctor embarks on a form of treatment which is still comparatively untried, with techniques and safeguards which are still in the course of development, or where the treatment is of particular technical difficulty . . . if the decision to embark on the treatment at all was justifiable and was taken with the informed consent of the patient, the court should . . . be particularly careful not to impute negligence simply because something has gone wrong.

SWABS AND THINGS – OPERATIONS GENERALLY

If a swab is left in the patient's body and causes damage (which may be only the necessity for an operation to remove it) the hospital will be liable. There are older cases which suggest the surgeon is not necessarily negligent in such a case, but in the first place the approach of the courts in those days is not likely to be followed now (the reluctance to find negligence which amounted to prejudice in favour of the doctor is far less marked) and, secondly, the issue was often the distinction between the liability of the surgeon and that of the hospital for negligence of the nursing staff, an issue which is no longer of any significance (save in the context of a consultant chosen and paid by the patient).

Thus the court was not willing to find negligence in *Mahon* v. *Osborne* [1939] 2 KB 14, and *White* v. *Westminster Hospital Board of Governors, The Times*, 26 October 1961; but did find negligence in *Dryden* v. *Surrey County Council and Stewart* [1936] 2 All ER 535, *James* v. *Dunlop* – referred to in *Mahon* v. *Osborne* (*supra*), *Hocking* v. *Bell* [1968] WN 21, *Urry* v. *Bierer*,

The Times, 15 July 1955, and *Cooper* v. *Nevill, The Times*, 24 March 1961.

Breaking a needle while giving an injection and leaving it in the patient without telling him was negligent: *Gerber* v. *Pines* (1933) 79 SJ 13.

Piercing the sciatic nerve when giving an injection for malaria was held to be negligent in *Caldeira* v. *Gray, The Times*, 15 February 1936.

Injecting cocaine instead of procaine was negligent in *Collins* v. *Hertfordshire County Council* [1947] KB 598.

It was negligent to inject pentothal when the patient was already anesthetised (the patient died): *Jones* v. *Manchester Corporation* [1952] 2 KB 852.

It was held to be negligent where a doctor failed to give penicillin for septicemia after a course of tetracycline: *Hucks* v. *Cole* (1968) 118 NLJ 469.

A surgeon was not guilty of negligence when, during an operation to improve for cosmetic reasons the appearance of an inveterately defective eye, he made a wrong cut, into the retina. The court said that notwithstanding the wrong cut he was exercising due skill, care and judgment: *White* v. *Westminster Hospital, The Times*, 26 October 1961.

A surgeon operating to remove granulated tissue adhering to the eardrum was not shown to have been negligent when partial paralysis resulted: *Ashcroft* v. *Mersey Regional Health Authority* [1983] 2 All ER 245.

A doctor administered to a patient who had a boil on his face and was in a very excited state the second part of a combined anti-cholera and typhoid injection. He was held not to have acted negligently even though the manufacturer warned that only healthy subjects should be injected, because there was no evidence of any foreseeable risk of injury arising since there was no finding that inoculation of an unhealthy person could cause or increase the risk of a stroke or similar neurological reaction: *King* v. *King* [1987] 1 *The Lancet* 991.

Vaginal swabs were negligently swapped in *G.* v. *North Tees Health Authority* [1989] FCR 53, so that a mother suffered nervous shock and her daughter protracted investigation over the consequent allegation that the daughter had been sexually abused (mother and child were each awarded £5,000).

The Court of Appeal increased the award from £8,000 to £20,000 for a woman who had been given the wrong blood transfusion (rhesus positive instead of negative) with the result that her child would be at risk in any future pregnancy (*Morgan* v. *Gwent Health Authority* [1988] 2 *The Lancet* 519). In *Roberts* v.

Johnstone [1989] QB 878 liability was admitted where the plaintiff was born with severe hemolytic disease due to failure to treat her mother for rhesus incompatibility.

In *Bentley* v. *Bristol and Weston Health Authority (No.2)* [1991] 3 Med LR 1 it was held that sciatic nerve damage resulting from a hip replacement operation had been caused by a degree of stretching of the nerve that was incompatible with the exercise of due care.

In the recent case of *Doughty* v. *North Staffordshire Health Authority* [1992] 3 Med LR 81 a plastic surgeon was held negligent for embarking on a series of cosmetic operations over many years starting soon after birth in an attempt to rectify a large facial birthmark. The judge was satisfied that at the relevant time there was no responsible body of medical opinion that would have approved of the decision to embark on that course of treatment.

INFECTION

Failure to isolate a patient from a woman suffering from puerperal fever was held to be negligent in *Heafield* v. *Crane, The Times*, 31 July 1937.

Failing to warn a patient before admitting her to a nursing home, that there had been a case of puerperal fever there, was held to have been negligent when the patient contracted that disease: *Lindsey County Council* v. *Marshall* [1937] AC 97 (a different decision was reached where a patient who was suffering from diphtheria contracted smallpox in hospital because he was not protected from contact with the infection. This decision was on the basis that the hospital had used the best system then available for dealing with such a situation (*Vancouver General Hospital* v. *McDaniel* [1934] WN 171)).

AFTER-CARE

A plastic surgeon was held to have been negligent for failing to make proper arrangements for his patient to contact him in the event of bleeding after discharge following an operation: *Corder* v. *Banks, The Times*, 9 April 1960.

It was not negligent for a surgeon to have failed to warn a woman after a sterilisation operation that there was a slight risk of future pregnancy and to advise her to use contraceptives: *Waters* v. *Park, The Times*, 15 July 1961.

Failing to communicate information about the patient's condition to those who are later to have the care of him may amount to negligence: *Bell* v. *Secretary of State for Defence* [1986] QB 322, where an army doctor failed to ensure that proper medical records were made available to the civilian hospital to which his patient, a soldier, was transferred.

And *Chapman* v. *Rix* [1994] 5 Med LR 239, where at first instance a hospital doctor was held to have been negligent for failing to communicate his findings upon examination of a stomach wound to the deceased's own doctor (the decision was reversed on appeal on the facts, but the principle remains valid).

In *Clarke* v. *Adams* (1950) 94 SJ 599, it was held to be negligent to have given a patient taking heat treatment an inadequate warning about the need to speak out if the machine got too warm. The fact that the warning given was in the standard form approved by the profession did not avail the defendant, as the court said it was in the circumstances inadequate.

A failure to warn of the danger of taking certain foods while on a particular drug regime would be negligent if the danger of such food had been publicised by the manufacturers of the drug or from some other source. This question was considered in *Buckle* v. *de Launay* [1970] 2 The Lancet 145, where on the facts it was found that the doctor had given an appropriate warning.

In *Cavanagh* v. *Bristol and Weston Health Authority* [1992] 3 Med LR 41 Macpherson J. held that the health authority had been negligent in not keeping tabs on the plaintiff after operations had failed to save the sight in his right eye. He went on to contract sympathetic ophthalmitis in the other eye and became totally blind. The judge found that if the health authority had monitored him they would have taken the decision in due course to enucleate the right eye which would probably have prevented the disease arising in the left eye.[1]

READING THE LITERATURE

It is a doctor's duty to keep reasonably abreast of medical knowledge, and for that purpose he needs to be aware of recent developments published in the medical press. But the doctor is not expected to read and ingest every available item. Thus in *Crawford* v. *Charing Cross Hospital, The Times*, 8 December 1953, a surgeon was not expected to know that a particular placing of a patient's arm during a blood transfusion was dangerous, as the only publicisation of that fact had been one article in a recent medical journal.

---

[1] For another recent case involving sympathetic ophthalmitis (*re* the duty to disclose the risk) see *Rogers* v. *Whittaker* [1993] 4 Med LR 79.

SELF-INFLICTED INJURY

Leaving a suicide-risk patient unobserved and with an open window behind his bed constituted lack of proper care, so that the hospital was liable when the patient got out of the window and threw himself off a roof. A high degree of surveillance was required in the case of patients with suicidal tendencies; the duty of care extended to a duty to protect the patient from the risk of self-inflicted injuries: *Selfe* v. *Ilford & District Hospital Management Committee* (1970) 114 SJ 935.

In *Lepine* v. *University Hospital Board* (1964) 50 DLR (2d) 225, affirmed (1965) 54 DLR (2d) 340, a hospital was held negligent for not having a constant watch on a patient suffering from a dangerous condition of post-epileptic automatism, who jumped from a window.

A patient of suspected suicidal tendencies managed to elude the nurses, went home and killed herself. The hospital was found not to have been negligent: *Thorne* v. *Northern Group Hospital Management Committee* (1964) 108 SJ 484.

There was no liability where a patient had attempted suicide after treatment and severely crippled himself. Lord Denning said that such actions ought to be discouraged as a matter of public policy: *Hyde* v. *Tameside Area Health Authority, The Times*, 16 April 1981.

Children require a specially watchful eye. Where a 7-year-old boy was left without supervision near an open window and fell out, the hospital was liable: *Newnham* v. *Rochester Hospital Board* (1936).

But where the injury occurs in a non-medical context, i.e. it does not give rise to considerations about care and treatment, the conclusion may be different. Thus a hospital was not negligent where a girl of nine injured herself when she ran into glass swing doors in the hospital, at a time when the orderly was momentarily absent. The hospital's duty in the non-medical context was said to be that of an ordinary prudent parent (*Gravestock* v. *Lewisham Group Hospital Management Committee, The Times*, 27 May 1955).

Liability was admitted where a three-month-old baby was not properly looked after in a steam tent and was scalded: *White* v. *Tilbury & South East Essex Hospital Management Committee*, unreported, 1964.

It was not negligent to leave a partially disabled child to manage a jug of hot inhalant in bed on her own: *Cox* v. *Carshalton Hospital Management Committee, The Times*, 29 March 1955.

There was no evidence, said the appeal court, to substantiate a finding of negligence where a psychiatric patient set herself alight with a box of matches (*Gauntlett* v. *Northampton Health Authority* (12 December 1985, CA)). See also *Hay* v. *Grampian Health Board* [1995] 6 Med LR 128 (preventable suicide attempt).

PSYCHIATRIC TREATMENT

Psychiatrists are very hard to sue successfully, because, however detrimental their attentions may be, lack of precise medical knowledge in this area of medicine usually prevents any causal connection being established between the treatment and the deterioration of the patient.

Furthermore, as psychiatry is not a science, and so little is known by the medical profession about the workings of the human mind, anything goes in the way of treatment, including drugging the patient, and, not so long ago, lobotomies and electro-convulsive therapy; so it is virtually impossible to get expert evidence to prove the treatment ill-advised. However, in *Landau* v. *Werner* (1961) 105 SJ 257, affirmed (1961) 105 SJ 1008, a psychiatrist who had social intercourse with a female patient was held to have acted in such a way as would be considered undesirable by the profession, especially as he knew that she had already fallen in love with him in the usual way of psychiatric patients. She later suffered a general deterioration in her mental condition and attempted suicide.

There was no liability when a mental patient who was receiving electro-convulsive therapy, a form of treatment which had at that time the approval of a considerable body of medical opinion (!), suffered a pelvic fracture on each side when the head of the femur was driven through the acetabulum: *Bolam* v. *Friern Barnet Hospital Management Committee* [1957] 1 WLR 582.

A practitioner recommending the admission to hospital of a mentally disordered patient under what is now the Mental Health Act 1983 owes a duty to the patient to exercise proper care and skill and is liable in damages for loss or injury arising from the failure to exercise that care (*de Freville* v. *Dill* (1927) 96 LJKB 1056). His duty 'is not merely a duty to take reasonable care in making inquiries, that is, in ascertaining the necessary data, but includes a duty to exercise reasonable professional skill in forming a conclusion from such data': *Everett* v. *Griffiths* [1920] 3 KB 163, 216, *per* Atkin L.J.

If a practitioner signs a certificate of insanity without making proper examination or enquiries and damage ensues to the patient, it was said as long ago as 1862 that an action lies (*Hall* v.

Semple (1862) 3 F & F 337). A recent case where it was clearly stated that recommendations by doctors for compulsory detention for medical treatment which were made without proper care could found an action for damages is *Routley* v. *Worthing Health Authority* (1983).

A wrongful regime imposed on a psychiatric patient could be the subject of a claim for damages (*Furber* v. *Kratter, The Times*, 21 July 1988).

The administration of Largactil, a strong sedative, to a distressed patient, which caused muscle stiffness, was not negligent (*Hughes* v. *Staunton*, High Court of Ireland, 16 February 1990, unreported).

DENTISTS

The same standard of professional care is naturally expected of a dentist as of a doctor (*Edwards* v. *Mallan* [1908] 1 KB 1002).

In *Fish* v. *Kapur* [1948] 2 All ER 176 a dentist who fractured the jaw of a patient whilst extracting a tooth and left part of the root still in the jaw was held not to have acted negligently (see also *O'Neill* v. *Kelly, The Times*, 15 December 1961, where a dentist who fractured a jawbone whilst attempting to remove a root by making use of a machine known as an elevator was cleared of negligence by Davies L.J. in a judgment that is as fine a bit of special pleading for the profession as one could hope to find).

But it was held to have been negligent where, after a jaw had been dislocated during extraction, the dentist failed to notice and treat the injury over the subsequent months of dental treatment (*Lock* v. *Scantlebury, The Times*, 25 July 1963).

In *Transewell* v. *Nelson, The Times*, 11 February 1959, a dentist who relied on a doctor's diagnosis of an abscess when the patient was in fact suffering from osteomyelitis was not negligent. It would have been otherwise if the dentist had been able to observe symptoms which should have told him the doctor's diagnosis was wrong.

Reference may also be made to *Nesbitt* v. *Holt* [1953] 1 DLR 671 (Canada), where a dentist was held to be negligent after his patient died of asphyxia, because he had not looked to see if a sponge was stuck in her windpipe; and to *Harrison* v. *Read* [1964] WAR 228 (Australia), where negligence was found in the use of an electrically driven carborundum disc that lacerated the underside of the patient's tongue. A similar approach was taken by Tudor Evans J. in *Sankey* v. *Kensington and Chelsea Area Health Authority* (2 April 1982, QBD).

In *Connor* v. *Fison-Clarke* (9 October 1987, QBD) a dentist was liable for faulty fitting of a bridge and poor occlusion of the lower teeth. This sort of complaint is usually impossible to prove as the patient will have been to a number of other dentists since the complained of treatment and it will be very hard to say who was responsible for what; also, dentists, far more than doctors, tend to gang up on anyone who sues, and then they will often refuse to treat the plaintiff, i.e. blacklist her.

In *Heath* v. *West Berkshire Health Authority* [1992] 3 Med LR 57 liability was established in respect of permanent damage to the lingual nerve during the removal of the lower left wisdom tooth. Compare *Christie* v. *Somerset Health Authority* [1992] 3 Med LR 75, where the judge concluded that a similar injury was negligently caused by retractor or burr when the disto-lingual bone was being removed.

In *Tomkins* v. *Bexley Health Authority* [1993] 4 Med LR 235 an orthodontist was held to be negligent during extraction of a wisdom tooth when the burr of the drill severed the lingual nerve.

VETS

Animal doctors get sued, too. A faulty operation on the foreleg of a promising racehorse that ended its athletic career resulted in an award of over £54,000 damages (*Shine* v. *Brown, Grant and Partners*, High Court, unreported, 21 February 1990). In *Fowlston* v. *Withan Land and Leisure Service Ltd, The Independent*, 2 May 1988, the Court of Appeal reversed the judge's finding of negligence where a mare had died as a result of a tear in her rectum sustained during an ultrasound scan to detect pregnancy.

A vet was obliged to pay over £1,000 damages to the owner of a Great Dane for negligent administration of anesthetic in a throat operation (*Crane* v. *Kynoch*, reported in *The Times*, 16 February 1991).

30 · Strict liability

SUMMARY

This chapter considers various contexts in which liability may attach in respect of a claim for a medical accident without the need to prove fault. These include the Consumer Protection Act 1987, the Vaccine Damage Payments Act 1979, and any proposed system of no-fault compensation.

THE CONSUMER PROTECTION ACT 1987

This Act came into force on 1 March 1988. Strict liability for damage caused is imposed on the producers and certain suppliers of any product falling within the Act and supplied after that date. The definition of 'product' is apt to cover medical products, equipment and drugs. It may also cover blood and blood-based materials.

Section 2 of the Act provides that where any damage is caused wholly or partly by a defect in a product (the relevant party) shall be liable for the damage.

This legislation, following the EC Product Liability Directive (85/374/EEC), was expected (wrongly, as it turned out) *inter alia* to put an end to the insuperable difficulties experienced by e.g. thalidomide victims in establishing negligence. One expected to have to prove that the drug had a defect (killing or deforming you, as many do, is suggestive of a defect), and that the patient suffered an injury from ingesting the drug (i.e. that his condition was not due to progress of his underlying illness). But one did not expect the so-called strict liability to be, as explained below, watered down to the point where it adds very little to ordinary principles of liability for negligence under the common law.

The supplier will be liable if he cannot name the producer. If he can identify the producer he will not be liable even if the producer cannot satisfy a judgment.

Defect: a product is deemed to have a defect if its safety is not such as persons generally are entitled to expect. This suggests a form of *res ipsa loquitur* in that the proof of the pudding may be said to be in the eating – you are entitled, one would hope, not to expect to be injured by a prescribed drug.

However, the Department of Trade does not seem to agree. They sounded a warning note about the variability of the safety factor in a 1985 explanatory (!) note:

The safety which a person is entitled to expect raises particularly complex issues in respect of medicinal products and adverse reactions to them. Establishing the existence of a defect in a medicine administered to a patient is complicated by the fact that not only is the human body a highly complex organism but at the time of treatment is already subject to an adverse pathological condition. In order to avoid an adverse reaction a medicine will have to be able to cope successfully with already faulty organs, disease and almost infinite variations in individual susceptibility to the effect of medicines from person to person. The more active the medicine, and the greater its beneficial potential, the more extensive its effects are likely to be, and therefore the greater the chances of an adverse effect. A medicine used to treat a life-threatening condition is likely to be much more powerful than a medicine used in the treatment of a less serious condition, and the safety that one is reasonably entitled to expect of such a medicine may therefore be correspondingly lower.

Why a drug that is intended to relieve a serious condition need be potentially lethal is hard to understand. How that is justified is even harder. But if you believe in drugs as the basic treatment for modern disorders, I suppose you can write such stuff without much trouble.

The 'development risks' defence: unfortunately a lot of the bite of this Act is taken away by the fact that the Government (who no doubt share the Department of Trade's belief in the wonders of modern drug therapy and/or find the pharmaceutical companies to be powerful – and wealthy – lobbyists) opted to enact the so-called 'development risks' defence, so that it is a defence to show that

the state of scientific and technical knowledge at the relevant time was not such that a producer of products of the same description as the product in question might be expected to have discovered the defect if it had existed in his products while they were under his control (s.4(1)(e)).

It appears that this provision has the effect of preserving the position at common law. If the producer is excused if he could not be expected to have discovered the defect, what point of strict liability is left? If he could have discovered it but did not, then, assuming it would have been reasonable for him to take steps to remedy it (which, with a potentially lethal drug as most of them are, would surely be the case), he would be negligent under the common law. All one can really say has been achieved for the patient by this complex legislation is that the burden of proof has shifted to the defendants to show that they were not 'negligent', i.e. they could not have been expected to know that the product was unsafe. That is not a negligible advantage to the plaintiff, but it is a far cry from strict liability without proof of fault.

In fact the defence that is given as an option in the EC Directive is not as wide as the formulation of the Act: the defendant is excused according to the Directive (Art.7(e)) if he proves 'that the state of scientific and technical knowledge at the time when he put the product into circulation was not such as to enable the existence of the defect to be discovered' – in other words there is no limitation, as to persons who could have discovered the defect, to producers of products of the same description. The United Kingdom is likely to find itself before the European Court for this transgression. Of the seven states that have legislated so far to embody the Directive into municipal law only Luxembourg has opted not to incorporate the development risks defence.

Limitation: an injured person has a three-year limitation period within which to issue his writ, on much the same principles as those that apply to a 'normal' action for personal injuries (see Chapter 28), subject however to an overall limitation period of ten years from the date of the relevant supplying.

The Act can usefully be invoked in the context of an otherwise routine medical negligence action where an instrument breaks during a procedure. It is usually impossible to show that the instrument was handled incompetently or that the hospital failed to inspect or maintain; so recourse may be had to the manufacturer or importer and the burden of disproof is on them.

NHS Circular

The DHSS produced a Circular (actually a Health Notice – see p. 43 for the distinction), HN(88)3, HN(FP)(88)5, which deals with the implications of this legislation for the NHS. First, hospitals are advised that a health authority may be liable as the supplier of a defective product to a patient unless either the producer or the authority's supplier can be identified. So records should clearly show from whom and when a product was obtained and to whom and when it was supplied, including any serial or batch number, the date of its issue to wards, clinics, etc., and it should be noted that all due warnings and instructions about use were passed on. Secondly, it is stated that the health authority may be liable as a keeper for damage from defective products that it uses, if its supplier or the producer show that the equipment has not been maintained, calibrated or used in accordance with the instructions. This is an added reason for keeping full records of such maintenance. Thirdly, the NHS may also be liable as a producer, e.g. of medicines, appliances, dressings, blood products, products from hospital pharmacies. So as well as taking great care in the manufacture the advice is to keep records which demonstrate conformity with proper standards.

The basic rule is to maintain clear, accurate and comprehensive records relating to the procurement, use, modification and supply of products, to be kept at least until the end of the ten-year period of limitation.

VACCINE DAMAGE PAYMENTS ACT 1979

This Act provides for a lump sum payment of £10,000 (increased in July 1985 to £20,000) to be paid, regardless of fault, to any person who has suffered severe (80%) disablement as a result of one of the specified vaccinations administered after July 1948. The claimant must have been vaccinated when under 18 years of age, except in the case of rubella or poliomyelitis. The Act was passed as a result of anxiety arising in the early 1970s over the possibility that the whooping cough vaccine, which, along with other vaccines, was being strongly urged on the populace by the Government, could cause brain damage. The Act is, however, of minor significance in the context of medical negligence and the no-fault compensation debate. The area in which it is operative is highly specialised and the compensation provided for a severely disabled person is minimal. It is really only a sop to those who may have been injured through following the Government's advice to be vaccinated, or, more usually, to their parents.

Causation has to be proved on the balance of probabilities to the satisfaction of the tribunal. It does not appear that the tribunal were particularly slow to find a nexus between the vaccination and the injury if the case appeared an appropriate one for compensation. However, the situation may well have suffered a sea-change in the light of the decision in *Loveday* v. *Renton* [1989] 1 Med LR 117, a common law action where the plaintiff sought, as a preliminary point, to establish that the whooping cough vaccine could cause brain damage. Stuart Smith J. found after a long and complex trial that it had not been established that the whooping cough vaccine was capable of causing permanent brain damage in young children. He said that all four of the suggested mechanisms for the nexus between the vaccine and the damage were improbable. He also added, *obiter*, that even if that nexus had been established the plaintiff would surely find it impossible to show that the GP had been negligent in vaccinating.

That same judge had already held in *Department of Health and Social Security* v. *Kinnear* (1984) 134 NLJ 886, that no action could be maintained against the Department for adopting in good faith a policy of whooping cough immunisation pursuant to the provisions of s.26 of the National Health Service Act 1946 (the legislation then in force).[1]

The child Loveday had also pursued compensation through the Vaccine Damage Tribunal in a long series of hearings: the tribunal and the appeal tribunal did not accept the nexus between injury and vaccination; the High Court ordered a rehearing before a different tribunal on the ground that the tribunals had not given proper thought to the matter. The new tribunal also refused an award. The High Court quashed that decision for certain procedural and evidential irregularities, but both it, and on appeal the Court of Appeal, refused to direct that the tribunal find the nexus established (*R.* v. *Vaccine Damage Tribunal, ex parte Loveday* [1985] 2 *The Lancet* 1137).

In *Bonthrone* v. *Millan* [1985] 2 *The Lancet* 1137, Scottish Court of Session, an action for negligence by a child against doctor and health visitor for administering the second dose of the pertussis vaccine despite an adverse reaction from the first, Lord Jauncey, dismissing the claim, said that, despite an earlier finding by a tribunal that injury had been caused to the pursuer by the second dose, there was no proved causal link between the injury and the vaccine (cf. *Bonthrone* v. *Secretary of State for Scotland* 1987 SLT 34).

Compare *Best* v. *Wellcome Foundation Ltd* [1994] 5 Med LR 81 where the Supreme Court of Ireland endorsed the judge's findings that there was at the relevant time a possibility, known to the defendants, that the pertussis component in the vaccine could in rare cases cause encephalopathy, that the tests carried out by the defendants in regard to the batch from which the injection in

---

[1] It is worth noting at this point that in fact Stuart Smith J. did not strike out the claims insofar as they alleged the giving by the DHSS of negligent and misleading advice to local health authorities regarding the circumstances in which such inoculation should be performed and the factors to be applied in determining whether a given individual should or should not be inoculated. The *Kinnear* decision was followed in part in the Scottish Court of Session in *Ross* v. *Secretary of State for Scotland* [1990] 1 Med LR 235, where a pursuer's direct case against the Scottish Home and Health Department alleging that she suffered brain damage as a result of being vaccinated against smallpox was dismissed because it was based on considerations of ministerial policy and matters of discretion and was, therefore, irrelevant in the absence of averments of bad faith. The *Kinnear* decision was distinguished in part in that the judge, Lord Milligan, said that that part of the *Kinnear* claim that was permitted to proceed appeared to be of an 'operational' nature and so not of assistance in his case. A similar decision on the main issue had been reached by Lord Grieve in the Scottish case of *Bonthrone* v. *Secretary of State for Scotland* 1987 SLT 34, where the pursuer's claim for injury allegedly sustained as a result of vaccination against whooping cough, diphtheria and tetanus without there having been given adequate warning of the risk of encephalopathy or other side effects had been struck out as attacking the ambit of exercise of a discretion rather than action taken to implement a discretionary decision.

question came were inadequate, and that they were therefore negligent in releasing the batch; but the Supreme Court also held that the judge's reason for rejecting the claim, namely that the evidence suggested that the plaintiff's first convulsion was not sufficiently proximate to the injection, was untenable. Therefore the plaintiff succeeded and a new trial on damages was ordered. It is understood that the action was later settled for a sum in the area of £2.75m. Those who have the UK conduct of the group litigation have recently secured a fresh grant of legal aid for further investigation on the ground of new evidence discovered.

NO-FAULT COMPENSATION

From time to time these days there are calls for the introduction of a no-fault system of compensation for those who are injured by medical accidents.[2]

A no-fault scheme would relieve doctors considerably, and advantage the patient from the strictly legal point of view that he would not have to prove that he received negligent care; but he would still have the difficult task of proving causation, a task growing daily more difficult in one particular and very important area of medical care (obstetrics), with the concerted efforts of certain parts of the medical profession to convince us that most cases of cerebral palsy at birth and other neurological injury are not due to perinatal injury but to congenital causes or events earlier in the pregnancy.

One riposte to the clamour for a no-fault scheme that is often stressed, for example, by Action for Victims of Medical Accidents, who would be the first to support any measure that promised to help injured patients and not merely bring comfort to doctors, is that the principle of accountability is being overlooked, and that there would be less incentive to maintain, let alone raise, standards if the question of fault was no longer to be investigated (AVMA advocate the creation of a Medical Inspectorate to monitor standards in the medical profession). One has also to be aware that the patient will often be more interested in publicising the failure of care and getting an admission of liability from the hospital than in obtaining financial compensation. One so often hears the patient say that her main purpose in bringing an action is to try to ensure that the same thing does not happen to any other patient.

---

[2] In October 1988 the Florida legislature introduced a scheme of no-fault compensation for 'birth-related neurological injury', the stated objective being that the obstetricians 'whom Florida so desperately needs' should return to the deserted delivery rooms. Virginia has a similar scheme in operation, but claims have been slow to be made.

And there are other considerations, I suggest, which need careful thought and investigation before one concludes that no-fault compensation would be a solution to the problems posed by the slow, anxious, uncertain and, as some would have it, unfair English litigious process.

It does seem to be assumed by those who call for a no-fault system that it would provide a simple and satisfactory solution to the perceived inadequacies and inequalities of the present fault-based tort system; any patient whose operation was not a total success, any child born handicapped, would receive substantial compensation (though it is not made clear where the money would come from). Reference is continually being made to the two no-fault systems of New Zealand and Sweden, as if what suits a sparsely populated, predominantly rural community where the pioneering spirit is still alive or a highly developed socialist state with a wide range of welfare benefits from cradle to grave would necessarily be appropriate here. This is wishful thinking, born, no doubt, of a genuine compassion for the innocent victims of misfortune and an understandable revulsion at the often titanic struggle that is involved in obtaining compensation under the present system. The first emotion makes us consider the rationale for compensating our fellow citizens for misfortunes that befall them, the second the procedure for so doing. It seems to be often overlooked that the first point is prior to the second, and needs to be clarified first.

The philosophy of compensation

It may be that the fault-based system is a hangover from the Victorian ideals of self-help and has no place in a modern welfare state, but it is not philosophically, even if it is politically, indefensible. A citizen has a right to expect that his fellows will conduct themselves with reasonable care in their dealings with him, and if they do not, and so cause him injury, then, given a breach of the duty of reasonable care, they will have to make good all his loss, insofar as that can be made good by money. But if he suffers one of the multifarious misfortunes that the vicissitudes of life are ever dealing us he has no right to demand that his fellows compensate him for that. He can always arrange his own insurance against such events.

That philosophy has perhaps a superficial attraction, if only for clarity and concision, but it takes no account of the theme of group endeavour which is the well-spring of the welfare state. One has to ask in what circumstances, as well as to what extent, should a citizen be compensated by his fellows for a misfortune, regardless of fault. Where he is injured giving his labour to the common weal there is clearly a case for compensation (hence industrial injury compensation). So, too, where he is injured acting on government recommendations or orders (hence the Vaccine Damage Payments Act 1979 and disability pensions for the armed forces). If he is willing to work but the state cannot find him work, or he would be working but for illness, his fellow citizens owe him a bare living. Examples can be multiplied.

The Pearson Commission suggested that no-fault compensation for motor accidents should be introduced (for the drunken or reckless driver, too?). This could be done without too much difficulty as the definition of injury through a motor accident is unlikely to give rise to much argument. But to what extent is it appropriate that medical misfortunes should be singled out as an area for compensation beyond the benefits that the welfare state already provides to ill or disabled citizens? Is it simply a practical suggestion because under the present tort-based system it is a particularly laborious and lengthy business to prove negligence against the medical profession, as well as unpleasant for all parties and hardly conducive to promoting good doctor/patient relations? Surely there is nothing particularly deserving of no-fault compensation in the medical misfortune, as opposed, say, to the misfortune of being struck by a falling branch or a tile dislodged unforeseeably by a high wind, or indeed the simple but all too common misfortune of an illness.

I maintain that a decision to permit no-fault recovery for medical misfortunes only has no philosophical justification and can only be defended on the basis that practical considerations demand it and society is ready to accept it. To be sure, one can wax indignant that the parents of a handicapped child may recover half a million pounds if they can prove, against all the odds, that some medical slip or other was made at or around the time of birth, whereas, if they cannot prove that then after years of hassle and heartache they will get nothing. But what if the handicap was congenital and not due to medical handling? Why should those parents not be similarly compensated? Why should the woman who has a heart attack under anesthesia receive a compensation and not the woman who has a heart attack walking down the road? I do not pretend to have a neat answer to these questions; I only ask that people think about this prior issue of the justification for a no-fault scheme in the medical context before proposing one.

The parameters of a no-fault scheme

It is not possible to decide what are the parameters for awarding compensation without at the same time being clear about what compensation you propose to award. We will assume agreement here that we are not trying to cover all injuries through accident, as in New Zealand, but only medical and drug-induced ones, as in Sweden.

It seems to be agreed that where the patient's condition is due to the progress of his disease, i.e. where medical intervention or omission did not contribute to it, there is no case for compensation, for that would be tantamount to compensating a person for becoming ill. That is the case in Sweden, where compensation is paid for injury or illness resulting from any procedure related to health care, and in New Zealand where 'accident' includes medical and surgical misadventure, although it was hoped originally to include compensation for illness *simpliciter*. So the amount of compensation is inextricably linked with the incidence of compensation.

But it is not necessarily every medical misfortune that falls to be compensated. What if the 'accident' was a recognised risk of the operation? The Swedish system does not cover misfortunes which were within the area of foreseeable risk of a medically justified act, though this is as much an 'accident' as an unforeseeable complication. It must be extremely difficult to show that an injury or adverse condition was not the natural progression of a disease or injury and also was not a foreseeable risk or side effect of treatment, but was in fact both the result of the treatment and a result that was not within the area of foreseeable risk. I would have thought that most medical 'accidents' came within the area of foreseeable risk, for there are always a number of risks attendant upon any medical intervention. In the case of drugs it may well be easier to show that the condition complained of was not a foreseeable consequence of taking the drug, as their capacity to injure is far-reaching and usually unknown, but it is likely to be difficult to prove that the drug caused the injury.

So we have got as far now as asking the advocates of a no-fault medical scheme to justify its introduction and define its intended scope. Now we ask them what sort of compensation they have in mind.

The amount of compensation

What will be paid to the victim of a medical accident? It is not presumably suggested that a high earner who comes out of a properly conducted operation unable to resume work because something went accidentally wrong should be paid what he would get in the tort scheme, say £50,000 times a multiplier of 15 equals £750,000, plus, say, a quarter of a million and more for private health care for the rest of his life, etc. Clearly the money is not available for this level of compensation. So it needs to be clearly understood that compensation under a no-fault scheme, however useful it may be to patients who cannot prove fault, would be very different from what it is under the tort-based system. It will probably involve a range of periodic payments, which top up or extend existing available welfare benefits (as in Sweden). Those who see the parents of handicapped children being awarded without proof of fault the sort of compensation that they would get if they proved fault are simply deluding themselves. And if that be so, one can see that a patient who is able to prove fault is not going to be satisfied with the no-fault level of compensation. Therefore the tort system should remain as an alternative, which only serves to emphasise my point that the no-fault scheme will do no more than extend the range of available welfare or similar benefits as and where need arises. (I find the treatment of this issue by the Pearson Commission somewhat disingenuous, as they seem to think that welfare benefits provide a more or less satisfactory scheme and level of compensation, a view which few who enjoy them would, I believe, endorse.)

But how extensive any increased benefits should be is unclear. For example, a handicapped child is likely already to receive all sorts of appropriate care and support in the field of therapy and education, as well as help at home for aids and equipment.[3] It is most unlikely that a 'no-fault' tribunal will be awarding thousands of pounds to the mother for nursing care or paying for the latest in electronic communication aids or trips to foreign remedial institutes, all of which are, if not standard, at any rate common items in tort-based awards. Advocates of these no-fault schemes need to be very clear about the sort of compensation that they envisage being paid, before they ask us to pay it. There are other possible solutions to some if not all of the unsatisfactory aspects of the present system, such as contingency fees, or a scheme of insurance against medical accidents, and these possibilities need to be taken into account in the general discussion.

Proposed legislation

The Labour Party produced a draft of a Compensation for Medical Injury Bill, creating a Compensation for Medical Injury

---

[3] This statement may be rather optimistic in the present climate of cutbacks.

Scheme, to be supervised by a Medical Injury Compensation Board: this would have provided unspecified compensation for medical injury that had caused death, more than ten days in-patient treatment or more than 28 days off work, but it excluded injury caused by a number of specified factors including reasonable diagnostic error, unavoidable complications of a proper procedure and the use of a drug in accordance with the manufacturer's instructions; so its ambit was substantially limited.

A second effort, called the NHS (Compensation) Bill, was refused a second reading by 193 votes to 81 in February 1991. It had been proposed by Mrs Rosie Barnes, MP. The drafting was inept but the ideas were interesting. The Board would assess compensation for NHS patients who suffered injuries due to 'mishap' during NHS care. 'Mishap', however, was nowhere defined save to say that it included but was not restricted to any act or omission which gave rise to an action at common law or for breach of statutory duty, and excluded any foreseeable or reasonable result of the medical care or the patient's pre-existing condition. It is not easy to know what was meant by a 'reasonable result', but presumably one should run the two epithets together and read 'reasonably foreseeable result'. The mishap would have to be such as to result in death, in-patient treatment for at least ten days, inability to engage in normal activities for at least 28 days, or significant pain, disability, harm, distress, or loss of amenity, or a reduction in life expectancy.[4]

New Zealand and Sweden

The New Zealand scheme covers all 'accidents'. An accident has to be unexpected and not to result from self-inflicted injury. Excluded is injury from disease, infection and the aging process, or such as occurs as a result of the normal and expected risks associated with medical treatment, or, be it noted, as a result of an omission to treat. Various reforms to the scheme have been proposed (partly because the scheme has run into financial difficulties), among them abolishing any award for pain, suffering and loss of amenity, so that the claimant would receive only periodic welfare payments.

Under the two Swedish schemes on the other hand, that for medical accidents and that for drug-related injury, 70% of the

---

[4] An interesting examination of the viability of a no-fault scheme has been published by the King's Fund Institute, under the title *Medical Negligence, compensation and accountability*.

compensation paid is for pain, suffering and loss of amenity. This is because the ordinary welfare benefits provisions are so extensive that the need for further payments is small. The schemes cover avoidable injury from medical intervention and diagnostic procedures, unavoidable injury from diagnostic procedures where the condition of the patient was not serious, injury from negligent diagnosis or due to faulty diagnostic equipment, accidental injury relating to the care received such as would not have happened in the patient's home (e.g. falling out of bed, slipping on the hospital floor), and injury from infection contracted during medical care provided the infection is not expected and unavoidable.

Arbitration

Some time ago, the Government unenthusiastically proposed an arbitration scheme for settling medical negligence claims, whereby written evidence and submissions would be adjudicated on by a tribunal without the parties being present. I cannot imagine any patient being satisfied with that system and it is unlikely to assume any significance. This half-hearted proposal seems to have been prompted by political considerations, by way of promised response to Labour's Bills.

The present position

Currently no-fault is staging something of a comeback, not because the well-recognised deficiencies of such a system have been overcome, but because the Government believes that, provided that it goes on to impose a ridiculously low ceiling on awards, as it has been trying to do recently for criminal injuries, the system will cost less than the current charge to legal aid and the NHS.[5]

---

[5] See also p. 462.

31 · Group litigation

SUMMARY

Group litigation, arising usually out of a disaster, is here to stay. New procedures are at last being devised by the judges, on an as yet ad hoc basis, to facilitate the process of litigation.[1]

Introduction

Group litigation, class action, representative action, multi-party litigation, disaster litigation – call it what you will, it is here to stay. There have been disasters before, but as with so much of the law, changes only occur when the mass consciousness of society is ready for them. Awareness of the possibilities of large-scale litigation following an event that has adversely affected a large number of people has increased in recent years. Whether disasters have themselves been more frequent in that period is a moot point – I doubt it (though events such as the aeroplane disasters of Lockerbie and the M1, the Hillsborough stadium disaster, the King's Cross underground fire, the Lewisham and Clapham train crashes, the Piper Alpha oil rig disaster, the Zeebrugge ferry accident, Opren, Myodil, the benzodiazepines, HIV-infected blood transfusions, the possibility of pertussis and other vaccine damage, *et al.*, give one pause for thought). The basic reason for the increase in mass litigation, I suggest, is not, or at any rate not simply, an increase in disasters, but the fact that the awareness of the possibility of litigation has developed. Also, in pharmaceutical cases, the recognition of the possibility of a connection between a certain drug and a widely appearing complaint arises more readily now, largely because the pernicious effect of most modern drugs is increasingly understood by the public; and the investigation of such connection and the possibility of negligence in putting the drug on the market, whether at all or without proper warnings, is more readily and more efficiently undertaken by increasingly experienced lawyers and para-legal workers. There was, of course, the thalidomide tragedy some

---

[1] The best current exposition of group litigation can be found in *The Journal of Personal Injury Litigation* [1994] p. 276 (by Mark Mildred). Reference can also be made to Powers and Harris, *Medical Negligence* (2nd edition) Chapter 14.

years ago; but, although that certainly served as a seminal event in the development of mass litigation, it took the intervening period to increase people's (and judges') awareness to the point where, now, there is a clear recognition of the need to develop both the court and the legal aid procedures to provide a suitable framework for handling group litigation.[2] Very little has as yet been done, and what has been done has been achieved by the persistent efforts of a small number of solicitors who have valiantly fought to process these mass claims as best they can and to convince the judiciary of the need for new rules. The creation of an official framework for group litigation is going to be one of the most important legal developments of the next few years.

Recognition by the judiciary

In the Myodil case of *Chrzanowska* v. *Glaxo Laboratories* [1990] 1 Med LR 385 (where the plaintiff claimed damages for an inflammation of the protective membranes of the spine – arachnoiditis – said to have been caused by a myelogram using the injected dye Myodil), Steyn J. said that the problem of the procedures to be adopted in group litigation under the English system of civil litigation should be investigated and it would be desirable that an outline procedure should be prescribed. If the courts did not have the power to devise new procedures to deal with such cases the system would break down. Our system of civil justice, said Steyn J., ought for the benefit of parties involved in civil litigation to prescribe at least in outline the procedures to be adopted. He said the 1990s might well witness an increase in group litigation (the judge had in mind as an important step the assigning of a particular judge to deal from an early stage with all the individual cases arising in any group litigation, as has been done in the past in complex litigation).

In the industrial deafness claim of *Horrocks* v. *Ford Motor Co.*, *The Times*, 15 February 1990, the Master of the Rolls had already said that the courts were entitled to devise new procedures for group litigation.

---

[2] From the short history of class litigation against pharmaceutical manufacturers we may note that the thalidomide litigation involved only the issue of negligence, not of causation, and had little recourse to the courts; the Eraldin litigation was avoided by a voluntary settlement scheme by ICI; the Primodos litigation was abandoned in 1982 as it was feared that causation could never be established; the Debendox litigation continues; in the Opren litigation almost all of the 1,500 claimants accepted the scheme of settlement offered in February 1988. The benzodiazepine litigation appears to have collapsed (see below).

In *Chapman* v. *Chief Constable of South Yorkshire, The Times*, 20 March 1990 (a Hillsborough stadium disaster claim), Steyn J. said that where a case involved multi-party litigation the 'sporting theory of justice' had no place. In such cases in the public interest the concept of a party being in control of the litigation ought, as far as possible, to be subordinated to case management techniques controlled by the court. This is the clearest statement yet of the desire, and presumably the intention, of the judiciary to adopt a radically new approach to the litigious process in the interests of group litigants.

RSC[3]

The only recognition of a class action in English rules of procedure is found in RSC O.15 r.12, i.e. representative proceedings. That would need radical development and restructuring if it were to serve for a modern group action (its most obvious deficiency being that it cannot accommodate a number of plaintiffs who would be entitled to differing amounts of damages on differing facts for differing injuries sustained in differing ways).

Handling group litigation

The solicitor who is willing to handle disaster litigation will need a whole office set aside for that purpose, with up-to-date equipment and specially recruited staff (one firm handling the Myodil litigation had already taken on a team of eight (ex-) nurses by the summer of 1989 to study the individual case records). He may also recruit a scientific co-ordinator to study the vast mass of documents that will be disclosed by the defendants (certainly in pharmaceutical cases, and possibly in others too) – see the section on the scientific co-ordinator in Chapter 7.

Two useful procedures are the test case, or preliminary issue, and the lead case, with co-ordinated arrangements (they are not mutually exclusive).

It was originally intended that *DHSS* v. *Kinnear, The Times*, 7 July 1984, be the test case on causation in the pertussis vaccine litigation (the point being whether the vaccine was capable of causing brain damage), but after a month of evidence an afternoon arrived when the only witness available to be called was the child's mother as no expert witness was in court at that time, and her evidence about her child's condition convinced her advisers that the case was no longer arguable. So it collapsed. The 'test'

---

[3] Rules of the Supreme Court, of course, not the Royal Shakespeare Company.

point had to be re-tried by special arrangement of the judge, Stuart Smith J., as a preliminary issue proper, so there would be no possibility of the 'individual' facts being ventilated. This was achieved by the case of *Loveday* v. *Renton* [1990] 1 Med LR 117, in which Stuart Smith J. held after a long and complex trial lasting 63 days that the plaintiff had not established that the vaccine was capable of causing brain damage (see p. 440). Clearly the test case is of only limited scope, for not many group actions will usefully admit of a single point, or a number of points, common to all the claimants, being decided first so as (probably) to bind all of them.

However, the experience of the benzodiazepine litigation, in which thousands of individual cases were processed at great expense before it became clear how many obstacles there were to proving causation and how few of the cases could successfully surmount them, suggests the need for some sort of preliminary hearings before costs escalate.

A plaintiff who seeks to proceed on his own case after a negative decision on a test case or a sample of cases runs the risk of having his action struck out as an abuse of the process of the court: see the industrial relations case of *Ashmore* v. *British Coal Corporation* [1990] 2 QB 238, and the reference therein by Stuart Smith J. at p. 1445 to his unreported decision in *Godfrey* v. *DHSS* (25 July 1988) where he struck out an action by a whooping cough vaccine claimant who sought to proceed despite the negative finding on causation reached in the *Loveday* case.

This is a new application of the rule of *res judicata*, but, if it be not right, it makes the decision in a test case of little effect, even nugatory. The situation would presumably be different if, as was not, according to the judge, the case in *Godfrey*, the claimant was able to show that he had collated reliable new evidence on the issue. Also, this situation should be distinguished from that where a mass settlement is negotiated with, say, a pharmaceutical company, and a claimant does not want to accept it: there is no power to force him so to do, at present – although the court always has an inherent power to strike out a claim for abuse of its process there is nothing to suggest that it would consider itself to be acting properly in striking out a claim for such a reason.

The benzodiazepine litigation

The ill-fated benzodiazepine litigation has shown the problems on causation (i.e. quite apart from proving generic negligence on the part of the manufacturers) that arise in any individual case. A plaintiff in a group pharmaceutical or similar action will normally have to prove:

(1) He took the drug over a certain period. This is usually ascertainable from the GP records.

(2) He suffered injury from the drug. This requires that the expert identify adverse effects suffered as caused by the drug or its withdrawal, and not by any other drugs that were being taken at the same time or by the progress of any underlying condition. If it is contentious as to what adverse effects the drug is capable of producing or how long those effects can continue, this will have to be researched and proved (by the generic team).

(3) He was worse off on the drug than off it. It is not clear whether it is sufficient for a claim to show merely that the patient suffered injury from the drug regardless of whether he would have been worse without it, albeit in a different way. Logic, and common sense, suggest that it is necessary to show that, overall, he suffered more on it than he would have off it.

(4) The manufacturers were in breach of their duty of care to him in marketing the drug at all, or, at least, in failing to give adequate warning of its dangers, such as physical or psychological dependence, or in failing to inform of its limited efficacy (in time or in effect). This is the big issue that takes the generic team and the para-legal workers volumes of research to establish.

(5) If such warning had been given, the plaintiff would not have been put on the drug, or at any rate only for so short and well-monitored a period that most of his injury would not have been sustained. This may be hard to establish if the relevant prescriber is unwilling or unable to confirm it.

(6) There was an alternative method of treatment (which includes no treatment at all – many of the patients who were almost automatically prescribed the minor tranquillisers would have been better off with a bit of counselling).

It was not for inability to prove negligence on the part of the pharmaceutical companies that this litigation failed, but because of the well-nigh insuperable obstacles to proving causation in most cases. The claim in respect of Valium, for example, failed very largely because the allegation was limited to the contention that warnings should have been given in 1973 of the dangers of addiction, but by then most of the claimants were already addicted. So what would have been the effect of warnings at that time? Could one really show that the patient would have been withdrawn from the drug? If so, there would have been a withdrawal syndrome in any event. And could one show that the patient would have been better off being withdrawn? It could be argued that he would then have coped better with the underlying pathology in one way or another, but could one hope to prove that?

This litigation has also provided a number of examples of the extensive authority allowed to the judge in charge of a group litigation.

In *A.B.* v. *John Wyeth & Brother Ltd* [1993] 4 Med LR 1 the Court of Appeal refused to interfere with the imposition by the judge of cut-off dates after which no further claims would be allowed to join the litigation even though this meant that most of the Halcion claimants would, through no fault of their own, be out of time. Steyn L.J. said:

. . . in my view the Court of Appeal ought to be particularly reluctant in group actions to interfere with a trial judge's procedural directions. The judge invariably has a much better perspective of the interests of all the parties and of the needs of efficient case management than the Court of Appeal can ever achieve. Moreover interference by the Court of Appeal with the trial judge's directions on one aspect will often upset the coherence of the entire structure of the litigation. In my judgment such appeals ought to be discouraged.

It is of note that the Lord Justice did not make clear whether this discouragement should extend to proposed appeals against unfair rulings.

In *Nur* v. *John Wyeth & Brother Ltd* [1994] PIQR 72 the judge had refused to permit after a cut-off date at the end of August 1992 any amendment of the medical report served with the pleading. Amendment had sought to be made in many cases in order to comply with the judge's earlier ruling of May 1992 whereby he required the medical report to specifically identify and substantiate all the symptoms pleaded by way of injury in the schedule of injury attached to the statement of claim. The Court of Appeal would not even grant leave to appeal. Rose L.J. said that it was within the discretion of the judge to make such an order, and that the striking out of claims that had not been put in order by the cut-off date was the inevitable concomitant. It is worth remarking that it was this order that effectively ended the litigation, because very few claimants had had the time to get their medical reports into the form that the judge had required. Indeed, no one had anticipated that he would deny a claimant the normal right of amendment merely because the cut-off date had gone by. The result, by design or accident, was that so few cases complied with the judge's requirement by the cut-off date that this expensive litigation became financially non-viable.[4]

---

[4] In *AB* v. *John Wyeth & Brother Ltd* [1994] PIQR 109 the Court of Appeal endorsed the judge's order in striking out claims against prescribers (as opposed to the basic claims

The future

However, enthusiasm (on the part of the lawyers, I mean, not of the judges) for group litigation remains undimmed. For example, actions are under way in respect of Debendox, Myodil, human insulin, steroids, anti-epileptic medication and not a few other drugs, not forgetting the potentially vastest of all group actions, the claim against the tobacco manufacturers for not warning of the dangers of smoking.

One has to wonder whether this new-found industry is a good thing (other than for the lawyers who specialise in it). The actions are mind-bogglingly expensive and extremely hard to win, and the compensation for each individual claimant is usually disappointingly modest. Although the practices of the pharmaceutical and other medical products companies are no doubt occasionally questionable and it is not hard, if one is so inclined, to depict them as callous commercial monsters, the fact remains that society is asking for drugs for all sorts of conditions and purposes, and in many respects we would be worse off without the fruits of these companies' researches (I would be reluctant to undergo even a minor tooth restoration without the assistance of one of their products). It must be understood, and accepted, that every drug has possible adverse effects, and it is usually not possible before marketing the product to ascertain the full range of possible side effects. That would simply take too long and be too expensive. The patient, it has to be said, has the stark choice between taking the risk of the drug or the risk of the pain or disease. This is not to say that the companies should not be accountable if they cut corners or distort or conceal test results, but to drum up a group action every time a drug or any other medical product is found to have side effects is doing no one (except the lawyers) any favours – and by no one I include the patient along with the taxpayer.

---

against the manufacturers of the tranquillisers). The court was obviously concerned at the apparent difficulties plaintiffs would face in establishing both liability and causation, as well as overcoming in the majority of cases a plea of limitation. The court said that in group litigation there was an inherent power to strike out, as vexatious and an abuse of process, claims in which the benefit to the plaintiffs in the event of success was likely to be extremely modest and the costs of the defence astronomical.

EPILOGUE

32 · Epilogue

THE FUTURE FOR MEDICAL NEGLIGENCE LITIGATION

The future of medical negligence litigation currently abounds in uncertainties. The present Government – and therefore all who represent it, including the Lord Chancellor's Department – is committed to cutting public expenditure, giving the impression of having scant regard for the needs of justice where they conflict with that prime objective. Already the Government has truncated the availability of legal aid and is doing its best to castrate the criminal injuries compensation scheme (the civil justice review being carried out by Lord Woolf does not, of course, come within this criticism, as one cannot imagine that judge being swayed by political considerations).

Medical negligence litigation is certainly expensive, principally because the cases are complex. The question of liability for a road traffic accident, for example, will usually raise far less difficult issues than liability for medical treatment. However, some particular causes of the expense can be identified and, one would hope, corrected. It is not a question of curtailing the procedure of investigation and judgment, with the result that uninformed decisions are given on inadequately prepared and presented cases. The traditional procedure for the preparation and presentation of a civil dispute is the best means of arriving at a just decision. What needs to be done is not to discard the procedure but to tighten it up. Let us not throw the baby out with the bath water.

Take three examples. A fair amount of time and money is wasted on fishing for claims, on defending good claims, and, by counsel, on taking every point possible, the bad as well as the good, and at great length.

Solicitors (or some of them) need to understand that they do not have the duty to do all in their power to uncover some sort of claim on behalf of every patient who consults them (nor, one could add, to dream up group actions). They should only begin to investigate if there appears to be a real possibility that the patient has suffered substantive injury as a result of medical mismanagement – and they should be reasonably willing to abandon a claim on receipt of appropriately negative responses from experts, rather than casting around for some other line to hang a case on.

They do not have a roving commission to investigate the whole of the medical history in the hope of latching on to something that could be fashioned into a claim with which, legally aided, they could worry the health authority into paying nuisance money. They should recognise those cases where they should decline to proceed, where the proposed claim is clearly untenable or the patient is simply having a general whinge. Most patients have a pretty clear idea of what their complaint is. There is no call for the solicitor to go beyond the area of complaint unless the indications are compelling. The lawyer should also bear in mind that the test for the propriety of proceeding on legal aid is whether one would advise a private client of moderate means to pursue the case.

As for the defence: the health authority and those acting for it must get their act together earlier. It will not do for them to put in a holding defence and then delay their investigations until a few months before trial. They must decide at an early stage whether the case is defensible and, if not, they must admit liability. They must be astute to recognise if they are being encouraged to defend by one of the small number of professional defence experts who make a living from defending the indefensible. The solicitor needs to exercise judgment and responsibility and not allow such a case to be pushed along to trial. Patients' solicitors almost invariably assess the quality of their experts and their opinions, not simply through fear of a wasted costs order but because they want to present a case that will win in court. It appears that health authority and trust solicitors almost never make such an assessment.

The third suggestion I make is probably impossible to realise, given the nature of the beast. Will counsel ever be willing to exercise an adequate degree of intellectual responsibility, or will they for ever be demonstrating the truth of Swift's aphorism:

Lawyers are a body of men bred from their earliest youth in the art of proving, by words multiplied for the purpose and in a language no other mortal understands, that black is white and white is black, according as they are paid.

If counsel were willing to speak concisely and make only the points that were worth making, cases would last half as long. This surely is what Lord Templeman had in mind when he said in *Ashmore* v. *Corporation of Lloyd's* [1992] 1 WLR 446 that pleadings should define the issues, be brief, chronological and consistent, and that counsel should not advance a multitude of ingenious arguments in the hope that out of ten bad points the judge would be able to fashion a winner. He was expressly critical of the tendency in some cases for legal advisers to make every point, conceivable and inconceivable, without judgment or discrimination.

Since I penned the above, the Practice Direction of January 1995 has appeared ([1995] 1 WLR 262). It provides in no uncertain terms that the court should limit the effusions of counsel, both their submissions and their cross-examinations. This should have the effect, *inter alia*, of avoiding, or rather averting, for example, the situation of a plaintiff claiming for nervous shock being detained in the witness box for five weeks (see *The Times*, 7 February 1995, page 35).

So what does the future hold? As described earlier, no-fault compensation may be staging a comeback. Medical arbitration is in the air. But it has to be understood that everyone has their own angle – government, doctors, arbitrators, patients' representatives. The government wants only to save public money. So it will support no fault as long as it can truncate the quantum of compensation as it has done with the criminal injuries scheme. It will approve cuts in legal aid for obvious reasons. It will support the unattractive conditional fee scheme pursued by the Lord Chancellor, whereby lawyers get an uplift to their fees if they win and nothing if they lose. It is unattractive because no lawyer will be prepared to investigate the difficult cases; lawyers cannot be expected to risk bankruptcy pursuing a case to trial knowing that if they do not win or get some sort of (any!) settlement they will be paid nothing for their work over the years of preparation and the week or so of the trial. Also, under this scheme the patient would still be liable for disbursements and for the defence costs if she loses, quite apart from the fact that the uplift on winning, which could well amount to a lot of money, would come out of her damages. The only perceived advantage appears to be that such a scheme would make no call on public funds.

Other possibilities have been mooted. The government would support a movement towards legal fees insurance (but the policy normally has an inadequate ceiling on costs). The government would support medical arbitration because, although the NHS trusts would still have to pay up if they lost, there would – just as with cases coming before the Criminal Injuries Compensation Board – be no legal aid available for preparation or representation. This, of course, means that the claim of the patient (bound to be far more complex and to cost far more to prepare and present than a CICB case) would not be properly prepared or presented.

Panels

Another interesting development is the Law Society medical negligence panel, and the legal aid board franchise scheme. No one yet knows how significant these two developments will be or how they will interact. Some sort of panel was certainly necessary in view of the number of incompetently processed cases that were continually coming to light. However the fear is that, given the strict criteria for admission to the panel, particularly the experience criteria, few solicitors will qualify, so that the work may become concentrated in the hands of a small élite, and the patient will have little choice of solicitor, particularly if the legal aid board decides to grant legal aid only to solicitors on the panel.

No-fault

A few years ago no-fault was all the rage, a star in the making. It was going to solve all the problems and iniquities of the current system. Patients were going to be compensated handsomely for medical accidents irrespective of fault. Doctors were going to be freed from the impossible pressures of being sued and would thus be free to devote their energies to curing the patient rather than to defensive medicine. Then someone asked where the money was going to come from to compensate all these unfortunates up to a reasonable level, and someone else pointed out that causation was at least as important in medical negligence actions as fault, and that would still have to be litigated. Yet someone else had the temerity to suggest that medical accountability was a good thing and that a system of no-fault would exclude that. Almost imperceptibly the audience for no-fault drifted away and it ended up on the back burner (or – not to mix our metaphors – a mere extra). (See also p. 442.)

However, it now seems to be making a comeback. This is not because the earlier objections have disappeared or been overcome. It is simply because this Government will do anything to save money, and if it can cobble together a system of small payments for unlucky patients this will save the new NHS trusts a lot of money (it may well be true that two or three successful £1.5m cerebral palsy claims could bankrupt a trust – unless they have access to a pool[1] – whereas such claims would not have had that effect upon a NHS-funded health authority). Having failed to get away (as yet) with its drastic reduction of compensation for criminal injuries, one wonders how confident the Government currently feels about creating a similar inadequate system for medical accidents.

---

[1] A pool is currently being set up by a special health authority under the aegis of the Department of Health.

Appendix I

Statutes, Regulations and Rules

Contents:

1. *Damages*

(a) Law Reform (Personal Injuries) Act 1948 (11 & 12 Geo. 6 c. 41)

Section 2. Measure of damages

. . .

(4) In an action for damages for personal injuries (including any such action arising out of a contract), there shall be disregarded, in determining the reasonableness of any expenses, the possibility of avoiding those expenses or part of them by taking advantage of facilities available under the National Health Service Act 1977, or the National Health Service (Scotland) Act 1978, or of any corresponding facilities in Northern Ireland.

Administration of Justice Act 1982 (1982 c. 53):

Abolition of certain claims for damages etc.

Abolition of right to damages for loss of expectation of life

1.–(1) In an action under the law of England and Wales or the law of Northern Ireland for damages for personal injuries –
  (a) no damages shall be recoverable in respect of any loss of expectation of life caused to the injured person by the injuries; but
  (b) if the injured person's expectation of life has been reduced by the injuries, the court, in assessing damages in respect of pain and suffering caused by the injuries, shall take account of any suffering caused or likely to be caused to him by awareness that his expectation of life has been so reduced.

(2) The reference in subsection (1)(a) above to damages in respect of loss of expectation of life does not include damages in respect of loss of income.

Abolition of actions for loss of services, etc.

2. No person shall be liable in tort under the law of England and Wales or the law of Northern Ireland –
  (a) to a husband on the ground only of his having deprived him of the services or society of his wife;
  (b) to a parent (or person standing in the place of a parent) on the ground only of his having deprived him of the services of a child; or
  (c) on the ground only –
    (i) of having deprived another of the services of his menial servant;
    (ii) of having deprived another of the services of his female servant by raping or seducing her; or
    (iii) of enticement of a servant or harbouring a servant.

Fatal Accidents Act 1976

3.–(1) The following sections shall be substituted for sections 1 to 4 of the Fatal Accidents Act 1976 –

. . .

Bereavement

1A.–(1) An action under this Act may consist of or include a claim for damages for bereavement.

(2) A claim for damages for bereavement shall only be for the benefit –
    (a) of the wife or husband of the deceased; and
    (b) where the deceased was a minor who was never married –
        (i) of his parents, if he was legitimate; and
        (ii) of his mother, if he was illegitimate.

(3) Subject to subsection (5) below, the sum to be awarded as damages under this section shall be £3,500. **[£7,500 for deaths from April 1991]**

(4) Where there is a claim for damages under this section for the benefit of both the parents of the deceased the sum awarded shall be divided equally between them (subject to any deduction falling to be made in respect of costs not recovered from the defendant).

(5) The Lord Chancellor may by order made by statutory instrument, subject to annulment in pursuance of a resolution of either House of Parliament, amend this section by varying the sum for the time being specified in subsection (3) above.

Claims not surviving death

Exclusion of Law Reform (Miscellaneous Provisions) Act 1934

4.–(1) The following subsection shall be inserted after section 1(1) of the Law Reform (Miscellaneous Provisions) Act 1934 (actions to survive death) –

"(1A) The right of a person to claim under section 1A of the Fatal Accidents Act 1976 (bereavement) shall not survive for the benefit of his estate on his death.".

(2) The following paragraph shall be substituted for subsection (2)(a) –
"(a) shall not include –
    (i) any exemplary damages;
    (ii) any damages for loss of income in respect of any period after that person's death;".

Maintenance at public expense to be taken into account in assessment of damages

5. In an action under the law of England and Wales or the law of Northern Ireland for damages for personal injuries (including any such action arising out of a contract) any saving to the injured person which is attributable to his maintenance wholly or partly at public expense in a hospital, nursing home or other institution shall be set off against any income lost by him as a result of his injuries.

(b) Supreme Court Act 1981 (1981 c. 54)

Powers

Orders for interim payment

32.–(1) As regards proceedings pending in the High Court, provision may be made by rules of court for enabling the court, in such circumstances as may be prescribed, to make an order requiring a party to the proceedings to make an interim payment of such amount as may be specified in the order, with provision for the payment to be made to such other party to the proceedings as may be specified or, if the order so provides, by paying it into court.

(2) Any rules of court which make provision in accordance with subsection (1) may include provision for enabling a party to any proceedings who, in pursuance of such an order, has made an interim payment to recover the whole or part of the amount of the payment in such circumstances, and from such other party to the proceedings, as may be determined in accordance with the rules.

(3) Any rules made by virtue of this section may include such incidental, supplementary and consequential provisions as the rule-making authority may consider necessary or expedient.

(4) Nothing in this section shall be construed as affecting the exercise of any power relating to costs, including any power to make rules of court relating to costs.

(5) In this section "interim payment", in relation to a party to any proceedings, means a payment on account of any damages, debt or other sum (excluding any costs) which that party may be held liable to pay to or for the benefit of another party to the proceedings if a final judgment or order of the court in the proceedings is given or made in favour of that other party.

(c) Administration of Justice Act 1982 (1982 c. 53)

Award of provisional damages for personal injuries

6.–(1) The following section shall be inserted after section 32 of the Supreme Court Act 1981 –

> **"Orders for provisional damages for person injuries**
> **32A.**–(1) This section applies to an action for damages for personal injuries in which there is proved or admitted to be a chance that at some definite or indefinite time in the future the injured person will, as a result of the act or omission which gave rise to the cause of action, develop some serious disease or suffer some serious deterioration in his physical or mental condition.
>
> (2) Subject to subsection (4) below, as regards any action for damages to which this section applies in which a judgment is given in the High Court, provision may be made by rules of court enabling the court, in such circumstances as may be prescribed, to award the injured person –
>> (a) damages assessed on the assumption that the injured person will not develop the disease or suffer the deterioration in his condition; and
>> (b) further damages at a future date if he develops the disease or suffers the deterioration.
>
> (3) Any rules made by virtue of this section may include such incidental, supplementary and consequential provisions as the rule-making authority may consider necessary or expedient.
>
> (4) Nothing in this section shall be construed –
>> (a) as affecting the exercise of any power relating to costs, including any power to make rules of court relating to costs; or
>> (b) as prejudicing any duty of the court under any enactment or rule of law to reduce or limit the total damages which would have been recoverable apart from any such duty."

(2) In section 35 of that Act (supplementary) "32A" shall be inserted before "33" in subsection (5).

(3) The section inserted as section 32A of the Supreme Court Act 1981 by subsection (1) above shall have effect in relation to county courts as it has effect in relation to the High Court, as if references in it to rules of court included references to county court rules.

(d) Administration of Justice Act 1982 (1982 c. 53)

PART III

POWERS OF COURTS TO AWARD INTEREST

Interest on debts and damages

15.–(1) The section set out in Part I of Schedule 1 to this Act shall be inserted after section 35 of the Supreme Court Act 1981.

(2) [Repealed by County Courts Act 1984, section 148, Schedule 4].

(3) The Crown Proceedings Act 1947 shall accordingly have effect subject to the amendment in Part III of that Schedule, being an amendment consequential on subsections (1) and (2) above.

(4) The provisions mentioned in subsection (5) below (which this section supersedes so far as they apply to the High Court and county courts) shall cease to have effect in relation to those courts.

(5) The provisions are –

    (a) section 3 of the Law Reform (Miscellaneous Provisions) Act 1934; and

    (b) in the Administration of Justice Act 1969 –

        (i) section 22; and

        (ii) in section 34(3) the words from "and section 22" onwards.

(6) The section set out in Part IV of Schedule 1 to this Act shall be inserted after section 19 of the Arbitration Act 1950.

Section 15.   SCHEDULE 1

INTEREST ON DEBTS AND DAMAGES

PART I

SECTION INSERTED IN SUPREME COURT ACT 1981

Power of High Court to award interest on debts and damages

35A.–(1) Subject to rules of court, in proceedings (whenever instituted) before the High Court for the recovery of a debt or damages there may be included in any sum for which judgment is given simple interest, at such rate as the court thinks fit or as rules of court may provide, on all or any part of the debt or damages in respect of which judgment is given, or payment is made before judgment, for all or any part of the period between the date when the cause of action arose and –

    (a) in the case of any sum paid before judgment, the date of the payment; and

    (b) in the case of the sum for which judgment is given, the date of the judgment.

(2) In relation to a judgment given for damages for personal injuries or death which exceed £200 subsection (1) shall have effect –

    (a) with the substitution of "shall be included" for "may be included"; and

    (b) with the addition of "unless the court is satisfied that there are special reasons to the contrary" after "given", where first occurring.

  (3) Subject to rules of court, where –

    (a) there are proceedings (whenever instituted) before the High Court for the recovery of a debt; and

    (b) the defendant pays the whole debt to the plaintiff (otherwise than in pursuance of a judgment in the proceedings),

the defendant shall be liable to pay the plaintiff simple interest at such rate as the court thinks fit or as rules of court may provide on all or any part of the debt for all or any part of the period between the date when the cause of action arose and the date of the payment.

  (4) Interest in respect of a debt shall not be awarded under this section for a period during which, for whatever reason, interest on the debt already runs.

  (5) Without prejudice to the generality of section 84, rules of court may provide for a rate of interest by reference to the rate specified in section 17 of the Judgments Act 1838 as that section has effect from time to time or by reference to a rate for which any other enactment provides.

  (6) Interest under this section may be calculated at different rates in respect of different periods.

  (7) In this section "plaintiff" means the person seeking the debt or damages and "defendant" means the person from whom the plaintiff seeks the debt or damages and "personal injuries" includes any disease and any impairment of a person's physical or mental condition.

  (8) Nothing in this section affects the damages recoverable for the dishonour of a bill of exchange.

County Courts Act 1984 (1984 c.28)

Interest on debts and damages

Power of county courts to award interest on debts and damages

  69.–(1) Subject to county court rules, in proceedings (whenever instituted) before a county court for the recovery of a debt or damages there may be included in any sum for which the judgment is given interest, at such rate as the court thinks fit or as county court rules may provide, on all or any part of the debt or damages in respect of which judgment is given, or payment is made before judgment, for all or any part of the period between the date when the cause of action arose and –

    (a) in the case of any sum paid before judgment, the date of the payment; and

    (b) in the case of the sum for which the judgment is given, the date of the judgment.

  (2) In relation to a judgment given for damages for personal injuries or death which exceed £200 subsection (1) above shall have effect –

    (a) with the substitution of "shall be included" for "may be included"; and

    (b) with the addition of "unless the court is satisfied that there are special reasons to the contrary" after "given", where first occurring.

(3) Subject to county court rules, where –

    (a) there are proceedings (whenever instituted) before a county court for the recovery of a debt; and

    (b) the defendant pays the whole debt to the plaintiff (otherwise than in pursuance of a judgment in the proceedings),

the defendant shall be liable to pay the plaintiff simple interest at such rate as the court thinks fit or as county court rules may provide on all or any part of the debt for all or any part of the period between the date when the cause of action arose and the date of the payment.

(4) Interest in respect of a debt shall not be awarded under this section for a period during which, for whatever reason, interest on the debt already runs.

(5) Interest under this section may be calculated at different rates in respect of different periods.

(6) In this section "plaintiff" means the person seeking the debt or damages and "defendant" means the person from whom the plaintiff seeks the debt or damages and "personal injuries" includes any disease and any impairment of a person's physical or mental condition.

(7) Nothing in this section affects the damages recoverable for the dishonour of a bill of exchange.

(8) In determining whether an amount exceeds –

    (a) the county court limit; or

    (b) an amount specified in any provision of this Act,

no account shall be taken of the provisions of this section or of anything done under it.

Income and Corporation Taxes Act 1988 (1988 c.1)

Interest on damages for personal injuries

329.–(1) The following interest shall not be regarded as income for any income tax purpose –

    (a) any interest on damages in respect of personal injuries to a plaintiff or any other person, or in respect of a person's death, which is included in any sum for which judgment is given by virtue of a provision to which this paragraph applies; and

    (b) [*Applies to Scotland only*].

(2) The provisions to which subsection (1)(a) above applies are –

    (a) section 3 of the Law Reform (Miscellaneous Provisions) Act 1934;

    (b) section 17 of the Law Reform (Miscellaneous Provisions) Act (Northern Ireland) 1937;

    (c) section 35A of the Supreme Court Act 1981;

    (d) section 69 of the County Courts Act 1984;

    (e) section 33A of the Judicature (Northern Ireland) Act 1978; and

    (f) Article 45A of the County Courts (Northern Ireland) Order 1980.

(3) A payment in satisfaction of a cause of action, including a payment into court, shall not be regarded as income for any income tax purpose to the extent to which it is in respect of interest which would fall within subsection (1) above if included in a sum for which a judgment is given or if decree for payment of it were included in an interlocutor.

(4) In this section "personal injuries" includes any disease and any impairment of a person's physical or mental condition.

(e) Practice Direction, 1 August 1984: special damages

QUEEN'S BENCH DIVISION

1. Time is too often wasted at the trial of personal injury actions because the parties do not try to agree the items of special damage, or to find out to what extent they disagree and why, until the hearing is imminent or has actually started. To avoid this happening, the practice set out in paragraph 2 is to be followed in future.

2. In any personal injury action in which the damages claimed consist of or include a claim for (a) loss of earnings, (b) loss of future earning capacity, (c) medical or other expenses relating to or including the cost of care, attention, accommodation or appliances, (d) loss of pension rights, particulars, where appropriate in the form of schedule, shall be prepared by the party making such claim and not later than seven days after the case appears in the Warned List in London shall be served on all other parties against whom such claim is made. Not later than seven days thereafter every party to whom particulars have been served shall indicate in writing whether and to what extent each item claimed is agreed and, if not agreed, the reason why not and any counter-proposals. When there is a fixed date for hearing, the plaintiff's particulars shall be served not less than 28 days before that date and the answer not later than 14 days thereafter. The failure by a party to comply with these requirements may be taken into account in deciding any question of costs.

3. In cases for hearing outside London the particulars referred to in paragraph 2 shall be served not later than the lodging of the certificate of readiness and the answer not later than 14 days thereafter.

1 August 1984   LANE C.J.

RSC O.18 r.12(1A)–(1C)

(1A) Subject to paragraph (1B), a plaintiff in an action for personal injuries shall serve with his statement of claim –
    (a) a medical report, and
    (b) a statement of the special damages claimed.

(1B) Where the documents to which paragraph (1A) applies are not served with the statement of claim, the court may –
    (a) specify the period of time within which they are to be provided, or
    (b) make such other order as it thinks fit (including an order dispensing with the requirements of paragraph (1A) or staying the proceedings).

(1C) For the purposes of this rule –
"medical report" means a report substantiating all the personal injuries alleged in the statement of claim which the plaintiff proposes to adduce in evidence as part of the case at the trial;
"a statement of the special damages claimed" means a statement giving full particulars of the special damages claimed for expenses and losses already incurred and an estimate of any future expenses and losses (including loss of earnings and of pension rights).

2. *Limitation*

Limitation Act 1980 (1980 c.58)

[*The sections reproduced below are printed as amended, where appropriate.*]

PART III

MISCELLANEOUS AND GENERAL

35. New claims in pending actions: rules of court
38. Interpretation

An Act to consolidate the Limitations Acts 1939 to 1980. [13th November 1980]

PART I

ORDINARY TIME LIMITS FOR DIFFERENT CLASSES OF ACTION

Time limits under Part I subject to extension or exclusion under Part II

Time limits under Part I subject to extension or exclusion under Part II

1.–(1) This Part of this Act gives the ordinary time limits for bringing actions of the various classes mentioned in the following provisions of this Part.

(2) The ordinary time limits given in this Part of this Act are subject to extension or exclusion in accordance with the provisions of Part II of this Act.

Actions founded on tort

Time limit for actions founded on tort

2. An action founded on tort shall not be brought after the expiration of six years from the date on which the cause of action accrued.

Actions founded on simple contract

Time limit for actions founded on simple contract

5. An action founded on simple contract shall not be brought after the expiration of six years from the date on which the cause of action accrued.

Actions in respect of wrongs causing personal injuries or death

Special time limit for actions in respect of personal injuries

11.–(1) This section applies to any action for damages for negligence, nuisance or breach of duty (whether the duty exists by virtue of a contract or of provision made by or under a statute or independently of any contract or any such provision) where the damages claimed by the plaintiff for the negligence, nuisance or breach of duty consist of or include damages in respect of personal injuries to the plaintiff or any other person.

(2) None of the time limits given in the preceding provisions of this Act shall apply to an action to which this section applies.

(3) An action to which this section applies shall not be brought after the expiration of the period applicable in accordance with subsection (4) or (5) below.

(4) Except where subsection (5) below applies, the period applicable is three years from –

    (a) the date on which the cause of action accrued; or
    (b) the date of knowledge (if later) of the person injured.

(5) If the person injured dies before the expiration of the period mentioned in subsection (4) above, the period applicable as respects the cause of action surviving for the benefit of his estate by virtue of section 1 of the Law Reform (Miscellaneous Provisions) Act 1934 shall be three years from –

(a) the date of death; or

(b) the date of the personal representative's knowledge;

whichever is the later.

(6) For the purposes of this section "personal representative" includes any person who is or has been a personal representative of the deceased, including an executor who has not proved the will (whether or not he has renounced probate) but not anyone appointed only as a special personal representative in relation to settled land; and regard shall be had to any knowledge acquired by any such person while a personal representative or previously.

(7) If there is more than one personal representative, and their dates of knowledge are different, subsection (5)(b) above shall be read as referring to the earliest of those dates.

Actions in respect of defective products

11A.–(1) This section shall apply to an action for damages by virtue of any provision of Part I of the Consumer Protection Act 1987.

(2) None of the time limits given in the preceding provisions of this Act shall apply to an action to which this section applies.

(3) An action in which this section applies shall not be brought after the expiration of the period of ten years from the relevant time, within the meaning of section 4 of the said Act of 1987; and this subsection shall operate to extinguish a right of action and shall do so whether or not that right of action had accrued, or time under the following provisions of this Act had begun to run, at the end of the said period of ten years.

(4) Subject to subsection (5) below, an action to which this section applies in which the damages claimed by the plaintiff consist of or include damages in respect of personal injuries to the plaintiff or any other person for loss of or damage to any property, shall not be brought after the expiration of the period of three years from whichever is the later of –

(a) the date on which the cause of action accrued; and

(b) the date of knowledge of the injured person or, in the case of loss of or damage to property, the date of knowledge of the plaintiff or (if earlier) of any person in whom his cause of action was previously vested.

(5) If in a case where the damages claimed by the plaintiff consist of or include damages in respect of personal injuries to the plaintiff or any other person the injured person died before the expiration of the period mentioned in subsection (4) above, that subsection shall have effect as respects the cause of action surviving for the benefit of his estate by virtue of section 1 of the Law Reform (Miscellaneous Provisions) Act 1934 as if for the reference to that period there were substituted a reference to the period of three years from whichever is the later of –

(a) the date of death; and

(b) the date of the personal representative's knowledge.

(6) For the purposes of this section "personal representative" includes any person who is or has been a personal representative of the deceased, including an executor who has not proved the will (whether or not he has renounced probate) but not anyone appointed only as a special personal representative in

relation to settled land; and regard shall be had to any knowledge acquired by any such person while a personal representative or previously.

(7) If there is more than one personal representative and their dates of knowledge are different, subsection (5)(b) above shall be read as referring to the earliest of those dates.

(8) Expressions used in this section or section 14 of this Act and in Part I of the Consumer Protection Act 1987 have the same meanings in this section or that section as in that Part; and section 1(1) of that Act (Part I to be construed as enacted for the purpose of complying with the product liability Directive) shall apply for the purpose of construing this section and the following provisions of this Act so far as they relate to any action by virtue of any provision of that Part as it applies for the purpose of construing that Part.

Special time limit for actions under Fatal Accidents legislation

12.–(1) An action under the Fatal Accidents Act 1976 shall not be brought if the death occurred when the person injured could no longer maintain an action and recover damages in respect of the injury (whether because of a time limit in this Act or in any other Act, or for any other reason).

Where any such action by the injured person would have been barred by the time limit in section 11 or 11A of this Act, no account shall be taken of the possibility of that time limit being overridden under section 33 of this Act.

(2) None of the time limits given in the preceding provisions of this Act shall apply to an action under the Fatal Accidents Act 1976, but no such action shall be brought after the expiration of three years from –

    (a) the date of death; or

    (b) the date of knowledge of the person for whose benefit the action is brought;

whichever is the later.

(3) An action under the Fatal Accidents Act 1976 shall be one to which sections 28, 33 and 35 of this Act apply, and the application to any such action of the time limit under subsection (2) above shall be subject to section 39; but otherwise Parts II and III of this Act shall not apply to any such action.

Operation of time limit under section 12 in relation to different dependants

13.–(1) Where there is more than one person for whose benefit an action under the Fatal Accidents Act 1976 is brought, section 12(2)(b) of this Act shall be applied separately to each of them.

(2) Subject to subsection (3) below, if by virtue of subsection (1) above the action would be outside the time limit given by section 12(2) as regards one or more, but not all, of the persons for whose benefit it is brought, the court shall direct that any person as regards whom the action would be outside that limit shall be excluded from those for whom the action is brought.

(3) The court shall not give such a direction if it is shown that if the action were brought exclusively for the benefit of the person in question it would not be defeated by a defence of limitation (whether in consequence of section 28 of this Act or an agreement between the parties not to raise the defence, or otherwise).

Definition of date of knowledge for purposes of sections 11 and 12

14.–(1) [Subject to subsection (1A) below,] in sections 11 and 12 of this Act references to a person's date of knowledge are references to the date on which he first had knowledge of the following facts –

    (a) that the injury in question was significant; and

    (b) that the injury was attributable in whole or in part to the act or omission which is alleged to constitute negligence, nuisance or breach of duty; and

    (c) the identity of the defendant; and

    (d) if it is alleged that the act or omission was that of a person other than the defendant, the identity of that person and the additional facts supporting the bringing of an action against the defendant;

and knowledge that any acts or omissions did or did not, as a matter of law, involve negligence, nuisance or breach of duty is irrelevant.

(1A) In section 11A of this Act and in section 12 of this Act so far as that section applies to an action by virtue of section 6(1)(a) of the Consumer Protection Act 1987 (death caused by defective product) references to a person's date of knowledge are references to the date on which he first had knowledge of the following facts –

    (a) such facts about the damage caused by the defect as would lead a reasonable person who had suffered such damage to consider it sufficiently serious to justify his instituting proceedings for damages against a defendant who did not dispute liability and was able to satisfy a judgment; and

    (b) that the damage was wholly or partly attributable to the facts and circumstances alleged to constitute the defect; and

    (c) the identity of the defendant;

but, in determining the date on which a person first had such knowledge there shall be disregarded both the extent (if any) of that person's knowledge on any date of whether particular facts or circumstances would or would not, as a matter of law, constitute a defect and, in a case relating to loss of or damage to property, any knowledge which that person had on a date on which he had no right of action by virtue of Part I of that Act in respect of the loss or damage.

(2) For the purposes of this section an injury is significant if the person whose date of knowledge is in question would reasonably have considered it sufficiently serious to justify his instituting proceedings for damages against a defendant who did not dispute liability and was able to satisfy a judgment.

(3) For the purposes of this section a person's knowledge includes knowledge which he might reasonably have been expected to acquire –

    (a) from facts observable or ascertainable by him; or

    (b) from facts ascertainable by him with the help of medical or other appropriate expert advice which it is reasonable for him to seek;

but a person shall not be fixed under this subsection with knowledge of a fact ascertainable only with the help of expert advice so long as he has taken all reasonable steps to obtain (and, where appropriate, to act on) that advice.

Actions in respect of latent damage not involving personal injuries

Special time limit for negligence actions where facts relevant to cause of action are not known at date of accrual

14A.–(1) This section applies to any action for damages for negligence, other than one to which section 11 of this Act applies, where the starting date for reckoning the period of limitation under subsection (4)(b) below falls after the date on which the cause of action accrued.

(2) Section 2 of this Act shall not apply to an action to which this section applies.

(3) An action to which this section applies shall not be brought after the expiration of the period applicable in accordance with subsection (4) below.

(4) That period is either –
    (a) six years from the date on which the cause of action accrued; or
    (b) three years from the starting date as defined by subsection (5) below, if that period expires later than the period mentioned in paragraph (a) above

(5) For the purposes of this section, the starting date for reckoning the period of limitation under subsection (4)(b) above is the earliest date on which the plaintiff or any person in whom the cause of action was vested before him first had both the knowledge required for bringing an action for damages in respect of the relevant damage and a right to bring such an action.

(6) In subsection (5) above "the knowledge required for bringing an action for damages in respect of the relevant damage" means knowledge both –
    (a) of the material facts about the damage in respect of which damages are claimed; and
    (b) of the other facts relevant to the current action mentioned in subsection (8) below.

(7) For the purposes of subsection 6(a) above, the material facts about the damage are such facts about the damage as would lead a reasonable person who had suffered such damage to consider it sufficiently serious to justify his instituting proceedings for damages against a defendant who did not dispute liability and was able to satisfy a judgment.

(8) The other facts referred to in subsection (6)(b) above are –
    (a) that the damage was attributable in whole or in part to the act or omission which is alleged to constitute negligence; and
    (b) the identity of the defendant; and
    (c) if it is alleged that the act or omission was that of a person other than the defendant, the identity of that person and the additional facts supporting the bringing of an action against the defendant.

(9) Knowledge that any acts or omissions did or did not, as a matter of law, involve negligence is irrelevant for the purposes of subsection (5) above.

(10) For the purposes of this section a person's knowledge includes knowledge which he might reasonably have been expected to acquire –
    (a) from facts observable or ascertainable by him; or
    (b) from facts ascertainable by him with the help of appropriate expert advice which it is reasonable for him to seek;
but a person shall not be taken by virtue of this subsection to have knowledge of a fact ascertainable only with the help of expert advice so long as he has taken all reasonable steps to obtain (and, where appropriate, to act on) that advice.

Overriding time limit for negligence actions not involving personal injuries

14B.–(1) An action for damages for negligence, other than one to which section 11 of this Act applies, shall not be brought after the expiration of fifteen years from the date (or, if more than one, from the last of the dates) on which there occurred any act or omission –
    (a) which is alleged to constitute negligence; and
    (b) to which the damage in respect of which damages are claimed is alleged to be attributable (in whole or in part).

(2) This section bars the right of action in a case to which subsection (1) above applies notwithstanding that –

(a) the cause of action has not yet accrued; or
(b) where section 14A of this Act applies to the action, the date which is for the purposes of that section the starting date for reckoning the period mentioned in subsection (4)(b) of that section has not yet occurred;
before the end of the period of limitation prescribed by this section.

PART II

EXTENSION OR EXCLUSION OF ORDINARY TIME LIMITS

Disability

Extension of limitation period in case of disability

28.–(1) Subject to the following provisions of this section, if on the date when any right of action accrued for which a period of limitation is prescribed by this Act, the person to whom it accrued was under a disability, the action may be brought at any time before the expiration of six years from the date when he ceased to be under a disability or died (whichever first occurred) notwithstanding that the period of limitation has expired.

(2) This section shall not affect any case where the right of action first accrued to some person (not under a disability) through whom the person under a disability claims.

(3) When a right of action which has accrued to a person under a disability accrues, on the death of that person while still under a disability, to another person under a disability, no further extension of time shall be allowed by reason of the disability of the second person.

(4) No action to recover land or money charged on land shall be brought by virtue of this section by any person after the expiration of thirty years from the date on which the right of action accrued to that person or some person through whom he claims.

[(4A) . . .]

(5) If the action is one to which section 10 of this Act applies, subsection (1) above shall have effect as if for the words "six years" there were substituted the words "two years".

(6) If the action is one to which section 11 or 12(2) of this Act applies, subsection (1) above shall have effect as if for the words "six years" there were substituted the words "three years".

(7) If the action is one to which section 11A of this Act applies or one by virtue of section 6(1)(a) of the Consumer Protection Act 1987 (death caused by defective product), subsection (1) above –
(a) shall not apply to the time limit prescribed by subsection (3) of the said section 11A or to that time limit as applied by virtue of section 12(1) of this Act; and
(b) in relation to any other time limit prescribed by this Act shall have effect as if for the words "six years" there were substituted the words "three years".

Extension for cases where the limitation period is the period under section 14A(4)(b)

28A.–(1) Subject to subsection (2) below, if in the case of any action for which a period of limitation is prescribed by section 14A of this Act –

(a) the period applicable in accordance with subsection (4) of that section is the period mentioned in paragraph (b) of that subsection;

(b) on the date which is for the purposes of that section the starting date for reckoning that period the person by reference to whose knowledge that date fell to be determined under subsection (5) of that section was under a disability; and

(c) section 28 of this Act does not apply to the action;

the action may be brought at any time before the expiration of three years from the date when he ceased to be under a disability or died (whichever first occurred) notwithstanding that the period mentioned above has expired.

(2) An action may not be brought by virtue of subsection (1) above after the end of the period of limitation prescribed by section 14B of this Act.

Fraud, concealment and mistake

Postponement of limitation period in case of fraud, concealment or mistake

32.–(1) Subject to subsections (3) and (4A) below, where in the case of any action for which a period of limitation is prescribed by this Act, either –

(a) the action is based upon the fraud of the defendant; or

(b) any fact relevant to the plaintiff's right of action has been deliberately concealed from him by the defendant; or

(c) the action is for relief from the consequences of a mistake;

the period of limitation shall not begin to run until the plaintiff has discovered the fraud, concealment or mistake (as the case may be) or could with reasonable diligence have discovered it.

References in this subsection to the defendant include references to the defendant's agent and to any person through whom the defendant claims and his agent.

(2) For the purposes of subsection (1) above, deliberate commission of a breach of duty in circumstances in which it is unlikely to be discovered for some time amounts to deliberate concealment of the facts involved in that breach of duty.

(3) Nothing in this section shall enable any action –

(a) to recover, or recover the value of, any property; or

(b) to enforce any charge against, or set aside any transaction affecting, any property;

to be brought against the purchaser of the property or any person claiming through him in any case where the property has been purchased for valuable consideration by an innocent third party since the fraud or concealment or (as the case may be) the transaction in which the mistake was made took place.

(4) A purchaser is an innocent third party for the purposes of this section –

(a) in the case of fraud or concealment of any fact relevant to the plaintiff's right of action, if he was not a party to the fraud or (as the case may be) to the concealment of that fact and did not at the time of the purchase know or have reason to believe that the fraud or concealment had taken place; and

(b) in the case of mistake, if he did not at the time of the purchase know or have reason to believe that the mistake had been made.

(4A) Subsection (1) above shall not apply in relation to the time limit prescribed by section 11A(3) of this Act or in relation to that time limit as applied by virtue of section 12(1) of this Act.

(5) Sections 14A and 14B of this Act shall not apply to any action to which

subsection (1)(b) above applies (and accordingly the period of limitation referred to in that subsection, in any case to which either of those sections would otherwise apply, is the period applicable under section 2 of this Act).

Discretionary exclusion of time limit for actions in respect of personal injuries or death

Discretionary exclusion of time limit for actions in respect of personal injuries or death

33.–(1) If it appears to the court that it would be equitable to allow an action to proceed having regard to the degree to which –

    (a) the provisions of section 11 or 11A or 12 of this Act prejudice the plaintiff or any person whom he represents; and

    (b) any decision of the court under this subsection would prejudice the defendant or any person whom he represents;

the court may direct that those provisions shall not apply to the action, or shall not apply to any specified cause of action to which the action relates.

(1A) The court shall not under this section disapply –

    (a) subsection (3) of section 11A; or

    (b) where the damages claimed by the plaintiff are confined to damages for loss of or damage to any property, any other provision in its application to an action by virtue of Part I of the Consumer Protection Act 1987.

(2) The court shall not under this section disapply section 12(1) except where the reason why the person injured could no longer maintain an action was because of the time limit in section 11 or subsection (4) of section 11A.

If, for example, the person injured could at his death no longer maintain an action under the Fatal Accidents Act 1976 because of the time limit in Article 29 in Schedule 1 to the Carriage by Air Act 1961, the court has no power to direct that section 12(1) shall not apply.

(3) In acting under this section the court shall have regard to all the circumstances of the case and in particular to –

    (a) the length of, and the reasons for, the delay on the part of the plaintiff;

    (b) the extent to which, having regard to the delay, the evidence adduced or likely to be adduced by the plaintiff or the defendant is or is likely to be less cogent than if the action had been brought within the time allowed by section 11, by section 11A or (as the case may be) by section 12;

    (c) the conduct of the defendant after the cause of action arose, including the extent (if any) to which he responded to requests reasonably made by the plaintiff for information or inspection for the purpose of ascertaining facts which were or might be relevant to the plaintiff's cause of action against the defendant;

    (d) the duration of any disability of the plaintiff arising after the date of the accrual of the cause of action;

    (e) the extent to which the plaintiff acted promptly and reasonably once he knew whether or not the act or omission of the defendant, to which the injury was attributable, might be capable at that time of giving rise to an action for damages;

    (f) the steps, if any, taken by the plaintiff to obtain medical, legal or other expert advice and the nature of any such advice he may have received.

(4) In a case where the person injured died when, because of section 11 or subsection (4) of section 11A, he could no longer maintain an action and recover damages in respect of the injury, the court shall have regard in particular to the length of, and the reasons for, the delay on the part of the deceased.

(5) In a case under subsection (4) above, or any other case where the time limit, or one of the time limits, depends on the date of knowledge of a person other than the plaintiff, subsection (3) above shall have effect with appropriate modifications, and shall have effect in particular as if references to the plaintiff included references to any person whose date of knowledge is or was relevant in determining a time limit.

(6) A direction by the court disapplying the provisions of section 12(1) shall operate to disapply the provisions to the same effect in section 1(1) of the Fatal Accidents Act 1976.

(7) In this section "the court" means the court in which the action has been brought.

(8) References in this section to section 11 or 11A include references to that section as extended by any of the preceding provisions of this Part of this Act or by any provision of Part III of this Act.

PART III

MISCELLANEOUS AND GENERAL

New claims in pending actions: rules of court

35.–(1) For the purposes of this Act, any new claim made in the course of any action shall be deemed to be a separate action and to have been commenced –

(a) in the case of a new claim made in or by way of third party proceedings, on the date on which those proceedings were commenced; and

(b) in the case of any other new claim, on the same date as the original action.

(2) In this section a new claim means any claim by way of set-off or counterclaim, and any claim involving either –

(a) the addition or substitution of a new cause of action; or

(b) the addition or substitution of a new party;

and "third party proceedings" means any proceedings brought in the course of any action by any party to the action against a person not previously a party to the action, other than proceedings brought by joining any such person as defendant to any claim already made in the original action by the party bringing the proceedings.

(3) Except as provided by section 33 of this Act or by rules of court, neither the High Court nor any county court shall allow a new claim within subsection (1)(b) above, other than an original set-off or counterclaim, to be made in the course of any action after the expiry of any time limit under this Act which would affect a new action to enforce that claim.

For the purposes of this subsection, a claim is an original set-off or an original counterclaim if it is a claim by way of set-off or (as the case may be) by way of counterclaim by a party who has not previously made any claim in the action.

(4) Rules of court may provide for allowing a new claim to which subsection (3) above applies to be made as there mentioned, but only if the conditions specified in subsection (5) below are satisfied, and subject to any further restrictions the rules may impose.

(5) The conditions referred to in subsection (4) above are the following –

    (a) in the case of a claim involving a new cause of action, if the new cause of action arises out of the same facts or substantially the same facts as are already in issue on any claim previously made in the original action; and

    (b) in the case of a claim involving a new party, if the addition or substitution of the new party is necessary for the determination of the original action.

(6) The addition or substitution of a new party shall not be regarded for the purposes of subsection (5)(b) above as necessary for the determination of the original action unless either –

    (a) the new party is substituted for a party whose name was given in any claim made in the original action in mistake for the new party's name; or

    (b) any claim already made in the original action cannot be maintained by or against any existing party unless the new party is joined or substituted as plaintiff or defendant in that action.

(7) Subject to subsection (4) above, rules of court may provide for allowing a party to any action to claim relief in a new capacity in respect of a new cause of action notwithstanding that he had no title to make that claim at the date of the commencement of the action.

This subsection shall not be taken as prejudicing the power of rules of court to provide for allowing a party to claim relief in a new capacity without adding or substituting a new cause of action.

(8) Subsections (3) to (7) above shall apply in relation to a new claim made in the course of third party proceedings as if those proceedings were the original action, and subject to such other modifications as may be prescribed by rules of court in any case or class of case.

(9) [*Repealed*]

Interpretation

    38.–(1) In this Act, unless the context otherwise requires –

    "action" includes any proceedings in a court of law, including an ecclesiastical court;

    "land" includes corporeal hereditaments, tithes and rentcharges and any legal or equitable estate or interest therein, including an interest in the proceeds of the sale of land held upon trust for sale, but except as provided above in this definition does not include any incorporeal hereditament;

    "personal estate" and "personal property" do not include chattels real;

    "personal injuries" includes any disease and any impairment of a person's physical or mental condition, and "injury" and cognate expressions shall be construed accordingly;

    "rent" includes a rentcharge and a rentservice;

    "rentcharge" means any annuity or periodical sum of money charged upon or payable out of land, except a rentservice or interest on a mortgage on land;

    "settled land", "statutory owner" and "tenant for life" have the same meanings respectively as in the Settled Land Act 1925;

    "trust" and "trustee" have the same meanings respectively as in the Trustee Act 1925; and

    "trust for sale" has the same meaning as in the Law of Property Act 1925.

(2) For the purposes of this Act a person shall be treated as under a disability while he is an infant, or of unsound mind.

(3) For the purposes of subsection (2) above a person is of unsound mind if he is a person who, by reason of mental disorder within the meaning of the Mental Health Act 1983, is incapable of managing and administering his property and affairs.

(4) Without prejudice to the generality of subsection (3) above, a person shall be conclusively presumed for the purposes of subsection (2) above to be of unsound mind –

    (a) while he is liable to be detained or subject to guardianship under the Mental Health Act 1983 (otherwise than by virtue of section 35 or 89); and

    (b) while he is receiving treatment as an in-patient in any hospital within the meaning of the Mental Health Act 1983 or mental nursing home within the meaning of the Nursing Homes Act 1975 without being liable to be detained under the said Act of 1983 (otherwise than by virtue of section 35 or 89), being treatment which follows without any interval a period during which he was liable to be detained or subject to guardianship under the Mental Health Act 1959, or the said Act of 1983 (otherwise than by virtue of section 35 or 89) or by virtue of any enactment repealed or excluded by the Mental Health Act 1959.

(5) Subject to subsection (6) below, a person shall be treated as claiming through another person if he became entitled by, through, under, or by the act of that other person to the right claimed, and any person whose estate or interest might have been barred by a person entitled to an entailed interest in possession shall be treated as claiming through the person so entitled.

(6) A person becoming entitled to any estate or interest by virtue of a special power of appointment shall not be treated as claiming through the appointor.

(7) References in this Act to a right of action to recover land shall include references to a right to enter into possession of the land or, in the case of rentcharges and tithes, to distrain for arrears of rent or tithe, and references to the bringing of such an action shall include references to the making of such an entry or distress.

(8) References in this Act to the possession of land shall, in the case of tithes and rentcharges, be construed as references to the receipt of the tithe or rent, and references to the date of dispossession or discontinuance of possession of land shall, in the case of rentcharges, be construed as references to the date of the last receipt of rent.

(9) References in Part II of this Act to a right of action shall include references to –

    (a) a cause of action;

    (b) a right to receive money secured by a mortgage or charge on any property;

    (c) a right to recover proceeds of the sale of land; and

    (d) a right to receive a share or interest in the personal estate of a deceased person.

(10) References in Part II to the date of the accrual of a right of action shall be construed –

    (a) in the case of an action upon a judgment, as references to the date on which the judgment became enforceable; and

    (b) in the case of an action to recover arrears of rent or interest, or damages in respect of arrears of rent or interest, as references to the date on which the rent or interest became due.

3. *Congenital Disabilities (Civil Liability) Act 1976*

(1976 c. 28)

An Act to make provision as to civil liability in the case of children born disabled in consequence of some person's fault; and to extend the Nuclear Installations Act 1965, so that children so born in consequence of a breach of duty under that Act may claim compensation.

[22nd July 1976]

Civil liability to child born disabled

1.–(1) If a child is born disabled as a result of such an occurrence before its birth as is mentioned in subsection (2) below, and a person (other than the child's own mother) is under this section answerable to the child in respect of the occurrence, the child's disabilities are to be regarded as damage resulting from the wrongful act of that person and actionable accordingly at the suit of the child.

(2) An occurrence to which this section applies is one which –

    (a) affected either parent of the child in his or her ability to have a normal, healthy child; or

    (b) affected the mother during her pregnancy, or affected her or the child in the course of its birth, so that the child is born with disabilities which would not otherwise have been present.

(3) Subject to the following subsections, a person (here referred to as "the defendant") is answerable to the child if he was liable in tort to the parent or would, if sued in time, have been so; and it is no answer that there could not have been such liability because the parent suffered no actionable injury, if there was a breach of legal duty which, accompanied by injury would have given rise to the liability.

(4) In the case of an occurrence preceding the time of conception, the defendant is not answerable to the child if at that time either or both of the parents knew the risk of their child being born disabled (that is to say, the particular risk created by the occurrence); but should it be the child's father who is the defendant, this subsection does not apply if he knew of the risk and the mother did not.

(5) The defendant is not answerable to the child, for anything he did or omitted to do when responsible in a professional capacity for treating or advising the parent, if he took reasonable care having due regard to then received professional opinion applicable to the particular class of case; but this does not mean that he is answerable only because he departed from received opinion.

(6) Liability to the child under this section may be treated as having been excluded or limited by contract made with the parent affected, to the same extent and subject to the same restrictions as liability in the parent's own case; and a contract term which could have been set up by the defendant in an action by the parent, so as to exclude or limit his liability to him or her, operates in the defendant's favour to the same, but no greater, extent in an action under this section by the child.

(7) If in the child's action under this section it is shown that the parent affected shared the responsibility for the child being born disabled, the damages are to be reduced to such extent as the court thinks just and equitable having regard to the extent of the parent's responsibility.

Extension of section 1 to cover infertility treatments

1A.–(1) In any case where –

(a) a child carried by a woman as the result of the placing in her of an embryo or of sperm and eggs or her artificial insemination is born disabled,

(b) the disability results from an act or omission in the course of the selection, or the keeping or use outside the body, of the embryo carried by her or of the gametes used to bring about the creation of the embryo, and

(c) a person is under this section answerable to the child in respect of the act or omission,

the child's disabilities are to be regarded as damage resulting from the wrongful act of that person and actionable accordingly at the suit of the child.

(2) Subject to subsection (3) below and the applied provisions of section 1 of this Act, a person (here referred to as "the defendant") is answerable to the child if he was liable in tort to one or both of the parents (here referred to as "the parent or parents concerned") or would, if sued in due time, have been so; and it is no answer that there could not have been such liability because the parent or parents concerned suffered no actionable injury, if there was a breach of legal duty which, accompanied by injury, would have given rise to the liability.

(3) The defendant is not under this section answerable to the child if at the time the embryo, or the sperm and eggs, are placed in the woman or at the time of her insemination (as the case may be) either or both of the parents knew the risk of their child being born disabled (that is to say, the particular risk created by the act or omission).

(4) Subsections (5) to (7) of section 1 of this Act apply for the purposes of this section as they apply for the purposes of that but as if references to the parent or the parents affected were references to the parent or parents concerned.

[Note: Section 1A was inserted by s.44(1) of the Human Fertilisation and Embryology Act 1990.]

Liability of woman driving when pregnant

2. A woman driving a motor vehicle when she knows (or ought reasonably to know) herself to be pregnant is to be regarded as being under the same duty to take care for the safety of her unborn child as the law imposes on her with respect to the safety of other people; and if in consequence of her breach of that duty her child is born with disabilities which would not otherwise have been present, those disabilities are to be regarded as damage resulting from her wrongful act and actionable accordingly at the suit of the child.

3.–(1) Section 1 of this Act does not affect the operation of the Nuclear Installations Act 1965 as to liability for, and compensation in respect of, injury or damage caused by occurrences involving nuclear matter or the emission of ionising radiations.

(2) For the avoidance of doubt anything which –

(a) affects a man in his ability to have a normal, healthy child; or

(b) affects a woman in that ability, or so affects her when she is pregnant that her child is born with disabilities which would not otherwise have been present,

is an injury for the purposes of that Act.

(3) If a child is born disabled as the result of an injury to either of its parents caused in breach of a duty imposed by any of sections 7 to 11 of that Act (nuclear site licensees and others to secure that nuclear incidents do not cause injury to persons, etc.), the child's disabilities are to be regarded under the subsequent provisions of that Act (compensation and other matters) as injuries caused on the same occasion, and by the same breach of duty, as was the injury to the parent.

(4) As respects compensation to the child, section 13(6) of that Act (contributory fault of person injured by radiation) is to be applied as if the reference there to fault were to the fault of the parent.

(5) Compensation is not payable in the child's case if the injury to the parent preceded the time of the child's conception and at that time either or both of the parents knew the risk of their child being born disabled (that is to say, the particular risk created by the injury).

Interpretation and other supplementary provisions

4.–(1) References in this Act to a child being born disabled or with disabilities are to its being born with any deformity, disease or abnormality, including predisposition (whether or not susceptible of immediate prognosis) to physical or mental defect in the future.

(2) In this Act –

    (a) "born" means alive (the moment of a child's birth being when it first has a life separate from its mother), and "birth" has a corresponding meaning; and

    (b) "motor vehicle" means a mechanically propelled vehicle intended or adapted for use on roads; [and references to embryos shall be construed in accordance with section 1 of the Human Fertilisation and Embryology Act 1990.]

(3) Liability to a child under section 1 [or 1A] or 2 of this Act is to be regarded –

    (a) as respects all its incidents and any matters arising or to arise out of it; and

    (b) subject to any contrary context or intention, for the purpose of construing references in enactments and documents to personal or bodily injuries and cognate matters,

as liability for personal injuries sustained by the child immediately after its birth.

(4) No damages shall be recoverable under [any] of those sections in respect of any loss of expectation of life, nor shall any such loss be taken into account in the compensation payable in respect of a child under the Nuclear Installations Act 1965 as extended by section 3, unless (in either case) the child lives for at least 48 hours.

(4A) In any case where a child carried by a woman as the result of the placing in her of an embryo or of sperm and eggs or her artificial insemination is born disabled, any reference in section 1 of this Act to a parent includes a reference to a person who would be a parent but for sections 27 to 29 of the Human Fertilisation and Embryology Act 1990.

(5) This Act applies in respect of births after (but not before) its passing, and in respect of any such birth it replaces any law in force before its passing, whereby a person could be liable to a child in respect of disabilities with which it might be born; but in section 1(3) of this Act the expression "liable in tort" does not include any reference to liability by virtue of this Act, or to liability by virtue of any such law.

(6) References to the Nuclear Installations Act 1965 are to that Act as amended; and for the purposes of section 28 of that Act (power by Order in Council to extend the Act to territories outside the United Kingdom) section 3 of this Act is to be treated as if it were a provision of that Act.

[Note: Sub-s. (4A) was inserted by s.35 of the Human Fertilisation and Embryology Act 1990, and the words in square brackets in sub-ss. (2), (3) and (4) were substituted by s.44 of that Act.]

Crown application

5. This Act binds the Crown.

Citation and extent

6.–(1) This Act may be cited as the Congenital Disabilities (Civil Liability) Act 1976.

(2) This Act extends to Northern Ireland but not to Scotland.

4. *The National Health Service*

(There is a mass of complex and much amended legislation on the NHS. This is not an encyclopedia, so I have selected just a few passages which I think could be of use and interest in and about the medical negligence action.)

(a) National Health Service Act 1977 (1977 c.49)

ARRANGEMENT OF SECTIONS

PART I

SERVICES AND ADMINISTRATION

Functions of the Secretary of State

Section
1. Secretary of State's duty as to health service.
2. Secretary of State's general power as to services.
3. Services generally.
4. Special hospitals.
5. Other services.

An Act to consolidate certain provisions relating to the health service for England and Wales; and to repeal certain enactments relating to the health service which have ceased to have any effect.   [29th July 1977]

PART I

SERVICES AND ADMINISTRATION

Functions of the Secretary of State

Secretary of State's duty as to health service

1.–(1) It is the Secretary of State's duty to continue the promotion in England and Wales of a comprehensive health service designed to secure improvement –
  (a) in the physical and mental health of the people of those countries, and
  (b) in the prevention, diagnosis and treatment of illness,
and for the purpose to provide or secure the effective provision of services in accordance with this Act.
  (2) The services so provided shall be free of charge except in so far as the making and recovery of charges is expressly provided for by or under any enactment, whenever passed.

Secretary of State's general power as to services

2. Without prejudice to the Secretary of State's powers apart from this section, he has power –

(a) to provide such services as he considers appropriate for the purpose of discharging any duty imposed on him by this Act; and

(b) to do any other thing whatsoever which is calculated to facilitate, or is conducive or incidental to, the discharge of such a duty.

This section is subject to section 3(3) below.

Services generally

3.–(1) It is the Secretary of State's duty to provide throughout England and Wales, to such extent as he considers necessary to meet all reasonable requirements –

(a) hospital accommodation;

(b) other accommodation for the purpose of any service provided under this Act;

(c) medical, dental, nursing and ambulance services;

(d) such other facilities for the care of expectant and nursing mothers and young children as he considers are appropriate as part of the health service;

(e) such facilities for the prevention of illness, the care of persons suffering from illness and the after-care of persons who have suffered from illness as he considers appropriate as part of the health service;

(f) such other services as are required for the diagnosis and treatment of illness.

(2) Where any hospital provided by the Secretary of State in accordance with this Act was a voluntary hospital transferred by virtue of the National Health Service Act 1946, and –

(a) the character and association of that hospital before its transfer were such as to link it with a particular religious denomination, then

(b) regard shall be had in the general administration of the hospital to the preservation of that character and those associations.

(3) Nothing in section 2 above or in this section affects the provisions of Part II of this Act (which relates to arrangements with practitioners for the provision of medical, dental, ophthalmic and pharmaceutical services).

Special hospitals

4. The duty imposed on the Secretary of State by section 1 above to provide services for the purposes of the health service includes a duty to provide and maintain establishments (in this Act referred to as "special hospitals") for persons subject to detention under the Mental Health Act 1983 who in his opinion require treatment under conditions of special security on account of their dangerous, violent or criminal propensities.

Other services

5.–(1) It is the Secretary of State's duty –

(a) to provide for the medical inspection at appropriate intervals of pupils in attendance at schools maintained by local education authorities or at grant-maintained schools and for the medical treatment of such pupils;

(b) to arrange, to such extent as he considers necessary to meet all reasonable requirements in England and Wales, for the giving of advice on contraception, the medical examination of persons seeking advice on contraception, the treatment of such persons and the supply of contraceptive substances and appliances.

(1A) It is also the Secretary of State's duty to provide, to such extent as he considers necessary to meet all reasonable requirements –

(a) for the dental inspection of pupils in attendance at schools maintained by local education authorities or at grant maintained schools;

(b) for the dental treatment of such pupils; and

(c) for the education of such pupils in dental health.

(1B) Schedule 1 to this Act shall have effect.

(2) The Secretary of State may –

(a) provide invalid carriages for persons appearing to him to be suffering from severe physical defect or disability and, at the request of such a person, may provide for him a vehicle other than an invalid carriage (and the additional provisions set out in Schedule 2 to this Act have effect in relation to this paragraph);

(b) arrange to provide accommodation and treatment outside Great Britain for persons suffering from respiratory tuberculosis;

(c) provide a microbiological service, which may include the provisions of laboratories, for the control of the spread of infectious diseases and to carry on such other activities as in his opinion can conveniently be carried on in conjunction with that service;

(d) conduct, or assist by grants or otherwise (without prejudice to the general powers and duties conferred on him under the Ministry of Health Act 1919) any person to conduct, research into any matters relating to the causation, prevention, diagnosis or treatment of illness, and into any such other matters connected with any service provided under this Act as he considers appropriate.

(2A) Charges may be made for services or materials supplied by virtue of paragraph (c) of subsection (2) above; and the powers conferred by that paragraph may be exercised both for the purposes of the health service and for other purposes.

(2B) The Secretary of State's function may be performed outside England and Wales, insofar as they relate –

(a) to holidays for patients

(b) to the transfer of patients to and from Scotland, Northern Ireland, the Isle of Man or the Channel Islands; or

(c) to the return of patients who have received treatment in England and Wales to countries or territories outside the British Islands.

(3) [*Repealed*]

(4) The Public Health Laboratory Service Board continues in being for the purpose of exercising such functions with respect to the powers conferred by paragraph (c) of subsection (2) above as the Secretary of State may determine.

(5) The Board shall continue to be constituted in accordance with Part I of Schedule 3 to this Act, and the additional provisions set out in Part II of that Schedule have effect in relation to the Board.

[Note: this section is printed as amended by the Public Health Laboratory Service Act 1979, the Health and Social Security Act 1984 and the Social Security Act 1988.]

(b) National Health Service and Community Care Act 1990 (1990 c.19)

Removal of Crown immunities

60.–(1) Subject to the following provisions of this section, on and after the day appointed for the coming into force of this subsection, no health service body shall be regarded as the servant or agent of the Crown or as enjoying any status, immunity, or privilege of the Crown; and so far as concerns land in which the Secretary of State has an interest, at any time when –

(a) by virtue of directions under any provision of the National Health Service Act 1977, the Mental Health (Scotland) Act 1984 or the Health and Medicines Act 1988 or by virtue of orders under section 2 or section 10 of the National Health Service (Scotland) Act 1978, powers of disposal or management with respect to the land are conferred on a health service body, or

(b) the land is otherwise held, used or occupied by a health service body, the interest of the Secretary of State shall be treated for the purposes of any enactment or rule of law relating to Crown land or interests as if it were an interest held otherwise than by the Secretary of State (or any other emanation of the Crown).

(2) In Schedule 8 to this Act –

(a) Part I has the effect to continue certain exemptions for health service bodies and property held, used or occupied by such bodies;

(b) the amendments in Part II have effect, being amendments consequential on subsection (1) above; and

(c) the transitional provisions in Part III have effect in connection with the operation of subsection (1) above.

(3) Where, as a result of the provision of subsection (1) above, by virtue of his employment during any period after the day appointed for the coming into force of that subsection –

(a) an employee has contractual rights against a health service body to benefits in the event of his redundancy, and

(b) he also has statutory rights against the health service body under Part VI of the Employment Protection (Consolidation) Act 1978 (redundancy payments),

any benefits provided to him by virtue of the contractual rights referred to in paragraph (a) above shall be taken as satisfying his entitlement to benefits under the said Part VI.

(4) Nothing in subsection (1) above affects the extent of the expression "the services of the Crown" where it appears in –

(a) Schedule 1 to the Registered Designs Act 1949 (provisions as to the use of registered designs for the services of the Crown etc.); and

(b) sections 55 to 59 of the Patents Act 1977 (use of patented inventions for the services of the Crown);

and, accordingly, services provided in pursuance of any power or duty of the Secretary of State under Part I of the National Health Service Act 1977 or Part I or Part III of the National Health Service (Scotland) Act 1978 shall continue to be regarded as included in that expression, whether the services are in fact provided by a health service body, a National Health Service trust or any other person.

(5) The Secretary of State may by order made by statutory instrument provide that, in relation to any enactment contained in a local Act and specified in the order, the operation of subsection (1) above shall be excluded or modified to the extent specified in the order.

(6) No order shall be made under subsection (5) above unless a draft of it has been laid before, and approved by a resolution of, each House of Parliament.

(7) In this section "health service body" means –

    (a) a health authority, within the meaning of the National Health Service Act 1977;

    (b) a Health Board or Special Health Board constituted under section 2 of the National Health Service (Scotland) Act 1978;

    (c) a State Hospital Management Committee constituted under section 91 of the Mental Health (Scotland) Act 1984;

    (d) a Family Health Services Authority;

    (e) the Common Services Agency for the Scottish Health Service;

    (f) the Dental Practice Board;

    (g) The Scottish Dental Practice Board; and

    (h) the Public Health Laboratory Service Board.

(c) National Health Service (General Medical Services) Regulations 1992 (92/635)

PART II

GENERAL

Scope and terms of services

3.–(1) The arrangements with doctors for the provision of general medical services which it is the duty of an FHSA under section 29 of the Act to make and, under section 15(1) of the Act, to administer shall include arrangements for the provision of –

    (a) all necessary and appropriate personal medical services of the type usually provided by general medical practitioners;

    (b) child health surveillance services;

    (c) contraceptive services, that is to say –

        (i) the giving of advice to women on contraception,

        (ii) the medical examination of women seeking such advice,

        (iii) the contraceptive treatment of such women, and

        (iv) the supply to such women of contraceptive substances and appliances;

    (d) maternity medical services; and

    (e) minor surgery services.

SCHEDULE 2

TERMS OF SERVICE FOR DOCTORS

General

3. Where a decision whether any, and if so what, action is to be taken under these terms of service requires the exercise of professional judgment, a doctor shall not, in reaching that decision, be expected to exercise a higher degree of skill, knowledge and care than –

    (a) in the case of a doctor providing child health surveillance services under regulation 28, maternity medical services under regulation 31 or minor surgery services under regulation 33, that which any general practitioner included in the child health surveillance list, the obstetric list or, as the case may be, the minor surgery list may reasonably be expected to exercise; and

    (b) in any other case, that which general practitioners as a class may reasonably be expected to exercise.

Services to patients

12.–(1) Subject to paragraphs 3, 13 and 44, a doctor shall render to his patients all necessary and appropriate personal medical services of the type usually provided by general medical practitioners.

(2) The services which a doctor is required by sub-paragraph (1) to render shall include the following –

    (a) giving advice, where appropriate, to a patient in connection with the patient's general health, and in particular about the significance of diet, exercise, the use of tobacco, the consumption of alcohol and the misuse of drugs and solvents;

    (b) offering the patients consultations and, where appropriate, physical examinations for the purpose of identifying, or reducing the risk of, disease or injury;

    (c) offering to patients, where appropriate, vaccination or immunisation against measles, mumps, rubella, pertussis, poliomyelitis, diphtheria and tetanus;

    (d) arranging for the referral of patients, as appropriate, for the provision of any other services under the Act; and

    (e) giving advice, as appropriate, to enable patients to avail themselves of services provided by a local social services authority.

(3) A doctor is not required by sub-paragraphs (1) or (2) –

    (a) to provide to any person contraceptive services, child health surveillance services, minor surgery nor, except in an emergency, maternity medical services, unless he has previously undertaken to the FHSA to provide such services to that person; or

    (b) where he is a restricted services principal, to provide any category of general medical services which he has not undertaken to provide.

Provision of services to patients

13.–(1) The services referred to in paragraph 12 shall be rendered by a doctor –

    (a) at his practice premises;

    (b) if the condition of the patient so requires –

        (i) at the place where the patient was residing when he was accepted by the doctor pursuant to paragraph 6 or, as the case may be, when he was assigned to the doctor pursuant to regulation 21, or, in the case of a patient who was previously on the list of a doctor in a practice declared vacant when the doctor succeeded to the vacancy, or

       (ii) at such other place as the doctor has informed the patient and the FHSA is the place where he has agreed to visit and treat the patient if the patient's condition so requires; or

     (iii) in any other case, at some other place in the doctor's practice area;

    (c) at such places and at such times as have been approved by the FHSA in his case, pursuant to paragraph 29.

Employees

28.–(1) A doctor shall, before employing any person to assist him in the provision of general medical services, take reasonable care to satisfy himself that the person in question is both suitably qualified and competent to discharge the duties for which he is to be employed.

(2) When considering the competence and suitability of any person for the purpose of sub-paragraph (1), a doctor shall have regard, in particular, to –

    (a) that person's academic and vocational qualifications;

    (b) the person's training and his experience in employment; and

    (c) any guidance issued by the FHSA pursuant to regulation 39.

(3) A doctor shall afford to each employee reasonable opportunities to undertake appropriate training with a view to maintaining that employee's competence.

Records

36. A doctor shall –

    (a) keep adequate records of the illnesses and treatment of his patients on forms supplied to him for the purpose by the FHSA.

5. *Discovery*

(a) Supreme Court Act 1981

Powers of High Court exercisable before commencement of action

33.–(1) On the application of any person in accordance with rules of court, the High Court shall, in such circumstances as may be specified in the rules, have power to make an order providing for any one or more of the following matters, that is to say –

   (a) the inspection, photographing, preservation, custody and detention of property which appears to the court to be property which may become the subject matter of subsequent proceedings in the High Court, or as to which any question may arise in any such proceedings; and

   (b) the taking of samples of any such property as is mentioned in paragraph (a), and the carrying out of any experiment on or with any such property.

(2) On the application, in accordance with rules of court, of a person who appears to the High Court to be likely to be a party to subsequent proceedings in that court in which a claim in respect of personal injuries to a person, or in respect of a person's death, is likely to be made, the High Court shall, in such circumstances as may be specified in the rules, have power to order a person who appears to the court to be likely to be a party to the proceedings and to be likely to have or to have had in his possession, custody or power any documents which are relevant to an issue arising or likely to arise out of that claim –

   (a) to disclose whether those documents are in his possession, custody or power; and

   (b) to produce such of those documents as are in his possession, custody or power to the applicant or, on such conditions as may be specified in the order –

     (i) to the applicant's legal advisers; or

     (ii) to the applicant's legal advisers and any medical or other professional adviser of the applicant; or

     (iii) if the applicant has no legal adviser, to any medical or other professional adviser of the applicant.

Power of High Court to order disclosure of documents, inspection of property etc. in proceedings for personal injuries or death

34.–(1) This section applies to any proceedings in the High Court in which a claim is made in respect of personal injuries to a person, or in respect of a person's death.

(2) On the application, in accordance with rules of court, of a party to any proceedings to which this section applies, the High Court shall, in such circumstances as may be specified in the rules, have power to order a person who is not a party to the proceedings and who appears to the court to be likely to have in his possession, custody or power any documents which are relevant to an issue arising out of the said claim –

   (a) to disclose whether those documents are in his possession, custody or power; and

(b) to produce such of those documents as are in his possession, custody
or power to the applicant or, on such conditions as may be specified
in the order –
   (i) to the applicant's legal advisers; or
   (ii) to the applicant's legal advisers and any medical or other
professional adviser of the applicant; or
   (iii) if the applicant has no legal adviser, to any medical or other
professional adviser of the applicant.

(3) On the application, in accordance with rules of court, of a party to any
proceedings to which this section applies, the High Court shall, in such
circumstances as may be specified in the rules, have power to make an order
providing for any one or more of the following matters, that is to say –

(a) the inspection, photographing, preservation, custody and detention of property which is not the property of, or in the possession
of, any party to the proceedings but which is the subject-matter of
the proceedings or as to which any question arises in the proceedings;

(b) the taking of samples of any such property as is mentioned in
paragraph (a) and the carrying out of any experiment on or with any
such property.

(4) The preceding provisions of this section are without prejudice to the
exercise by the High Court of any power to make orders which is exercisable
apart from those provisions.

Provisions supplementary to ss. 33 and 34

35.–(1) The High Court shall not make an order under section 33 or 34 if it
considers that compliance with the order, if made, would be likely to be
injurious to the public interest.

(2) Rules of court may make provision as to the circumstances in which an
order under section 33 or 34 can be made; and any rules making such provision
may include such incidental, supplementary and consequential provisions as the
rule-making authority may consider necessary or expedient.

(3) Without prejudice to the generality of subsection (2), rules of court shall
be made for the purpose of ensuring that the costs of and incidental to
proceedings for an order under section 33(2) or 34 incurred by the person
against whom the order is sought shall be awarded to that person unless the
court otherwise directs.

(4) Sections 33(2) and 34 and this section bind the Crown; and section
33(1) binds the Crown so far as it relates to property as to which it appears to
the court that it may become the subject-matter of subsequent proceedings
involving a claim in respect of personal injuries to a person or in respect of a
person's death.

In this subsection references to the Crown do not include references to Her
Majesty in Her private capacity or to Her Majesty in right of Her Duchy of
Lancaster or to the Duke of Cornwall.

(5) In sections 33 and 34 and this section –
   "property" includes any land, chattel or other corporeal property of
any description;
   "personal injuries" includes any disease and any impairment of a
person's physical or mental condition.

(b) Rules of the Supreme Court

24/7 Order for discovery of particular documents (O.24, r.7)

7.–(1) Subject to rule 8, the Court may at any time on the application of any party to a cause or matter, make an order requiring any other party to make an affidavit stating whether any document specified or described in the application or any class of document so specified or described is, or has at any time been, in his possession, custody or power, and is not then in his possession, custody or power when he parted with it and what has become of it.

(2) An order may be made against a party under this rule notwithstanding that he may already have made or been required to make a list of documents or affidavits under rule 2 or rule 3.

(3) An application for an order under this rule must be supported by an affidavit stating the belief of the deponent that the party from whom discovery is sought under this rule has, or at some time had, in his possession, custody or power the document, or class of document, specified or described in the application and that it relates to one or more of the matters in question in the cause or matter.

24/7A Applications under s.33(2) or 34(2) of the Supreme Court Act 1981 (O.24, r.7A)

7A.–(1) An application for an order under section 33(2) of the Act for the disclosure of documents before the commencement of proceedings shall be made by originating summons in Form No. 10 in Appendix A and the person against whom the order is sought shall be made defendant to the summons.

(2) An application after the commencement of proceedings for an order under section 34(2) of the said Act for the disclosure of documents by a person who is not a party to the proceedings shall be made by summons, which must be served on that person personally and on every party to the proceedings other than the applicant.

(3) A summons under paragraph (1) or (2) shall be supported by an affidavit which must –
  (a) in the case of a summons under paragraph (1) state the grounds on which it is alleged that the applicant and the person against whom the order is sought are likely to be parties to subsequent proceedings in the High Court in which a claim for personal injuries is likely to be made;
  (b) in any case, specify or describe the documents in respect of which the order is sought and show, if practicable by reference to any pleading served or intended to be served in the proceedings, that the documents are relevant to an issue arising or likely to arise out of a claim for personal injuries made or likely to be made in the proceedings and that the person against whom the order is sought is likely to have or have had them in his possession, custody or power.

(4) A copy of the supporting affidavit shall be served with the summons on every person on whom the summons is required to be served.

(5) An order under the said section 33(2) or 34(2) for the disclosure of documents may be made conditional on the applicant's giving security for the costs of the person against whom it is made or on such other terms, if any, as the Court thinks just, and shall require the person against whom the order is made to make an affidavit stating whether any documents specified or described in the order are, or at any time have been, in his possession, custody or power and, if not then in his possession, custody or power, when he parted with them and what has become of them.

(6) No person shall be compelled by virtue of such an order to produce any documents which he could not be compelled to produce –

    (a) in the case of a summons under paragraph (1) if the subsequent proceedings had already been begun, or

    (b) in the case of a summons under paragraph (2) if he had been served with a writ of *subpoena duces lecum* to produce the documents at the trial.

(7) In this rule "a claim for personal injuries" means a claim in respect of personal injuries to a person or in respect of a person's death.

(8) For the purposes of rules 10 and 11 an application for an order under the said section 33(2) or 34(2) shall be treated as a cause or matter between the applicant and the person against whom the order is sought.

[Note: this rule was inserted by SI 71/1269 and amended by SI 75/911, SI 82/1111 and SI 90/1689.]

29/7A Inspection, etc., of property under ss. 33(1) and 34(3) of the Supreme Court Act 1981 (O.29, r.7A)

7A.–(1) An application for an order under section 33(1) of the Act in respect of property which may become the subject-matter of subsequent proceedings in the High Court or as to which any question may arise in any such proceedings shall be made by originating summons and the person against whom the order is sought shall be made defendant to the summons.

(2) An application after the commencement of proceedings for an order under section 34(3) of the Act in respect of property which is not the property of or in the possession of any party to the proceedings shall be made by summons, which must be served on the person against whom the order is being sought personally and on every party to the proceedings other than the applicant.

(3) A summons made under paragraph (1) or (2) shall be supported by affidavit which must specify or describe the property in respect of which the order is sought and show, if practicable by reference to any pleading served or intended to be served in the proceedings or subsequent proceedings, that it is property which is or may become the subject-matter of the proceedings or as to which any question arises or may arise in the proceedings.

(4) A copy of the supporting affidavit shall be served with the summons on every person on whom the summons is required to be served.

(5) An order made under the said section 33(1) or 34(3) may be made conditional on the applicant's giving security for the costs of the person against whom it is made or on such other terms, if any, as the court thinks just.

(6) No such order shall be made if it appears to the court:

    (a) that compliance with the order, if made, would result in the disclosure of information relating to a secret process, discovery or invention not in issue in the proceedings, and

    (b) that the application would have been refused on that ground if:

        (i) in the case of a summons under paragraph (1), the subsequent proceedings had already begun, or

        (ii) in the case of a summons under paragraph (2), the person against whom the order is being sought were a party to the proceedings.

[Note: this rule was inserted by SI 71/1269 and is printed as amended by SI 71/1955 and SI 82/1111.]

(c) Access to Health Records Act 1990

CHAPTER 23

ARRANGEMENT OF SECTIONS

Preliminary

Main provisions

Supplemental

An Act to establish a right of access to health records by the individuals to whom they relate and other persons; to provide for the correction of inaccurate health records and for the avoidance of certain contractual obligations; and for connected purposes.   [13th July 1990]

Preliminary

1.–(1) In this Act "health record" means a record which –
   (a) consists of information relating to the physical or mental health of an individual who can be identified from that information, or from that and other information in the possession of the holder of the record; and
   (b) has been made by or on behalf of a health professional in connection with the care of that individual;
but does not include any record which consists of information of which the individual is, or but for any exemption would be, entitled to be supplied with a copy under section 21 of the Data Protection Act 1984 (right of access to personal data).

   (2) In this Act "holder", in relation to a health record, means –
   (a) in the case of a record made by, or by a health professional employed by, a general practitioner –
      (i) the patient's general practitioner, that is to say, the general practitioner on whose list the patient is included; or
      (ii) where the patient has no general practitioner, the Family Practitioner Committee or Health Board on whose medical list the patient's most recent general practitioner was included;

(b) in the case of a record made by a health professional, for purposes connected with the provision of health services by a health service body, the health service body by which or on whose behalf the record is held;

(c) in any other case, the health professional by whom or on whose behalf the record is held.

(3) In this Act "patient", in relation to a health record, means the individual in connection with whose care the record has been made.

2.–(1) In this Act "health professional" means any of the following, namely –

(a) a registered medical practitioner;

(b) a registered dentist;

(c) a registered optician;

(d) a registered pharmaceutical chemist;

(e) a registered nurse, midwife or health visitor;

(f) a registered chiropodist, dietician, occupational therapist, orthoptist or physiotherapist;

(g) a clinical psychologist, child psychotherapist or speech therapist;

(h) an art or music therapist employed by a health service body; and

(i) a scientist employed by such a body as head of a department.

(2) Subsection (1)(a) above shall be deemed to include any person who is provisionally registered under section 15 or 21 of the Medical Act 1983 and is engaged in such employment as is mentioned in subsection (3) of that section.

(3) If, after the passing of this Act, an order is made under section 10 of the Professions Supplementary to Medicine Act 1960, the Secretary of State may by order make such consequential amendments of subsection (1)(f) as may appear to him to be necessary or expedient.

(4) The provisions of this Act shall apply in relation to health professionals in public service of the Crown as they apply in relation to other health professionals.

Main provisions

3.–(1) An application for access to a health record, or to any part of a health record, may be made to the holder of the record by any of the following, namely –

(a) the patient;

(b) a person authorised in writing to make the application on the patient's behalf;

(c) where the record is held in England and Wales and the patient is a child, a person having parental responsibility for the patient;

(d) where the record is held in Scotland and the patient is a pupil, a parent or guardian of the patient;

(e) where the patient is incapable of managing his own affairs, any person appointed by a court to manage those affairs; and

(f) where the patients has died, the patient's personal representative and any person who may have a claim arising out of the patient's death.

(2) Subject to section 4 below, where an application is made under subsection (1) above the holder shall, within the requisite period, give access to the record, or the part of a record, to which the application relates –

(a) in the case of a record, by allowing the applicant to inspect the record, or, where section 5 below applies, an extract setting out so much of the record as is not excluded by that section;

    (b) in the case of a part of a record, by allowing the applicant to inspect an extract setting out that part or, where that section applies, so much of that part as is not so excluded; or

    (c) in either case, if the applicant so requires, by supplying him with a copy of the record or extract.

(3) Where any information contained in a record or extract which is so allowed to be inspected, or a copy of which is so supplied, is expressed in terms which are not intelligible without explanation, an explanation of those terms shall be provided with the record or extract, or supplied with the copy.

(4) No fee shall be required for giving access under subsection (2) above other than the following, namely –

    (a) where access is given to a record, or part of a record, none of which was made after the beginning of the period of 40 days immediately preceding the date of the application, a fee not exceeding the maximum prescribed under section 21 of the Data Protection Act 1984; and

    (b) where a copy of a record or extract is supplied to the applicant, a fee not exceeding the cost of making the copy and (where applicable) the cost of posting it to him.

(5) For the purposes of subsection (2) above the requisite period is –

    (a) where the application relates to a record, or part of a record, none of which was made before the beginning of the period of 40 days immediately preceding the date of the application, the period of 21 days beginning with that date;

    (b) in any other case, the period of 40 days beginning with that date.

(6) Where –

    (a) an application under subsection (1) above does not contain sufficient information to enable the holder of the record to identify the patient or, in the case of an application made otherwise than by the patient, to satisfy himself that the applicant is entitled to make the application; and

    (b) within the period of 14 days beginning with the date of the application, the holder of the record requests the applicant to furnish him with such further information as he may reasonably require for that purpose,

subsection (5) above shall have effect as if for any reference to that date there were substituted a reference to the date on which that further information is so furnished.

4.–(1) Where an application is made under subsection (1)(a) or (b) of section 3 above and –

    (a) in the case of a record held in England and Wales, the patient is a child; or

    (b) in the case of a record held in Scotland, the patient is a pupil,

access shall not be given under subsection (2) of that section unless the holder of the record is satisfied that the patient is capable of understanding the nature of the application.

(2) Where an application is made under subsection (1)(c) or (d) of section 3 above, access shall not be given under subsection (2) of that section unless the holder of the record is satisfied either –

    (a) that the patient has consented to the making of the application; or

    (b) that the patient is incapable of understanding the nature of the application and the giving of access would be in his best interests.

(3) Where an application is made under subsection (1)(f) of section 3 above, access shall not be given under subsection (2) of that section if the record includes a note, made at the patient's request, that he did not wish access to be given on such an application.

5.–(1) Access shall not be given under section 3(2) above to any part of a health record –
    (a) which, in the opinion of the holder of the record, would disclose –
          (i) information likely to cause serious harm to the physical or mental health of the patient or of any other individual; or
         (ii) information relating to or provided by an individual, other than the patient, who could be identified from that information; or
    (b) which was made before the commencement of this Act.
  (2) Subsection (1)(a)(ii) above shall not apply –
    (a) where the individual concerned has consented to the application; or
    (b) where that individual is a health professional who has been involved in the care of the patient;
and subsection (1)(b) above shall not apply where and to the extent that, in the opinion of the holder of the record, the giving of access is necessary in order to make intelligible any part of the record to which access is required to be given under section 3(2) above.
  (3) Where an application is made under subsection (1)(c), (d), (e) or (f) of section 3 above, access shall not be given under subsection (2) of that section to any part of the record which, in the opinion of the holder of the record, would disclose –
    (a) information provided by the patient in the expectation that it would not be disclosed to the applicant; or
    (b) information obtained as a result of any examination or investigation to which the patient consented in the expectation that the information would not be so disclosed.
  (4) Where an application is made under subsection (1)(f) of section 3 above, access shall not be given under subsection (2) of that section to any part of the record which, in the opinion of the holder of the record, would disclose information which is not relevant to any claim which may arise out of the patient's death.
  (5) The Secretary of State may by regulations provide that, in such circumstances as may be prescribed by the regulations, access shall not be given under section 3(2) above to any part of a health record which satisfies such conditions as may be so prescribed.

6.–(1) Where a person considers that any information contained in a health record, or any part of a health record, to which he has been given access under section 3(2) above is inaccurate, he may apply to the holder of the record for the necessary correction to be made.
  (2) On an application under subsection (1) above, the holder of the record shall –
    (a) if he is satisfied that the information is inaccurate, make the necessary correction;
    (b) if he is not so satisfied, make in the part of the record in which the information is contained a note of the matters in respect of which the information is considered by the applicants to be inaccurate; and
    (c) in either case, without requiring any fee, supply the applicant with a copy of the correction or note.
  (3) In this section "inaccurate" means incorrect, misleading or incomplete.

7.–(1) A health service body or Family Practitioner Committee shall take advice from the appropriate health professional before they decide whether they are satisfied as to any matter for the purposes of this Act, or form an opinion as to any matter for those purposes.

(2) In this section "the appropriate health professional", in relation to a health service body (other than a Health Board which is the holder of the record by virtue of section 1(2)(a) above), means –

(a) where, for purposes connected with the provision of health services by the body, one or more medical or dental practitioners are currently responsible for clinical care of the patient, that practitioner or, as the case may be, such one of those practitioners as is the most suitable to advise the body on the matter in question;

(b) where paragraph (a) does not apply but one or more medical or dental practitioners are available who, for purposes connected with the provision of such services by the body, have been responsible for the clinical care of the patient, that practitioner or, as the case may be, such one of those practitioners as was most recently so responsible; and

(c) where neither paragraph (a) nor paragraph (b) above applies, a health professional who has the necessary experience and qualifications to advise the body on the matter in question.

(3) In this section "the appropriate health professional", in relation to a Family Practitioner Committee or a Health Board which is the holder of the record by virtue of section 1(2)(a) above, means –

(a) where the patient's most recent general practitioner is available, that practitioner; and

(b) where the practitioner is not available, a registered medical practitioner who has the necessary experience and qualifications to advise the Committee or Board on the matter in question.

Supplemental

8.–(1) Subject to subsection (2) below, where the court is satisfied, on an application made by the person concerned within such period as may be prescribed by rules of court, that the holder of a health record has failed to comply with any requirement of this Act, the court may order the holder to comply with that requirement.

(2) The court shall not entertain an application under subsection (1) above unless it is satisfied that the applicant has taken all such steps to secure compliance with the requirement as may be prescribed by regulations made by the Secretary of State.

(3) For the purpose of subsection (2) above, the Secretary of State may by regulations require the holders of health records to make such arrangements for dealing with complaints that they have failed to comply with any requirements of this Act as may be prescribed by the regulations.

(4) For the purpose of determining any question whether an applicant is entitled to be given access under section 3(2) above to any health record, or any part of a health record, the court –

(a) may require the record or part to be made available for its own inspection; but

(b) shall not, pending determination of that question in the applicant's favour, require the record or part to be disclosed to him or his representatives whether by discovery (or, in Scotland, recovery) or otherwise.

(5) The jurisdiction conferred by this section shall be exercisable by the High Court or a county court or, in Scotland, by the Court of Session or the sheriff.

9. Any term or condition of a contract shall be void in so far as it purports to require an individual to supply any other person with a copy of a health record, or of an extract from a health record, to which he has been given access under section 3(2) above.

10.–(1) Regulations under this Act may make different provision for different cases or classes of cases including, in particular, different provision for different health records or classes of health records.

(2) Any power to make regulations or orders under this Act shall be exercisable by statutory instrument.

(3) Any statutory instrument containing regulations under this Act or an order under section 2(3) above shall be subject to annulment in pursuance of a resolution of either House of Parliament.

11. In this Act –

"application" means an application in writing and "apply" shall be construed accordingly;

"care" includes examination, investigation, diagnosis and treatment;

"child" means an individual who has not attained the age of 16 years;

"general practitioner" means a medical practitioner who is providing general medical services in accordance with arrangements made under section 29 of the National Health Service Act 1977 or section 19 of the National Health Service (Scotland) Act 1978;

"Health Board" has the same meaning as in the National Health Service (Scotland) Act 1977;

"health service body" means –

(a) a health authority within the meaning of the National Health Service Act 1977;

(b) a Health Board;

(c) a State Hospital Management Committee constituted under section 91 of the Mental Health (Scotland) Act 1984; or

(d) a National Health Service trust first established under section 5 of the National Health Service and Community Care Act 1990 or section 12A of the National Health Service (Scotland) Act 1978;

"information", in relation to a health record, includes any expression of opinion about the patient;

"make", in relation to such a record, includes compile;

"parental responsibility" has the same meaning as in the Children Act 1989.

12.–(1) This Act may be cited as the Access to Health Records Act 1990.

(2) This Act shall come into force on 1st November 1991.

(3) This Act does not extend to Northern Ireland.

6. *Evidence*

(a) Civil Evidence Act 1972 (1972 c.30)

[*The sections reproduced below are printed as amended, where appropriate.*]

ARRANGEMENT OF SECTIONS

Section

An Act to make, for civil proceedings in England and Wales, provision as to the admissibility in evidence of statements of opinion and the reception of expert evidence; and to facilitate proof in such proceedings of any law other than that of England and Wales.   [12th June 1972]

Application of Part I of Civil Evidence Act 1968 to statements of opinion

1.–(1) Subject to the provisions of this section, Part I (hearsay evidence) of the Civil Evidence Act 1968, except section 5 (statements produced by computers), shall apply in relation to statements of opinion as it applies in relation to statements of fact, subject to the necessary modifications and in particular the modification that any reference to a fact stated in a statement shall be construed as a reference to a matter dealt with therein.

(2) Section 4 (admissibility of certain records) of the Civil Evidence Act 1968, as applied by subsection (1) above, shall not render admissible in any civil proceedings a statement of opinion contained in a record unless that statement would be admissible in those proceedings if made in the course of giving oral evidence by the person who originally supplied the information from which the record was compiled; but where a statement of opinion contained in a record deals with a matter on which the person who originally supplied the information from which the record was compiled is (or would if living be) qualified to give oral expert evidence, the said section 4, as applied by subsection (1) above, shall have effect in relation to that statement as if so much of subsection (1) of that section as requires personal knowledge on the part of that person were omitted.

Rules of court with respect to expert reports and oral expert evidence

2.–(1) If and so far as rules of court so provide, subsection (2) of section (2) of the Civil Evidence Act 1968 (which imposes restrictions on the giving of a statement in evidence by virtue of that section on behalf of a party who has called or intends to call as a witness the maker of the statement) shall not apply to statements (whether of fact or opinion) contained in expert reports.

(2) In so far as they relate to statements (whether of fact or opinion) contained in expert reports, rules of court made in pursuance of subsection (1) of section 8 of the Civil Evidence Act 1968 as to the procedure to be followed and the other conditions to be fulfilled before a statement can be given in evidence in civil proceedings by virtue of section 2 of that Act (admissibility of

out-of-court statements) shall not be subject to the requirements of subsection (2) of the said section 8 (which specifies certain matters of procedure for which provision must ordinarily be made by rules of court made in pursuance of the said subsection (1)).

(3) Notwithstanding any enactment or rule of law by virtue of which documents prepared for the purpose of pending or contemplated civil proceedings or in connection with the obtaining or giving of legal advice are in certain circumstances privileged from disclosure, provision may be made by rules of court:

  (a) for enabling the court in any civil proceedings to direct, with respect to medical matters or matters of any other class which may be specified in the direction, that the parties or some of them shall each by such date as may be so specified (or such later date as may be permitted or agreed in accordance with the rules) disclose to the other or others in the form of one or more expert reports the expert evidence on matters of that class which he proposed to adduce as part of his case at the trial; and

  (b) for prohibiting a party who fails to comply with a direction given in any such proceedings under rules of court made by virtue of paragraph (a) above from adducing in evidence by virtue of section 2 of the Civil Evidence Act 1968 (admissibility of out-of-court statements), except with the leave of the court, any statement (whether of fact or opinion) contained in any expert report whatsoever in so far as that statement deals with matters of any class specified in the direction.

(4) Provision may be made by rules of court as to the conditions subject to which oral expert evidence may be given in civil proceedings.

(5) Without prejudice to the generality of subsection (4) above, rules of court made in pursuance of that subsection may make provision for prohibiting a party who fails to comply with a direction given as mentioned in subsection (3)(b) above from adducing, except with the leave of the court, any oral expert evidence whatsoever with respect to matters of any class specified in the direction.

(6) Any rules of court made in pursuance of this section may make different provision for different classes of cases, for expert reports dealing with matters of different classes, and for other different circumstances.

(7) References in this section to an expert report are references to a written report by a person dealing wholly or mainly with matters on which he is (or would if living be) qualified to give expert evidence.

(8) Nothing in the foregoing provisions of this section shall prejudice the generality of section 75 of the County Courts Act 1984, section 144 of the Magistrates' Courts Act 1980 or any other enactment conferring power to make rules of court; and nothing in section 75(2) of the County Courts Act 1984 or any other enactment restricting the matters with respect to which rules of court may be made shall prejudice the making of rules of court in pursuance of this section or the operation of any rules of court so made.

Admissibility of expert opinion and certain expressions of non-expert opinion

3.–(1) Subject to any rules of court made in pursuance of Part I of the Civil Evidence Act 1968 or this Act, where a person is called as a witness in any civil proceedings, his opinion on any relevant matter on which he is qualified to give expert evidence shall be admissible in evidence.

(2) It is hereby declared that where a person is called as a witness in any civil proceedings, a statement of opinion by him on any relevant matter on which he

is not qualified to give expert evidence, if made as a way of conveying relevant facts personally perceived by him, is admissible as evidence of what he perceived.

(3) In this section "relevant matter" includes an issue in the proceedings in question.

Interpretation, application to arbitration, etc., and savings

5.–(1) In this Act "civil proceedings" and "court" have the meanings assigned by section 18(1) and (2) of the Civil Evidence Act 1968.

(2) Subsections (3) and (4) of section 10 of the Civil Evidence Act 1968 shall apply for the purposes of the application of sections 2 and 4 of this Act in relation to any such civil proceedings as are mentioned in section 18(1)(a) and (b) of that Act (that is to say civil proceedings before a tribunal other than one of the ordinary courts of law, being proceedings in relation to which the strict rules of evidence apply, and an arbitration or reference, whether under an enactment or not) as they apply for the purposes of the application of Part I of that Act in relation to any such civil proceedings.

(3) Nothing in this Act shall prejudice:

    (a) any power of a court, in any civil proceedings, to exclude evidence (whether by preventing questions from being put or otherwise) at its discretion; or

    (b) the operation of any agreement (whenever made) between the parties to any civil proceedings as to the evidence which is to be admissible (whether generally or for any particular purpose) in those proceedings.

Short title, extent and commencement

6.–(1) This Act may be cited as the Civil Evidence Act 1972.

(2) This Act shall not extend to Scotland or Northern Ireland.

(3) This Act, except sections 1 and 4(2) to (5), shall come into force on 1 January 1973, and sections 1 and 4(2) to (5) shall come into force on such day as the Lord Chancellor may by order made by statutory instrument appoint; and different days may be so appointed for different purposes or for the same purposes in relation to different courts or proceedings or otherwise in relation to different circumstances.

[Note to s. 6: ss. 1 and 4(2)–(5) of this Act have been brought into operation for the purpose of, inter alia, proceedings in the Supreme Court and in the county court, other than proceedings in bankruptcy: for the relevant commencement orders, see SI 74/280 and 1137.]

(b) Rules of the Supreme Court

ORDER 38

EVIDENCE

I. GENERAL RULES

General rule: witnesses to be examined orally

1. Subject to the provisions of these rules and of the Civil Evidence Act 1968 and the Civil Evidence Act 1972, and any other enactment relating to evidence, any fact required to be proved at the trial of any action begun by writ by the evidence of witnesses shall be proved by the examination of witnesses orally and in open Court.

[Note: this rule is printed as amended by SI 69/1105 and by SI 79/1542.]

Evidence by affidavit

2.–(1) The Court may, at or before the trial of an action begun by writ, order that the affidavit of any witness may be read at the trial if in the circumstances of the case it thinks reasonable so to order.

(2) An order under paragraph (1) may be made on such terms as to the filing and giving of copies of the affidavits and as to the production of the deponents for cross-examination as the Court thinks fit but, subject to any such terms and to any subsequent order of the Court, the deponents shall not be subject to cross-examination and need not attend the trial for the purpose.

(3) In any cause or matter begun by originating summons, originating motion or petition, and on any application made by summons or motion, evidence may be given by affidavit unless in the case of any such cause, matter or application any provision of these rules otherwise provides or the Court otherwise directs, but the Court may, on the application of any party, order the attendance for cross-examination of the person making any such affidavit, and where, after such an order has been made, the person in question does not attend, his affidavit shall not be used as evidence without the leave of the Court.

Exchange of witness statements

2A.–(1) The powers of the Court under this rule shall be exercised for the purpose of disposing fairly and expeditiously of the cause or matter before it, and saving costs, having regard to all the circumstances of the case, including (but not limited to) –
- (a) the extent to which the facts are in dispute or have been admitted;
- (b) the extent to which the issues of fact are defined by the pleadings;
- (c) the extent to which information has been or is likely to be provided by further and better particulars, answers to interrogatories or otherwise.

(2) At the summons for directions in an action commenced by writ the Court shall direct every party to serve on the other parties, within 14 weeks (or such other period as the Court may specify) of the hearing of the summons and on such terms as the Court may specify, written statements of the oral evidence which the party intends to adduce on any issues of fact to be decided at the trial.

The Court may give a direction to any party under this paragraph at any other stage of such an action and at any stage of any other cause or matter.

Order 3, rule 5(3) shall not apply to any period specified by the Court under this paragraph.

(3) Directions under paragraph (2) or (17) may make different provision with regard to different issues of fact or different witnesses.

(4) Statements served under this rule shall –
- (a) be dated and, except for good reason (which should be specified by letter accompanying the statement), be signed by the intended witness and shall include a statement by him that the contents are true to the best of his knowledge and belief;
- (b) sufficiently identify any documents referred to therein; and

    (c) where they are to be served by more than one party, be exchanged simultaneously.

(5) Where a party is unable to obtain a written statement from an intended witness in accordance with paragraph (4)(a), the Court may direct the party wishing to adduce that witness's evidence to provide the other party with the name of the witness and (unless the Court otherwise orders) a statement of the nature of the evidence intended to be adduced.

(6) Subject to paragraph (9), where the party serving a statement under this rule does not call the witness to whose evidence it relates, no other party may put the statement in evidence at the trial.

(7) Subject to paragraph (9), where the party serving the statement does call such a witness at the trial –

    (a) except where the trial is with a jury, the Court may, on such terms as it thinks fit, direct that the statement served, or part of it, shall stand as the evidence in chief of the witness or part of such evidence;

    (b) the party may not without the consent of the other parties or the leave of the Court adduce evidence from that witness the substance of which is not included in the statement served, except –

        (i) where the Court's directions under paragraph (2) or (17) specify that statements should be exchanged in relation to only some issues of fact, in relation to any other issues;

        (ii) in relation to new matters which have arisen since the statement was served on the other party;

    (c) whether or not the statement or any part of it referred to during the evidence in chief of the witness, any party may put the statement or any part of it in cross-examination of that witness.

(8) Nothing in this rule shall make admissible evidence which is otherwise inadmissible.

(9) Where any statement served is one to which the Civil Evidence Acts 1968 and 1972 apply, paragraphs (6) and (7) shall take effect subject to the provisions of those Acts and Parts III and IV of this Order.

The service of a witness statement under this rule shall not, unless expressly so stated by the party serving the same, be treated as a notice under the said Acts of 1968 and 1972; and where a statement or any part thereof would be admissible in evidence by virtue only of the said Act of 1968 or 1972 the appropriate notice under Part III or Part IV of this Order shall be served with the statement notwithstanding any provision of those Parts as to the time for serving such a notice. Where such a notice is served a counter-notice shall be deemed to have been served under Order 38, rule 26(1).

(10) Where a party fails to comply with a direction for the exchange of witness statements he shall not be entitled to adduce evidence to which the direction related without the leave of the Court.

(11) Where a party serves a witness statement under this rule, no other person may make use of that statement for any purpose other than the purpose of the proceedings in which it was served –

    (a) unless and to the extent that the party serving it gives his consent in writing or the Court gives leave; or

    (b) unless and to the extent that it has been put in evidence (whether pursuant to a direction under paragraph (7)(a) or otherwise).

(12) Subject to paragraph (13), the judge shall, if any person so requests during the course of the trial, direct the associate to certify as open to inspection any witness statement which was ordered to stand as evidence in chief under paragraph (7)(a).

A request under this paragraph may be made orally or in writing.

(13) The judge may refuse to give a direction under paragraph (12) in relation to a witness statement, or may exclude from such a direction any words or passages in a statement, if he considers that inspection should not be available –

(a) in the interests of justice or national security,

(b) because of the nature of any expert medical evidence in the statement, or

(c) for any other sufficient reason.

(14) Where the associate is directed under paragraph (12) to certify a witness statement as open to inspection he shall –

(a) prepare a certificate which shall be attached to a copy ("the certified copy") of that witness statement; and

(b) make the certified copy available for inspection.

(15) Subject to any conditions which the Court may by special or general direction impose, any person may inspect and (subject to payment of the prescribed fee) take a copy of the certified copy of a witness statement from the time when the certificate is given until the end of 7 days after the conclusion of the trial.

(16) In this rule –

(a) any reference in paragraphs (12) to (15) to a witness statement shall, in relation to a witness statement of which only part has been ordered to stand as evidence in chief under paragraph (7)(a), be construed as a reference to that part;

(b) any reference to inspecting or copying the certified copy of a witness statement shall be construed as including a reference to inspecting or copying a copy of that certified copy.

(17) The Court shall have power to vary or override any of the provisions of this rule (except paragraphs (1), (8) and (12) to (16)) and to give such alternative direction as it thinks fit.

[Note: this rule is printed as substituted by SI 92/1907.]

Evidence of particular facts

3.–(1) Without prejudice to rule 2, the Court may, at or before the trial of any action, order that evidence of any particular fact shall be given at the trial in such manner as may be specified by the order.

(2) The power conferred by paragraph (1) extends in particular to ordering that evidence of any particular fact may be given at the trial:

(a) by statement on oath of information or belief, or

(b) by the production of documents or entries in books, or

(c) by copies of documents or entries in books, or

(d) in the case of a fact which is or was a matter of common knowledge either generally or in a particular district, by the production of a specified newspaper which contains a statement of that fact.

Limitation of expert evidence

4. The Court may, at or before the trial of any action, order that the number of medical or other expert witnesses who may be called at the trial shall be limited as specified by the order.

Order to produce document at proceeding other than trial

13.–(1) At any stage in a cause or matter the Court may order any person to attend any proceeding in the cause or matter and produce any document, to be specified or described in the order, the production of which appears to the Court to be necessary for the purpose of that proceeding.

(2) No person shall be compelled by an order under paragraph (1) to produce any document at a proceeding in a cause or matter which he could not be compelled to produce at the trial of that cause or matter.

IV. Expert Evidence

[Note: this Part (rr.35 to 42) was added to O.38 by SI 74/295 and rr.37 and 38 come from SI 87/1423 (1.8).]

Interpretation

35. In this Part of this Order a reference to a summons for directions includes a reference to any summons or application to which, under any of these Rules, Order 25, rules 2 to 7, apply and expressions used in this Part of this Order which are used in the Civil Evidence Act 1972 have the same meanings in this Part of this Order as in that Act.

Restrictions on adducing expert evidence

36.–(1) Except with the leave of the Court or where all parties agree, no expert evidence may be adduced at the trial or hearing of any cause or matter unless the party seeking to adduce the evidence:

    (a) has applied to the Court to determine whether a direction should be given under rule 37 or 41 (whichever is appropriate) and has complied with any direction given on the application, or

    (b) has complied with automatic directions taking effect under Order 25, rule 8(1)(b).

(2) Nothing in paragraph (1) shall apply to evidence which is permitted to be given by affidavit or shall affect the enforcement under any other provision of these rules (except Order 34, rule 5) of a direction given under this Part of this Order.

Direction that expert report be disclosed

37.–(1) Subject to paragraph (2), where in any cause or matter an application is made under rule 36(1) in respect of oral expert evidence, then, unless the Court considers that there are special reasons for not doing so, it shall direct that the substance of the evidence be disclosed in the form of a written report or reports to such other parties and within such period as the Court may specify.

(2) Nothing in paragraph (1) shall require a party to disclose a further medical report if he proposes to rely at the trial only on the report provided pursuant to Order 18, rule 12(1A) or (1B) but, where a party claiming damages for personal injuries discloses a further report, that report shall be accompanied by a statement of the special damages claimed and, in this paragraph, "statement of the special damages claimed" has the same meaning as in Order 18, rule 12(1C).

Meeting of experts

38. In any cause or matter the Court may, if it thinks fit, direct that there be a meeting "without prejudice" of such experts within such periods before or after the disclosure of their reports as the Court may specify, for the purpose of identifying those parts of their evidence which are in issue. Where such a meeting takes place the experts may prepare a joint statement indicating those parts of their evidence on which they are, and those on which they are not, in agreement.

Disclosure of part of expert evidence

39. Where the Court considers that any circumstances rendering it undesirable to give a direction under rule 37 relate to part only of the evidence sought to be adduced, the Court may, if it thinks fit, direct disclosure of the remainder.

Expert evidence contained in statement

41. Where an application is made under rule 36 in respect of expert evidence contained in a statement and the applicant alleges that the maker of the statement cannot or should not be called as a witness, the Court may direct that the provisions of rules 20 to 23 and 25 to 33 shall apply with such modifications as the Court thinks fit.

Putting in evidence expert report disclosed by another party

42. A party to any cause or matter may put in evidence any expert report disclosed to him by any other party in accordance with this Part of this Order.

Time for putting expert report in evidence

43. Where a party to any cause or matter calls as a witness the maker of a report which has been disclosed in accordance with a direction given under rule 37, the report may be put in evidence at the commencement of its maker's examination in chief or at such other time as the Court may direct.

Revocation and variation of directions

44. Any direction given under this Part of this Order may on sufficient cause being shown be revoked or varied by a subsequent direction given at or before the trial of the cause or matter.

7. Procedure (RSC)

O.6 r.8(1)–(2A) (duration and renewal of writ)

8.–(1) For the purposes of service, a writ (other than a concurrent writ) is valid in the first instance –
- (a) if an Admiralty writ *in rem*, for 12 months,
- (b) where leave to serve the writ out of the jurisdiction is required under Order 11, for 6 months,
- (c) in any other case, for 4 months

beginning with the date of its issue.

(1A) A concurrent writ is valid in the first instance for the period of validity of the original writ which is unexpired at the date of issue of the concurrent writ.

(2) Subject to paragraph (2A), where a writ has not been served on a defendant, the Court may by order extend the validity of the writ from time to time for such period, not exceeding 4 months at any one time, beginning with the day next following that on which it would otherwise expire, as may be specified in the order, if an application for extension is made to the Court before that day or such later day (if any) as the Court may allow.

(2A) Where the Court is satisfied on an application under paragraph (2) that, despite the making of all reasonable efforts, it may not be possible to serve the writ within 4 months, the Court may, if it thinks fit, extend the validity of the writ for such period, not exceeding 12 months, as the Court may specify.

O.18 r.12(1A)–(1C) (provision of medical reports)

(1A) Subject to paragraph (1B), a plaintiff in an action for personal injuries shall serve with his statement of claim –
- (a) a medical report, and
- (b) a statement of the special damages claimed.

(1B) Where the documents to which paragraph (1A) applies are not served with the statement of claim, the Court may –
- (a) specify the period of time within which they are to be provided, or
- (b) make such other order as it thinks fit (including an order dispensing with the requirements of paragraph (1A) or staying the proceedings).

(1C) For the purposes of this rule –
"medical report" means a report substantiating all the personal injuries alleged in the statement of claim which the plaintiff proposes to adduce in evidence as part of his case at the trial;
"a statement of the special damages claimed" means a statement giving full particulars of the special damages claimed for expenses and losses already incurred and an estimate of any future expenses and losses (including loss of earnings and of pension rights).

O.18 r.19 Striking out pleadings and indorsements

19.–(1) The Court may at any stage of the proceedings order to be struck out or amended any pleading or the indorsement of any writ in the action, or anything in any pleading or in the indorsement, on the ground that –
- (a) it discloses no reasonable cause of action or defence, as the case may be; or
- (b) it is scandalous, frivolous or vexatious; or
- (c) it may prejudice, embarrass or delay the fair trial of the action; or
- (d) it is otherwise an abuse of the process of the Court;

and may order the action to be stayed or dismissed or judgment to be entered accordingly, as the case may be.

(2) No evidence shall be admissible on any application under paragraph (1)(a).

(3) This rule shall, so far as applicable, apply to an originating summons and a petition as if the summons or petition, as the case may be, were a pleading.

O.24 r.16 Failure to comply with requirement for discovery, etc.

16.–(1) If any party who is required by any of the foregoing rules, or by any order made thereunder, to make discovery of documents or to produce any documents for the purpose of inspection or any other purpose fails to comply with any provision of that rule or with that order, as the case may be, then without prejudice, the case of a failure to comply with any such provision, to rules 3(2) and 11(1) the Court may make such order as it thinks just including, in particular, an order that the action be dismissed, or, as the case may be, an order that the defence be struck out and judgment be entered accordingly.

(2) In any party against whom an order for discovery or production of documents is made fails to comply with it, then, without prejudice to paragraph (1) he shall be liable to committal.

(3) Service on a party's solicitor of an order for discovery or production of documents made against that party shall be sufficient service to found an application for committal of the party disobeying the order, but the party may show in answer to the application that he had no notice or knowledge of the order.

(4) A solicitor on whom such an order made against his client is served and who fails without reasonable excuse to give notice thereof to his client shall be liable to committal.

O.26 (interrogatories)

Discovery by interrogatories

1.–(1) A party to any cause or matter may in accordance with the following provisions of this Order serve on any other party interrogatories relating to any matter in question between the applicant and that other party in the cause or matter which are necessary either –

    (a) for disposing fairly of the cause or matter, or

    (b) for saving costs.

(2) Without prejudice to the provisions of paragraph (1), a party may apply to the Court for an order giving him leave to serve on any other party interrogatories relating to any matter in question between the applicant and that other party in the cause or matter.

(3) A proposed interrogatory which does not relate to such a matter as is mentioned in paragraph (1) may not be administered notwithstanding that it might be admissible in oral cross-examination of a witness.

(4) In this Order,

        "interrogatories without order" means interrogatories served under paragraph (1);

        "ordered interrogatories" means interrogatories served under paragraph (2) or interrogatories which are required to be answered pursuant to an order made on an application under rule 3(2) and, where such an order is made, the interrogatories shall not, unless the Court orders otherwise, be treated as interrogatories without order for the purposes of rule 3(1).

(5) Unless the context otherwise requires, the provisions of this Order apply to both interrogatories without order and ordered interrogatories.

Form and nature of interrogatories

2.–(1) Where interrogatories are served, a note at the end of the interrogatories shall specify –

    (a) a period of time (not giving less than 28 days from the date of service) within which the interrogatories are to be answered;

    (b) where the party to be interrogated is a body corporate or unincorporate which is empowered by law to sue or be sued whether in its own name or in the name of an officer or other person, the officer or member on whom the interrogatories are to be served; and

    (c) where the interrogatories are to be served on two or more parties or are required to be answered by an agent or servant of a party, which of the interrogatories each party or, as the case may be, an agent or servant is required to answer, and which agent or servant.

(2) Subject to rule 5(1), a party on whom interrogatories are served shall, unless the Court orders otherwise on an application under rule 3(2), be required to give within the period specified under rule 2(1)(a) answers, which shall (unless the Court directs otherwise) be on affidavit.

Interrogatories without order

3.–(1) Interrogatories without order may be served on a party not more than twice.

(2) A party on whom interrogatories without order are served may, within 14 days of the service of the interrogatories, apply to the Court for the interrogatories to be varied or withdrawn and, on any such application, the Court may make such order as it thinks fit (including an order that the party who served the interrogatories shall not serve further interrogatories without order).

(3) Interrogatories without order shall not be served on the Crown.

Ordered interrogatories

4.–(1) Where an application is made for leave to serve interrogatories, a copy of the proposed interrogatories shall be served with the summons or the notice under Order 25, rule 7, by which the application is made.

(2) In deciding whether to give leave to serve interrogatories, the Court shall take into account any offer made by the party to be interrogated to give particulars, make admissions or produce documents relating to any matter in question and whether or not interrogatories without order have been administered.

Objections and insufficient answers

5.–(1) Without prejudice to rule 3(2), where a person objects to answering any interrogatory on the ground of privilege he may take the objection in his answer.

(2) Where any person on whom ordered interrogatories have been served answers any of them insufficiently, the Court may make an order requiring him

to make a further answer, either by affidavit or on oral examination as the Court may direct.

(3) Where any person on whom interrogatories without order have been served answers any of them insufficiently, the party serving the interrogatories may ask for further and better particulars of the answer given and any such request shall not be treated as service of further interrogatories for the purposes of rule 3(1).

Failure to comply with order

6.–(1) If a party fails to answer interrogatories or to comply with an order made under rule 5(2) or a request made under rule 5(3), the Court may make such order as it thinks just including, in particular, an order that the action be dismissed or, as the case may be, an order that the defence be struck out and judgment be entered accordingly.

(2) Without prejudice to paragraph (1), where a party fails to answer ordered interrogatories or to comply with an order made under rule 5(2), he shall be liable to committal.

(3) Service on a party's solicitor of an order to answer interrogatories made against the party shall be sufficient service to found an application for committal of the party disobeying the order, but the party may show in answer to the application that he had no notice or knowledge of the order.

(4) A solicitor on whom an order to answer interrogatories made against his client is served and who fails without reasonable excuse to give notice thereof to his client shall be liable to committal.

O.33 r.4(2A) (split trials)

(2A) In an action for personal injuries, the Court may at any stage of the proceedings and of its own motion make an order of the issue of liability to be tried before any issue or question concerning the amount of damages to be awarded and –

(a) notwithstanding the provisions of Order 42, rule 5(5), an order so made in the absence of the parties shall be drawn up by an officer of the Court who shall serve a copy of the order on every party; and

(b) where a party applies within 14 days after service of the order upon him, the Court may confirm or vary the order or set it aside.

Appendix II

Drafts and Precedents

Contents:

Draft letter (to hospital or GP) requesting disclosure of the medical records

The following is the short form – it is usually as effective as the longer form (the vital points are a rough indication of what the complaint is and the authority for the disclosure from the client):

Dear ....

                          Our client: ....

We act under a legal aid certificate no .... dated .... on behalf of the above-named, who was a patient at your hospital [who received treatment at your hospital] [who was under the care of your GP practice] between .... and ....

Now set out very briefly the treatment complained of and the possible grounds for complaint.

Please send all the medical records you hold concerning our client (we will pay your reasonable copying charges). We enclose our client's authority for the disclosure.

Yours faithfully,

....

The longer form is:

Dear ....

                          Our client: ....

We act under a legal aid certificate no .... dated .... on behalf of the above-named, who was a patient at your hospital [who received treatment at your hospital] [who was under the care of your GP practice] between .... and ....

Now set out details of the treatment complained of and its apparent consequences to the client.

It is in these circumstances that we are applying to you for voluntary disclosure of the medical records. We cannot of course be specific about the allegations that may be made, but it seems to us that there are good grounds for considering a claim for [*here set out the nature of the possible complaints e.g. negligent diagnosis / negligence in the operation / failing to warn of the risks of the operation / failure of nursing care / premature mobilisation / premature discharge etc., etc.*].

We take the view, therefore, that your Authority [you] and our client are likely parties to subsequent proceedings for damages for personal injuries in the High Court and that you have in your possession documents that are likely to be relevant to issues in the proceedings. We therefore ask you to furnish us with all medical, nursing, anesthetic, surgical and medication records and notes, together with the records and notes from any other treatment or investigation undertaken; all laboratory and other test reports, X-ray films, records and reports, all consent forms and all clinical and other correspondence, and any accident reports and memoranda [*for even greater specificity you can ask for all the medical records set out on the enclosed schedule and attach a schedule culled to suit the case from the schedule which follows this letter – I say culled because you do not want to be seen to ask, for example, for the partogram in a geriatric case – this could lose you street credibility!*].

We undertake to preserve the confidentiality of the records and to use them only for the purpose of the proposed claim. We will accept either the originals, in which case we undertake to take proper care of them and to return them to you with all due speed, or legible and properly photographed copies, for which we will pay your reasonable copying charges.

If you provide copies, please ensure that all sheets comprising a single document are stapled together and that the sheets are in some semblance of order. Please ensure that any dates that appear at the edges of any document are not cut off by the photocopier – this is often a vital omission. Please also supply a list of the disclosed documents, to avoid the possibility of arguments later about what we were sent. We reserve our right to inspect copies against the originals in your possession.

We are sure we do not need to tell you that we will not accept disclosure to a nominated medical adviser only.

Please tell us if you have passed any relevant documents to any other party, and, if so, identify the party. Please also undertake to preserve in their entirety, pending production, inspection and trial, all relevant documents.

We must ask you to signify your consent to this disclosure within three weeks from today, and thereafter to provide the records within at most another four weeks, failing which we are instructed to apply to the court without further delay.

Please let us know, with full particularity, if you are likely to blame anyone else for any part of the injury suffered by our client.

We would prefer to name only your Health Authority and not the Regional Health Authority as defendants in any application for pre-action discovery or any subsequent action for damages. Could you kindly confirm to us that it is agreed with the Regional Health Authority that all relevant documents which are or have been in their possession, power and control will be deemed to be within your power and control; also that all staff involved in the treatment of our client will be deemed for the purposes of any proceedings taken by our client to be, if they are not in fact, employed by you, so that any vicarious liability that might otherwise be imposed on the Regional Health Authority will be discharged by you.[1]

Finally, we enclose a letter of authority for this disclosure from our client.

Yours faithfully,

. . . .

---

[1] Be aware, however, of the imminent demise of the RHAs.

For the schedule, if you want to do it that way, a more or less full list of potential documents would be as follows:

A & E record card; GP's referral letter; admitting doctor's notes of examination; consent forms; ward doctor's clinical notes; operating and anesthetic records; intensive therapy records; Kardex (daily nursing notes);

laboratory request forms and subsequent reports on blood and other bodily samples; ultrasound scan reports, photographs and videotapes; ECG (electrocardiograms) and reports thereon;

temperature, pulse, blood pressure and respiration charts; fluid balance charts; blood balance charts; blood transfusion records; drug prescription records (once only and continuing sheets); heart injury charts; X-ray request forms, plates and reports; theatre registers and casualty registers; cardiac cerebral function record, perfusionist records;

doctors' own files; health visitor records; all correspondence, internal memoranda, directives and circulars; accident memoranda, reports and all documents relating to any relevant untoward incident.

For particular cases there will be additional records, e.g. in maternity cases there will be some or all of the following:

The co-operation card (if the hospital has a copy) and all antenatal records; partogram; [*the vital*] CTG traces (cardiotocograph); progress of labour chart; community midwifery records.

Draft letter of instruction to the expert

How much detail you put in the letter will depend on how experienced the expert is at providing these reports. A very few need virtually no instruction. For the average expert the important points to make are, in my view, that he should set out the chronology of events with relevant extracts from the medical records (referring to the page number of the record in the bundle), that he should identify any area of substandard care (do not use the word 'negligence'), and that he should appreciate the importance of causation so that he will understand he has to detail the consequences, if any, of any substandard care. You can explain the Bolam principle if you like, but I think that may only serve to confuse at this stage [see Chapter 9 for a fuller discussion]. It is as well to make it clear that you want a full report and not merely responses to any questions that you may have raised – it is not up to us to identify the issues that need addressing.

Dear Dr ....

Our client: ....

Following our telephone conversation in which you kindly agreed to provide a report for us on the treatment received by our above-named client at ....
[by ....] on [over the period] .... we now enclose copies of the medical records that we have obtained from ...., together with a statement from our client. We have sorted and paginated the records, and please ensure that you give the page number when referring to or commenting on the records, so that we can follow your reasoning and conclusions more closely. Let us know if any records appear to be missing.

The short facts of the matter appear to be as follows .... Our client's dissatisfaction arises from the fact that ....

It is in these circumstances that we ask you to review the whole of the treatment received by our client and to identify any area or aspect where in your view the treatment fell below the standard which our client had a right to expect.

Another way to put it is to ask if any of the care or treatment constituted in your view unacceptable medical practice or an unacceptable level of care (we do not ask specifically for a finding of 'negligence', though you are free, if you wish, so to condemn any aspect of the management).

In respect of any item of substandard care, we will need to know with as much precision as possible how that may have affected the outcome for our client. When we say 'may have' we mean 'on the balance of probabilities', i.e. more likely than not (sometimes expressed as '51%'!) – certainty, or even near-certainty, is not required.

Your report should give the chronology of the matter as far as relevant by reference to the records and setting out any important entries, and then contain your conclusions as to the standard of care afforded the patient and the consequences to him, whether temporary or enduring, of any failure of care.

If you would be assisted by a report from any other specialty or by an examination of our client please let us know.

We hope you will forgive us if, in addition to providing your report as you deem appropriate, we ask you to help us by specifically answering the following questions (we hardly need say that we do not want your report merely to comprise answers to our questions – they are probably far from comprehensive!):

[*put here any questions that you feel are relevant, but do not overdo it!*]

If you do examine our client could you please let us have a short report specifying the various aspects of injury caused him by any substandard care, i.e. a short report on condition and prognosis, as we are obliged to serve such a report with the statement of claim. Your main report, i.e. that on liability, will not be disclosed without your consent.

We are grateful to you for your kind attention in this matter and look forward to receiving your report in due course.

Yours faithfully,

....

Draft originating summons for pre-action discovery

In the High Court of Justice   1992 ....

Queen's Bench Division

In the matter of section 33 of the Supreme Court Act 1981

and in the matter of RSC Order 24 r.7A[2]

Between

XX   plaintiff

and

XXX   defendants

The plaintiff claims against the defendants on the ground that they are a likely party to subsequent proceedings to be brought by him in this court for damages for personal injuries and are likely to have or to have had in their possession, custody or power documents relevant to issues likely to arise out of the claim, and he seeks the following orders against them:

1. That the defendants make and serve on the plaintiff's solicitor within 28 days a list verified by affidavit sworn by a properly authorised officer of the defendants, stating whether any documents, including all medical, nursing, anesthetic, surgical, and medication records and notes together with all records and notes from any other investigation and treatment undertaken, laboratory and other test reports, X-ray films, records and reports, all consent forms and all clinical and other correspondence relating to the plaintiff are in their possession, custody or power, and if any such documents were in their possession, custody or power but are no longer, identifying them and their present whereabouts.
2. That the defendants produce to the plaintiff's solicitor within 28 days such of the above-named documents as are currently in their possession, custody or power with leave granted to the plaintiff's solicitors to pass them on to the plaintiff's medical advisers.
3. That all costs of and occasioned by this application be the plaintiff's in any event etc.

....

You may, alternatively, request the medical records "as set out on the attached schedule", and attach a suitable schedule as set out above in connection with the letter asking for disclosure.

---

[2] In the County Court the appropriate references are section 52 of the County Courts Act 1984 and CCR Order 13 r.7.

Draft affidavit in support of application for pre-action discovery

In the High Court of Justice   1992 No.

Queen's Bench Division

In the matter of section 33 of the Supreme Court Act 1981

and in the matter of RSC Order 24 r.7A[3]

Between

XX	plaintiff
and	
XXX	defendants

I, ...of ...., MAKE OATH and say as follows:

1. I am a partner in the firm of ...., and I have the conduct of this action on behalf of the above-named plaintiff.

2. I make this affidavit in support of the plaintiff's application for pre-action disclosure of all the relevant medical records. [*Now explain in summary form the nature of the case and the complaint.*]

3. I have asked the defendants for voluntary disclosure of the medical records, but they have not consented. Copies of the relevant correspondence are now produced and shown to me marked "AB 1".

4. I wish to take expert advice on various aspects of the plaintiff's potential claim. I expect the parties herein to be parties to any subsequent action in this court for personal injuries on one or more of the following grounds: [*e.g. improperly advising the plaintiff to undergo the operation, failing to warn him of the risks involved, negligence in the operation itself.*] Accordingly I respectfully ask for an order for disclosure in the terms of the summons herein.

5. I respectfully submit that the defendants' failure to consent to disclosure should be penalised by an order for costs against them.

SWORN etc.

---

[3] See preceding footnote.

Draft summons for directions

[This is capable of variation; the main point is to secure a timetable, and one whereby witness statements are exchanged before medical reports and there is some provision for the plaintiff's expert[s] to provide a secondary report on liability by way of reply to the defendants' expert report, and also to provide supplementary reports on condition and prognosis nearer the time of trial. Paragraph 4 could be useful in an appropriate case, but it is hardly used as yet.

Paragraph 5 (courtesy of Peter Latham) is intended to clarify formally the customary position where the medical records are put in an indexed file and placed before the judge as agreed but the parties are free to challenge the accuracy of any particular record if they wish (see further as to the summons in the main text in Chapter 13).

Note that if chronological difficulties may arise from taking the date of setting down as the trigger for the timetable, you can take the date of the order on the summons instead.]

1. The plaintiff and defendants do respectively within 21 days hereof serve a list on the other stating what documents are or have been in their possession custody or power relating to the matters in question in this action, and there be inspection of the documents within seven days of service of the said lists.

2. The plaintiff and the defendants do serve by way of mutual and simultaneous exchange signed statements of witnesses of fact relevant to liability issues of negligence and causation of injury within four months from the date of notice that the action is set down for trial. No such witness to be called at trial without leave of the trial judge unless his or her statement has been served in accordance with this direction. For the avoidance of doubt the witness statements to be disclosed include the statements of investigating and treating doctors and ancillary hospital staff dealing with matters of primary fact and recollection but excluding any expert opinion of that witness that it is proposed to rely on. Such statements to be agreed if possible. Where a party fails to comply with this direction he shall not be entitled to adduce evidence to which this direction relates without leave of the court.

3.(a) The plaintiff and the defendants do mutually and simultaneously disclose by way of exchange medical reports on liability issues as to the alleged negligence and causation of injury within six months from the date of notice the action is set down for trial [*or* within two months of the above exchange of witness statements having been effected]. Such medical evidence be limited to [three] witnesses for each party. The parties be at liberty to call [three] expert medical witnesses on the said liability issues limited to those witnesses whose reports have been disclosed in accordance with this direction. If either party proposes to rely on further reports dealing with issues arising out of primary disclosure, such reports to be served not later than two months before the trial.

(b) The plaintiff and the defendants do mutually disclose by way of exchange medical reports relating to the plaintiff's present condition and prognosis to be agreed if possible and if not such medical evidence to be limited to [two] witnesses for each party. No such witness to be called at trial without leave of the trial judge unless the substance of his or her evidence has been disclosed within six months of the date upon which the action is set down for trial, save that supplementary reports on condition and prognosis (from any expert who has already provided a first report on condition and prognosis) which merely update the position may be relied on at trial if served up to one month before trial.

(c) The plaintiff and the defendants do mutually disclose by way of exchange reports relating to the assessment of quantum to be agreed if possible and if not such evidence to be limited to [two] witnesses for each party. No such witness to be called at trial without leave of the trial judge unless the substance of his or her evidence has been disclosed within six months of the date upon which the action is set down for trial.

(d) If any expert witness proposes to rely in his or her report or in evidence in chief at trial on any textbook, article or other published item in any expert or any other learned journal or any unpublished learned work a list of such material is to be served on the other party no less than 56 days before the date of trial.

[4. The parties' medical experts do meet on a date to be fixed but not later than 21 days before trial with a view to isolating the issues then in dispute between the parties. The experts to prepare a joint statement indicating those parts of their evidence on which they are and those on which they are not agreed.]

5. Under RSC O.38 r.3(2)(b) and (c) all relevant statements and entries in books and documents from the .... Hospital concerning the plaintiff as a patient therein shall be admissible in evidence at the trial (saving all just objections) as evidence of contemporary records of the events in question but without admission of the truth of their contents by production of the original records of the events or such copies as may be the best surviving evidence without the need to call the maker(s) of such statements or entries.

6. The plaintiff do serve an [updated] schedule of special damages not later than two months before the date of trial, the defendant to be at liberty to serve a counter-notice and the plaintiff to be at liberty to serve a supplementary schedule of special damages but not later than one month before the trial.

7. The action to be tried in London, judge alone, category B, estimated length of trial .... days, to be set down within three months.

8. Costs of this application to be costs in cause.

Draft interrogatories

In the High Court of Justice   1992 C. No. 161

Queen's Bench Division

Between

                                    XX   plaintiff

                                    and

                                    XXX   defendants

Interrogatories: Plaintiff to Defendants

1. Did the operation of 4 June 1990 carry any risk of injury (a) from the anesthetic administered, (b) from the treatment accorded to the plaintiff's back, (c) arising in some other and, if so, what way?
2. If so, what was the nature and degree of each such risk?
3. Did anything (a) unusual, (b) unexpected, (c) untoward, (d) dangerous to the patient, (e) life-threatening occur in or about the said operation?
4. If so, what precisely was it, when precisely did it occur, and which of the above epithets properly describe it?
5. Precisely what action was taken by the medical team upon such occurrence?
6. What drugs, and in what quantities, and precisely when, were administered to the plaintiff during the course of the said operation?
7. How long was the plaintiff unconscious?
8. For how long were attempts made to intubate the plaintiff?
9. Were they successful?
10. If not, why not?
11. Who was present during the said operation?
12. Who was in charge during the said operation?
13. What were the medical qualifications of the medical personnel present at the operation?
14. How many such operations had the surgeon in charge already performed and when and where?
15. How many such operations had the senior anesthetist attended in that capacity before the said operation, and when and where?

[As indicated in the main body of the text, the possible range of interrogatories is very large, depending on the view as to admissibility taken by the Master. What questions arise to be asked will depend on the circumstances of the case and the points made by your expert's report. Note the new rules on interrogatories (see Chapter 12).]

Appendix III

Action for Victims of Medical Accidents

AVMA was set up in 1981 by Peter Ransley as a direct result of the reaction he received to the first screening of his television play *Minor Complications*, which depicted the difficulties faced by the victim of a medical accident.

The aims of AVMA have been to try to change what were perceived as the ingrained attitudes among the health professionals, so that they might adopt a more positive approach to easing the path of the injured party in whatever direction was most helpful to him or her; to establish appropriate procedures for dealing with the needs of victims of such accidents and the accountability of those responsible for the accident; and to give personal help to victims in order to ensure that they understood what had happened and were able to secure the assistance they needed whether by way of financial compensation or otherwise.

For those lawyers who have recently come into the field of medical negligence it is probably difficult to appreciate that, when AVMA was founded, victims of medical accidents had nobody to whom to turn and there were few if any lawyers competent to help because medical negligence as a specialty did not exist.

AVMA has come a long way since then, and has had a major influence both on the development of the conduct of medical negligence litigation and the skills of lawyers and on the approach of health professionals and the health care establishment towards medical accidents. It has offices at Bank Chambers, 1 London Road, Forest Hill, London SE23 3TP (tel. 0181 291 2793) where there is a staff of 22. It has dealt with more than 17,000 cases. All enquiries are dealt with personally by one of the case-workers.

After a careful assessment, which often involves considerable research, clients with a potential claim for medical negligence are referred to one of the 80 or so solicitors (personally by name, i.e. not by firm) who AVMA knows will process the case properly, and thereafter AVMA continuously monitors the progress of the case.

Another vital role that AVMA performs is the monitoring of medical experts' input; and it keeps up-to-date information on suitable experts, details of which, together with other valuable guidance, such as the analysis of medical reports, it makes available for a moderate annual fee to members of its Lawyers Resource Service. It is in fact the monitoring of experts which it is able to do with the feedback from its membership which exceeds 950 firms, and the extensive additional information and continuous support it provides to lawyers, which now includes membership of LAWTEL, that differentiates AVMA's service from the various 'directories' that are increasingly appearing. AVMA has been instrumental in creating a body of lawyers who are expert in processing the medical negligence action; one still reads (or comes across in one's own practice!) horror stories where a possible claim is ruined by an inexpert lawyer, but this should happen less and less as the work of AVMA is assimilated more widely by the legal profession. The establishment of the Law Society's medical negligence panel is a measure of the extent to which this has already happened.

Since 1989 AVMA has run a high-powered two-day conference for medical negligence practitioners (and it runs or is involved in other conferences which, because of its contact with practitioners, are always particularly relevant to their needs); it publishes a useful quarterly journal which is now incorporated in a major publication on clinical risk; it runs medical courses for lawyers which are a fundamental requirement for membership of the Law Society's panel, as well as holding regular meetings for its regional Lawyers' Support Groups where useful lectures and discussions take place.

In 1990 AVMA was awarded a small annual grant from the DOH. This, together with the fact that its Chief Executive is a member of that Department's working party on mediation in medical negligence claims, is a further indication of the progress AVMA has made in achieving recognition for its ideas.

Currently the main thrust of AVMA's work is concerned with standards and accountability, since it sees that as the best way to improve the situation for victims. It is campaigning, with the Association of Community Health Councils for England and Wales, for the introduction of a Health Standards Inspectorate that will investigate complaints and accidents and award compensation as well as set and enforce standards in the profession (it is hoped that one would then see the end of the inadequate exercise by the General Medical Council of its disciplinary function).

Additionally AVMA is becoming increasingly involved with the Health Service on the important subject of risk management, running courses in which it can use its experience of helping victims to teach those responsible for dealing with complaints and risk management what the needs of patients are in that area.

AVMA's aim is not to make things difficult for the health care professionals but to ensure that the patient gets a fair deal, and part of that fair deal is that – to preserve (or even improve) standards – doctors and other professionals must be accountable for their actions (hence, incidentally, AVMA's opposition to a no-fault scheme for compensation for medical injuries without a parallel scheme for accountability as envisaged by its Inspectorate).

Appendix IV

Here is a list of common abbreviations and hieroglyphs, reproduced by kind permission of Ann Winyard.

Common hieroglyphs

+ + +	much/many
#	fracture
Δ	diagnosis
Diff. Δ or ΔΔ	differential diagnosis
℞	treatment
J° (no jaundice)	nil/nothing/no
↑	up, increasing
N, →	constant, normal or lateral shift (e.g. of apex of heart)
↓	down, decreasing
⊥	central (of the trachea)
1/7	one day
2/52	two weeks
3/12	three months
T38.6°C	temperature 38.6
T − 14	term (i.e. date baby due) less two weeks
T + 7	term plus one week
35+4/40	35 weeks and 4 days
37+3/40	37 weeks and 3 days

Common abbreviations

AAL	Anterior axillary line
ATCH	Adrenocorticotrophic hormone
AE	Air entry
AFB	Acid fast bacillus (TB)
AFP	Alpha-fetoprotein (maternal serum and occasionally amniotic fluid levels tested in pregnancy to screen for neural tube defect in fetus)
AJ	Ankle jerk (reflex: see also BJ, KJ, SJ, TJ)
Anti-D	This gamma globulin must be given by injection to Rhesus negative mother who delivers/aborts Rhesus positive child/fetus to prevent mother developing antibodies which could damage a subsequent Rhesus positive baby

Apgar	Apgar score: means of recording baby's condition at birth by observing and 'scoring' (0, 1 or 2) 5 parameters
A/V	Anteverted
BJ	Biceps jerk (reflex: see AJ)
BNF (plus date)	British National Formulary (prescriber's 'bible' supplied free to all NHS doctors). New edition each year. You can buy one (about £10 from medical bookshops)
BO	Bowels open
BP (plus date)	British pharmacopoeia
BP	Blood pressure
BS	(a) Breath sounds
	(b) Bowel sounds
	(c) Blood Sugar
c̄	With (Latin: cum)
C_2H_5OH	Alcohol
Ca	(a) Carcinoma/cancer
	(b) Calcium
Caps	Capsules
CAT scan	Computed axial tomograph
CNS	Central nervous system
CO	Complaining of
CO_2	Carbon dioxide
COETT	Cuffed oral endotracheal tube (see COT and ETT)
COT	Cuffed oral tube (endotracheal tube used for ventilating a patient who cannot breath unaided)
CPD	Cephalo-pelvc disproportion (baby too big to fit through pelvis)
CSF	Cerebro-spinal fluid
CTG	Cardiotocograph (trace during labour of baby's heart and mum's contractions)
CVA	Cerebro-vascular accident (stroke)
CVS	Cardio-vascular system
Cx	Cervix
CXR	Chest X-ray
DNA	(a) Did not attend
	(b) Deoxyribonucleic acid
D & V	Diarrhoea and vomiting
DOA	Dead on arrival
DVT	Deep vein thrombosis
Dx	Diagnosis
ECG	Electro-cardiogram/graph (electric heart recording)
ECT	Electro-convulsive therapy
EDC	Expected date of confinement
EDD	Expected date of delivery
EEG	Electroencephalogram/graph (brain scan)
ERCP	Endoscopic retrograde choledochopancreatico/graphy/scopy
ERPC	Evacuation of retained products of conception
ESR	Erythrocyte sedimentation rate (blood)
EtOH	Another code for alcohol
ETT	Endotracheal tube (see COT above)
FB	Finger's breadth

FBC	Full blood count
FBS	Fetal blood sampling (carried out during labour to check baby's condition)
FH	Family history
FHH	Fetal heart heard
FHHR	Fetal heart heard regular
FHR	Fetal heart rate
FLK	(Used by pediatricians) Funny looking kid
FMF	Fetal movements felt
FSE	Fetal scalp electrode
FSH	(a) Family and social history
	(b) Follicle-stimulating hormone (produced in pregnancy)
GA	General anesthetic
GFR	Glomerular filtration rate
GIT	Gastro-intestinal tract
GTT	Glucose tolerance test (for diabetes)
GUT	Genito-urinary tract
Hb	Hemoglobin (blood)
HPC	History of presenting complaint
HS	Heart sounds
HVS	High vaginal swab
Hx	History
ICS	Intercostal space (usually as xICS, where x = a number from 1 to 11)
IJ	Internal jugular vein
IM	Intramuscular
IVI	Intravenous infusion (drip)
JVP	Jugular vein pressure
K	Potassium
KJ	Knee jerk (reflex: see AJ)
kPa	Kilopascal, approximately 7.5 mmHg
L	Litre
LA	Local anesthetic
LFTs	Liver function tests
LIH	Left inguinal hernia
LMP	Last menstrual period
LN	Lymph node
LOA	Left occiput anterior (position of baby's head at delivery: see also LOP, ROA, ROP)
LOC	Loss of consciousness
LOL	Left occipitolateral
LOP	Left occiput posterior (see LOA above)
LSCS	Lower segment cesarean section (the 'normal' type of cesarean)
LSKK	Liver, spleen and kidneys
mcg	Microgram
MCL	Mic clavicular line
µg	Microgram
mg	Milligram
mist	Mixture
ml	Millilitre
mmHG	Millimetres of mercury (pressure)
mMol	Millimol

N & V	Nausea and vomiting
Na	Sodium
NaHCO₃	Sodium bicarbonate (alkaline substance: inter alia given to counteract metabolic acidosis following oxygen deprivation)
NAD	Nothing abnormal diagnosed/detected
NBM	Nil by mouth
ng	Nanogram
NG	Carcinoma/cancer (neoplastic growth)
NLM	Nice looking mother
NMCS	No malignant cells seen
NOF	Neck of femur
N/S	Normal size
O₂	Oxygen
OA	Occipito-posterior
P	Pulse
π	Period
Pco₂	Partial pressure of carbon dioxide (normally in blood)
PERLA	Pupils are equal and react to light and accommodation
PE	(a) Pulmonary embolism
	(b) Pre-eclampsia
PET	Pre-eclamptic toxemia
pg	Picogram
pH	Negative log of hydrogen ion activity: 'acidity and alkalinity' scale. Low is acidic. High is alkaline. pH7 is about neutral.
PH	Past/previous history
PID	(a) Pelvic inflammatory disease
	(b) Prolapsed intervertebral disc
PMH	Past/previous medical history
PN(R)	Percussion note (resonant)
PO₂	Partial pressure of oxygen (normally in blood)
POH	Past/previous obstetric history
po	Per os (by mouth)
pr	Per rectum (by the rectum)
prn	As required – of, e.g., pain killers
pv	Per vaginam (by the vagina)
RBC	Red blood cell (erythrocyte)
Rh	Rhesus (blood type, can cause problems in pregnancy if mother is Rhesus *negative* and father Rhesus *positive*)
RIH	Right inguinal hernia
ROA	Right occiput anterior (see LOA above)
ROL	Right occipito-lateral
ROM	Range of movement
ROP	Right occiput posterior (see LOA above)
RS	Respiratory system
RTI	Respiratory tract infection
s̄	Without (Latin: sine)
S/B	seen by
S/D	Systolic/diastolic (heart and circulation)
SH	Social history

SJ	Supinator jerk (reflex: see AJ)
SOA	Swelling of ankles
SOB (OE)	Short of breath (on exertion)
SOS	(a) si opus sit (if necessary)
	(b) see other sheet
SROM	Spontaneous rupture of membranes (labour)
SVC	Superior vena cava
SVD	Spontaneous vaginal delivery
SVT	Supraventricular tachycardia
TCI 2/52	To come in, in 2 weeks' time
TGH	To go home
THR	Total hip replacement
TIA	Transient ischemic attack
TJ	Triceps jerk (reflex: see AJ)
TVF	Tactile vocal fremitus
U & E	Urea and electrolytes (biochemical tests)
URTI	Upper respiratory tract infection
UTI	Urinary tract infection
VE	Vaginal examination
VF	Ventricular fibrillation
VT	Ventricular tachycardia
V/V	Vulva and vagina
WBC	White blood corpuscle/white blood cell count
XR	X-ray

[Author's note: there are some others that one is less likely to find now that the patient has easy access to her records, such as:

FOC	Fat old cow
HGAC	Haven't got a clue
SOF	Silly old fool.

I have even heard of, though never actually seen, **TTFO** (told to ....off).]

Appendix V

Hippocratic Oath

This oath, taken at the time of graduation by medical students at some universities, dates back to the 4th century BC. It was handed down as part of the *Hippocratic Collection*, a philosophy developed by the Greeks from the writings of Hippocrates and others, from which the whole of their science grew. One version of the oath states:

I will look upon him who shall have taught me this Art even as one of my parents. I will share my substance with him, and I will supply his necessities, if he be in need. I will regard his offspring even as my own brethren, and I will teach them this Art, if they would learn it, without fee or covenant. I will impart this Art by precept, by lecture and by every mode of teaching, not only to my own sons, but to the sons of him who taught me, and to disciples bound by covenant and oath, according to the Law of Medicine.

The regimen I adopt shall be for the benefit of my patients according to my ability and judgement, and not for their hurt or for any wrong. I will give no deadly drug to any, though it be asked of me, nor will I counsel such, and especially I will not aid a woman to procure abortion. Whatsoever house I enter, there will I go for the benefit of the sick, refraining from all wrongdoing or corruption, and especially from any act of seduction of male or female, of bond or free. Whatsoever things I see or hear concerning the life of men, in my attendance on the sick, or even apart therefrom, which ought not to be noised abroad, I will keep silence thereon, counting such things to be as sacred secrets.

Index